The Venture of Islam

To consider mankind otherwise than brethren, to think favours are peculiar to one nation and exclude others, plainly supposes a darkness in the understanding.

—John Woolman

The Venture of Islam

Conscience and History in a World Civilization

MARSHALL G. S. HODGSON

VOLUME ONE

THE CLASSICAL AGE OF ISLAM

THE UNIVERSITY OF CHICAGO PRESS
CHICAGO AND LONDON

To John U. Nef
and to the memory of
Gustave E. von Grunebaum
in admiration and gratitude

Some of the material in these volumes has been issued in a different form in *Introduction to Islamic Civilization* (volumes 1, 2, 3, Copyright © 1958, 1959 by The University of Chicago), in *A History of Islamic Civilization* (Copyright © 1958 by Marshall G. S. Hodgson), and in an earlier version of *The Venture of Islam* (volumes 1, 2, Copyright © 1961 by Marshall G. S. Hodgson).

The University of Chicago Press, Chicago 60637
The University of Chicago Press, Ltd., London

Printed in the United States of America

International Standard Book Numbers: 0-226-34677-3 (3-vol. set); 0-226-34678-1 (vol. 1); 0-226-34680-3 (vol. 2); 0-226-34681-1 (vol. 3)

Library of Congress Catalog Card Number: 73-87243

86 85 84 83 82 81 80 79 6 5 4 3 2

CONTENTS

VOLUME I

CHARTS

VOLUME I

Book One

Book Two

MAPS

VOLUME I

Marshall Hodgson and *The Venture of Islam*

Marshall Goodwin Simms Hodgson died suddenly on June 10, 1968, in his forty-seventh year, before he had finished this and other works. At the time of his death the manuscript for the first four of the six books of *The Venture of Islam* had been submitted to a publisher as final (although minor editing and footnote attribution still remained to be done); he had reworked much of Book Five; and he had indicated revisions wanted in Book Six. Many of the charts and diagrams were only sketches, and there were only general descriptions of the intended maps. A much shorter version of the work, resembling *The Venture of Islam* in its general form, had existed for a number of years, used and sought after by graduate and undergraduate students alike. It had started as a brief outline, some chapters consisting of only two or three pages or not yet even written. He constantly wrote, withdrew what he had written, rewrote, and sought criticism from his colleagues near and far. He was simultaneously at work on a world history, and he often remarked that he hoped readers would some day have both available, for he had long been convinced that any historical development could only be understood in terms of the historical whole, and that whole included the entire canvas of human history. Although several hundred pages of manuscript for his world history exist, most unfortunately it apparently cannot be published, for to put it in meaningful form would mean that it was no longer his work. A number of the world history's basic assumptions and points of view can be found in *The Venture of Islam,* however, particularly in the various sections of the 'Introduction to the Study of Islamic Civilization', originally planned by Hodgson as appendices to the entire work. He was an indefatigable and fastidious worker, with definite ideas of his own. Although continually seeking advice from everywhere, he was yet adamant that no publisher's editor would alter his text.

It was with considerable trepidation that I agreed to see this work through the press after his death. I had worked with him, even sharing his office for a time, and had taken over the course in the history of Islamic civilization at the University of Chicago, a course that he had created and that we had for two years jointly taught. *The Venture of Islam* had originated to meet the needs of that course; but concurrently Hodgson recognized that much he had to say went far beyond any ordinary text. He always hoped the book would appeal to the educated layman as well as to the specialist and the beginning student; he thought he could reach all three in the one work, and it was thus that he wrote.

He kept voluminous notes, and he had written out for himself many directions; there were numerous complete charts as well as sketches and designs for others. The same was true for illustrations, which unfortunately because of cost have had to be eliminated. I saw my task to be as light-handed as possible, and to preserve the manuscript as completely his. Therefore, there is a more detailed text, and there are more charts and maps for the first two-thirds of the work than for the last third. His writing style, particularly, is unaltered; there were places in the manuscript where he had deliberately changed to a greater complexity from an earlier, less detailed style. Always his aim was to pack as much meaning as possible into a sentence or a paragraph, while keeping it so circumscribed as to include only what he wanted. Some of his neologisms may not be attractive; more than most other writers, however, he has made his readers aware of the traps one may fall into when giving a word or concept familiar in one culture an apparently similar connotation in the context of another culture. His world history would have had central to it such concerns. I followed his notes where I could. Since he opted for different spellings and even in some cases different terminology later in his writing, I have tried to bring some consistency there. In a few instances he altered traditional dates to other, less usual chronology; these dates I have left. Only where a few notes in brackets are found in Book Six has my presence intruded. I hope and believe the work is his, purely and directly, and that I have done nothing to alter it.

No one who was associated with Marshall Hodgson remained unmoved by who he was and the scholarship he stood for. He was a lesser-known giant among better-known scholars. His Quaker background provided him with a quiet gentleness backed by absolute resolution when necessary; perhaps more than for most teachers, the kind of person he was informed the classes he taught, especially those in Qur'ān and Ṣūfism. No narrow specialist, he found in his work with the intellectually wide-ranging Committee on Social Thought at the University of Chicago a satisfaction rivaling that afforded by his Islamic study and teaching.

It is impossible here to make the acknowledgments he would have made if he were alive. Leading Islamic scholars throughout the world read portions of his work. He was able to take few leaves from his teaching and his administrative duties to devote entirely to research; but one or two precious opportunities did occur. Help also came from friends, and especially his students. I would like to acknowledge simply by name help graciously and eagerly offered me by his colleagues and students: Professors William H. McNeill, Muhsin Mahdi, and the late Gustave von Grunebaum for valuable counsel; graduate students Harold Rogers, Marilyn Robinson Waldman, William Ochserwald, and George Chadwick, now all launched on careers of their own; and many others too numerous to mention.

Most of all, the countless hours Marshall Hodgson's wife, Phyllis, devoted to the whole work over the years under the most trying of circumstances cannot be left unacknowledged. Her example, as his, remains for the rest of us a monument.

REUBEN W. SMITH

Callison College
University of the Pacific

Publisher's Note

Reuben Smith's account of his own contribution to the posthumous realization of Marshall Hodgson's monumental work is far too modest. Over a period of at least four years he gave uncounted hours, which he might otherwise have spent on his own research and writing, to the difficult task of finishing his colleague's work. For this selfless devotion, and for his never-failing good humor in answering countless questions, the University of Chicago Press wishes to thank Mr. Smith on behalf of all students and other readers of these volumes.

When the University of Chicago Press acquired *The Venture of Islam* from a commercial publisher, all the text had been set in type by Unwin Brothers Limited in England and galleys had been proofread by Mr. Smith. Decisions remained to be made concerning the charts and the maps. After consultation with Mr. Smith, the Press decided to include all the charts originally planned by Marshall Hodgson except a very few incomplete or peripheral ones. The titles of the charts are Hodgson's, as are the concepts and the contents, as nearly as we could reproduce them.

A tentative list of map titles had been drawn up by Smith from Hodgson's notes and references in the text. Using this list and drawing on his wide knowledge of the field as well as his understanding of Hodgson's aims and point of view, John E. Woods, of the Department of History of the University of Chicago and currently one of the professors teaching the course in Islamic civilization, drafted all the maps included in these volumes. From his drafts, the Cartographic Division of the University of Wisconsin provided the final versions.

The indexes to all three volumes were compiled by Yusuf I. Ghaznavi, graduate student at the University of Chicago, with the assistance of his wife, Huricihan, a former student of Hodgson. Mr. Ghaznavi also adapted Hodgson's original Glossary to the three-volume format so that the user of each volume would have definitions of the unfamiliar words at hand.

The decision to make these volumes available singly as well as in a set necessitated a few changes from Hodgson's original plan. In a series of 'Appendices' Hodgson had set forth his views on the meaning of Islamic terms, transliteration, personal names, dates, historical method, and other important aspects of his work. Since familiarity with this material enhances the reader's understanding of the entire work, we decided to move it all to the beginning of Volume I, changing only the title, from 'Appendices' to 'Introduction to the Study of Islamic Civilization'. Cross references in the text to the 'Appendices' have (we hope all of them) been changed to refer to the Introduction. Hodgson conveniently arranged his 'Selective Bibliography for Further Reading' in chronological sections that enabled us to divide it into the three relevant parts, and accordingly, each volume has its own 'Selective Bibliography'. General works are all listed in Volume I. The question of the Glossary was more difficult. Convenience of the reader again indicated the desirability of a glossary in each volume, even though many words would appear in all three. Finally, while Hodgson supplied titles for each of his six 'books' and for the work as a whole, he did not envisage its being divided into three volumes; from terminology he used elsewhere, we have provided titles for the separate volumes.

The University of Chicago Press is pleased to be able to bring *The Venture of Islam* to the many students and friends who have long awaited its publication and regrets only that Marshall Hodgson himself is no longer here to share that pleasure.

The Venture of Islam

Introduction to the Study of Islamic Civilization

On making sense of Islamicate words, names, and dates

The thoughts of a people distant in time or space cannot be at all deeply shared without our becoming acquainted with things and ideas important to them but of which we have had no exact equivalent. As far as possible, one wants to read the works themselves in which the thoughts have been expressed; in these, even in translation, the special concepts and categories of the writers, as well as the personalities and places referred to, must be reproduced (if the translation is serious) in forms alien to the usual flow of English, no matter how much the resources of English may have been adapted or even twisted to do duty for what remain alien conceptions.

The same is, in some degree, true of any work treating of the alien civilization. The serious reader must be prepared to think in novel ways. To this end, he must be prepared to absorb as readily as possible a whole range of new concepts and terms. Otherwise he cannot expect to profit seriously by a study of the culture; at most he will receive an impression of exotic quaintness, romance, or incongruity which does no justice to the human reality.

Though Islamicate culture has been expressed in many languages essentially unrelated to each other, much terminology and customary practice has been common to them all. For instance, technical terms in religion and also in some other fields have commonly been derived from the Arabic or in some cases from the Persian, as have been Western terms from Latin and Greek. Just as is the case with Christian names, Muslim names form to a large degree a common stock that reappears substantially the same in every Muslim country. The manners of dating an event or of heading a letter tend to be constant, and of course the use of Arabic script. It is important to feel as much at ease as possible with all this.

The problem is complicated by the fact that in many cases writers about Islamdom as well as translators have been very inconsistent in their renderings of names and concepts. The reader will find the same term presented in many utterly different guises. The various sections of this Introduction give a number of aids for negotiating the resultant maze. Ways of transliterating from various Islamicate languages are outlined, with suggestions of how the reader can refer from one system to another if he reads different authors; Muslim personal names are grouped into common types, with suggestions for keeping them apart; the Muslim calendar is explained; short essays are offered on problems of studying a civilization; recurrent technical terms are briefly defined. Leaving most detail to the following special sections, I believe it necessary at this point to emphasize reasons for using exact transliteration, and to offer some suggestions of how the systems used in this work may at the same time assist approximate pronunciation.

Why transliteration?

Transliteration is the rendering of the spelling of a word from the script of one language into that of another, in this case from the 'Arabic' alphabets used in Islamicate languages into the 'Latin' alphabet used in English. Transcription is the rendering of the sound of a word so that a reader can pronounce it. Ideally, transliteration should include as much transcription as possible. When an original script is unfamiliar, transliteration is necessary first of all in the case of names, which by their nature cannot be translated and yet must be clearly recognizable and distinguishable from any names like them; and secondly in the case of technical terms, when the concept they represent is not present in another language and it is important to refer to it with precision.

In this second case of technical terms there is room for difference in the degree to which *transliteration* is used as compared with a rough *translation*. Different writers draw the line at different points. A word that some will transliterate, others will try to translate by more or less equivalent English words, either because they attach less importance to precision in that given case, or because they hope to attach a technical meaning to a special English word or pair of words. Thus the concept expressed in all Islamicate languages as شريعة is not present in English. If it is translated as 'law' the reader is misled, because it covers much that we do not call 'law' and fails to cover much that we do call 'law'. Even if we use a compound term (as is often advisable), 'Sacred Law', the reader will be misled unless he is given a full explanation that this is something quite different from what the term 'sacred law' might ordinarily lead him to expect. In *The Venture of Islam* the concept here being referred to has a special importance; hence for exactness it is rendered, according to its sound in Arabic, by the transliteration (which is also a close transcription), *Sharî'ah*, and it is explained in detail. The like is done with a number of other important terms that occur frequently. In this way, so far as a term carries any meaning at all, it will be that assigned it in the explanation and not one derived from overtones attaching to previously known English terms. In addition, it is unmistakable which original term is referred to; whereas arbitrary translations, varying according to the writer, often leave the careful reader in doubt.

If a system of transliteration used for names and for terms is consistent and exact it saves everyone much time and effort in the long run. Above all, any system must be reversible; that is, such that the original *written* symbols (which are far more constant than the pronunciation) can be reconstructed with certainty from the transliteration. Second, it should so far as possible at the same time be a transcription, such that the careful reader will pronounce the word more or less recognizably in oral communication. Finally, it should require as few diacritics as possible so that, if they are omitted, confusion will be held to a minimum; the diacritics that are used should be common ones, available on the average academic or professional copyist's typewriter.

Diacritics are, however, necessary. Since letters of one language usually have no exact equivalent in the alphabet of another language, the choice of English letters to render Arabic or Persian letters must be rather arbitrary. Some alien letters can be rendered more or less happily by existing English letters: for instance the Arabic ت sounds not unlike the English T. The sound of others is unlike any sound in English; but they are usually in the same phonetic category with some other sound, just as the G in *gave* is related to the C in *cave*. For such we can sometimes use digraphs, like TH for the Greek Θ; but sometimes we must invent a new English letter that is rather like an existing English letter of related sound. Thus for the Arabic ط we invent arbitrarily a new letter Ṭ, because to the native speaker of English that Arabic letter is rather like T in sound. It must be noted that T and Ṭ are quite as distinct from each other as C and G (in fact, G was originally formed in the same way, simply by adding a stroke to C). The added part—a dot, a stroke, or whatever—of the new letter is the *diacritical mark*, and is sometimes omitted in printing (just as in certain Latin inscriptions both G and C are written as C, without the stroke). But properly speaking, the diacritical mark is not something extra, to be omitted at will; it is an essential part of a new letter.

It might seem as if exact reconstruction of the original were of importance only to the scholar who knows the original language.[1] In fact, it is of importance to the ordinary reader also. He needs to know whether the *scharia* he comes across in one writer is the same concept as the *shareeah* he finds in another writer (it is); or whether *Hassan* and *Hasan* are likely to be one man or two. (*Ḥassân* and *Ḥasan* are two quite different names; but newsmen, who have no exact system, often write them both 'Hassan'.) That otherwise educated persons seem to be helpless in the face of exact transliteration and fail to profit by it does not show that on this point human nature is perverse but only that Western education is remiss. The only way that this can begin to be remedied is for scholars to set a good example and form better habits in their readers.

[1] It is sometimes said that specialists do not need exact transliteration and non-specialists cannot use it. This is not so. Outside of a very narrow subspecialty in which he has full first-hand acquaintance, even the Arabist or Persianist will come across names first in secondary works, commonly in a Western language; yet he will want to know the original. Without diacritics he cannot distinguish *'Âlî* from *'Alî*, *Ḥâkim* from *Ḥakîm*, *ẓâhir* from *zâhir*, *'Âmir* from *Amîr*. To assume that the non-specialist can have no use for exact transliteration suggests condescension; for it implies that he will read only the one book on the subject, and so have no occasion to refer across from the usage of one book to that of another, nor need to straighten out the names he comes across.

If all writers used a single consistent system, the problem of identifying transliterated names would be much reduced. If that is impossible, then if each author's system is at least exact, and he explains it (as careful authors do) in a note or in his preface, a reference to the prefaces of the two works will usually tell the reader whether or not one spelling is the equivalent of the other.

Strictly speaking, it might be enough if the writer put the exact forms only in the index, to avoid the cost of diacritics in the text. But this sacrifices the advantage of accustoming the eye to the correct form rather than an ambiguous one, as well as being a nuisance to that reader who wants to read a passage uninterruptedly and yet be sure of references as he goes along. Since careful writers now spell 'Cézanne', 'Tübingen', 'Saint-Saëns', 'Charlotte Brontë', 'façade', 'Provençal', 'Potëmkin', Arabic and Persian words should also be spelled with diacritics. The careless reader should not begrudge the careful one such precision. Nevertheless, in those cases where a well-known name has already achieved a *uniform* rendering in English, it is generally regarded as unnecessary to include it in the system of transliteration since common Anglicized forms such as *Cairo* or *Damascus*—like *Naples* or *Quebec*—are unambiguous. This is especially appropriate where the most frequent context of the term in English will be other than special discussions of Islamicate materials: in other words, situations that do not require special new thought habits. A rough rule is that common English usage should be retained when a term refers to something easily recognized and presently existing, such as a great city.[2] (To allow for Anglicized accentuation, diacritics may sometimes be dropped when an English termination is added to words so common that they have already shown the exact spelling in the simple form.)

[2] It is worth noting that non-technical, 'popular' forms are subject to a steady erosion, however much uniformity they may have achieved. Specialists will tend to use the technical transliteration, first in special monographs and then by habit in their general works. Once a majority of the specialists are using the technical transliteration in general works, the rest tend to follow; and one generation later, the non-specialists are likely to follow the usage of the specialists. Thus the name of the Prophet was once, for non-specialists, usually *Mahomet*; this was almost universally replaced among non-specialists by what used to be the technical transliteration of the specialists, *Mohammed*; but meanwhile, a more sophisticated technical transliteration had supervened among the specialists, *Muḥammad*; now this (shorn of its diacritic) is beginning to replace the older form also among non-specialists.

For those who would like to maximize continuity in the English literary tradition, it is hard to know where to try to stem the tide. Once the technical form has become the more common among specialists—e.g., *Qur'ân* for *Koran*—it is probably too late. Very few terms regarding the past seem destined to retain a non-technical form, perhaps only those prominent in European history and where the technical form requires a major shift in pronunciation and not just in spelling (*Ottoman* for *Osmanlî*, *Caliph* for *Khalîfah*). Current geographical terms, on the other hand, have a better chance despite the tendency of some cartographers to put all names into native form, even *Roma* and *Napoli*.

Some general suggestions for pronunciation

Transliteration is required in this work chiefly from four languages, Arabic, Persian, Ottoman Turkish, and Urdu, each of which has used a form of what was originally the Arabic alphabet. Of these, Arabic words will most often be met because, for the sake of uniformity, technical terms (whatever the linguistic context) will be rendered only in a single form, that of their original language, which is most often Arabic.

The letters used in this book for transliterating Arabic and Persian can be pronounced recognizably enough by a beginner if he renders the vowels as in Italian (a = ah, e as in bet, i = ee, o = oh, u = oo), and the consonants in the commonest English way. Long vowels (â, î, û) should be held extra long, and may receive the stress. The consonants must be pronounced unvaryingly; thus s is always hissed, and h is always pronounced, even in words like *Mahdî* or *Allâh* (but not in digraphs like th, sh, ch pronounced as in English). Beginners may pronounce the dotted or lined letters like the undotted ones, but must keep them separate in the mind or similar names may be confused. Aw is like ou in *house*; dh is th in *then*; ʼ(*hamzah*) and ʻ(ʻ*ayn*) are consonants which are not always distinguishable to the Anglophone ear and can be overlooked in pronouncing.

The same rules of thumb may also be used for the other languages, except for Urdu (and Indo-Persian), where a short a is like u in *but*; and a combination of h with a consonant often is not a digraph but must be pronounced as an aspirate; that is, th is not pronounced as in *nothing*, but somewhat as in *at home;* and dh somewhat as in *ad hominem*. Ottoman Turkish names may be treated like the Persian except that ö and ü are pronounced as in German (French eu and u). Modern republican Turkish has a Latin alphabet of its own, several letters of which must be learned ad hoc (see the section following); but apart from these, the usual system will serve—vowels as in Italian, consonants as in English. The same guide will serve at least roughly for any other foreign names to be encountered.

It is wise for the beginner to use *no stress at all*, but to pronounce each syllable with equal fullness (unless he *knows* that a given syllable is to be stressed).

Certain Muslim names are often spelled in English in two portions, which are, however, essentially inseparable. Beginners (and journalists) often drop the first portion, treating the latter portion as a 'last name' to be used alone. This is like referring to MacArthur as 'Arthur'. Abû-Yazîd, for instance, is a quite different figure from Yazîd, Ibn-Saʻd from Saʻd, and ʻAbd-al-Malik from Mâlik. (Still worse than calling ʻAbd-al-Malik 'Malik' is the complementary error of treating the ' ʻAbd-al-' as if it were an independent 'first name': forms like 'Abdul', 'Abul', or 'Ibnul' when thought of as separable names are barbarisms that are not even formed in the original script, let alone actually used.) In this work such compound names will be hyphenated;

but many writers separate them without even a hyphen, and the beginner may well learn to restore the hyphen mentally, to avoid endless confusion.

TRANSLITERATION

Transliteration from Islamicate languages, especially from Arabic, has been increasingly uniform in scholarly works in English. Yet even now writers differ; books written in the last century and the beginning of this century show a great variety of systems (and lack of system). A serious reader who goes beyond one or two books must gradually become used to the chief older variations as well as the the main modern systems.[3]

As suggested in the preceding section of this Introduction, there are three practical requirements in transliteration: *written reversibility*, that is, one should be able to reconstruct the original written form from the transliterated form; *oral recognizability*, that is, the reader's pronunciation should be well enough guided to allow oral recognition by someone who pronounces properly; and *resistance to accident*, that is, if diacritics are changed or lost, either by chance or for economy, confusion should remain minimal. To fill all three requirements, there must be a separate system from each language into each language. Arabic and Persian, for instance, not only pronounce the same letters very differently, but they are two different languages. Hence they require not just distinguishing transcriptions but separate transliterations.[4] Some scholars interested only in written reversibility have tried to use a single system for transliteration into all languages using Latin script.

[3] Detailed differences in transliteration continue to be multiplied. For instance, Cowan, in editing the translation of Hans Wehr's *Dictionary of Modern Written Arabic*, as late as 1961 introduced two new symbols. Variations are often not accompanied by a justification, and they may only increase the general problem. By retaining, for extraneous reasons, the old dj and k, the second edition of the *Encyclopaedia of Islam* lost an opportunity to provide a final settlement of transliteration of Arabic, at least, into English.

[4] Once there was an attempt to transliterate all Semitic alphabets by one system (Wellhausen); this included Arabic and by extension Persian, Turkish, etc. Then an attempt was made to transliterate uniformly all languages using the Arabic alphabet. In addition to the difficulty of maintaining some semblance of transcription for the other Islamicate languages, such as Persian, 'uniform transliteration' foundered on the fact that Urdu (Hindustani) was written in two alphabets (which were thus handled differently); and either the Islamicist's way of writing Urdu had to look too clumsy in comparison with the alternative, or his way of writing Arabic had to be so denatured as not to stand comparison with the transliterations for other Semitic languages. But there is an even more serious dimension when an alphabet-to-alphabet system instead of a language-to-language system is pressed. If Persian or Turkish is felt as a language in its own right, a 'uniform transliteration' point of view can become offensive, because not only pronunciation but certain syntactical practices of Persian, for example, are made to seem merely an 'exception' to the rules for Arabic. In a general work, such a misapprehension must be avoided. Uniform transliteration implies more concern with philology than with lay intelligibility. The philologian can easily learn to convert from the system of one language to that of another, while the layman needs assistance barely to pronounce.

The problem is, the same Latin-script letter can have a very different value in English, for example, from its value in French. Though scholars could work with some international system of transliteration, the lay reader would find it quite difficult, and it seems useful to have separate transliteration systems for the widely used languages, systems that incorporate as many elements of transcription as possible. Scholars can learn the French or German transliteration systems, say, in the same way they learn any other novelty in French or German. And the lay reader will be encouraged to continue his reading.

A careful writer will generally list the letters he uses for transliteration in the regular order of the Arabic (or Persian, etc.) alphabet or else refer to some other publications he follows where such a list is to be found. To correlate a term in one work with that in another, the reader will need to refer the letters back to the respective lists; from their position there he can tell whether they form the same term or a different one. The regular order is used in the following tables, with the preferable transliterations indicated and some alternatives added.

Transliteration from Arabic

English	*International*	*Encyclopaedia of Islam*	*Approximate 'Literary' Pronunciation*	*Alternatives Sometimes Used*
ʼ			glottal stop; as between the two words in 'me?! angry?'	often omitted
b			English b	
t			like English t	
th	ṯ	t̲h̲	English th in *thin*	t; ts
j	ǧ	dj	English j	g (in Egypt)
ḥ			pharyngeal h ('guttural')	h
kh	ḫ	k̲h̲	German and Scots ch, Spanish j (nearer h than k)	x; k̲
d			like English d	
dh	ḏ	d̲h̲	English th in *this*	d; ds
r			rolled (trilled) r	
z			English z	s
s			hissed s (in *this*)	ss
sh	š	s̲h̲	English sh	sch; ch
ṣ			velar s ('emphatic')	ss; s
ḍ			velar d ('emphatic')	dh; d
ṭ			velar t ('emphatic')	th; t
ẓ			velar z ('emphatic')	z
ʻ			glottal scrape; to Anglophones difficult to pronounce; sometimes omitted	

English	*Inter-national*	*Encyclopaedia of Islam*	*Approximate 'Literary' Pronunciation*	*Alternatives Sometimes Used*
gh	ġ	<u>gh</u>	voiced equivalent of kh above	g
f			English f	ph
q		ḳ	uvular k ('guttural')	c; k
k			English k	
l			English l (in *live*)	
m			English m	
n			English n	
h			English h	
w			English w	
y			English y (as consonant)	
a			short a as in *cat* or *ask* (according to position)	e
i			short i as in *bit*	e
u			short u as in *full*	o
â			long a as in *father*; sometimes as in *fat* (but held long)	au, o
î			long i as in *machine* (but held long)	ee
û			long u as in *rule* (but held long)	oo, ou
aw	au		English ow in *how*	ow, ou
ay	ai		English ai in *aisle* (or in *ail*)	ey, ei

The transliteration in the table marked 'English' is that usually used in English-language scholarly publications.[5] In this system some digraphs are

[5] The 'English' system is close to that of the *Encyclopaedia of Islam* except that it uses j as simpler than dj, and q rather than ḳ because the latter is more expensive and is confused with k if the dot happens to be lost. The system would have been better if instead of dots it had used the European accent marks available in every printer's fount and on every academic typewriter. When such a replacement is made little confusion results; and in fact, in some contexts cedillas are regularly substituted for the dots. The system would also have been better if for ' something else had been used. But in this work, we follow usual practice, for to introduce a new system without expectation of getting it generally adopted is merely to add to confusion. In the vowels, either a macron or a circumflex has been used to indicate length. The circumflex is preferable as available in ordinary founts and academic typewriters. Scholars might well rethink the problem of diacritics and their general availability, for we are entering a period of widely disseminated, inexpensively reproduced works, especially works produced directly from typescript by offset duplication. (Thus also the old feeling that a given diacritic should have only a given value universally, which led to using macrons invariably for length and dots for all velar consonants including q, must yield before the typewriter and the widening phonetic horizons of our time.) The long vowels might have been better rendered aa, iy, uw, to avoid confusion on the loss of diacritics, to

used (e.g., th or sh). In some publications such digraphs are joined by a bar placed below the pair; when the bar is not used, the rare cases where the two signs do not form a digraph are indicated by separating them, for instance, with an apostrophe.[6] (Thus t'h would indicate the pronunciation of *at home*.) The most important deviation from these letters still found in English scholarly works reflects the dislike of digraphs by some purists, who replace them with the letters listed as 'international' because they are widely used in Europe. The *Encyclopaedia of Islam*, edited in more than one language, has perpetuated a further complication for the two 'English' choices of j and q. In older works and in journalistic writing the variations in transliteration are numerous and often based on French phonetic patterns even though appearing in English language works. The scholarly systems of other Western languages tend to be similar to the English except for characteristic variations in the case of digraphs; e.g., English sh is French ch or German sch; English j is French dj or German dsch.

In addition to the regular consonants, which in the Arabic script appear uniformly, and the vowels, several other peculiarities of Arabic spelling must be rendered. Here variations arise from the nature of Arabic writing. The usual Arabic form as it is written gives less than is needed for sure identification of a term; for instance it leaves out most 'short' vowels which all transliteration systems supply. Moreover, transliteration with too great attention to transcription may confuse the non-specialist reader as to actual word elements. Any system must admittedly be a compromise, but it seems better to emphasize the element of reversibility.

The most important points of scholarly compromise are two. One Arabic consonant is not included in the order of the Arabic alphabet, a certain h marked like a t, sometimes pronounced h and sometimes t. It occurs only after an a at the end of a word. In this work it is rendered h after short a, t after long â; by many it is omitted at least after short a or rendered by t before the article of a following word.[7] Thus for our *Kûfah*, some write *Kûfa*. The

stress the long pronunciation, and to bring out root letters in the latter two cases; a nuance of Arabic spelling which distinguishes between û and a hypothetically different yw is irrelevant to the needs of transliteration. But I follow usual practice.

[6] Some philologians find a digraph unsound pedagogically. Despite added expense and the diminished oral recognizability and resistance to accident, they prefer to multiply diacritics. If persuaded to use digraphs at all, some will use a ligature to make the digraph artificially a single unit. But typing a ligature when one is also underlining for italics presents difficulties; moreover, the apostrophe should still be used when the letters do not form a digraph (such as s'h), to warn the interested but unpracticed lay reader that normal English pronunciation does not hold.

[7] In this case, consistent clarity would call for a preceding diacritically marked vowel, preferably a specially marked a, but such a letter has not been adopted. The use of -ah is better than plain -a because it avoids confusion with -â or -à when the diacritics are dropped (for instance, distinguishing Ḥîrah from Ḥirâ'), a confusion far more likely than that with an -ah where the h is radical. It also avoids confusion with the -a of grammatical endings when a whole phrase is transliterated and the endings included. The use of -ât is a concession to widespread pronunciation habits, and overlaps no more than would -âh.

second compromise is that the Arabic article *al-* is in certain cases 'assimilated' to the noun that follows, the l being pronounced like the initial letter of the noun.[8] Writers attempting to preserve a closer transcription render the article *ar-* or *as-* before r or s, etc., so as to assure a more exact pronunciation; but many writers, and this work follows such a system, render the article with an l, however it is pronounced, because in this case mispronunciation will cause little confusion and the l identifies the article for the layman (and also answers to the Arabic script form the librarian must learn to recognize). Thus I write al-Shâfi'î, not ash-Shâfi'î, which is yet how it is pronounced.

Minor points that call for notice are the following. Some final vowels written long in Arabic but pronounced short are here transliterated as long, but some writers make them short. In the case of a final -a written with a -y in Arabic, I distinguish it as -à, while some write it as an ordinary long -â. Consistently with the ordinary rules for vowels and consonants, I write certain forms -iyy- and -uww-; but some make these -îy-, -ûw-. An exception is usually made for the ending which by normal rules would be -iyy; here I write -î, to conform with Persian, Turkish, and Urdu, as well as the Arabic vernaculars, in all which the same ending occurs; thus I write al-Bukhârî, not al-Bukhâriyy. But a few writers make it simply -i; others restore partial consistency with -iy. Hamzah (') at the start of a word is always omitted. Grammatical endings omitted in pausa are always dropped.

Transliteration from Persian, Turkish, and Urdu

In this work I transliterate technical terms throughout in a single form, usually the Arabic, but the Persian or Turkish when the original form is Persian or Turkish. Names of persons and countries will naturally vary from language to language.[9] But in other writers' works even technical terms, originally Arabic, will often be met with in a Persian form or in still other forms, including the modern romanized Turkish or an adaptation of it. For instance, in such works *ḥadîth* may appear as *ḥadîs*. Accordingly, the reader should consider the following notes when reading such works, and he may find they apply to the Arabic words he encounters as well as to the other languages.

For the other Islamicate languages transliteration poses certain special problems. It has been less well systematized by scholars, and this is particularly true for Persian, from which (and not directly from Arabic) the Turkish and Urdu and several other languages derived their alphabets.

[8] The 'assimilating' letters are d, ḍ, dh, l, n, r, s, ṣ, sh, t, ṭ, th, z, ẓ.

[9] As in European languages Maria, Marie, and Mary represent the same name in different guises, so Ḥusayn, Ḥoseyn, Hüseyin represent a single name in Arabic, Persian, and Turkish. As between Arabic and Persian, at least, the equivalence is easy to trace by comparing the equivalent letters in transliteration; but for most purposes the etymology of a name is unimportant to the layman.

Islamicists who are better Arabists than Persianists often treat Persian words exactly as if they were Arabic, only adding four letters: p, ch, zh, g. (Zh is pronounced like s in pleasure; for ch, pronounced as in church, č may be substituted by those who avoid digraphs in Arabic; and for zh, ž.) Since Persian is full of words and names derived from Arabic, and it is often difficult to decide whether a given name belongs in fact to an Arabic or a Persian context, such a policy has the advantage of making a decision unnecessary, and from the point of view of alphabetic reversibility (ignoring transcription) seems to work well enough.

But Persian is a separate language. Its alphabet has its own rules and is better rendered by a distinctive system, though preferably differing from that for Arabic as little as possible. Unfortunately, for transliterating Persian, especially with a view to at least partial transcription, no one system has been generally accepted. The following list gives the preferable systems and some alternatives. (Standard forms for Arabic are shown in parentheses.)

(th) (dh) (ḍ) (ṭ) (ẓ) (w)
’ b p t s̤ j ch ḥ kh d ẕ r z zh s sh ṣ ẓ ṯ z̤ ‘ gh f q k g l m n v h y
s̄ z̄ z ṭ ẓ
(E.I.:) dj č [ż, ẕ] (E.I.:) ḳ
a i u â î û aw ay ah -i
e o i u ow ey eh -e, -ye
ou, au ei, ai e, a

The first row represents the most widely used system, apart from the Arabizing system mentioned above. It has the awkward disadvantage (in addition to diacritics inconvenient on the typewriter, especially when underlining) of using ẓ for a character different from the Arabic character ẓ is used for. A newer system, whose points of difference are shown on the second line, restores ṭ and ẓ to the same use as for Arabic and eliminates the conflict over ẓ. (Bracketed forms are alternatives to z.)[10]

In the newer system, all diacritics (save that for the long â vowel) represent non-phonetic distinctions—that is, distinctions in Persian spelling that make no difference in the Persian pronunciation. Hence it fits in with one tendency in transliterating from Persian which ignores all non-phonetic distinctions in Persian pronunciation and so, being essentially a sort of transcription, could almost avoid diacritics altogether. The first line of vowels indicates transliteration practice close to Arabic; the second line indicates trans-

[10] This system, adopted by the Library of Congress, seems to carry most authority at the moment. The Library of Congress has decided to use a bar under the ẕ instead of the ż suggested by its expert and used elsewhere (e.g., by the editors of the Turkish version of the *Encyclopaedia of Islam*). The ż is wanting in most printing founts and is apt to be blurred; but the ẕ is in conflict with usage in the older system as well as being awkward when a word is underlined to italicize. If a single dot over the ż be deemed inconvenient on the typewriter, it may be easily replaced by an apostrophe or by diaeresis, as the macron may be replaced by circumflex and the dot under by cedilla. All these should be available on an academic typewriter.

literation suggesting a closer transcription. On the third line, are shown some further variants that are sometimes used.

In this work, I follow the newer system (s̄, z̄, etc.) in rendering consonants, choosing ż as clearer than z. But because the vowels of the newer system have appeared so rarely in scholarly work, and would be badly out of place in Indo-Persian anyway, I have retained the vowel system that is closer to the Arabic (using also ê, ô in Indo-Persian), except for the Persian linking vowel, rendered -e, -ye. The net result is that for Persian words I spell Arabic-derived names as if in Arabic except for four consonants (w:v; th:s̄; dh:z̄; d:ż). Compounds from Arabic are run together (and the article assimilated) rather than separated with hyphens.[11]

All Persian consonants are pronounced nearly as in English, ignoring the diacritics (which make no difference in Persian pronunciation), except that kh and gh are as in Arabic, and q is often like gh (it is so transliterated by some). S is always hissed, g is always hard as in *go,* zh is like z in *azure,* w after kh is silent. Vowels are pronounced as in Arabic, except that long â tends toward our a in *all*; short i is rather like e in *bed*; aw is au in *bureau*. Final -ah has the value of e in *bed*, with h silent. In certain words û was formerly ô, and î, ê; those words are still so pronounced in India and are so rendered for Indo-Persian.

Specifically Turkish and especially Urdu names are relatively infrequent in this work. Modern republican Turkish is naturally to be rendered according to the modern Turkish Latin alphabet, used since 1928 in the Turkish Republic (the Turks of the Soviet Union have used other forms of the Latin and Cyrillic alphabets). There most consonants are pronounced approximately as in English except that c is our j; ç is our ch; ğ is standardly a barely-sounded approximation to Arabic gh; j is the French j (z in *azure*); ş is our sh. (S of course is hissed, g is hard.) The vowels are a, e, i, o, u, as in Italian, with variations; ö, ü, as in German (French eu and u); and i without a dot (sometimes marked with a circle or a half-circle)—a slightly stifled vowel found also in Russian.

But the republican alphabet cannot readily be extended to the other Turkic languages or even to Ottoman Turkish, partly because its characters conflict with English values and with the system used for Persian and Arabic, and so would be confusing outside a clearly restricted context.

For the Ottoman Turkish, which used the Arabo-Persian alphabet, our

[11] Modern Iranians consistently prefer the e and o, which make the diacritic on î and û unnecessary, though perhaps useful where the reader does not know if a name is Arabic or Persian. But the vowel u is phonetically more accurate in most cases than o, as is sometimes i than e. Both i and u are usual in scholarly work dealing with premodern periods and occur frequently toward the beginning of words (hence determining alphabetic position in indexes). It seems justifiable to suggest that e (and ey) and o (and ow) be substituted for i and u only when diacritics are to be dropped altogether—a seemingly no longer justifiable practice. As to compounds, they are misleading to untutored readers if printed separately, and the value of indicating their origin disappears in a second language.

system for Persian will do as a base for the consonants, with the addition of a form of g pronounced n (originally ng), rendered in this work ñ; and replacing q with ḳ, which eliminates a large class of deviations from modern Latin and Cyrillic norms. However, pronunciation varied greatly from place to place and from time to time; in some words g was pronounced y, ż and ṭ were pronounced d, etc.; final plosives were usually unvoiced. Spelling varied also. In some of these cases, it is conventional to follow the Istanbul pronunciation rather than the spelling. Often, but not always, the distinction between ḳ and k, ṣ and s, ṭ and t, is shown in transliteration by the vowel context; in such cases, the diacritic may be dropped. The vowels are best shown by those of the republican Latin alphabet; Arabic aw becomes ev, ay becomes ey. The three Perso-Arabic long vowels, however, are still distinguished in quality (not quantity) and can usefully be so marked, but usually need not be. (The editors of the Turkish version of the *Encyclopaedia of Islam* have devised the following system for representing the Ottoman Turkish: ʼ b p t s̠ c ç ḥ ḫ d z̠ r z j s ş ṣ ż ṭ ẓ ʻ ğ f ḳ k g ñ l m n v h y.)

Other Turkic languages of Persian script are in this work usually assimilated to Ottoman Turkish or to Persian as seems appropriate, partly because it is often hard to reconstruct the actual pronunciation of a name in its own form of Turkish.

Transliteration from Urdu (an Islamicate language of India) cannot be considered without reference to the received system for Hindi in the Sanskrit alphabet, for the two are substantially a single language. The older Persian transliteration (in which Arabic ḍ became ẓ) was developed with the needs of Urdu in mind and is still the prevailing system for Urdu if there is one. For Urdu transliteration requires, in addition to the characters for the Persian letters, vowels in ê and ô and five consonants: four 'retroflex' consonants, written (as for Hindi) ṭ, ḍ, ṛ (all different from anything in Arabic), and a sign for vowel nasalization, ṅ (or n̲ or tilda over the vowel). Many consonants in Urdu appear in an aspirated form, that is, accompanied by an h that represents a puff of breath after the stop and not the formation of a fricative. Thus th must be read as a strong t, and so for dh, ṭh, ḍh, ph, bh, kh, gh, chh, jh, ṛh. Hence kh and gh, as digraphs, can within the Indic context come to stand for two different consonants each: the fricative kh and gh as in Persian and Arabic, and the aspirated kh and gh. (Duplication for th and dh does not occur in that context.) The digraphs can be joined by a bar beneath them when they form a fricative, and not when they form an aspirate. (For Hindi, English ch is often written plain c, and aspirated ch, sometimes transliterated chh, is written ch.)

For the purposes of this work, it seems simpler to transliterate Urdu, when necessary, by the same system as used for Persian, only adding the retroflex t́, d́, ŕ (as in the *Encyclopaedia of Islam*), ṇ (and nasal ṅ). (The fricative k̲h̲ and g̲h̲ may be so underlined; but this merely distinguishes the one digraph from the other, for aspirate kh and gh are equally digraphs and must not be confused with what could be marked k'h, g'h discussed in the section on Arabic transliteration.) Except for retroflexes, aspirates, and nasalization, pronunciation of consonants is much as in Persian (commonest English sound, with diacritics ignored). Vowels are as in Arabic except: a like u in *cut*, ay like a in *bad*, aw as in *awe*, ê as in *they*, ô as in *over*.

As to other languages, there is little occasion to transliterate from them in this work and when occasion arises it will be done, so far as possible, on one of the following bases. Sometimes there is an agreed scholarly convention which can be followed. When there is a standard modern romanized form, that will do even for earlier times; or the transliteration may follow a Cyrillic script. Sometimes names will be assimilated to one of the above four languages, when they appear in such a context. The transliteration of the four languages into English in this work is therefore (for the reasons given in text and notes):

Arabic:	ʼ	b		t		th	j		ḥ	kh	d		dh	r		z		s	sh	ṣ	ḍ	ṭ	ẓ	ʻ	gh	f	q	k			l	m	n		w	h	y
Persian:	ʼ	b	p	t		s̄	j	ch	ḥ	kh	d		z̄	r		z	zh	s	sh	ṣ	ż	ṭ	ẓ	ʻ	gh	f	q	k	g		l	m	n		v	h	y
Urdu:	ʼ	b	p	t	t́	s̄	j	ch	ḥ	k̲h̲	d	d́	z̄	r	ŕ	z	zh	s	sh	ṣ	ż	ṭ	ẓ	ʻ	g̲h̲	f	q	k	g		l	m	n	ṅ	v	h	y
Ottoman Turkish:	ʼ	b	p	t		s̄	j	ch	ḥ	kh	d		z̄	r		z	zh	s	sh	ṣ	ż	ṭ	ẓ	ʻ	gh	f	ḳ	k	g	ñ	l	m	n		v	h	y

Arabic:	a	i	u	â		î		û	aw	ay	-ah	
Persian:	a	i	u	â		î		û	aw	ay	-ah	-e, -ye
Urdu:	a	i	u	â	ê	î	ô	û	aw	ay	-ah	
Ottoman Turkish:	(a e i o u ö ü ı â î û)											

By such systems, transliteration for all the languages is fully reversible (except some details of Turkish); does not conflict with that for Arabic (except in the Urdu aspirates th, dh); allows for a fair degree of oral recognizability; offers a minimum of difficulty in being adapted to typewriters and printers' founts; and suffers minimal loss of recognizability if diacritics are dropped. The systems used in this work deviate from the second edition of the *Encyclopaedia of Islam* as follows:

in all languages: -ah for -a, q for ḳ (except Turkish), j for d̲j̲; no digraph bars (unless in Urdu);
in Persian, Urdu, Turkish: s̄ for t̲h̲, z̄ for d̲h̲, *ż* for ḍ, v for w, ch for č, -e(-ye) for -i, and assimilation of article and compounds (*-uddîn* etc.);
in Indo-Persian and Urdu also: ê, ô;
in Turkish from Arabic also: the Turkish vowels.

MUSLIM PERSONAL NAMES

Many of the personal names to be met with in Islamicate materials will seem long and forbidding to the beginner and hard to sort out. This is natural in the case of an alien civilization; the only complete remedy for the difficulty is long familiarity. Nevertheless, the reader can take note of certain classes of personal names which he can learn to identify. If he can recognize what is similar in these names, he can then more easily concentrate on their distinguishing features when he meets them in his reading, and so keep them apart.

Muslim personal names have been mostly of Arabic, Persian, or Turkish origin, even in countries with quite different languages; the Arabic element is especially strong. Other languages are of course locally represented, as in Malaysia or Africa. The basic approach to personal naming has been by and large the same everywhere. Until modern times very few people in Muslim countries had 'family' names. The commonest way of naming was threefold: first, a 'given' name, received at birth; then the given name of the father; and finally, if necessary, one or more descriptive names, such as one indicating the man's city of origin or his occupation or perhaps his ancestry, his family. In addition, a man of position commonly had one or more honorific names, often bestowed by a ruler. In several times and places there have been, to all intents and purposes, two given names: a specifically Muslim name, usually of Arabic derivation, alongside one of local derivation; an ordinary name alongside one honorific in form; or, among Arabs, a *kunyah* (explained below) alongside an ordinary name. Usually only one or the other of these was much used.

No one of these various names has necessarily been the 'filing name'—the one by which one would look up the man in a card catalogue or in a telephone directory. What part of the total appellation is to be used for such quick reference has been a matter of convenience—sometimes whichever of a man's names was the least common among his fellows. For instance, suppose a man's given name is Aḥmad, his father's name is 'Alî, and he is known as Zinjânî because he comes from Zinjân. There are dozens of Aḥmads in any Muslim city, and dozens of 'Alis; but very few men from the small place of Zinjân—so the least ambiguous way to refer to the man (except as regards other men from the same place) is *Zinjânî*. Often there have been two or more such names by which a man was known, perhaps in different circles. Accordingly, in referring to a man it is best for the beginner to follow the lead of whatever author he is depending on, and in cases of doubt to use a combination of as many names as necessary.

There are several elements, found especially in names of Arabic origin, which form an inseparable part of certain sorts of names, and which the student should learn to recognize. *Al-* is simply the definite article, 'the', and occurs with a great many names. Before certain consonants the *l* is assimilated to the consonant, being pronounced—and in some transliterations written—r, s, d, etc. (Cf. the section on Transliteration.) In some cases the *al-* can be either present or absent, indifferently. It is usually omitted in indexing. *Abû* originally meant 'father of', but has come to be, in effect, merely an element in a man's name: any given name can be added to it, the combination forming a single new name. Among the ancient Arabs this was used as a sort of epithet or honorific, the *kunyah,* in addition to the more personal name, e.g., Abû-Bakr. (*Abû-* in Persian and Turkish sometimes becomes *Bû-* or *Bâ-*.) *Umm-* has the place in women's names of *Abû* in men's, e.g., Umm-Kulthûm.

The letter b is short for *ibn,* meaning 'son of' (or for *bint,* 'daughter of') which is often used in Arabic between one's given name and the father's name—and further between the father's and grandfather's names, and the grandfather's and great-grandfather's, and so on up the line, which is sometimes traced very far in giving a man's full appellation. 'Ibn-N . . .' sometimes becomes simply a family name. In languages other than Arabic, and in many modern Arabic lands, the *ibn* is usually not used. On the other hand, in Persian its place may be taken by the suffix *-zâdah*; in Turkish by the suffix *oğlu,* which commonly form family names. Sometimes these are interchanged; thus Ibn-Taqî = Taqî-zadeh.

N.B.: Such elements as *Ibn-* or *Abû-*, as well as certain other prefixed (or suffixed) words like *'Abd-*, *cannot be dropped* from a name without basically changing it. In this work they will be hyphenated.[12]

Classes of names to be spotted and kept distinct (this is in no sense an exhaustive list of types of names—it includes only easily recognizable types):

I. Names of prophets as given names:

Most of the Biblical heroes are recognized as prophets by the Muslims, and their names, in Arabic form (sometimes further modified in other languages), are commonly used. (Christians and Jews in Islamicate lands have used special variants of some of these names.) Examples are: Ibrâhîm = Abraham; Ismâ'îl = Ishmael; Isḥâq = Isaac; Ya'qûb = Jacob; Yûsuf = Joseph; Mûsà = Moses; Hârûn = Aaron; Dâ'ûd = David; Sulaymân = Solomon; Yaḥyà = John; Maryam = Mary; 'Îsà = Jesus. In addition, there are several prophets not mentioned in the Bible, notably Muḥammad himself, whose name is very commonly used.

II. Names from favoured Arabic roots: notably

(*a*) in ḤMD, three consonants which enter the formation of words having in common some notion of 'praise', thus Muḥammad, Aḥmad, Maḥmûd, Ḥamîd, etc.;

[12] The use of the hyphen in compound proper names is called for because of the Anglo-Saxon habit of isolating the last element in any personal appellation as a primary, 'last name'. (The use of the hyphen can help to eliminate a remarkably prolific source of confusion in beginners.) Subordinate and inseparable elements in names include: *Ibn-, Bint-, Umm-, Abû-, Nûr-, Gholâm-, Mamlûk-, 'Abd-, Dhû-, Sibṭ-*; and of suffixed words: *-qoli, -bandeh, -bakhsh, -dâd, -zâdeh, -oğlu.* Many other compounds are similarly used as names. In some cases, the subordinate part of the name can be dropped almost at will or else may be used alone; but the hyphen is appropriate wherever the last element in the name cannot properly be used by itself; the reader should not overlook it.

(*b*) in ḤSN, forming words having in common some notion of 'good', thus Muḥsin, Ḥasan, Ḥusayn, Ḥassân, etc.;
(*c*) in S'D, forming words having in common some notion of 'happiness', thus Sa'd, Sa'îd, Mas'ûd, etc.;
(*d*) in ZYD, forming words having in common some notion of 'growth', thus Zayd, Yazîd (Yaziyd), etc.;
(*e*) in 'MR, forming words having in common some notion of 'life', thus 'Amr, 'Umar, etc.

III. Names in *'Abd*:

The word *'abd* means 'slave of', and is prefixed to epithets of God, to form single, indivisible given names. Thus, 'Abd-al-Qâdir, 'Slave of the Almighty'. (Hence such names cannot be split up, as sometimes happens in the press.) Other common names of this class are 'Abd-al-Rahmân (or Abdurrahman, in another spelling), and the common 'Abd-Allâh (more usually, 'Abdullâh).

Other words meaning 'slave' are used in the same way: thus the prefixes *Mamlûk-* and *Gholâm-* and the suffixes *-bandeh* and *-qoli*. Often these are attached to the name of a prophet or an imâm rather than of God.

IV. Names in *-Allâh*:

Analogous to the above class of names are those ending in *-Allâh* (or sometimes other divine names) with various first elements (or, sometimes, suffixes); thus, Ḥamd-Allâh, 'Praise-God'. Sometimes similar compound names are formed with a prophetic name; thus, Nûr-Muḥammad, 'Light of Muḥammad'.

V. Names in *-al-dîn, -al-dawlah, -al-mulk*:

These were originally titles but have often become simply given names. For example, *-al-din* (or *-eddin*) means 'of the religion': thus, Quṭb-al-dîn, 'Pole of the religion'; *-al-dawlah* (or *-eddaula*) means 'of the dynasty': thus, Mu'izz-al-dawlah, 'Strengthener of the dynasty'; *-al-mulk* means 'of the kingdom': thus, Niẓâm-al-mulk, 'good order of the kingdom'. N.B.: These three post-fixed elements *sometimes can be dropped* without deforming the name beyond recognition.

VI. Names in *Mu-*:

A majority of Arabic participles start with M, and especially with Mu; and a great many names, originally often honorifics, are in participle form. This is true of the reign names of most of the 'Abbâsid caliphs: Manṣûr, Ma'mûn, Mu'taṣim, Mutawakkil, Mu'taḍid, Mustanṣir. Often these start with *Mut-* or *Must-*, which form participles in whole sets of verbs. It is the letters following the initial *mu-*, that must be taken note of in order to keep names of this class apart.

VII. Names in *-î*:

This is the common termination, taken over into several Islamicate languages, indicating origin or relationship. A person from the town Shîrâz is *Shîrâzî*; a person from India (Hind) is *Hindî*; a protégé of a man called Sa'd is *Sa'dî*; a descendant of 'Uthmân is *'Uthmânî*; a member of the tribe of Kindah is *al-Kindî*. (The Turkish equivalent ending is -li or lî, -lu, -lü.)

Constantly repeated, but not easy to classify by sight, are various other personal names of Arabic origin (masculine: 'Alî, Ja'far, Ḥabîb, Ḥamzah, Ṣâliḥ; feminine: Fâṭimah, Zaynab, etc.), of Persian origin (Fîrûz, Bahrâm, etc.), of Turkish origin (Arslân, Timur, etc.), and of still other origins.

Sometimes various titles are used as parts of purely personal names—for instance Malikshâh, in which *malik* is Arabic and *shâh* Persian for 'king'. More common is the use of titles or titular elements to replace a personal name, or used inseparably with it. Among such titles are *mîr* (*amîr*), *beg, khân, mîrzâ, shaykh, shâh, âghâ,* (*âqâ*), etc. Some titles have a special significance: *shâh* as prefix often means 'saint', as suffix, 'king'; *mîrzâ* as suffix means 'prince', as prefix, 'sir'; *sayyid* or *sharîf* is used for a descendant of Muḥammad; *ḥâjj*, or *ḥâjjî*, for one who has made a pilgrimage, not necessarily to Mecca.

In various languages, the same name can sometimes be scarcely identifiable: thus Muḥammad becomes Meḥmed (or Mehmet) in Turkish, Maḥmadu in West Africa. In the Russian empire, Muslims themselves have commonly replaced *-î, -oghlu, -zâdeh* by *-ev* or *ov*; or simply added the latter (Russian) endings to names as they stand. Muslims in India have often Anglicized their names in ways answering to vague norms of English pronunciation; thus Syed for Sayyid, Saeed for Sa'îd; more generally, ay = y, î = ee, û = oo, and short a becomes u. In French colonies, Muslims Gallicized their names: s = ss, û = ou, g = gu, etc.

THE ISLAMICATE CALENDARS

An era is a system of numbering years from a given base year—thus the year 1 of the common Christian era is the year in which Christ was supposedly born. The year 1 of the Islamic era is that of the *Hijrah* (H.), in which Muḥammad moved from Mecca to Medina and effectively established the Muslim community. That year corresponds to the last part of 622 and the first part of 623 of the Christian, or Common, era (CE).

In contrast to the case with most eras, the 'years' of the Islamic era are not true solar years—complete rounds of the seasons—but are lunar 'years' of twelve 'true months', twelve periods from new moon to new moon. Since a true month has only 29 or 30 days, twelve such months fall short of a solar year by about eleven days. Most lunar calendars that have used true months have kept themselves in line with the solar year by adding an extra month every three years or so. This was forbidden in the Qur'ân, and in consequence a date in the Islamic 'year' has no fixed relation to the seasons; a given festival, for instance, will pass from summer to spring to winter and autumn and back to summer again three times within a long lifetime. Accordingly the Islamic calendar, while it has been used for ritual and historical purposes, has almost always and everywhere been accompanied by a different, a 'secular' calendar, one of solar years, which could be used for fiscal and other practical purposes. These secular Islamicate calendars have been numerous but have never had much prestige, and few of them have been in use long enough, or reckoned systematically enough, to serve for historical purposes. Except in recent times, when the secular calendar used has usually been the Gregorian or modern international calendar, no such auxiliary solar calendar has seriously rivalled the Islamic lunar calendar in general acceptance.

Because the Islamic era does not reckon by solar years even approximately, it is not possible, as it is in the case of other eras, simply to add to the Islamic date the difference in years between the two starting points (622), in order to get the date in the Christian era. If one does not have a conversion table, there is a quick method of finding the date to within a couple of years. Because of the shortness of Islamic 'years', an Islamic century is accomplished in three years less than a century of solar years; hence the Islamic dates are always gaining on the Christian at the rate of three in a hundred years. At year 1 of the *Hijrah* there was a difference of six centuries plus 21 years—Christian year 622. At year 100 there was a difference of six centuries plus 18 years (100 + 618 = Christian year 718); at year 200, of six centuries plus only 15 years (815 CE). By the year 700 the difference is just six centuries—Christian year 1300. After that, it is a difference of six centuries *minus* so many years. Accordingly, the approximate date in the Christian era can be found by adding to the Islamic date 600 years plus three years for every century before 700 (H.), or minus three years for every century after 700 (H.).

For the arithmetically inclined, a somewhat more exact date can be gained with the formula $G = H - \frac{H}{33} + 622$ (G = Gregorian date, H = *Hijrah* date).[13] The Islamic date of a Gregorian year can be found with $H = G - 622 + \frac{G - 622}{32}$. It must be remembered that such formulae give only the year during which the corresponding year began—the greater part of the latter year may have coincided with a year succeeding the one given.

The months of the Islamic year traditionally have been determined by actual observation of the new moon. Hence the same month had different numbers of days in different years and even in the same year in different

[13] Somewhat easier to use might be the formula stated in the following terms: $G = H - .031\,H + 622$.

places; this makes exact dating precarious unless the week-day is also known (for the Islamic calendar included the seven day week as well as the month). Under some régimes mathematical means, such as alternating the months thirty, twenty-nine, thirty, and adding 'leap years' by various systems, were used to make the calendar more predictable. The months are in order: Muḥarram, Ṣafar, Rabî' I, Rabî' II, Jumâdà I, Jumâdà II, Rajab, Sha'bân, Ramaḍân, Shawwâl, Dhû-l-Qa'dah, Dhû-l-Ḥijjah.

Since the month began with the sighting of the new moon in the evening, the day was made to begin at sunset.

The most common month names of the solar Islamicate calendars are (with appropriate Gregorian equivalents)

for Arabic:

Nîsân (April), *Ayyâr* (May), *Ḥazîrân* (June), *Tamûz* (July), *Âb* (August), *Aylûl* (September), *Tishrîn al-awwal* (October), *Tishrîn al-thânî* (November), *Kânûn al-awwal* (December), *Kânûn al-thânî* (January), *Shubâṭ* (February), *Adhâr* (March);

for Persian:

Farvardîn (March–April), *Urdî-bihisht* (April–May), *Khurdâd* (May–June), *Tîr* (June–July), *Murdâd* (July–August), *Shahrîvar* or *Shahrîr* (Aug.–Sept.), *Mihr* (Sept.–Oct.), *Âbân* (Oct.–Nov.), *Âẕar* (Nov.–Dec.), *Day* (Dec.–Jan.), *Bahman* (Jan.–Feb.), *Isfand* (Feb.–March).

HISTORICAL METHOD IN CIVILIZATION STUDIES

Historical humanism

Unless a scholar is content to accept his categories (and hence the questions he can ask and hence the answers he can arrive at) as given by the accidents of current predispositions, he cannot escape the obligation of justifying his selection of units for study, which means justifying his point of view. Such a justification, in turn, must imply an explicit stand on his role as a scholar. If there were unanimity in these matters, they might be left tacit—at least, if the given scholar were in accord with the rest. Fortunately, several quite different viewpoints guide historical studies generally, and Islamic studies in particular, in our present world.

Historical studies have been called 'idiographic' as describing dated and placed particulars, as do many phases of geology or astronomy, in contrast to 'nomothetic' studies such as physics and chemistry, which are supposed to lay down rules to hold regardless of date. This distinction has its usefulness so long as one bears in mind certain considerations sometimes forgotten. Firstly, whether the objects of the questions are dated or dateless, the questions themselves (as befits a cumulative public discipline) ought to be, in some degree, of timeless significance to human beings: sometimes perhaps leading to manipulative power, but always leading to better understanding of things that matter to us humanly.[14] Moreover, any discipline, ideally, should not be defined exactly by the category of the objects it studies nor even by the methods it uses, and still less by the form of its results—though empirically these may be useful indices, especially in interpreting the various academically recognized fields of inquiry which have grown up largely by historical accident. Ideally, a discipline needs to be set off just to the degree that there is a body of interdependent questions that can be discussed in relative autonomy from other bodies of questions, at least according to some one perspective. In a discipline so set off, it cannot necessarily be decided in advance just what forms of questions will prove to be required or what sorts of methods will prove necessary to answer them effectively. From this point of view, if there is a field of historical studies (as I believe) and not merely a group of several fields, it can be nothing less than the whole body of questions about human cultural development, about human culture in its continuity over time; and here we cannot rule out a potential need to develop relatively dateless generalizations, for instance about what may be possible in cultural change, such generalizations are not simply derivable from any other discipline as such, yet they are necessary for studying what is timelessly important about the dated and placed events of human culture.

These considerations being understood, then it can be said that historical studies of human culture are preponderantly 'idiographic' in the sense that even their broader generalizations are usually not dateless, in contrast to certain kinds of nature study, and perhaps in contrast also to certain kinds of social studies of human culture, designed to refine analysis of any given society at any given time. Moreover, in any case, historians' questions are concerned ultimately with the dated and placed, and when (as they must) they ask questions that are undatable within the historical context, it is for the sake of elucidating particulars which *are* dated and placed, however broad in scope, and not vice versa. The dated and placed events are not mere examples, not mere raw material for dateless generalizations.

But I am concerned here with a further distinction. Within the body of questions about culture in its continuity over time, even when the focus of interest is admittedly on the dated and placed as such, one can still distinguish historical viewpoints further in terms of what sort of date-bound questions are regarded as primary, the answer to which is the goal of the inquiry; and what sort are regarded as subordinate, yielding information which will help in answering the primary questions. On this basis we may

[14] Increased predictability through the 'lessons' of history, and hence increased power of manipulation, may sometimes supervene through historical study; but it is surely not its true purpose. On the other hand, prediction as a *means of verification* sometimes plays an essential role in historical inquiry. This is not, of course, prediction of 'the future'—that is not the proper purpose of any scholarly or scientific discipline—but prediction of future evidence, which may come in the form of laboratory experiments, of field surveys, or (in the case of history) of newly found documents.

distinguish two sorts of historian, 'typicalizers' and 'exceptionalizers'. In practice, the distinction is one of emphasis: the 'exceptionalizer' is concerned with all that concerns the 'typicalizer', or he ought to be; and despite his principles, the 'typicalizer' generally finds himself involved in points he might feel should concern the 'exceptionalizer' alone. Nonetheless, the two viewpoints can issue in the use of differing units and categories in defining the field of study. I believe that in pre-Modern civilization studies, at any rate, the more inclusive view that I am labelling 'exceptionalizing' cannot be left out of account if the humanly most significant questions are to be got at. It is on this principle that I have constructed this work.

Some historians, relatively 'typicalizing' in viewpoint, intend primarily to articulate intelligibly their chosen portion of the total cultural environment as it impinges by way of interacting events on the present human inquirer. They intend to present that environment as it is structured in space and time (asking, in effect, how things came to be as they are now) much as an astronomer studies the particular structure, in space and time, of the solar system. Some may even hope that their work may ultimately serve chiefly to elucidate dateless regularities of culture change, not tied to any dating or placing (at least within the particular span of time and place which human culture as a whole presupposes). Such historians, if fully consistent, must be concerned first with the typical, and then with the exceptional only as it serves to make clear (or perhaps account for) what is or has been typical. If they study a state, or a novel, or a sect, they will study it primarily as typifying, or at least causing, general political or aesthetic or religious patterns—at least the patterns of the time, and perhaps preferably those of all time.

On the other hand, from what may be called a more humanistic viewpoint, the reason for studying the typical is rather that thereby we may be better able to appreciate the exceptional, seeing more fully in just what way it is exceptional. We need to know works of artists or acts of statesmanship which are typical of a period just so that we may the better place the excellent, the outstanding.[15] We study Islamdom as a whole, as a great complex historic event, as well as the various less extensive events that compose it, not primarily as examples of something more general but as something unrecurrent and unrepeatable, and as having importance precisely for that reason. In consequence, we can be as concerned with the great failures as with the great successes, and as concerned with the potential moral implications of an act as with its immediate outcome.

Such inquiry remains legitimate public inquiry, and not just private

[15] This is not reducible to aesthetic criticism, of course, let alone to straight moral judgment. The difference between the art historian and the art critic—and the corresponding difference in other fields than art—is a matter of the historian's concern with culture as such in its dimension of continuity over time. But such a concern cannot do away with the sense of greatness; it rather puts it in perspective.

antiquarianism, to the extent that the exceptional events were in some sense or other outstanding in the context of mankind generally, and not just for private individuals or groups. Events evidently meet this test when they have altered the context of routine human life in their time, insofar as no region or period of human life has, in the long run, been so isolated that it has not had its effects in turn on the rest of us. On this level, the 'exceptionalizer' is at one with the 'typicalizer'. But he wants to add a further dimension.

It is not merely as events have altered the natural or the socio-cultural context that they can have exceptional significance. So far as there is moral or spiritual solidarity among human beings, apart from physical confrontations at any given time, the fate of each people is relevant to all human beings whether or not it had permanent external consequences otherwise. It is, then, also, and perhaps above all, as events and acts have altered the moral context of human life that they are of universal significance, for they have set irreplaceable standards and norms, and they have posed distinctive challenges and established moral claims which as human beings we dare not ignore. Herodotus wrote his history, he said, to preserve the memory of the great deeds done by the Greeks and the Persians: unrepeatable deeds that have an enduring claim to our respect. Those deeds cannot be imitated, though they may be emulated and in some sense perhaps surpassed. But even now we dare call no man great whose deeds cannot somehow measure up to theirs. Once having known those deeds, the world can never be quite the same for us again: not because of what they may tell us of *what* we are, may tell us statistically about the potentialities of our hominid species; but because they add to our understanding of *who* we are, of what we are committed to, as human beings, what is worthy of our wonder and our tears.

We are speaking here of such events and acts as form human cultural institutions on the level of public action. We are dealing with peoples—or, more accurately, with groups of men and women at least relatively autonomous in culture. Purely individual exploits may have something of the same quality, but they are meaningful on a different level and their student is the biographer, not the historian. Yet it is especially in this 'exceptionalizing' perspective that persons' ideal norms and expectations and even the special visions of individuals can be crucial. For they prove to be the mainsprings of creativity at the interstices of routine patterns, when exceptional circumstances arise and something new must be found to do. This is how, in fact, the would-be 'typicalizer' finds himself dragged into matters more suited to the programme of the 'exceptionalizer'.

Clearly, the serious 'exceptionalizer'—despite the doubtful example of some scholarly story-tellers—necessarily needs to understand all that the most 'social-scientific' of the 'typicalizers' will want to be studying. Always, of course, visions and ideals can come into play only within the leeway allowed by the human interests (material and imaginative) of those less concerned with ideals. Ultimately all historical 'why's' must be driven back (often in the form of 'how could that have become effective?') to circumstances of hominid natural and cultural ecology—the circumstances which determine that what would otherwise be the individual random 'accidents' that shape history will not simply cancel each other out but will be reinforced and cumulatively lead in a single direction.[16] However irrational human beings may be, in the long run their irrationalities are mostly random. It is their rational calculations that can be reinforced in continuing human groups and can show persisting orientation and development—even when they are calculations on misconceived presuppositions.[17] Hence group interests have a way of asserting themselves. Group interests seem ultimately based in ecological circumstances in general and, more particularly, in that cumulative development of cultural resources which the essential internal instability of cultural traditions assures will be likely, in the long run, to be ever more elaborated and so to require ever new adjustments.

But such ecological circumstances merely set the limits of what is possible. Within those limits, the personal vision has its opportunity. For when habitual, routine thinking will no longer work, it is the man or woman with imagination who will produce the new alternatives. At this point, the concerned conscience can come into play. It may or may not prove adequate to the challenge. But in either case, it is such personal vision that is the most human part of human history.

Hence the humanistic historian must concern himself with the great commitments and loyalties that human beings have borne, within which every sort of norm and ideal has been made explicit; and he must concern himself with the interactions and dialogues in which these commitments have been expressed. Hence, for an 'exceptionalizing' historian with such intentions, it is Islamdom as a morally, humanly relevant complex of traditions, unique and irreversible, that can form his canvas. Whether it 'led to' anything evident in Modern times must be less important than the quality of its excellence as a vital human response and an irreplaceable human endeavour. In this capacity, it would challenge our human respect and recognition even if it had played a far less great role than, in fact, it did play in articulating the human cultural nexus in time and space and in producing the world as we find it now.

On scholarly precommitments

Because of the central role, in historical studies, of human loyalties and commitments, the personal commitments of scholars play an even greater

[16] It is for this reason that every 'why this?' presupposes at least one 'why not that?' 'Might-have-beens' are built into the inquiry of any historian, whether explicit or not, just as they are built into that of any other scholar or scientist.

[17] On the self-determination of each new generation—as against 'blind tradition'—compare the section on determinacy in traditions, below.

role in historical studies than in other studies, a role that stands out in special relief in Islamics studies.

On the most serious levels of historical scholarship—where the human relevance of major cultural traditions is at issue, such as that of religious or artistic or legal or governmental traditions, or even that of whole civilizations—historical judgment cannot be entirely disengaged from the basic precommitments of inquirers. Indeed, it is not necessarily desirable that it should be: the very issues can arise only as we are humanly deeply engaged. Inquiries by pure specialists, seeking only to straighten out this or that detail brought up by some greater scholar who *was* humanly engaged and had discussed the great issues, may bring useful clarifications but often miss the main points. Precommitment can lead the unwary—and often even the most cautious scholar—to biased judgment. Bias comes especially in the questions he poses and in the type of category he uses, where, indeed, bias is especially hard to track down because it is hard to suspect the very terms one uses, which seem so innocently neutral. Nevertheless, the bias produced by precommitment can be guarded against; the answer to it cannot finally be to divest ourselves of all commitments, but to learn to profit by the concern and insight they permit, while avoiding their pitfalls.

Such basic precommitments are always to a degree idiosyncratic in really serious scholars; yet the deeper they are, the more fully they are likely to be rooted in one of the major cultural traditions of ultimate overall commitment. In fact, certain of these traditions have loomed especially large in determining the viewpoints of the masters of Islamics studies, who have done the most to set the problems and the framework within which other Islamicists have worked. I shall mention five, three old and two new. The Christian tradition—in Catholic or in Protestant form—has been deeply determinative for many Western scholars, as has Judaism for still others. More recently, increasing numbers of scholars committed to the Islamic tradition—Sharî‘ah-minded or Ṣûfî—are making their contributions to scholarship in the field. The pitfalls that await scholars committed to any of these traditions are evident enough in such scholars' work, at least to any scholar of a rival commitment. It is no guarantee of balanced insight, to be a Muslim, nor of impartiality, to be a non-Muslim. Alongside these older traditions, and representing precommitments leading to the same sorts of pitfalls as lurk in commitment to Christianity or Islam, we find Marxists on the one hand and dedicated Westernists on the other. I call 'Westernists' those whose highest allegiance is to what they call Western culture, as the unique or at least the most adequate embodiment of transcendent ideals of liberty and truth. They usually share, to some degree, a Christian viewpoint on Islam, insofar as the Christian tradition has been so central to Western culture, however much personally they may reject the claims to allegiance of Christianity in itself. Not all Islamicists are consciously committed to one of these major allegiances; but for many who are not, the alternative is not genuine independence and objectivity. Commonly the alternative, rather, is more limited horizons and shallower awareness, together with unconscious and hence unanalyzed piecemeal commitment to partisan viewpoints which, in those consciously committed, are subject to conscious review and control.

Accordingly, the problem of how one may legitimately go about studying Islam from within a commitment to another great tradition—and in particular how to go about studying it from within a Christian commitment—is no by-problem of interest only to a few scholars who by exception are religiously inclined. It is central to the whole scholarly problem. Jean-Jacques Waardenburg, in *L'Islam dans le miroir de l'Occident: comment quelques orientalistes occidentaux se sont penchés sur l'Islam et se sont formés une image de cette religion* (The Hague, 1963), has demonstrated how the work of the formative Islamicists Ignaz Goldziher, Christiaan Snouck Hurgronje, Carl Becker, Duncan MacDonald, and Louis Massignon was in each case intimately and pervasively marked by the basic precommitments of these men (though he does not use the concept 'Westernist'). The cultural allegiance of the serious scholar is crucial in his work. This is not to say that it is impossible to study fairly one religious tradition from within another, as has sometimes been suggested. Ultimately all faith is private, and it is often far easier for congenial temperaments to understand each other across the lines of religious or cultural tradition than it is for contrasting temperaments to make sense of each other's faith even when they follow the same cult and utter the same creed. We are primarily human beings and only secondarily participants in this or that tradition. Nevertheless, not only the scholars' cultural environment at large but their explicit precommitments, which brought the greater of the scholars to their inquiry in the first place, have determined the categories with which they have undertaken their studies. Only by a conscious and well-examined understanding of the limits of these precommitments and of what is possible within and beyond them can we hope to take advantage of our immediate humanness to reach any direct appreciation of major cultural traditions we do not share—and perhaps even of traditions we do share.

Where we compare the Occident and Islamdom in general, and Christianity and Islam in particular, such awareness is especially essential. There has been a tendency, among those Christians who have been willing to concede spiritual validity to Islam at all, to see Islam as, in one way or other, a truncated version of Christian truth: all or virtually all the truth to be found in Islam is to be found in Christianity, but Christianity leads beyond that truth to a crowning essential truth that eludes the Muslim's grasp. Correspondingly, Muslims have historically seen Christianity as a truncated or perverted Islam. But such a comparison is, on the face of it, unsound at least for historical purposes. It can hardly be intelligible, to those Christians or Muslims having such views, how it can be that intelligent, sensitive, and upright persons can prefer Islam to Christianity, or vice versa, once they have been exposed to the appeal of both.

In sensitive hands, some such approach can have suggestive results, indeed. The most attractive such interpretation of Islam from the Christian side is surely that of Louis Massignon, set forth allusively in a number of his articles, such as 'Salmân Pâk et les prémices spirituelles de l'Islam iranien', *Societé des Etudes Iraniennes*, vol. 7 (1934), and in his several articles on the Seven Sleepers; he saw Islam as a community in spiritual exile, veiled from the divine presence, yet through that very exile charged with a special witness to bear. (Giulio Basetti-Sani, *Mohammed et Saint François* [Commissariat de Terre-Sainte, Ottawa, 1959], has developed part of Massignon's idea in his beautiful and knowledgeable, if not very scholarly, book, which forms a suggestive contribution to a modern mythology.) A less poetic, though still sensitive, approach to Islam in Christian terms is offered by Eric Bethmann's *Bridge to Islam* (Nashville, Tenn., 1950) and by the works of Kenneth Cragg. Yet it remains true that the ultimate judgments such approaches presuppose are suspect. A serious exploration of any one religious tradition in its several dimensions could consume more than one lifetime, and it is not to be expected that many persons can genuinely explore two. If this fact helps account for so many intelligent persons not seeing the truth as the apologist sees it, it also suggests that the apologist too is deceiving himself if he thinks he is qualified to judge the rival tradition. A view of Islam as a Christianity manqué, or the reverse, however elegantly formulated, must be received with great scepticism.

But the readiest alternatives, among those willing to concede some truth to a rival tradition, are equally unsatisfactory for making a comparison. One may resort to syncretistic assimilation, as if superficially similar elements in the two traditions could be identified; but this is bound to falsify one tradition or both—if only by not recognizing the genuineness of the demand, at the heart of each, for exclusive historical commitment. For instance, in both traditions there is a demand for moral behaviour on the basis not of arbitrary human custom but of divine revelation; and at least in broad areas, the moral norms implied in the two revelations are much alike. Yet for Christians, being based in revelation means being in response to redemptive love as it is confronted through the presence of a divine-human life and the sacramental fellowship of which that is the source. For Muslims, being based in revelation means being in response to total moral challenge as it is confronted in an explicit divine message handed on through a loyal human community. The two senses of revelation not only contrast to one another: they exclude one another categorically. Yet to abstract from them is to make pointless both the Christian and the Muslim demand for a revealed morality over against human custom.

To avoid the over-explicit identifications of syncretism, one may resort frankly to reducing both traditions to some lowest common denominator—a formless mysticism or a vague appeal to the common goodwill of mankind. But in practice this means appealing to the prestige carried by the great traditions, on behalf of something that can rise above the level of impotent platitudes only as the quite private viewpoint of an individual.

The two traditions, as such, must be recognized as incompatible in their demands, short of some genuinely higher synthesis presumably not yet available to us. And we must retain this sense of tension between them without interpreting the one by the standards of the other. This may be accomplished, in some degree, through a comparison of the two structures, of what sorts of elements tend to get subordinated and what tend to get highlighted. In such a perception, those committed and those with no commitment can join, provided each maintains a sensitive human awareness of what can be humanly at stake at every point. But this is possible only so far as the elements chosen can be evaluated in some independence. This is an ideal only approximable at best. Hence even the best comparison cannot be regarded as providing an objective basis for ultimate judging between traditions. Yet it may make more understandable the special strengths of Islam—and its weaknesses—in the given historical circumstances.

I have developed this point about the irreducible incompatibility of any two traditions of faith somewhat more in detail in my 'A Comparison of Islam and Christianity as Frameworks for Religious Life'; but there I did not develop adequately what I feel must be the basis for mutual comprehension among religious traditions: growth within tension, through persistent dialogue. (That article was published in *Diogenes*, 1960, but in so mangled a form that it cannot be suggested for reading. The reprint by the University of Chicago Committee on Southern Asian Studies, reprint series No. 10, contains a fuller text and a list of essential corrigenda to the printed portion of the text.)

On defining civilizations

In civilization studies—the study of the great cultural heritages (especially those dating from the pre-Modern citied ages)—what may be called a 'civilization' forms a primary unit of reference. Yet the specification of such units is only partly given by the data itself. In part, it is a function of the inquirer's purposes.

Once society has become fairly complex, every people, even each sector of the population within what can be called a people, has had a degree of cultural self-sufficiency. At the same time, even the largest identifiable group of peoples has never been totally self-sufficient. Even the cultural patterns so large a group have in common will show interrelations with those of yet more distant peoples. Social groupings have intergraded or overlapped almost indefinitely throughout the Eastern Hemisphere since long before Islamic times. If we arrange societies merely according to their stock of cultural notions, institutions, and techniques, then a great many dividing lines among pre-Modern civilized societies make some sense, and no dividing line within the Eastern Hemisphere makes final sense. It has been effectively argued, on the basis of the cultural techniques and resources to be found there, that all the lands from Gaul to Iran, from at least ancient classical times onward, have formed but a single cultural world. But the same sort of arguments would lead us on to perceive a still wider Indo-Mediterranean unity, or even (in lesser degree) the unity of the whole Afro-Eurasian citied zone. In these circumstances, any attempt to characterize a less extensive 'civilization' requires adopting an explicit basis on which to set off one body of peoples from another as a civilization; but too often such groupings have been taken as given, on extraneous grounds, and characterizations have then been attempted without regard to the basis on which the grouping was made.

We have yet to develop an adequate analysis of cultural forms for studying the pre-Modern citied societies. Anthropologists have acquired some sophistication in dealing with non-citied societies, and some of them have extrapolated their methods into citied societies. Sociologists have learned to study Modern Technical society, and generally societies of the Technical Age in the light of it. But far too few since Max Weber have systematically explored the periods and areas between—that is, from Sumer to the French Revolution. This is partly because the lack of a tenable framework of world history, which would supply an elementary sense of the proportions and interrelations of the field, has hampered any comparative studies there. Anything may be compared with anything else, but fruitful comparisons require relevantly comparable units of comparison, which can be assured only through a sound sense of overall context. In consequence, the questions posed about the pre-Modern civilizations, and in particular about the Islamicate, have often been irrelevant or misleading, and the answers they yield have been beside the point or positively false.

It may be noted here that this lack of a proper world-historical framework has probably arisen at least in part for want of a proper framework for scholarly co-operation. What are commonly called 'Oriental studies' form the larger part of what are better called 'civilization studies', including the European heritage along with the others, since fundamentally the same methods are involved in all cases, and the historical problems are all interrelated. It is absurd for scholars in Islamics studies to be sharing conferences with those in Chinese studies more readily than with those in Medieval European studies.

It has largely been philologians who have—by default—determined our category of 'civilizations': a civilization is what is carried in the literature of a single language, or of a single group of culturally related languages. This notion has been presupposed by Carl Becker, Gustave von Grunebaum, and Jörg Kraemer, for instance. It is not, in fact, a bad notion, to the extent that my definition of a civilization in terms of lettered traditions is sound. But it is not the same as what I am suggesting; it needs to be refined. In crude form it has led, for instance (as we shall be noting), to an approach in which everything carried in Arabic, including pre-Islamic pagan Bedouin customs, is regarded as native and ancestral to the civilization that later expressed itself largely in Arabic; while materials in Syriac, for instance, produced in the mainstream of cultural development under the earlier Muslim rulers and leading directly to central features in the urban life of the civilization, are regarded as 'foreign' to it, and as 'influencing' it when their ideas were 'borrowed' into it at the point when their exponents began to use Arabic. The resulting picture of cultural development is, I believe, erroneous. In principle, a field of study such as 'whatever culture happens to be attested in Arabic documents' can be legitimate; but its relevance is limited. If, for instance, we deal not with Islam but with Arabic as our point of departure, so regarding Iranians as outsiders, we think of Bedouin notions as 'surviving' while Iranian ones 'influence' the later culture from outside. The Arabic culture of the High Caliphate then takes on two traits: (*a*) suddenness; (*b*) a derivative character, as largely 'borrowed'. What a difference in tone, if rather we should look at the problems posed by an overlay of Arabic 'borrowing' upon Iranian and Syriac 'survivals'! Accordingly, we must respect the challenge presented by men like Toynbee, who defines his civilizations according to criteria based on inner cultural development. When he divides what has been called 'Islamic' civilization among three different civilizations, I believe he is in error, but he reminds us that if we make it a single civilization we must give some reason why.

The reason for distinguishing a 'civilization' cannot be a single, universal one, however; it must almost be special to each case. For no more than language does any other one criterion necessarily determine a grouping that will be worth studying as a major large-scale culture. Even a localized culture, at least on the level of citied and lettered life, cannot be defined simply in terms either of component traits or of participant families. In cross-section, a culture appears as a pattern of lifeways received among mutually recognized family groups. Over time, it may be more fully defined as a relatively autonomous complex of interdependent cumulative traditions, in which an unpredictable range of family groups may take part. It forms an overall setting within which each particular tradition develops. But even within one relatively local culture, some traditions—a given school of painting, say, or a particular cult—may come to an end, and new ones may take their places. It is not possible to distinguish, in any absolute sense, authentic or viable from unauthentic or unviable traits in a culture, or even authentic from unauthentic traditions. Yet a culture does have a certain integrality. The consequences and the meaning of any given trait, inherited or newly introduced, will depend at any given time on what implications it has for the ongoing interaction, the dialogue or dialogues into which it fits (or which it confuses). The consequences and ultimate meaning of any given particular tradition will in turn depend on its implications for the cultural setting as a whole. These implications will be more decisive, the more they touch the most persistent and widely ramified features of the culture. Over time, then, what sets off a culture as an integral unity in some degree is whatever makes for cultural continuity in that particular culture.

On the wider and more rarefied level of what may be called a 'civilization', cultural identity is even more problematic and what will make for continuity is even less predictably formulable. We may indeed describe the most likely situations in general terms which may seem to settle the matter. If we may call a 'civilization' any wider grouping of cultures in so far as they share consciously in interdependent cumulative traditions (presumably on the level of 'high culture'—of the relatively widely shared cultural forms at the urban, literate level of complexity and sophistication), then the shared traditions will be likely to centre in some range of 'high' cultural experience to which the cultures are committed in common. This may be a matter of literary and philosophical as well as political and legal values carried in lettered tradition, with or without explicit allegiance to a given religious community. (Usually, lettered tradition is indissociable from the continuity of written language; yet there need not be cultural identity except marginally between two groups, especially in different periods, using the same language. Many would refuse to put ancient Attica and Christian Byzantium in the same civilization just because both used Greek and even read Homer. What matters is the dominant lettered traditions, with their attendant commitments, in whatever language.) When such major lettered traditions, then, are carried in common, often there will be a continuity likewise in social and economic institutions generally. All cultural traditions tend to be closely interdependent. Often the integration within one area has been so marked and the contrasts between that area and others so strong that at any given time a demarcation line has been quite clear, and that line has tended to perpetuate itself. Thus we get, especially in cross-section, the impression of clearly marked civilizations parcelling out among themselves the Eastern Hemisphere.

But this apparent clarity should not persuade the historian to take his categories for granted. There will always be 'borderline' and 'anomalous' cases which are quite as normal as the major groupings. It would be hard to place such peoples as Georgians and Armenians unequivocally within any one major 'civilization'. In any case, it cannot be clear in advance what sorts of life patterns will in fact be found to be shared among the peoples forming what can be called a 'civilization'. Each civilization defines its own scope, just as does each religion. There may even be several sorts of basic continuity which may overlap in range. Thus, depending on one's viewpoint, Byzantine culture may be seen as continuing the ancient Hellenic tradition, or as part of a Christendom briefer in time but wider in area; and in each case there is a genuine and effective continuity on the level of 'high culture' and its commitments. Hence over a time span it often becomes a matter of choice—depending on what sort of lettered traditions one specially wants to inquire into—which among several possible delimitations will prove most suitable. Then the scholarly treatment of the 'civilization' must differ with the grounds for singling it out.

On determinacy in traditions

However a civilization be defined, it must not be hypostatized, as if it had a life independent of its human carriers. The inherited cultural expectations at any given time form part of the realities that members of a given society must reckon with. They even put limits on what the most alert of those members can see in their environment. But they have no effect except as they interact with the actual environment and the immediate interests of all concerned. The determinacy of tradition is limited, in the long run, by the requirement that it be continuingly relevant in current circumstances.

Continuing relevancy is crucial to recall especially when cross-cultural comparisons are being made. For instance, in an attempt to understand why it was in the Occident that, eventually, technicalized society arose, scholars have looked to the state of the Occident in the centuries preceding the transformations. This can be done along two lines: by studying the special circumstances of the time when the transformations began and the special opportunities open to Occidentals at that time; or by studying inherent differences between Occidental culture and other cultures. In the latter case, a comparative study of the High Medieval Occident with its contemporaries is fundamental.

It is this latter case that has seemed the easier in the past. An adequate framework of overall world history was lacking as a basis for studying the special characteristics of the time of the transformation itself, whereas the chief other societies were just well enough known as isolated entities to allow specious global generalizations to be made about their cultural traits, traits which could be contrasted to subtle traits traceable in the more intimately understood Occident. Moreover, studying inherent traits in the Occident did have undeniable relevance to a related question, often confused with the question why it was the Occident that launched Modernity. The special form that modern technicalization took, coming where it did, certainly owes much to special traits of the Occident in which it arose. Since without adequate world-historical inquiries it is hard to sort out what has been essential and what accidental in technical Modernity, studies of what was special to Occidental culture as such, which were assured at least some success in accounting for the shape of Modernity as it actually arose, were mistakenly supposed to have succeeded in accounting for where and when it arose. Accordingly, scholars have been tempted to invoke, in accounting for the advent of Modernity, the determinant effect of a fortunate traditional attitude or combination of attitudes in the pre-Modern Occident. Complementarily to that, often enough, they have invoked the 'dead hand of tradition' to explain the 'failure' of other societies such as the Islamicate, which are then compared, to their disadvantage, with the pre-Modern Occident. The circumstances of the time when Modernity was launched have been relatively neglected.

All attempts that I have yet seen to invoke pre-Modern seminal traits in the Occident can be shown to fail under close historical analysis, once other societies begin to be known as intimately as the Occident. This applies also to the great master, Max Weber, who tried to show that the Occident inherited a unique combination of rationality and activism. As can be seen here and there in this work, most of the traits, rational or activist, by which he sought to set off the Occident either are found in strength elsewhere also; or else, so far as they are unique (and all cultural traits are unique to a degree), they do not bear the weight of being denominated as so uniquely 'rational' as he would make them. This applies to both Occidental law and Occidental theology, for instance, where he partly mistook certain sorts of formalism for rationality, and partly simply did not know the extent among Muslims, for instance, of a probing rational drive. But when the several traits prove not to be so exceptional, the special combination of them that he invoked as decisive loses its cogency.

It must also be noted that his method, as such, sometimes did not push quite far enough. He sometimes depicted the attitudes he found as if they were standing facts with automatic consequences, rather then processes that never remain quite the same and have regularly to be renewed. Accordingly, he could neglect the historical question of what it was that *kept* the attitude in being once it had arisen; and so he failed to see the full range of its interaction with other things, including with its own consequences.

The question of the relation of pre-Modern Occidental culture to Modernity is a specially intriguing case of a much wider problem: the relative role in historical development of traditional culture and of the current play of interests. When it becomes clear that long-range historical change cannot be adequately interpreted in terms of the initiative of great men or of direct geographical or racial causation; and when interpretation through the evident moral level of the leading classes or even through immediate economic interests proves to require explanation in turn of why the moral level or the economic interests were as they were; then recourse can be had to explanation by unevident but seminal culture traits. These seminal traits are supposed to have latent implications, not visible in the earlier course of the society, the consequences of which unfold at a later stage of the society's development—if it may be assumed that the society has a determinate course of development. Of the several sorts of seminal traits invoked, the most commonly appealed to are inherited attitudes of mind, evaluations of what is good and what bad. Thus in contrast to an Occidental inclination to rationalize and to reinvest is posited an eternal Chinese inclination to tao-ize and to become gentry; whereupon the failure of the Chinese to carry through an industrial revolution is ascribed to their successful families' not persisting in industry, but turning to other, more honoured, careers. (If the Chinese *had* been the first to fully industrialize, they might have accounted for this also by their wealthy families' tendency to become gentry—and so to sell their industries to ever new blood, willing to innovate.)

I am sure that seminal traits may exist, though it is hard to pin them down. But any evaluation of their historical effects must take into account the full ecological setting of a given generation—that is, all the conditions (including both geographically and socially given resources as well as current interrelations with other groups) that would determine the effective advantage of various possible lines of action and hence of attitudes that might be adopted. Ideally, one should determine the points at which, under the given conditions, additional investment of money, time, intellectual effort, etc., would yield diminishing returns. Such calculations would have to take into account natural, man-made, and demographic resources, technical and scientific alternatives available, and social institutions as given to that generation, including patterns of expectation, and what *at that time* these expectations depended on (that is, what it was that, at that time, might have altered them). Such a listing would have to include the *consequences* of ancestors' attitudes; but under the circumstances facing any given generation, the consequences of those attitudes need not come to the same thing as the attitudes themselves. Even the outcome, in a given setting, of child-raising techniques—the area where an unconscious past seems likely to weigh heaviest—can vary strongly.

Attitudes like 'individualism', 'sense of personal vocation', or 'world-negation' are hard to define closely enough for such purposes. It is easier to trace the particular tokens of such attitudes; and these can come to take on quite opposite implications in a new setting. Thus the expectation in the USA, that each nuclear family should have its own lawn-surrounded house, which originally was doubtless a bulwark of certain aspects of individual independence, can lead, in certain sorts of 'organization-man' suburbia, to bolstering social involvement and conformity. Or the exclusivity of the Qur'ân, with its rejection of the reliability of Jewish and Christian religious witness, could contribute (by way of the self-containedness of the Qur'ânic exegesis) to the special universalism and tolerance of divergent traditions (and not only of those of the People of the Book), which characterize some strains of Ṣûfism.

Indeed, whatever the situation may be in non-lettered societies, in every complex society most relevant attitudes are to be found either among the multiplicity of variant and practical traditions, or within that lettered tradition that has maximum prestige. Most temperaments and most possible facets of experience that are to be found in any major tradition can be found in corresponding traditions elsewhere. Accordingly, tradition can account for almost anything. Thus for a time it was sought to prove that basic familistic attitudes would prevent the Chinese from turning Communist; now the Chinese bureaucratic heritage is shown to have made the Chinese peculiarly susceptible to Communism.

Accordingly, it is wise to posit as a basic principle, and any deviation from which must bear the burden of proof, that *every generation makes its own decisions*. (This is perhaps a partial application of Ranke's principle that all generations are morally equidistant from God.) A generation is not bound by the attitudes of its ancestors, as such, though it must reckon with their consequences and may indeed find itself severely limited by those consequences in the range of choices among which it can decide.

The difference between major traditions lies not so much in the particular elements present within them, but in the relative weighting of them and the structuring of their interplay within the total context. If this structuring remains relatively constant (in the very nature of tradition, it cannot remain absolutely so), it will be because the predisposing conditions remain relatively constant, and because they are further reinforced by the institutionalizing of attitudes appropriate to them. Such institutionalizing can indeed be crucial in making the predisposing conditions fully effective: e.g., the mercantile bias of the Irano-Semitic cultural traditions, already so visible in the development of the monotheisms, was given fully free play only under the auspices of Islam. The triumph of Islam was made possible by its special adaptation to that bias, but its triumph in turn allowed that bias to determine the subsequent course of Irano-Semitic history. Nevertheless, the consequences of such institutionalization cannot reach very far in independence of the predisposing conditions. They can allow a tendency already the strongest in the field to become fully effective, and they can then reduce fluctuations that might result from variations in the underlying conditions, so that a temporary or a local deviation from the general norm will not produce a total cultural disruption. But if altered basic conditions long persist, the corresponding attitudes and their institutionalization will soon be changed to match.

Historical change is continuous and all traditions are open and in motion, by the very necessity of the fact that they are always in internal imbalance. Minds are always probing the edges of what is currently possible. But even apart from this, we are primarily human beings with our personal interests to pursue, and only secondarily participants in this or that tradition. Any tradition must be regularly reinforced by current conditions so that it answers to current interests or it will perish by drying up—or be transformed into something relevant. Whatever unity of patterning we may be able to discover, as to primacy of orientations or as to validation of norms of organization—whatever sense of common style we may find in the culture, that is—may be very pervasive and persistent and yet be essentially fragile. As soon as new positive possibilities open up, the unity of patterning is quickly vulnerable. To the extent that a homogeneous and compelling style is attained, in fact, it must be regarded as a delicate flower, not a tap root; it is not something imposed by cultural necessity, though the range of potentialities may be given so, but something achieved by creative effort.

A special word has to be said about one of the crudest, yet remarkably pervasive forms of hypostatizing a cultural tradition—or, in this case, a whole series of them. The misimpression that 'the East' has latterly been awaking from a 'millennial torpor' is still remarkably widespread. It results, of course (like the term 'East' itself), from the profound ignorance of world history not only among modern Westerners but among others as well, whose eager vaunting of the antiquity of their institutions was taken at face value by Westerners.

We may single out two types of scholar who have reinforced the misimpression. Western tourists, whose moods played a large role even in scholarship, easily mistook the exotic for the immemorial, and were necessarily blind to subtler institutional changes. Their impressions, then, were dignified into learnèd theses, sometimes of a racialist hue, by scholars bemused by the spectacular progressiveness of their own West, and ready to write off other societies as irrelevant. Reading back the recent Western pace of activity into the earlier Occidental past by a foreshortening of time-spans in the distance, and unaware that in other parts of the world there was a comparably active past, Western scholars assumed that the comparatively slow pace of technical and intellectual development which they could perceive in the nineteenth-century world abroad amounted to no development at all, and marked a difference of race and place rather than one of age.

But other Western scholars—well represented in 'area studies'—have confirmed the misimpression by an opposite error. While more or less recognizing the comparability of pre-Modern Western and non-Western societies as to degree of cultural activity, they have blanketed all pre-Modern areas under the common term 'traditional', the misleading tendency of which we have already seen, as if all had been asleep together (save in certain periods of undeniable florescence)—rather than all awake together. As we have noted, the degree to which pre-technicalized and even pre-literate peoples have been bound by the 'dead hand of tradition' has been greatly exaggerated. Among Muslims, at any rate, the major institutions of each age can be shown to have their own functional justification in their own time: Muslim social decisions, even under the conservative spirit, were made not primarily out of deference to the past but as meeting concrete practical interests of dominant social groups. Whether it is the 'East' or the 'pre-Modern' that is being misperceived, the postulate of essential changelessness obscures the important question of how the particular posture in which various peoples happened to be at the moment of the Transmutation affected their destiny under its impact. There is too ready an answer to the question of why 'reform' efforts so often failed: the 'tradition-bound' lands were ruled by blind conservatives. Some are thus spared the trouble of discovering what very practical and alert statesmen those 'tradition-bound' men often were ... except in the case of the Japanese, who are gratuitously labelled 'good imitators'.

On the history of Islamics studies

Only gradually have scholars come to recognize the relevance of the scholar's perspective in delimiting his field, enough to make the perspective conscious and so keep it relatively under control. Historically, scholars' notions of 'Islam' as a field have been rather arbitrarily determined by a series of political and other extraneous circumstances. These notions still have their consequences. Almost all stages of the historical development of modern Islamics[18] studies are represented in the works that an inquirer must still consult in the library. What is more, many of these stages are still represented in studies made in the mid-twentieth century. Hence even the relatively casual student of things Islamic should be aware of the history of Islamics studies. This will allow him better to appreciate the relevance of the individual scholarly studies to whatever his own interests are, as well as put him on guard against various endemic but avoidable errors that have come to prevail in the field.

Because of the cultural circumstances of the Modern Technical Age, Western scholarship has been the chief channel for studies of a Modern type in the Islamics field at least until very recently. Western scholarship entered the Islamics field above all by three paths. First, there were those who studied the Ottoman empire, which played so major a role in modern Europe. They came to it usually in the first instance from the viewpoint of European diplomatic history. Such scholars tended to see the whole of Islamdom from the political perspective of Istanbul, the Ottoman capital. Second, there were those, normally British, who entered Islamics studies in India so as to master Persian as good civil servants, or at least they were inspired by Indian interests. For them, the imperial transition of Delhi tended to be the culmination of Islamicate history. Third, there were the Semitists, often interested primarily in Hebrew studies, who were lured into Arabic. For them, headquarters tended to be Cairo, the most vital of Arabic-using cities in the nineteenth century, though some turned to Syria or the Maghrib. They were commonly philologians rather than historians, and they learned to see Islamicate culture through the eyes of the late Egyptian and Syrian Sunnî writers most in vogue in Cairo. Other paths—that of the Spaniards and some Frenchmen who focused on the Muslims in Medieval Spain, that of the Russians who focused on the

[18] On the use of the term 'Islamics', see the section on usage in Islamics studies below.

northern Muslims—were generally less important. All paths were at one in paying relatively little attention to the central areas of the Fertile Crescent and Iran, with their tendency towards Shî'ism; areas that tended to be most remote from Western penetration. Unless perhaps in Russia, studies of the central areas still tend to be neglected except for the earliest centuries; Islamdom is rarely seen from such a perspective.

For a long time, in any of the paths it took, Modern Western scholarship was largely a matter of translating the results of pre-Modern Muslim scholarship and adapting them into Occidental categories. Improvement in Western scholarship was largely a matter of moving from later, secondary Muslim sources to earlier, more nearly primary ones; new editions of more ancient texts tended to be the most important scholarly events. At the same time, the Western scholarly viewpoint changed in response to shifts in viewpoint which took place during the nineteenth century among Muslims themselves: shifts which emphasized the importance of the early Arabic period and the Sharî'ah associated with it (as against the more recent Persianate and Ṣûfî tendencies, which were being rejected as decadent). Both these currents of change tended to emphasize the earlier periods and the Arabic documents as the object of the best scholarly work and the focus of scholarly interpretations. In consequence (especially with the decline of Istanbul in international importance after 1918), the Cairene path to Islamic studies became the Islamicist's path par excellence, while other paths to Islamics studies came to be looked on as of more local relevance: via Istanbul one became an Ottomanist, for instance, but no longer a scholar of Islamics as such.

All this, then, reinforced the Arabistic and philologistic prejudices which resulted anyway from several European tendencies: the interest in a Semitic 'race' (set over against an Indo-European 'race' represented by the West) which was expected to illuminate the Semitic Biblical background; the interest in 'origins' of supposedly isolable cultural entities, with which nineteenth-century Western scholarship was obsessed; the concern with Mediterranean (and hence largely Arab) Islamdom, as nearest to Europe and most involved with its history; and the philological tendency to learn Arabic as the most essential linguistic resource and to stop there rather than going on seriously to other languages. This Arabistic and philological bias is reflected in book after book and article after article; not least in the *Encyclopaedia of Islam*, where many entries discuss more the word (usually in its Arabic form even if it is derived, say, from Persian) than the substance; and present data for Egypt and Syria as if for Islamdom as a whole. (For a consideration of the problem of getting past this situation, see the section on usage below.)

Meanwhile, however, other changes had been modifying Western historical scholarship generally, and with it Islamics studies. It is especially in the twentieth century that Islamicists have been going beyond the results of older Muslim scholarship to pose their own questions and derive their own answers from the documents, now pulled apart as bits of evidence rather than copied as authorities. More slowly, scholars are learning even to get beyond categories derived from the Occident, partly by learning to use with more precision categories used by Islamicate writers themselves, and partly by learning to use relatively neutral categories disciplined by wider studies of world history and of human society and culture generally. This task is as yet far from complete, however, even in the work of the best scholars.

Apart from this, present-day Islamics studies still suffer from the philologism of their past. Their Arabistic bias, with the neglect of the more central Islamicate areas, is only gradually being overcome. (Yet with the dropping of the training in general Semitic studies that Arabists used to have, a great advantage of the old philologism is being undermined: its ability to integrate Arabic with older Semitic—especially Hebrew and Aramaic—studies and sometimes even with older Iranian studies.) Perhaps even more important, Islamics studies have tended to be concerned, above all, with high culture, to the neglect of more local or lower-class social conditions; and within the high culture, to be preoccupied with religious, literary, and political themes, which are most accessible to a philological approach. Hence it is important to point out such journals as *Comparative Studies in Society and History* and *Social and Economic History of the Orient*, which have stressed other sides, and in both of which Gustave von Grunebaum has taken a leading role in encouraging a good contribution to Islamics studies. Claude Cahen has been the most effective Occidental writer on social and economic questions in many dispersed articles, to be traced down through the *Index Islamicus*.

I will here illustrate the problems that arise from too great a reliance on a philological outlook by way of offering some caveats on the work of scholars on the period immediately before and after the rise of Islam, when lack of broadly based data encourages an unhistorical use of what there is.

The special role of old Arab families has given rise (in combination with certain more extraneous circumstances) to a tendency on the part of many scholars to interpret the development of Islamicate civilization from an Arab, even an Arabian point of view. Identifying 'Islamic culture' as 'culture appearing in the Arabic language', they will treat all pre-Islamic Arabian elements (i.e., those found in the Arabian peninsula) as native to Islamic culture, and will think of an Arabian Bedouin folkway as 'lost' or 'dropped' if it is not found among later Muslims in the Fertile Crescent. Correspondingly, they will treat Syriac, Persian, or Greek cultural elements as 'foreign' imports into Muslim Arab life, despite the fact that they formed the ancestral traditions of most of the Muslim population, and even of most of the educated and culturally privileged section of that population. The term 'pre-Islamic' for some scholars means strictly 'pre-Islamic Arabian', not pre-Islamic from Nile to Oxus generally wherever Islam was established.

When one focuses attention, as one often must, on the Arab Muslims and especially on the creatively concerned minority among them, this standpoint is largely relevant; for from the standpoint of the ruling Arabs, and even of their more ardent converts, everything non-Arabian was 'foreign'. What the observer might call the Arabs' gradual assimilation into the established cultural patterns among which they came to live appeared to the Arabs, rather, as a gradual assimilation of external cultural elements into an on-going essentially Arab society. It is a legitimate question, how such non-Arabian elements were assimilated among Arab families.

But if one is to understand the larger scene in terms of which even the concerned men of old-Arabian family were working, this Arab-centred or 'Arabistic' viewpoint can be misleading. Unfortunately, this Arabistic approach has, in fact, often been carried too far by philologists, for whom the language group (in this case, Arabic) is the key unit of all historical study, and for whom the origin of terms is occasionally more fascinating, or at least more accessible, than the origin of the actual institutions to which they are applied. In fact, this approach may be called the conventional one; it has often imposed its terminology even on those who might otherwise be relatively free of it. Yet if not balanced with other points of view, the Arabistic viewpoint can put developments into a false light, arousing false expectations and raising false questions. The reader of studies in the field must be ever on guard against being misled in this way; the Arabistic bias in studies of early Islam has been remarkably hard for even the best scholars to get past.

For instance, if comparisons of conditions before and conditions after the advent of Islam are made between pre-Islamic Arabia on the one hand and Syria or Iran in Islamic times on the other, they can be revealing of what happened to those families that formed the Arabian element in the new Islamic societies. But since those families had undergone not merely Islam but also a major migration and a great rise in social status, any comparison may not tell much about Islam itself or its culture, unless it is balanced with comparisons between pre-Islamic Syria, say, and Syria under Islam; and between pre-Islamic Arabia and Arabia itself in Islamic times. Otherwise, differences may appear to result from Islam which are matters of politics and of geography. Yet such balancing has rarely occurred in published work.

To such a philological bias is often added the old unexamined assumption of identity among the three ethnic criteria: patrilinear race, language, and cultural heritage. 'Arabs' by language and 'Muslims' by heritage are often identified, even at much later historical periods, as almost a single category, in which Arabian 'race' is thought of as normal, even though it is acknowledged that the 'exceptions' have been far more numerous than the 'normal' cases, such 'exceptions' being duly noted as such. At this point, historical inquiry can be seriously thrown off. Writers are to be found, for instance, asking how Greek elements entered (as non-Arabian) from 'outside' not merely into a few Arab families but into the whole Arabic-using society from Nile to Oxus, in which (in fact) they were already present by inheritance; while the same writers fail to inquire how such elements were avoided for so long in the education of upper-class Muslims. This latter question in turn leads to the wider and more serious question (which too purely philological a scholar will scarcely know how to set about asking), how the Arabic language and with it so much of the Arabian background managed to emerge as a cultural framework in a society where they were so greatly disadvantaged. How did Arabian foreign elements—alien at several points even to Islam itself as conceived by Muḥammad—come to receive such relatively ready acceptance among the Semitic and Iranian peoples?

The answer partly lies in the development of those peoples themselves. The Islamicate civilization may be seen as the latest phase of the Irano-Semitic culture which goes back, in the lands from Nile to Oxus, to Sumerian times. The very vision of Islam grew out of that heritage; even the mercantile-nomad understanding which led to the Arab conquest was not entirely alien to it. Islam as an Arab creation was able to come to flower in those wider lands because it answered to circumstances that were already determinative there. The Irano-Semitic cultural traditions showed a long-term tendency, within what remained overall an agrarian-based cultural context, to shift from a more agrarian base for high culture toward a more mercantile base for it. What was distinctive in Islamicate civilization grew largely from the special role in it of traditions linked to the mercantile classes. It brought to culmination what had long been developing.

The antidote to the Arabistic bias ought to lie in marshalling the data on the rest of the society other than the few Arabian families. But unfortunately, this has not proved easy. The few ambitious attempts to do it, moreover, have themselves suffered from a philological approach in a different form.

Sâsânian religious and social history must be reconstructed from archaeological and indirect textual sources, with very few major literary witnesses from the period itself. Aramaic, Greek, or Armenian texts view affairs largely from the outside and marginally. The Pahlavî texts are often suspect as having been edited, at least, in Islamic times, or they must even be reconstructed from Arabic and Persian translations and adaptations. Even when we do have undoubted Pahlavî texts from Sâsânian times, the original script was so tricky and the manuscript tradition has been so defective that reading the texts must be left to philological specialists. In consequence, few scholars have entered the field and those who have been tempted to indulge in rather wild philological speculation, building much on shreds of verbal detail. Since Arthur Christensen's work, for instance, two of the most spectacular writers have been Robert Zaehner (notably, *Zurvan, a*

Zoroastrian Dilemma [Oxford, 1955]), and Franz Altheim, who summarizes in *Utopie und Wirtschaft: eine geschichtliche Betrachtung* (Frankfurt/Main, 1957) the more questionable results of his more detailed work (with Ruth Stiehl), *Ein asiatischer Staat: Feudalismus unter den Sasaniden und ihren Nachbarn* (Wiesbaden, 1954). Both illustrate the pitfalls of philological limitations even in their excellences.

Zaehner's work is very informative in detail and suggestive in some correlations, yet he needs to point out the difference between a verbal formulation and its existential, experiential meaning in real life between the doctrine of a religion and the mood of a poem. Consequently, his description of the evolution of Zervanism, which seems to have been a Mazdean school of thought which did not survive, is unconvincing in detail, for one can usually think of less improbable explanations of the particular points. I thus find it unconvincing as a whole. The like tends to be true of his work in Islamics studies, where he takes a few schematic notions and builds a whole typology of faith on the presence or absence of them in the verbal formulations of a given thinker.

Altheim's work is likewise informative and often suggestive; but here again far too much is built on single reconstructions of textual passages, while human probability is flaunted. Nûshîrvân's tax measures on the surface, as Altheim points out, generalized taxation in money rather than in kind and therefore suggest an increasing strength in the monetary and mercantile aspects of the economy. But by a series of ingenious and most improbable correlations, Altheim finds, even in this, evidence for the reverse: Nûshîrvân's taxation was introducing control of the economy rather than mercantile market freedom; his lesser dependence on the traditional landed gentry likewise meant closer controls of the society, and—by creating a new lesser gentry—put the central government in more immediate dependence on the land. The whole, Altheim maintains (by way of weak evidence on castle building and anachronistic misconstruction of Muḥammad's work), led to strengthening of the non-monetary 'natural' economy and so (by interaction with Byzantium) to the Middle Ages. At almost every point, a more adequate awareness of post-Axial agrarianate-level social conditions as such would have suggested better alternative interpretations.

Both Zaehner's and Altheim's systems make such sense as they do by incorporating certain uncriticized preconceptions about world history which allow them to overlook alternative possibilities in their philological reconstructions. Zaehner speaks, without a word of apology, of a Zoroastrian 'church', of 'orthodoxy', of 'sects' of which he takes for granted his Zervanism must be one, though he gives no grounds for supposing that such phenomena, in the sense he presupposes, were in fact present in that period. Altheim, correspondingly, takes for granted the underlying stereotypes of 'Orient' and of 'Middle Ages', without which his scheme would have no plausibility. His 'Orient' or 'East' is an eternal entity, from ancient times down to the present Soviet Union, always basically backward and irrational but capable of learning from the essentially rational and progressive 'West' and of learning so well as to force or drag the latter into a Dark Age. For him, Mazdak was an ancient Marx, the forerunner of Islam as was Marx of the Soviet system. This parallelism is again made easier by a stereotype: it has become conventional to refer to Mazdak and other reformers as 'communistic', advocating 'community' of property and of women. This terminology Altheim continues to use although he himself makes it clear enough that neither community of property nor community of women was involved, but rather their redistribution, in certain cases, to other private individuals. He seems never to have thought through these various stereotypes to consider what their meaning could really be. Such confusion as to basic historical categories plagues Islamics studies all through, but is nowhere so clear cut (or so disastrous) as in the Sâsânian period. The general scholar is forced, even more than in the Islamic periods, to reconstruct by educated guesswork for want of adequately grounded scholarly guidance.

USAGE: REVISIONISM IN SCHOLARLY TERMINOLOGY

If one must consciously choose and face the implications of one's approach to a civilization, so must one also choose and face the implications of one's terms, selecting them relevant to the questions one is asking. In using such words as 'Oikoumene' and 'Axial Age', 'Islamdom' and 'Islamicate', I have preferred to introduce new usages or adopt relatively rare ones rather than use terminology now conventional. I have done this with reluctance, recognizing that the historian, like the philosopher, has a special obligation to be intelligible to the layman because of the human immediacy of the questions he is dealing with. Nevertheless, some special terms and usages are necessary. In many disciplines, scholars would not dream of taking their terminology from the street. Even if they do not fully succeed in agreeing upon a given set of terms, they recognize that it is essential for each writer to use his terms with precision, and that an attempt to accommodate oneself to popular usage as reflected in a dictionary must be disastrous. Too often, historians (especially in the field of Islamics) still try to avoid recognizing such a necessity and are satisfied to be guided by whatever is 'common practice'. They note that often terminological discussion can descend into pettifogging, and that the nature of their field prevents historians from building up a single total body of terminology in which all cases are provided for. They hope, therefore, that terminology will take care of itself; but it does not. The responsibility remains for selecting minimally misleading terms and for defining them precisely.

Terms are the units by which one constructs one's propositions. The terms one uses determine the categories by which one orders a field—or at least all those categories that are not the immediate focus of one's inquiry. The categories one presupposes, then, necessarily delimit the questions one can ask—at least all the constants implied in the questions, apart (again) from the special point of focus. The questions posed, in turn, determine what answers will ultimately be reached when the questions, as posed, are pursued. The story of scholarly error is largely one of questions wrongly put because their presuppositions were wrong; correspondingly, the story of scholarly achievement can almost be summed up in successive refinements of terminology.

There are two approaches to conventional misusages: the admonitionist approach and the revisionist. The admonitionists, admitting a given usage or practice is misleading, prefer to maintain the continuity of communication which even false conventions make possible, but to add a warning that such and such a usage or categorization must not be taken in the most likely way. The revisionists prefer to replace outright the conventional misusage (or biased categorization) with a sounder one.

Those who have not had time to verify that the conventional error is as unmitigated as the revisionists claim, or that the offered replacements are not themselves tainted with unanticipated further error, almost necessarily incline to wait and meanwhile have recourse to a caveat. But even some who grant that the revisionist point is quite sound may feel that the advantages of change do not outweigh the disadvantages which come with any break with continuity.

As will appear especially from my defence of the term 'Islamicate', in the section below on usage in Islamics studies, in this work I have been insistently and almost without exception revisionist where I saw occasion arise. Whatever concessions need to be made, I feel that the categories and terms arising from the Arabistic bias in particular need drastic revision. But there are other cases where conventional misusages tend to reinforce natural misconceptions. For instance, to put 'land assignment' (or 'land grant' in some situations, perhaps) in place of the usual term 'fief' in the conventional discussions of what is admittedly miscalled 'Islamic feudalism' will usually have one of two effects. Where the discussion happens to be sound, the change throws the points being made into sharper relief—and often makes many of the clarifications prove superfluous. But remarkably often it shows up inadequacies and even absurdities in the conventional discussion and its presuppositions. In the latter case, to hide from the consequences of a more accurate usage, on the grounds of convention, does not serve good scholarship.

The most common conventional errors tend to be bias-reinforcing errors, which is, perhaps, just why they are clung to. With such errors, human nature is such that a caveat does very little good. It is more than the divided human attention can do to keep in mind a caveat that runs against one's favourite presuppositions if those presuppositions are constantly reinforced by the very terms one uses. In such a case, new terms and new practices alone can take effect; the old, even amended, cannot usually transcend themselves. In any case, in Islamics studies and in civilization studies generally, the inadequacy of our studies up to this point is so great that an attempt to maintain continuity is doomed to failure: we are still almost in the 'pre-historic' period of scholarship. Continuity with old first approximations is bound to be of minimal value.

In fact, historians have already used some care in glaring cases. In the field of Islamics we have got rid almost altogether of 'Moorish' and 'Turanian' and 'Saracen' among specialists because each of these terms had come to carry, as a category, implications too hopelessly confused for reform to seem worthwhile. But far more debris remains to be cleared away. For instance, in the case of terms for areas, European historians would not think of analyzing past conditions in terms of current political boundaries, positing a historic Switzerland, Austria, Germany, Belgium, and France in their mid-twentieth-century limits; yet many Islamicists try to discuss past periods in terms of 'Persia', 'Afghanistan', 'Syria and Palestine', and even 'Lebanon', all of which refer to strictly modern entities, at least in the meaning usually assigned them. We must face the fact that such terminology will not do. It will not do in discussing particular historical events where, fortunately, it is often possible to refer to territorial states of the time. But it will also not do when describing long-term developments and trends in given areas, for current boundaries rarely set off areas with any such inherent unity as will allow for useful discussion. We must reconcile ourselves to using area terms based not on the political situation of any period, but on more enduring criteria relevant to the discussions at hand.

To take one unusually illustrative example, the coastlands between the Mediterranean and the Syrian desert shared much in common and often need to be referred to as a body. If we do not use the term 'Syria' for that area—including what is currently Lebanon, and Palestine in its old, largest definition, but excluding the eastern parts of what (by French fiat) is now the Syrian republic—we must invent some other term. Most writers recognize this fact, but—accepting current political usage of terms as pre-emptive—try to express themselves somehow by means of them. First off, though, the name 'Israel' cannot be used in any designation because of current implied connotations. Even a periphrasis in 'Syria including Lebanon and Palestine', however, is not only too clumsy but inaccurate, since it does not exclude enough. The compound 'Syria and Palestine', tacitly including current Lebanon in 'Syria' (since on the interwar maps they were both coloured French) is a formation not purely political in inspiration. Partly it reflects Western sentiment about the special place of Palestine, which was to be set apart from the rest of Syria; but in net effect it amounts to an interwar compromise which exaggerates the place of southern Syria in the Islamicate scene without satisfying those who go purely by today's political map. Hence some decide to degrade the old term 'Levant' to mean only this smaller area; but then we will have to provide somehow for the wider usage which 'Levant' used to serve; and in any case we will be faced by French restriction of 'Levant' still further to cover just the two states under French mandatory control. Such yielding to current political and sentimental fashions in the end usually leads nowhere. Sometimes political fiats and the language of the street must simply be defied and terms be used on the basis of historical needs alone. In this case, unless some other term can be found which the politicians will not proceed to steal, it seems best to continue to use the term 'Syria' in the old sense it most often had before 1918, which happens to be just the sense we need. We may indeed concede 'geographical Syria' or 'the Syrian lands' or the like for the noun, as avoiding a clash; but the adjective anyway must remain 'Syrian'. The reader must be told to adjust himself! In other cases, special terms must be invented. Sometimes I have had recourse to adding the article, where an original Arabic article has made it appropriate, to indicate reference to a geographic area rather than a modern state; e.g., 'the Iraq' for the more southerly part of the current Iraqi state. But here, as with phrases in 'lands' or 'area', there is no help for the adjective.

USAGE IN WORLD-HISTORICAL STUDIES

In the broad field of world history, the terminology of the street is especially misleading, for it reflects consistently a strongly ethnocentric Western view, radically distortive of the reality. The major terms for area and period will suffice as illustrations. The periodization in 'Ancient', 'Medieval', and 'Modern' has been attacked by innumerable historians as inadequate for a fair long-run view even of European history; and while it is sufficiently vague so that at least the second and third terms seem adjustable to any area, yet overall it is still more distortive of the world scene than of the European. Far worse is the geographical terminology. 'Europe', 'Asia', and 'Africa' referred initially to the north, east, and south hinterlands of the Mediterranean. When the sub-Saharan region is lumped with the southern littoral of the Mediterranean, and everything east as far as China and Japan with the Levant, the resulting monstrosities would look like bad jokes were they not made use of every day (even for statistical purposes) as if they were real entities with real characteristics of their own. As it is, they are vicious historical distortions. 'Europe', if taken loosely, is a more defensible concept; yet attempts to trace an eastern 'boundary' for Europe through the Aegean (the two sides of which have always had basically the same cultural and historical features) and along the Urals (which have never once served as either a political or a cultural boundary) would also be easily dismissible were they not taken seriously and even inscribed on popular maps.

The reason such terms persist, of course, is that on one level they do serve a use. In the case of 'Europe' and 'Asia', at least, the artificial elevation of the European peninsula to the status of a continent, equal in dignity to the rest of Eurasia combined, serves to reinforce the natural notion, shared by Europeans and their overseas descendants, that they have formed at least half of the main theatre (Eurasia) of world history, and, of course, the more significant half. Only on the basis of such categorization has it been possible to maintain for so long among Westerners the illusion that the 'mainstream' of world history ran through Europe. (The acceptance of such terms by non-Westerners too is a sign of their continuing cultural dependence on the West.) The other major pair of popular world-historical conceptions, 'West' and 'East' (or 'Orient') form a variant on the pair 'Europe' and 'Asia' and serve the same function of reinforcing Western ethnocentric illusions.

It is, of course, precisely because of this strongly emotive unconscious function that the careful pre-Modernist historian, at least, should never use the concepts 'Asia' or 'Orient' but should refer precisely to the more limited area he actually has in mind (the area is always in fact more limited, if he is not just indulging in uncritical generalizations). But unfortunately it is often just historians who have been misled most drastically into false statements because they take those categories seriously. The key point is to *say what one means:* 'Semitic', 'Islamicate', 'Indic', 'Indic and related', 'Far Eastern', perhaps sometimes 'Indic *and* Far Eastern'; or else 'exotic', 'alien to the Occident', 'non-Western', perhaps 'Islamic and Monsoon Asian', 'non-Western civilized'; or else 'indigenous', 'local', 'non-technicalized', or just 'other'! Even in the Modern period, when the non-Western citied lands have had something in common precisely in not being 'Western', the terms 'Orient' and 'East' have connotations sufficiently unfortunate in *several* ways to make them suspect, though I find the term 'West' useful in the Modern period for all those on the 'European' side of the development gap.

My world-historical terminology is made clear, for the most part, as I go along. Many of the terms or phrases I use in a distinctive sense are also listed in the Index or the Glossary. Here I can explain a few choices.

The Occident is for me precisely western or Latin Europe and its overseas settlements. If I mention the 'European region', it is with reference to the extended northern hinterland of the Mediterranean, including the Anatolian peninsula; if, especially in compounds, I use 'Europe' for short, in a pre-Modern context, at least, I have in mind the same region. In a Modern context I may use it for European Christendom instead. The term 'Indic region' likewise seems safer, when convenient, than just 'India' for the areas southward of the Pamirs and Himalayas; and it is less pretentious than the politically retroactive 'Indo-Pakistan subcontinent'. The (Eurasian) 'Far East' I use for the area of primary Chinese cultural influence—including (for instance) Vietnam but not Cambodia. I have chosen the term 'Oikoumene', in a sense similar to that latterly used by Alfred Kroeber not just as an area term but to refer to the Afro-Eurasian agrarian historical complex as having a distinctive interregional articulation in an ever growing area; there seems to be no other term for this complex at all. (The form 'Oikoumene' allows better than 'Ecumene' for an adjectival form distinct from 'ecumenical'.) The term 'citied society' (i.e., containing cities, as distinct from 'urban' which refers to the cities themselves) has the advantage over 'civilized' of avoiding, in certain contexts, any invidious implication of degrees of refinement of manners; for most purposes it suffices without further modifiers. The term 'agrarianate' (cf. note 3 in chapter 1 of Book One) has the advantage over phrases like 'pre-modern' or 'traditional' of being distinctly set off, as well from Modern technicalistic as from pre-agricultural society. The single antithesis 'traditional-modern' not only oversimplifies historically what is chosen as a contrast to 'Modern' but underplays the dynamic nature of what is commonly thought of as tradition, and it definitely ignores the active role of 'tradition' in the most Modern society. The articulation of the long 'Agrarian Age' from Sumer to the French Revolution as pre-Axial, Axial, and post-Axial suits most general purposes for which terms like 'Medieval' would serve and gets round the question whether to include the world-historical period from Columbus to the French Revolution under the label 'Medieval', since from a world viewpoint it is undeniably still post-Axial Agrarian, though within the Occident it initiates Modernity. The important though shorter periods required within the post-Axial, such as the age of the dominance of the confessional faiths, can be referred to *ad hoc*.

Modern

Various terms are now used in referring to the distinctive complex of cultural traits that have played a decisive role in human society since about the generation of 1789. Most of such terms are appropriate in one context or another. A first set of terms depends on the recentness of these traits and on the fact that they do not remain constant, but must always be brought further up to date. The age characterized by these traits (together with that period which, within the Occident, can be regarded as leading up to them) is usually called 'Modern'; the traits can be summed up as 'Modernity', and adoption of them, as 'Modernizing'. A second set of terms refers to the high degree of economic exploitation of resources which is also a fundamental characteristic. A society lacking the traits in question is called 'undeveloped' or 'underdeveloped' and the acquisition of such traits is called 'development', which properly should refer strictly to technical development as applied to exploitation of resources, but can be generalized to all the necessarily related traits. A third set of terms has a more precise application. Because a key trait is technical rationality in the sense of subjecting all behaviour to calculation according to presumedly objective ends without interference from arbitrary tradition, the acquisition of the traits generally can be called 'rationalization'. Finally, some refer to acquisition of the traits in question as 'Westernization' because they were first developed in western Europe, and because acquisition of them appears to make any group seem like western Europeans.

In this study, usage on this point needs to be more effectively differentiated than is customary. Use of the term 'modern' commonly presupposes use of the term 'traditional' as a lumping term for all social forms not characterized by the given complex of traits. This latter usage is very unfortunate in as much as within the 'non-Modern' social forms there are often important distinctions between what is and is not traditional, even in the sense of the term—i.e., immemorially customary—intended by those who use it. For instance, there has been a dynamic distinction between the Sharîʿah of the textualistic ḥadîth-minded ʿulamâʾ, always fighting popular ways, and more 'traditional' custom which tended to continue popular ways; and such a distinction may be of crucial import just in the present context. Again, common current usage can result in calling 'traditional' certain political or economic patterns that are clearly not characteristic of a 'Modern' form of society in our special sense, but which may have developed only in the nineteenth century and in response to the presence of 'Modern' conditions in the environment. Such usage invites confusion on a very crucial aspect of the history of our times by confounding these latter-day intrusions or expedients with more genuinely 'traditional' traits. But even the term 'Modern', though useful in many contexts where it happens to be unambiguous, is not satisfactory as a precise technical term for the traits in question, if only because it is so often necessary to distinguish between what is up to date and what is out of date at any given point *within* the process of Modern change. Though in this work I do sometimes use 'Modern' (capitalized) to refer to what more properly I call 'technicalistic' or 'of the Technical Age', yet it seems best as far as possible to retain 'modern' for the up-to-date as such, using it in a more epochal sense ideally only when it contains just that specific element of relativity and even of normative implications—in other words, the element, indeed, normally implied in the word.

Terms like 'development', 'rationalization', and 'industrialization' (which likewise are occasionally used loosely to cover the whole wider process) also will better be restricted to their more precise meanings—that is, respectively, technical development of whatever degree, technical rationalization, and the preponderance, over other sectors of the economy, of technically developed industry. The first two terms, technical 'development' in some degree, and 'rationalization', can then usefully refer not only to phases within technicalism but even to isolated situations of a very pre-Modern date, not organically related to the complex of Modern times at all. As to 'Westernization', the broad use of such a term implies a *parti pris* on the question—crucially open for us—of how much the complex of traits in question may be dissociable from the rest of Western culture, in particular from the pre-modern Occidental cultural heritage. I prefer to restrict the term to an explicit adoption of Western traits *as Western* rather than simply as Modern.

Technicalistic, Technical Age

I prefer to use special variants on the root 'technical' when it is important to be precise. The term 'technicalized', corresponding to 'industrialized' but applicable to technical development not only in manufacturing but in agriculture, administration, science, and so on, will suffer neither semantic loss nor serious obscurity if it is used to characterize the several sectors or the whole of *a society in which the dominant elements are on a level of social organization where in intellectual and practical activity, calculatively rationalized and specialized technical procedures form an interdependent and preponderant pattern.* Denmark, which may not be primarily industrialized as a society, is highly technicalized in this sense. Then I shall use the word 'technicalistic' to refer to patterns of thought or activity appropriate to or functionally associated with technicalized processes.

Just as the term 'agrarianistic' cannot safely be used of all developments which characterized the agrarianistic societies, so the terms 'technicalization' and 'technicalism' will not exhaust all the traits legitimately associable with Modern times. Above all, certain moral qualities which may have been necessary to launch technicalization in the first place, or the cultivation of which may be facilitated by its presence and consequences, cannot be subsumed under 'technicalism'. I prefer cautiously to refer to them as typical of or associated with the *age* of technicalism, the period since technicalistic patterns became crucially dominant in the world at large. The period thus comes after the generation during which technicalization came into full effect in at least some aspects of some west European societies with the Industrial (1785) and the French (1789) Revolutions, which was also the generation of the establishment of European world hegemony. For convenience I call this succeeding age (down at least to the present) the 'Technical Age', since an age can be named merely for a dominant feature and no one is likely to find the term misleading in this brief form. As a term for an age it refers to the time-period the world over, whether any given land was actually being technicalized then or was merely suffering (or even fortunately escaping) the backwash effects of technicalization elsewhere. Correspondingly, when I use the term pre-Technical, it refers generally to the time-periods that precede the Technical Age; it does not refer to non-technicalized, or technically underdeveloped, countries or sectors within the Technical Age. This allows me, as the less precisely used 'Modern Age' and 'pre-Modern' would not, to keep in focus the overall historical situation as well as the internal state of development in any given place. It will be obvious that the *terminus a quo* of the Technical Age is at the same time the *terminus ad quem* of the Agrarian Age.

West, Occident, Europe

I use the term 'West' in discussing conditions of the Technical Age; I do not use it before. I must distinguish it from my use of the terms 'Europe' and 'Occident'.

The term 'West' is often very loosely used, even if not quite so misleading as the term 'East'. It can cover at least five different historical groupings of lands and peoples. All too often a statement proper to one of these groupings is taken implicitly as applying to another, with consequent confusion. (The confusion usually occurs in tendentious ways.) 'West' refers (1) originally and properly to the western or Latin-using half of the Roman empire; that is, to the *west Mediterranean lands*. By extension, (2) it can refer to the *west European lands* generally, more precisely to the western or Latin Christian countries north of the Mediterranean (in the Middle Ages and since) which traced their heritage back to the Roman empire. In this usage it will normally exclude those west Mediterranean lands which turned Muslim. By a further extension, (3) the overseas settlements of the *west European peoples anywhere*, in the Americas and the Antipodes, can be included. It is in these latter two senses that the term 'Occident' is used in this work: to designate the peoples of Western (originally Latin) Christendom, including in more modern times their overseas settlements. (The term 'Occident' is less popularly used in English and so has some chance of being captured for a precise purpose.) The term 'West' is also sometimes used (4) for *all European Christendom*, usually including all the peoples of European origin (both in the European region and in their extra-European settlements); that is, both the original west Europeans and the east Europeans from whom the term 'west' originally distinguished them. It is by a curious extension of this usage that selected portions of ancient Greek history are commonly included (retroactively) in a 'Western' history which otherwise is chiefly only Occidental in the narrower sense (so that the Merovingians and *not* the Byzantines are made to appear as 'Western', with the consequent implication of being heirs of ancient Greece!). For such purposes, the terms 'European' or 'Christian European' are more appropriate, at least for the period before the Technical Age, when extra-European settlers were still obviously Europeans. But for the strictly Modern period, I use the term 'Western' for this purpose so as to include unequivocally the extra-European settlers. Finally, (5) sometimes all Afro-Eurasian *civilized lands west of the Indus* may be included, that is, roughly both Europe and the Middle East; for such a purpose, 'west Eurasian' or 'Irano-Mediterranean' is preferable.

The term 'Europe', in contrast to the term 'West', has come to have a specious exactitude, referring to the most westerly peninsula of Eurasia, with the associated islands and an arbitrarily designated part of their continental hinterland, usually bounded at the Urals. This precise area, however, has at no time ever formed a cultural or political entity to any degree at all. I have used the vaguer term 'European region' or 'European lands' to cover an area similar to this but forming at least in pre-Modern periods a historically truer grouping: the lands north of the Mediterranean (from Anatolia to Spain) with their hinterland northward (including into the Russian plains), and without always excluding such related lands as the Maghrib. The term 'Europe' then can take on a more usefully precise political and social meaning only in Modern times, when it refers to the west European stages plus those east European states that had assimilated to them; i.e., until recently, the Christian states.

Accordingly, in Book Six, I still use 'Occident' to refer to the ex-Latin Europeans and their overseas settlers, and 'European' in the general regional sense of the lands north of the Mediterranean. But I also use 'Western' to refer to all European Christendom and its extra-European extensions, and 'Europe', in a political sense, to refer to the Christian European states and their organizations.

Yet another recent usage of 'West' comes back to a west-east division within Europe, but rather different from the old one: the 'East' is the Communist bloc, and the 'West' then becomes the non-Communist Western bloc. In a general historical context it will be easy to refer to 'Western-bloc' powers when this is intended.

'East Roman empire', 'Byzantine'

After the capital of the Roman empire was finally settled in Constantinople (following a period when Rome, in any case, had not been the actual capital), many authors call the empire 'East Roman' or 'Byzantine'. The term 'Byzantine' becomes useful at least to distinguish the ruling classes, though it is most appropriate only after the Arab conquests, when Latin practically disappeared. But the term 'East Roman' can be misleading in a more general historical perspective. It does not happen to refer, like 'Eastern Han', to the shift of the capital from a western to an eastern location; rather it refers to the frequent appointment, during more than a century, until 480, of an autonomous co-emperor in the western provinces. This used to be misconstrued as marking the creation of two contemporaneous empires, an 'East Roman' and a 'West Roman'. The 'West Roman' was then tacitly identified with the Roman empire proper—partly because it included the original Roman territories, but more because the historians, as west Europeans, were chiefly interested in the western provinces.

Accordingly, when during the fifth century most of the western provinces temporarily escaped imperial control, never to be fully reconstituted as a group, this was thought of as the 'fall of the Roman empire' (dated specifically in 476, a date poorly chosen in any case). And, in fact, Gaul and Britain, on whose history most Western historians have tended to centre, were not reoccupied; so the imperial power does end locally there in the fifth century. Thereafter by such scholars the continuing main body of the Roman empire has been called the 'East Roman empire' and has been thought of as distinct from the 'Roman empire' proper; so that even the re-establishment of imperial authority in the more important of the western provinces in the sixth century has sometimes been thought of not as a restoration but as an expansion of a different empire—'the East Roman empire at its largest extent'. Commonly used historical atlases so label their maps. But we must be continually reminded that Gaul and Britain were marginal to the empire as such, and the whole western half of the empire was in most ways less important than the eastern half. From the viewpoint of the society and culture of the empire as a whole, there was no beginning 'division' into east and west, and the major transitions come not in the fifth but in the third and the seventh centuries. To refer to the later undivided empire as 'East Roman' is to retroject Occidental independence into too early a past and to obscure the continuity of the empire as a whole. It can confuse our sense of the Roman heritage in the Mediterranean basin as it confronted the first Muslims, as well as distort our sense of the early relations between Islamdom and the Occident.

The Westernizing world-map projections and atlases

The Muslims in ages past had an image of the world noticeably more balanced than that of the west Europeans. Maps in certain Western history books labelled 'the known world' represent, of course, not the world as known in more advanced and cosmopolitan centres, but as known to the literate public of western Europe. Given the peripheral location of the European peninsula, the Occidentals' image of the world might be expected to have been eccentric. Their division of the old world was not into seven parts, as was the Muslims', but into only three, centred on the Mediterranean Sea (the lands north of it were Europe; those south of it, Africa; those east of it, Asia). Such a distribution was naturally totally inappropriate to the hemisphere as a whole.

Yet it did serve admirably to set off the little European peninsula as a unit comparable to the great land masses. The Medieval ethnocentric classification was preserved and subsequently written into the modern Western map of the world, just as was the equally ethnocentric conception 'Orient'. Its absurdity was disguised by the increasingly widespread use of a drastically visually distortive world map, the Mercator projection, which by exaggerating northward manages to make an artifically bounded 'Europe' look larger than all 'Africa', and quite dwarf that other Eurasian peninsula, India. In this way all the 'well-known' cities of Europe can be included, while the unfamiliar cities of India can be omitted. When the Mercator projection is decried for distorting Greenland—as if Greenland mattered so much—mapmakers can resort to a remarkable compromise: a projection like Van der Grinten's preserves the basic ethnocentric distortion, continuing to exaggerate Europe at the expense of the other main historical cultural centres, but without exaggerating so much the barren far north. Even in historical atlases, maps of the world tend to be visually distortive, and they almost invariably place the Atlantic and Europe in the centre. In our day, such maps, putting the White men's lands on so much larger a scale and in so much more prominent a position than the Coloured men's lands, may fittingly be called 'Jim-Crow' world maps. But the idea is much older than modern racialism. Such maps represent visually how pre-Modern yet continuing popular notions can persist into even Modern scholarly usage.

The disastrous effect that distortive map images can have has been recognized in modern military thinking, where the Second World War forced at least airmen to use 'global' maps so as to think imaginatively. Unfortunately, many Islamicists, like other scholars, have unconsciously allowed their physical image of Islamdom to be distorted by the popular maps that are all about them. They continue to be influenced by European-centred ways. Yet Islamicists, at least, could very usefully take their geographical terms and their 'world image,' and even their 'maps of the known world' from pre-Modern Islamdom. An atlas so oriented would be of great value in reinforcing the proper views presented in carefully written works.

USAGE IN ISLAMICS STUDIES

'Islamics', 'Islamicist'

When the object of a body of studies is people who themselves make studies, it can on occasion be useful to distinguish, in terms, between the studies and their object, which is not done in phrases like 'Islamic studies', 'Islamic scholar', 'Chinese studies', 'Chinese scholar', equally used for studies about or by Muslims or Chinese. Hence the use of slightly pretentious terms like 'Sinology', 'Sinologist', and 'Islamology' or 'Islamics', and 'Islamicist'. Though I use the term 'Islamics' I feel it does not yet distinguish clearly enough between studies of Islam as such and studies of Islamdom. The hospitality of English for appositional phrases permits constructions at once simpler and more unmistakable: 'China studies', 'China scholars', 'Islam studies', 'Islamdom studies', 'Islamdom scholars'—a form adaptable at will to any desired delimitation of field. But despite the self-evident clarity of such phrases, I hesitate to introduce them—at least before the term 'Islamdom' has established itself.

'Islamdom', 'Islamicate'

The use of the unwonted terms 'Islamdom' and 'Islamicate' requires a more extended defence. I plead that it has been all too common, in modern scholarship, to use the terms 'Islam 'and 'Islamic' too casually both for what we may call religion and for the overall society and culture associated historically with the religion. I grant that it is not possible nor, perhaps, even desirable to draw too sharp a line here, for (and not only in Islam) to separate out religion from the rest of life is partly to falsify it. Nevertheless, the society and culture called 'Islamic' in the second sense are not necessarily 'Islamic' in the first. Not only have the groups of people involved in the two cases not always been co-extensive (the culture has not been simply a 'Muslim culture', a culture of Muslims)—much of what even Muslims have done as a part of the 'Islamic' civilization can only be characterized as 'un-Islamic' in the first, the religious sense of the word. One can speak of 'Islamic literature', of 'Islamic art', of 'Islamic philosophy', even of 'Islamic despotism', but in such a sequence one is speaking less and less of something that expresses Islam as a faith.

Accordingly, it should avoid confusion, to distinguish the two current meanings of 'Islam' conceptually by means of distinct terms. If one speaks of 'Islamic law', for instance, one may mean the Sharîʿah; but if one is comparing law, as a dimension of cultural life, with 'Islamic' art or literature, one should include the non-Sharʿî legal patterns on a level with the 'non-religious' literature and art. Otherwise one gets a false balance. But too rarely is the non-Sharʿî law, in fact, included. Without a distinction of terms, such a confusion, which may originate in the chances of what material is available to scholarship, tends to persist unnoticed. Thus there are several studies of 'Islamic international law' which (taking 'Islamic' in the first, narrower, sense) deal with the Sharʿî principles of the relation of the caliphate to non-Muslim states. But it seems to have occurred to few to study that other 'Islamic international law', not explicitly religious but characterizing the civilization as such, a law which governed, above all, relations among 'Islamic' states. Yet the latter, and not the Sharʿî 'international' law, is what would culturally correspond to most of what we call 'Islamic art', or 'Islamic literature', or 'Islamic science'; and, indeed, to Western 'international law'.

In fact, the need for a distinction is rather urgent. It would be easy to show that not only beginners but even scholars have found themselves falling into outright error because they have not kept the two current senses of the word 'Islam' distinct. A study of 'Medieval Islam' or of 'Modern Islam' may be primarily a study of religion, or it may be a study of an overall culture in which religion simply takes its place; or it may be a mixture, sections of it differing according to different sources of information. It has happened, for instance, that the same discussion referred to 'Medieval Islam' in a broader cultural sense and to 'Modern Islam' in a more specifically religious sense, and that the fact went unobserved that different discussants, or the same discussant at different times, were referring to different matters in the two cases. The results can be most misleading. Bernard Lewis has suggested that the adjective 'Islamic' be used in the second, the cultural sense, and the adjective 'Muslim' in the first, the religious sense. But it does not appear that this usage will be maintained; and indeed there is some advantage in distinguishing between 'Islamic' as an adjective 'of or pertaining to' Islam as either an idealized or a historical cumulative tradition of faith, and 'Muslim' as an adjective 'of or pertaining to' the Muslims, insofar as they accept that faith—a slight distinction, but sometimes a useful one, and one that comes easily.

I have come to the conclusion that the problem can be solved only by introducing new terms. The term 'Islamdom' will be immediately intelligible by analogy with 'Christendom'. 'Islamdom', then, is the society in which the Muslims and their faith are recognized as prevalent and socially dominant, in one sense or another—a society in which, of course, non-Muslims have always formed an integral, if subordinate, element, as have Jews in Christendom. It does not refer to an area as such, but to *a complex of social relations*, which, to be sure, is territorially more or less well-defined. It does not, then, duplicate the essentially juridical and territorial term, 'Dâr al-Islâm'; yet, in contrast to 'Muslim lands', it is clearly collective—frequently an important point. Sometimes the phrase 'the Islamic world' is used much in this sense. I prefer not to use it for three reasons: (*a*) in compound phrases where 'Islamdom' can be a useful element, the three-word phrase can become clumsy; (*b*) the phrase itself uses the term 'Islamic' in too broad a sense; (*c*) it is time we realized there is only 'one world' even in history. If there is to be an 'Islamic world', this can be only in the future.

On the other hand, if the analogy with 'Christendom' is held to, 'Islamdom' does not designate in itself a 'civilization', a specific culture, but only the society that carries that culture. There has been, however, a *culture*, centred on a lettered tradition, which has been historically distinctive of Islamdom the *society*, and which has been naturally shared in by both Muslims and non-Muslims who participate at all fully in the society of Islamdom. For this, I have used the adjective 'Islamicate'. I thus restrict the term 'Islam' to the *religion* of the Muslims, not using that term for the far more general phenomena, the society of Islamdom and its Islamicate cultural traditions.

The noun 'Islamdom' will presumably raise little objection, even if it is little adopted. (I hope, if it is used, it will be used for *the milieu of a whole society* and not simply for the body of all Muslims, for the Ummah.) At any rate, it is already felt improper, among careful speakers, to refer to some local event as taking place 'in Islam', or to a traveller as going 'to Islam', as if Islam were a country. The adjective 'Islamic', correspondingly, must be restricted to 'of or pertaining to' Islam *in the proper, the religious, sense,* and of this it will be harder to persuade some. When I speak of 'Islamic literature' I am referring only to more or less 'religious' literature, not to secular wine songs, just as when one speaks of Christian literature one does not refer to all the literature produced in Christendom. When I speak of 'Islamic art' I imply some sort of distinction between the architecture of mosques on the one hand, and the miniatures illustrating a medical handbook on the other—even though there is admittedly no sharp boundary between. Unfortunately, there seems to be no adjective in use for the excluded sense—'of or pertaining to' the society and culture of Islamdom. In the case of Western Christendom we have the convenient adjective 'Occidental' (or 'Western'—though this latter term, especially, is too often misused in a vaguely extended sense). 'Occidental' has just the necessary traits that 'West Christian' would exclude. I have been driven to invent a term, 'Islamicate'. It has a double adjectival ending on the analogy of 'Italianate', 'in the Italian style', which refers not to Italy itself directly, not to just whatever is to be called properly Italian, but to something associated typically with Italian style and with the Italian manner. One speaks of 'Italianate' architecture even in England or Turkey. Rather similarly (though I shift the relation a bit), 'Islamicate' would refer not directly to the religion, Islam, itself, but to the social and cultural complex historically associated with Islam and the Muslims, both among Muslims themselves and even when found among non-Muslims.

The pattern of such a double adjectival ending, setting the reference at two removes from the point referred to, is sufficiently uncommon to make me hesitate. But there seems no alternative. In some contexts, but only in some, one can refer without ambiguity to the 'Perso-Arabic' tradition to indicate 'of or pertaining to' Islamdom and its culture, for all the lettered traditions of Islamdom have been grounded in the Arabic or the Persian or both. In other cases, one might use a periphrasis involving the terms 'traditions/ culture/ society of Islamdom'. One cannot, speaking generally, call Swedish 'a Christian language'; and if one were debarred from calling it an 'Occidental' language, one could not say simply that it is 'a language of Christendom', which might in some contexts seem to imply that it was to at least some extent used throughout that extensive realm; but one might say it is 'a language of the culture of Christendom'. Likewise, it is hardly accurate, despite certain West Pakistani claims, to call Urdu an 'Islamic' language, in the strict sense. (It was the insistence of some Muslims on treating it that way, and opening a meeting on fostering Urdu with Qur'ân readings, that drove Urdu-loving Hindus away from it and may, in the end, have meant the ruin of Urdu in its motherland.) If one could not refer to it as 'Islamicate', one could yet say it was a language 'of the culture of Islamdom'. One cannot refer to Maimonides as an Islamic philosopher, but one could say, without being seriously misleading, that he was a philosopher in the Perso-Arabic tradition or, still better, a writer in the philosophical tradition of Islamdom. But there is a limit to such periphrases. Eventually, it is stylistically less clumsy to use an explicit term. Moreover, such a term may have valuable pedagogical uses, its very presence militating against the confusions which periphrases would avoid in the writer but not necessarily in his readers.

It may be noted that some, not only Arabs and Western Arabists, but latterly even some non-Arab Muslims (for the historical reasons noted elsewhere), might use the term 'Arabic'—especially in such a case as that of Maimonides. But—to take the case of philosophy—this is ruled out because, for one thing, some important representatives of that tradition wrote in Persian. In fields other than scholarship and philosophy—in politics or art, say—the idea becomes even more patently absurd, despite the bias in favour of it among certain scholars. The term 'Arabic' must be reserved for that subculture, within the wider society of Islamdom, in which Arabic was the normal language of literacy; or even, sometimes, to the yet smaller sphere in which Arabic-derived dialects were spoken. Indeed, the Western temptation to use this term with a wider reference springs from historical accidents that have tended falsely to identify 'Arab' and 'Muslim' in any case. To use the term 'Arabic' then, would not only be inaccurate, it would be one of those erroneous usages that reinforce false preconceptions—by far the most mischievous sort of error, as I have noted in the section on historical method above.

'Middle East', 'Nile to Oxus'

For this region I will not usually use the term 'Middle East' but one or another phrase in 'Nile to Oxus'—'from Nile to Oxus' (generally implying inclusively), for instance, or 'between Nile and Oxus' if what is meant is some given spot in or portion of the area; or occasionally 'in the Nile-to-Oxus region'. The term 'Middle East', which seems the best phrase of those more commonly used, has a number of disadvantages. It is, of course, vague, being used for so limited a region as that of the eastern (or even northeastern) Arab lands plus Israel (the presence of the latter is probably the occasion for having recourse to such a vague term for so limited an area); and it has been used for so extensive a region as that stretching from Morocco to Pakistan, and sometimes including a number of Muslim peoples even further afield. It can, of course, be defined at will; but overtones remain, especially overtones implying an Iran of present-day political bounds.

Its principal disadvantage stems from its relatively exact military usage, where it originated. It cuts the Iranian highlands in half—the western half ('Persia') having been assigned to the Mediterranean command, the eastern half ('Afghanistan') to the Indian command. Since the Iranian highlands are of primary importance in the region that is basic to Irano-Semitic and Islamicate history, such a usage is completely unacceptable. Unfortunately, the military usage as to the eastern limits of coverage has become standard in a great many works using the phrase 'Middle East', and for many readers it comes to imply an area that is, on balance, more westerly than our history requires. Since for Westerners there is anyway a temptation to see everything from the shores of the Mediterranean, the more easterly parts becoming foreshortened as it were, a phrase that has the virtue of explicitly running counter to that temptation is to be preferred.

The phrase 'Nile to Oxus' has the further virtue of being eminently concrete: if one means 'Egypt', say, or 'Egypt and Syria', or some other relatively restricted area (as many do in fact, even when they believe they are using the term 'Middle East' in an inclusive sense) one may hesitate to make too sweeping a generalization if forced to ascribe it explicitly to all the lands from Nile to Oxus.

Another disadvantage of the term 'Middle East' is that it implies it is part of some 'East'—that is, all civilized lands but the Occidental, taken as somehow forming a civilization or a region to which something distinctive may be ascribed, set off as one entity against the 'West' as another. That sort of Western ethnocentrism is discussed in the preceding section on usage in historical studies. The same objection applies to the term 'Near East', which has the further disadvantage of shifting the focus to a yet more westerly zone than 'Middle East' usually does. The absurd phrase 'Near and Middle East', a compromise sometimes used, has the disadvantages of both phrases and the advantages of neither.

From the point of view of the Oikoumene as a whole, 'Middle West' might do, but would anyway not be so immediately intelligible as 'Nile to Oxus'. The phrase 'West Asia' (which seems gratuitously to exclude Egypt from a region where historically it commonly belongs if it belongs to any region beyond itself) has the disadvantage of perpetuating the notion of 'Asia' as a 'continent', a notion that is merely a variant on the Western ethnocentrism of the term 'East'. The Germans commonly use the term 'Orient' for the area from Nile to Oxus. This usage might be both unexceptionable and convenient if only that word did not have far different connotations for English-speaking readers—and also among Germans, to judge by the frequency with which German writers use it in both a strict and an extended sense even in the same discussion.

It will be noted that western Anatolia does not lie between Nile and Oxus, but lies on the contrary along the northern shores of the Mediterranean. This has been its location in all periods, from the time of the ancient Lydians who patronized Delphi to the time of Atatürk.

For the most important complex of cultural traditions in the region from Nile to Oxus, I use the phrase 'Irano-Semitic', which refers to the cultural traditions, both on the folk level and on that of the high culture, rather than to the area as such. The two terms have only for a brief time, if ever, been geographically coextensive, for the area in which the Irano-Semitic culture prevailed in its various periods steadily expanded. For an explanation of my usage of that phrase, see note 9 in chapter I of Book One.

'Arab'

The term 'Arab', *'arab,* as noun and adjective, has been used on at least five levels. (1) It has referred—perhaps originally—expressly to the Bedouin, the nomads and especially the camel nomads of Arabia. (But careful usage has preferred a special term, *a'râb,* for them.) This has at times been the commonest usage of the term in Arabic. However, to render the Arabic *'arab* in such cases by our 'Arab', as some writers do when translating, is bound to be confusing and is to be avoided. The reader must be on the alert for such a usage in older translations. When a pre-Modern Arabic writer, such as Ibn-Khaldûn, said something uncomplimentary about *'arabs,* he was usually speaking only of the Bedouin. (2) Then it has referred to all those claiming descent from or old cultural identification with the Bedouin or their language, including of course the 'settled Bedouin'. In this use, it has historically sometimes had an implication of 'Muslim', since the early Muslims were Arab in rather this sense; but the early jurist Abû-Yûsuf, using it in this sense, included also some Christians and Jews. (3) The next extension was to all those peoples speaking Arabic-derived dialects, whatever their relations to Bedouin traditions or to Islam; in this sense, whole peasant populations can be called Arabs. (However, those among whom the literate have used some other than the standard Arabic alphabet—for instance the Maltese and some other non-Muslim groups, especially Jews—have commonly, but not always, been excluded.) This latter sense is essentially a modern one. In using it in this work I am retrojecting it, for convenience' sake, upon a set of groups which might not have recognized that they formed a common category; it is analogous to having a common term, 'Latins', for all the Romance-speaking peoples. It must not, therefore, be lent any 'national' overtones: in this sense, 'the Arabs' have moved toward forming a nation only recently. However, it is the commonest modern usage and it must be remembered that in this sense the Arabs are mostly neither Bedouin nor tribal; they are, in large majority, peasants, living in villages and closely tied to the land. (4) It has further been used where the normal language of literacy was the classical Arabian, or Muḍarî, Arabic—whether the home vernacular was Arabic-derived or quite unrelated. Usually this usage has been restricted to the individual level. Persons who wrote in Arabic but whose own language was Persian or Spanish or Turkish or Kurdish have been included in what is called collectively 'the Arabs'. Where whole peoples have possessed literacy only in Arabic—e.g., the Somalis—this usage has not usually applied. But even at best the usage is very dubious; it is sounder to say something like 'the Arabic writers'. (5) Finally, there are to be found authors who will seem to use the term for all peoples among whom Arabic is used at least in ritual. This is never done consistently; but it seems to be the implied definition when a book on the modern Arabs, for instance, includes, as illustrations of past Arab achievements, pictures of the Tâj Maḥall in India or of illustrations to Persian poetry. Such a usage is thoroughly confusing and unacceptable.

'Allâh'

We properly use the same English word for the object of worship of all who are recognized as monotheists—the various sorts of Christians and Jews, as well as many persons of other faiths. Normally we leave untranslated a proper name, such as 'Zeus' or 'Odin', when we think of the divinity in question as distinct from (and lesser than) the monotheists' One God. To use 'Allâh' in English can therefore imply, accordingly, the notion that Muslims honour something different from what is honoured by Christians and Jews (and Stoics and Platonists and so forth), and presumably something imaginary: as if they believed that it was some mythical god called 'Allâh', *rather* than God, the Creator. This is essentially a dogmatic position and can be allowed only in those ready to admit its theological implications. Sometimes Muslims writing in English use 'Allâh' instead of 'God', generally with a like distinction in mind, but with the implications reversed—implying more or less consciously that the 'God' which Christians and Jews worship is not really true in the full sense, so that Muslims must be distinguished as worshipping 'Allâh'. Sometimes, to be sure, the usage merely reflects an understandable zeal for the Arabic text of the Qur'ân.

On the other hand, in philological and historical contexts it is sometimes useful to distinguish a particular figure with lineaments envisaged by particular groups in particular forms. In this case, just as it is sometimes convenient to refer to 'Yahweh' in discussing the early Hebrew conception of God, so it can be convenient to refer to 'Allâh' in corresponding circumstances.

'Ḥadîth report', 'Tradition'

The term *ḥadîth* has often been translated 'tradition', in the sense of the Latin *traditio*, something handed from one to another, used of certain alleged unwritten laws and teachings in Jewish and Christian theology. When scholars were Latinists and theologians and when it was considered proper to interpret an alien culture in terms of one's own concepts, the rendering 'tradition' was doubtless convenient. Now, however, it is felt to be important to understand a culture in its own terms. In English, the word 'tradition' implies not only a contrast to anything written, but anonymity and imprecision. The ḥadîth reports, however, are not a matter of vague custom but of explicit statements, *texts*, early put into writing; frequently just *contrary to custom;* and always *naming* both the transmitters and the original source. Since there is also, of course, tradition among Muslims, in the English sense of the word—and since that tradition is often to be contrasted to ḥadîth—such a term as 'narration' or 'report' seems a far more convenient rendering for *ḥadîth* if the term is to be translated at all. Hence in this work I refer to ḥadîth *reports* and ḥadîth *reporters* (or *transmitters*) where conventionally writers have referred to 'Traditions' and 'Traditionists'; I refer to the ḥadîth *corpus* where conventional writers have referred to 'Islamic Tradition'.

A term like 'report' is also philologically more accurate, for *ḥadîth* means 'new' and then reported 'news', 'narration' (and finally even 'conversation'). Moreover, theologically, the analogy with Christian 'tradition' is technically unsound. In exact usage, the term *ḥadîth*, 'report', is explicitly distinguished from *sunnah, sunan,* 'custom(s)', and from *ijmâ*, 'consensus'; it is a *report* of sunnah. It is the term *sunnah* that would be more properly compared to the Christian 'tradition'—at least sunnah when supported by ijmâʿ, consensus, *whether the sunnah happens to be supported by ḥadîth reports or not*.

But what matters is not so much the philological accuracy of the rendering as its scholarly consequences. By using the term 'report', I have left the words 'tradition' and 'traditional' open for more appropriate uses—which will sometimes correspond to *sunnah* in its more general sense ('living' tradition, in the works of Joseph Schacht), but will more often refer to still other cases of the basic cultural phenomenon described in the Prologue. Thus I can avoid giving occasion to certain confusions that are too common in the scholarly literature as it is. Too many writers seem to suppose that Muslim traditional lore and ḥadîth lore, Muslim traditional law and Sharʿî law, were the same, or would have been the same if the Muslims in question had been 'true' Muslims. Or at least many writers suppose that ḥadîth lore and the law based on it were always 'traditional' in some ordinary English sense, even if they did not form the whole tradition. Often writers will use 'tradition' and 'traditional' freely in their ordinary sense in the same discussion where they use these words for ḥadîth reports, without specially marking the contrast. But such ways of thinking and writing make nonsense of all the Sharʿî reformers from al-Shâfiʿî to Abd-al-Wahhâb. But these men were all attacking actual Muslim custom and *tradition* in the name of (often obscure) *texts, naṣṣ*, which were commonly in fact innovative. They could claim to represent tradition, in the crucial cases, only in a very tenuous sense even if one grants them all their presuppositions: that is, in the sense that those few who followed a lone but exalted precedent, contrary to all custom, were maintaining the only tradition that really counted. In fact, the ḥadîth reporter was not, as such, a traditionalist but a *textualist* (or perhaps by intention a *revivalist*—in the exact sense of that term) and was often quite as much opposed to the truly tradition-minded as to any rationalist.

The needless confusion invited by using the term 'Tradition' for a report has been seen by a number of scholars, who have tried to avoid it by capitalizing the word when used in its 'technical' sense. This might work if it were not that the confusion is weighted; the usage is one of those insidious misusages which reinforce erroneous tendencies already present among us, and which therefore cannot be counteracted with a mere footnote warning. For unfortunately the ḥadîth-minded Muslims themselves insisted that the ḥadîth reports did represent the only tradition that ought to be valid for a Muslim, and moreover a tradition unbroken from the time of the Prophet himself. Until the work of Ignaz Goldziher, Islamicists tended to believe this without examination; even since his time they have been tempted, as philologians, to look on the ḥadîth textualist party among Muslims—the party most easily traceable by philological methods—as in all cases and in all periods the partisans of the 'true' Muslim tradition, in the ordinary sense of that word, even if they acknowledged that some 'traditions' were in fact later than was claimed. This has led them to overlook the anti-traditionalist function of ḥadîth reports in forming the early law, and to think of Ḥanbalîs and Ẓâhirîs, who clung especially to ḥadîth reports, miscalled 'traditions', as the most *traditionalist*—not merely the most *textualist*—of the schools: a serious misconception. And it has led them, if at all alert, to having to have recourse to needlessly cumbersome excursuses to explain, apropos of Muslim Modernist movements, that ḥadîth reports ('Tradition') form only a part of the actual Islamic tradition; that a stress on such reports may or may not indicate what is ordinarily called traditionalism in a man; that, in fact, a strict ḥadîth-mindedness, now as ever, may well imply an anti-traditional orientation in several respects.

Practically any discussion involving the role of ḥadîth reports will illustrate the potential and often actual confusion that results from using the rendering 'Traditions'. Too often not only the unwary general reader but the scholar himself falls victim. It is true that Islamicists, like other scholars, tend to have their own traditionalism (in the common sense), but scholars know that when a usage is not merely unfortunate but actively misleading, it must be abandoned, however painful the effort to do so and however hallowed the usage is by age.

An example may serve to pinpoint the difficulty. George Makdisi, in an article cited in chapter III of Book Three, shows that the conventional picture of Ash'arism as becoming 'orthodox' in the Earlier Middle Period will not stand up. But he does not escape the conventional picture otherwise, for he identifies traditionalism among early Muslims with adherence to ḥadîth reports; and then he finds himself puzzled by his own results in consequence. This picture of Islamic history was almost certainly reinforced by his use of the term 'Tradition' for a ḥadîth report; at any rate, his terminology did nothing to alert him to the confusion.

He begins with a remark that it would be only natural—on the basis of general history of religions—to expect (as in the usual scholarly image of Islamic development, based on the Ash'arî apologists) an early division between 'traditionalists' and 'rationalists', which would then be later bridged by a mediating 'orthodoxy' (the Ash'arî kalâm). In saying this, he seems to identify the 'traditionalists' in the general sense with his 'Traditionists', the ḥadîth-reporters and especially the Ahl al-Ḥadîth—and, of course, the 'rationalists' with the Mu'tazilîs (as against the Ash'arîs).

But, in fact, since both the 'kalâm men' and the 'ḥadîth men' had at first been, in different ways, partly opposed to the living tradition of Marwânî times, to call the ḥadîth men 'traditionalist' in any broad sense is to misrepresent them (though, to be sure, it was their own misrepresentation); the Mu'tazilîs had as good a claim to be called traditionalist, their 'rationalism' (in defence of the older tradition) being no more anti-traditional than was the textualism of the ḥadîth men (or than the 'rationalism' of the Ash'arîs). To the extent that the ḥadîth men succeeded in gaining popular support, their subsequent conflict with the kalâm men (Mu'tazilî or Ash'arî) was a secondary development not to be expected to answer to any universal primitive experience in religious traditions.

Indeed, Makdisi goes on to note that in Islam the pattern he expected to see did not fulfill itself after all. But such an observation loses its point if one gets outside the framework set by the identification of ḥadîth reports with Islamic tradition. Without such an identification, he might have been led to see that what he had to deal with were three, not two, universal types of phenomena in religious history—traditionalism, 'rationalism', and *textualism* (allowing, but only for the moment, the legitimacy of a term like 'rationalism' for the argumentative viewpoint of the kalâm men). He then might have seen the whole range of Islamic textualism in a different light—which might not have altered his immediate conclusions, but would surely have given them an ultimately different and more fruitful meaning. Avoidance of the term 'Tradition' for a hadîth report and of 'Traditionist' for a reporter would not by itself have led to new insights, but it might have helped avoid taking old misconceptions too much for granted.

'Sect', 'firqah'

The common term used in the the pre-Modern Arabic and Persian languages for any grouping of people according to their opinions was *firqah*. This has been translated 'sect', but it rather rarely answers to the modern English notion of 'sect'. Usually it should be rendered by nothing stronger than 'school of thought'. Often it is used to refer to a single teacher and his disciples, with reference to one minor point of doctrine. In such a case there is no question of a body of persons sharing a common religious allegiance such that their overall religious life is led among themselves and apart from others, as is implied in a 'sect'.

The Muslim historians of doctrine always tried to show that all other schools of thought than their own were not only false but, if possible, less than truly Muslim. Their works describe innumerable 'firqahs' in terms which readily misled modern scholars into supposing they were referring to so many 'heretical sects'. These histories of doctrine have been called, not unfairly, 'heresiographies', which, however, is rather a description of their tendencies than an exact designation of their contents. But to use the word 'sect' wherever a Muslim writer used the word *firqah* produces odd misconceptions. A person could maintain a given viewpoint on the imâmate, one on questions of metaphysics or kalâm, and one on fiqh law; he could be, for instance, a Jamâ'î-Sunnî, a Mu'tazilî, and Ḥanafî. Beginners, and (unfortunately) not only beginners, have sometimes been confused as to how so many Ḥanafîs, whom he knows to be Sunnîs, could belong to the supposedly rival 'sect' of the Mu'tazilah. In so prominent a case the confusion can be relatively easily laid to rest; but the elevation of many less well-known viewpoints on one or another issue into full-blown 'sects' has peopled with strange ghosts the history of Muslim rebellions and urban factions as well as the history of doctrine.

Note that the conventional distinction between 'orthodox' Islam and 'the sects' is at best dubious. For my usage of the terms 'Sunnî' and 'Jamâ'î', see the discussion in chapter I of Book Two.

NOTE ON TRANSLATING

A translation must be judged according to the purposes of the given translator. It is possible to distinguish three usual sorts of translation: re-creative, explanatory, and precise study translations. In bibliographical references I have identified translations accordingly, when necessary.

The translator's purpose may be to re-create a work so as to enrich a second literature with a work having approximately the same effect as the original. Sometimes the effect intended is very close to the original effect, sometimes it is an analogous effect. One may then draw inspiration from such a model without being tied to those features of it that are relevant only within its original setting. Such a translation of poetry will aim to be poetic; with prose, such a translation will be more or less a paraphrase, with one or another degree of 'modernization', if necessary, to make it easily readable. Ideally, this kind of translation should be by someone who is an artist in his own right. If the effect aimed at is something like the original effect, it is *possible* for a re-creative translation to be useful, even for the scholar, in evoking the elusive flavour of the whole work. But it is necessarily impressionistic in two senses. It gives a calculated impression to a new audience, and it renders only those nuances of the original that the translator wishes the reader to see relevance in. In any case, for scholarly purposes, a re-creative translation can never substitute for the original.

The translator's purpose may be to explain and interpret a work—using the occasion of rendering it into a second language for much the same task that would be served by a commentary in the original language. Such an explanatory translation, if cautiously done, will stay fairly close to the text, but it almost necessarily changes the mood of the work, since words in the second language grow out of different conceptualizations from the words of the original language, and the translated text itself, no matter how many notes accompany it, tends to sway the understanding of the reader. Most of the current 'serious' translations of belles-lettrist (poetry and literary prose) works seem to fall into the explanatory category of translation, but with nuances of the re-creative. Thus, though an explanatory translation may be exceedingly useful to the scholar, it still cannot dependably replace the original.

The translator's purpose may be, finally, to reproduce the information carried by the original work, for the purposes of special study by those who cannot read the original language. Such a translation attempts to provide an equivalent communication of the original which readers can then interpret for themselves. For study purposes, the translation has to be maximally precise. Special study through translation is legitimate so long as few even among scholars can master the ever-increasing number of languages in which significant work has been or is being done. Precise study translations are generally most appropriate for scriptures, scientific theses, technical philosophy, chronicles, and secondary scholarly essays, though this sort of translation in fact has its place in many other kinds of material. With ingenuity and, of course, a complete control of what is routine grammatical pattern or idiom and what is personal choice in the original writer, precision can often be combined with great elegance of translation, as has been shown in Islamics studies by H. A. R. Gibb.

For almost all scholarly purposes, re-creative translation is out of place. On the other hand, all scholars have to admit their reliance on translations. In the first place, no scholar can command all the languages now necessary for him to read in, no matter how specialized his own field. But even more important, no one person can grasp all the implications of a work—especially not of a masterpiece—which may be of importance to another reader. The translator must find an equivalent for every personal turn of phrase of the original, however superfluous it may seem, and must leave ambiguities, so far as possible, ambiguous. Such a translation almost necessarily requires a certain number of explicitly technical terms and a few footnotes or square brackets to pinpoint untranslatable implications. (Need it be added that a precise translation in this sense cannot be an overly literal one? Sometimes the most exact rendering of a Persian word or even a phrase may be, in English, a comma or a semicolon.) The crucial test of the success of a precise study translation is that, although the translation is free of the syntax of the original language as such, yet the most natural retranslation of it into the original language will give back the original form, without precisions or omissions.

Unfortunately, our supply of re-creative and explanatory translations is larger than our supply of good precise translations for study. This springs partly from an inclination of some persons to downgrade the importance of translating, and partly from a natural desire of translators to be creative in their own right. But even from the scholar's viewpoint, let alone the lay reader's, the lack of usable translations is a major handicap to serious work and proper understanding.

The Islamic Vision in Religion and in Civilization

Muslims are assured in the Qur'ân, 'You have become the best community ever raised up for mankind, enjoining the right and forbidding the wrong, and having faith in God' (III, 110). Earnest men have taken this prophecy seriously to the point of trying to mould the history of the whole world in accordance with it. Soon after the founding of the faith, Muslims succeeded in building a new form of society, which in time carried with it its own distinctive institutions, its art and literature, its science and scholarship, its political and social forms, as well as its cult and creed, all bearing an unmistakable Islamic impress. In the course of centuries, this new society spread over widely diverse climes, throughout most of the Old World. It came closer than any had ever come to uniting all mankind under its ideals.

Yet the 'civilization of Islam' as it has existed is far from being a clear expression of the Islamic faith. From the first, pious Muslims themselves differed as to what the 'best community' should be like. The Islamic vision of what mankind might be has been seen and interpreted variously: no one ideal has ever fully prevailed among the Muslims. Moreover their efforts, such as they were, to build a good society often produced actual results strikingly different from what anyone had anticipated. Some of the greatest triumphs of culture under an Islamic aegis have been such as many devoted Muslims could not look on with favour; and while Islam has seen some outstanding successes which all could acclaim, it has seen failures at least as outstanding. Those who have undertaken to rebuild life in Islamic terms have ventured on an enterprise with a high potential reward—that of winning through to the best that is open to mankind; but with correspondingly great risks of error and failure.

Muslims have yet to implement the Qur'ânic prophecy fully in all its implications. But they have perennially renewed their hopes and efforts to live the godly life not only as individuals but as a community. In every age, pious Muslims have reasserted their faith, in the light of new circumstances that have arisen out of the failures and also of the successes of the past. The vision has never vanished, the venture has never been abandoned; these hopes and efforts are still vitally alive in the modern world. The history of Islam as a faith, and of the culture of which it has formed the core, derives its unity and its unique significance from that vision and that venture.

It may be doubted how relevant to historical reality such ideals can be. Can in fact a world society be effectively built on allegiance to a vision of the divine? Or must society evolve almost regardless of the ideals or concerns of any individuals—nay, create and destroy those ideals according to the play of more casual interests? Certainly, as we shall see, the conscious planning of idealists has played no great direct role in the social evolution of the Muslim peoples. Yet the presence of the Islamic ideals (whatever their cause) has made the crucial difference between the existence of a society that can be called 'Islamic', on the one hand, and—what might presumably as readily have been—the perpetuation of earlier traditions in new forms, experiencing no doubt much of what came to pass under the sign of Islam but without the peculiar genius which sets off the 'civilization of Islam' as an object of our interest, our admiration, or our fear.

THE IMPLICATIONS OF THE ACT OF ISLÂM

The vision quite naturally, as it is taken seriously in a human mind, unfolds and materializes itself into a whole complex of life patterns, a whole culture. Primitively, the term 'islâm' refers to the inner spiritual posture of an individual person of good will. The word *islâm* in Arabic means the act of submitting to God. (The word *muslim*, 'submitter', is a participle from the same verb.) That is, it means accepting a personal responsibility for standards of action held to have transcendent authority. In this sense, many persons who have admittedly had no part in the historical community of Muḥammad—among them, all the Hebrew prophets and Jesus and his first disciples—have been regarded by Muslims as having accepted islâm. In any religious tradition, it is an inward stance in individuals (varying intimately, of course, from individual to individual) that lies at the heart of all the ritual and myth. It is this elementary islâm, a personal acceptance of godly ideals, which stands at the heart of Islamic religion, and from which it receives its name.

But the term 'Islam' (capitalized) has come to refer also more generally to the whole social pattern of cult and creed which, at least for the pious, follows from or even grows out of the personal islâm of the individual devotee; that is, to the 'religion' in the historical sense. The various elements of the historical religion can be seen as depending more or less directly on the act of islâm of the individual believer. Some seem to follow almost by logical necessity; and while others seem to be connected with it only indirectly or even by arbitrary association, apart from it they would be felt to be meaningless. From the most essential religious avowals through the realms of uniform cult and law to the most localized and incidental custom, all can be derived in this perspective from islâm, and all can be included in Islamic beliefs and ways. In particular, the historical Islamic beliefs about the due place of human beings in the cosmos and what they should do there can be seen as stemming logically from the act of islâm; then all else can be derived from these.

Islamic belief has a reputation for being easily understood and while under careful study it turns out to have its due share of complexity, in fact its most essential elements can be set forth rather simply. It is the very point of islâm to own the supremacy of one single God, Who is identified as the God of Abraham and of Moses and of Jesus, and Whose name in Arabic is *Allâh.*[1] To make this supremacy meaningful, faith must specify. God is the Creator of the world and of mankind in it; and He will finally bring the world to an end and, reviving at the Last Judgment all men and women that have ever lived, will punish them in Hell or reward them in Paradise according to whether they have obeyed His will in their lifetimes. To give God's supremacy concrete content, faith must specify further. God has sent prophets, such as Moses and Jesus, to summon various peoples to obedience, which consists in worshipping Him alone and in dealing justly with one's fellow men. The last and greatest of these prophets, whose message is to all the world and supersedes that of any previous prophet, was Muḥammad of Arabia (d. 632 CE), whose precepts and example all men and women are henceforth bound to follow, individually and collectively.

Insofar as much of the morally most decisive human activity is group activity, Muslims must work together as a body. But to work together the faithful must recognize one another. True inward islâm cannot be perceived from without. Hence for social purposes one must judge by its most elementary consequences. Whoever declares that 'there is no divinity but God, and Muḥammad is the messenger of God' (the *shahâdah*) has usually been reckoned a Muslim and a member of the Islamic *Ummah,* the community of the faithful, with appropriate rights and responsibilities in common undertakings. Thus from a fundamental private attitude of soul is derived a concrete social body and a precise formula of belief to define membership in it.[2]

All this must be worked out in massive detail if people are to move from the general ideal to its actual implementation in the midst of the innumerable complexities of living. In the course of doing so, Muslims move still further from the inward core of personal Islam to a vast body of social conventions, perhaps accepted by most believers rather out of hereditary loyalty than from any fresh personal idealism.

Above all, the commands of God must be known in detail. Muḥammad's message is embodied in permanent written form. The Qur'ân ('Koran' is a different spelling of the same word) is the collection of the revelations, word for word, which God made to Muḥammad; it has been accepted as literally the words of God, and every Muslim must know some of it by heart. *Ḥadîths* are reports of the sayings and doings of Muḥammad (primarily), as related by

[1] Normally, *Allâh* is to be translated as 'God', just as is (for instance) the Greek *ho Theós* in appropriate contexts. *Allâh* is, in fact, the Arabic equivalent of *ho Theós* not only for Muslims but also for Christian Arabs, just as 'God' is the English equivalent. To use *Allâh* in English in referring to the object of Muslims' worship (and not the Arab Christians') is to imply that Muslims and Christians (or Jews) do not have the same object of worship; a position not to be adopted lightly. See the note on *Allâh* in the section on usage in Islamic history in the Introduction.

[2] For the pronunciation of unfamiliar terms and names, see the Introduction.

his associates (or perhaps by his representatives); if authenticated, they have commonly possessed almost equal authority with the Qur'ân itself. The Qur'ân and certain collections of ḥadîth reports together have formed the Muslim scriptures; on their basis Muslim religious scholars, called *ulamâ*, have set forth in detail what obedience to God means in daily life. (The 'ulamâ' are not, properly speaking, priests, but teachers; for every Muslim is authorized to perform all rites, not just the 'ulamâ'.) Their rules of correct practice came to be called the *Sharî'ah;* in principle it covers every possible human contingency, social and individual, from birth to death.

Central among the commands of God are those which provide for the cult—the outward expression in symbolic acts of the individual's devotion. A socially established faith does not spring simply from a private personal exaltation, but consecrates generally imposed social obligations; appropriately, then, devotion, if not to the ideals, at least to their practical consequences, is expressed largely in group activity: notably in the ritual worship at the central cult building, the mosque. Much of the cult, however, even in its group expression, is carried on outside the mosque; much of it, though socially sanctioned, is left to the family or the individual—for instance, the requirement of circumcision. At this level the cult merges insensibly, by way of private etiquette, into every sort of family custom, from styles of personal grooming and cooking recipes to casual superstition. Almost any custom which he recognizes as valid is likely to be associated by an unlearnèd Muslim at least vaguely with his faith—as happens in the case of other religions also. Thus a modern Indian Muslim may exchange his European-cut street clothes for a more old-fashioned costume before going to the mosque, feeling the latter costume to be more 'Islamic'; though such a change is not prescribed by Islamic law, and the older costume itself is simply representative of the part of India he lives in and is not found in other Muslim lands.

In its narrowest sense, 'religion' can be identified with the cult itself and with the credal beliefs which are required to give the cult meaning; for it is only at this level that religion as a social institution usually reflects unmistakably a concern with the central impulse of submission to God, without admixture with other sorts of social interests. Yet religion, in a more meaningful sense, goes beyond cult into every realm, most particularly all moral life, to just that degree to which its initial impulse is taken really seriously.

Accordingly, the cult requirements are but the most obvious of a wider range of social practices associated more or less closely with Islamic religion, sometimes set forth in a uniform Sharî'ah law but often varying greatly from place to place. Most directly tied to Qur'ân and ḥadîth reports is a general system of ethics, which has included a wide body of law of personal status, of criminal sanctions, and of commerce—never applied exclusively or in its entirety, but always present to the tender conscience. The sense of membership in a world-wide community with a historical mission has been very strong, and the obligation of Muslims to help one another has been an explicit part of the faith, particularly in the case of *jihâd,* a war against non-Muslims sanctioned in certain circumstances by religion. Almost as closely tied in with religion have been certain social customs, such as the practice (never universal, and now perhaps in course of disappearing) of keeping women in strict social segregation from men. Less closely tied to religion is the use of the Arabic script for writing whatever local language the Muslim uses—a practice, almost universal in pre-Modern times, which helped to set off a series of 'Islamic' cultural languages from sometimes almost identical 'non-Islamic' ones. Still further from a religious prescription is the development of certain typically 'Islamic' decorative patterns of a complex linear type, especially the 'arabesque', often involving ornamental use of the Arabic script, whether in mosques or in buildings unrelated to the cult. With such features we are gradually leaving the realm of what are clearly points of Islamic religion as such and moving into the wider realm of culture at large.

Associated with Islam by extension comes to be a whole vocabulary of art motifs, not merely the arabesque but even related figural styles; a customary expectation of certain social and political forms and standards; above all, a classical body of literature ranging, by slight gradations, from devotional and legal works through works of theological disputation to works of pure metaphysics and natural science; from the history of the Prophet and his community through works of moral edification and general information to every sort of belles-lettres in prose and verse. All were written under the sign of Islam and, to a remarkable extent, all have managed to justify themselves as in some way contributing to the fully Islamic life; they have been carried wherever Muslims have gone and, transmitted from generation to generation, have formed the common background of literary culture shared among all Muslims of cultivation, those who maintained the norms of Islamic society. Not only what may be called the religion proper, then, but the whole social and cultural complex associated with it—indeed, at the most extreme extension, the totality of all the lifeways accepted among any Muslims anywhere—may be looked on as Islam and seen as a self-contained whole, a total context within which daily life has proceeded in all its ramifications. All can, in some sense, be derived as consequent upon the initial posture of *islâm,* of personal submission to God.

As the accompanying chart of the twentieth-century distribution of Muslims shows, though Islam now counts only about a seventh of the world's population, it is unique among the religious traditions for the diversity of the peoples that have embraced it. It began among Arabs in a hot and arid climate, but very early became international and has since taken root in the coldest north and in the wettest tropics. Yet everywhere it went there has been a continuous pressure toward persuading all Muslims to adopt like standards, like ways of living, based on the Islamic ideals prevailing at a given time. There has never been any central world organization of Muslims after the first generations. But even now everywhere Muslims are noted for

Twentieth-Century World Distribution of Muslims

Areas	Numbers of Muslims*	Proportion of Muslims to Total Population	Chief Languages Spoken by Muslims†	Climate
Arab countries: Arabia, the Fertile Crescent, Egypt and Nile Sudan, Maghrib (Libya to Morocco)	*c.* 96,000,000(?) (about ⅕ of world total)	Great majority Muslims; Christian and/or Jewish minorities in most countries	*Arabic* (in various vernaculars), some Berber	Arid, largely desert with fertile areas; rarely far from sea; among the earliest lands of Semitic civilization
Iranian highlands: Iran (and Azerbaijan), Afghanistan, Tajikistan	*c.* 47,000,000(?)	Almost entirely Muslims by heritage; some Christian, Jewish, and Zoroastrian minorities	*Persian*, Pashto, Baluchî, Kurdish, Turkish	Arid highlands, continental climate
Southeast Europe: Turkey (Anatolia), the Balkans, Crimea	*c.* 38,000,000	Muslim majority in some parts, otherwise majority is Christian; Jewish minority; in 20th century, largely redistributed by religion	(*West*) *Turkish*, Slavic, Albanian, some Greek	Relatively well-watered, temperate; at the seaways of ancient Hellenic culture
Central Eurasia and Russia: Volga basin, Siberia; Kazakhstan, Uzbekistan, Turkmenistan, Kirghizistan; Sinkiang	*c.* 18,000,000(?)	Along Volga and elsewhere, minority among Christians; in Republics, almost entirely Muslim by heritage before recent Russian and Chinese influx	(*East*) *Turkish*, in various forms	Cold, continental, largely arid save in north

Indic lands: Indus Valley, Ganges plain, Bengal, Deccan, south India, Ceylon	*c.* 160,000,000 (110 m. in Pakistan, 50 m. in India—over ¼ of world total)	Majority, in those areas which became Pakistan; minority elsewhere among Hindus, Christians, Sikhs; 20th-century redistribution by religion in Panjâb; Muslims about ¼ of all Indic population	*Urdu*, Panjâbî, Kashmîrî, Bengalî, Gujarâtî, Sindhî, Telugu, Tamil, Malayalam	Hot, monsoon area; in the fertile plains of ancient Sanskritic culture
Malaysia and Indochina: From Burma to Indonesia and the Philippines	*c.* 111,000,000(?) (over ⅕ of world total)	Great majority, in most of islands; minorities in Indochinese lands divided among Buddhists and some Hindus and Christians	*Malay* (Indonesian), Sudanese, Javanese, Cham	Hot, humid, islands and peninsulas
China: All provinces but especially Kansu and Yünnan	*c.* 15,000,000(?) or more	Minority among Buddhist-Taoists	Chinese	From arid continental to humid mountains and coast
Sub-Saharan Africa: East coast, western and central Sudan, and scattered	*c.* 42,000,000(?)	Almost entirely Muslim in large parts, shading to a minority divided among animists and (now) Christians	Swahili, Hausa, Somali, etc.	Hot, often well-watered
Elsewhere: The Americas, the South Seas, west Europe, etc.	*c.* 1,500,000	Minorities, usually very small	Various	Various

* Figures for most areas are very inexact. Cf. Louis Massignon, *Annuaire du monde musulman, 1954* (Paris, 1955). These figures have, for the most part, been projected on data given in that volume, with some allowances made which become clear from its pages.

† Major literary languages of Islamdom before the 20th century are italicized.

their keen consciousness of the world Muslim community; they are moved by a sense of universal Muslim solidarity, and maintain in the most diverse geography not only the essential distinctive Islamic rites—including the great common pilgrimage to Mecca where all nations may meet—but also, to some degree, a sense of a common cultural heritage.

At any given time, in any pious mind, Islam could thus seem a timelessly integral ideal whole. Islam as such could not change, though its practice might here and there be more or less corrupted. Such a viewpoint is not purely a subjective illusion. Insofar as Islam, as a religious teaching, can be legitimately formulated as an integrated overall doctrine based on crucial beliefs about the nature of existence (in particular, on a belief about the Creator implied in the basic act of islâm), then to that extent it imposes its own limits on its own future. Such a doctrine, though it may undergo some further development or, more likely, corruption cannot be too radically altered in substance or in spirit without the original teaching itself being denied, and therefore a new ground for faith being implicitly required.

Within a given social context, at least, this integral view may well hold. The Sharîʿah law, for instance, in the form it has taken, as a comprehensive corpus of life regulations, nowadays seems tied to certain outdated social assumptions. Many Muslims would like to 'Modernize' it. But it has yet to be shown how far it will be possible for modern Muslims to modify the Sharîʿah in its more fundamental presuppositions without, in effect, abandoning any serious allegiance to the traditional ḥadîth reports on which it is based. Yet the ḥadîth reports have served to interpret the Qur'ân ever since the Qur'ân ceased, at Muḥammad's death, to be its own continuing interpreter; it is questionable, then, how far the ḥadîth reports can, at this date in history, be separated off from the Qur'ân as dispensable, without decisively abandoning hope of grounding life on the Qur'ân and in the islâm it calls for.

In a less precisely formulable way, the same is true of the culture generally, of the overall complex of lifeways associated with the religion. In any culture can be seen a distinctive manner of fitting life together, which gives it a distinctive tone or style. New ways introduced either from within or from outside may be assimilated to the cultural style and fit in easily; or they may prove incompatible with it and arouse endless difficulties, occasioning a round of readjustments throughout the culture or even disrupting it altogether (as has happened with some non-literate peoples which disintegrated when their members met modern lifeways they could not learn to cope with). An integral conception of Islam as a total culture highlights its distinctive style, its cultural integrality as an indissolubly coherent whole, by tracing all its ramifications to what seem to be indispensable foundations. One is forewarned of points of incongruity and strain in the cultural fabric. On occasion, what comes to be lived as Islam, in particular cases, does violate the integrality of Islamic life: that is, it proves inconsistent with more fundamental cultural presuppositions of Islam, as Islam has been developed; and it is bound to produce a conflict, therefore, which will require some sort of psychological or historical resolution. In some sense, Muslim life has had an integral character as Islamic, not to be violated with impunity.

THE DIALECTIC OF A CULTURAL TRADITION

What has been felt as Islam, however, considered historically, in all its ramifications and even in its most central implications, has of course varied enormously. The very comprehensiveness of the vision of islâm as it is unfolded has insured that it can never be quite the same from one place or one time to another.[3] Empirically, any particular formulation of what the fundamental consequences of the act of islâm must indispensably include, would find serious Muslims to reject it—as would a corresponding attempt with regard to any other religious tradition. Still more would this be the case for the culture generally. For historically, Islam and its associated lifeways form a cultural tradition, or a complex of cultural traditions; and a cultural tradition by its nature grows and changes; the more so, the broader its scope.

Tradition can cease to be living, can degenerate to mere transmission. A recipe for a holiday pastry may be 'traditional' in the sense merely that it is transmitted unaltered from mother to daughter for untold generations. If it is merely transmissive, a sheer habit, then any change of circumstances may lead to its abandonment, at least once the mother is gone. But if it is vital, meeting a real need, then the tradition will be readjusted or grow as required by circumstances. A living cultural tradition, in fact, is always in course of development. Even if a pattern of activity remains formally identical in a changed context, its meaning can take on new implications; it can be gradually, even imperceptibly, reconceived. A pastry first made when all foods were prepared at home inevitably becomes something very different when it alone is home-made, though exactly the recipe be used. To cling to the recipe then requires, or perhaps produces, a new point of view toward the pastry. But even without so drastic a change in circumstances, the recipe and its use will prove to have a history. Even in primitive life, over the millennia or even only the centuries, fuel differed, or water, or the quality of the utensils. Eventually, if the tradition was genuinely alive, some cook found that the recipe itself could be improved on in the changed conditions. As she did so, she was

[3] Wilfred C. Smith, in *The Meaning and End of Religion* (New English Library, 1966), has pointed out that the very notion of '*a* religion', as an integral *system* of belief and practice held to be either true or false, is relatively recent as compared with the notion of 'religion' as an aspect of any one person's life, which may be more or less true as that person is more or less sincere or successful. Even in the Irano-Semitic sphere, where 'religions' were earliest and most sharply set off as self-contained total communities, the notion of 'a religion' as a *system* was slow to prevail and has become dominant only in quite modern times. He suggests that what we generally have to deal with are cumulative traditions through which religious faith has been expressed. I am indebted to him for sharpening my awareness here.

not abandoning the tradition but rather keeping it alive by letting it grow and develop.

Living societies seem never to have been actually static. With the advent of citied and lettered life, this dynamic aspect of cultural tradition was intensified; or, rather, the living tradition-process was speeded up and became more visible, so that generation by generation within each tradition there was a conscious individual cultural initiative in response to the ever-new needs or opportunities of the time. It is in what is called 'high culture', in relatively widely shared cultural forms at the literate, urban level, that social tradition has unmistakably shown itself as a process of change. Yet even in 'folk culture', the culture of peasants or even of non-lettered peoples, cultural traditions share substantially the same dynamic force which is more visible in high culture.[4]

In general, then, but especially in the high culture of pre-Modern citied societies, which has been the primary milieu of Islam, we may describe the process of cultural tradition as a movement composed of three moments: a creative action, group commitment thereto, and cumulative interaction within the group. A tradition originates in a creative action, an occasion of inventive or revelatory, even charismatic, encounter: for instance, the discovery of a new aesthetic value; the launching of a new technique of craftsmanship; a rise to a new level of social expectation, one man of another; the assertion of a new ruling stock or even the working out of new patterns of governing; or, in the case of religion, an occasion of fresh awareness of something ultimate in the relation between ourselves and the cosmos—that is, an occasion of spiritual revelation, bringing a new vision. In accepting the Qur'ân and its challenge, Muhammad and his followers opened themselves to vast new considerations of what life might mean, which relegated their former concerns to frivolity; their act of acceptance was thus intensely creative.

Such occasions are creative partly through the quality of the objective event itself, in which there must be something which genuinely answers to universally latent human potentialities. The human impact of the Qur'ân as a sheer piece of writing is undeniable. At the same time, the occasions are creative equally through the particular receptivity of their public, of those who take up the creative event and what it has produced and assign it value, finding in it something which answers to their particular needs or interests, material or imaginative, so that it becomes normative for them. The Qur'ân spoke not only in the language of but to the personal and social needs of a particular group of Arabians, of Meccans and Medinese, with particular social and moral problems. By their responses, positive and negative, they built concrete meaning into what might otherwise have remained on the verbal level as

[4] Throughout this chapter, I have tried to take advantage of the increasing sophistication of anthropologists about cultural processes; but since I am dealing, as a historian, primarily not with folk culture but with high culture, I have had to develop my own theoretical framework here.

general exhortations and observations. Without such response, which indeed is presupposed in the later portions of the Qur'ân itself, it could at most have become a striking but otherwise inconsequential piece of literature. This double aspect of the creative action is nowhere more crucial than in the religious life, where revelatory possibilities are doubtless latent in many an event that passes almost unnoticed; but revelatory experience occurs only when enough persons are ready to receive the impact of a given event and allow it to open their eyes.

The second moment of a cultural tradition is group commitment arising out of the creative action: the immediate public of the event is in some way institutionalized and perpetuated; that is, the creative action becomes a point of departure for a continuing body of people who share a common awareness of its importance and must take it into account in whatever they do next, whether in pursuance of its implications or in rebellion against them. Such was long the case of Occidental artists vis-à-vis Italian Renaissance painting, for instance. In a tradition of liberal education built around an agreed-on core of classics, the commitment becomes even more binding, still more so in a tradition of law. At its most effective the commitment becomes an allegiance. Thus Islam could be defined as commitment to the venture to which Muḥammad's vision was leading; which meant, concretely, allegiance to Muḥammad and his Book and then to the continuing community of Muḥammad, or at least (later) to a supposed faithful remnant of that community. The allegiance came to be marked by such symbolic gestures as utterance of the shahâdah, the formula of Muslim belief, or performing worship toward the *qiblah*, that is, toward Mecca; which acts have been sufficient to establish a person as committed to the social and juridical consequences of being a Muslim, whatever the extent of his inward islâm.

This group commitment retains its vitality through cumulative interaction among those sharing the commitment; above all, through debate and dialogue, as people work out the implications and potentialities latent in the creative event to which they are bound. In the arts, the solution of one problem—itself arising from within the artistic tradition—is witnessed by other artists, who may adopt it or respond to it with alternative solutions; and these solutions open up new opportunities and new artistic problems in their turn. In philosophy and in science, the transmission of what has been done and found, especially in the case of the great initiators like Plato or Ptolemy, is but the preliminary essential to the continuing cumulative dialogue, the response and counter-response, which is the purpose of such transmission and without which the transmission itself will gradually cease. The like is true of the inventive and elaborative development of an economic order; and above all of political life, built of the thrust and parry of contrasting interests, each party striving to turn the accumulated heritage of a major state formation to its own advantage, and in doing so shifting the pattern of the heritage which the next special interest will work through.

The implications of an initial event may be relatively particular and functional—may have reference to the development of historical circumstances as the community faces them. Once the early Muslims had conquered the region from the Mediterranean through Iran, a common corpus of law and custom was required if the community was to hold together and maintain its position: some sort of Sharîʻah law was needed. And if this was to be worked out in harmony with the experience that had brought the Muslims together and assured them of their highest ideals, building a Sharîʻah could require, in turn, the discovery of ḥadîth reports, of reports about the earliest Muslims, which could relate the Qur'ânic challenge to the practical needs of the subsequent empire. Gradually, over centuries, pious Muslims building one on another's work found such ḥadîths and created such a Sharîʻah. Much of their work meant coming to terms at least as much with their own society as with the Qur'ânic challenge.

Or else the implications of the creative event may be relatively universal and logical—may stem, that is, from the very nature of the event, from its inherent potential for enlarging the resources of any human beings seeking truth in their lives. Thus whatever may have led a man to commit himself initially to Muḥammad's community (and it was likely to have been much less than a total apprehension of Muḥammad's own vision), this public commitment necessarily led him further in the direction of that islâm which is the private affair of the soul; and of seeking an articulate conception of prophecy and of God, such as would make intelligible the islâm he found himself being led towards. It was in dialogue, in an exchange of insights and of objections with others in a like situation, that he came to realize what sense of himself and of the universe would serve and what would not. In such searching, he might be confronting something in Islam, and perhaps something in the human spiritual condition, more or less relevant under any circumstances.

Relatively circumstantial and functional or relatively inherent and logical, in either case the implications of the initial commitment could be worked out fully only as the initially creative vision was confronted ever afresh from a new perspective in the course of cumulative interaction and dialogue among those to whom the initial events were meaningful.

But not only does a developing interaction arise out of an initial point of creativity; that interaction, that dialogue, itself is made up of a sequence of creative actions and of commitments stemming from them—secondary actions, secondary commitments, up to a point, but genuine actions, encounters and discoveries, all the same. Rather than being an ideally fixed pattern which might almost be deduced from the initial creative event, supplying a determinant body of ideas and practices, a cultural heritage forms a relatively passive setting for action. Within that setting, any given juncture may bring a fresh turn of orientation; or at least its outcome will be relatively unpredictable, for the same setting will allow for varying sorts of actions according as circumstances, temperaments, and problems vary.

Thus, within the dialogue launched by the advent of Islam, almost from the start there came to be conflicting sets of presuppositions about what Islam should involve, each producing its own commitment and its own dialogue. Around the charismatic figure of 'Alî, companion of Muhammad and the fighting man's hero, the common soldier's sense of Islamic justice crystallized, even in the first generation, against what were felt to be the backslidings of a wealthy clique which had got control of the Muslims' conquests for its own benefit. This sentiment, sealed in the blood of rebellion, issued in a deep loyalty to 'Alî and later to his house. The resulting movement was called *Shî'ism*. The bulk of the Muslims were felt to have gone astray in rejecting 'Alî's leadership, only a faithful remnant holding to the original vision. Generation by generation, the widest possible implications of such a loyalty in such a remnant were worked out among the Shî'î Muslims, implications for social justice not merely in the soldiers' cause but in all fields, and (since life is whole) implications also for the personal devotional life, for metaphysics, and for the whole range of Islamic concerns. At the same time, the stirring and demanding experience of forging an effective unity among the Muslim community, despite such partisan pressures as that of the Shî'îs, was yielding a contrasting loyalty, called *Sunnism:* a loyalty to the Muslim community as it had come historically to be constituted, despite all its faults. This loyalty likewise had its pervasive implications, gradually worked out in a long dialogue among the Sunnî Muslims.

Thus arose within the Islamic setting two differing sub-traditions, sub-settings for dialogue, within which the implications of the original advent of Islam were being worked out in contrasting ways. And each secondary dialogue, like Islam itself, began with a point of creativity: within each, it was duly noted that there was something divinely guided or even revelatory —though of course not in the same degree as in the Qur'ân itself—in the position of 'Alî, the hero, or in that of the Ummah, the general community, respectively. As may be seen from the map of the distribution of Shî'îs, the two contrasting traditions have endured to the present. (In our day more than a quarter, perhaps a third, of the Muslims in the central lands of 'old Islam' from Nile to Oxus are Shî'îs. The rest there—as well as most Muslims in the more outlying lands—are chiefly Sunnîs, who therefore form nine-tenths of the Muslims in the world at large.)

THE DIVERSITY OF ISLAM IN THE NEXUS OF GENERAL HISTORY

As the Islamic tradition developed within its own terms, it was likewise interacting with other cultural traditions which were already present among the populations in which Islam was adopted. No tradition is isolable from others present in the same social context. (A culture, indeed, may be defined as a complex of interdependent traditions.) A creative event in any sphere of life is likely to have consequences in many fields; in any case, the interaction and

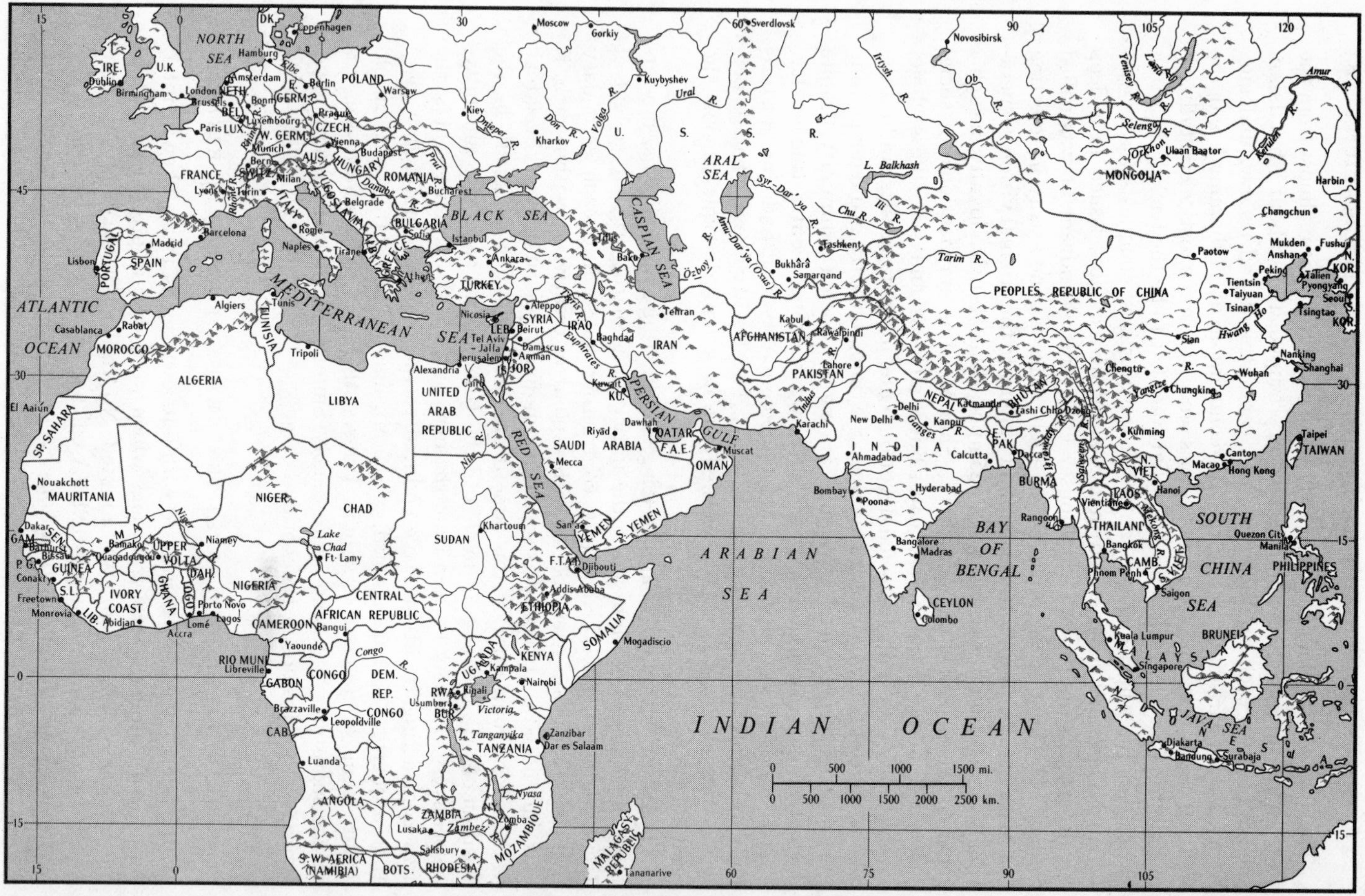

Countries of the Afro-Eurasian landmass, 1970

dialogue in religious or artistic or political or scholarly settings overlap and merge because the important problems that arise are rarely so technical that only one sort of tradition proves relevant. The sub-traditions into which Islam seemed to divide, even when mutually hostile as were those of the Shî'îs and Sunnîs, were not in fact exclusive; it was common for an individual Muslim, almost from the start, to share to some degree in both of these. Still less did people cease to take part, when they became Muslims, in the other ongoing traditions which moulded their lives, except in the few cases where the commitment involved was explicitly incompatible with the Muslim commitment: as in some, but not all, aspects of other religious traditions. For the rest, Islam found itself in a vital and multiple cultural environment. It was only as it entered into these other dialogues, in fact, that it could become significant for cultural life at large.

The artistic traditions of which Muslims found themselves at first patrons and later also practitioners had been launched in pre-Islamic times. Only as Muslims (rather gradually) found special viewpoints toward elements in these traditions—viewpoints suggested as readily by their particular social situation as by any more strictly Islamic inspiration—did the continuing development of those traditions introduce any features that might be called Islamic. The same is true of scientific and philosophical traditions, of traditions of commerce and of crafts and of public administration, even of pious legend and of ascetic practice. Always the presence of Islam made itself felt only gradually as Muslims discovered points at which it would be relevant within the settings provided by the various other traditions.

Such a difference as that, often noted, between Islam in a majority-Muslim environment (such as the Arab lands) and Islam in a minority-Muslim environment (such as India) is not, then, a matter of the degree to which Muslims are Muslims. It cannot be reduced to the difference between stale custom and enforced alertness, as an Indian Muslim might suggest; or between inbred mastery and latter-day imitation, as some Arab Muslims might feel. It will also be the difference between two equally genuine responses to the overall spiritual challenge carried in the Islamic dialogue in the midst of two different cultural environments. Indian Muslims, for instance, would read at least some books by other Indian Muslims, being stimulated by the special Indian problems those writers were contending with; and would respond positively or negatively to the creative experiences to which the writers bore witness. Arab Muslims likewise had their own subordinate dialogue with its own special Arab problems and encounters.

When we look at Islam historically, then, the integral unity of life it seemed to display when we looked at it as a working out of the act of islâm almost vanishes. In such ever-renewed dialogues, among settings formed apart from Islam at all, is not anything possible provided only it possess a certain general human validity? We can no longer say that Islam eternally teaches a given thing, or that another thing is necessarily a corruption of Islam. Such judgments a believer may feel himself able to make, but not a historian as such. At a given time, in a limited milieu, perhaps, Islam may form a relatively delimited and inviolable pattern. But over time, and especially on a world scale, any particular formulation of thought or practice is to be seen as the result of how the ever-changing setting formed by the Islamic tradition is reflected in particular circumstances and in relation to all the other cultural traditions present.[5]

Even the persistent pressure which has existed toward some sort of unity or uniformity among Muslims everywhere is not to be seen as an inevitable attribute of Islam as such. Rather, it arose out of the relationships which held, at various times, between the ongoing Islamic tradition and the other cultural traditions among which it was developing. In the time of the first Arab conquests, the sense that the Qur'ânic vision demanded some sort of unity among the war bands of the faithful was sufficiently expressed in a demand for a single supreme authority among them, a caliph who would lead their worship and their wars. The notion of a caliph was never abandoned, but later—when most Muslims were merchants or craftsmen or peasants—it became merged in the ancient notion of the disinterested royal arbiter among the several classes of a settled society; eventually Muslims could admit several caliphs at once. Muslims by then, however, represented numerous differing cultural traditions; those who were concerned to fulfill the Qur'ânic vision, accordingly, found it necessary to demand a new sort of unity: a unity in the customs of social intercourse, on which could be built in common a just society. Still later, under the disruptive impact of Modern times, a third sort of demand for unity seemed required. Tendencies toward what has been called 'pan-Islamic' sentiment have represented a hope that the various peoples of Islamic faith, having found themselves in a common subjugation to the Modern West, would co-operate politically in their common interests, however diverse they remained culturally.

What then is Islam? Can we study it as a meaningful whole? Is it more than the name for a hope, and a few common symbols? Clearly, yes: but only in the way that any cultural tradition, whatever its internal contradictions, is a whole. However diversely it develops, or however rapidly, a tradition does not lend itself indifferently to every possible opinion or practice. It imposes limits which are none the less enduringly effective for being impossible to formulate

[5] Not every scholar, and certainly not every Muslim, will be happy with so strong a limitation as I put on the existence of any eternal 'true' Islam. It is conventional, in fact, for scholars to distinguish more and less 'true' or 'genuine' Islam among the various forms which Islamic consciousness has taken; they often label some forms 'orthodox' and use other categories, implicit and explicit, which presuppose such distinctions. There is a certain validity in such usages, but only, I think, when very carefully circumscribed. Partly, of course, it is a matter of definitions. I have used 'Islam' in the way which, it seems to me, most genuinely answers to its prevailing usage in ordinary contexts. Here there can be more practical accord than on the level of global theory. Perhaps my usage should always tacitly presuppose some such adjective as 'historical', as against 'ideal' or 'metaphysical'.

in advance. Dialogue within a group, indeed any dialogue, is scarcely possible if everything is put in question at once. If a new insight is to come at one point, it can be clarified only against a background of received insights, held for the moment as if they were constant, or at most shifted only in perspective. The same is true of any sort of interaction: an innovation at one point is feasible only if it can be assumed that at least some other points will remain fixed. At any given time a minimal cultural integrality can be assured at least by those features of the cultural setting which even those men take for granted who think they are out to change everything. Over the generations, innovations may indeed appear at any point. Yet so long as there is a common commitment to an initial point of departure which all acknowledge, and to the continuing body of persons which shares that acknowledgement, the dialogue will retain common features, even though these are not necessarily those most visible at any given time. For to the extent that the dialogue is cumulative, every later comer having to reckon both with the point of departure and with the later debate, there will needs be a common vocabulary of ideas (or of art forms or institutional principles or whatever) which will include somehow all generations concerned. It is this integrality of dialogue that can provide an intelligible framework for historical study.

THE UNITY OF ISLAM AS A RELIGIOUS TRADITION, AND ITS LIMITS

We can distinguish two levels on which there has been effective continuity in such dialogue among Muslims over the centuries: that of religion and that of civilization. Throughout this work, we will be dealing with a religious tradition and with a civilization; we must clarify briefly here what we mean by religion and what by a civilization; and what sort of relations can exist between them. Cultural continuity among the Muslims is most visible on the level of what we call 'religion'. The Islamic religious tradition, for all its diversity, has retained a certain integrality; distinctly more so than, say, Christianity or Buddhism. But we will find that this religious unity among Muslims is but one expression of a wider cultural unity. This wider cultural unity is historically, doubtless, the more fundamental.

The religious unity must be recognized first; and among Muslims it already carries with it much—but by no means all—of the realms of culture that in some other contexts might not be considered religious at all. At the very least, all Muslims must come to terms with the Qur'ân; and in doing so they must not only talk in part a common language, but must find themselves faced with at least partly common challenges. Hence the whole range of what appears under the Islamic name can be relevant to seeing the full implications, positive and negative, of a personal commitment to its founding events and their latent challenges. But because even the most diverse Muslims have sometimes read not only the Qur'ân but each other's subsequent books, the tradition has had, in fact, more integrality than this minimum. Consequently, any serious questions about that commitment, its implications, and even its historical development will prove interdependent; the tradition must, then, be studied as a whole.

As we have seen, this religious commitment and dialogue carried far. It concerned not merely a corner of people's lives, reserved for moments of special exaltation or of special despair. It reached pervasively into daily living. How far it reached, we must see. For we cannot arbitrarily set off the sphere of 'religion' in general in advance, even if we give it a broad mandate; we cannot assume that such-and-such a type of activity must be 'religious' and other types of activity not. Indeed, so variable is the sphere of 'religion' in different cultures that a common term for all that we call 'religious' is really justifiable only by invoking a series of extended meanings.

In a person's life, we can call 'religious' in the most restricted sense (in the sense of 'spiritual'), his ultimate cosmic orientation and commitments and the ways in which he pays attention to them, privately or with others. Properly, we use the term 'religious' for an ultimate orientation (rather than 'philosophical' or 'ideological'), so far as the orientation is personally committing and is meaningful in terms of a cosmos, without further precision of what this may come to. In an Islamic context, this has meant, in effect, a sense of cosmic transcendence, and we may apply the word, more concretely, to efforts, practical or symbolical, to transcend the limits of the natural order of foreseeable life—that is, efforts based on hope from or struggle toward some sort of 'supernatural' realm.[6] Then we may call 'religious' (extending the term a bit) those cultural traditions that have focused on such cosmic commitments: cumulative traditions of personal responses to presumed possibilities of transcending the natural order. Such traditions take off from events people have found to be revelatory of such possibilities. But in common usage the term is extended still further. A person's actual 'religious' life does not necessarily consist in creative cosmic commitment; it consists in his participation in religious traditions as given to him—in any aspect of them, whether he personally cares much for the initial spiritual impulse, or carries on only those aspects of the tradition that were secondary to and supportive of the primary

[6] For some purposes, one can apply the term 'religious' wherever an experience of the numinous or a notion of the transcendent (commonly linked thereto) becomes life-orientational. But in different life-orientational traditions, and even within the same tradition, the numinous-transcendent can play very different roles, or be absent even in primary moments. Hence, for the purpose of classifying the traditions (if one must), a more general definition will help: one can apply the term 'religious' to any life-orientational experience or behaviour in the degree to which it is relatively most focused on the role of a *person in an environment felt as cosmos*. Any developed life-orientational outlook, however much oriented to culture or history to the exclusion of concern with natural cosmos, deals with personal life and has some interpretation of the cosmic whole; but the term 'religious' would not be applied to the central experience and behaviour of, e.g., Marxism, since, in contrast, say, to 'atheistic' Buddhism, the relation person-cosmos plays a relatively slight role there.

spiritual commitment. For historical purposes, it is not very feasible or even desirable to separate out these different extended usages.

Accordingly, though what we call the 'religious' traditions have been centred on such ultimate commitments, they have not—as actual historical traditions—been reducible to them. Whatever its central concern, Islam has come to imply much else besides, not necessarily deducible from its concern with transcendence; and as a historical tradition, Islam must be seen integrally in its own terms, constituted by all these diverse things. It is not because Islam embraces a certain cultural sphere but because, in the spheres it does embrace, it happens to put central an effort toward transcendence, or toward cosmic meaning, that we call the Islamic tradition 'religious', and participation in it 'religious behaviour'. Even narrowly conceived as cult and creed, Islam contains far more than—and also less than—what we might suppose was necessarily implied in an effort toward transcendence: in, for instance, the direct personal act of islâm. It can be religious behaviour, for instance, to extol one's own religious heritage—in this case Islam—and to denigrate other people's; but this need not indicate a very lively sense of personal submission before the God who created all. Indeed, Islam may be highly cultivated, for social or intellectual reasons, by persons who have had little such religious experience of their own. (We must also, of course, be ready to recognize on their own merits the norms of all the sub-traditions that diversely developed Islam—all the contrasting positions that were 'Islam' to one or another group of Muslims.)

The reader will find that Islam, rather more than Christianity, tended to call forth a total social pattern in the name of religion itself. None of the great religious traditions of this type has been content with occasional acts of worship in consecrated buildings—all have hoped to form men and women's daily attitudes and conduct. In principle, any religious allegiance might make demands on every aspect of life to such a degree that a religious body could constitute a complete society, its way of life a self-sufficient culture. But Islam especially has tended to make this kind of total demand on life. In many spheres, not only public worship but such spheres as civil law, historical teaching, or social etiquette, Muslims succeeded quite early in establishing distinctive patterns identifiable with Islam as religion.

But even Islam could not be total. Even in these preferred spheres, specifically Islamic patterns rarely prevailed exclusively; and in many other spheres, such as trade or poetry, the articulated religion had to be content to lay down limits which the merchant or poet should not overstep. Otherwise, these aspects of culture were cultivated, in substantial autonomy from any particular religious allegiance. What was religion and, in particular, what was Islam, was always, if diversely, kept consciously distinct from the total culture of Muslim society. In even the most pious man's life there was much that he could not call religious.

The wider cultural life of Muslims, their civilization, had its own historical integrality, which was not simply an extension of the specifically religious unity of Muslims. Indeed, this wider cultural complex included the Islamic religious life as but one facet, albeit a central one. For around the actual Islamic religious tradition was formed, historically, an overall culture not restricted to what was 'religious', even granting the wide sphere claimed for Islam as religion. It was not only the Qur'ânic challenge and its consequences that Muslims confronted together, but also a whole series of historical events and problems in every sphere of life. In Islamic times, to an important degree, the arts and sciences (for instance) of Muslim Turks and Persians, of Muslims of Egypt and of India, were interdependent; moreover, they were clearly distinct from those of lands outside the Muslim sphere even when they defied the religious convictions of most pious Muslims. Further, since the cultural traditions which together made up the civilization associated with Muslims often depended little, directly, on the Islamic tradition as such, they were by no means restricted to Muslims. Many non-Muslims—Christians, Jews, Hindus, etc.—must be recognized not only as living socially within the sphere of the Muslim culture; they must be recognized as integral and contributory participants in it, engaging actively in many of its cultural dialogues. At the same time, some groups ardently Muslim in religion (for instance, in China) were only limitedly influenced culturally by this cultural complex. The scope of the historical civilization, then, was not only distinct from the religion as to field of activity; it was not even coextensive with it in time and space, and as to the populations involved. Here we have, then, a second, more inclusive level on which cultural traditions carried by Muslims form an interrelated whole to be studied as such.

This wider level of integrality, however, has been profoundly influenced by the religious level, especially among Muslims, not because it is an extension of it but because of the strategic position in which the carriers of the religious vision have found themselves within the civilization, notably in the high culture which gives definition to a civilization in the most meaningful sense of that term.

A CIVILIZATION AS EXPRESSION OF FORMATIVE IDEALS

In this work we shall speak more of masterpieces of art, and dynastic policies, of religious geniuses, and scientific discoveries, than of everyday life on the farm and in the kitchen. Hence we will include in our scope those peoples among whom a few privileged men shared such masterpieces and discoveries, however much those peoples differed among themselves in farmwork or in homemaking. This may seem like arbitrary preference for the spectacular. I believe it answers to a legitimate human need to understand ourselves. In any case, we must be clear as to what we are doing, and its consequences.

The wider culture associated with Islam has been as highly differentiated and heterogeneous as any; has been, in fact, the sum of many cultures, or at least of aspects of them. The peoples concerned, flourishing from the time of Muḥammad in the seventh century to the present, have extended in space over half of the Eastern Hemisphere of our globe. They have been correspondingly diverse in language, climate, historical situation, and national culture patterns. It is such a compound culture that we call 'a civilization': that is, a relatively extensive grouping of interrelated cultures, insofar as they have shared in cumulative traditions in the form of high culture on the urban, literate level; a culture, that is, such as that of historical India or Europe taken as cultural wholes. Such groups of peoples have varied greatly among themselves and yet have shared broadly cultural and historical experiences differing decisively from those of more distant peoples. Thus the diverse peoples of India cherished in common the Sanskritic traditions, and those of Europe the Greco-Latin. In the field of pre-Modern Afro-Eurasian history a number of such broader cultural complexes have existed, not necessarily covering without remainder the whole field of citied and lettered life, yet by and large dominating the more local cultures.

There are many ways of grouping into 'civilizations' what is in fact an endless chain of interrelated local cultural life. We must know why we make the selection we do. Often one may make alternative combinations according to what questions one is concerned with. Thus the civilization that united the lands from Nile to Oxus in the Islamic period could be regarded, for some purposes, as no independent cultural body but simply the latest phase in a long-term Irano-Semitic civilization continuous from the time of the ancient Sumerians. The cultural traditions associated with Islam in India, then, would be regarded as forming part of an equally continuous Indic civilization, complicating it and relating it to the lands from Nile to Oxus, yet still regionally bound. This makes obvious sense on the level of everyday life. Even on the level of high culture, Islamic faith, for instance, is part of a longer tradition. In particular, the creative events at the founding of Islam were themselves part of an ongoing monotheistic tradition. They took place within the setting formed by the dialogue that was working through the implications of the ancient Hebrew prophetic discoveries; they formed a response to challenges presented historically in that dialogue at the point when Muḥammad was drawn into it. In the Islamic dialogue, the same basic monotheistic commitment persisted, though the particular allegiance was new. The like was true of many other facets of high culture even though new languages were used.

If one is concerned primarily with socio-economic institutional evolution, conscious or unconscious, especially with that of the more local social units, such regional groupings may provide the most intelligible fields of study. (Grouping by region, itself, would offer a number of alternatives: for instance, instead of distinguishing between Europe on the one hand and the 'Middle East' from Nile to Oxus on the other, one might, especially in some periods, distinguish a Mediterranean region from a region centred round the Iranian plateau.) But if one is concerned primarily with the more conscious commitments of human beings and with their public actions in the light of those commitments, as historians traditionally have been, a grouping by traditions of high culture will be more relevant than one by socio-economic regions.

When we speak of a great civilization, we mean above all a consciously cultivated human heritage—and only secondarily a collection of folkways or of sociological raw data. In the study of any culture, of course, intellectual, economic, artistic, social, political aspects all have their role; ruling classes, peasant villagers, city artisans, bands of vagrants, all must be taken into account in interpreting it. But in studying a given civilization our first interest is in those aspects of culture that have been most distinctive of it; that have been most interesting and humanly significant in their variation within its own sphere of space and time as well as in their diverging from other forms of culture. During much of history, at least, this has meant the artistic, philosophic, scientific life, the religious and political institutions, in general all the more imaginative activities among the more cultivated of the population. It is in terms of these aspects of culture that we do commonly distinguish the great civilizations from one another. And in the long run, these aspects can be decisive even for the common people who are scarcely aware of them.

This fact is especially relevant among the Muslims. Wherever it went, Islam entered into the local cultural complexes carried by local ethnic groups, as one tradition among the complex of interdependent traditions which go to make up a local culture. But these local cultures might have nothing else in common. It is not on this level that the wider culture (religious and non-religious) associated specifically with Muslims was articulated. Such a wider culture was carried primarily on the level of 'high culture', rather than folk culture: that is, on the urban, literate level and more particularly on the level of the cultivated circles who were direct or indirect beneficiaries of the land revenues and who participated in the large-scale institutions that imposed a social order wider than that of family or village unit.[7] It is this culture—including, of course, its religious components—that we are to study in this work. A civilization in this sense will normally be defined by a continuity of lettered traditions: that is, of literature in the widest sense of the word, including (for instance) religious or scientific literature. Hence our field, in studying the civilization associated with the Muslims, will be delimited not by geography—as, for instance, the culture of the 'Middle East' in one or another acceptance of that term—but rather by the lines of development of the high cultural traditions, wherever they lead us.[8]

[7] Edward Shils, in 'Charisma, Order, and Status', *American Sociological Review*, 30 (April 1965), 199–213, suggests how much the high culture (his 'central value system') rests on the chariṣma attributed to it because it represents an inclusive social order felt to be just.

[8] What the civilization is that we associate with Muslims, and what its position is in world history, have been discussed from many viewpoints; but rarely in an adequately comprehensive world-historical perspective or with sufficiently flexible categories. Among the best discussions have been three which form a sequence. Carl H. Becker, in *Vom*

Such a definition of our field can have subtle consequences. It makes for a special way of viewing religion, for instance. In the historical developments that mark a civilization so defined, religion almost inevitably plays a key role; but not necessarily so much because of the inertia of folk habits as because of its place in the consciences of a concerned minority. For the ideals of a minority can be specially seminal on the level of high culture.

Any civilization, as a delimitable complex of cultural traditions, has been constituted by standards of cultural valuation, basic expectations, and norms of legitimation, embodied in its traditions. In the high culture, these are carried partly in lettered traditions directly, and partly in other traditions, such as social and artistic ones, associated with the lettered traditions. It is the more far-reaching standards of legitimation that have served as the most dependably persistent cultural traits, endowing a civilization with such cultural integrality, such distinctive style, as it has had. What sets off most clearly one civilization in our sense, from another, then, is not so much any general stock of cultural ideas and practices—easily borrowed from one people to the next—as these formative ideals. Such a cultural heritage has been carried not only by all of the upper, educated classes, but even, to a lesser degree, by still wider sections which have absorbed something of its outlook, down to the ordinary peasants. But within this mass, a much smaller group has played a special role: those who have taken the more articulate and far-reaching ideals of the heritage as a personal responsibility, which they must themselves realize. This concerned minority for whom cultural or spiritual ideals are a major driving force are not usually the men of immediate power. But at every crossroads, they are the men of cultural initiative—it is within the framework they have clarified that new cultural choices must commonly be made.

At least in pre-Modern times, the most important focus of persistent cultural ideals has often tended to be in religion. In religion, the impact of the creative, revelatory events has tended to stand out most strongly from the continuing dialogue in which their implications were being worked out; hence religion could provide unusual continuity in the dialogue itself. Moreover, even more than in the aesthetic or the political spheres, the circle of responsive con-

---

Werden und Wesen der islamischen Welt: Islamstudien, Vol. I (Leipzig, 1924), Part I, 'Zur Einleitung', brought out, among other things, that the pre-Modern Christian and Muslim societies lived by largely common cultural resources. This point was developed in a new direction by G. E. von Grunebaum, in *Medieval Islam* (University of Chicago Press, 1946 [2nd ed. 1953]), who stressed the parallelism of their world views. Jörg Kraemer, in *Das Problem der islamischen Kulturgeschichte* (Tübingen, 1959), has recently reviewed the questions suggestively, attempting to balance the 'Hellenic' character of the culture with other elements. Unfortunately he, like most scholars, still presupposes untenable notions about a fictitious 'Orient', which lead much of his argument astray. He fails to see that the data he cites to support the 'Oriental' character of Islamicate culture illustrate instead the indivisibility of the Afro-Eurasian historical complex as a whole, which included the Occident.

For further development of my own thoughts on defining civilizations, see the section on historical method in the Introduction, especially the subsection on civilizations.

frontation that spreads out from religion tends to be comprehensive of all life. A new aesthetic impulse may affect science in some degree, or have economic repercussions as fashions change. A new political impulse can reach further, can carry in its train economic decisions, aesthetic ideals, or the very tone, sometimes, of private life caught up in the pride of a new allegiance. A fresh sense of impact from whatever it may be in the cosmic presence that is seen as transcending the natural order may be felt strongly by only the concerned minority. But if these take it seriously, it can touch every point in the natural order of human affairs: it can reorient people's aesthetic sense, their political norms, their whole moral life, and with these everything else that can be seen to matter. A religious commitment, by its nature, tends to be more total than any other. Perhaps especially among Muslims, religious vision has often proved decisive at just the points that are historically most interesting. Moreover, that vision proved sufficiently potent to ensure that Muslims formed a single great civilization of their own.

Among Christian or Buddhist peoples, religion has indeed been very central also. But it has informed the culture of Christian Occidentals and of Christian Abyssinians, for instance, almost entirely in isolation from each other, so that there is no single civilization associated with Christianity. Nor is there one civilization associated with Buddhism. But—despite the vaster areas covered —those who participated in the tradition of Islamic faith, so far as they developed any culture of their own at all, never lost contact with each other: their cultural dialogues were always intermeshed. The bonds of Islamic faith, indeed especially the irrepressible transcendent ideals implied in the root meaning of islâm, with their insistent demand for a godly transformation of all life, have been so telling in certain crucial aspects of the high culture of almost all Muslim peoples that we find ourselves grouping these peoples together across all their different regions, even apart from considering other facets of high culture. Islam offered creative impulses that ramified widely throughout the culture as a whole, even where it was least religious. It is largely around the central Islamic tradition that the concerned and the creative built and transmitted a common set of social and, above all, literary traditions; these were carried in many languages but looked largely to the same great classics, not only religious but secular, and especially to the norms which they express, applicable to all aspects of life. Thus Islam helped to knit together peoples who otherwise might have remained remote, or have drifted apart if they were close to begin with. Through the greatest diversity of forms (as the chart giving an overview of the history may suggest), these traditions (religious and otherwise) have maintained a decisive continuity. Hence in studying these peoples there is special urgency for studying as a body, and hence primarily on the level of the high culture, the civilization given definition by the lettered traditions in which Islam held a central place.[9]

[9] The student will find that differences in scholars' notions of what it was they were studying have left a profound impress upon the works which anyone must read if he is to

In studying the history of Muslims, obviously, we need distinct terms for the religious tradition on the one hand and for the more inclusive civilization on the other. Unfortunately, we have not had such terms in the past. The terms 'Islam' and 'Islamic' have often been used in both senses. But these two terms are clearly appropriate only to the realm of religion. If we speak in this work of 'Islamic' art or literature, then, we will be referring to religious art or literature within the traditions of Islamic faith, in the same sense as we refer to 'Christian' art or literature. We will require a different term for the cultural traditions of the civilization at large, when we are not restricting our reference to religion. The various peoples among whom Islam has been predominant and which have shared in the cultural traditions distinctively associated with it may be called collectively 'Islamdom', as forming a vast interrelated social nexus. The distinctive civilization of Islamdom, then, may be called 'Islamicate'.

The civilization could have been given some other name than one derived from Islam; in fact it has, in some contexts, been referred to appropriately as the 'Perso-Arabic' civilization, after the two chief languages in which it has been carried. But because of the pre-eminent role played in it by Islam and by Muslims, it has most commonly been called the 'Islamic' civilization. It will be convenient to retain such a usage here, only adding the double ending (*-icate*) to avoid an ambiguity that has proved all too common. In some cases, the distinction is unimportant, and the choice between the terms 'Islamic' and 'Islamicate' may be a matter of emphasis. But on occasion it is essential to point up the distinction between those traditions associated relatively closely with the act of islâm and its spiritual implications, and those traditions that were associated with Islam more indirectly, through forming a part of the overall civilization in which Muslims were leaders. The form 'Islamicate' has the advantage of being almost self-defining: if it appears in a context where it is contrasted to 'Islamic', it is clearly not just the same as 'Islamic' but does relate somehow to what is Islamic. This is approximately the effect intended.[10]

ISLAMICATE CIVILIZATION AS HUMAN HERITAGE

The Islamicate culture of the past has, of course, been very important in influencing the present condition of mankind. It is naturally the major influence from the past among the widespread Muslim peoples of our time; moreover, it has had notable effects, for good and for ill, in still wider areas, such as much of India and of Europe, where Muslims once ruled. The civilization remained actively creative within its own terms until the moment when a

---

pursue even casually any given line of interest in the Islamics field. In the paragraphs on the history of Islamics studies in the Introduction is a brief sketch of the major orientations and biases which the reader should learn to be aware of and, if necessary, discount.

[10] For an explanation of my choice of the terms 'Islamdom' and 'Islamicate', see the section on usage in Islamics studies in the Introduction.

Overview of the History of Islamdom

Late Sâsânî and Primitive Caliphal periods, *c.* (485)–692	*The intrusion of Islam into Irano-Semitic society and the genesis of a new social order.* In Iran, in the Fertile Crescent, in Arabia, the way was being prepared, as it turned out, for the new order. First came the shaking up of the old Sâsânî political order; but the central event of the period was the advent of Muḥammad and his followers' rise to power from Nile to Oxus and even beyond.
High Caliphal Period, *c.* 692–945	The first period of Islamicate civilization proper: *A classical civilization under the Marwânî and earlier ʿAbbâsî caliphates.* Islamicate society formed a single vast state, the caliphate, with an increasingly dominant single language of science and culture, Arabic. The Islamic religion was being given its classical formulation; Muslims, Christians, Jews, and Mazdeans were renovating and weaving together the lettered traditions of several pre-Islamic backgrounds into a creative multiple flowering.
Earlier Middle Islamic Period, *c.* 945–1258	*Establishment of an international civilization spreading beyond the Irano-Semitic areas.* The great expansion of Islamicate society was based on a decentralization of power and culture, in many courts and in two major languages, Persian and Arabic. Unity was maintained through self-perpetuating social institutions which outgrew the caliphate and encouraged high-cultural sophistication and a synthesis of the lettered traditions that had been developed in the High Caliphal Period.
Later Middle Islamic Period, *c.* 1258–1503	*The age of Mongol prestige: crisis and renewal in the Islamicate institutions and heritage.* Despite devastation and conquest of the central Islamicate lands by a vigorous pagan movement, the Islamic norms reimposed themselves and hemisphere-wide expansion continued. The Mongol challenge launched a new political tradition and new horizons in high culture in the central areas, forming a Persianate culture from the Balkans to Bengal and influential even more widely.
Period of Gunpowder Empires, *c.* 1503–1789	*Flowering of Persianate culture under major regional empires.* The political and cultural impetus of the Mongol age was developed in regional empires with relatively regional cultures, especially in three: one primarily European, one centered in the old Islamic lands, one Indic. It was the height of Islamic material world power. The aesthetic and intellectual creativity and prosperity faded, however, before the new Occident in the course of a basic transformation.
Modern Technical Age, *c.* 1789–present	*The Islamic heritage caught up in the Modern technicalistic world.* Under the impact of a new world order carried by the Modern West, the world-historical conditions of the Islamicate civilization have disappeared. Instead of a continuing comprehensive society, we have a heritage which several peoples share within a wider social order where Muslims form a minority, a minority disadvantaged by just those events which, creating the new order, brought prosperity to the new West.

transformed Modern Occident put all pre-Modern heritages in question. Until that time the Muslims and their society played a pivotal role in world history as a whole, both negatively and positively; hence in almost every part of the Old World—and in the New World cultures derived therefrom—even where Islam never prevailed, at least some elements of the local culture have been traceable to Islamicate sources. Through its manifold influence on the Medieval Occident, particularly in the realms of science and technical skills, the older Islamicate culture had a significant share even in the far-reaching cultural transformations which the Modern Occident has introduced to our present world.

Important as it has been for its effects on the course of history, Islamicate civilization may be still more important for us as illustrating the evolution of a civilization as such. As we follow the traditions of that civilization in their many forms and many spheres of activity, from a time before there could be said to have been an Islamicate civilization at all, we are presented with an instructive instance of a major civilization as an evolving, historical phenomenon. Every degree of integration and disintegration, of freshness, maturity, decadence, and revival is illustrated in the most varied historical patterns. Moreover, the roots of Islamicate civilization are largely the same as those of Occidental civilization: the urban commercial tradition of the ancient Fertile Crescent, the Hebrew religious challenge, the classical Greek philosophical and scientific culture. Hence for Westerners (and for all who at least partly share now in the Occidental heritage), the Islamicate forms a sister civilization, like yet very different; acquaintance with it can throw a special light, by way of comparisons and contrasts, on Occidental civilization in particular as well as on the nature of civilizations as such.

Comparisons between the Islamicate culture and the Occidental are inevitable and very worthwhile. But one caution must be kept in mind. It is not ordinarily legitimate to compare pre-Modern Islamicate institutions and cultural patterns with those of the Modern West, and to treat that comparison as if it were primarily one between different *peoples*. Such a comparison is more likely to be one between *ages*. In recent centuries, enormous changes have supervened in the Occident; changes which produced their counter-effects almost immediately, and are now having their analogues elsewhere, in the Muslim and in other non-Western countries. Serious comparisons between the Muslim peoples and the West should be made with this fact in mind. Pre-Modern Islamicate ways can be compared with those of the pre-Modern Occident; and those aspects of society in Islamdom in which the Modern changes have taken positive effect can be compared, within measure, with the Modern West. But it is illegitimate to regard as 'Western'—in contrast to 'Islamic'—such traits as clock sense among workers, or democratic social expectations, or even subtler characteristics often cited; for these traits were mostly as absent in the pre-Modern Occident as in pre-Modern Islamdom, and may in the future prove as congenial to Muslim peoples as they now seem to be to Western.

But from a more deeply human point of view, perhaps neither the far-reaching historical effects of Islamicate civilization, nor its value as illustrating the nature of civilization in general, is so important as is the inherent marvel of what it built, and even of what it dared try to build. Our fundamental purpose must be an understanding of the human achievements of the civilization in their own terms. It is with this intention that our field of study has been delimited here, and the place of everything in it assessed. The place of the civilization in the world-historical chain of events, and its usefulness as an example of what culture can be, come out naturally and necessarily as we try to understand what is special to the human endeavours that have been tied together by the presence of the Islamic vision. In studying Islamicate civilization, we will be concerned with society and culture as the context in which concerned individuals have worked, especially Muslim individuals, and as the handiwork which exhibits in varying ways the intended and unintended results of their work and of their vision.[11]

Even in terms of evident relevance for current personal life among Modern humans, the Islamicate heritage is rich. Its visual arts, for instance, include surely the greatest ever known in which the element of sheer visual design could be given priority over all other considerations. Its literatures, richly unmatched in their most distinctive genres, are perhaps unparalleled in—among other things—their mastery of the esoteric as a dimension of human experience. Its philosophical and scientific and religious thought has not merely made a lasting contribution to subsequent knowledge; much of it presents continuing points of enduring challenge. As we watch the unfolding of the civilization as a whole we will gain, at the same time, essential background for appreciating the monuments of Islamicate culture which can still enrich our understanding and our life. For it is only in their total context, in the setting of the developing cultural institutions which formed them, and of the hopes and fears they embodied, that the monuments can come fully alive for us: works of architecture and painting, literary masterpieces, philosophical systems, expressions of religious insight, and, above all, living religious and social institutions among millions of mankind. Perhaps the latter sort is the most important of all the monuments of Islamicate civilization, if only because the Islamicate society represents, in part, one of the most thoroughgoing attempts in history to build a world-wide human community as if from scratch on the basis of an explicitly worked out ideal.

But important as is the heritage of Islamdom to us as presenting resources for our current cultural ventures, the great human venture which Islam has been is even more important, for Modern mankind, as a venture: as it was in itself then. If the Modern Technical Age is to remain human, it cannot overlook the trust that our ancestors have left with us. Our past cannot be mere

[11] For a fuller presentation of the historical viewpoint which I have used in this work, see the section on historical method in the Introduction, especially the subsection on historical humanism.

matter for a more or less curious utilitarianism, like iron deposits, say, on the moon. Islamicate culture is supremely important because it represents the highest creative aspirations and achievements of millions of people. Whoever we are, the hopes, the triumphs, and the failures too of any human beings are properly of concern to us; in the moral economy of mankind they are also our own hopes and failures. In studying and sharing in them we know ourselves better, understand better who we truly have been and are, we human beings.

BOOK ONE

The Islamic Infusion: Genesis of a New Social Order

Isaiah answered. I saw no God, nor heard any, in a finite organical perception; but my senses discover'd the infinite in every thing, and as I was then persuaded, & remain confirm'd, that the voice of honest indignation is the voice of God, I cared not for consequences but wrote.

—*William Blake*

I

The World before Islam

The Islamicate was unique among the great civilizations of its time in failing to maintain the earlier lettered traditions of its region. Elsewhere, the masterpieces of the first millennium BC continued to form the starting point for intellectual life. Right up to Modern times, the classical Greek and Latin (and even ancient Hebrew) masters were read in Europe, their contemporary Sanskrit and Prakrit masters in the Indic regions, the Chinese in the Far East. In Islamdom, on the contrary, the Semitic and Iranian literatures of the preceding periods were gradually replaced by Arabic, and later Persian, during the early centuries of Islam. Except in special little groups they died out, relatively little surviving even in translation. Indirectly, elements of the old lettered traditions persisted strongly in the new; but the great ancient works were mostly unknown to Muslims in the original or in translation. Instead, the Muslims developed their own classical models afresh. On the conscious literary level where the consciences of cultivated persons are engaged, the coming of Islam, then, marked a breach in cultural continuity unparalleled among the great civilizations we have come to know; a breach which can help to produce an impression of youthfulness—or of immaturity—on observers more at home in civilizations with a longer explicit heritage.[1] The breach with the older regional heritage was later emphasized still more when the Islamicate civilization, again uniquely in its time, became so widely dispersed over the hemisphere that it ceased to be associated exclusively with a single region and became dominant even in the heartlands of the older Greek and Sanskritic traditions.

Yet the Islamicate society was not only the direct heir, but in significant degree the positive continuator of the earlier societies in the lands from Nile to Oxus. By geography and in point of human and material resources, it was ultimately heir to the civilized traditions of the ancient Babylonians, Egyptians, Hebrews, Persians, and their various neighbours; more particularly, it was heir to the traditions expressed in the several Semitic and Iranian languages cultivated during the centuries immediately preceding Islam, traditions which in turn had built on the more ancient heritages. In their more routine dimensions, life and thought did not greatly differ in the earlier Islamic

[1] For a discussion of this and other circumstances—especially the accidents of Western scholarship—which have helped produce in outsiders a sense of aridity in the Islamicate civilization, see my 'Islam and Image' (a discussion of Muslim iconophobia) in *History of Religions*, 3 (1964), 220–60.

centuries from what they had been in the later pre-Islamic ones. Numerous details in the culture of the Islamic period—art motifs, social customs, the presence of minority religions such as the Christian—make sense only in terms of the earlier cultures which first produced them. What is more, the Muslims inherited also in large measure the problems, the opportunities, and the temptations of their ancestors in the region. Even those aspects of the civilization which were most strikingly new—for instance, the Muslim religion itself—were formed in the context of the earlier Irano-Semitic traditions. The goals to be set, the norms to be abided by, had been adumbrated long before.

Hence the achievements of the Muslims, in the unexpressed implications of their writings or their art, in the deeper problems solved in their institutions, often presuppose the continuing lifeways formed before Islam in the whole region; to savour these achievements, even to assess their uniqueness, one must recall the motive forces of that earlier life. What differed under Islam was largely the relative weighting of different elements in the culture, the balance among them. In working out that new balance, the impulses which formed Islamicate culture proved to be exceptionally comprehensive and self-sufficient.

Even these impulses go back into pre-Islamic times, however. With the proclamation of Islam in Arabia, or at latest with the subsequent Muslim conquests, a new subculture, a new complex of cultural traditions, appeared within the existent Irano-Semitic societies. But this was not yet in itself the Islamicate civilization, though its heritage later formed the decisive element in defining that civilization. As to the substance of social traditions—basic expectations, knowledge, and even taste—others of the many heritages which went into forming the civilization were commonly more decisive in it than the heritage of the nascent Muslim community. The actual civilization, then, took time to form. Even as to the Islamic contribution itself, it was only with time that the developing Islamic traditions could penetrate into the various aspects of the existing high cultural life of the times sufficiently for it to take on identifiably Islamicate forms. But much that was to be associated explicitly with the Islamicate civilization arose less from interaction with the Islamic traditions themselves than from independent new developments within the older traditions. Some of these were well launched long before Islam.

Accordingly, we must recognize an ill-defined period of gestation of the Islamicate civilization, when its characteristic traditions were taking form and being brought together. This period began long before (and ended a considerable time after) the crucial event—the life of Muḥammad—which marked the beginning of the new subculture. Here we will try to trace, in this pre-Islamic background, the developments that gradually sharpened within it in the direction of Islamicate culture. We will begin by recalling certain long-enduring overall social traits which have now very nearly vanished, but which must be borne in mind at all times in appreciating any work of Islamicate culture.

The culture of agrarian-based society

We necessarily possess some image of society and culture in civilized lands before the Modern Technical Age—an image usually influenced at least vaguely by Karl Marx or Max Weber and their masters. In order to specify effectively what was distinctive in the Islamicate development, I shall have to single out points in pre-Modern social structure that were crucial to that development as I see it in this work; and then to define a term that will (I hope) bring to mind the particular complex of phenomena I find relevant—which does not coincide exactly with those that Marx or Weber have brought into view.

When men first built cities and extended an urban governmental authority over the surrounding villages, they posed in a new form the dilemma between social privilege and equal justice. In the valleys of the Euphrates, Tigris, and Kârûn, and of the Nile, and in several neighbouring lands, the city dwellers, especially the wealthier among them, enjoyed a substantial share of whatever was produced in the countryside, beyond what the peasants themselves needed so as to keep going. This was the 'revenue' of the lands. It was regarded as at the disposal of whoever wielded power locally, and served to support those who performed such essential functions as storing grain against the day of bad harvests, maintaining internal order, defending the area against outside predators, and, directly or indirectly, an increasing variety of other specialized tasks ranging from the propitiation of natural forces to the importation of exotic objects, such as metal, which all had need of.

Those who controlled the revenues patronized all that was refined in cultural life above the level of village subsistence; and the quality of this culture tended to depend directly on the material prosperity of its well-to-do patrons. Thus it was the wealthy who patronized the fine crafts which, in the cities, produced beautiful objects of leather and cloth and wood, as well as of bronze and silver and gold, for ornamentation and for all everyday purposes; whatever came under the hand or the eye of the wealthy was a specially designed work of art. The craftsmen passed on their methods from father to son; the methods included as much the aesthetic standards, and even the particular aesthetic forms, as they did the physical technique, from which indeed the forms were inseparable. The excellence of the result depended largely on the quality of materials used, the amount of time the craftsman could spend on a piece, and the degree of discipline of the craft tradition; all these depended in turn on the patrons. When the revenues from the land were great, when the wealthy who received them could use them in security to gratify their tastes, and when those tastes in turn had been cultivated through lifetimes of high standards, the craftsmen were able to develop their skills and put forth their best efforts. If, on the other hand, times were troubled, and for some reason the wealthy could not collect much revenue from the peasants, or could not use it freely for their private tastes, the quality of craft work was likely to decline.[2]

It was in the cities likewise that more monumental art was produced—fine massive buildings, and the statuary and other carving and painting that went with them. Enormous effort was commonly put into temples which, as expressions of the honour paid by the community to the gods, were to the interest of all, or at least all in the cities; commonly the temples represented the best that men's resources could achieve. At the same time, the homes and courts of rulers and of well-to-do individuals were likewise built as sumptuously as such individuals could command. Finally, it was in the cities, and among those released by wealth or office from the everyday labour of the peasant, that people produced a refined literature of ritual and of myth and legend; a literature which finally came to enshrine a sense of personal conscience in the face of the cosmos. Such monumental literature, like the monumental architecture, was often devoted to magnifying rulers also, whom indeed it was sometimes difficult to distinguish from the more natural Powers.

All these arts of civilization, then, were dependent on the patronage and appreciation of a limited number of privileged persons in the cities. As in the case of handicrafts, when wealth failed to concentrate peacefully in their hands, standards of excellence declined. Their wealth, in turn, depended on the subjection of the bulk of the population, especially the peasants.

Most persons who troubled to compare the state of the great and the lot of the peasants, or other lesser beings, were content to observe that a mere peasant, rude and uncultivated from his childhood, had all that was due him if he had just enough to live on. Yet, very early, voices were raised in doubt. One of the arts of civilization was the art of legally enshrined justice; a ruler might pride himself not only on a magnificent palace, or on a magnificently composed record of his awesome exploits, but also on a reputation as a giver of just laws. As the cultivation of a personal conscience came to the fore among the civilized arts, the pride of justice might be expected to loom ever larger.

At first it was the temple that was the focus of whatever high culture there

[2] It has seemed necessary to try to delineate, here and in later chapters, a number of traits general to pre-Modern life. Increasingly, attitudes and presumptions of an earlier age become strange to us; even circumstances that seemed self-evident as late as fifty years ago have become unintelligible to younger readers unless they are specially reminded of their occasions. Yet all historical judgment is made through comparison, explicit or implicit. If non-comparable items are used as the basis for such comparison, the results are false. In Islamics studies a range of false assumptions has arisen about politics, religion, literature, progress and decadence, and so on, derived from various phases of Western experience on the basis of just such false comparisons. Questions have been put, on the basis of supposed comparability to Modern Western situations, which are irrelevant in the pre-Modern Islamicate context; conversely, truly pertinent questions have too often been overlooked. To know what must be explained as special to Islamicate society, we must recognize what was usual to pre-Modern society generally. Even scholars have too frequently been misled on such points; other readers will have yet greater need of being reminded of the broader context.

was. At the temples in ancient Sumeria, where urban life began in the fourth millennium BC, the work of controlling the local flooding and providing for the drought of the Mesopotamian alluvial plain was carried on under the learnèd priests, who in turn disposed of the surplus. It was they who sent out traders to bring in exotic goods necessary to the developing exploitation of the plain, fertile but lacking in minerals and even stone. When disputes arose with rival towns, perhaps over control of the trade, they organized the fighting men. But then as warfare became more elaborate—each town trying to outdo the others—military affairs and the general control of the town fell into the hands of non-priestly specialists: kings and their dependents. The royal court became a second focus of high culture alongside the temple, and was based like it upon agricultural production. Its revenue, in whatever form it took it, may be called taxes, which came chiefly from the land. Much more gradually, at last, the traders too became independent merchants, doing business on their own account and gaining enough profit to share, if more modestly and indirectly than temple or court, in the revenue of the land. When this happened, rich merchants too became patrons of the arts and the market became a third focus of high culture.

All three foci of high culture depended on the condition of agriculture. The basis of temple and court was agrarian in that their wealth and power presupposed chiefly arrangements concerning agricultural production. The market depended on agriculture less directly than did temple or court, for the traders brought goods from afar subject to other hazards than that of the local weather, and (provided there were sufficient stored savings) sold their goods in lean years as in fat. Yet, in the long run, the merchants too depended on the state of agriculture and their profits presupposed the peasants' surplus. Even when, as in Syria, mercantile city-states arose which depended primarily on distant trading by sea and land, their trade depended so intimately on the agrarian societies about them that both morally and materially they too lived ultimately from the peasants. Even the pastoralists, including the desert nomads, who depended on the agriculturists for much of their food and goods, were part of the same social complex. Accordingly, the type of social order which was introduced into the agricultural regions (and the areas dependent on them) with the rise of cities may be called *agrarian-based* or (to be more comprehensive) *agrarianate citied society*. (I say 'citied', not 'urban', because the society included the peasants, who were not urban though their life reflected the presence of cities.)

We shall use the phrases 'agrarianate' society or culture to refer not just to the agrarian sector and the agrarian institutions immediately based on it, but to the whole level of cultural complexity in which agrarian relations were characteristically crucial, which prevailed in citied societies between the first advent of citied life and the technicalizing transformations of the seventeenth and eighteenth centuries. The term 'agrarianate', in contrast to 'agrarian', then, will refer not only to the agrarian society itself but to all the forms of society even indirectly dependent on it—including that of mercantile cities and of pastoral tribesmen. The crucial point was that the society had reached a *level of complexity associated with urban dominance*—in this sense, it was 'urbanized'—but the urban dominance was itself *based, directly or indirectly, primarily on agrarian resources* which were developed on the level of manual power: based on them not in the sense that all must eat but that (since most production was agricultural) the income of crucial classes was derived from their relation to the land.

The culture of agrarianate citied society can be characterized as a distinct type in contrast both to the pre-literate types of culture that preceded it and to the Modern technicalistic culture that has followed. In contrast to pre-citied society—even to agricultural society before the rise of cities—it knew a high degree of social and cultural complexity: a complexity represented not only by the presence of cities (or, occasionally, some organizational equivalent to them), but by writing (or its equivalent for recording), and by all that these imply of possibilities for specialization and large-scale intermingling of differing groups, and for the lively multiplication and development of cumulative cultural traditions. Yet the pace of the seasons set by natural conditions imposed limits on the resources available for cultural elaboration; moreover, any economic or cultural development that did occur, above the level implied in the essentials of the symbiosis of town and land, remained precarious and subject to reversal—in contrast to the conditions of Modern times, of our Technical Age, when agriculture tends to become one 'industry' among others, rather than the primary source of wealth (at least on the level of the world economy as a whole).

We must recognize the great diversity within what we call 'agrarianate' society, both as to the level of complexity it reached and as to the forms of elaboration to be found in different areas. Fundamental changes took place everywhere, especially during what we call the Axial Age (800–200 BC). At that time, letters ceased being the monopoly of a priestly scribal class and became widespread among a section of the bourgeoisie, and correspondingly the character and pace of development of the lettered traditions changed; and at the same time, the overall geographical setting of historical action was transformed, being articulated into vast cultural regions spanning the hemisphere among them.

Yet because of their common agrarian basis, pre-Axial Age and post-Axial Age society everywhere shared certain basic ranges of opportunity for historical action, and corresponding limitations on it. Productivity could be multiplied through the proliferation of specializations in crafts and crops, made possible by the centring of surplus resources in cities; but not beyond the level at which the power of animals and of the natural elements could work. Social organization could allow for a diversity of personal roles well beyond that possible in pre-literate societies; but not such as to escape a severe social stratification, in which the great majority remained excluded from regular participation in political and high-cultural life. In particular, citied life implied an accelerated pace of historical change, of those actions and events that change the presuppositions of everyday life, to the point where the individual could become conscious of such change and of the possibilities of his own actions changing the life conditions of future generations. Among other things, therefore, a social conscience became a more likely possibility. Yet in society on the agrarianate level, basic change remained the exception and innovation, in principle, an occasional matter, in contrast to the Modern Age, when innovation has become institutionalized. Historical and moral consciousness, that is, escaped the anonymity of the locally immemorial and could even envisage a vast geographical scene of action; but it could not escape the sense that the past was per se authoritative, nor achieve a trans-cultural world-wide perspective.[3]

Cosmopolitan and mercantile tendencies in early agrarianate society

Within the limitations of cultural resources on the agrarianate level, change was steady and far-reaching; and from very early such changes were interdependent across a large part of the Afro-Eurasian landmass. Local societies were less and less independent in their cultural development.

Agrarian-based citied society determined the main features of historical development throughout an increasingly major portion of the Eastern Hemisphere: that is, in those regions which together went to make up what the Greeks called the 'Oikoumene', the 'inhabited quarter' of the world. The Greeks conceived the Oikoumene as a geographically fixed area between Atlantic and Pacific and between the equator and the uninhabitably cold north; but if we define it in terms of the peoples the Greeks would have included explicitly or implicitly, we must regard it as a historically developing complex. As agriculture and the associated domestication of animals spread through the

[3] The term 'agrarian' can properly refer to an agricultural order in which property relations are disposed with reference to the sort of stratification and organization most commonly associated with the presence of cities as key political and economic centres and foci of historical initiative. So soon as cities developed, the agriculture—and also the primitive commerce and industry—in their vicinity were thus subjected to urban influence; but always on an agrarian basis. The term 'agrarianate' seems comprehensive enough, so understood, to include within itself both urban life of this sort, which presupposed the economic resources concentrated by agrarian tenures as its mainstay (at least if one sees any given urban life in its total economic setting); as well as such peripheral economic forms as independent pastoralism, which also presupposed at least agricultural society, and generally, in practice, the citied agrarian-based form of it. Alternative terms seem all unsatisfactory for our purposes. 'Pre-Modern civilized' or 'pre-Modern citied' life fails to bring out the positive urban-agrarian character of the social order itself.

The tendency in modern area-studies to lump all pre-Modern society as 'traditional' is subject to many serious objections, which will appear abundantly in the course of this work; not the least of them is that it fails to bring out the startling historical contrast between conditions before and after the development of citied and lettered life. It also presupposes a definition of 'tradition' that reduces it to immemorial prescriptive custom, and thus drastically misrepresents the nature of culture on the agrarianate level.

Afro-Eurasian landmass, all the peoples involved came to be historically interrelated to some degree, tied into the trade network and subject to at least the indirect impact of the historical developments that arose in the citied regions in the older agricultural areas. All these peoples, even when south of the equator, may be included as making up the historical Afro-Eurasian Oikoumene. This Oikoumene remained the setting of most historical life in the hemisphere down to Modern times, when agrarianate society ceased to be the determining form of society in the world at large, being superseded by Modern technicalized society by the end of the eighteenth century. We may call the period when agrarianate society was historically dominant, within the range of the Oikoumene, the 'Agrarian Age' (lasting from the time of Sumer down to the seventeenth and eighteenth centuries), in contrast to the Modern 'Technical Age' since the eighteenth century.

The history of all the peoples of this vast area was affected more and more by the interrelations in the Oikoumene. Over the centuries, the areas within the Oikoumene that were organized under urban rule expanded. New luxuries were discovered and coveted, traders sought out more distant sources of supply, and armies followed them to impose a more secure authority. New techniques were developed in production—and in organization. Nowhere was all this felt more than among the many peoples of the Fertile Crescent and the neighbouring lands, who lived in the very midst of the Oikoumene.

These peoples, among whom Islam was to develop, were increasingly linked together, even apart from wider contacts across the Oikoumene. At first, they were the foremost example of the development of a cosmopolitan regional high culture. Several peoples had come to use the cuneiform script of the Sumerians, and among them all, the Sumerian lettered tradition (cultivated especially by the priests) tended to be influential: to this extent, they formed a single multinational civilization which can most conveniently be called the 'Cuneiform'. Meanwhile, political units became larger. Among Sumerians and Akkadians, Hurrians, Hittites, Urartians, and many others, territorial kingdoms arose which learned effectively to control from a central capital the politics of many cities; and then great empires arose, in which even such larger nationalities were mingled and sometimes even dispersed. Under the relatively restricted sway of the Hittites, then under the widespread empire of the Assyrians, the populations of whole cities were transported from one land to another for reasons of state. People came to have a wider perspective on matters taken for granted in local societies. They could see more readily how limited were local assumptions in craftways and in political patterns and even in points of conscience. The cosmopolitanism of the future Irano-Semitic cultural tradition was being launched.

The consequences of such a development were expressed in a shift in social alignments. In the eighth and seventh centuries BC, the Assyrians were perfecting their imperial power by a combination of horsemanship, of cruel terror, of moral earnestness, and of administrative efficiency. It was the administrative efficiency that was probably most decisive, for it spread a single set of high-cultural standards everywhere. Local traditions were perpetuated—most notably in the worship of the gods; but increasingly they receded before common traditions expressed in a new common administrative language, Aramaic. Unlike earlier languages, Aramaic did not share the priestly Cuneiform tradition, which from this time gradually lost its power; it was, however, Semitic, like the most important of the Cuneiform languages. It became the language (especially in the Fertile Crescent) first of the merchants and of city life generally; from there it came to be used by the clerks at the courts (if not in the temples)—and at last even among the peasantry. Other languages continued for some centuries as local rural dialects (and as the medium of religion and science among the learnèd); but the more dominant elements of the Fertile Crescent and the nearby highlands were becoming, with one regional layman's language, substantially one diversified people, and shared many common expectations.

It was not only in language that the growing power of the merchants and clerks appeared. Even the Cuneiform literatures of the time reflect a growing sense of personal individuality which most probably catered to the tastes of the market more than to either temple or court. Perhaps a symptom of the mood of many people of the time can be seen in the striking development of astrology in this period. The movements of the stars had long been studied in Babylonia for their bearing, among other things, on the fate of kings. There developed, beginning about this time, in the Cuneiform Babylonian language of the priests (who still monopolized such matters), a more systematic, 'scientific' cultivation of mathematical astronomy. But by the end of the Axial Age it was directed no longer merely toward understanding the fate of kings, and so of their kingdoms at large, but also toward understanding the fate of ordinary individuals (presumably, wealthy ones), as individuals and apart from the common destiny of peoples.

The florescences of the Axial Age and the articulation of cultural regions

The old Cuneiform lands with their new practical Aramaic were not alone in these tendencies. As, with trade, the citied regions in the Oikoumene had constantly spread, the market had become a major focus of high culture also elsewhere. In other areas too, scholars became concerned with individual destiny. For partly unknown reasons, the different citied regions of the Oikoumene, even when there was no direct commercial contact (as between China and the Indo-Mediterranean regions) developed along parallel lines. At any rate, as is well known, toward the middle of the first millennium BC everywhere men grew prosperous and new social and economic ways proliferated, especially in matters mercantile; for instance, coinage, as a means of ready financial exchange under complex conditions, seems to have been developed roughly simultaneously, toward the seventh century, in Anatolia, in northern India, and in China. In the same widely distant parts of the Oikoumene appeared unexampled works of intellectual creativity which proved decisive for all subsequent high-cultural life. Cumulatively, all this amounted to great bursts of creative and many-sided cultural innovation, launching many new traditions of high culture: that is, to unparalleled cultural florescences. We may adopt for this period, roughly 800–200 BC, the term used by the philosopher Karl Jaspers, 'Axial Age', on account of its subsequent historical importance.[4] The age can be called 'Axial' not merely because—as the chart of the place of Islam in world chronology shows—it comes at the middle of the citied Agrarian Age, but because it resulted in an enduring geographical and cultural articulation of the citied zone of the Oikoumene into regions.

One of the most significant outcomes of these florescences was, in fact, the establishment of new and comprehensive complexes of high-cultural tradition, such as the Cuneiform had once formed. These were carried now in laymen's languages: the Aramaic was perhaps the first but also the least fully developed of these. The areas where the new lettered traditions developed came to form core areas: areas within which the greater part of all new high-cultural development was to be found thenceforth, or at least that which was at all widely propagated. Among them, these core areas tended to give a lead to the high-cultural life of the whole Oikoumene during the rest of the Agrarian Age.

At the expense of a certain schematizing, Afro-Eurasian citied history thenceforth can be presented as the interdependent and more or less parallel development of four major complexes of civilized traditions: the European complex, with its core area from Anatolia to Italy along the north of the Mediterranean Sea, and with Greek (and Latin) as classical languages; the complex in the region from Nile to Oxus, centred in the Fertile Crescent and the Iranian highlands, and carried chiefly in a series of Semitic and Iranian languages; the Indic, in the Indian area and the lands to the southeast of it, with Sanskrit (and Pali); and the Far Eastern, in China and its neighbouring lands.[5] As these regions were all in contact, there was much mutual influence and even sharing of common heritages, for instance in commerce and art, in religion and in science.

Still more important, perhaps, than simple borrowing among the regions was their common historical context. The culture of each of the regions was constantly expanding its sway beyond its original centres; thus jointly they extended in all directions, millennium by millennium, the overall field of

[4] I have found it necessary to use a number of new terms in this work; and other terms I have defined in a way alien to the daily newspaper (e.g., such a geographical term as 'Syria', which refers to the whole area between the Sinai peninsula and the turn of the Anatolian peninsula). For a defence of my policy, see the section on revisionism in scholarly terminology in the Introduction.

[5] For an explanation of my usage of such general terms as 'European' and 'Indic', see the section on usage in world historical studies in the Introduction.

The Place of Islam in the Chronology of World History

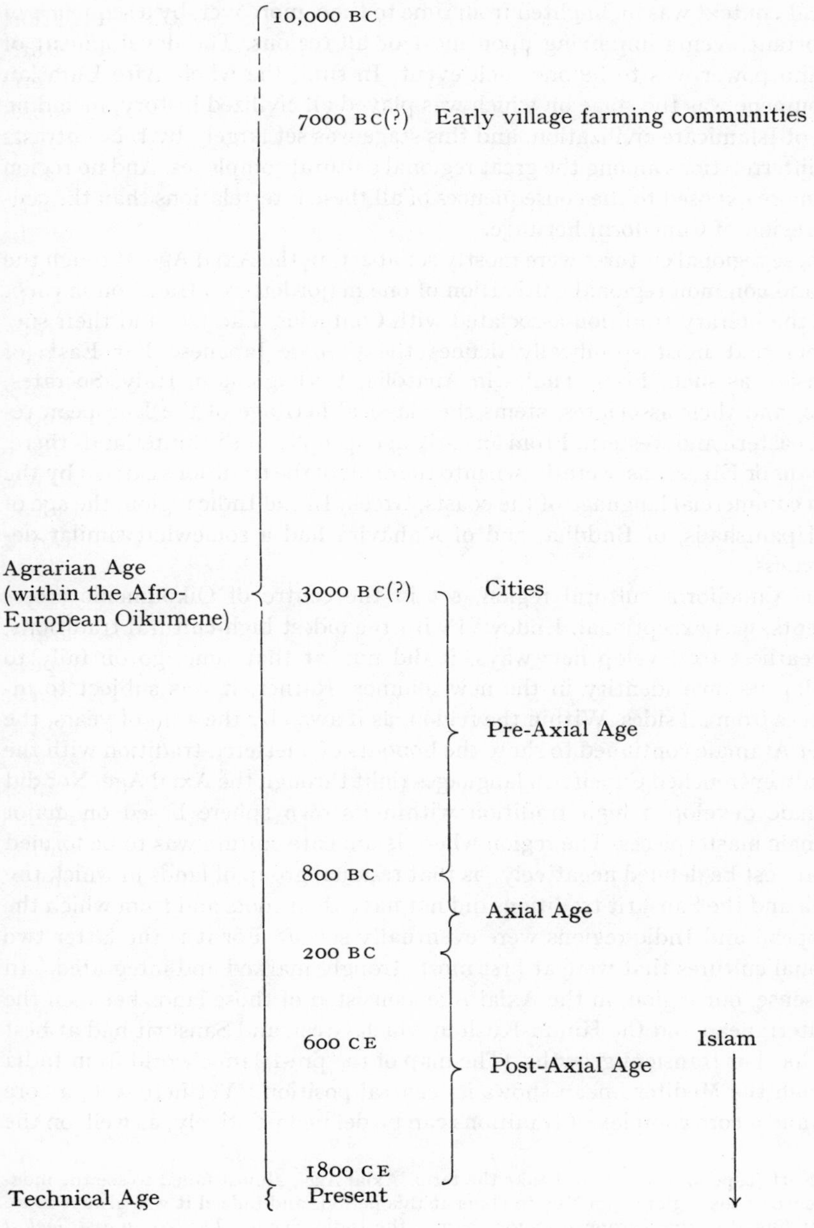

mercantile endeavour and of civilized history. All shared in a cumulatively increasing geographical network of commercial and cultural interchange and in a cumulative multiplication of techniques of all kinds. The common historical context was highlighted from time to time, moreover, by a sequence of important events impinging upon most or all regions. The development of Muslim power was to be one such event. In sum, the whole Afro-Eurasian Oikoumene was the stage on which was played all civilized history, including that of Islamicate civilization, and this stage was set largely by the contrasts and interrelations among the great regional cultural complexes. And no region was more exposed to the consequences of all these interrelations than the central region of Cuneiform heritage.

These regional cultures were mostly set apart, in the Axial Age, through the rise and common regional cultivation of one major lettered tradition in each. It is the literary tradition associated with Confucius, Lao-tze, and their successors that most specifically defines the Chinese-Japanese Far East (of Eurasia), as such. From Thales in Anatolia, Pythagoras in Italy, Socrates, Plato, and their associates, stems the classical heritage of the European region, eastern and western. From an early age, peoples of the hinterlands there, Lydians or Etruscans, were drawn into the orbit of the traditions carried by the main commercial language of the coasts, Greek. In the Indic region, the age of the Upanishads, of Buddha, and of Mahâvîra had a somewhat similar decisiveness.

The Cuneiform cultural region, set in the centre of Oikoumenic cross-currents, was exceptional. Endowed with the oldest high-cultural traditions, and earliest to develop new ways, it did not, at that time, go on fully to develop its own identity in the new manner. Rather, it was subject to influences from all sides. Within the region, as if awed by the aura of years, the newer Aramaic continued to share the honours of a lettered tradition with the already entrenched Cuneiform languages right through the Axial Age. Nor did Aramaic develop a high tradition within its own sphere based on major Aramaic masterpieces. The region where Islamicate culture was to be formed can almost be defined negatively: as that residual group of lands in which the Greek and the Sanskrit traditions did not have their roots and from which the European and Indic regions were eventually set off. For it is the latter two regional cultures that were at first most strongly marked and integrated.[6] In this sense, our region, in the Axial Age, consisted of those lands between the Mediterranean and the Hindu-Kush in which Greek and Sanskrit had at best only local or transient growths. (The map of the pre-Islamic world from India through the Mediterranean shows its central position.) Yet here, too, a core area and a core complex of traditions can be defined positively, as well, on the

[6] Karl Jaspers, from whom I take the term 'Axial Age', almost failed to see the independence of the region from Nile to Oxus at this period; and indeed it was always more closely linked to the European region than to the Indic. See his *The Origin and Goal of History* (Yale University Press, 1968).

basis of regional creativity which took place in the Axial Age; though this was not necessarily in Aramaic.

As in the other areas, it was concern with the private individual as personal, as independent in some degree from the group of which he formed a part, that increasingly exercised the great prophets who arose in the Axial Age, notably Zarathushtra (Zoroaster) in Iran and the Biblical prophets among the Hebrews. The prophets spoke to human beings in the name of a supreme and unique God, not reducible within any image, visible or mental, but expressing a moral dimension in the cosmos; they demanded unconditional allegiance from each person to this transcendent vision. Zarathushtra and his successors preached the duty of each individual personally to take part in a cosmic struggle between good and evil, justice and injustice, light and dark; a struggle in which finally light and truth must be victorious. On the personal level, the individual's duty was to be expressed in purity of life; on the social level, in maintaining a just balance among agrarian social classes. The Hebrew prophets, in Palestine and later in Babylonia, called men and women to the love of a Creator-god elevated above any nation, who would exact unusually severe standards precisely of those he most favoured, but promised them in the end compassion and fulfillment, when they should be prepared to worship him in full moral purity. These prophets founded strong literary traditions in old Iranian[7] and, above all, in Hebrew (and thence later in Aramaic), expressing and developing their visions. Though, at the time, these traditions were politically submerged and none found general intellectual acceptance, they gradually became the most sacred heritages—developed in greatly diverse ways—of an increasingly large proportion of the people of the Fertile Crescent and the Iranian highlands; ultimately they quite replaced the Cuneiform as well as any local heritages.

Accordingly, at least indirectly, the Axial Age launched the distinctive traditions also of the fourth region, what is commonly called the 'Middle East'. This region may be defined for our purposes, roughly, as the lands from the lower Nile valley to the Oxus basin, inclusive.[8] The core area of the region was limited to the Fertile Crescent and the Iranian highlands, where Cuneiform languages and Aramaic were used: from the Axial Age on through Islamic times, it was books written in this limited area that were read beyond it, or

[7] We have no dependable evidence of written texts in the Zoroastrian tradition before Arsacid (Parthian) times; the transmission of the key compositions may have been oral, though writing was known in eastern Iran in the Achaemenid period and the tradition seems to have grown (and retained distinctions of language) rather as it might have if written. It is not clear what was the role of a priest like Saêna (who is mentioned prominently as an upholder of truth), either as a transmitter or as a relatively independent presenter of moral challenge; but one must doubt whether Zarathushtra was the only significant prophetic figure.

[8] I prefer not to use the term 'Middle East' for this region, as it is misleading in more than one way, and I refer instead to the 'lands from Nile to Oxus' or even to the 'Nile-to-Oxus region'. I have explained my usage in the section on usage in Islamics studies in the Introduction.

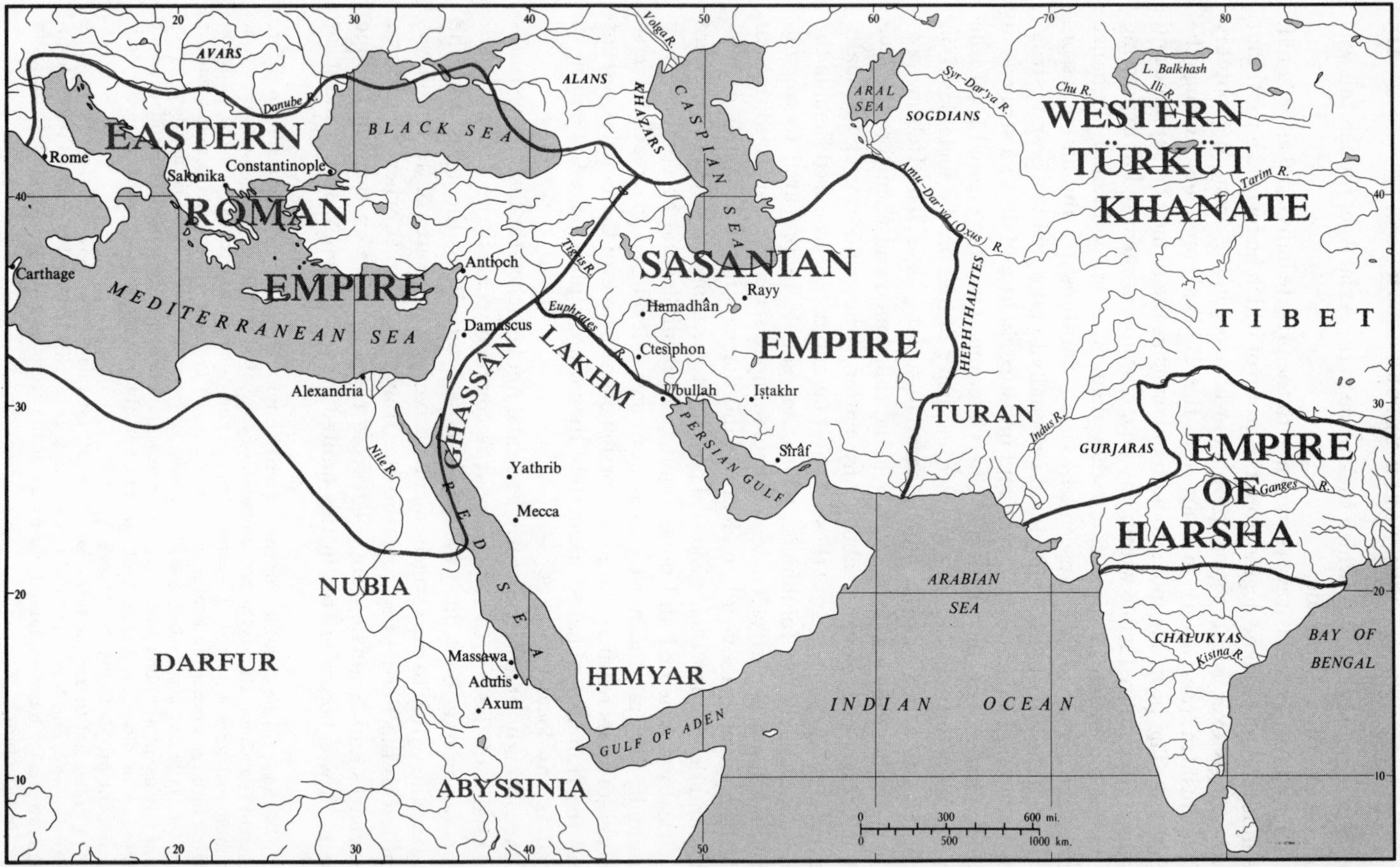

The central Mediterranean through India, *c.* 600 CE

institutions introduced there that were imitated elsewhere, and only rarely the reverse. Here the literary traditions founded by the Iranian and Hebrew prophets provided the most creative imaginative stimulus, giving rise subsequently to related traditions such as those of the Christians and the Manicheans. Already within the Axial Age there was enough influence of one tradition or another to suggest a common name for the group. The languages of these traditions were largely Semitic and Iranian, and we may call the regional culture so represented, somewhat loosely, the 'Irano-Semitic'.[9]

Personal conscience and the new society

In all four regions, the innovating thinkers shared certain orientations, perhaps as a result of similar experiences during the mercantile expansiveness of their time and because of the intermingling of peoples then (at least from the Mediterranean to India). Very often, in any case, the cultural setting in which they spoke was that of the market; it was rarely that of the temple. They all spoke to the aroused individual conscience and founded their appeals on the basis of individual, rational responsibility. Beyond that, however, the forms in which they posed the problems, and naturally the answers they came to, though there was much overlapping, differed radically in their most characteristic presuppositions. The Indic thinkers concerned themselves above all with exploring the resources of the self, developing subtle and comprehensive ways of understanding and mastering its unconscious recesses; they sometimes sought to transcend injustice (as in the Gîtâ) by making irrelevant the terms in which the question was posed. The Hellenic thinkers explored, above all, external nature; even after Socrates' and Plato's emphasis on the moral nature of the individual, the starting point of a philosophic synthesis normally remained a system of nature as a whole; justice (as in the *Republic*) must be founded in cosmic harmony, in which different sorts of individuals will play different parts. The Irano-Semitic prophets analyzed neither the inner self nor the outer world. If they analyzed anything, it was history itself; the Hebrew writers, especially, developed a majestic awareness of moral progression in

[9] I prefer the term 'Irano-Semitic' for this cultural complex to 'Middle Eastern' (if only because the latter phrase can be far too inclusive for this purpose); and to the ubiquitous 'Oriental', which even in the most circumscribed German usage includes too much. I see, indeed, no special need for a common term for all cultural traditions from Nile to Oxus except insofar as the phrase 'Irano-Semitic' is in fact applicable; that is, until the date when other traditions lost their autonomy and the whole regional culture became, in fact, Irano-Semitic predominantly.

But I do not understand 'Irano-Semitic' in a genetic sense. I am not concerned here to sort out—if that be possible—the remoter Iranian, Semitic, and Hellenic origins of various cultural elements. Here I am concerned with how they developed as an interrelated complex of cumulative traditions. For this purpose, the Semitic and Iranian peoples formed a *relative* cultural unity over against the Greek and Latin-speaking peoples. The relative amount of Hellenic elements in Gnosticism, for instance, interests me here less than its development—in whatever language—within the overall context of Irano-Semitic traditions.

history (not, of course, of 'progress' as such). The prophets summoned the personal conscience to confront a cosmic moral order, which expressed itself in the contingencies of social history; the struggle for justice was a matter of historical action. For their more consistent followers, interpersonal, egalitarian justice became the supreme value in civilized life, even, if need be, at the expense of the arts and accomplishments of luxury.

The developments of the Axial Age bore fruit in a new type of political structure—and again earliest and least completely between Nile and Oxus. The Assyrian military empire had collapsed, overwhelmed by the hatred of many peoples for its cruelties. But after an interval, in the sixth century BC even more of the lands from Nile to Oxus were absorbed into the Achaemenid Persian empire, which united in peaceful interchange the many peoples from the Aegean to the Indus. Under it the Aramaic merchants received full mercantile freedom, and Aramaic became the chief administrative tongue even throughout Iran. The Persians were careful to make no such violent breach with old local traditions as had the Assyrians; perhaps they no longer needed to, for the peoples had by now learned something of how to live in an international society. They preserved traditionally developed institutions everywhere so far as was still possible, without introducing important new social principles; but they proclaimed with new insistence the supreme duty of maintaining truth and justice, a duty imposed upon those privileged to rule. Such an ideal was proclaimed even in their monumental art which, in contrast to the Assyrian portrayal of generals destroying their enemies, commonly presented the king in his court as lord of peoples. Many among these peoples, in fact, like the Jews who were benevolently restored to their homeland, learned to revere the Great King as guarantor of peace and prosperity against interference by any lesser powers throughout the lands.[10]

In each of the great regions there was a tendency, as from Nile to Oxus, for political power to be built on an increasingly wide territorial basis, with the consent and support of the cities of diverse peoples, who found a common interest in the order such a power provided as their interrelationships became increasingly complex. Empires were built, typically over all the core area, at least, of each of the four regions, carrying not only military control but also a degree of social and cultural unity. Such empires were made possible by the considerable economic and social development that had taken place in each region during the Axial Age. They tended to found themselves, at best, on some elements of the best philosophic thinking of their respective regions. The

[10] For an overview of ancient cultural life between Nile and Oxus, two volumes are especially convenient: Henri Frankfort, *The Birth of Civilization in the Near East* (London, 1968) and Henri and H. A. Frankfort, John A. Wilson, and Thorkild Jacobsen, *The Intellectual Adventure of Ancient Man* (University of Chicago Press, 1946—also in paperback as *Before Philosophy*, Pelican Books). Gordon Childe, *What Happened in History* (Pelican Books, 1942), is rather out of date but still a suggestive review of a longer period. The master summary of present knowledge is now volume one of the Unesco-sponsored *History of Mankind* (New York, 1963).

Maurya empire in northern India made use of Buddhist thought; the Ch'in-Han empire of China was founded by anti-traditionalist theorists, and then depended increasingly on Confucian standards; the Roman empire of the Mediterranean built its law largely on Stoic assumptions about mankind, and its social order generally on the ideals of Hellenic city life developed in the time of the classical thought.

The regional tradition developing more weakly from Nile to Oxus suffered a peculiar complication upon the fall of the Achaemenid Persian empire. Its conqueror, Alexander, represented not Aramaic nor even prophetic but Hellenic culture; that is, the civilization centred in the northern coastlands of the Mediterranean. Hellenic merchants and mercenaries had played an increasing, though subordinate, role already within the Achaemenid empire. But for several centuries after Alexander, Greek culture and its carriers held a more or less dominant position in much of the region. Throughout the central area of the Irano-Semitic traditions, in the Fertile Crescent and the Iranian highlands (as well as in Egypt), Greek cities, with Hellenic traditions and expectations, flourished side by side with cities whose traditions continued Aramaic and even Cuneiform patterns of life. In many areas the Hellenic element was the more powerful.

This Hellenic strength came less from military force than from cultural attraction. The Seleucid dynasty, which ruled after Alexander's death, was explicitly Hellenic and depended upon cities formed in the first instance of Greek colonists, scattered everywhere between Nile and Oxus. But the Parthian Arsacid dynasty, which soon succeeded it in the greater part of its territories, was Iranian by tongue; yet it too was avowedly (at least at first) a protector of Hellenic culture. Hellenic culture, minimally diluted with local colour, enjoyed a near-monopoly of respect in the cosmopolitan big cities; the old Cuneiform (and Hieroglyphic) traditions gradually died out, and not Aramaic but Greek took their place as vehicle of the more highly cultivated literature. The four or five centuries after Alexander, as far east as the Oxus as well as in the Mediterranean basin, are reasonably called the 'Hellenistic' age.

The eventual results of this superposition of Hellenic culture upon the Irano-Semitic and Egyptian are still in debate. One thing is certain. The whole tradition of natural science, centring on mathematics and astronomy, which had been founded largely on ancient Babylonian data and which even in Seleucid times was being developed simultaneously in Babylonian Cuneiform and in Greek, gradually came to be indissolubly associated with the Hellenistic aspect of culture in the region; the fortune of natural science henceforth depended upon that of the Hellenic elements there. This situation was perhaps decisive for the subsequent course of Islamicate civilization on its intellectual side.

In any case, the region from Nile to Oxus did remain distinct, culturally, from the European region, where Hellenic culture—in Greek or in Latin, and even when Christianized—became the basis of all high-cultural tradition, such as there was. The lands from Nile to Oxus were highly varied, and one cannot say either of Egypt (where city life was especially Hellenized) or of the Oxus basin (where Sanskritic influence was strong) a good deal that can be said of the areas between. Yet the various lands in the region were closely interrelated; to some degree they underwent a common destiny. I think this resulted at least partly from the role of the mercantile classes in the regional life.[11]

The position of the Nile-to-Oxus region in the Oikoumene

We have seen that the assertion of a regional identity between Nile and Oxus was problematical, despite a certain amount of common history and culture. It remained so even in Islamic times—though by then it was no longer the Irano-Semitic traditions that were submerged by their neighbours, but rather those traditions were overflowing throughout the hemisphere. It is not really clear how our region came to have so anomalous a history. But we may guess a part of it.

A distinctive high-cultural pattern in the region from Nile to Oxus was surely encouraged by two geographical features of the region: its focal commercial position in the Oikoumene and its relative aridity. These need not have come into play in the origin of the distinctive patterns. Doubtless the Irano-Semitic prophetic traditions originated in at most a few centres, points where creative leadership was able to evoke unusually potent social and intellectual norms, able to command wide human assent and imitation. It is possible, for instance, that the uniquely creative tradition of the Hebrew people was the outcome of a phenomenon rare in all Oikoumenic history: an enduringly successful peasant revolt (like those which launched the

[11] It will be seen that I have been presupposing here a conception of civilization in some ways more allied to that of Childe, say, or his disciple Turner, than to that of Spengler or Toynbee. I see no necessary life-pattern in the formation of a civilization, and I was willing to discuss the advent of a regional cultural integration among Semites and Iranians without considering whether this was or was not a 'new civilization': it was sufficient to analyze it as a complex of cultural traditions in a new phase. Nevertheless, I feel that practically all the analytic devices that Toynbee, in particular, introduces into his system have their validity: a creative minority can indeed, given favourable circumstances, develop cultural patterns that will spread even at the expense of highly developed rival patterns; and they can then evoke hostile reactions in those peoples among whom they have been received. In particular, I see sufficient integrality in the culture of a region to take seriously the phenomenon that both Spengler and Toynbee—building on those historians who have contrasted the 'Greek' and the 'Semitic' spirit—have cited as abnormal in this region: the seeming suppression by a Greek overlay of an indigenous cultural life, which later reasserted itself (and most fully with Islam). But I do not think that such a phenomenon can be reduced to general rules covering such cases on that level. Certainly one cannot simply refer to latent spirits, either racial or cultural. One must establish what it was, in a given case, that made an area receptive to alien patterns; what gave it continuing interests calling for patterns alternative to the new dominant ones; and what positive circumstances finally made possible the emergence of such alternatives.

remarkable Druze and Swiss peoples). In that case, the covenant would represent the agreement of the rebels leagued against city domination, and Joshua's campaigns would represent help brought to the peasants west of Jordan by those initially successful in the east (perhaps, as in the Druze case, under ideological leadership from Egypt).[12] In such revolutionary events could have been revealed a deity not only ethical but supremely historical—a trait uniquely characteristic of the god of the Hebrews. The implications of such a conception of deity, even for urban conditions, would gradually be unfolded in the dialogue of the tradition (as I have pointed out in the Prologue). Then such insights, once they had become established, could win assent far beyond the original historical community. Yet whatever was the source of the Hebrew tradition, in any case new viewpoints could become widely dominant only in a general setting which would favour their survival as compared with other viewpoints. In the case of the prophetic traditions, one can speculate that this setting was found among the Semitic and Iranian mercantile classes more consistently than among either the peasants or their landlords; then it gained its force from the ecology of the region.

The citied traditions of the region were first based on the agriculture of the rich Mesopotamian alluvial plain, which required considerable investment in controlled irrigation to be fully used; and to a lesser extent on Egypt (whose irrigation required less management). For a long time, the wealth and hence power of the regional empires was derived largely from the alluvial agriculture; in the Mesopotamian plain, especially, investment became more and more elaborate after the Axial Age, in part through the resources of centralized imperial power. Even elsewhere, agriculture was the major source of revenue; associated with the court in profiting from it was a great class of landholders who, as cavalry (sometimes followed by peasants from their lands as infantry), provided much of the military manpower the ruling courts depended on. But, except perhaps in exploiting the alluvial plain, there was an early limit to any increase in the agricultural resources on which the landholders' position depended.

The region from Nile to Oxus forms the central portion of the great Arid Zone stretching across the Afro-Eurasian landmass from the Sahara through the Gobi deserts. Some large portions of it, as can be seen on the map of physical conditions from Nile to Oxus, are pure desert—expanses of sand and rock or of salt flats, where there is so little vegetation that neither humans nor animals can live. Some few scattered districts, on the other hand, such as the coastlands south of the Caspian, receive a great deal of rain, are naturally heavily forested, and when cleared support a lush rainfall agriculture. But most of the region is neither desert nor well watered but arid, in the sense

[12] George E. Mendenhall, 'The Hebrew Conquest of Palestine', *The Biblical Archaeologist*, 25 (1962), 66–87, sets forth an alluring theory which has the virtue at least of making intelligible the long-run story in ways that the supposition of a mass invasion and settlement by pastoralists (itself improbable) never can.

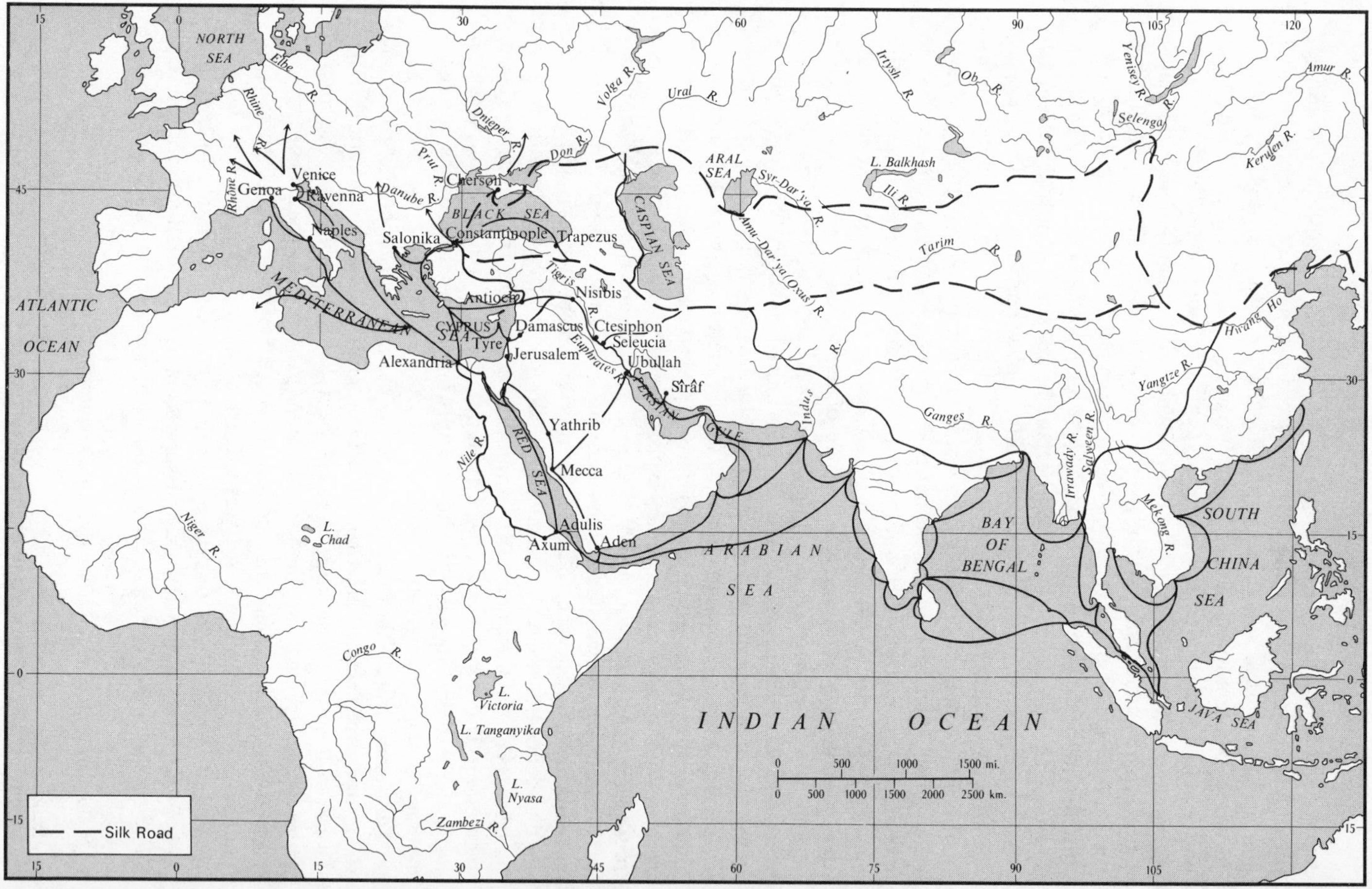

Trade routes of the seventh and eighth centuries

that water is the most decisive limiting factor in supporting life: the more water there is, the more vegetation; the more vegetation, the more animal and human life.

There are three types of terrain in an arid region: that where there is enough scattered rainwater to produce sporadic vegetation for grazing, but where settled agriculture in any one spot is impossible; that where rain in a given spot is predictable enough to warrant planting crops—which, however, are always in danger of failing if the rain fails; that where water is available in concentrated amounts from some source other than local rain—as from geological strata which trap water falling over a large area and then can be tapped by wells, which serve to irrigate the fields. The latter sort of terrain is called an oasis and may be large enough to include many villages and a city or two. The same effect is produced when water is available from rivers fed by distant rains: in this sense, the whole lower Nile valley can be called one large oasis.

As compared with better-watered regions—including the greater part of all three of the other focal regions of high culture in the Oikoumene—aridity reduced the resources and solidarity of those in any given area whose wealth was in land. Within the cultivated terrain the yield was insecure in the rain areas; and the irrigated areas, which required continuous investment, were widely scattered for the most part, forming only a small part of the total land surface. Then between settled agricultural areas or around them there was terrain good only for herding grazing animals; and this terrain was often so extensive that the herdsmen could not retain a village as base but had to take along their families and develop a full-time social and cultural existence of their own, as nomads in some degree. Such herdsmen yielded little or no revenue. Moreover, they sometimes posed a source of social power which might rival that of the agrarian gentry. (Of course, there have been many sorts and degrees of nomadism and of combinations of pastoralism with agriculture.) In any case, over any given large territory human life was concentrated in favoured spots rather than distributed at all evenly, so that it took more overall land space to support a given population. Agricultural groups tended to be far apart, and those who could be wealthy on an agrarian basis were relatively few in any given place.

In contrast to the limits on expansion in agriculture, there seemed to be no limits on potential expansion in commerce. Perhaps in part because it was the point of origin of the Oikoumenic agricultural complex, but more enduringly because of the Afro-Eurasian configuration of seas and mountains, the Fertile Crescent and its surrounding lands offered juncture points for more long-distance trade routes than were concentrated in any other comparable region. From a port (like Baṣrah) at the head of the Persian Gulf, for instance, commercial relations were possible, directly or through neighbouring (Mediterranean or Iranian) centres, with all the major regions of the Oikoumene; something impossible from a port in any of the other regions, as can be seen from the map of trade routes in the Afro-Eurasian Arid Zone. Nowhere did merchants have more opportunity to become cosmopolitan in outlook—and to gain wealth through entrepôt trade whatever the local or even regional state of prosperity. Over the millennia, as the Afro-Eurasian Oikoumene and the area of citied commerce in it expanded, the long-distance trade throughout the hemisphere became not only larger in sheer bulk but more varied. To the steady accumulation of technical refinements in the lands of old civilization was added the development of special resources in the newer areas—such as the spices of the Malaysian archipelago; which areas then became themselves commercial centres instead of mere way stations. Cumulatively, long-distance trade bulked, millennium by millennium, larger in the economies of the various regions; the potential opportunities of merchants, particularly those at the crossroads between Nile and Oxus, became correspondingly larger.

The fundamental economy of the region from Nile to Oxus remained agrarian-based and the absolute proportion of the wealth of the society going to landholders remained larger than that going to merchants. But with the relatively low concentration of agrarian wealth and the relatively high concentration of mercantile opportunities, it is possible that merchants in several countries there (whether or not themselves engaged in distant trade) were able to acquire a relatively larger proportion of the civil wealth than could merchants in most agrarian-dominated areas; and over the region as a whole, in any case, they were probably a bit less completely dependent on the local landed gentry economically. Increasingly over the centuries there was opportunity for the high culture focused on the market to become more autonomous and even more influential in the society as a whole. The form that such influence took (as compared with mercantile influence elsewhere) was governed, in turn, by the effects of the early advent of agriculture and of urbanization in the region (and of its physical openness to widespread military operations and imperial constructions). An imperial tradition of long standing accentuated the cosmopolitanism, but militated against its embodiment in any sort of civic particularism. These tendencies were pushed yet further in the Islamic period. (We will study them in more detail in Book Three.)

It was doubtless a mercantile potentiality that, at one stage of Oikoumenic development, made it possible for Greek culture to gain such a hold in the region. It was doubtless the special conditions under which cosmopolitanism developed between Nile and Oxus that produced a very different sort of mercantile life there as the Oikoumenic complex matured and the region's role in it became greater. In any case, in the field of religion, at least, the mercantile classes were sometimes able to set the tone for whole peoples. From Nile to Oxus, then, religious history especially took a distinctive turn after the Axial Age, as we may see outlined in the chart showing the rise of confessional religion (pp. 126–27).

The confessional religious allegiances

Largely under the relative peace assured by the great empires that were built following the Axial Age, and in part growing out of the great ideas as well as the social ferment of that age, came the beginnings of a series of movements which are spoken of as the great historical religions—the 'universal' or 'confessional' religions. From an intellectual élite, the sense of challenge to the individual conscience was generalized among the urban and finally (at least superficially) even the rural masses. Sometimes the thoughts of great figures such as the Buddha or Isaiah came to be directly accepted, in principle, as the creative springs of the new traditions and as sources of inspiration among even illiterates. Often new figures and new leadership intervened, launching relatively independent traditions. In either case, insights were woven into a system, dramatized in exclusive myth and cult, and equipped with popular organization and sanctions. The old local cults were subsumed under the new allegiances, or were replaced.

By the early centuries of the Christian era were thus established, all across the citied zone of the Afro-Eurasian Oikoumene, organized religious traditions which, in contrast to most of the previous religious traditions, made not tribal or civic but primarily personal demands. They looked to *individual* personal adherence to ('confession' of) an explicit and often self-sufficient body of moral and cosmological *belief* (and sometimes adherence to the lay *community* formed of such believers); belief which was embodied in a corpus of sacred *scriptures*, claiming *universal* validity for all men and promising a comprehensive solution of human problems in terms which involved a *world beyond death*. Beyond this very general framework, the several allegiances contrasted as greatly as possible. Especially those originating between Nile and Oxus, in the prophetic traditions, contrasted in almost every possible way with those originating in northern India, which ultimately shared with them the adherence of most of the Oikoumene. But they all filled the same sort of social role.

By the fourth and fifth centuries CE, these religious allegiances were not only generally prevalent; the stronger of them, in their several areas, were able to establish their representatives in some degree of political power. An official form of Christianity achieved exclusive status in the Roman empire; Zoroastrian Mazdeism gained a comparable status in the Sâsânian (Persian) empire, though had it to tolerate stronger rivals. Vaishnavism and Shaivism (which together issued in modern Hinduism) vied for royal favours in the Indic lands and southeast overseas. Buddhism vied with a Buddhist-influenced neo-Taoism for power in China. Even allegiances with fewer adherents could dominate a court (like Jainism) or even control a kingdom now and then, as did Rabbinical Judaism (at this time a proselytizing body like the others) and Manicheanism. The origin of the latter illustrates the general mood. It was founded in the third century in the Iraq, not to win over pagans

The Development of Confessional Religion in the Irano-Mediterranean Region, *c.* 650 BC–632 CE

THE AXIAL AGE AND FOLLOWING CENTURIES

Throughout the citied area of the Afro-Eurasian landmass arise movements of independent thought, forming *classical literatures*, which become the norm in *culturally unified regional empires*, in which then spread the *confessional religions* (characterized by an expectation of individual adherence on the basis of scripture)

c. 650–550 BC	Zarathushtra (Zoroaster) and Jeremiah and others, in Iran and Syria, as major *prophetic figures* demand ethical confrontation of cosmos and history, while Thales and Pythagoras and others in Greek Anatolia and Italy as pioneering *philosophers* pursue rational investigation of human and cosmic nature; both prophets and philosophers figuring as critics and reformers of established nature cults
538–331 BC	The *Achaemenid Persian empire* provides a single tolerant and prosperous sovereignty from the Aegean to the Indus; Zoroastrian tradition penetrates the priestly caste of Magi
433 BC	Nehemiah restores *Jewish worship at Jerusalem* on a prophetic basis, launching the Jewish community as a people founded on faith in scripture
399 BC	*Socrates dies* martyr to philosophy at Athens, becoming hero of Greek humanistic idealism in its many schools
333–328 BC	Alexander establishes *Greek supremacy* in the former Achaemenid lands, initiating a long confrontation of the Irano-Semitic prophetic with the Hellenic philosophic traditions
c. 200 BC–200 CE	The Mediterranean basin is dominated and then ruled by the philhellenic Romans, under whom *Hellenistic municipal culture* is standardized, while the philhellenic Parthians dominate the Iranian highlands and the Mesopotamian plain; common cults offering personal salvation spread in all these areas
30 CE	The *Christian community* is founded in Syria, universalizing the appeal of the Jewish divinity

THE SÂSÂNIAN EMPIRE TO THE DEATH OF MUḤAMMAD

Representatives of the confessional religions, from ocean to ocean, achieve social authority and power, rivalling each other for exclusive positions

226–642	The *Sâsânian empire* replaces the Parthians in Iran and the Mesopotamian plain, fosters urban prosperity with relative centralization

273	*Mânî dies,* founder of the otherworldly Manichean faith, and friend of the Sâsânî emperor
285	After crises (235–268) in which the Roman city loses its Mediterranean power, the *Roman empire* is bureaucratically reorganized with its capital at the Thracian straits (from 330, at Constantinople); Christianity persecuted as anti-social; rival cults encouraged
275–292	In the reign of Bahrâm II, at latest, *Zoroastrian Mazdeism* is given an official central organization in the Sâsânian empire, and is allowed to persecute dissenters
324–337	In the reign of Constantine I, *Christianity* gains an official position in the reorganized Roman empire, and subsequently becomes legally enforced
485–531	In the reign of Qubâd, Zoroastrianism and the Sâsânian aristocracy are torn by *Mazdak's attempted egalitarian reform*
c. 525	Christian *Abyssinians occupy the Yemen,* in alliance with Romans, ending Jewish kingdom (which had persecuted Christians)
527–565	In the *reign of Justinian,* Roman power and cultural magnificence reach a peak, while the last Pagan school is closed (529) and Christian orthodoxy is enforced
531–579	In the *reign of Nûshîrvân,* Sâsânian power and cultural magnificence reach a peak, with the crown triumphing over the nobility; heresies against Zoroastrian orthodoxy are stamped out
c. 550	Final *break of the Ma'rib* dam in the Yemen, symbolizing the decline of the south Arabian agricultural society and the predominance of pagan Bedouin patterns in the Arabian peninsula
603–628	Last great *war between the Roman and Sâsânian empires,* in which the forces of both are badly depleted, but political status quo is restored. Restoration of the True Cross to Jerusalem (629) symbolizes triumph of Christian over Zoroastrian empire—and over Jews and heretics
622–632	*Muḥammad,* an Arab of Mecca, sets up a religiously organized society in Medina, and expands it over much of the Arabian peninsula to march with and even locally replace Sâsânian and Roman power

(that is, adherents of the older types of religion) but to restore the pure truth which was felt to have been already corrupted in all the other popular confessional religious bodies. Almost everywhere, alongside the dominant religious bodies, there were minority groups ready to challenge the established group if given the opportunity. Forms of Buddhism and of Christianity were especially widespread. Taken together, these religious allegiances, extremely varied as they were in their approaches, achieved in common one grand result: they eliminated (or took over and transformed) the old tribal and civic cults, replacing them for public purposes with their own rites; and they accustomed the people of most of the Oikoumenic citied zone to expect every serious individual to acknowledge at least some sort of life-orientational tradition of universal claims as ultimate authority in his life. In the western parts of the zone, they even accustomed people to expect some such religious allegiance to be not merely patronized but enforced officially by governments.

The Irano-Semitic religious traditions, which generally prevailed in the western part of the Oikoumene, were of two families. What we may call the 'Abrahamic' religious communities, chiefly Jewish or Christian in various forms, could be traced back to the tradition of the Hebrew prophets; they generally recognized the act of faith of Abraham as their point of origin or as their classic model. Among communities of Magian-Mazdean affiliations, the most important was that of the Zoroastrian Mazdeans, who worshipped the good Creator-god as Ahura Mazdâh; Zoroaster was their great prophet.[13] The Abrahamic traditions were expressed primarily in Semitic tongues and flourished especially in the Fertile Crescent; those of Mazdean affiliations, primarily in Iranian tongues and on the Iranian highlands. (Cf. the map of language and religion.) But despite quite separate origins in Axial times, even then the two prophetic traditions had begun to merge; by post-Axial times, the two sets of traditions cannot be fully marked off from each other. The traditions influenced one another and even converged; some groups cannot clearly be placed in one family or the other. A different criterion is probably more important for distinguishing among the Irano-Semitic confessional religions, a criterion which only partly coincides with the distinction between Abrahamic and Mazdean: their degree of populism.

The role of populism in the Irano-Semitic monotheisms

Some of the religious traditions emphasized more than did others what we may call 'populism': that is, concern for the ordinary moral needs and cap-

[13] It is conventional to refer to this family of traditions as 'Iranian', but such a term carries unwarranted ethnic implications (and has misled some into supposing that other traditions, such as Islam, have not really belonged in Iran) and is not exact anyway. A reference to Magian-Mazdean affiliations covers all the traditions relevant here. It is becoming common to refer to those who applied to themselves the term *Mazdayasnian*, as 'Mazdean' (for brevity) rather than 'Zoroastrian'; accordingly, I reserve the latter term for such aspects of the tradition as can be identified with Zarathushtra.

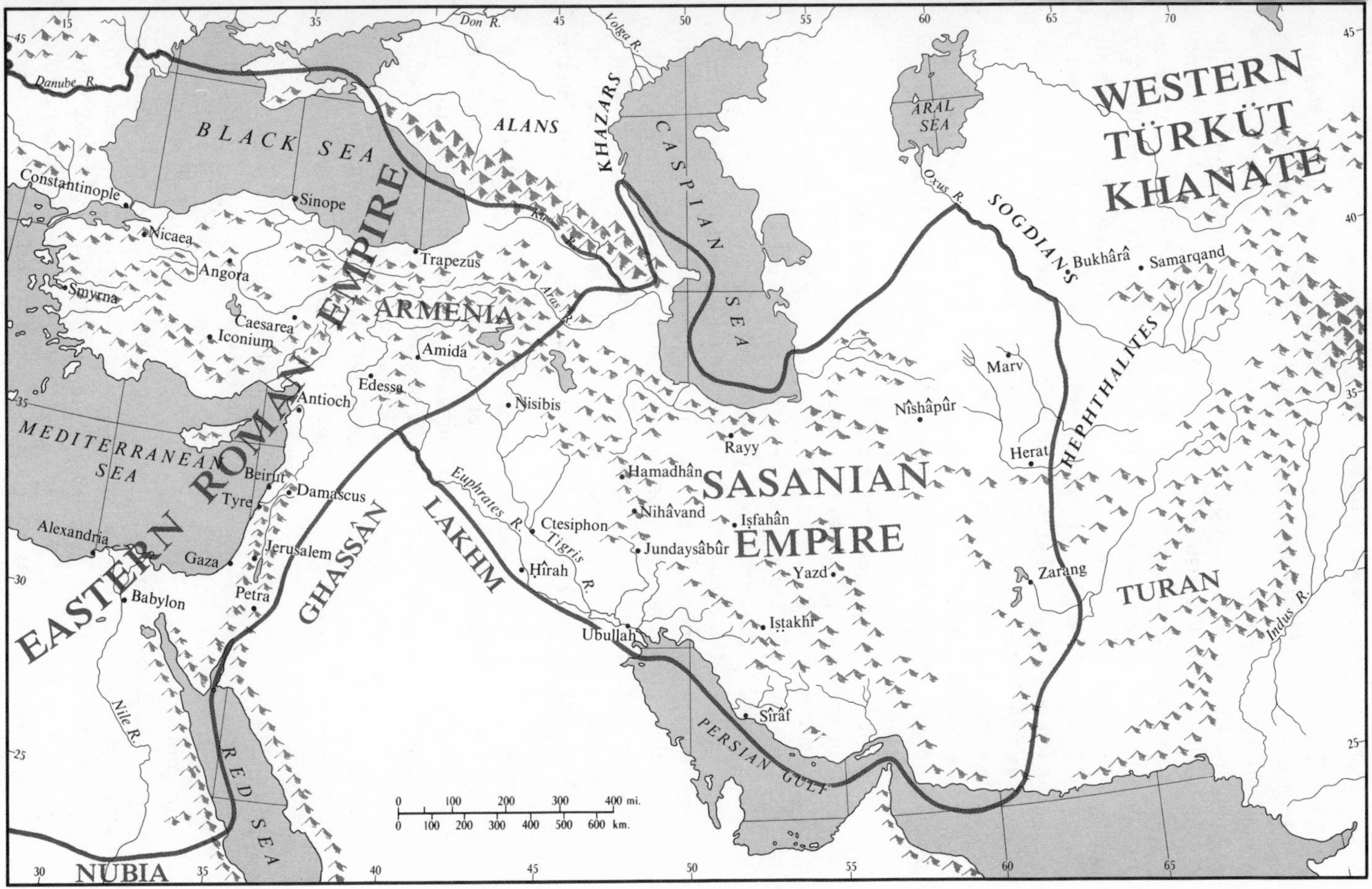

The lands from Nile to Oxus before the rise of Islam

abilities of the common people, as contrasted to the highly privileged classes; or at least for what the religious specialists deemed appropriate to the common people. All the confessional religious traditions may be called somewhat populistic in that they tended to cast their doctrines and their moral standards into forms intelligible to the ordinary person. But among some of the Irano-Semitic religious communities, populist values were stressed even to the condemnation of any other values. I suggest that this emphasis seems to have answered, in part, to the sense of propriety that prevailed among mercantile classes when they distinguished themselves from the more aristocratic tastes of the landed families. Merchants, preoccupied with their steady daily tasks, necessarily felt themselves to be ordinary folk as compared to the court and the landed aristocrats who had the wealth and leisure to set the cultural tone to which all other classes were tempted to aspire. An assertion of their own dignity must mean a certain rejection of that aristocratic culture that lured or mocked them.

This is not to say that mercantile classes must be, or were then, always populistic in orientation; but that populism was specially appropriate to merchants when they were not the highest class, and yet were sufficiently autonomous to form their own standards. The sorts of individual whose imaginative responses looked to the moral needs of common people had a better chance, in a mercantile context, that their concerns would be reinforced by a corresponding response in others. In the dialogue that formed the traditions, their interpretations proved not only abstractly attractive but also relevant to the material interests shared by all; hence while every moral view might gain a hearing exceptionally according to temperament, this one would gain a hearing from all, and come to dominate the common expectations cultivated in the tradition.

Populism, at any rate, was strongest in the traditions that predominated in the Semitic Fertile Crescent, where the long-distance trade routes were concentrated more intensely than in the Iranian highlands, and presumably the relative cultural autonomy of the market was strongest. Accordingly, populism was strongest among the Abrahamic traditions, carried chiefly in the Semitic languages, as the chart of cultural and religious orientations points out. But the populistic emphasis could appear in either the Abrahamic or the Mazdean family of religious traditions.

The overall outlook of both Abrahamic and Mazdean traditions may be summed up as looking to justice in history through community. All the prophets had stressed just action as the highest religious activity. In contrast to the traditions of Indic origin especially, preoccupied with individual self-awareness, the Irano-Semitic traditions (populistic or not) centred attention on problems of interpersonal justice. Such an emphasis was crystallized in the central doctrine of the Last Judgment at which every individual would be forever rewarded in Paradise or punished in Hell according as he had done good or evil in his lifetime. In contrast again to the Indic traditions in which right

Cultural and Religious Orientations between Nile and Oxus

Language and area:	SEMITIC, IN FERTILE CRESCENT, the home base of	IRANIAN, IN THE HIGHLANDS, the home base of
Religious tradition:	ABRAHAMIC traditions (JEWS, CHRISTIANS, MUSLIMS, etc.); more often identified with	MAZDEAN (and/or MAGIAN) traditions (ZOROASTRIANS, etc.); more often identified with
Relative social class strength:	MERCANTILE classes, who were less outweighed by agrarian interests there, and congenial (but not exclusively) with	AGRARIAN LANDED classes, who outweighed the merchants there, and congenial (but not exclusively) with
Cultural and religious tendencies:	POPULISM, MORALISM, and the EGALITARIAN COMMUNITY	ARISTOCRATIC TASTE and the HIERARCHICAL COMMUNITY

and wrong were to be balanced out in an indefinitely continued series of reincarnations, in the Irano-Semitic traditions each person had one lifetime, one period of responsible moral choice, which was irrevocably decisive. One's moral decisions now determined one's eternal fate without appeal.

On the social level, such an outlook made for a strongly positive evaluation of history. As in the individual life, so in the life of communities, what happened was irreversible and determined all future history one way or the other. There could be no question of an infinite round of cycles in which gods and humans were equally caught up. The way of the world in general and the course of history in particular were governed by the purposes of one supreme God, who expressed Himself in personal will and judgment, over and above the regularities and recurrences of nature. The course of events itself was not a matter of impersonal destiny but stood under His judgment: He was protagonist in a cosmic drama with a beginning and an end, in which the just cause finally would triumph. In the Mazdean tradition, He was temporarily limited by a counter-creator, author of evil; in the Abrahamic traditions, by a less exalted enemy, the Devil; but these figures did not share His ultimate cosmic status and were not, in any case, to be worshipped. Hence these faiths can all be called 'monotheistic', as calling for the worship of a single dominant figure. Any lesser cults that might be tolerated, as directed to angels or saints, remained (in principle) subordinated to the one primary cult.

One responsible lifetime; one transcendent God—and one righteous community. To assert the priority of the moral universe over the natural called for all three. With the cause of justice would triumph also the people which had identified itself with that cause. What might seem like a tribal and parochial heritage from pre-Axial times was transformed, in the monotheistic traditions, into an assertion of social and hence historical responsibility. The Jews were to bear witness, among the peoples, to the lordship of God; whoever did not join in the common witness but stood alone not only forfeited the moral guidance the community could give him but was directly unfaithful to the covenant made with God. The people of Ahura Mazdâh were to help Him clear the world of evil; who stood aside was a traitor. The cults of the old gods of nature were superseded and even excluded by those of the new ethical and historical God. The difference was expressed in a tendency for the new cults to use less palpable symbols of the Transcendent, such as fire, rather than the old fleshly images which answered well enough to gods of the visible world; for the true symbol and expression of the divine presence was the community itself. Monotheism might be defined by the worship of one God; it became effective in history when the worshippers formed one people.

But this overall monotheistic scheme could be interpreted in a spirit more populistic or less so. The ideal of justice, to begin with, could be interpreted in harmony with an aristocratic social order. For the official Mazdeism of the Sâsânian empire, agriculture was the noblest of ordinary occupations; but it was only the landed gentry, who depended on it financially, that formed the best of social classes, as its military defenders. The peasant was, in principle, more greatly respected than the merchant or craftsman, but he was not expected to prove noble nor yet to understand the subtleties of religion, which were reserved to a still higher body of hereditary and aristocratic priests. In the cosmic drama, the priests, together with the landed gentry as a military force, had the major part to play.

Yet Max Weber is surely justified in linking especially to merchants the type of religion which stresses the ethical demands of deity more than its role in ensuring the round of the agricultural seasons.[14] The demand of the prophets for just dealing, originally perhaps of agrarian inspiration, could be readily interpreted in terms of trade and contracts; so interpreted, it was more immediately relevant to the market than any cult of nature deities invoked to assure fertility and the recurrence of the immemorial natural order. The monotheistic traits of the Mazdean tradition were always threatened by compromise on the top social levels: Sâsânian state religion was never very pure. It was when shaped by the populism of mercantile elements that what was distinctive in the overall scheme of Irano-Semitic confessional religion stood out most sharply against the general background of agrarian-based culture. Nurtured in urban life, the monotheistic emphasis on an ethical God was accentuated into an interpersonal moralism in maximum contrast to the sympathetic ritual and even magic retained in the cult of the gods of nature.

In Judaism and related traditions, in which merchants held a much higher position than in the Mazdean tradition, social justice accordingly took on implications more challenging to the established order. It tended to be, above all, egalitarian justice, the justice of the market, with every person equal before the law. To be sure, marked equality, given the initial inequalities in human nature, tends to issue in its own sort of social inequalities. The demand for a more radical egalitarian justice, for effective equality among social classes, was not always pressed very far by merchants who found themselves forming, after all, a privileged class themselves. Still, several of the Abrahamic traditions (and even some religious traditions of quite different backgrounds elsewhere in the Oikoumene) reflected initially an active sense of the equal dignity and ultimate rights of the less privileged classes in society. Over the centuries, within each Irano-Semitic religion, tradition tended to develop again and again reformed versions in which such egalitarian justice was commonly stressed and some degree of practical implications drawn from it. On the whole, however, as they became established the religious leaders found ways to justify accepting the social order for the present, with at best secondary modi-

[14] Max Weber's analyses are—in the nature of his purpose—schematic; even so, they offer suggestions for possibilities to be alert for rather than universal rules governing what can and what cannot happen. However unhistorical his discussions may be, they offer an invaluable starting point for any attempt at analysis of the interrelations of various social phenomena in particular cases. It is unfortunate that he said so little about Islam. His 'Religions-sociologie', in *Wirtschaft und Gesellschaft* (Tübingen, 1921–22) has been translated as *The Sociology of Religion* (London, 1965).

fications. Any guilt felt for present unjustifiable privilege and good fortune was to be assuaged by charitable actions and benevolent deeds; while the social injustice itself was found to be a transient matter, counterbalanced, or even eventually eliminated, in the cosmic order as a whole.

The populistic temper

The populistic spirit of the market was expressed more effectively in developing the prophetic ethical bent into a full-scale personal moralism: that is, insistence on justice and equality in interpersonal relations even at the expense of any other sort of cultural value, such as those more imaginative values which exceptional individuals or even whole privileged classes are sometimes pleased to foster. The ordinary individual must be an honest man, whose duty is to do what is useful rather than what is decorative, what helps himself and others in the tasks of daily living rather than what embellishes that living or even interrupts it. Aristocrats might indeed have the leisure to exalt the creative, the adventurous, the tasteful; to value exceptional achievement in activities demanding special skill and talent. It was appropriate for the aristocrat to aim at personal distinction in himself and to prize it in others, including the learnèd among the priests. As to the merchant, he too was no unsophisticated peasant; he had a high culture of his own. Yet he could not normally look to the personal distinction which could come with a socially more privileged position, nor even to the luxurious display which lavishly patronized the arts. His culture must express itself through perfection in the common duties.

The high culture of the market, therefore, emphasized more moderate virtues: not personal courage or political or artistic virtuosity, but the 'bourgeois virtues', thrift, sobriety, and, above all, respect for law and order. What would require special talents and luxurious expense—the science presupposed in alchemy and in astrology, the art used in monumental sculpture and painting, the extravagance displayed in silk and gold—was already suspect as inaccessible to the ordinary man. Carried into the realm of religion, this attitude reinforced the specifically spiritual objections that also arose to some of these things because of their association with the old nature gods. In general, such an outlook made for neglect of grand aesthetic ceremonial in favour of the moralism encouraged in, say, the Talmud. At most, by way of special distinction, what the populistic temper could admire was an ascetic virtuosity, requiring no lush resources beyond a personal self-discipline.

Just as for the populistic temper the monotheistic ethical emphasis led to egalitarian moralism, maximally uncompromising in its contrast to nature cults, so the monotheistic cosmic drama was concretized into immediate human history, for the course of which each individual could be responsible. The sense of cosmic drama could become still more definitive if set loose from any analogy which tied it to the dramatic sequence of the seasonal year, and therefore to the natural order in which the landed aristocrat triumphed; it could be interpreted entirely in terms of will and action, of bargain and fulfillment of the bargain. In this perspective, what mattered in the historical drama was the action and fate of the religious body as such, as a group of responsible individuals. Such a religious group was made up of, and should even—if possible—be led by common people, as the world reckons. It must be egalitarian; its adherents were essentially equal in status. Among the Jews, even priesthood was in doubt: whoever was most learnèd and pious was rabbi, a strictly lay leader. History required the human involvement of all. Finally, a populistic temper could heighten the claims of the one religious community. The aristocrat found his dignity through his place in the natural order of society, where the common person counted for little. But in the community of faith, the aristocrat's dignity need not matter; here the common person could count, in principle, as much as any other. Since the decisive historical responsibility was undertaken by the religious community as a body, all human beings were called on individually to support it. The individual could do nothing worthwhile outside it. Such a body was not only one of a kind, but total in its claims. Ideally, every individual ought to live his spiritual life entirely within its norms. With populism, then, the exclusive demands of the religious body, too, became more comprehensive, universal, and uncompromising. There was one true faith and all else was false.

Nowhere was the tendency for the lay population to be partitioned out among the confessional religious bodies, as belonging exclusively and decisively to one or the other of them, stronger than in the region from Nile to Oxus. Even the more aristocratic-minded of the monotheistic traditions fell into this tendency (perhaps by reaction to the others), if less rigidly than the more populistic ones. Farther east, the religious specialists, even at the height of their power, were never able to persuade everyone to declare an allegiance to one system and only one. Though the more pious usually became convinced that truth was entirely, or at least most perfectly, expressed in one or another of the religious traditions, many of the ordinary population seem always to have been inclined to respect equally the representatives of all the more popular traditions. In the European region, the religious traditions which first introduced the new religious pattern were likewise usually tolerant of multiple adherence; in any case, a person remained first a Roman and was only secondarily an adherent of one of the new cults. Even when a single religious tradition—one of Semitic origin, to be sure—did win official and exclusive status, it soon became so integral a part of the general culture that to be a Roman and to be a Christian of the official church became almost equivalent. Between Nile and Oxus, on the other hand, the rise of the confessional allegiances soon meant the organization of the whole population into many mutually exclusive rival religious bodies; that is, into *communities* which were religious rather than primarily territorial. It was as socially unthinkable to be associated with two or more such communities as to be associated with none.

Not everyone could be forced into the standard recognized communities. In the environment of the prophetic monotheistic tradition, and stimulated by Hellenic thought and notably by Plato's sense of philosophic wisdom, arose a diverse movement, the most distinctive tradition in which is called 'Gnosticism', because, it sought to liberate the soul from the darkness and falsehood of material body through cosmic illuminative *knowledge, gnosis*. Gnostics and those spiritually kin to them assumed that the universe was in all details, as well as in its whole, humanly meaningful (whether positively or negatively), and not merely an aribitrary creation of God for His own unfathomable purposes; but the meaning lay not in the apparent structure of objects and sequence of events but in a hidden truth that lay behind them, of which they were the traces or perhaps the symbols. To fathom and realize the hidden meaning of the universe, then, was the true calling of human beings; this would occur in a process of purification and enlightenment of the individual soul, which was itself a part of a cosmic process of enlightenment in which the whole universe was moving toward a truer condition, when its hidden meaning would become manifest. Accordingly, the external conditions of the world, including the popularly received religious traditions, were of little significance save as they pointed the seeking soul toward the inward truth that lay behind them. It was individual enlightenment that mattered; and this was typically to be achieved not so much through a community allegiance as through discipleship to a wiser individual who had already achieved enlightenment, and whose enlightenment in turn came from discipleship to his predecessor—and so on backward in a chain of discipleship to one who had received direct revelation. For all that, the several movements of this type ended by forming little religious communities or sects of their own.

The Gnostic movement and its spiritual kin were especially prevalent (among a seeking section of the population) in the region from Nile to Oxus, in Egypt and the Semitic lands and probably in Iran; but much of their writing there was done in Greek and it was very influential also in the Greek and even Latin European lands. It was in the early centuries after the Axial Age that these several élite religious traditions took form, and many Gnostic sects were associated with one of the major popular religious traditions, notably Christianity. But the most popular of the movements of this family (though it was not a Gnostic sect in the exact sense) formed a fully independent community: Manicheanism, which we shall meet again. All these movements shared a number of common traits, despite their diversity, which allow them to be characterized in common in relation to the best known of them, the Gnostic (though indeed some movements which in this perspective can be associated with Gnosticism had, in other respects, more in common with some other group of traditions than with the Gnostic traditions). Or perhaps we should say that tendencies of a Gnostic type, together with terminology typical of the movement, were very widespread, so that traces can be found in almost all religious movements of the time in the Irano-Semitic lands.

Whether in esoteric or, more usually, in exoteric form, it was in terms of religious communities that the Nile-to-Oxus region was maintained as one of the four core areas of high culture after the Axial Age. When the Semitic and Iranian traditions were overlaid by the Hellenic traditions, they received little support from common administrative or even commercial continuity. Rather than in a common classical language, the persistence of an independent high-cultural orientation was expressed, above all, in the various religious communities, comprehensive as they were and demanding exclusive total loyalty. Eventually, each major religious community tended to cultivate its own more or less localized literary language, usually some form of Aramaic or Iranian. In each of these languages the traditions going back to the prophets of the Axial Age were more or less independently developed. Commonly, selected writings from those prophets were retained, at least in translation; sometimes the tradition was reformulated entirely. Greek long remained the most widespread common language of high culture in most of the region between Nile and Oxus, but—outside of certain explicitly Hellenic cities and (in the Roman provinces) certain elements in the upper classes—it was increasingly limited to circles concerned with philosophy and science; and even these subjects were increasingly cultivated in the Aramaic and Iranian languages of the various religious communities.

The confessional empires

The cultural independence of the Iranian and Semitic peoples from the Hellenic cultural sphere was at best imperfectly expressed, on the political side, in the Parthian Arsacid empire of Iran and the Iraq, which had succeeded outright Hellenic (Seleucid) rule except where Rome took over (in Syria). But in the third century CE, with the increasing predominance of the confessional religions, both Roman and Parthian empires were transformed in such a way as to give the Irano-Semitic traditions more complete expression (though not necessarily yet in their most populistic form).

In the Mediterranean, the old empire of the Romans was replaced, after a period of near anarchy, by a structure based more equally on all the Mediterranean peoples, with a capital, Constantinople, nearer the centre of economic life and of the old Hellenic culture than Rome had been. It was then that the reconstructed Roman empire adopted a new confessional religion, Christianity. It was this altered Roman empire into which, later, Islam came.

Greek was the empire's chief cultural language, though the Latin of its western provinces was long maintained throughout the empire as the language of law and in some other spheres. The classics looked to by both Greek and Latin provinces of the empire (including, of course, large elements in Syria and Egypt) were the Greek masters, from Homer to Aristotle; and the political and social ideals were still, even when in fact the emperors were almost absolute masters, traceable to the ideals of liberty and civic virtue of the ancient

Greek polis. Since the beginning of the fourth century, however, the empire had been officially Christian. Though the Christian New Testament was written in Greek, Christianity had its origin in the Semitic Fertile Crescent. (Only gradually did the Christian bodies of Syria and Egypt form themselves into communities distinct from the official church of the more Hellenic and Latin parts.) The spirit of Christianity—and the massive institution of the church—had long competed strenuously against the main classical Greek tradition for the allegiance of the ruling classes. Hence the Christian triumph marked a new era. Hellenistic art, philosophy, even science and law were remoulded under Christian influence in the Roman provinces as well as farther east. It was in this form that they reached the Muslims.

By the time of Muḥammad the most striking feature of the Roman empire was its support of the Christian church over a vast area, even though in a form that had become unpopular in Syria and Egypt (and among some elements even in the Maghrib). In his time, the Roman empire had lost a good many provinces in the west, holding there only southern Spain, the Maghrib (North Africa), parts of Italy (including Rome), Dalmatia, and islands like Sardinia and Sicily; but it still controlled the seas; and in the east its hold on the Balkan and Anatolian peninsulas, Syria, and Egypt was practically intact.[15]

Meanwhile, in the same third century which saw the reconstruction of the Roman empire in the Mediterranean lands, the Parthian dynasty was replaced in the Iraq and Iran by the militantly Iranian dynasty of the Sâsânian Persians.[16] As becomes clear on the chart of the origins of the Islamicate culture, the Sâsânian empire was the great rival of the later Roman empire to the east, and the chief predecessor of the caliphal state. The Sâsânian capital was Ctesiphon on the Tigris, near what was to be the Muslim Baghdad and about forty miles from what had been the ancient Babylon. The Sâsânian Persian nobility looked back to the ancient Achaemenid Persian empire as its model. The Sâsânian territories were not so broad as the Achaemenid had been, particularly in the west where, far from extending into Europe, they did not include even Syria and Egypt. These latter two provinces continued—under protest, to be sure—to be ruled by the Roman empire, and hence by the

[15] It is important to remember that the Roman empire which the Muslims confronted was not an 'Eastern Roman Empire' but the continuation, though weakened, of the whole empire in the Mediterranean as a unity (compare the section on world-historical usage in the Introduction).

[16] The Sâsânian ruling class is often referred to as 'Persian', as is also the empire itself, because the origin of the dynasty was in Fârs, ancient Greek *Persis* in southwest Iran, as was that of the Achaemenids; and the official language was Pârsîk, 'Middle Persian', miscalled 'Pahlavî'. This usage of the term 'Persian' to refer to a connection with Fârs, in whatever age, is related to but distinct from a usage of the term commoner in this work: to refer to the Fârsî, 'New Persian' language and the extensive populations using it, whether or not under a dynasty from Fârs. Provided the term is used with care, the two usages need not conflict: the first is for pre-Islamic times, the second for Islamic times. When it is carelessly used, however, considerable confusion can result. (Cf. Note 3 in the Ṣafavî chapter below, Book V, chap. 1.)

The Origins of Islamic Culture in Its World Context, 226–715

Western Europe	From Nile to Oxus	India	China
	226 Foundation of Sâsânian empire in Iran and the Iraq on a more centralized basis than the preceding empire, the Parthian		**220** End of Han dynasty, which had founded tradition of united Chinese state
	285 Reorganization of Roman empire in Mediterranean basin on a more centralized basis after military chaos		
314 Latin Christians recognize primacy of the bishop of Rome (pope) among themselves		**320** Gupta dynasty founded, patrons of north Indian cultural florescence	
430 Death of Augustine, premier Latin theologian			**386–534** Northern Wei dynasty. Turkic patrons of Buddhism in north China
486 Merovingian Franks rule in Gaul (replacing last Roman governors)	**485–498** First reign of Qubâd, Sâsânid patron of anti-aristocratic reformer Mazdak		
496 Conversion of Clovis of Gaul to Roman Christianity	**540–562** Wars between Justinian the Great of the Roman empire and Nûshîrvân the Great of the Sâsânian empire		
568–571 Roman empire loses much of the interior of Italy (for second and final time) to the Lombard barbarians	**589–628** Khusraw Parvîz, Sâsânî ruler, under whom Egypt, Syria, Anatolia are taken from Rome (*c.* 611–627), then lost		**589** Reunion of Chinese empire under Sui dynasty
590–604 Gregory the Great, pope at Rome (still under imperial rule from Constantinople)	**622–632** Muḥammad rules at Medina and founds Muslim polity among the Arabs	**606–647** Harsha rules last major Hindu empire of north India	**618** T'ang dynasty continues the Chinese political and commercial resurgence
	644 Death of ʿUmar, who directed the most decisive Arab conquests, from Egypt to western Iran		
	661 Death of ʿAlî; the disrupted Arab state is reunited by Muʿâwiyah		
	692 ʿAbd-al-Malik re-establishes the Arab state, after renewed disruption (from 680), on basis of Syrian power		
714–741 Charles Martel restores strength to Frankish kingdom and defeats Arabs in northern Gaul	**715** Death of al-Walîd, under whom Arabs occupied Spain and Sind		

chief carriers of the Hellenistic traditions as modified by Christianity. Nevertheless, the greater half of the Fertile Crescent was Sâsânian, as well as most of the Iranian highlands; that is, the majority of the centres of Irano-Semitic culture; while from time to time Sâsânian power extended beyond the mountains in the north and east, around the coasts of Arabia, and for a moment to Syria, Egypt, and even Anatolia.

There were two chief languages of high culture in the Sâsânian domains, one each of the Iranian and Semitic families, as had been the case in the Achaemenid empire and as was to be the case under Islam. Of the Iranian tongues, Pahlavî (properly Pârsîk)—spoken in the highlands, especially Fârs in the southwest—was the official language of the court and of Mazdean religion. It was in Pahlavî that translations from Indic literature made themselves most felt. Of the Semitic tongues, a form of Aramaic called (eastern) 'Syriac', used especially by the Nestorian Christians of the Iraq, was the chief carrier of the Hellenistic traditions apart from Greek itself. Many works, especially on natural science, were translated from Greek into Syriac; and some also into Pahlavî. (The Nestorian church, opposed to the official Roman, Chalcedonian, church, was commonly favoured by the Sâsânian empire, among its Christian subjects, as being in natural opposition to the Roman empire.)

But (in some contrast to the older Achaemenid—and especially to the subsequent Islamic—situations) the two chief languages carried largely different cultural traditions. Moreover, several other literary languages were also used in the region as a whole, partly based on religious communities and partly on local traditions, as in the Syr-Oxus basin to the northeast. In particular, other forms of Aramaic were used by Jews and by other Christians, including those across the boundary in the Roman empire who yet dissented from the established church of the empire. (The dissenting church in Egypt used the local Coptic tongue.) Sâsânian Iraq was the centre of Jewish life throughout the Oikoumene; there the Talmud was being compiled (in a form of Aramaic). Jews formed a substantial part of the population of the cities and countryside of the Iraq.

Though the Sâsânian court looked to the ancient Achaemenid empire as a model, the new empire was far from a restoration of the old, for the older empire had naturally not embodied all the cultural forms that had later resulted from the ferment of its own time, the Axial Age. Into the Sâsânian ideas of culture and the good society entered many traditions not only from Achaemenid times but sometimes traceable back even to the ancient Babylonians. The Sâsânian hope for a universal absolute monarch, whose disinterested power could curb all lesser ambitions and allow peace and justice to the ordinary population, thus went back to Achaemenid experience. Yet even the ideal of the grand monarchy was no repetition of the tolerant Achaemenid overlordship. It had inherited the large-scale economic initiative of the Hellenistic monarchies (the name of Alexander played as great a role in the Iranian as in the Roman imagination); and its concern with central power reflected, perhaps, dissatisfaction with too loose a central control under the later Parthians. Sâsânian absolutism was a distinctively post-Axial political order, typical (in essentials) of the imperial regimes of the time. Above all, it was supported by an official confessional religious allegiance, which made for cultural unity in the empire at least among the ruling classes.[17]

About the time that Christianity was being established in the Roman empire, Mazdeism was being given a corresponding position in the Sâsânian realm by early rulers of the dynasty. In this tradition, men revered Zoroaster as a supreme prophet, and his poetic compositions, the Gâthâs, afforded perhaps the most creative impulses taken up in it. Ahura Mazdâh was worshipped as lord of light and truth in the struggle of creation against darkness and falsehood. At the same time, in coming to offer a comprehensive religious pattern, the tradition had built upon much else as well. It centred on the learning and the ritual offices of a hereditary priestly class, the Magi, guardians of the temples in which a sacred fire was kept burning as a symbol of the light of Ahura Mazdâh, and in which the several angelic expressions of divine truth, 'Good Thought' and other guardian spirits, were duly invoked and honoured. On the official level, the Magi had to tolerate quite a pantheon of old gods, in fact. In the life of the more scrupulously pious, the faith expressed itself most strikingly in a minute and comprehensive concern for purity—for physical ritual purity, and for the purity of a truthful mind.

As we have noted, official Mazdeism was agrarian-oriented and aristocratic in temper. Justice was to be found in a well-ordered hereditary class society, in which each class was to have its own dignity and its own reward. The peasants were honoured as performing the most essential tasks in the production of basic needs—the cultivation of the sacred earth, to bring forth nourishment for life. Yet they were justly to yield what of their product they did not need for their own lives to the landholders, the government officials, and the Magi themselves; the privileges of these latter were justified by their functions in maintaining order, defending against alien predators, and mediating between humans and the divine. Other privileged groups seem to have had less dignity in the official system—the urban merchants and craftsmen, caterers to the desires of the rulers and priests for cultivated luxuries. In theory, the more frivolous arts of civilization (but not the priestly art or the art of government, regarded as cosmically useful) were given little place, and their representatives regarded almost as parasites. In practice, because a privileged position was

[17] On the Sâsânian empire—and generally on the Fertile Crescent and Iran in the thousand years before Islam—we are more poorly informed than perhaps on any other major lettered historical period. On the Mazdean religious tradition, see Jacques Duchesne-Guillemin, *La religion de l'Iran ancien* (Paris, 1962), especially the bibliographical discussion in the chapter called 'Histoire des études'. For a survey of the Sâsânian empire see Arthur Christensen, *L'Iran sous les Sasanides* (2nd ed., Copenhagen, 1944), somewhat uninspired but indispensable. For comments on making use of the work of Zaehner and of Altheim, two of our most creative scholars in dealing with the period, but whose works are subject to great caution, see the section on the history of Islamics studies in the section on historical method in the Introduction.

granted to some, those who created the luxuries of privilege were indirectly justified also.

Populism in the Sâsânian empire

The Parthian empire had been a relatively loose association of regional governments and semi-independent cities, among which the central dynasty had failed to prevent frequent warring. Probably wealth was less concentrated than in some other periods and we have little evidence of great monumental cultural works. Nevertheless, it seems to have been a time of considerable vigour, both economically and in arts and letters. The foundations then laid come to spectacular fruition under the Sâsânians.

In the Sâsânian period, peace was usually maintained within the empire. Monumental works of building and sculpture, technically masterful and beautifully expressive of empire, bear witness to great concentration of wealth—that is, great prosperity for the privileged (which might or might not be accompanied by prosperity for the ordinary peasants, of course). Economic development was twofold. On the one hand, agrarian investment reached its peak in the Mesopotamian alluvial plain, with massively large-scale irrigation and a steady increase in the agricultural population. On the other hand, mercantile trade was extended and industry fostered; for instance, both the import of silk from China and its working within the empire. Cities increased in wealth and importance; the Sâsânian monarchs were notable as founders of cities and protectors of trade.[18]

The mercantile development represented in part a response to the ever-quickening pattern of trade throughout the Afro-Eurasian Oikoumene. Direct trade by sea and land between China and the Indo-Mediterranean regions opened up only at the end of the Axial Age, yet quickly became important commercially and financially. Trade elsewhere in the Southern Seas (the seas of the Indian Ocean and eastward) had likewise expanded, as had trade both north of the Mediterranean in Europe and south across the Sahara. The peoples from Nile to Oxus not only took full advantage of their crossroads. They helped develop the new fields of trade. It was in this period that Greek, premier commercial language at the end of the Axial Age in many parts, was displaced in favour of elements from the Fertile Crescent. Along the central Eurasian trade routes, it was Iranian and Semitic culture and religion that came to dominate locally even more than Chinese or Indic. Along the west and especially southwest coasts of India, it was in this period that Christian and even Jewish populations—settled or converted from the Persian Gulf area—began to become numerically important. In the west Mediterranean and its hinterland, the same elements—'Syrians' and Jews—became carriers of mer-

[18] On the prosperity of Sâsânian Iran and Iraq, see Thorkild Jacobsen and Robert M. Adams, 'Salt and Silt in Ancient Mesopotamian Agriculture', *Science*, 128 (1958), 1251–58.

cantile culture to the point that even under local Christian rule Judaism proved to have great attractiveness for converts. Our region was becoming the mercantile heartland of the Oikoumene.

It should perhaps not surprise us, then, that especially in the Fertile Crescent the agrarian-based imperial powers should find themselves challenged by populistic movements (sometimes, at least, of a mercantile cast) expressed in the confessional communities. In the midst of all the prosperity, religious conflict became a major theme of social life. Not all dissident religious groups were subversive. Of the numerous sects of Gnostic type that had arisen especially in Jewish and Christian contexts, at least some seem to have been relatively populistic in temper, expressing clear social protest, but not rebellious. The same may be said, it seems, of the Buddhist groups found in much of the empire and in the Syr-Oxus basin (in fact, Buddhism seems in its own way to have been as populistic as any of the other confessional traditions). It was early in the Sâsânian period that the Manicheans attempted their vigorous synthesis of all previous revelations in a system of Gnostic type, and spread their gospel wherever the Iranian and Semitic merchants went. For a time, Manicheans, and evidently representatives of other movements also, hoped to win the Sâsânian monarchy to their support. But after official Mazdeism came to be clearly established, unrecognized communities were allotted an inferior position or not tolerated at all; the Sâsânian empire proved committed to the agrarian gentry which provided it with its primary armed forces—heavy cavalry. It became clear that a shift in the religious—and political—establishment could be made only through an overthrow of Mazdean power.

There were evidently several movements which combined religious innovation with social protest against the privileged classes. The most effective of these was that of Mazdak: a leader who seems to have won the monarch himself to a programme of popular semi-egalitarian justice against landed privilege. Despite the relatively centralized and bureaucratic structure of the Sâsânian state, the old noble families had inherited a great deal of independence from Parthian days; weaker kings were ruled by them, and stronger kings had to carry on a constant struggle to assure the enforcement of central policy. In the latter part of the fifth century, the monarch Qubâd (Kavâd) was evidently persuaded for a time to try to undermine the nobles' growing power by supporting Mazdak's movement to destroy or cripple the grander forms of social privilege in the name of ascetic spiritual fraternity. Many nobles lost much of their property (and even their superfluous wives), and commoners were raised to high positions. For some years, the state was in great turmoil.

In his later years, Qubâd abandoned the movement, and his successor, Khusraw Nûshîrvân, led a reaction. Mazdak and many of his followers were massacred, the old official Mazdeism was restored, and the nobles given back their privileges. But evidently their old position was not fully regained. The nobles' power to disregard central authority was, at least temporarily, reduced; Nûshîrvân seems to have been the strongest king of the dynasty. He used the opportunity to reorganize the whole empire, setting taxation on a more commercial basis; in particular, he seems to have increased state investment in the Iraq alluvial irrigation agriculture. It was probably in his time that investment there reached its absolute peak.

Thus financially buttressed, Nûshîrvân was evidently in a position to develop a stronger central army, supported by taxes rather than levies of the gentry. We know as yet too little of the reign, but one source of recruitment for that army was pastoral Arab tribesmen, who were independent of links to the agrarian gentry, accustomed to fighting, and easily accessible from the Iraq. The Arab pastoralist society was, of course, inherently fragmented, so that reliance on Arab soldiery (even if still tribally organized) seemed to pose no political threat comparable to that posed by the gentry. (Within a few years after Nûshîrvân's death, however, the Arabs were interfering in the succession.) Thus the court and its military and civilian bureaucracy, with perhaps the co-operation of some of the wealthier mercantile elements of the cities, presumably gained a certain independence of the landed nobility, and perhaps even outweighed it. Nûshîrvân was subsequently revered as the model king of a model dynasty, the supreme exponent of royal justice. Muḥammad was born in his day, Muslims were proud to note. The centralizing, urbanizing tendencies which had distinguished Sâsânian times from the start came to a climax under his rule.

Nûshîrvân's time is traditionally made also the peak of Sâsânian literary culture. Monumental history of ancestral legend and royal deeds paralleled the monumental visual art. In a lighter vein, courtly literature seems to have cultivated a wide-ranging curiosity; and Hellenistic culture was revived, notably at the school of medicine and philosophy at Jundaysâbûr in Khûzistân (the southeastern part of the Mesopotamian plain); some Greek philosophers were attracted there for a time when Justinian closed the schools at Athens. Its science and philosophy found favour even among some Mazdean priests, who developed their theology in terms of it. But the most important source of intellectual stimulus at this time was northern India. In the first centuries of our era, there was a broad extension of Indian commerce and Indian ideas, to about the same extent, though over a somewhat different area, as Hellenic ideas had spread in the last centuries BC. It was this movement which had carried Buddhism, at the hands of active missionaries, to wide popularity in eastern Iran and central Eurasia before it spread throughout the Eurasian Far East. (Whether, indeed, the early Indic development of monkish ways accounts for the spread of various sorts of monasticism even in the Mediterranean basin during these centuries is not fully clear.) Under the Sâsânian empire, and especially in its last century, Indic ideas in science and the arts became popular. About this time Indians had made notable advances in mathematics, especially over the Babylonian and Greek foundations they had largely built on, as well as, it seems, in medicine; this seems to have been at least partially appreciated in Sâsânian scholarly circles. Wider circles accepted Indicism to the point of making popular lighter Indian literature in translation, and such a cerebral Indian game as chess.

In the early centuries of our era the civilized lands west of India were all overshadowed culturally, if not ruled directly, by the Sâsânian and Roman empires. By and large, the effective area of the Sâsânian empire tended to be slightly smaller than that of the Roman, but they met as equals. Despite the internal problems of both empires with dissident communities, they maintained impressive rival power structures, each claiming (in principle) universal authority. The two empires struggled repeatedly with each other along their frontier on the upper Euphrates, often giving only grudging attention to other opponents; in the case of the Romans, to the Germanic and Slavic peoples of inner Europe, in the case of the Sâsânian Persians, to the Turkic states of central Eurasia. In Muḥammad's lifetime they waged the most destructive of all the wars waged against one another in all their centuries of fighting, and at his death both empires were financially and politically exhausted.[19]

[19] Gustave von Grunebaum has saved me from some errors in this vast field, where I am ill at ease (but he cannot be blamed for the persisting errors or biases, here or elsewhere).

II

Muhammad's Challenge, 570–624

The lands from Nile to Oxus would most certainly have changed somehow in the eighth and ninth centuries, even without the intervention of Islam. The Sâsânian empire, perhaps under a new dynasty, might indeed have succeeded in taking Syria and Egypt (if not the Maghrib) permanently from the Roman empire and might have developed, in Syriac (Aramaic) and Pahlavî (Iranian), a culture not unlike what developed in fact among the Muslims in Arabic and Persian. Such a culture might have been carried fairly widely in the hemisphere; for some elements of the Iranian and Semitic traditions were already being carried into Europe and India. But it is hard to conceive of such a renewed Syriac-Pahlavî civilization as having developed all the homogeneity and expansive vitality which were manifested under Islam. Arab tribes might even have taken a hand in establishing the new dynasty which would have succeeded to the Sâsânian, yet by all analogies we must suppose that ordinarily they would have been rapidly assimilated to the more cultured settled population, forgetting in time their remarkable but limited Bedouin poetry, learning to speak some sort of Aramaic, and adopting one or another of the existent forms of Christianity. One ingredient, the presence of Islam, would seem to have made the vital difference, making possible a truly new civilization, based on uniting the bulk of the population of the region into one religious community.

Among the most important elements in the background of the Islamicate civilization, then, is the development of Islamic religion and of the community which carried it. This was the work of a number of remarkable men, starting with Muḥammad himself. The community was built up first within the general Arabian culture and then, after its sudden conquests, as a ruling community scattered thinly throughout the Aramaic- and Iranian-speaking lands and far beyond. Within the community there were sharp disagreements about what its character was to be, and many struggles among the contending parties. The Muslim religion and community that resulted from these struggles could not have been foreseen by any human means; yet they bear the impress of the vigorous minds and devoted spirits that went into their formation.[1]

[1] William McNeill, in his *Rise of the West* (University of Chicago Press, 1963), did me the honour of referring to an early (and very incomplete) version of this work as an important source for his own thinking about Islam and the Islamicate civilization. This is flattering, for I regard McNeill's book as very important in the sense that it is the first genuine world history ever to be published (the first to present the history of citied peoples as a single overall historical complex, with primary attention to interrela-

Bedouin-based culture in Muḥammad's time

Between the Roman and Sâsânian empires, and increasingly important in their wars and their commerce, was the vast bloc of Bedouin Arabia. This was not simply the Arabian peninsula as such. Bedouin Arabia was that area of the peninsula in which the customs founded on camel-nomadism prevailed: primarily the north, west, and centre. These were arid steppe lands, interspersed with great reaches of rock or of sand, visited in winter and especially spring with sporadic rains that awoke transient vegetation. The steppes were dotted with oases, where the earth formations brought water fairly close to the surface in sufficient amounts so that regular irrigation could maintain a more or less extensive agriculture in limited and isolated areas. From the spotty seasonal vegetation, and from springs and wells that could be dug even where no oasis was possible, by keeping frequently on the move, herdsmen could maintain their animals, supplementing their milk and occasional flesh (and what they could get by hunting) with the wheat and dates that agriculturists could raise in the oases. The agriculturists, in turn, though hemmed in by the desert, could get needed animals from the herdsmen and also any specialized products that required bringing from a distance. But such a pattern of living presupposed the domesticated camel, alone capable of forming the basis for large-scale pastoral life in such deserts.

The camel does not seem to have been domesticated early, not before the second millennium before our era. Only after long experience in breeding camels for transport would some pastoral groups, relying less on sheep and more on camels, have been able to move out into the more arid regions at a distance from the settled areas of the Fertile Crescent, followed step by step, presumably, by the necessary agriculturists in the oases. Independent pastoralism may have begun not long after agriculture itself—that is, a life based on herding in which the herdsmen are not members of a village community, herding the village animals, but rather form permanent social units of their own independent of any particular village. But camel nomadism deep in the desert was a highly specialized form of life, presupposing special technical and even social skills. We cannot surely identify camel nomads, that is, Bedouin, until the beginning of our era. By then, the tradition was well established, at least in the margins both of Syria and of the Yemen, and it unfolded its consequences rapidly from that time on.[2]

---

tions among the societies, and without unduly excessive attention to one society), Unfortunately, I find myself occasionally disagreeing with McNeill (beyond this fundamental point) both as to basic theory and as to the interpretations of the several civilizations; and particularly as to his interpretation of Islam and Islamdom. Many of my points of disagreement both on world history generally and on Islam will become obvious in the course of this work.

[2] I owe to H. A. R. Gibb's lectures my attention's being drawn to the significance of the chronology of camel pastoralism, as well as to numerous other points in this part of the work. The chronology itself is still in doubt.

Once camel nomadism had developed, it carried potentialities of a major social force. Camels allowed their herders greater mobility than other pastoral animals, being able to endure longer than ordinary animals without food and even water, and so to travel farther between watering places. But the wild ass is almost as tough, and faster; the hunting people who tamed it could range even more freely than the camel men. It was crucial that the camel was also a great beast of burden: it was unrivalled, except by the elephant; and it yielded good milk; through its various qualities it not only sustained its owners but found a ready market. Such economic advantages enabled a heavier concentration of people to live from camels than could live, say, from wild asses; but with equal independence from agrarian controls. This gave the Bedouin a potential predominance over not only the desert oases but even the nearby reaches of the settled countries, allowing them not merely to trade (which was essential) but, under favourable circumstances, to exact tribute. If there were governments strong enough to refuse tribute, then the qualities that Bedouin life developed in the men and their ready-made transport equipment and their numbers made them welcome soldiers for those same governments—which could prove an alternative path to social power.

The Bedouin necessarily developed their own distinctive type of social organization. Originally adapted to herding, it could be maintained more or less in other situations too. In fact, by the sixth century even parts of western Arabia that had once been little more than extensions of the settled life of Syria or the Yemen, living under kings, had been absorbed into the Bedouin life; even people settled in the agricultural oases or in commercial towns tended to be organized as 'settled Bedouin', to keep camels, and to think of themselves as if they were in principle pastoralists.

This sixth-century Bedouin and Bedouin-based Arabian culture differed from that of the more agriculturally developed of the lands on the agrarianate level in its presuppositions for historical action. Bedouin-based society presupposed the wider agrarian-based society of which it was essentially an extension; and hence looked to an agrarianate level of high or learnèd culture, if to any. It did not escape the overall historical limitations imposed by the fact that the bulk of the resources on which any large-scale historical endeavour must be based were limited by the agricultural resources on which wealth and leisure were ultimately based. Yet within these limitations, Bedouin-based culture posed a special variant case. With all pastoralists on roughly the same economic level, there might be wealthier or more respected families, but relative to more agrarian societies there was little class stratification and concentration of wealth—the herdsmen could not be so readily exploited as could a peasantry—and hence also a lack of many aspects of learnèd high culture within the Bedouin communities.

The relative equality among Bedouin was reinforced by their tribal organization, such as independent herdsmen have commonly developed; that is, hereditary economic and social solidarity among smaller or larger groups of families, not based either on territorial proximity or on directly functional relations, yet sharing a common responsibility in good and bad fortune. In this way, families were associated in larger groups for general economic purposes, and these in turn in still larger ones for political strength. Groups on every level possessed internal autonomy, but were likely to be grouped with yet others in still larger associations. (We call the larger—and more tenuous—of these groups 'tribes'. Smaller groups are sometimes called 'clans'.) At every level, these groups defined themselves in terms of a real or fictive common descent, though newcomers might be adopted into them. No man who had sufficient kin could want for protection and status.

That the herdsmen were nomads does not mean, of course, that they wandered indifferently according to their fancies. Each larger grouping—normally, what we call a tribe or some division thereof—possessed its own recognized pasturing grounds; even within these grounds, major movements might be made in massed armed groups. But the camel nomadism of Arabia was less closely tied to fixed grazing grounds and seasonal itineraries than most nomadism elsewhere. There remained a good deal of leeway for unpredictable wandering by smaller groups and even individuals, which helped give a tone to the Bedouin social ways. Each tribe, almost each clan or group of families, was sovereign; led by its chief, chosen partly for his family descent and partly for his personal wisdom, each group defended its own grazing rights in its own area, or attempted to better its position at others' expense. Each group had to take decisions in which all might participate and which repeatedly could mean life or death for all adult males of the group.

Such a society rejected authoritarian political forms and based itself instead on individual prowess and prestige and on close lineage group loyalties. Besides leadership in fighting, the chief might serve to arbitrate disputes or he might be custodian of the group's sacred symbols; but others might serve in either of these roles. In any case, he had no authority to coerce the acceptance of his position by any family. Every man was free in the last resort to depart at will with his dependents. In the absence of any common court of justice, intergroup restraint was maintained by the principle of the retaliatory blood-feud: an injury by an outsider to any member of a group was regarded as committed against the whole group by the whole group to which the outsider belonged; the injured group's honour required that it exact from the other group in retaliation an equivalent—normally an eye for an eye, a life for a life (though commutation in goods might be accepted)—or more, if the injured group regarded itself as above the level of the other. But if the retaliation were regarded by the other group as excessive, it in turn was honour-bound to retaliate again—till the feud could somehow be stopped.[3]

[3] W. Robertson Smith, *Kinship and Marriage in Early Arabia* (London, 1885) chaps. I and II, conveniently presents the nature of the Arabian tribes and their genealogies. Modern Bedouin life is studied from the viewpoint of its political potentialities—in any period—by Robert Montagne, *La civilisation du désert* (Paris, 1947).

From time to time, especially in association with some sedentary power, such large agglomerations of tribes could be formed acknowledging common leadership, that the chieftain at the top, normally basing himself at least in part on urban revenues, could take on something of the role of a king. But such kingship was founded, even so, on tribal presuppositions. Unlike a tribal chieftain, the king could have orders carried out by his own agents with relatively little regard to group sentiment; but his power was based on the lineage ties of a tribe, which ultimately he could not flout. Such kingdoms were precarious in their power at best.

The camel nomads were the élite of the more arid parts of Arabia. In addition to their camels, they often had horses which they pampered and used for specialized raiding purposes; more humble but more economically useful were sheep and goats. But the dignity of a tribe was likely to be in inverse proportion to its dependence on the smaller animals; for sheep-herders had to stay near the agricultural lands, and necessarily found themselves at the mercy of those more mobile than themselves. The pure camel-herders, more mobile and resourceful than either agriculturists of the oases or other pastoralists, felt that they had, and they were widely conceded to have, greater prestige than any other people of the area. Even when more settled groups did not actually descend from Bedouin who had taken over the oases by superior force, they looked to Bedouin traditions as the most honourable to follow.

The camel nomads called themselves *'Arab*. And the earliest appearances of the term seem to connect it with camel-herders as such. But, presumably in consideration of the nomads' prestige, the term *'Arab* came to mean not only Bedouin proper, still herdsmen, but also settled Bedouin who would still have camels but who lived from the date palms and grain of the oases or were engaged chiefly in commerce. Hence the dominant population of the peninsula came to be called 'Arab and their language (a form of Semitic differing somewhat from the Aramaic of the Fertile Crescent) 'Arabic'. (Subsequently, *'arab* has been used in Arabic itself in several senses, some of them quite extended. Here we will use 'Arab' to refer to any person whose parental tongue is derived from the Arabic of the Peninsula. 'Arabic' is used with reference to the language itself, and 'Arabian', of course, only with reference to the Peninsula proper, not to the Arabs generally.)[4]

The economic life of the Bedouin tribes, while immediately a matter of herding or (when they settled in oases) of agriculture, was ultimately dependent on an extensive system of trading and raiding. The herding groups always depended on agricultural groups for essential food or equipment, notably for grain and dates to supplement camel's milk and meat; beyond this, a more long-distance trade brought in luxuries like wine or skilled singing (slave) girls, in which all tribes desired to share. Thus the nomads became involved in

[4] For the several ways in which the term 'Arab' has been used among scholars—which must be kept distinct when one reads their works—see section on usage in Islamics studies in the Introduction.

the commerce between the Mediterranean lands and the Southern Seas. Tribes near trade routes furnished camels for transport, escorted traders, or even traded on their own. Others shared in the booty by raiding the more fortunate. The occasional towns, accordingly, as nodes of the trade, formed a focus of tribal aspirations. They enjoyed an influence based on wealth and prestige, which was not, however, necessarily expressed in any political domination.

The Arabs in international politics

The Arabs were proud of their independence, blazoned in glorious tribal genealogies. But once the Bedouin society was fully developed, then both politically and economically their life was constantly entangled with that of the great empires around them, on whose commerce their own trading and raiding depended. As the map of Arabia shows, Bedouin Arabia lay between three agricultural lands: the Iraq, Syria, and the Yemen. ('Umân, relatively infertile, cut off from the main mass of the Arabs by the wastes of the Empty Quarter, and giving only on the south Iranian deserts, counted for little.) Syria and the Iraq formed the main portions of the Fertile Crescent, the long-standing home of the Semitic cultural traditions. The Yemen, since about 1000 BC, had been the site of agrarian kingdoms of a Semitic language (south Arabian) and of a culture related to that of the Fertile Crescent but distinctive. (The kingdoms there had left a more recent memory of greatness than the Semitic kingdoms of the Fertile Crescent, a memory cherished by tribes with Yemeni associations.) The Yemen throve partly on agriculture, which had been declining, and partly on trade, which had been growing more important over the millennia, between the Southern Seas and the north. Like the Fertile Crescent, it was Christian and Jewish in religion, but it had a more important pagan sector than had survived in the Fertile Crescent.

Each of the three lands was connected with what may be called a political hinterland—a highland region which tended, in the sixth century, to dominate it. Behind the Iraq lay the Iranian highlands, homeland of the Sâsânian empire. Syria had long been ruled by an empire based in the Anatolian highlands—and more generally, in the Greek-using peninsulas of the north Mediterranean. For the Yemen, the Abyssinian highlands were less important. The Abyssinian citied culture itself had derived originally fairly directly from that of the Yemen, though it had struck independent roots and developed a distinct language and its own dominant Christian church. But the Abyssinian monarchy—commonly in alliance with the Roman empire—had cultivated commercial and political pretensions which had culminated in an occupation of the Yemen by Abyssinian forces, which had ruled there autonomously until overthrown by the Sâsânians at the end of the century.

The Bedouin were playing an ever larger part in the life of all three surrounding lands, and hence of the empires which dominated them. The greater part of the Yemen, by the sixth century, seems to have been Arabic-speaking:

the south Arabian language died out soon after the rise of Islam, though traces of the dialects have persisted. There were many Arabic-speakers also in Syria, and they played a role in the Iraq. This was partly due to the normal tendency for population distant from cities, and less subject to the great scourges of life on the agrarianate level, to fill in the recurrent gaps in the more

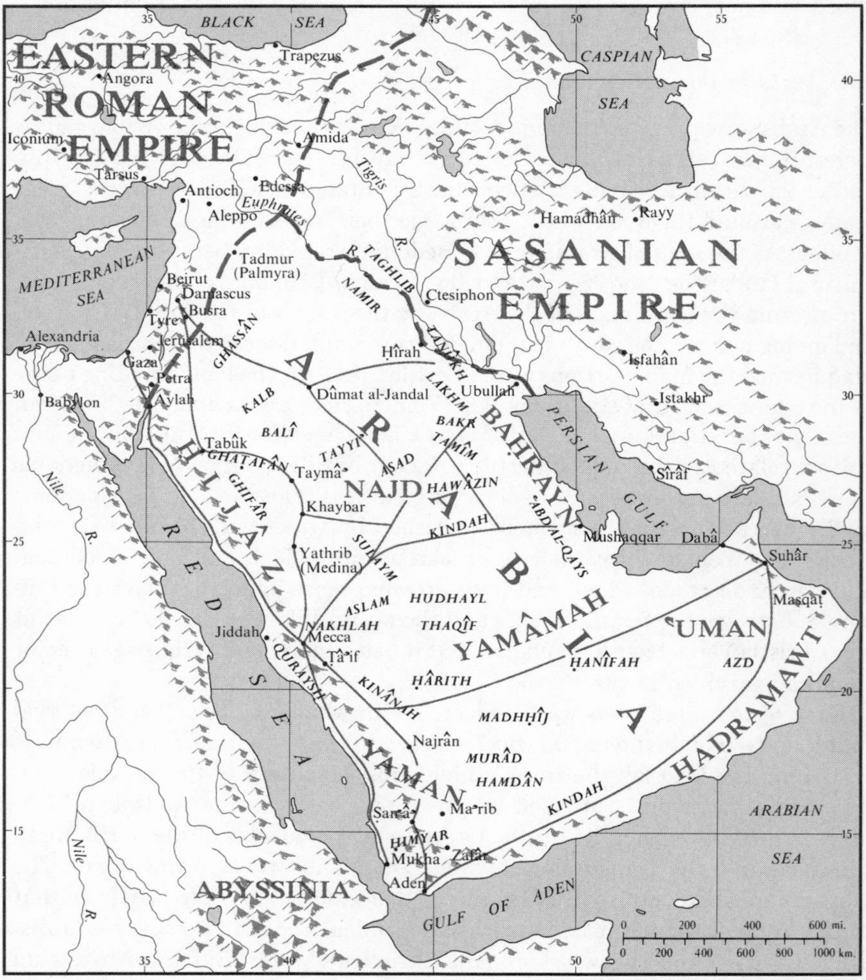

Towns and tribes in Arabia in the time of Muhammad

settled population. It was also due to the active initiative of the Bedouin Arabs as traders and as soldiers. The trade routes north and south along the west Arabian littoral were of long standing; in late centuries they were no longer controlled by Yemenis or by Aramaic-users based in Syria, but by Arabs of Bedouin background. Newer trade routes across Arabia in the middle and around the northern fringes—skirting conventional customs stations and perhaps river pirates—were also in Arab hands, and important enough to enter Roman-Sâsânian treaties. When Muḥammad was growing up, much of the transit trade between the Indian Ocean and the Mediterranean basin was passing through Arabian overland routes. This may have been due partly to the long sequence of wars between the Roman and Sâsânian empires, which encouraged the enterprise of neutral merchants who could bypass troubled frontiers; it was made possible, however, by the full development of the technique of camel transport, which began to replace the donkey or the ox-drawn wagon for long-distance hauls. Moreover, Arabs were becoming mercenaries and allies in the great power struggles.

All three lands had their political projections into the Bedouin Arab complex. At the end of the fifth century, the Yemeni kingdom was supporting a great tribal grouping in central Arabia, under the lead of the Kindah tribe; presumably it should have acted for Yemeni interests in trade and perhaps politically to balance Roman and Sâsânian power, but just then the Yemen was occupied by the Abyssinians. The Kindah power broke up almost immediately. But soon the Sâsânian and Roman empires were each sponsoring, and subsidizing, their own Bedouin tribal kingdoms. On the southern borders of Syria, the Romans gave high title to the Ghassânids, partly expecting protection from raiding by other tribes, partly as an Arab arm in their power struggle with the Sâsânians, in which the lands south of the Fertile Crescent, like the mountainous region north of it, offered opportunities for gaining competitive advantages. The Sâsânians financed the Lakhmid kings at Ḥîrah near the Euphrates, at the end of an Arabian trade route to the Iraq; these controlled tribes far to the south and the northwest and had great prestige even in central Arabia. The Lakhmid was the strongest and most enduring of the Bedouin kingdoms, till after 602 the Sâsânians took direct control of Ḥîrah and its military resources. But even apart from these kingdoms, Arabs were serving as mercenaries at least in the Roman armies. The Lakhmid forces seem to have been sufficiently well placed to have helped decide a contested succession to the Sâsânian throne. The development of camel nomadism had reached a point where it was impinging importantly on the surrounding lands.

The Arabs had surely been in touch with each other, over the whole of Bedouin Arabia, from the time when nomadism was fully developed. But it was under the stimulus of the international competition that was pouring money into the Arab kingdoms, and doubtless partly because of the prosperity of the Bedouin trade routes, that in the fifth and sixth centuries the rudiments of an Arabic high culture grew up. The first Arab merchant-kings had used Aramaic as their formal tongue. Ghassânids and Lakhmids were proud to use Arabic. There was surely always tribal poetry, but in these centuries the poetry reached a peak of formal specialization.

The supreme cultural expression of the tribal life—again whether among the nomadic Bedouin tribes or in the towns—was a highly cultivated body of poetry in a standard all-Arabian form of Arabic, sometimes called *muḍarî* or 'classical' Arabic. Very early, poetry was connected with the transient Kindah kingdom. Later the most important poetic centre was the Lakhmid court, which rewarded panegyrics grandly. The patterns of metre and of sense in these poems were highly stylized and the individual poets were given great recognition as tribal spokesmen. Despite a tendency to kingly patronage of distant poets, even the Lakhmid chiefs shared in this tribal mood. Each new poem was soon carried throughout Arabia by professional reciters, especially if it bore some relation, as it commonly did, to the greater intertribal feuds. For at this time—perhaps not unrelated to the wider commerce—a network of feuds and political struggles tended to involve the whole of Arabia in a single political complex, if a rather incoherent one.[5] The Arabs had their common sagas and common heroes, and their common standards of behaviour worthy of a Bedouin.

The Meccan system

The Quraysh Arab tribe at Mecca made a special place for themselves in this Arab society. The most important trading centre of western and central Arabia was Mecca in the Ḥijâz. It was at the junction of two major routes. One went south and north, through the mountainous Ḥijâz from the Yemen and the Indian Ocean lands to Syria and the Mediterranean lands; the other, of less importance, went east and west from the Iraq, Iran, and the central Eurasian lands to Abyssinia and eastern Africa. As compared to Tâ'if and other central Ḥijâz localities in the same area, Mecca was relatively unpromising; unlike Tâ'if, it had no great oasis—that is, sufficient underground water was not tapped there to form a watered agricultural area. It had sufficient water to satisfy many camels, however; it was protected by hills from Red Sea pirates; and it possessed a respected shrine to which pilgrimage was made.

Some generations before Muḥammad, under the leadership of one Quṣayy

5 On the condition of pre-Islamic Arabia, and especially of the Ḥijâz, see Henri Lammens, *Le Berceau de l'Islam: l'Arabie occidentale à la veille de l'hégire*, vol. 1, *Le Climat —Les Bédouins* (Rome, 1914), especially part III, 'Les Bédouins'; and Henri Lammens, 'La Mecque à la veille de l'hégire', in *Mélanges de l'Université St.-Joseph*, 9 (Beirut, 1924), 97–439.) In using Lammens, the reader must beware of Lammens' over-scepticism; often Lammens' doubts leave the evidence hanging in mid-air, and sometimes he exaggerates (e.g., in introducing modern commercial terminology). The standard historical work will now be Jawâd 'Alî, *Ta'rîkh al-'Arab qabl al-Islâm* (6 vols., Baghdad, 1951–57). Frants Buhl, *Muhammeds Liv* (Copenhagen, 1903), translated as *Das Leben Muhammeds* (Leipzig, 1930), has a lucid and judicious chapter describing relevant conditions, 'Forholdene i Arabien ved Tiden for Muhammeds Optraeden'. Sidney Smith, 'Events in Arabia in the Sixth Century', *BSOAS*, 16 (1954), 425–68, is useful on dating. See also Giorgio Levi della Vida, 'Pre-Islamic Arabia' in *The Arab Heritage* ed. Nabih A. Faris (Princeton University Press, 1944)—a skilful summary of what we do and do not know about the history of pre-Islamic Arabia as a whole; note that the translator has misrendered some words so badly that they can be misleading to the unwary reader at important points.

and with the aid of tribes along the route to Syria, a tribe had been brought together, called Quraysh, to take over the springs at Mecca and the shrine from other Bedouin. The Quraysh were organized on Bedouin principles, without a king or any other municipal institutions beyond the clan councils; they used an assembly of notables of all the clans for non-binding consultation. The threat of blood-feud guarded the peace. But ever since Quṣayy's time, the Quraysh had maintained solidarity (not without some clans gaining a position of more influence than others) and had made effective use of their resources. They controlled the north-south trade and grew rich by it. To do so, they had also to win a secure diplomatic (and warlike) position among the tribes of the Ḥijâz, which was then bolstered with a financial position—leading tribesmen became their creditors. For they engaged not only in the long-distance trade, but in local trade in western Arabia; they had fostered the pilgrimages (and accompanying fairs) made at certain seasons to Mecca itself and to a neutral spot not far away ('Arafât), as well as other markets held in the region. They became the dominant partners in an alliance with the Thaqîf tribe of nearby Tâ'if, where leading Meccans had summer houses. In the course of all this, they had acquired prestige as a tribe of dependable and independent honour.[6]

Their position was institutionalized in religious forms. The fairs took the form of pilgrimages, and to protect the traffic at those times the Meccans established sacred truce months, four a year, which a large number of tribes observed. To settle the times of the sacred months, the Meccans maintained a calendar of their own, equally widely used. Internally, their solidarity was maintained through the worship at the Ka'bah, a rectangular building which formed the object of the Meccan pilgrimage (*ḥajj*). This worship seems to have embodied a somewhat unusual development of the Arab paganism.

Among a world of minor spirit beings (*jinn*), the Arabs distinguished a number of more serious divinities, often as protectors of particular tribes; each was associated with a shrine at some given locality, a tree or a grove or a strangely formed rock (or sometimes with a sacred stone or other object carried ceremoniously by the worshipping tribe). The greatest divinities were likely to be associated also with stars. People supplicated or propitiated them with special rites in view of some worldly hope or fear. Back of these active divinities was a vaguer figure, Allâh, 'the god' par excellence, regarded as a Creator-god and perhaps as guarantor of rights and agreements which crossed tribal lines. But, as with many 'high gods', he had no special cult.[7]

[6] Julius Wellhausen, *Reste arabischen Heidentums* (2nd ed. Berlin, 1897; also in *Skizzen und Vorarbeiten*, Heft 3), section 'Mekka, der Hagg, und die Messen', discusses the reasons for Mecca's importance. For the commercial position of the Quraysh and their political relations, see Lammens 'La Mecque à la veille de l'hégire', especially chaps. I–III and XIII–XV. (But beware exaggerations.) Irfan Kawar, 'The Arabs and the Peace Tready of AD 561', *Arabica*, 3 (1956), 181–213, brings out some suggestive points about the Arab commercial context of Meccan activity.

[7] On the pagan Arab cults, see Wellhausen, *Reste arabischen Heidentums*, especially the final section; but note that the conception of a supreme creator-god need not be explained linguistically, for such figures are widespread.

In the Ka'bah were gathered the sacred tokens of all the clans of Mecca; it thus merged their several cults into one. Qur'ânic testimony shows us that the Ka'bah was presided over by Allâh, presumably in his capacity as guarantor of agreements among the tribes, and hence as guarantor of the pilgrimage as well as of the agreements among the Meccan clans. If Allâh still had no special cult, at any rate in Mecca he thus came into special prominence. (It seems that even Christian Arabs made pilgrimage to the Ka'bah, honouring Allâh there as God the Creator.) The special role of the Ka'bah as shrine of joint pagan worship was not limited to the Meccans. In addition to the sacred tokens of the Meccan clans, other tribes in alliance with the Quraysh were encouraged to bring their tokens and fetishes there, so as to join in a common sacredness. A number of the more active divinities seem to have received special honour at Mecca: notably three goddesses (Allât, al-'Uzzà, and Manât) who were widely worshipped among the Arabs and in particular had shrines in the neighbouring districts with which the Meccans had close relations. Worshippers honoured the Ka'bah by circling it a fixed number of times on foot, and touching the sacred stones built into it: particularly the Black Stone in one corner. Near it sprang a sacred well, called *Zamzam*. It was the centre of a hallowed area, extending all round Mecca, in which fighting was taboo even when it was not a truce month.

Mecca was located approximately equidistant from the three spheres of power around Bedouin Arabia. Midway between Syria and the Yemen, it was about equally distant from the long arm of Sâsânian power to the northeast. Perhaps only at such a distance from the agrarian lands could so thoroughly independent and Bedouin a system have arisen. A major task of the Quraysh—on their own behalf and perhaps also on behalf of the tribes of their allies—was to maintain the independence of their zone. Both Romans and Abyssinians had made expeditions to the area (the Sâsânians had not, and it is clear that the Quraysh rather favoured the Sâsânians over either Rome or Abyssinia). When a Jewish dynasty came to power in the Yemen, Abyssinia, as Christian ally of Rome, had finally intervened to overthrow it, on the pretext of halting persecutions of Christians, but perhaps also on account of the Sâsânian and anti-Roman sympathies shared by many Jewish groups, even in Syria. The Abyssinians seem to have sent expeditions as far north as Medina against Jewish settlements along the trade route. The Abyssinians in turn were ejected by Sâsânian forces, evidently gladly received in the Yemen. In Muḥammad's lifetime, an attempt by one of the Quraysh to forge links with Byzantium (and possibly rise to power in Mecca himself) was frustrated by Meccan insistence on neutrality.

The corollary of maintaining political neutrality was to maintain neutrality among the religious allegiances that disputed among themselves the lands from Nile to Oxus and the Fertile Crescent in particular. This was not necessarily easy. Bedouin Arabia was a prime mission field offering opportunities to casual merchants or to solitary monks. Arabs were keenly aware of those venerable agrarianate high cultures in which they as Bedouin had little share, and in particular of the confessional communities that played so prominent a part in urban civilization. Some Arab tribes had even adopted for themselves, to some degree or other, one of these religious allegiances in place of the not very lively tribal paganism of their ancestors. We may surmise that the rest of the Arabs could not long resist conversion to one or another such religious allegiance. Perhaps only the want of a single allegiance that would automatically command adherence had allowed them to linger.

In the area around Bedouin Arabia the confessional traditions, all of the Irano-Semitic monotheistic type, proliferated as diversely as anywhere in the Nile-to-Oxus region. Most widespread was Christianity, which in a variety of mutually hostile forms prevailed in the Mesopotamian plain (Nestorian and Jacobite Christianity), in Syria (Jacobite, Armenian, and Chalcedonian Christianity—the latter being the official Christianity of the Roman empire, later split into Roman Catholic and Greek Orthodox), in Egypt (Coptic and Chalcedonian), and in Abyssinia (Coptic). Judaism and Christianity were also especially strong in the Yemen in the far south. On the east coasts of Arabia, Zoroastrianism was also important. In most of Bedouin Arabia, and especially in the Ḥijâz, the mountainous area of the west in which are Mecca and Medina, none of the confessional allegiances had yet become prevalent. Bedouin Arabia, never incorporated till then into the great agrarian empires that had risen and fallen north of it for so long, was a still pocket of paganism, where the commonest form of religion was the old worship of local and tribal spirits. But all the main religious allegiances were represented there; even in the Ḥijâz there were some Christians and a great many Jews. When Muḥammad preached a religion of one God, of prophets, and of Hell and Paradise, the terms he used could be understood by many Arabs, even among the pagans.

Yet Muḥammad may have been in the one place where paganism was still most vital. As the camel nomads began to play a role in the agrarian lands and in international politics, the Quraysh of Mecca were playing a role not only influential but politically and religiously unique among them. In contrast to the precarious pyramiding of tribal agglomerations with a king-like chieftain at the top, they had been able to base a reasonably effective political order on the solidarity of one tribe, and its prestige. And this was cemented in an equally independent religious system, likewise based on Bedouin ways, and equally neutral to all the confessional religious allegiances. The Meccans seem to have offered the only effective Bedouin-based alternative to assimilation to the settled cultures.[8]

[8] Joseph Chelhod, *Introduction à la sociologie de l'Islam: de l'animisme à l'universalisme* (Paris, 1958) is not about the sociology of Islam as a religious tradition, but about the development of religious consciousness in Muḥammad and his compatriots, in their social context. Chelhod builds upon Lammens' work very suggestively, stressing the evolution of Mecca itself in the Ḥijâz; unfortunately, his racialism leads him to misconceive the course of subsequent Islam; and even on the proper subject of his book, his arguments are mostly very tenuous. See the excellent study by Gustave von

Muḥammad becomes a prophet

Abû-l-Qâsim Muḥammad b. 'Abd-Allâh[9] was a substantial and respected merchant in Mecca. He had grown up an orphan, under the care of an uncle in unprosperous circumstances; but he was of an established family (the Banû Hâshim), members of the Quraysh, the ruling tribe of Mecca. He had shown his competence as a trader in the service of a well-to-do widow, Khadîjah, some years his senior, whom he subsequently married. By her he had four daughters (and evidently sons who died in infancy), whom he was able to marry into prominent families.[10] He was known in Mecca as *al-Amîn*, 'the trustworthy'.

In his thirties, if not earlier, Muḥammad seems to have become preoccupied with questions of how to live a serious life in truth and purity. He apparently listened to all who had something to say about the meaning of human life in this world and he meditated intensely in periods of retirement in a cave (on Mount Ḥirâ') outside the town. He did not dissociate himself from the rites and customs of the Quraysh, which indeed continued dear to him. But he sought something which they lacked.

We shall be talking a good deal about religion in this work, for it pervaded every aspect of Islamicate culture. I must make clear my point of view on it.[11] It may be said that the religious impulse is ninety per cent wishful thinking. Wishful thinking is, indeed, rooted deeply in us. Unlike other animals, human beings live by their illusions: our very words, it has been said, point to what is in fact not there. Human beings alone are artists. Over and beyond the immediate stimulus and response, we want every moment to make sense in some larger whole which our lives form: people cannot stand living with sheer absurdity. If we refuse to make a conscious choice of what sense to make of life, we are told, we will in practice adopt some pattern of sense unconsciously and without consideration. Hence even intelligent people may persuade themselves to believe almost anything that seems to make hopeful sense of life. And since life is largely a tissue of miseries, we are under pressure to discover some sense which will give the misery a positive meaning. The logic of wishful thinking,

---

Grunebaum, 'The Nature of Arab Unity before Islam', *Arabica*, 10 (1963), 5–23, on the pre-Islamic Arabs and the conditions that allowed Mecca to play a special role among them.

[9] The abbreviation 'b.' stands for *ibn*, 'son of'; for a fuller explanation, see the section on personal names in the Introduction.

[10] On Muḥammad's connections and the status of families in Mecca, see W. Montgomery Watt's *Muhammad at Mecca* (Oxford, 1953), chaps. I.2 and II.3.

[11] I am personally a convinced Christian, of the Quaker persuasion, but neither here nor earlier do my general formulations on the nature of religion represent Christianity as such. If they represent anything, it is the sort of considerations that have been developed in the modern discipline of religion studies in the works of such scholars as Rudolf Otto and especially Mircea Eliade; not without influence from the anthropological tradition (e.g., Bronislaw Malinowski, Paul Radin), the sociological (e.g., Emile Durckheim), certain psychologists (e.g., Carl Jung), and philosophers (e.g., Ernst Cassirer, Wm. James, Albert Camus).

then, is not to be despised: that if something is possible (though proof or disproof is unattainable), and if it is desirable, then it may be presumed true until disproven.

But what is remarkable about human beings, in distinction from other animals, is what we have done with our illusions—with our free imaginations. Artists deal, in a sense, with illusion; but if they are disciplined, they can evoke reality by way of the illusion. In religion also a disciplined imaginative response can touch reality. The component of sheer wishful thinking in religion is large, but is still not the whole of it. What is most interesting about religion is not the wishful thinking as such, but the creative insights that come along with it, which open new possibilities of human meaningfulness and expression. To identify these expressions of religion in particular, the observer must sometimes penetrate into motives and implications not immediately apparent to outsiders in the words used in religious discourse. But this need not mean distortion. What serious and intelligent persons over many generations, and in preference to many available alternatives, have held to be significant rarely turns out, on close investigation, to be trivial.

Despite Quṣayy's measures, the prevailing religious climate in Mecca was still not far removed from the Bedouin paganism round about. Relations with fetishes or with deities were chiefly on the basis of bargaining—for this offering I give you, lord, you will give me that favour in return. This was little removed from magic. Lots were cast at the Ka'bah to foretell fortunes, and vows and sacrifices were made to assure successes. A sense of loyalty certainly there was; but there seems to have been little higher moral challenge. Even the special presence of the Creator-god Allâh did not carry far. No meaning or goal was added to a man's life other than what he already had as a tribesman.

But a different sort of spiritual attitude was also represented at Mecca, an attitude associated with monotheistic religion. Foreigners who were settled in Mecca, or just passing through, were attached to a number of Christian and perhaps Jewish communities and to other monotheistic communities of a 'Gnostic' type such as were then common in Syria; Meccans were aware that such religion was supported by the great empires, and knew that some important Arab tribes adhered to it en bloc. Apparently none of the representatives of monotheism whom Muḥammad knew in Mecca was very well-versed in his faith. The terminology used in the Qur'ân, as well as other details, reflects traditions from a variety of religious communities but presupposes no intimate understanding of any of them.[12] Nevertheless, even an ill-trained adherent of any monotheistic group could convey at least the possibility that a

[12] Whatever one thinks of the provenance of the Qur'ân, its language is designed explicitly to be intelligible to Arabs. Hence we may gather from it what sort of concepts could be expected to be intelligible to Muḥammad and his contemporaries. That is, we can learn from it with assurance what ideas were circulating in Mecca at the time. It is only those ideas of which the Qur'ân would make use.

man's life must be measured by larger than tribal standards—that his actions counted as those of a human being, not just a tribesman; that to be good they must accord with the nature of the world as a whole, not just with personal or tribal interests; and that accordingly only at a summing up of the world's whole history could any man's life be seen in its proper light.

There were a few other men of the Quraysh in Muḥammad's time who were attracted to monotheism; they seem to have worked out, perhaps each for himself, some sort of private faith—later tradition called them the 'Ḥanîfs'. From these, Muḥammad was distinguished by a crucial event. Toward the age of forty, during one of his retirements in Mount Ḥirâ', he heard a voice and saw a vision which summoned him to offer worship to the God who had created the world, the God of the monotheists, to Allâh whom the ordinary Arab honoured but had no cult for. Encouraged by his wife, Khadîjah, he accepted the summons as coming from God Himself. Thereupon, he received further messages which he interpreted as divine revelation, and the worshipful recitation of which formed a major element of the new cult. The messages collectively were called the *Qur'ân*, which means 'recitation'. For a time, only his wife and a few close friends shared the cult with him. But after some years the messages demanded that he summon his fellow Quraysh to the worship of God, warning them of calamities to come if they refused. From a private monotheist he was to become a prophet to his people.

We know far less about Muḥammad than was once supposed. On the face of it, the documentation transmitted among Muslims about his life is rich and detailed; but we have learned to mistrust most of it; indeed, the most respected early Muslim scholars themselves pointed out its untrustworthiness. But we do know a great deal more about him than, for instance, about Jesus. The evidence about Jesus is almost exclusively contained in the four Gospels and in a letter by Paul. The more they are analyzed, the less dependable the Gospels prove to be. Even the recorded sayings of Jesus can be shown to have been heavily edited at least in some Gospels. As to the personal spirituality of Jesus we have only the thinnest evidence. We may surmise that he was sincere; but we are already in the realm of conjecture when we try to say what he was sincere in. We tend to choose as characterizing him those episodes that are most touching, or most distinctive and unlikely to have been common stock. This is probably a sound instinct, but it is dangerous from a scholarly viewpoint; at the least, it must be checked on the basis of other texts from the period, which are only just becoming available. In the case of Muḥammad, though we must use a large amount of conjecture, we can base it on reasonably objective scholarly principles. We can rely on the text of the Qur'ân itself as direct evidence—though that text is habitually ambiguous in any concrete references it makes. To interpret the Qur'ân, we are forced to resort to reports collected several generations later; but even among these, we are not entirely at a loss: we can probably rely on those reports which can be shown not to grind the axe of any particular later party, provided such reports fit reasonably well into a coherent picture that emerges from them all as a body. And most important, we can often rely on the background detail which the reports take for granted as known to all. Hence, though what I have to say about Muḥammad is largely conjecture, yet it can be responsibly offered.

About Muḥammad's call, we may say this. First, Muḥammad accepted the summons to the new cult: that is, he himself believed. This in itself was a decisive act of faith. And then he did more: he accepted the role of prophet to his people. This acceptance required not only unwavering faith in the validity of his cause, but high courage; for it necessarily brought on him the scorn and ridicule and mistrust of most of the men about him. For them, such a claim was at best absurd—and at worst likely to be a cloak for private ambition, perhaps connected with some Roman plot to control the Ḥijâz trade through a local puppet, such as the Quraysh had had to resist before. Muḥammad's positive response to what he found himself confronted with, then, was his great creative act. Before he summoned others, he himself had accepted the consequences of his faith and staked his life on it.

A prophet is one who speaks for a god—who utters whatever messages from the god are divinely laid upon him (not necessarily, of course, nor even primarily, messages regarding the future). The impulsion to speak as a prophet has been variously felt; it has ranged from institutionalized rituals, in which abnormal physiological states are induced out of which dark words come, to the expression of consciously personal insights by 'inspired' poets. Muḥammad's standard for prophecy was, in principle, the experience and action of the old Hebrew prophets. But he knew nothing of them directly. His own experience was evidently very personal.

He found himself gripped in a distinctive physical condition and therein becoming conscious of ideas which he did not recognize to be his own. The physical stress seems to have been sometimes sufficiently violent that he required wrapping up and he then sweated profusely; sometimes it was far milder. (On the basis of some aspects of the detailed Muslim descriptions, the moments of revelation have been very conjecturally likened to epileptic seizures.) At such times he might be unconscious or at least abstracted. The form in which the ideas came seems to have varied still more than his physical condition. On certain occasions, presumably at the very start, we have the evidence of the Qur'ân that there was not only audition but ocular vision; notably, according to reports, a waking vision of a gigantic being on the horizon—on every horizon to which Muḥammad turned his eyes—who spoke to him the words he must say. Usually, however, there were simply auditions: Muḥammad heard words spoken or—in milder cases—some sort of tinkling sound, to which, on his arousing, a meaning was attached.

The words which he then uttered were written down with care—he used a number of 'secretaries'—and were memorized by the pious. They were retained especially by the 'Qur'ân-reciters', followers of his who specialized in reproducing and teaching the whole of the constantly growing Qur'ân.[13] The various bits of revelation were arranged in *sûrahs* ('chapters'), some of which represented a single revelation but most of which were added to from time to time—often new passages being inserted in the midst of old.

A variety of incidents show that neither the occasion nor the content of the revelations was under Muḥammad's conscious control. After the earliest revelations, there was a long period when he received none at all and became severely depressed, doubting the truth of his own call—he was supported, above all, by Khadîjah's continuing reassurance. Later, Muḥammad came to expect a revelation at need. Accordingly, he was badly embarrassed on at least one occasion when for days a required divine decision failed to come—an experience he interpreted as designed to humble him.

The experience of being gripped as by an outside being, as well as the ecstatic rhyming prose in which especially the earlier revelations took form, seemed to the Arabs like the similar outbursts of a soothsayer, *kâhin*. These men were regarded as possessed by *jinn*, sprites, who put their utterances into their mouths. On a higher level, the respected poets, though they suffered no state of seizure and what they uttered was in a far more developed literary form, were regarded also as inspired by jinn. The words of both soothsayer and poet were regarded as preternatural and possessing hidden powers. Muḥammad was at great pains to distinguish himself from either soothsayer or poet; to insist it was no transient and irresponsible jinn that possessed him, but a cosmic representative of the Creator-god Himself, an angel. (Eventually he identified the angel as Gabriel.) Muslims have made a point ever since of denying the Qur'ân to be poetry in the technical sense, *shi'r*, as practiced by the ancient Arab poets.

Monotheism and personal moral responsibility

At first it does not seem to have been clear that the new cult was incompatible with the existing cults in which the Quraysh took part. In the new cult, portions of the Qur'ân were recited periodically to the accompaniment of bowings and prostrations in honour of Allâh. This was called the *ṣalât;* as a form of adoration it was reminiscent of Syrian Christian practice. Just as even Christian Arabs could take part in the ḥajj pilgrimage, the first Muslims, adding their special practices, need not otherwise have made any notable break with Quraysh customs. But from the first, the new cult set off its devotees as

[13] The Qur'ân-reciters (Qâri') are sometimes called 'Qur'ân *readers*' in English, but this is misleading. They were often illiterate and in any case were not engaged in 'reading' the Qur'ân in the modern sense of taking in the meaning of a written text before one. (Unfortunately, there are still Muslims who speak of 'reading' the Qur'ân—or other text!—when they mean merely declaiming it: uttering the appropriate sounds, with or without sight of the printed page, without necessarily attaching any meaning at all to the individual sounds uttered. In this sense, some claim to 'read' Arabic without knowing a word of the language.)

pledged to a new vision of life. The early portions of the Qur'ân contain numerous moral injunctions, urging purity, chastity, and generosity. The specific moral ideals were in no case unprecedented and rarely departed from moral norms upheld, in principle, in the older Bedouin society. (The Qur'ân made no attempt to lay down a comprehensive moral system; the very word for moral behaviour, *al-ma'rûf*, means 'the known'.) What was new was the conception of the place of these norms in a man's life.

In the Qur'ân, the immensity of the human situation is brought out in the descriptions of the Last Day, thus (LXXXI, 1–14):

When the sun shall be darkened, when the stars shall be thrown down, when the mountains shall be set moving, when the pregnant camels shall be untended, when the savage beasts shall be stampeded,[14] when the seas shall be set boiling, when the souls shall be coupled, when the buried infant shall be asked for what sin she was killed, when the scrolls shall be unrolled, when the skies shall be stripped off, when Hell shall be set blazing, when Paradise shall be brought near,—a soul shall know what it has produced.

There is a moral condemnation of infanticide here, but not by way of introducing a new commandment nor even of reinforcing an old one. Rather, female infanticide, which was a natural consequence of the tribal emphasis on males and of its disregard of the individual as such, is pointed to as showing what sort of thing the godless soul 'has produced'—the quality of a life which is without God.

In the Qur'ân it was early made clear that human beings face a fundamental moral choice. They cannot hover half way. On the one hand, they may choose to stand in awe of their Creator and accept His moral demands. In this case, God, in His mercy, will guide those who are faithful, making them upright and pure. Or human beings may, on the contrary, turn away from their Creator; becoming absorbed in their private wishes of the moment, and praying the various godlings for success in them. In this case, God will likewise turn away from them, and they will become wicked, petty men and women. For a human being cannot choose to be pure at will (a sad fact too readily experienced!); he does not control his own ways, but can achieve moral purity only by the power of God.[15] The fundamental choice, then, appears in the Qur'ân as overwhelmingly crucial: to turn to God and worship Him, or to turn from Him to one's own desires. All else in the moral life will follow from this choice.

[14] Stampeded by fear, as Richard Bell suggests—literally, 'driven together'. The scrolls, further on, are of course the records of persons' lives. I have based my renderings on A. J. Arberry's but have departed from him freely so as to stay closer to the direct simplicity of the original. (For Bell, Arberry, and other Qur'ân translators, see the section on translations of the Qur'ân in the Selective Bibliography.)

[15] This account of predestination in the Qur'ân seems to answer the tenor of the whole, Maurice Gaudefroy-Demombynes, *Mahomet* (Paris, 1957), p. 357, suggests that Qur'ân XCII, 5–13, may express this idea succinctly. Certainly the usual interpretation of it makes it improbably thin in moral content.

Muḥammad was convinced that this choice determined the whole worth of a person's life. As did the other monotheists, he believed that this fact would be made inescapably manifest in a final cosmic catastrophe, when the world would be destroyed and all human beings would be visibly judged by God Himself, those who had already died being restored to life for judgment. Then those who had been faithful to God would be rewarded with all good things the human heart delights in while those who had turned away would be punished with all evil things the heart dreads. The Qur'ân painted both the rewards and the punishments in vivid colours—the blessèd would dwell in beautiful gardens with delicious fruits and charming damsels; the damned would burn frightfully in fire, swallowing nauseous refuse. The likelihood of the great final catastrophe was supported by descriptions of lesser catastrophes that had overtaken individual peoples which had rejected the summons of prophets sent to them; for instance, the people of Noah. Doubters were reminded that such a catastrophe, and the resurrection of the dead for judgment, were entirely within the power of the God who had made the world and who had formed each man and woman in the womb in the first place. But the coming of the great Day was assured for Muḥammad, finally, by its having been announced in the messages sent to Muḥammad and to all previous monotheistic prophets as well. The same revelation which insisted on the choice between the commands of the Creator and one's own desires also warned of the final Judgment in which the choice would be vindicated; Muḥammad could not doubt any portion of the total message.[16]

Accordingly, Muḥammad insisted on the moral responsibility of human beings. Life was no matter of play, it called for sober alertness; men dare not relax, secure in their wealth and their good family and their numerous sons—all these things would avail nothing at the Judgment, when a person's own personal worth would be weighed; humans must live in constant fear and awe of God, before whom they were accountable for every least deed. To be sure, God is merciful: if a person were truly turned toward Him, slips could be forgiven in view of his human weakness; but a carelessness which neglected God Himself for the transient delights He had given would not be forgiven.

The Qur'ân puts the human situation in powerful images, drawn from Biblical and Talmudic lore but reworked to express the vision of Islam. God

[16] Very often, scholarly interpreters of the Qur'ân have stressed the *source* of various notions which appear in it. For our purposes, it is more useful to look for their *meaning within the Qur'ân*. The Qur'ân could speak only in terms of the language and the concepts which Muḥammad and his followers already possessed with which to receive its message. These were limited, on the whole, to what was to be found in the monotheistic traditions. To understand a given reference, one must take note of the assumed context first: e.g., to see the meaning of references to the Last Judgment, we must recognize that the notion of the Judgment as an event in time was *given* by the monotheistic tradition. Then one must see what the Qur'ân does with this—what *direction* the notion is pushed in. It is only this which can yield its *meaning*, morally and humanly. The same, of course, holds for all the Qur'ânic tales, whether Biblical or not. Their deviation from the Biblical form is relevant primarily as pointing up the message they are to carry.

offered to the heavens the trust of keeping faith, and they refused; He offered it to the mountains, and they said they were not strong enough; but human beings undertook it. When the angels heard that God was creating mankind, they objected. Why should God place in the earth creatures which would simply fill it with injustice and bloodshed? But God insisted He knew what He was doing. He taught Adam the names of all things (we would say Adam received the faculty of rational discrimination), then He challenged the angels to tell what things were; when they found they had to be taught this by Adam, they acknowledged God was doing something beyond their understanding. Indeed, God insisted that they all bow down and do obeisance to Adam and all did so save Iblîs (Satan), who was too proud. Thereafter, Iblîs was permitted to tempt humans to evil, and those who did not sincerely turn from him to God would succumb. Then God drew forth all future generations of mankind from the loins of Adam and confronted them with the demand, 'Am I not your Lord?' They acknowledged Him each one and were tucked back in, to come forth in due time to be tested, whether they would maintain the faith or no.[17]

The responsibility to obey God is thus imprinted in human nature, the Qur'ân tells us, but by people's carelessness the truth is forgotten—unless warners come from God, prophets (*nabî*) who will bring to humans messages from God such as Muḥammad brought, whereby men and women may be reminded of their duty. The figures appealed to by the various monotheists had been such prophets, bringing to their several peoples the same reminder of their duty toward God. Many of them had performed wonders, deeds beyond normal human powers, which authenticated their messages by showing that they were supported by the same Being who performed the wonders of creation and Who alone could be expected to produce wonders of a truly high order. Thus Jesus, with the permission of God, gave life itself (to clay birds, as told in an apocryphal gospel), a wonder especially distinctive of the Creator and therefore unmistakably marking His intervention. Muḥammad himself claimed no wonder but the Qur'ân itself; this, however, he regarded as undeniable. He challenged any man to produce its like; and (like any great creative work) it has in fact proved inimitable. Nevertheless, it is clear from the Qur'ân that the divine message ought to be acknowledged without need for any such evidentiary miracles. Those who are blinded by their delight in transient things, and hence subject to the suggestions of Iblîs (who can whisper his temptations to the heart, though he has no power of himself to mislead us), will reject any prophet, however well evidenced. But those who have guarded themselves from such blindness will recognize the truth as soon as they are reminded of it by the warnings of a prophet. The prophet's mission, therefore, is in the first instance simply to utter the warnings as God gives them to him.

[17] Qur'ân, xxxiii, 72; ii, 30–34 (28–32); xxxviii, 71–85, xvii, 61–65 (63–67); vii, 172 (171).

At least latent in Muḥammad's message from the beginning was the idea that there is only one true object of worship, only one God; that all other godlings are not just secondary but absolutely false, and their cults wicked. For a time, Muḥammad may have preached the new cult without insisting on the overthrow of any of the old cults; once he even tried to find a place for a cult of the greater, Meccan goddesses as intermediaries, subordinate to that of Allâh; yet, before long, insistence on the exclusive cult of God alone became the central dogma of Islam.[18]

As Muḥammad confronted both his opponents and his own followers with the new message, and as its implications were lived through, it became clear that no concessions could be made. If Judgment was to be total and final, the Judge must be utterly transcendent, incommensurate with all that was to come under His judgment. There could be no intermediaries, no half-gods. And if people genuinely made the fundamental moral choice of turning to God for His guidance, they should not turn back to the petty cults which were there to serve only their lusts. The various monotheists agreed in imposing such a ban, and the ban became the crucial test of whether a person had become a *muslim,* whether he was undertaking the obligations of faith. The essential step in joining the Muslim community came to be abandonment of idolatry (*shirk,* literally association of something else with God); that is, any cult of beings other than the Creator-god.

The monotheistic communities whose representatives Muḥammad looked to as worshippers of the Creator-god had developed complex theories about the divine realm. The elements of an elaborate supernatural apparatus seem to have played a considerable part in Muḥammad's thought also, particularly at first. The Qur'ân presupposes acquaintance with various cosmic figures and objects. It mentions, for instance, angels, the Spirit (*Rûḥ*), the Word (*Qawl*), the Command (*Amr*); several heavens, the divine Throne, and heavenly books —the latter recording not only human destiny, but men's and women's deeds in the world and the divine message itself (from which the Qur'ân comprises only excerpts).[19] On the other hand, Muḥammad seems not to have been acquainted with the more central doctrines of the New Testament—those of divine incarnation, of suffering, sacrificial love, of redemption; nor to have been acquainted with the major literary prophets of the Hebrew Bible, such as Isaiah or Jeremiah. Nevertheless, he seems to have become less concerned, in time, with the supernatural apparatus, and to have centred into an outlook far more in harmony with the great Hebrew prophets than with the sectarianism, often of Gnostic type, whose terminology and sacred tales he knew. It is as if he had been led back of the popular imagery that was visible to him, in the chance representatives of monotheism he encountered, to the grand themes of the old prophets whose personalities had not seized the popular

[18] On the 'Satanic verses' and on the early evolution of Muḥammad's mission, cf. Watt, *Muhammad at Mecca,* chap. V.1.

[19] On the Qur'ânic cosmology cf. Gaudefroy-Demombynes, *Mahomet,* pp. 292ff.

imagination, but whose basic insight still formed the solid groundwork under all the later luxuriant overgrowth.

Muḥammad, with the Qur'ân, presented a potent challenge to everyone at Mecca: a challenge to rise to a level of personal moral purity such as it had occurred to few to dream of. He presented it as a real possibility for human beings, indeed a necessity if they were not to risk offending the very structure of the cosmos in which they found themselves. And he presented it in a concrete, tangible form in which, by an act of will, they could adopt the new ideal practically.

Muḥammad founds a religious community

When Muḥammad began to preach publicly his new cult, particularly when he began to oppose the old cults, most men of the Quraysh naturally ridiculed and opposed him; but he won many converts, especially among the younger men. Some converts were slaves or tribeless persons, but most were from the less powerful Quraysh clans, and a number were among the less well-placed younger men in the very top families. With the development of Mecca as a commercial and financial centre, the moral standards of Bedouin society no longer served well. Though the Quraysh seem to have kept the dangerous custom of feuding under control at least within Mecca, a type of economic inequality had arisen between man and man which threatened tribal solidarity and in any case undermined the Bedouin ideal of generous manliness in which wealth was a welcome but relatively transient distinction. In Mecca, as the individual began to act more freely in his own private interest, the tribal expectations came to fit less well. Particularly those who were disadvantaged in the new, more individualistic pattern welcomed a moral conception which could restore something of the older moral security in a form adapted to individualistic, commercial life. To this end, Islam was highly appropriate. Muḥammad's creative act of accepting prophethood thus found a public capable of responding to it.

It was not only his message that mattered, however; Muḥammad's personality backed up the message. He was able to convert and hold the loyalty of diverse sorts of outstanding and able men. As the chart of Muḥammad's relatives shows, he won their respect on the most intimate level. Two youths of his own household, whose conversion may no doubt be ascribed to his private influence, grew into exceptionally strong leaders. His uncle, Abû-Ṭâlib, had entrusted one of his sons, 'Alî, to Muḥammad to raise; 'Alî as a boy may have been the first male to accept Muḥammad (i.e., the first person after Khadîjah); as a man he proved a powerful warrior, winning in his own person an almost fanatical loyalty from many men. Almost as early a convert was Zayd b. Ḥârithah, a freedman of Muḥammad, whom he adopted for a time as a son, and who was later a trusted general for Islam.

One of the earliest converts from other clans was Abû-Bakr b. Abî-Quḥâfah,

Muḥammad's Relatives

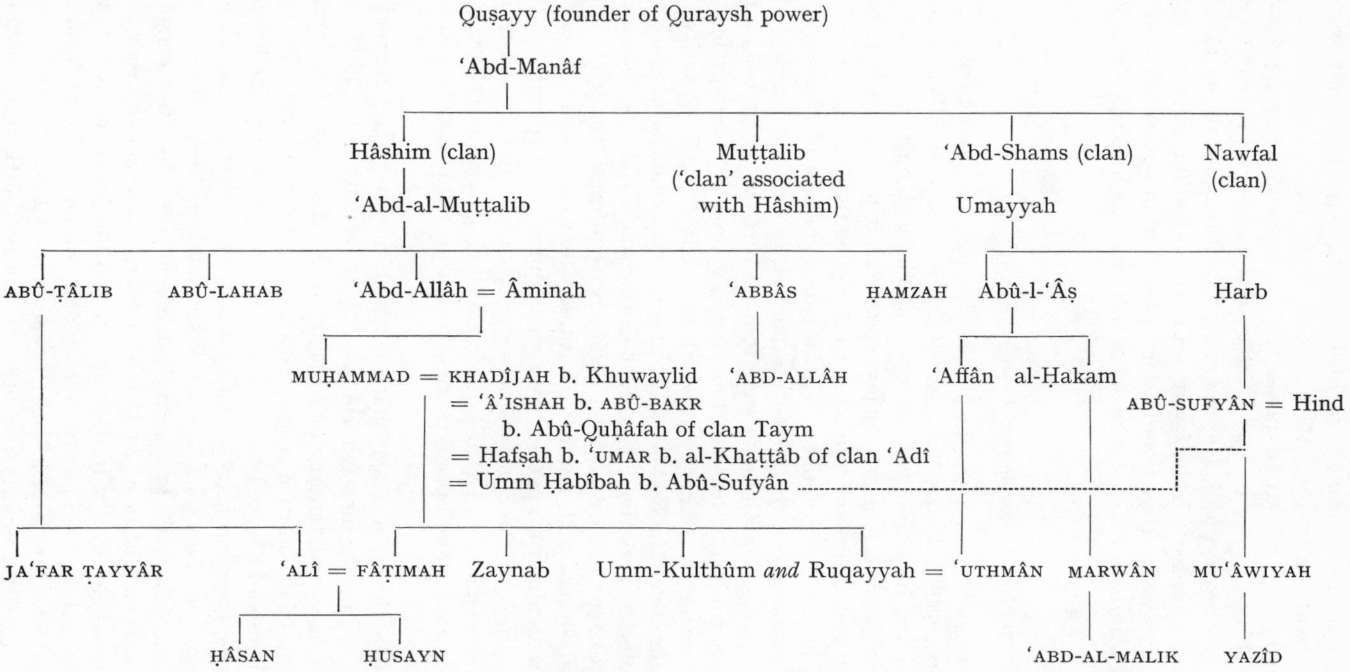

Names of those who played an important role in Muḥammad's lifetime or afterwards are in capitals.

Most men shown had more sons than those mentioned.

Muḥammad, 'Alî, and others had more wives than those mentioned.

a well-to-do merchant (though not among the very wealthiest), who acted somewhat as Muḥammad's faithful lieutenant, devoted his wealth unhesitatingly to the cause, always showed a cool good judgment and an admirable impartiality, and won abiding general respect among the Muslims. 'Uthmân b. Maẓ'ûn, also an early convert, contrasted with Abû-Bakr in having independently become something of an ascetic monotheist before Muḥammad's preaching and seems to have continued, even while loyal to Muḥammad, as something of a leader on his own; he is listed as chief of those Muslims who went to Abyssinia to escape persecution. 'Uthmân b. 'Affân (who was to become a caliph), was a retiring and deeply pious member of one of the best families of Mecca. 'Abd-al-Raḥmân b. 'Awf was a clever businessman; it is said that later, on arrival penniless in Medina, he refused an offer of property from a Medinese friend, took a trifling item to the market place, and quickly traded himself into a good supper—afterward becoming quite wealthy.

'Umar b. al-Khaṭṭâb was impulsive, almost fiery, but intensely committed to whatever won him. He is said to have been talking of killing Muḥammad out of zeal for the Meccan godlings one day, when he was told for the first time that his sister had herself become a Muslim; going to her in a rage, he found her engaged in reading a portion of the Qur'ân—and on reading it himself he was impressed, and converted; thereafter he forced the Quraysh to let him perform Islamic worship publicly at the Ka'bah itself, which was not tolerated before, and all the Muslims could do so likewise. His uprightness was never doubted; on occasion he chided Muḥammad himself. His sternness is said to have been such that levity which was tolerated in Muḥammad's own presence was suppressed if 'Umar appeared. After Muḥammad's death, he governed the Muslims with genius during their greatest conquests.

Islam soon became more than a private cult; it became an issue dividing the town. Muḥammad demanded that all Mecca join his cult and abandon all others, on pain of divine chastisement. This demand created something of a dilemma. Though in principle Muḥammad was but one of the faithful, distinguished from the others only as recipient of the Revelation and as specially charged to warn the rest, in practice he could not but be more. The lines of commitment which tied together the new group, and which tied the new group as a whole to Muḥammad, had an emotional and moral strength which could well rival that of a weakened tribal solidarity. Muḥammad, as prophet, could readily seem the authorized interpreter of the moral implications of the message which he brought, and therefore have an authority over the faithful. Muḥammad and his followers always distinguished between the Revelation from God and Muḥammad's own decisions. For years some of his strongest and closest followers were inclined to come to their own conclusions as to what the new faith implied in given situations. Nevertheless, Muḥammad showed himself a man of good personal judgment and when the demands of faith began to conflict with accepted standards at Mecca, he naturally came into a position of leadership among the faithful.

After some years of the preaching in Mecca, the Qur'ân revelations began to recount the experiences of former (usually Biblical) prophets with the peoples to whom they were sent. As in earlier monotheism, the divine challenge was taking historical form. The cosmos of the Qur'ân was intensely human and even social; if a single sequence of historical unfolding does not emerge as in the Hebrew Bible, despite its adumbration in the first part of sûrah II (for the Qur'ân rejected the idea of a chosen people), yet we feel a strong sense of common human destiny. In these historical stories, the prophet came to figure as something like the head of a community of faithful, set off against their opponents; the story of Moses was a favourite. The stories, of course, reflected Muḥammad's own circumstances in Mecca and therefore gave divine sanction to what was becoming increasingly evident: that for the Quraysh to accept the new cult of Allâh would mean accepting not merely the moral demands of the Creator, but also the political lead of Muḥammad himself. In the nature of prophecy, a transcendent universality appealing to the individual conscience was inescapably linked to concrete relationships with a particular human group and its leader.

The tribal forms of Meccan life allowed no more for municipal than for monarchical institutions. Hence when Muḥammad preached repentance and the worship of the God of the great empires round about, there was no government to jail him as a traitor or even as a public nuisance; nor for his followers to seize and reform. Instead, the struggle between the reformers and their opponents took the form of personal manoeuvres and of family and clan oppositions. In such a struggle, the Muslims, distributed as a minority among many clans, were at a disadvantage. There was a certain measure of personal persecution. The weakest of Muḥammad's followers, especially slaves, who had no clan to retaliate against any who might do them harm, were molested by the more zealous enemies of Islam, and occasionally tormented painfully; Muḥammad himself was sometimes insulted in ways hard for an Arab to bear. One of Muḥammad's uncles, called in the Qur'ân *Abû-Lahab* (the 'flame man', as doomed to Hell) was one of the most vehement in fighting the movement. But the Banû Hâshim as a whole, led by Muḥammad's uncle Abû-Ṭâlib, loyally stood by their clansman Muḥammad, even though most of them did not accept his cult; threat of retaliation from them, accordingly, prevented any direct personal injury to Muḥammad. The same seems to have held good for most of the better-placed faithful, though some may have suffered considerable loss through financial pressures, for which retaliation was not provided under the Bedouin code of honour.

Two years after the mission was made public, some Muslims (about eighty) began to emigrate to Christian Abyssinia, across the Red Sea, where they could expect (and did find) asylum among monotheists. A few became Christian and stayed there, but most subsequently returned to Mecca or (later) to Medina when Muḥammad was established in that oasis. Their motive was in part to escape from persecution but they may also have been expected to form a base for some sort of wider plan envisaged by Muhammad.[20] Such a project would be the first instance of Muḥammad's attempting measures on a political plane toward a solution of the dilemmas presented by his becoming a prophet; in any case, the adventure illustrates how quickly his followers were becoming an autonomous group, with its own destinies as such.

Perhaps three years after the mission was made public, the other clans of the Quraysh, failing to persuade the Banû Hâshim to cease protectingMuḥammad, joined in a boycott of the Banû Hâshim, refusing to have commercial relations with them. The Banû Hâshim held out against this for two or three years till there arose sufficient disunity among the Quraysh for the boycott to be given up. But shortly after this, in about 619, Abû-Ṭâlib, Muḥammad's protector, died and Muḥammad's position with the Banû Hâshim became more questionable. At the same time, he lost his wife Khadîjah, who had been a major spiritual support to him. Muḥammad began taking active steps to find a more satisfactory base for his work.

A visit to neighbouring Ṭâ'if proved fruitless; he was abused and driven away. Returning to Mecca, he was able only with difficulty to assure himself protection from families outside the Banû Hâshim (now, it seems, led by his enemy Abû-Lahab) so as to remain provisionally in Mecca. He seems to have been greatly discouraged. He was gratified to feel that a number of jinn (sprites) who happened to be listening as he recited the Qur'ân were converted, and he seems to have made a good deal of a dream vision which he was granted, in which he visited Heaven, or possibly Jerusalem, city of the prophets. (This vision was later greatly elaborated among Muslims, as the *mi'râj*, and given a central place in Muḥammad's legend.) Muḥammad's insistence on such things seems to have scandalized some of his followers and to have contributed to their defection during these years.

He may have regarded his mission, till then, as directed chiefly to his own people, the Quraysh, just as other prophets had been sent to their own people (though at all times any human being who was present was certainly included, for the message was in its nature universal). Clearly, however, most of the Arabs, being pagans and not monotheists, were equally in need of the message, and now he preached to all who would listen at the great fairs in the vicinity of Mecca. In 620, about a year after Khadîjah's death, he met (at 'Aqabah, on the pilgrimage) with a handful of converts from Yathrib (afterwards called Medina), an agricultural oasis about two hundred miles north of Mecca; the next year they returned with a few more and not only declared themselves Muslims but pledged themselves to obey Muḥammad in any wholesome command; in 622 six times as many were at hand to reinforce the pledge, promising Muḥammad and his Meccan followers protection if they came to Medina. In the same year, Muḥammad sent most of his followers, rather more

[20] For possible implications of the migration to Abyssinia, cf. Watt, *Muhammad at Mecca*, chap. V.2.

than seventy, to move one by one to Medina, and finally went himself. (This move, or 'migration', was called in Arabic the *Hijrah*.)

Pressure against the Muslims had been mounting in the last year or so. There was some sort of effort to prevent Muḥammad's leaving at the last when it was realized what was afoot—the Muslims subsequently, at least, interpreted it as a plot to kill him. Muḥammad and Abû-Bakr, his lieutenant, fled by night and hid in a cave till the search had slackened (away from their protectors at Mecca, but not yet at Medina, they would presumably have been fair game). Then they made the long trip secretly, till at the outskirts of Medina the local converts came to meet them and receive Muḥammad as their chief.

The Ummah achieves autonomy

To the Medinese, such a step was a solution to pressing problems. Medina had evidently been developed or restored as an agricultural oasis (notably raising date palms) by Jewish Arab tribes; apart from their religion, these tribes shared the same culture as the other Arabs, though presumably at least the nucleus had immigrated from farther north, originally being Aramaic-speakers from Syria. With the adoption of Judaism had come sufficient of the Jewish law to provide good order. In recent generations, however, other clans had settled there, still pagan, who had not adopted Judaism. Their Bedouin ethical system of 'honour' had plunged the settled clans into ever more intense feuds; in Muḥammad's time they had lined up in two main tribes, 'Aws and Khazraj, who had come to a deadlock such that no man was safe outside the limits of his own fields. Living among Jewish tribes, even the pagans at Medina had come to recognize and no doubt to respect monotheistic religion. In Muḥammad's message, many saw an opportunity to adopt a monotheistic cult of their own which would at the same time introduce a new type of moral sanction and a neutral leader to represent and apply it as arbiter of the deadlocked quarrels. Thus they added to the public which was proving capable of responding to the Revelation. Even those pagans who were little interested in the new faith could welcome a neutral arbiter to restore peace.[21]

To Muḥammad, the move to Medina was not merely an escape from an untenable immediate position in Mecca. It was an opportunity to build a new order of social life such as the development of his faith had more and more obviously demanded. The cult of Allâh as Creator demanded, in the first instance, a personal devotion to moral purity; but personal purity implied a just social behaviour: generosity to the weak and curbing the licence of the strong.

[21] On conditions in Medina and the relations among Jews and pagans, cf. Wellhausen, 'Medina vor dem Islam', in *Skizzen und Vorarbeiten*, vol. 4 (Berlin, 1889); but his assurance that most of the Jews must have come from Palestine seems based partly on racialist presuppositions. Clearly, conversion to Judaism meant a sharper break with Bedouin tradition than did conversion to Christianity, but descendants of converts were capable of acquiring both settled habits and Talmudic learning.

Moreover, it was fully recognized that a person's moral life is usually less a function of his good resolutions than of the level of actual expectations around him. It must be society and not just individuals that should be reformed. The Qur'ân makes it sufficiently clear that the new way is for everyone, not just for moral heroes, by praising almost as much those who urge others to a virtue as those who practice it themselves. The new life must be lived by a society at large.

This called for more than exhortation to be good; it became clear that Muslims could not rest content to be irrelevant deviants in a society founded on contrary principles. Sooner or later, the challenge of the Qur'ân was bound to require the creation of a just polity as the natural outgrowth and context of the personal purity it required. Obviously, no pagan who did not accept the challenge could have remained neutral to such claims in the long run. Whatever the personal circumstances, the pagan Quraysh could not have tolerated a movement which attacked the principles of their social order and suggested an alternative sort of moral sanction for behaviour and especially for social authority. So long as the Muslims stayed as a minority in Mecca there would have been deadlock at best.

Muḥammad and his followers had been gradually emerging in Mecca as something like a new tribal formation (possibly, on this level, analogous to what happened when the Quraysh had been first gathered by Quṣayy). Each man retained his loyalties to his inherited clan; but (and here Quṣayy's example was departed from) he was coming to have overriding loyalties to the new grouping, based not on family ties but on individual acceptance of the faith which Muḥammad preached. The word Muḥammad used for the new grouping was *Ummah*—a word which he had used of a people to which a prophet had been sent (such as the Meccans), but which now was applied to such of that people as did respond to the prophet and so formed a new community with him. In the negotiations with the Medinese Muslims, Muḥammad claimed explicitly an authority over the religious community which had become in-increasingly implicit already even among his Meccan followers. He did not yet make the same demands among non-Muslims, of course, but the political autonomy of the Muslims allowed them to establish at least a certain level of social expectations among themselves. Moreover, as *ḥâkim*, judge-arbiter, among even those Medinese who were not Muslims, Muḥammad was able to extend something of the new spirit outside the Ummah proper even before the whole of Medina merged into the Islamic group.

The life of the new Ummah was to be marked by a pervasive new moral tone, derived from the individual's relationship to God, but maintained (as moral standards must be, save perhaps in the case of 'moral athletes') by the expectations prevalent in the group as a whole and given form in their corporate life. The new tone was contrasted to a moral orientation associated with both Bedouin pastoral life and with the settled Bedouin pagans. These had stressed, above all, individual and group pride and point of honour—

pride in birth, pride in one's wealth or prowess, pride which led, when crossed, to an unremitting, pitiless vengefulness; to a passionate and heedless (if sometimes magnificent) pursuit of self-centred, inherently trivial ends. Even those who might prefer a different way of responding to life were dragged into the pattern by the voice of public opinion, urging vengeance as the most practical means of justice, and praising transient delights of drink and sex in which to forget the pettiness and pointlessness of a life which time would sweep away.

To the heedless pettiness of men, which Islam presented as sheer ingratitude (*kufr*) to their Creator, Islam contrasted humility, generosity, and a serious purpose of carrying out the demands of God in a pure life. To the passionate vengefulness of men, Islam contrasted patient restraint and mercifulness. Some of these virtues had, indeed, been recognized and extolled by the wiser among the Bedouin, though humility and restraint in carnal pleasures had not; but the accent in any case had been different. Islam was to reinforce in its community life the godly virtues, provide more just alternatives to the relentless feud, and remove all persuasion to what were newly felt as vices.

The contrast was summed up in key words. The old heedlessness of God was termed *kufr*, 'ingratitude' or 'denial', to be replaced by submission to Him, *islâm;* the old harsh passions were summed up as *jâhiliyyah*, to be replaced by trust and faithfulness to God, *îmân*. (In later times, *kufr* became a theological term for whatever was incompatible with Islam, and *Jâhiliyyah* became a historical term for the age before Islam appeared.)[22] And the new moral order, like the old, was not to be merely a personal ideal but the effective norm of a total, responsible, social environment.

When it was disentangled from the clans at Mecca, and so could form a political unit of its own, the Muslim Ummah at first still took an essentially tribal form. In Medina, Muḥammad was the acknowledged commander of the Muslims, both those of Mecca (called *Muhâjirûn*, 'emigrants') and those of Medina (called *Anṣâr*, 'helpers'). He was also, more generally, arbiter among all the social groups at Medina. This position was established in a document (sometimes rather grandiosely called the 'constitution of Medina') in which the mutual obligations of the adhering clans were set forth, and all Medina was included by way of clan alliances. But at first his primary role lay among the Muslims as such and especially his own Meccans. His Meccans, the Muhâjirûn, lacked resources when they arrived; they became the guests of the Medinese Anṣâr, with certain of whom, to begin with, he paired them as brothers. Almost immediately, he began sending the Muhâjirûn out to raid the trading caravans of the Quraysh.

Raiding was, of course, the normally received procedure whereby the less well-placed Arab tribes recouped their disadvantages from the more fortun-

[22] On the relation between the moral tone of the pagan Arabs and Islam, cf. Ignaz Goldziher, 'Muruwwa und Dîn', in his *Muhammedanische Studien*, vol. 1 (Halle, 1889); Watt, *Muhammad at Mecca*, chap. III, 3, 4; Toshihiko Izutsu, *The Structure of Ethical Terms in the Koran* (Keio University, 1959).

ately placed. In leaving Mecca, the Muhâjirûn had broken their ties with their own clans there, abandoning claims to protection by them; they now formed, in effect, a clan or tribe of their own; that they should raid (if they could) those with whom they no longer had any agreements was taken for granted. Muḥammad, however, felt the step nevertheless required justification in terms of the new moral orientation. He pointed out therefore that the Quraysh were not merely declining to become Muslims themselves; they were actively opposing the divine order with their persecution of Muslims and their interference with the public practice of Islam. This was not just a private grief of the Muhâjirûn, but a public cause on which the eternal fate of others hung; it was right to fight the Quraysh till they should no longer place obstacles in the way of those who might otherwise become Muslims.

In particular, there were two outstanding motives for launching the raids, which set them off from the normal Arab raiding. In the first place, they were a means, important if not absolutely necessary, for Muḥammad's own men to gain an independent economic position at Medina, without which the life and social order of the new community there must remain artificial. (Perhaps also such raids, once they became effective, might form an outlet for the passions of the Medinese, debarred henceforth from the old feuding; but it is doubtful if Muḥammad would have acknowledged such a motive as being independently valid.) Secondly, the raids were to humble the pride of the Quraysh, perhaps in anticipation of coming acts of divine displeasure—or even as part of those acts, as it might appear when fighting came to be commanded in the Qur'ân itself. It may have been that Muḥammad already had the aim of ruining their trade and reducing them to a recognition that in Islam they were meeting something bigger than they supposed, with which they must come to terms even to survive in the present life.

The first raids were unsuccessful. The first success was that of a small party which attacked (at Nakhlah, near Mecca) a caravan during a sacred truce month, killing one man and bringing home the booty. It is unclear how far Muḥammad was directly responsible for the violation of the truce month, but he may have anticipated it; the event proved to be a scandal at Medina, which was calmed only by a revelation in the Qur'ân that while violation of the truce was bad, persecution of the faith was worse and justified the violation. Muḥammad then allowed the booty to be accepted. This act deepened the breach between the Muslims and the Quraysh to a breach with the whole of pagan Arab culture, and particularly the Meccan system, of which the truce months were a primary symbol. The primacy of Islam over all old customs was asserted; in effect, no bond or tie of pagan society need hold, in the Islamic community, unless explicitly acknowledged anew within Islam. In the following years this principle was implemented consistently. Whatever crimes a man had been guilty of, even against Islam, when he adopted Islam the slate was wiped clean. And just as a Muslim could not be punished for what had gone before, so he could not profit by attachments with the past: he retained his own property, indeed, but could inherit nothing from a pagan relative. Thus the Ummah of Islam was proclaimed wholly independent.

Muḥammad's acceptance of the success at Nakhlah despite the qualms of his followers may be thought of as a mark of courageous consistency in which he discerned, without flinching, the complete implications of his mission and carried them through as occasion presented itself. Had he compromised here, he might well have been reducing his Ummah to the status, in practice, of but one more competing tribe within a common pagan moral framework. In the clarity and single-mindedness of aim here displayed surely lay much of his genius. At the same time, the inherent dilemma in Muḥammad's mission found here concrete expression. Through the prophet, transcendent truth was brought into men's and women's lives by being embodied in the work and fortunes of a given human community, which was limited by given circumstances. It could thus take practical effect. But the raid at Nakhlah was not simply a break with a superstitious custom, hallowed by pagan cults but inconsistent with a new wider truth. Since there is no indication that the Muslims had previously declared or implied that they would not respect the truce months, it was also an outright act of treachery which Muḥammad accepted, and perhaps had to accept, as occasion for consummating the moral independence of Islam.[23]

Muḥammad establishes a new polity

The success at Nakhlah seems to have encouraged a large turnout at the next raid, in which many Anṣâr Muslims from Medina also participated. The caravan from Syria which was its object got by safely, but the raiders, some 315 men, found themselves at the wells of Badr face to face with a relieving force from Mecca at least twice their size. Good generalship on Muḥammad's part, and presumably good discipline among the Muslims as well as high enthusiasm, won them a smashing victory. Several leading men of the Quraysh, opponents of Islam, as well as many lesser Meccans were dead or prisoners. Muḥammad regarded the victory of so few, over a numerous foe of such high prestige, as being the result of divine intervention. It seemed to seal the independence of the Muslim community and its ability to survive, and indeed to fulfill some foretaste of the doom with which the Quraysh were threatened. In later years. to have been present at Badr, at the first triumph of Islam as an organized body, was like a patent of nobility. Later converts might be attracted by success, but the men of Badr had been converted when Islam was weak and they had held firm during its leanest years.

Henceforth the other Arabs, especially the nomads, must regard the Mus-

[23] On moral implications of the Nakhlah raid, cf. W. Montgomery Watt, *Muhammad at Medina* (Oxford, 1956), chap. I.3; also X.2.But the sacredness of the truce months was surely not merely a matter of superstitious fear of retribution.

lims as challengers to and potential inheritors of the prestige and the political role of the Quraysh. Muḥammad found himself in a position to attack some Bedouin tribes which proved unfriendly; thus he gained booty and also a freer hand against the Quraysh. And within a year a whole Quraysh caravan had been captured. From then on, a primary activity of the community was raiding and warfare, as its influence (and, later, conversion to Islam itself) was extended. The warfare culminated eventually, but did not end, with the surrender of Mecca itself.

Directly after Badr, Muḥammad expelled the Jewish clan of Banû Qaynuqâʿ from Medina. This was in part an admission of defeat and a countermeasure thereto. Muḥammad had won his converts among the gentile clans and his first authority was in the gentile sector of Medina. But he had always expected that monotheists, whether Christians or Jews, ought to welcome his message and give him support in his work among the pagans. But just as serious Christians could not accept a timeless monotheism stripped of the Incarnation, so most Jews could not accept a universalism in which their history as the chosen people lost its unique significance. Moreover, Muḥammad's versions of Biblical, Talmudic, and apocryphal Christian stories were too patently incoherent, and sometimes garbled, to win the respect of those who already possessed the older sacred books. There was little to encourage them to hail Muḥammad as prophet even to their pagan neighbours.

When Muḥammad found that the Jews of Medina denied his prophethood and ridiculed his misapprehensions of Biblical stories, he was deeply disappointed. More, he was threatened. As interpreters of monotheism, the Jews had undoubted seniority over the Muslims and were already respected in Medina. As long as they challenged his authority, a single bad turn of fortune might make his position untenable. Together with numerous smaller groups of Jews, there were four important clans which were mostly or entirely Jewish; of these, two held some of the best date groves in the oasis and a third, the Banû Qaynuqâʿ, comprised the craftsmen and retail tradesmen in the market at the heart of Medina. These three latter clans, at least, were in a sufficiently strong position to hold aloof from Muḥammad's arrangements. Muḥammad took advantage of a fracas between some Muslims and the Banû Qaynuqâʿ (in which it chanced that a Muslim had begun the violence). He besieged them in their strongholds till they agreed to leave Medina with their property, but to abandon their arms. (Expulsion or migration of whole clans, either within an oasis or to great distances, had been of quite frequent occurrence in Arabia and at Medina in particular, as an outcome of tension among neighbours.) Numbering perhaps two thousand adults, the Banû Qaynuqâʿ migrated to Jewish settlements further north.

The expulsion of the Banû Qaynuqâʿ consolidated within Medina the prestige Muḥammad had gained at Badr vis-à-vis the Quraysh and the Arabs at large. He did not leave it at that. From this point on, at least, he was building no longer just a new tribe but a more developed polity, in which both Muslims and non-Muslims at Medina were to be subsumed on the basis of their common social life. While adherence to his leadership, at least apart from the Muhâjirûn, remained as yet voluntary, and from time to time even some professing Muslims refused to go along with him, his position as general arbiter had taken on weight. He now uncontestedly spoke for Medina as a whole. His chief rival among the Medinese, Ibn-Ubayy, who had tried to intercede for the Banû Qaynuqâ', had been rudely discomfited. Islam, under Muḥammad's leadership, formed henceforth the ruling community in Medina and dissenters found themselves at best tolerated. We do not know when any given provision was inserted into the agreement called the 'constitution of Medina', but it was appropriate to the spirit of this period that it contained a ban on any Muslim's helping an infidel against another Muslim.

Not everyone who now proclaimed himself a Muslim was wholehearted. Ibn-Ubayy became the leader of a group whom Muḥammad called the 'waverers' (*munâfiqûn*, sometimes rendered 'hypocrites'), who gave Muḥammad trouble for several years. But he never gave them a chance to turn against him openly. It was soon expected that all those who had been pagans, at least, would now be Muslims; and Jews were expected to recognize Muslim primacy. Meanwhile, the market place had become vacant, ready to be occupied by Muḥammad's Meccans, who could thus gain a surer economic position.

The new position appeared most clearly in the cult. In the quarrel with the Jews it became clear that Islam not only was distinct from paganism but, even within monotheism, formed an independent religious system, parallel to and distinct from Judaism and Christianity. Whereas up to this point Muḥammad had expected his cult to conform by and large to that of the Jews (for instance, in praying toward Jerusalem and in observing certain fasts), now the Muslim cult was set off markedly. Learning that Abraham was considered the common ancestor of Israelites and of Ishmaelite Arabs, he pointed out that Abraham was faithful to God though he was neither Jewish nor Christian, having lived before either Moses or Jesus. Muḥammad's cult was to be like that of Abraham.

This decision sprang from two principles both very marked in the Qur'ân, which now came into their own. First was the principle of worshipping God alone. Pure religion need be bound by no communal limitations—as Abraham himself was bound by none. Muḥammad proclaimed himself the *ummî* prophet, that is, the prophet of those who had no sacred book—who belonged to none of the established religious communities. This referred in the first instance to his being an Arab. But it carried implications. The Irano-Semitic dilemma of conflicting religious communities, which could become specially clear to the thinking person in that mission field which was Bedouin Arabia, was to receive its solution through a community that rejected the exclusivities of the old communities and went back to the very font of the monotheistic tradition. In principle, one cult was as good as another; wherever one turned his face, the

Qur'ân pointed out, there was God. A cult was instituted only to meet human requirements; what mattered, as the Qur'ân tirelessly stressed, was a person's acceptance of God Himself, not his adherence to anything lesser (e.g. sûrah VI, 160 ff.). This casual attitude toward any particular formulation of cult or law is illustrated in the Qur'ânic assurance that not only earlier revelations were accommodated to their people's needs, but even within the present revelation, God may set aside one verse of the Qur'ân, and its injunctions with it, and then a better will be given in its place.

Yet once instituted, of course, a command could not be ignored by those who adhered to the new community; and to worship God properly, one had to be in a guided community. The independence of the Meccan religious system and the central place in it of the Creator-god Allâh now proved a point of departure for a new interpretation of monotheism that might transcend the communal divisions of the older monotheistic traditions in a concretely practical way. Abraham and Ishmael were naturally presumed to be the founders of the chief shrine of Ishmaelite Arabia, the Ka'bah at Mecca, which was therefore in origin dedicated only to the true God; the tribal fetishes there were subsequent contaminations. One of the sacred stones near the Ka'bah was—then or later—specially dedicated to Abraham (the *Maqâm Ibrâhîm*). The bowings and prostrations of the formal worship, the *ṣalât,* were commonly done at least three times a day in unison, normally at the prayer ground (mosque) at the Prophet's home. Now Muslims were told to perform this worship in the direction not of Jerusalem but of the Ka'bah. They were also to look forward to performing the ḥajj, the annual pilgrimage in the Meccan area, as a ceremony instituted in principle by Abraham. Elements of the cult were derived also, however, from the experience of the new community itself. The month of Ramaḍân, in which the Qur'ân is said to have been first revealed and in which the battle of Badr was certainly won, was likewise instituted as a time of fasting superseding the time of the Jewish fasts. Islam thus became ritually independent of previous monotheisms.

The essentials of the new society were the new relations in it between human beings and God and between one human being and another. But the society was held together by the Prophet; his position was indispensable and unique. The chief of a tribe, in view of his authority as commander in war, and also as responsible for various obligations in maintaining the tribe's position and honour, conventionally received a fourth of the booty taken in a tribal raid. Muḥammad, in a somewhat analogous position, received a fifth of any booty, which he was to use for community purposes such as the relief of the poor or the conciliation of new converts, and over the dispensing of which he had complete authority. Also like some of the greater tribal chiefs, who had numerous wives, Muḥammad was authorized to have numerous simultaneous wives beyond the four to which his followers were limited. Muḥammad seems to have used his marriages to cement political relations, so that this privilege was, like the fifth of the booty, essentially a political one. (Only one of his wives was a virgin when he married her, 'Â'ishah, and in no case are social and political reasons for a marriage not traceable.)

In harmony with their importance, his wives were to receive special respect from the public. They were to live secluded, receiving their visitors (who were many, on account of their supposed influence with Muḥammad) only from behind a curtain, rather than face to face. After Muḥammad's death they were not to marry again but were to be honoured as mothers of all the faithful. Despite their political significance and the social hedge with which he had to surround them, his wives meant much to Muḥammad personally as well. Their various quarrels produced his gravest personal emotional crises; the trace of more than one of his marital complications is left in the Qur'ân. None of them ever took the place of Khadîjah; in any case, he tried to treat them all on an equal basis without favouritism. But his best-beloved was Abû-Bakr's daughter, 'Â'ishah, whom he married at nine years old and who was always the liveliest of them all. With her he seems always to have unbent. Indeed, despite his special position, Muḥammad seems to have lived a quite simple and modest life without any luxury, by and large accessible and affable with the lowliest, delighting in laughter and in children.

An attack on Muḥammad was felt as an attack on Islam, which he represented. Muḥammad had deeply resented a number of individuals who had abused him publicly, especially in verse. (Poetry was held in great respect by the Arabs, being felt not only as the primary means of building one's own and destroying one's opponent's morale, but even as something of almost magical powers.) By existing Arab custom, Muḥammad owed no obligation to persons with whom he had no treaty. Shortly after the victory at Badr, he encouraged some of his followers to assassinate, among these detractors, a certain man and a woman to whom the assassins were closely related (and on whose account, therefore, they were not subject to blood-feud).

Beginnings of a new society and culture

Supreme within its own territory and spiritually independent, Islam could begin to develop its own social order in earnest. It was scarcely as yet an independent culture in most respects, to be sure; but increasingly many aspects of culture among the Muslims were differentiated in the new social context. This was sometimes a matter of detail. Muslims were forbidden pork (here Bedouin and Jewish feeling seem to have converged) and gaming and intoxicants or at least the imported wine (this was in part a measure of social discipline).[24] Most noticeable was a new system of assuring the security of the

[24] The Bedouin may have had no objection to wild boar meat, but domesticated pig was never suited to pastoralism and probably always had peasant associations. The history of prejudice about animals like the pig and the dog will not be satisfactorily elucidated till we are able to see how probably diverse motives converged and were reinforced by continuing circumstances; circumstances which can include ethnic pride, but cannot include any inherent racial sentiment, too often invoked by scholars at present.

weak against the strong. Feuding among Muslim clans was forbidden and equal penalties strictly proportioned to the offences were substituted, to be exacted under the eye of Muḥammad as God's representative. At the same time, the financially weak were also provided for by the collection of *zakât*, a tax on possessions. This 'alms' tax grew out of a practice of alms-giving for self-purification, *zakât;* it was organized in Medina as the financial basis of group life (along with Muḥammad's fifth of the booty) as well as to serve individual justice: its proceeds were normally used at Muḥammad's discretion, like the fifth of the booty, either for the common cause or for the needs of the poor, the traveller, and others in like case. Both the legally fixed criminal penalties and the centrally distributed alms helped give individuals a status independent of clan associations, and so could foster individualistic culture traits.

Perhaps at the heart of any social structure is its family law. Certainly in the Medina community it was in this field that the most explicit innovations were made; so far as the Qur'ân contains legislation, it largely regards family relationships. The regulations were made piecemeal during the rest of Muḥammad's life, but here again the tendency was persistently toward asserting individual rights on the basis of equality before God. We are not perfectly acquainted with marriage practices among the pre-Islamic pagan Arabs, but it is clear they varied greatly. In some cases the man acquired the woman very nearly as property and brought her to live with his own clan; in some cases the man seems to have retained but a casual relation to his woman, who remained completely dependent on her parental clan.[25] What dignity either a man or a woman had in the family relationship depended on status at birth, family circumstances, and wealth.

At the centre of Muḥammad's family arrangements were the Qur'ânic rules on marriage, which universalized one existing type of Arab marriage, with modifications. The nuclear family—man, wife, and children—was stressed as a self-sufficient unit, with every marriage given equal status at law. This was largely achieved through strengthening the position of the individual adult male. The man retained wide authority over the wife to the exclusion of either his family or hers. The children were to be the husband's, who was responsible for maintenance of wife and children. Inheritance was to be primarily within the immediate family, not diffused through the clan. The degrees of relationship within which marriage could not take place were stressed and even multiplied—with the effect that it was less easy for a married couple to be absorbed by multiple ties within a wider household; thus relationship by fosterage

[25] Watt has some suggestive, but not altogether proven, theses on the meaning of traces of matrilocal practices at Medina, *Muhammad at Medina*, chap. VIII.2. For a more general discussion of family law, see J. Wellhausen, 'Die Ehe bei den Arabern', in *Nachrichten von der königlichen Gesellschaft der Wissenschaften zu Göttingen*, no. 11 (1893), pp. 431–81. Corrections by Gertrude H. Stern, *Marriage in Early Islam* (London, 1939), are not always reliable; in particular, her sampling could provide little evidence for absence of polygyny, which is everywhere rare save among the wealthy.

(many of the Quraysh had their children nursed by foster mothers, that is, wet-nurses) was made equal to relationship by blood. At the same time, the integrity of the natural family was protected against the introduction of fictive relationships which might be independent of whether children had been reared together: adoptive relationship, which the Arabs frequently created between adults, was allowed no status at law. If a man formed more than one sexual partnership—as sometimes happened among the wealthiest Arabs, as elsewhere—each partnership must be given equal status with the first, up to the number of four; each marriage, that is, must have the same tight-knit character. More casual unions (with free women) were strictly forbidden, save possibly in special cases.

At the same time, wives and daughters were given a stronger position than they had had in those Arab marriages on which the Muslim form of marriage was modeled. In Bedouin society the man had often given the bride's family a 'bride-wealth', *mahr*, when taking his bride. In Mecca this had often been given to the bride herself and this became the Muslim law. A substantial mahr helped assure the woman's position. Under Islam, part of the male prerogative as provider for the family was the right of divorce (though women also might —at least later—sometimes initiate divorce); but if a man divorced he could not regain his mahr. Nor could he make use of his wife's property during the marriage, but must maintain her from his own resources. Both wives and daughters inherited from their men, though sons, having to maintain new families of their own, were given twice as much as daughters. The insistence on the personal dignity of every individual, male or female, was illustrated in the prohibition of infanticide, which had borne especially on infant girls.

In one case Muḥammad and the Qur'ân permitted an inequality of status in the family to continue, though mitigated. As everywhere till recently, men and women could own other men and women as property, though even such slaves were allowed certain rights. Muslims were not permitted to enslave Muslims, but outsiders could be enslaved. A man was permitted, in particular, to take his female slaves as concubines, despite Muḥammad's general disapproval of other than strict marital unions. Slaves were for the most part war captives, commonly children who had been sold far away from their tribes and so had no family when they grew up except that of their owners. Since in Arabia no one could well exist without family and clan, slaves could not usually expect to separate from their owners altogether; what they could look to was an improvement of their status within the owner's family. This was encouraged; the freeing of slaves was suggested as a common penance for breaches of duty; then the ex-slave would be freely attached to his former owner. But Muḥammad did not compromise the principle of the solid nuclear family by encouraging slaves to be adopted into it and receive the full right of sons.

One further aspect of family law received special attention in the Qur'ân, personal etiquette. The privacy of the home was to be respected and a modest decorum was to be observed by both men and women outside the home.

Though the rules laid down in the Qur'ân were not very precise, they served to support respect for individuals in their independent private lives. After Muḥammad's time, however, these rules became the starting point of a social code of very different import.

The Qur'ân and the community experience

As the Muslim community developed, the character of the Qur'ânic messages altered. The earlier portions of the Qur'ân commonly have an ecstatic character, suggesting with great beauty the solemn majesty of the divine and pointing up the awesomeness of the Revelation itself. These lyric solemnities gave way to exalted but often rather prosaic exhortation and commentary. The Qur'ân served at once as the inspiration of Muslim life and the commentary on what was done under that inspiration; its message transcended any particular circumstances yet at the same time served as a running guide to the community experiences, often down to seemingly petty details. It was filled with repeated exhortations to support the community efforts, notably the military excursions, and with regulations of community procedure, especially in regard to marriage. Even particular crises were sometimes resolved by decisions on disputed points or justifications of lines of action. At one point, Muḥammad's best-beloved wife, 'Â'ishah, was accused of infidelity to him by a faction hostile to her, in circumstances where no judgment, pro or con, could rest on other than an estimate of her character. After a time of agonized doubt, the Qur'ân pronounced in her favour. But at the same time it brought a rule requiring four witnesses in such an accusation—and upbraiding those who had spread the cruel accusation without proof. A factional episode was written into the Qur'ân: and with it, moral observations on the episode which carried beyond it.

The Qur'ân did not generally initiate social policies as such. Here it was left to Muḥammad personally to act. The 'constitution of Medina', which settled the position of the several elements in Medina when Muḥammad established himself there, was the work of Muḥammad, not of the Qur'ân. Time and again, crucial decisions were left to Muḥammad in his own person. Even at the crisis of Ḥudaybiyah when, as we will see, the Quraysh stopped a much heralded pilgrim expedition to Mecca, and Muḥammad's wisdom was doubted by his closest followers, the Qur'ân did not intervene to dictate a course of action. It concerned itself especially with individuals and with their individual consciences. For instance, it did not order the burdensome expedition to Mu'tah (toward Syria), which most Muslims would have liked to resist. But it dealt individually with the cases of three slackers who had failed to join the expedition despite being sincere Muslims. Nevertheless, it steadily supported Muḥammad's policies, solving problems that arose out of them—for instance, the distribution of booty—and above all it urged the supreme importance of loyalty to the common cause as this was determined by Muḥammad.

Throughout the Qur'ân, the transcendent point of reference in all this human confusion was kept vividly before the mind, and a tone of grandeur was maintained. In the whole monotheistic tradition, on its more populistic side, ethics tended to be thought of in terms of the market—thus the protection of orphans was, in the first instance, protection of their property; hence the Qur'ân freely uses market terminology—partly by way of familiar analogy (the faithful strikes a good bargain with God), but partly by way of introducing the transcendent inextricably into daily life. But the manner of using mundane references ennobled them. Even when the question of 'Â'ishah's adultery is discussed, for instance, the very wording of the Qur'ân —word order and proportion, overtones, sonority—combines to keep the discussion on such a level that the dignity carries the sordidness with it, rather than the reverse; a quality that hardly can come through in translation. The wholeness of its vitality gives the Qur'ân a certain self-sufficiency. As the embodiment of an independent Islam, the Qur'ân needed no supplementing from the older revelations. It became a many-sided, vivid, and intimate possession mirroring the spiritual hopes and needs of each of the faithful and above all bringing to ever new focus their common destiny as it unfolded.

Because of its intimate interaction with the day-to-day destinies of the community, the Qur'ân cannot be read as a discursive book, for abstract information or even, in the first instance, for inspiration. The sequence of its bits and pieces is notoriously often lacking in clearly logical order or development. Even the stories it recounts come not as consecutive narratives but rather in the form of reminders of episodes which are often presumed to be known to the audience—reminders which point up the implications of the episode for faith with little concern otherwise for continuity—as if he who did not know the story should ask someone to tell it him before approaching the Qur'ân's commentary on it. Hence many non-Muslims have found it a jumbled and incoherent mass, ridden with repetitions, and have been at a loss to fathom why Muslims regard it as supremely beautiful. It must not be read through but rather be participated in: it must be recited, as an act of self-dedication and of worship. The Qur'ân presents at every point one great challenge: to accept the undertaking of faith. To recite it truly is to be accepting and affirming that undertaking. Then its beauty can be responded to line by line and one will delight in the juxtaposition, whatever the immediate subject, of all its main themes within any given passage. The repetitious phrases remind one of the total context in which a given message must be understood: in even a small part of the Qur'ân, the act of worship can be complete.

By and large, the Qur'ân did not emphasize the mysterious or the exceptional after the earliest period. It never lost the sense of majesty, indeed. Even the relatively late 'light verses' of the Sûrah (Chapter) of Light, revealed at Medina, illustrate an intense aspect of Muḥammad's piety: they liken God to an ethereal, supernally pure Light in images which can suggest a true mystical experience. Yet the dominant tone of Muḥammad's piety was to suffuse everyday life with a powerful sense of transcendently divine requirements. In the same Sûrah of Light, side by side with the most lyrical descriptions of divine luminosity and of the desperate state of those who have lost divine guidance, come simple exhortations, 'Perform the ṣalât, pay the zakât, and obey the Messenger; perhaps so you will find mercy. Do not think that those who are ungrateful [to God] can frustrate [Us] on the earth; their sheltering place is the Fire, a bad destination'. And then immediately come details to encourage propriety in the household—bringing a sober, sensible discipline to a community of ordinary people: 'You who are faithful, have those who are in your possession [slaves] and those who have not reached puberty ask you leave at three times [before coming in]: before the dawn ṣalât, and when you take off your clothes at midday, and after the evening ṣalât, three times of privacy [lit., nakedness] for you. Neither you nor they are at fault, apart from then, when going about among yourselves. So God makes clear to you [His] signs. And God is knowing, wise.'

In the opening sûrah of the Qur'ân, the Fâtiḥah, we find a typically sober expression of the community's reverent hope and fear of God:

In the name of God, the Merciful, the Compassionate: Praise belongs to God, Lord of all being; the Merciful, the Compassionate; Master of Judgment Day. Thee we serve, on Thee we call for help. Guide us in the straight path, the path of those whom Thou art bounteous to, not those whom anger falls on, nor those who go astray.

Muḥammad has been called 'the prophet armed'. This scarcely distinguishes him from a number of other prophets, beginning with Moses. It is more helpful to say that he was the prophet of the Ummah, of the confessional community. The religious community had moved increasingly toward becoming the framework of all high culture between Nile and Oxus. Despite his rejection of the ultimacy of any one community's law—or perhaps because of the creative freedom which this insight allowed him in building a new and purer community form, it was Muḥammad's achievement to fulfill this communal tendency at least in a single instance. His community at Medina formed nearly the total framework of culture and society there. But the regional tendency could be thus fulfilled at all only because Muḥammad's community was not designed simply to redeem the elect from the world, leaving to the Devil those who failed to respond to its vision. It was designed to transform the world itself through action in the world.

But such a vision led inevitably to the sword. When those whose interests will suffer by reform also wield power, maintaining jointly sufficient force to put down any individual objections, reform will require changing the basis of power. In the twentieth century, Gândhî has brought to the fore methods of creative non-violence for producing basic changes in social power. But short of these methods, a serious intention of social reform has commonly implied at least readiness on the part of the reformers to use physical compulsion to meet and overcome the compulsion used by those already in power. That is, it has implied readiness to wage war—and to commit all the violence and deceit this necessarily entails.

It is not just a Christian squeamishness, I think, that points to Muḥammad's military measures as a central problem in his prophethood. Every virtue carries with it its own characteristic defects, every perception of truth is accompanied by its own temptations to falsehood. In any tradition, greatness is in part to be measured by success in overcoming the peculiar failings which necessarily accompany the peculiar excellences of the tradition. Christianity has its own pitfalls. A peculiar test of Islam lies in how Muslims can meet the question of war. In the loyalty and risk of warfare, a man used to find the supreme virtue of dedication to a goal beyond himself to the point of readiness to give up his life. But warfare—apart from the acts of individual injustice it necessarily involves (since individuals are treated as elements in a mass)—is at the same time the supreme expression of that claim to exclusive validity for one's own position, which must be fatal to the open search for truth. Such a claim to exclusivity has been, indeed, a standing temptation of all the monotheistic communities. Muḥammad's prophethood, in fulfilling the monotheistic tendency toward a total religious community, at the same time left his community confronted with that temptation to a spirit of exclusivity that went with any vision of a total community and that received appropriate expression in warfare. The resulting problems came to form a persistent theme of Muslim history.

III

The Early Muslim State, 625–692

Muḥammad had created a new local polity, founded on his prophetic vision. But almost immediately that polity took on far-reaching international dimensions. Very soon it was contesting power within Arabia not only with the Quraysh but with both the Byzantine and the Sâsânian empires. Having through these contests, made itself a general Arab polity, in the succeeding two generations it extended its sphere over the neighbouring lands in monumental struggles between the Muslim Arabs and the two imperial powers. These the Arabs replaced, forming an established empire and organizing in Arab and Islamic terms the life of the whole region from Nile to Oxus as well as much of the west Mediterranean basin. The campaigns which created the Arab empire were epic achievements.

But decisive struggles were equally required among the Arabs themselves at each step in the formation of the empire. Only so could what started as a loose association in the Ḥijâz, built around a charismatic individual, be transformed into a massive and permanent state administering a complex agrarianate civilization. At every turn, crucial decisions were made determining the character which the Islamic polity was to take for the future. Ultimately, this character, in turn, determined what impact Islam was to have on the society it had conquered. It was the internal development which ensured that the conquests should have any permanent significance.

Muḥammad builds an Arab commonwealth between the Byzantine and Sâsânian empires

While Muḥammad was creating a new social order at Medina, he was also actively extending his influence beyond his chosen oasis. Indeed, it was this militancy that both made possible and, at least in some measure, formed the character of the Medina society. As can be seen from the chronology of Muḥammad's lifetime, once he was established at Medina decisive events followed one another very quickly. The relatively slow preparation at Mecca bore fruit with great rapidity, first at Medina itself and then at Mecca and in all Bedouin Arabia.

The Quraysh were duly alarmed at the position Muḥammad had achieved at Medina after Badr. It was clear that Muḥammad might possibly ruin their

Chronology of Muḥammad's Lifetime

Events in Muḥammad's Life	Related Events
?570 Birth of Muḥammad	**?575** Sâsânians occupy the Yemen, expelling Abyssinians
	579 Death of Khusraw Nûshîrvân, greatest Sâsânî monarch, leaving his empire at war with Romans
?580 Confederacy of the Fudûl formed in Mecca to counterbalance more powerful clans	**580** Ghassânîs, Byzantine-sponsored Arabs, burn Ḥîrah, capital of Sâsânî-sponsored Lakhmid Arab kingdom in the Iraq desert
?585–590 War of Fijâr—Quraysh involved in a breach of a sacred month in fighting Bedouin	
?590— 'Uthmân b. Ḥuwayrith attempts (in vain) to lead Mecca under Byzantine paramountcy	**582–602** Reign of Mauritius, Roman emperor, who bolsters the crumbling empire; brings the Ghassânîs in Syrian desert under more direct control
?595 Muḥammad marries Khadîjah; four daughters from this marriage	**589–628** Reign of Khusraw Parviz, Sâsânî monarch
	591 After a revolt, Khusraw is restored by the Romans, with whom he makes peace
	602 Lakhmid Arab kingdom put under control of a Sâsânî resident; soon after, it breaks up
	602–610 Phocas, incompetent general, overthrows Mauritius and is attacked by Khusraw
610 (or earlier) Muḥammad has first revelation	**610–641** Reign of Heraclius, who reorganizes Roman empire
	?611 Day of Dhû Qâr: an Arab tribal group defeats a Sâsânian force near Ḥirah
613 (or earlier) First public preaching	**612–614** Sâsânians occupy all Syria with aid of Jewish uprisings, remove the "True Cross" from Jerusalem to Sâsânian capital
615 (or earlier) Emigration of some Muslims to Abyssinia	**615** Sâsânians occupy Anatolia as far as Chalcedon opposite Constantinople
616–619 (or earlier) Boycott of the Banû Hâshim	
?617 Battle of Bu'âth at Yathrib (Medina)—stalemate between 'Aws and Khazraj groups	

?619 Death of Khadîjah and Abû-Ṭâlib; Muḥammad seeks support in Ṭâ'if	**619** Sâsânians occupy Egypt
621 First agreement at 'Aqabah with Medinan converts	
622 Larger agreement at 'Aqabah, and Hijrah to Medina	**622–625** Heraclius invades Sâsânian realm via the Armenian highlands
624 Expedition of Nakhlah, first bloodshed; Battle of Badr, Muslim victory against odds; Qaynuqâ' Jews expelled from Medina	
625 Battle of Uḥud: Quraysh fail to suppress Medina despite a victory; Jews of al-Naḍîr expelled	
626 First expedition to Dûmat al-Jandal, between Syria and the Iraq	**626** Avars from across the Danube, cooperating with Sâsânians, besiege Constantinople unsuccessfully
627 Meccans besiege Medina (campaign of al-Khandaq, the Ditch); Qurayẓah Jews are massacred	**627** Heraclius campaigns in Mesopotamia
628 Treaty of Ḥudaybiyah: truce with Quraysh; Khaybar Jews are subjugated	**628** Heraclius is victorious near Ctesiphon, Sâsânian capital, and Khusraw Parviz is assassinated; peace is made (status quo ante)
629 Peaceful pilgrimage to Mecca; first expedition to Mu'tah, toward Ghassân territory on Syrian border, following Sâsânian evacuation	**629** Sâsânians evacuate former Roman provinces; Romans refuse to renew subsidy to Ghassân in Syrian desert; plague carries off Khusraw's son—thereupon, 629–632, numerous claimants, including two women, enthroned in Sâsânian empire
630 Muslims occupy Mecca; defeat Bedouin at Ḥunayn; temporarily abandon siege of Ṭâ'if; massive expedition to Tabûk south of Syria, against Ghassân	**630** Heraclius restores the "True Cross" to Jerusalem
631 Deputations from many parts of Arabia accepting Islam, including Ṭâ'if and the Sâsânî-connected Yemen	
632 Muḥammad's "farewell" pilgrimage; Musaylimah appears as prophet in Yamânah in central Arabia; Muḥammad's death	**632** Yazdagird III succeeds to the Sâsânian throne

trade with Syria (and therefore with the Yemen as well); discredit them among the Bedouin, on whose respect their whole system depended; and make their position in barren Mecca untenable. The following year they organized a major campaign against Medina. They collected all available Meccan resources for the expedition. Arrived at the Medina oasis, they set about cutting the new grain, standing in the ear, and so forced the Medinese to abandon the strongholds to which they were inclined to retire and to come out to a pitched battle. Muḥammad took a strong position against a hill, Uḥud, at the northern side of the oasis. (Some of the 'waverers' preferred to sit the battle out, even so.) Muslim tradition has it that what promised to be a victory was changed to defeat because some of Muḥammad's men, posted to guard the flank, broke away against his orders to join in the plundering. A Meccan cavalry captain called Khâlid saw the opening and turned the tide. Muḥammad himself was wounded, but he held his ground and became the centre of a rally at the hill.

The Quraysh were overjoyed at their victory. Their women had followed the army to encourage it, as was common on major occasions, and they celebrated the victory after their fashion. Indulging in unusual excess, Hind, wife of the leader, Abû-Sufyân, tore the liver from the body of the fallen Ḥamzah, Muḥammad's uncle and an early convert, and bit into it; for Ḥamzah, one of the heroes at Badr, had there killed her father.

With the Muslim army still partially intact, however, and with some forces in Medina not yet engaged, the Quraysh evidently did not feel strong enough to attack the Medinese strongholds; they withdrew with some restoration of prestige but without subduing Muḥammad.[1] Muḥammad took advantage of their departure to exile a second Jewish clan, the Banû Naḍîr, whom he suspected of hostile designs; when they refused to leave on the same terms as the Banû Qaynuqâʿ, retaining ownership of their palm groves, he besieged their strongholds and forced them to leave and forfeit their palm groves also. Outside Medina, Muḥammad assured himself of the co-operation or at least neutrality of any tribal groups who stood to gain by friendliness with Medina, and he continued his raiding.

Two years later, when it became clear that Muḥammad was becoming stronger rather than weaker, the Quraysh made a still greater effort. They summoned all the Bedouin allies still left them, adding that strength to the full local strength of Mecca. They thus admitted that Meccan strength by itself could not put down Muḥammad. The campaign had to be decisive, or even the potential ultimate strength of the Quraysh would prove insufficient and prestige might be irrecoverably lost. The cumbrous coalition this time arrived

[1] Frants Buhl, *Muhammeds Liv* (Copenhagen, 1903), p. 251 (p. 256 of the German translation), suggests that the failure of the Quraysh to follow up Uḥud resulted from their lack of statesmanly vision, which let them be satisfied with formal vengeance for Badr. The case is conjectural, but in view of the leadership which some of the same Quraysh later took in major Muslim conquests, W. Montgomery Watt's analysis of the event followed here, is more convincing. Similar dilemmas arise in interpreting many events of Muḥammad's life.

later, after harvest, and the Medinese could not be lured from the more built-up part of the oasis and their strongholds there. To neutralize the Meccan and Bedouin cavalry (the farmers of Medina had few horses), Muḥammad had a ditch dug across the more vulnerable sectors. For about a month the ditch was successfully defended in a series of skirmishes and the fighting was restricted to what could be done on foot. Then some of the Bedouin were persuaded to abandon the Quraysh, and the whole company faded away. Muḥammad's blockade of Meccan trade was confirmed. From this point on, the Quraysh had defensively to await Muḥammad's moves.

The one Jewish clan in Medina that still resisted Islam and Muḥammad's leadership, the Banû Qurayẓah, had remained neutral during the defence of the ditch but had negotiated with the Quraysh. The exiled Jewish clans had been very active in supporting the Bedouin coalition in favour of the Quraysh. When the Quraysh departed, Muḥammad attacked the Banû Qurayẓah, refused to allow them to depart into exile like the Banû Naḍîr, and insisted on unconditional surrender. In Arab expectations (as among many ancient peoples), when enemy captives were taken, the women and children were enslaved but adult males were killed or held for ransom, as they were not dependable as slaves. Muḥammad now allowed no ransom but insisted that all the men, about six hundred, be killed.

Muḥammad had been able to set up a new moral order in Medina and had been able to defend it against the Quraysh attacks. But even so it was not self-sufficient. In a society where the Bedouin set the moral norms of all, a single oasis could not long maintain, by itself, quite contrary standards. More specifically, Mecca might for now be neutralized; but so long as the Meccan system still stood on its pagan foundations, any other system in the area was precarious. If Muḥammad was to create a totally responsible moral environment for his Muslims, he must Islamize the Meccan system itself. Consciously or not, what he proceeded to do would be sure to have that result—and more.

Muḥammad's first public preaching had taken place in the midst of a war between the Sâsânian empire and the Roman—a war in which at that time Syria was being occupied by the Sâsânians. The occupation was a major calamity for the Byzantines: not only was the territory devastated by the armies as they occupied it, but large numbers of the most crucial personnel were deported to old Sâsânian territory—for instance, many of the inhabitants of Jerusalem. Even beyond Syria, Constantinople itself was besieged. For the Quraysh, the occupation and devastation put in question their trade, of course, but also their neutrality. What had been a strong but distant empire had now moved closer—both in the Yemen and in Syria. What Muḥammad had in mind we cannot know, but if all his expeditions that now followed had been as successful as were those against the Quraysh, he would have been gathering into his system not only the elements which had gone to make up the Meccan system, but also the Arabs at the northern and southern ends of the main Meccan trade route—taking them away from either Abyssinian or Sâsânian or

Byzantine control and aligning them with the trading cities of the Ḥijâz. If this alignment had in fact succeeded, it would have created a power from Syria to the Yemen which might conceivably have defied both Byzantines and Sâsânians, even if the latter continued to hold the main part of Syria.

From his base in Medina, and presumably building upon the ties of alliance that already existed between various Medinese clans and some of the neighbouring Bedouin tribes, Muḥammad had been systematically building up Bedouin connections to rival those of the Quraysh. If not a full allegiance to Islam, the Bedouin accepted at least alliance with the Muslims and some recognition of Muḥammad's leadership. This was accomplished partly by direct conversion; partly, when some anti-Muslim act gave occasion, by punitive raiding (in parties ranging from a dozen to several hundred). But mostly it was by diplomacy. Muḥammad played on differences between factions in a clan or a tribe as well as offering the more direct advantages that might come from the friendship and perhaps the arbitration of a neutral Medina and, later, from sharing in the Muslim raids. Thus the system of security among clans, which he had built in Medina, was extended into considerable territory beyond the oasis.

The setback at Uḥud had not long interrupted this policy. Gradually it became clear that Muḥammad was aiming at converting all accessible Arabs to his faith, not merely those who had had links to the Quraysh; or at least at tying them to his society by bonds that would assure peace and security among all the Arabs, such as would be congenial to the new Islamic ideals; and most especially the Arabs to the north—toward Syria. The year after Uḥud, a Muslim expedition into the Syrian desert underlined his interest in the Syrian Arabs. Gaining them over would mean, in the first instance, disrupting the Meccan trade with Syria. But there was more. The tribes in that direction had been accustomed to varying degrees of Byzantine political influence, many becoming more or less Christian as well. Since Syria had passed under Sâsânian administration, the Sâsânian-Byzantine rivalry seemed ended in favour of the Sâsânians. Muḥammad, however, did not believe the Sâsânian victory was final. In the Qur'ân, their subsequent defeat was predicted at the very moment of their victory. (In 622, in fact, Heraclius had invaded the Sâsânian empire through the Armenian highlands; by 625, the year of Uḥud, he was ready to make a full push to the heart of the empire, where, indeed, by 628 he was entirely successful. He forced the Sâsânians to restore the status quo ante.) But meanwhile, Muḥammad's systematic efforts in the direction of Syria suggest that he was hoping ultimately not only to replace the Quraysh in the central Ḥijâz, but also (outbidding the Sâsânians) to replace Byzantium, and its Christian allegiance, among the Arabs further north.

In Medina, after the Meccan failure before the ditch, Muḥammad presided without open opposition over a society of Muslims, with a certain number of Jews remaining in a more or less autonomous dependent relation to the various Muslim clans. Among the tribes outside Medina, most were pagan and were increasingly required to become Muslims as a condition of entering into league with Muḥammad and into his security system. But, especially on the way to Syria, many were more or less Christian, and in the oases most were Jewish. From these allegiances there was little conversion. Many of the oasis dwellers, who had been shown to be incorrigibly inimical, were reduced to dependence by military expeditions, beginning in the year following the defence of the ditch, and were forced to turn over part of their crops henceforth to Medina. In contrast, some Christian-oriented Bedouin tribes who were willing to work with Muḥammad were accorded, it seems, a status as equal allies. Yet Muḥammad was always acknowledged as commander of the joint enterprises.

Accordingly, Muḥammad's society came to include both Muslims and non-Muslims in various degrees of membership. It had long since ceased to be just a new tribe of the faithful, or even a local voluntary association. It was becoming a complex and extensive society of heterogeneous elements, more fully organized than had been the Meccan system (both religiously and politically); the political structure which Muḥammad was building for it was by now clearly a state, like the states in the nations round about Arabia, with an increasingly authoritative government, which could no longer be ignored with impunity. Muḥammad sent out envoys, who taught the Qur'ân and the principles of Islam, collected the zakât, and presumably arbitrated disputes so as to keep the peace and prevent feuding. The Muslims of Medina thus undertook to bring into being throughout much of the Ḥijâz, and even beyond it, a way of living which should be just and godly. They depended fundamentally, to be sure, on the willingness of a majority to accept the system for the sake of its more immediate benefits in peace among themselves and strength against rivals outside. But the ideal was to be established whether with or without the active co-operation of the various tribes.

Mecca is taken

Such a system could not, however, well be completed or even survive without including Mecca and exploiting the trade route between Syria and the Yemen: without actually replacing the Meccan system. In 628, toward the end of his sixth year in Medina, Muḥammad marched with perhaps a thousand or more men to Mecca with the stated aim of taking part in the annual ḥajj pilgrimage. After tense negotiations at Ḥudaybiyah outside Mecca, he signed a treaty with the Quraysh: the Muslims would withdraw this year (it took all Muḥammad's charisma to hold his men to this renunciation), but the following year the Quraysh would evacuate their own city long enough to allow the Muslims to make the pilgrimage without hostile contact. Temporarily, at least, the Muslims would control even the Meccan shrines. The treaty could seem highly favourable to the Quraysh: Muḥammad allowed them a ten-year truce, during which their trade would be unhindered. But the Quraysh had to permit their

Bedouin allies to leave them and join Muḥammad—which, indeed, some of them promptly did. Given the atmosphere of high prestige that Muḥammad already had, his tribal system in the Ḥijâz was, in effect, tacitly being accorded Quraysh approval; and the old Meccan system was being allowed to lapse. Yet in the negotiations Muḥammad had demonstrated a friendly, even generous attitude to Mecca. The Quraysh could be assured that they would hold a high position in his system if they should enter it.

In the year following Ḥudaybiyah, Muḥammad completed his subjugation of certain major Ḥijâz oases. The pilgrimage was duly made as arranged. On the reoccupation of Syria by the Byzantines in 629, he sent a major expedition (3000 men) to Mu'tah at the southern tip of Syria, which made a show of force.

Then in 630, in Muḥammad's eighth year at Medina, Muḥammad interpreted a skirmish between some Bedouin allies of the Quraysh and of the Muslims as a breach of the treaty by the Quraysh. Collecting all his Bedouin allies, he marched to Mecca with an enormously increased host—some ten thousand men. After the death of many leading men at Badr, Abû-Sufyân (of the Umayyad clan) had become the most prominent leader among the Quraysh. Since the breach of the truce, he had evidently been attempting to arrange some settlement by personal negotiation; now he came to Muḥammad's camp, reluctantly became a Muslim, and returned to Mecca announcing that Muḥammad would grant a general amnesty if he were permitted to enter the town as master. The Quraysh agreed. There was little resistance when Muḥammad marched in. He received the peaceful submission of almost all his old enemies; a handful were proscribed, chiefly for public insults against him in verse.

The Muslims had now inherited the position in Arabia of the Quraysh. The Quraysh immediately joined Muḥammad in an expedition against those Bedouin who still resisted, and they were so generously rewarded out of the spoils that Muḥammad's older followers were inclined to complain. Most of the Bedouin were forced to submit very soon, and submission now meant full acceptance of Islam. The idols, sacred stones, and shrines of godlings in Mecca and in all the areas dependent on Mecca were destroyed. Before long, Ṭâ'if, Mecca's rival and partner as a trading city, which had at first successfully resisted a siege, found itself isolated and forced to submit likewise.

The year after the taking of Mecca is known as the year of deputations. Representatives from tribes all over the Ḥijâz and Najd arrived to come to some understanding with the new power. In some cases, whole tribes were ready to adopt Islam. Often just one faction within a tribe seems to have come seeking support against its rivals. There were a few deputations from almost every part of Arabia, even areas remote from the Ḥijâz such as the Baḥrayn mainland and 'Umân. An important part of the Yemen, where Sâsânian control seems to have become weak during the wars, submitted, notably the Christian town Najrân; as monotheists, the people of Najrân were permitted to acknowledge the political control of Muḥammad without abandoning religious allegiance to their own prophet, Jesus.

The tribes toward Syria in the northwest, however, were mostly still unready to submit; after the Sâsânian defeat, they seem to have renewed their ties with Byzantium. Muḥammad seems to have been more concerned about them than about any of the others and his remaining military efforts were mostly directed against them. From the time of the Sâsânian withdrawal, those who submitted to Muḥammad were given very good terms, while those who refused had heavy tribute laid on them when they were overwhelmed. A year after taking Mecca, Muḥammad led his largest expedition, perhaps 30,000 men, against the Banû Ghassân, the chief defenders of Byzantine interests on the Syrian frontier, with indecisive results.

At the next ḥajj pilgrimage to Mecca, those Arabs who remained pagan were forbidden to appear thenceforth. Then in 632 Muḥammad made the pilgrimage in person, establishing the forms of the pilgrimage which were to hold in Islam. In the Islamic system, as in the Meccan system, the pilgrimage had a prominent place; but in being Islamized, its cult was more sharply focused. It was intertribal no longer because it assembled tokens from all the tribes but because its cult far transcended any tribe—even the Quraysh. Though observances at several secondary places were retained, these were all made to depend upon the primary visit to the Ka'bah, the house of Allâh founded by Abraham and Ishmael. The Muslims kissed the Black Stone in the corner of the Ka'bah no longer as embodying some godling, but as a symbolic act of allegiance to God, who had sent both Abraham and Muḥammad to guide mankind.

A few months later, in the midst of equipping another expedition toward Syria, Muḥammad was taken with illness and died in the arms of 'Â'ishah. He was buried at the spot where he had died.

The genesis of a new regional culture

The period that followed was naturally of supreme importance in forming the Islamicate civilization. But our interest in it here is for the elements going to form a civilization which in itself did not exist till later, rather than for the general cultural life of the time in itself. Throughout the period of genesis, before and for a time after Muḥammad, the mainstream of religious, artistic, intellectual, and commercial life in the region from Nile to Oxus continued to reflect the ascendancy of earlier cultural allegiances. In the light of Islamicate cultural developments, it is only a limited range of what was happening, in all this period, which stands out as specially pregnant for us. Within this range we often include events equally significant for their own cultural setting as for Islamicate development: thus certain evolutions in the pre-Islamic Roman and Sâsânian empires, in whose territories the Islamicate civilization developed, were decisive under Islam also. But sometimes, though we exclude much that loomed large at the time, we include events which at the time possessed little significance for the dominant cultural life of the age. For instance, the culture of pre-Islamic Arabia, also crucial later under Islam, was in its own time marginal; to the rise of an artful but not highly rich or diversified tradition of Bedouin poetry, neither Greeks nor Aramaeans nor Persians of the time would have had reason to pay much attention.

Even the emergence of Islamic faith and the expansion of Arab control, which introduced ultimately decisive new traditions into the whole cultural situation, had at the time a limited impact and might have seemed transient and superficial. From the perspective of the older civilizations, the minority community of Muslims did not then represent, despite their power, the highest or most significant levels of culture; it is only in retrospect that they become a major focus of our attention.

This minority group presents one point of overriding interest. They represented consciously and intentionally a new tradition set over against the great traditions of ancient civilization. Gradually some of them began to imagine replacing the former societies of all mankind with a new society based on their new ideals. At length, we have something approaching a total social experiment—perhaps one of the few really major ones in history. To be sure, this did not begin to mature till the very end of the period; with its maturing, we enter the realm of Islamicate civilization proper. But its seeds were present in the small group of primitive Muslims.

In the formation of the civilization, therefore, a small group of concerned Arab families, with more or less Arabian habits of thinking, were peculiarly important. What the Irano-Semitic traditions of the settled lands did to modify their expectations and life-patterns, against their pre-Islamic Arabic background, had lasting effects among Muslims generally. At the same time it must not be forgotten—as too often it is—that from a broader historical viewpoint the Arabs were essentially foreigners being assimilated into an ongoing cultural pattern, which they helped to modify, partly through some bits and pieces of their own older heritage, but chiefly through two things equally new to all concerned: their catalytic presence as a new ruling class; and Islam itself, of which they were the carriers. What we are dealing with here is the history of the whole Irano-Semitic historical complex and its transformations; we deal with the internal history of the new ruling class only as it is relevant thereto.[2]

[2] Failure to recognize the minority role of the Arabian families in the social development of the time has resulted in one of the most distortive tendencies in all Islamics studies, what may be called the Arabistic bias, which has pervasively twisted the analysis not only of the early period but of all Islamicate history. Among other results is a recurrent notion that Islamicate civilization was 'sudden' in appearance and flowering—as if it had no direct background save the Arabian desert, and all else were 'borrowed' and quickly incorporated by nomads. Compare a more explicit analysis of the bias, toward the end of the section on the history of Islamics studies in the Introduction under 'Historical Method'. See also my 'Unity of Later Islamic History', *Journal of World History*, 5, (1960), especially pp. 880–82.

The establishment of the caliphal state

In pursuit of a new and total moral order, Muḥammad had reconstituted most of the elements of the Meccan system of the Quraysh in a new, broader system, which, however, maintained and even extended the neutral independence of the Quraysh on both the political and the religious levels. But this social labour had been largely personal to himself. The Qur'ân, as such, had supported this side of his work, but its emphasis was on the more individual level. It had, typically, provided for no political contingencies on the Prophet's death.

The first question that arose on Muḥammad's death was whether any state should survive it at all. Islam was a personal relation of men and women to God. It had been preached by a prophet, indeed, and so long as he lived it could be presumed he would provide the safest guidance to God's will. On his death, each group of men that had accepted Islam could be expected to find its own way to obey God; unless, indeed, God sent other prophets to be followed, as might well be anticipated. The Qur'ân referred to numberless prophets and gave no clear indication that Muḥammad was to be the last of them. Indeed, more than one monotheistic prophet had actually appeared in recent years, in tribes beyond Muḥammad's main sphere of action, presumably inspired by Muḥammad's example. The most prominent of these was Maslamah (called in scorn 'Musaylimah'), among the Banû Ḥanîfah in central Arabia; if Muḥammad had denounced him in his lifetime, Maslamah's followers could suppose it was because Muḥammad was jealous that revelation should come to any other than himself; after Muḥammad's death, they could have little doubt of the part of one who would be faithful to God. Others also might think to turn to him.

Of the Bedouin tribes that had submitted to Muḥammad, many felt themselves free of any further obligation and, with or without new prophets to turn to, refused to send any further zakât to Medina; many others seem to have waited only to see what Muslims at Medina and Mecca would do, for the power of the Quraysh, at least, had not been negligible even apart from Muḥammad. At Medina itself there was consternation and indecision. The Anṣâr, the Muslims of Medina, were soon suggesting that they should choose a leader for the Muslims of Medina and the Quraysh should choose a leader for those of Mecca.

Such were the most obvious resolutions of the crisis. But some men had a more ambitious conception of Islam and of the Ummah community Muḥammad had created. Islam was not merely a matter of each individual's obeying God; it was a compact in which all Muslims were bound to each other as well. This compact did not cease with the Prophet's death; the pattern of life he had instituted could be continued under the guidance of those who had been closest to him, the earliest Muslims. Any who separated from the core of the Muslims at Medina were in fact backing out of Islam itself; they were traitors to the cause of God for which Muhammad and his followers had so long been fighting.

That cause was still to be fought for, and demanded a single chief to whom all would be loyal.

Abû-Bakr and 'Umar are credited with persuading the Muslims of Medina to this audacious viewpoint. They broke in among the assembled Anṣâr leaders and called for unity: 'Umar promised his loyalty to Abû-Bakr, and the Anṣâr soon followed suit, as did the Quraysh. With the two towns thus determined to maintain Muḥammad's polity, the demand was extended to the Bedouin. To subdue them, Muslim energies were thrown into the wars of the *Riddah*, of the 'Apostasy', as it came to be called on the ground that the recusants had apostatized. The Muslims found a general of genius in a latter-day convert from the Quraysh, Khâlid b. al-Walîd, who had distinguished himself as an enemy at the battle of Uḥud. Recalcitrant tribes were attacked in several quick campaigns and reduced to obedience. But Muḥammad's system had been reaching out to clans and factions in tribes much further afield. Such factions could not remain as they were; they had either to be vindicated or left in the lurch. In the snowballing impetus of enthusiasm, many tribes in which only a minority faction had recognized Muhammad—and even some where none at all had done so—were now forced to acknowledge Islam and pay zakât to the collectors from Medina. The several new prophets that had arisen were declared false—from this time on it was held that there could be no prophet after Muḥammad, a doctrine then equivalent to asserting the unity of Muslims. It was the community organized at Medina that was to be the acknowledged authority in Islam, and it was Muḥammad's associates there whose decisions were to be accepted in all matters of common concern. At the same time, all the Arabs, as Muslims, were to be essentially equal under the terms of that leadership. Within less than two years the power of the Muslim community, so reconstituted, was far more widespread than it had been under Muḥammad.

Thus were ruled out two possible outcomes of Muḥammad's challenge. One could have imagined a continuing wave of prophetic leadership, inspired men in the several tribes carrying on Muḥammad's tradition in a Bedouin Arabia fragmented but confirming its cultural independence. Or one could have imagined an assimilation of Muḥammad's mission to the Hebrew Bible, which would have led eventually to its submersion in a wider Jewish tradition. The affirmation of Muḥammad's political construction meant instead that the Arabs would be both united and independent. But this unity could prove feasible only through carrying conquest into the lands about, for which central leadership was required.

Before the campaigns to subdue the Bedouin were completed, some of the Arabs were already launching raids against the Sâsânian and Byzantine empires. Muḥammad himself had been planning a major expedition toward Syria at the time of his death, which was duly sent ahead. Though it withdrew after making a demonstration, it was followed up late in 633 with several smaller raiding bands into southern Palestine. The frontier Arabs of Syria were no longer being subsidized by the Byzantines, whose funds were exhausted; they put up little resistance. In contrast to the Byzantine penury, it was excessive bureaucratic prosperity that had tempted the Sâsânians to weaken their Arab ties by abolishing the subsidized Lakhmid Arab kingdom on their frontier and undertaking to control their dependent Arabs directly. Some independent northeastern Arabs had already (notably in 610) had some success against the Sâsânians; they likewise now launched a raid on the frontier of the Iraq. They now had the co-operation and, as operations increased in scale, accepted the leadership of the Ḥijâz Muslims. Under the bold and far-sighted generalship of Khâlid b. al-Walîd, the raids against the exhausted empires proved successful and yielded much booty. In particular, Ḥîrah, the former Lakhmid capital, was occupied. Various tribal groups came together to share in the work. The leadership of the Medina Muslims was the only common arbiter making possible the large-scale co-operation necessary; the participating Arabs accepted it and called themselves Muslims. As soon as the raids northward were well advanced, there was no longer any question of pagan Arabian tribes refusing to acknowledge Islam.

In the following years, the leadership at Medina had two cares: to spread a more serious Islam among the tribes and to organize the raids on the empires into expressions of Muslim power. For the first purpose, Qur'ân-reciters were sent, as they had been under Muḥammad, to teach the Arabs the essentials of Islamic faith. (Tribes already Christian, however, were not expected to become Muslim.) But such teaching merged with the second objective: to organize the Arabs and lead them on campaigns. The moral and financial solidarity implied in the Qur'ânic teaching became the foundation of the military expansion. In carrying out the second objective, the Medina Muslims made a further major decision by 635. From raids for booty or for, at most, a border lordship over the nearby peasantry, the campaigns were extended into a full-scale conquest of the settled lands. Henceforth the Muslims aimed at occupying their cities and replacing their governments with Muslim government.

There was no attempt at converting the peoples of the imperial territories, who practically all adhered to some form of confessional religion already. Islam was felt to be primarily, if not exclusively, meant for Arabs, and only within the Peninsula was there any sense that all ought to be Muslims. Yet even Christian Arab tribes were still allowed to participate actively in the conquests. In the chiefly non-Arab agricultural lands, the object was not conversion but rule. The limited example of Muḥammad in subjecting settled Jews and Christians in western Arabia was extended beyond Arabia to all lands within reach. The superiority of Islam as religion, and therefore in providing for social order, would justify Muslim rule: would justify the simple, fair-dealing Muslims in replacing the privileged and oppressive representatives of the older, corrupted allegiances. The caliphal state was no longer simply an Arabian commonwealth but was a vehicle of conquest beyond Bedouin Arabia, and depended on that conquest for its financial and psychological existence.

Chronology: Abû-Bakr to ʿAbd-al-Malik, 632–692

632–656	Military occupation of the empires, directed from Medina
632–634	Caliphate of Abû-Bakr: Arab tribes are defeated in the Riddah wars, establishing the leadership of Medina in a single Muslim society, in which all Arabia is incorporated
634–644	Caliphate of ʿUmar: Most of the Fertile Crescent, Egypt, and much of Iran are conquered, and the patterns of military settlement and of finance of the Islamic régime are set up
644–656	Caliphate of ʿUthmân: Conquests continue northward, eastward in Iran, and westward from Egypt, but with the enormous enrichment of privileged families at Medina and Mecca, jealousies and discontents divide the Muslims; the Qur'ân text is standardized for the sake of unity
656–661	The first fitnah: ʿUthmân is murdered, and in civil wars ʿAlî, established at Kûfah and at first widely recognized as caliph, gradually loses Muslim allegiance; Medina is abandoned as capital, and factions are organized, especially that of the intransigently puritan Khârijîs (658)
661–683	The Sufyânî Umayyads:
661–680	The Umayyad Muʿâwiyah is caliph at Damascus, relying on Syrian Arab power and Muslim desire for unity; conquest is resumed, especially in the Mediterranean (with a powerful fleet); internal discontents are restrained by threat of force; Ziyâd b. Abîh governs former Sâsânian areas
680–683	Muʿâwiyah's son Yazîd succeeds (idea of hereditary rule is implied) and ʿAlî's son, Muḥammad's grandson, Ḥusayn is killed at Karbalâ', in an attempted rising of Kûfah in the Iraq—his death becomes symbol for partisans of ʿAlid rule
683–692	The second fitnah: On Yazîd's death, Ibn-Zubayr restores Medina as capital; but at Marj Râhiṭ (684) the Umayyads regain Syria under Marwân, and Mukhtâr al-Thaqafî at Kûfah (685–687) tries to establish the rule of the family of ʿAlî; under Marwân's son ʿAbd-al-Malik (685–705), in civil wars, the Umayyads regain control of all Islamic provinces

The conquest of the Sâsânian empire

In 634, two years after Muḥammad, his lieutenant Abû-Bakr had died, leaving ʿUmar as his acknowledged successor. ʿUmar may have been responsible for the decision to occupy the agricultural provinces; in any case, he carried it out systematically. Some initial successes in 635, especially in Syria where even Damascus was occupied for a time, may have been due to the force of surprise. In 636 the Roman army in Syria—not the main army of the empire, of course—was destroyed at a point well chosen by the Muslims on the Yarmûk river; the Arab auxiliaries, forming a major portion of the Roman army, having gone over to the Muslims at a crucial point. Most of the Syrian cities then capitulated with little struggle. This encouraged the Muslims to make a more concerted and highly organized effort against the Iraq. In 637 the main army of the Sâsânians was destroyed at Qâdisiyyah, guarding the Euphrates. Presumably it was after this battle that the Sâsânian Arab auxiliaries went over to the Muslims. Most of the cities of the Iraq then capitulated. In the Iraq, among the cities surrendered was the capital of the empire, Ctesiphon, where little resistance was offered. By 641, when the Roman emperor Heraclius died, practically all of the Aramaic-speaking lowlands had been occupied, including the Jazîrah (Mesopotamia proper) in the north and the Kârûn (Dujayl) valley in Khûzistân.

The Roman provincial power in Syria and the central Sâsânian power in the Iraq seem to have lost all morale and to have collapsed without serious attempts at internal co-operation or regrouping. In Syria, at least, this appears to have resulted from the apathy not only of the peasants but even of the urban populations, who in the Agrarian Age participated somewhat in the privileges of rule and would normally obstruct usurpation by an alien group. The large body of Syrian Jews had long been persecuted by the Christian empire, and had actively assisted the Sâsânian conquest; but they had no more reason to trust the Muslims than the Byzantines. But the majority of Syrian Christians were likewise persecuted, for they refused to accept the Greek church leadership which held power at Constantinople, and the creed of the Council of Chalcedon which that leadership wanted to enforce. The Syrians mostly preferred to support a religious community of their own with Aramaic leaders, who adopted a Monophysite creed and seem to have been supported by the Sâsânians. Even an attempt at a neutral creed under Heraclius, when he reoccupied the land, had issued only in more persecution. At the same time, the imperial (Greek) church, which had allowed some of its treasure to be used during the former war, demanded to be repaid and forced an unusually severe rate of taxation. When the imperial army was broken, the city populations accepted individual treaties with the Muslims (stipulating a lower rate of taxation) and received them in friendliness. The Greek-speaking landlord class withdrew to the Anatolian highlands and never came back.

In the long run, the collapse of the Sâsânians in the Iraq was still more decisive. Especially since Nûshîrvân, a large part of the Mesopotamian alluvial plain had become virtually a state farm, in the 'Sawâd', where the revenues were not allowed to be diverted to private landholders. It was maintained by a massive irrigation system which was no longer manageable on a piecemeal basis as irrigation there once had been and still was, to some degree, even in earlier Sâsânian times. This had formed the physical basis for the centralized army and hence for the centralized, bureaucratic empire. Now, only close and continuous central administration could keep it in order at all. A central collapse would mean ruin throughout large agricultural tracts—and must confirm the disaster to the central treasury. But following the Sâsânian defeat in the last war with Rome, several years had passed in political chaos as various claimants to the throne and factions in the army fought for the prize of power;

different Sâsânian provinces were run almost in independence by the generals. A major shift in the Tigris bed seems to have created permanent swamps in the lower Iraq and ruined much farmland there even before the war was concluded. It is just possible that the changes in land formation were already

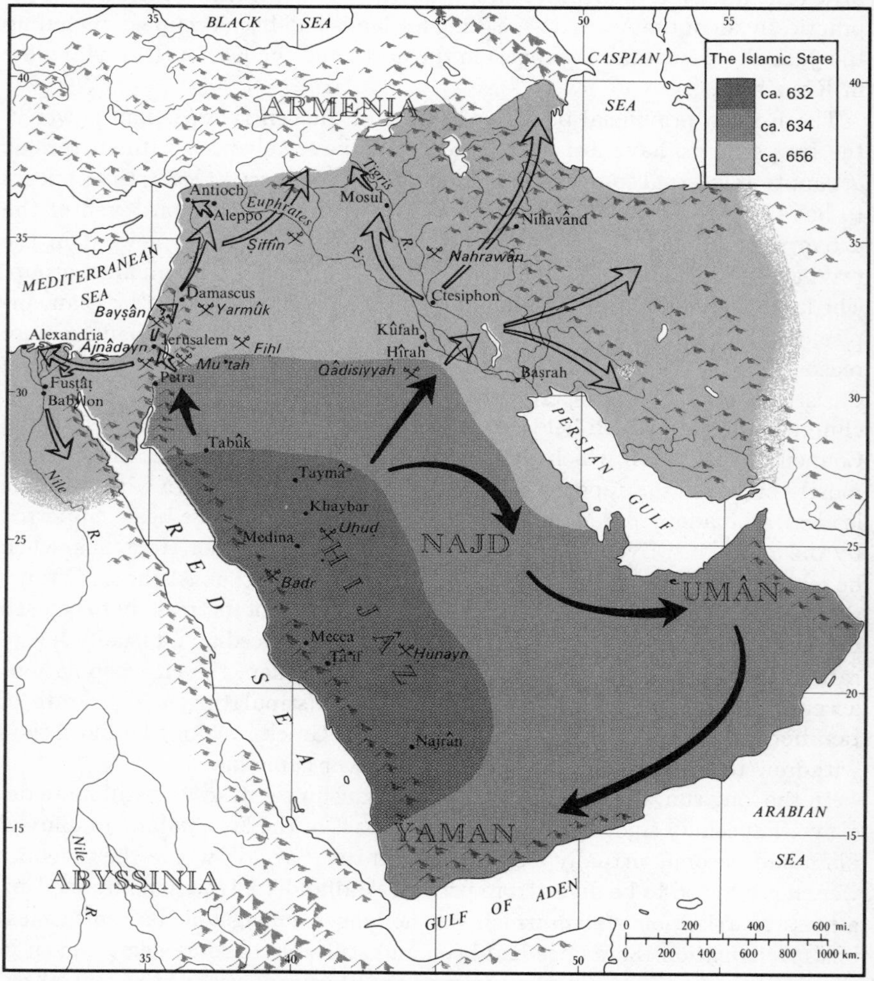

Conquest of the Fertile Crescent and adjacent lands to 656

beginning which eventually made much of the alluvial plain inherently harder to irrigate than it was earlier. But the political disruption alone was enough to account for unprecedented disaster conditions in the Iraq. This disaster, in turn, made it more difficult for the winner in the civil wars (Yazdagird III, in

632) to impose his authority. Nûshîrvân's policies had ended, at least for the moment, in collapse.[3]

Even apart from the disorders, the population of the plain could have little interest in holding the state lands for one government rather than another. The majority of people there were Christian and Jewish, or Manichean, and had suffered disabilities under the Mazdean hierarchy. The Sâsânian upper agrarian classes did not have a personal interest—or following—in the plain; they seem to have been based chiefly on the Iranian highlands. The most important part of the Sâsânian soldiery with a local interest in the Iraq were Arabs—some of them having been lately deprived of their autonomy. When the Sâsânian forces made a strategic withdrawal to the highlands, then, the Sâsânian nobility went with them; the Sâsânian Arab soldiery went over to the independent Arabs; and neither the peasantry nor the urban populations that remained offered resistance to the new military masters.

When Arab possession of the Fertile Crescent had been assured, a wholesale migration of tribes from all parts of Arabia poured in, men bringing their families along, to join the victorious armies. These soon provided enormous army potential. The families were lodged in military bases quickly built on the edge of the desert, and armies were sent into all neighbouring lands. The first expedition beyond the Aramaic lowlands began late in 639 into Egypt, well known to the Meccans for its wealth. In Egypt, the Coptic inhabitants had likewise resisted the Greek imperial church in the name of a Monophysite Christian creed and had been most bitterly persecuted since the evacuation of the Sâsânians. During 641, most of the country was occupied, and in 642 even Alexandria, the local Roman capital. Within a few years, Egypt was supplying the Ḥijâz with tribute grain as it had been supplying Byzantium.

In 641 began the advance into the Roman and Sâsânian highlands. Despite some initial reverses, Mu'âwiyah (son of Abû-Sufyân, former leader of the Quraysh), as governor of Syria, was able in the next few years to raid not only into Cilicia (southeast of the Taurus mountains) but far into the Anatolian peninsula, reaching Amorium by 646; but he was unable to occupy much territory beyond Melitene permanently, and by 647 was reduced to destroying fortresses in Roman territory which, for the time being, he could not expect to hold.

But the most important advances were into Sâsânian territory from Baṣrah and especially Kûfah. It was to these centres that the bulk of the new Arab immigration came, swamping the older, more city-disciplined, elements that had known Sâsânian rule and Sâsânian service from the time of the Lakhmids of Ḥîrah; whereas the corresponding older elements continued to predominate

[3] Robert M. Adams, *Land behind Baghdad: A History of Settlement on the Diyala Plains* (University of Chicago Press, 1965), a study of irrigation agriculture in the Diyâlah plain (just east of Baghdad) from Sumerian times to the present, provides important archeological evidence for the collapse; though nothing can be absolutely proven for particular years, and our reconstruction of events must remain partly conjectural. The same study is of fundamental importance for economic history throughout the Islamic period.

in Syria. The army sent into ʿIrâq ʿAjamî, the main plateau area of western Iran, overcame a major Sâsânian army at Nihâvand in 641; by 643 the main cities of the province had capitulated. Deprived of their capital and of the state income from the alluvial plain, the Sâsânians seem to have been unable to concert their forces. In contrast to the Byzantines, whose main reserves and administrative headquarters were intact at distant Constantinople, the Sâsânians were thereafter reduced to piecemeal resistance on a provincial basis. Eventually, their whole empire was overrun and the Arabs inherited their major resources and political potentialities. In this way, the Arabs' success in the Iraq made it possible for them to form an enduring new empire despite their ultimate failure to overcome the Byzantines in the latters' homelands.

The Bedouin Arabs had conquered readily enough the three surrounding countries—the Yemen, already partly subordinated in Muḥammad's own time, no longer closely held by either Sâsânians or Abyssinians, and in any case half-Arabized long since; Syria, at odds with its Byzantine rulers in an upsurge of Semitic monotheistic communal spirit against a Hellenizing ruling class that had long lost the creative spirit of the polis; the Iraq, where, as in Syria, Arabs already formed a major military element and which, in any case, no longer possessed its own independent dominant classes. Egypt also fell readily as, like the Iraq, it had no military force of its own and was open to control by the strongest neighbour. It can even be suggested that—without its being planned so—many Syrian elements, and perhaps also Yemeni, co-operated readily enough with the Islamized Meccans, with whom they had long been in trading relations; it is as if there was set up a Yemen-Mecca-Syria axis which was strong enough to dominate both Egypt and the Iraq with its military and commercial power. The Syrians seem readily enough to have co-operated with at least their immediate Meccan governors: if it was the desertion of the only military element among the Monophysites— the Arab auxiliaries—that gave Syria into Arab hands, it was the almost immediate co-operation of the non-Arab Syrian shipping which allowed the Arabs to appear as a naval power almost from the start, defeating the seriously truncated Byzantine naval forces. Leading Meccan merchants lost little time in penetrating, as privileged competition, the Iraq particularly; but it is not clear whether they did so with any active Syrian support. But conquest of the hinterlands of these three neighbouring countries was another matter. In such efforts, only special circumstances could allow an Arab success.

The Arabs very early sent an expedition against Abyssinia, a naval expedition which was wrecked. Wisely, they made no further attempts. The Abyssinians formed a reasonably strong power, still intact, for the conquest of the Yemen had scarcely touched them; there was no reason to expect that they would offer the Arabs even a beachhead. Even the Nile Sudan, which had not been integrated into the Roman empire and so retained its own social order intact, and where there was no prior Arab base, successfully resisted invasion. As to the Byzantines, their power was based on the north Mediterranean

Chronology: The Arab Conquests, 632–655

632–633	Death of Muḥammad brings about Riddah wars; Abû-Bakr brings back to Muslim allegiance Arab tribes whose primary allegiance was to Muḥammad's political leadership; battles fought in many different parts of Arabia; fighting groups push out of Arabia to northwest and northeast
633	Ḥîrah, Sâsânian fortified town near the Euphrates river, taken
634	Byzantine force defeated in S. Syria
635	Damascus taken, followed by some other Syrian cities
636	Battle of Yarmûk, near the Jordan river, crushes a strong Byzantine army commanded by the emperor's brother, who is killed; Syria thenceforth lies open; Damascus retaken
637	Battle of Qâdisiyyah, near Ḥîrah, crushes a strong Sâsânian army commanded by the principal general Rustam, who is killed; Iraq west of the Tigris lies open; Sâsânian capital of Ctesiphon taken
638	Jerusalem taken; Baṣrah, Kûfah founded as garrison towns
640	Caesarea (Palestinian seaport) finally taken; no Byzantine power remains in Syria; Egypt invaded (end of 639); Khûzistân taken
641	Mosul taken; no Sâsânian power remains west of the Zagros mountains; battle of Nihâvand in central Zagros opens that area by destroying remaining Sâsânian army; Babylon in Egypt (site of later Fusṭâṭ and Cairo) taken
642	Alexandria taken; Barqah (Tripolitania) raided (642–643); raids toward Makran coast, southeast Iran (643)
645–646	Alexandria retaken by Byzantines; retaken by Muslims
c. 645—	Muslims engage fleets from Egypt and Syria; Muslim sea power begins
c. 647	Tripolitania taken
649	Cyprus taken—first important Muslim sea operation
649–650	Persepolis taken—chief city of Fârs and Zoroastrian religious center
651	Yazdagird, last Sâsânî ruler, assassinated in Khurâsân
652	Armenia mostly subjugated; Byzantine fleet repulsed off Alexandria; Sicily pillaged; treaty made with Nubia, south of Egypt
654	Rhodes pillaged
655	Combined Muslim fleets shatter principal Byzantine fleet off southwest Anatolian coast; emperor in command barely escapes

peninsulas, which were oriented to the sea and formed a viable unity without Syria and even Egypt. To conquer the Anatolian highlands would have required an overwhelming force ready to occupy every town without offering any reason for the local privileged classes to prefer an alien rule; it is doubtful if the taking of Constantinople itself would have produced results even so permanent as the Crusaders' taking it in 1204. The Iranian highlands, on the contrary, were linked closely to the Iraq. An integral part of the Arid Zone, those inland highlands had been closely tied to the irrigated river basins on their flanks, especially to that of the Oxus on the north and to that of the Tigris-Euphrates on the west (the Indus basin was separated by barriers from the main parts of the plateau). The capital of an Iranian empire had regularly gravitated to the Mesopotamian lowlands, from Susa to Ctesiphon. The mutual involvement of Iranian and Semitic traditions was almost a given, in the common arid setting; it was part of this more comprehensive, persistent pattern, that the Iranian state had come to depend for its financial integrity on the Iraqi Sawâd.

Hence, of the three empires in the midst of which the Meccans and their allies had maintained their neutrality, it was only the Sâsânian they were able to conquer—when they combined the full force of the Qur'ânic revelation with the potentialities of the expansive camel nomadism. Having conquered that empire, they were able to conquer also, beyond it, nearby lands which had not, or had not lately, been subordinated to it. It was political reasons that gave them the Sâsânian empire: particularly the current Sâsânian crisis, and then the collapse of Sâsânian power when bereft of its capital. But these political reasons were expressions of the more enduring cultural reasons for the persistent unity of the Irano-Semitic cultural territories between Nile and Oxus, and their differentiation from the more purely Greek territories of the peninsulas. Only in the Maghrib and Spain were the Arabs able to conquer distant areas without reference to the Sâsânian power base; but there they stimulated and gave guidance to a separate movement, that of the Berbers, which had its own momentum.

'Umar's organization of conquest

In contrast to the Christian or even the Mazdean situation, no explicit distinction between religion and state could be made among the Muslims. As already in Muḥammad's time, the head of the major undertakings of the Muslims was at once head of the Muslim community and head of the whole society which it controlled. But it was within the framework of the Muslim Arab community that the course of the whole society was to be worked out. As in Muḥammad's Ḥijâz, non-Muslims were mostly relegated to the position of tolerated dependents; they were left to organize their own autonomous life under the protection and overriding control of the Muslim community. The governing conceptions and ideals of the dominant Arab community were defined by

Islam. The Islamic institutions were thus at first designed simply as practical expressions of the various aspects of Muslim Arab life. What Arabian customs were already satisfactory were accepted—and with the conquests, the same applied to patterns of relation between rulers and ruled in the agrarian lands. Customs contrary to the new faith were replaced.

The central problem in Muḥammad's time had been to replace a system of feuding within a society, in favour of a common life under a single arbiter. Under 'Umar the same problem was renewed under new circumstances—to bring some common discipline among the rather lawless occupiers of the conquered territories. Muḥammad's solution, to provide for a central distribution of funds to those at a disadvantage and a central settlement of disputes by a divinely sanctioned moral standard, was to be adapted and extended. The problem for 'Umar, and for the Medinese whom he represented, was to define the nature of the authority at such a centre.

Abû-Bakr had been known as the representative of Muḥammad, his *khalîfah* (Anglicized as 'caliph'). His had been essentially an emergency status. The term continued to be used of 'Umar, but he later chose for formal use the title *amîr al-mu'minîn*, commander of the faithful. The only binding authority the Arabs had recognized was that of the military commander on the march to new pastures or at war. Though the Qur'ân enforced the idea of a community, in which individual pious action was completed by joint action in the cause of God, it provided directly for no government other than that of the Prophet himself. The only position, therefore, that could be felt to be legitimate was still that of military commander, with authority correspondingly limited. 'Umar saw this as his position. But war was the business of the community for the present and such a position opened a wide scope of responsibility.

The Muslims accepted him as commander of the community in any matter wherein each man could not act for himself. This position of command rested on personal prestige; and in this case, on a religious prestige. Since any group action beyond tribal interests was a matter for religion, we may say that it was precisely in religious matters that he was successor, 'caliph', to the Prophet; certainly his decisions were to be consistent with what Muḥammad had shown of God's will. Of course, since he received no revelations from God, he had no independent religious authority; it was only current political questions that he was to decide on this religious basis. In any case, his authority depended on his personal closeness to the precepts and example of Muḥammad and on his being personally recognized at Medina—and on that account also by the bulk of the Muslims at large—as in fact representing Muḥammad's way.

'Umar's position, then, religious and military as it was, was based on person-to-person relationships, as had been Muḥammad's. But with the vast increase in the number of persons in the community, even among the ruling Arabs (to say nothing of the subject peoples), the organization which he set up had to be less immediately personal. It was, in fact, an institution capable of operating apart from the immediate intervention of any given individual. This organization was centred in an army *dîwân*, a register of all the Muslims of Medina and Mecca and of the conquering armies (and their descendants). The booty from the conquest was to be distributed in individual pensions to the men (and sometimes women) listed in the dîwân, according to their rank therein. Some prominent Muslims received revenue from particular tracts, but most received their share through the dîwân system.

This system recognized that conquest was the keynote of the Muslim state, and helped perpetuate this situation. With distribution of booty as the most attractive physical resource of the state, it was obviously desirable to continue the conquests; and though this may not have been ʿUmar's intention, yet the conquests did continue and no doubt helped with their heady results to make ʿUmar's arrangements workable. But ʿUmar also provided for the area already conquered to continue in the condition of conquered possessions. Movable booty had been distributed among the armies at the moment of conquest—with the Prophetic fifth of the booty reserved to the disposition of the caliph for the benefit of the poor and for other state concerns. But immovable booty—the land revenues or 'taxes'—was mostly not divided up, but kept (as *fay'*) as a single source of income to be doled out to the conquering Arabs and their descendants (in principle) from the centre, to which a fifth was sent outright. Each Arab was to receive his due as it was apportioned by headquarters through the army dîwân, though actual finances were largely handled in the provinces.

The Arabs—even if they wanted to—were not to settle down in the old cities as new landlords (garrisoning had been tried in Ctesiphon, the Sâsânian capital, with demoralizing effects). They and their children were to remain in garrison towns (*miṣr*, pl. *amṣâr*) of their own as a separate conquering class, living on the tribute allotted by pensions. Each garrison town was situated for maximum military effectiveness—normally near enough to the desert that a potential retreat thither remained open. Kûfah, in the region of Ctesiphon (and not far from the old Ḥîrah of the Lakhmid Arab kingdom), and Baṣrah, between the desert and the ports of the Persian Gulf, were the two garrison towns in the Iraq, from which expeditions were launched to the furthest points east; Fusṭâṭ (the future Old Cairo) at the head of the Nile delta was built as the capital of Egypt and headquarters for expeditions further west. Only in Syria, where the occupying Arabs had already formed close local ties before the conquest, was the main centre an old city, Damascus, rather than a new garrison town. From there, expeditions were launched northwest against the one great remaining enemy, Byzantium.

But as Muslims, the Arabs were not merely an army of occupation. They were also representatives of God's good order among mankind, founded on adherence to His revelation. In each garrison town, and in each city where Muslims settled a garrison, a mosque was built, which was at that time a simple enclosure, usually roofed over at one end, suitable for mass assemblies. There the faithful came together to perform public worship (*ṣalât*), especially the Friday midday worship. The pattern of the Friday service seems to have echoed that of the Jewish and Christian services (the latter having been based on the former) in the general order of worship; for instance, the *khuṭbah* (sermon) was divided into two parts, answering, in the older rites, to a reading of scripture first and a less sacred reading or sermon afterwards; and it preceded the ṣalât proper, as did scripture reading, the Eucharist. (In details, such as that the leader should hold a staff when speaking, it even reflected old pagan Arabian practices.) But in total effect, the services expressed the new Muslim vision: thus the *khuṭbah* sermon focused not on ancient scripture, but on the living Muslim community equally in each of its two parts. The Qur'ân was used extensively, but it was uttered by every individual, sometimes at individual choice. (Compare the chart of the Muslim public cult and the diagram of the ṣalât.)[4] The mosque was also used for any other public activity that was called for.

Centred on its mosque and kept in order by its commander, each garrison town formed a self-sufficient Muslim community, dominating and living from the district under its military control; in the process, it moulded its own people into an Islamic pattern. In each garrison was appointed a commander representing the caliph and hence charged with leading the ṣalât worship and the military expeditions undertaken from there, and with managing the tribute collected. He was expected to keep the garrison in order, settling disputes among the faithful in a spirit of justice and in accordance with the Qur'ân where that applied. 'Umar needed as administrators men who were able to handle the Bedouin, most of whom (especially those not from a Syrian or Ḥîran background) were unused to outside controls; men who at the same time were able to see the long-term problems of finance and administration in agrarian territory. Such he could find among the Quraysh—and among their allies the Thaqîf of Ṭâ'îf—but sometimes at the price of their showing less than the highest Islamic morality in their personal lives.

Despite the weaknesses of some of his governors, 'Umar stressed Islam as the basis of Arab life. Muḥammad had left many questions open in the developing life of Medina. For the life of the Muslim garrison towns, full of new converts and tempted by undreamed-of wealth from the tribute, 'Umar had to establish sharp and clear standards to prevent rapid demoralization. He sent Qur'ân-reciters as missionaries to the garrison towns, but did not leave it all to the Qur'ân. He seems to have decided what the essential minimum common

[4] For a description in English of the primary Islamic cult, cf. Arthur Jeffery, *Islâm: Muhammad and His Religion* (New York, 1958), section V, 'The Duties of Islâm', consisting largely of descriptive and explanatory passages from standard Muslim authors. He translates *ṣalât* (worship) as 'liturgical *prayer*', a common rendering. For greater detail, see Edwin E. Calverley, *Worship in Islâm* (2nd ed. London, 1957)—largely a translation of a treatise by the great Muslim scholar, Ghazâlî.

The Public Cult as It Had Developed by Marwânî Times

Ṣalât (five times each day: before dawn, after noon, mid-afternoon, before sunset, mid-evening):
summoned to by the
Adhân = call to worship (in Arabic)
carried by the voice of the
Muezzin (mu'adhdhin) = chanter of the Adhân,
stationed in the
Minaret (manârah) = tower at the mosque;
it is performed, however, *anywhere*, only after
Wuḍû' = ritual ablutions (i.e., washings of face, arms, and feet)
and while facing in the direction of the
Qiblah = direction of the Ka'bah, the shrine at Mecca
(i.e., for the majority of Muslims in the twentieth century, more or less toward the *west*, not east)
reciting Arabic phrases, especially taken from the Qur'ân, including the
Shahâdah = statement of Islamic belief, and the
Takbîr = 'Allâhu akbar', 'God is Great';
and composed of two or more
Rak'ah = a sequence of bowing and prostrations;
or else the ṣalât is
performed in a
Mosque (masjid) = any place set aside for ṣalât,
in a group lined up in rows and led by an
Imâm (leader), with whose performance of the ṣalât the others keep time,
facing the
Miḥrâb = niche in the wall toward the Qiblah.

Fridays (yawm al-jum'ah):
midday ṣalât performed by all adult males in a
Jâmi' = special mosque ('cathedral mosque') for the whole local community,
with, following the ṣalât, a
Khuṭbah = sermon (in Arabic, and later in set form)—including mention of the name of the recognized Muslim ruler—
preached by the caliph or his governor (later substituted by the *Khaṭîb*, sermonizer) from the
Minbar = a series of steps on which to stand ('pulpit').

Yearly:
Ramaḍân = ninth lunar month, month of daylight fasting,
at end of which is celebrated the
Lesser 'Îd ('îd al-fiṭr), with a special morning group ṣalât,
followed in the twelfth month by the
Ḥajj = pilgrimage to Mecca in full form, with special rituals at Mecca and in its vicinity,
at end of which is the
Greater 'Îd ('îd al-aḍḥâ), celebrated both at Mecca and everywhere,
with a special morning group ṣalât, and with ritual animal sacrifices.

ritual for all should be, where Muḥammad had scarcely had time to do so by example even if he had cared to make such a prescription: for instance, in imposing the ḥajj as an obligatory duty. According to later Muslim tradition, at least, ʿUmar tightened up the family law, insisting (in principle) on severe punishments for adultery; forbidding an old Arabian practice of temporary marriage (not far from prostitution) which Muḥammad seems to have tolerated; and giving the slave concubine a more secure status if she became pregnant. In general, he insisted on rigorous discipline (being especially hard on drunkenness) and discouraged by his own example and probably by other regulations the luxury among the Arabs that was a natural consequence of the conquered wealth. Helped by other high-minded associates of the Prophet, he made of Islam a puritan standard for the Arab soldiery.

This religious character of the Arab community was presupposed in ʿUmar's army dîwân as clearly as was its conquering character. The dîwân gave a clear social status to all the Muslim Arabs, even those defeated in the Riddah wars, alongside the original community in Medina and Mecca; a social status, in turn, based not on descent but on faith. The tribesmen were, by and large, set off according to tribe; for tribes had converted as units; yet where appropriate, each Arab could be given his place individually. The prime criterion was one of priority in accepting Islam. This naturally, in practice, gave pre-eminence to the Muslims of Medina, especially since time priority was assessed in broad categories; but any tribesman who happened to have been an early convert—or to have performed signal services—could have due recognition. Muḥammad's wives and family were given a special place as closest to him. Thus the whole Arab community was sorted out according to a strictly Muslim criterion. The state was centred in Medina and founded on the religious prestige of Muḥammad; but it included as integral members the whole ruling class of Arabs scattered over the conquered provinces.

The spirit of the new order was symbolized in the era which ʿUmar adopted: it dated from the Hijrah of Muḥammad, when he broke with the tribal past and went to Medina to set up a new order. The very term *hijrah* was likewise applied to the migration of an individual or a tribe to the new military camp-cities: in joining the active Muslim community, each individual repeated for himself the essential step which had launched the Muslim community as a whole. Along with the new era, ʿUmar also consecrated a lunar calendar, which in itself implied a break with the environment; for (knowingly or not) in the calendar he ignored the seasonal year, interpreting an ambiguous Qur'ânic decree of the last years of Muḥammad's life as ruling out any accommodation of the lunar cycle to the seasons. Hence the Islamic 'year', which is a pure twelvemonth, has been about eleven days short of the true seasonal year and neither the calendar year nor its festivals have coincided with the necessities of pastoral or agricultural life—or with the course of other calendars.

The first fitnah wars

'Umar died in 644 at about 52 years of age, leaving a panel of Medinese leaders to choose his successor; jealous of each other, they chose the weakest among themselves, 'Uthmân b. 'Affân, the pious early convert and son-in-law of the Prophet. Under 'Uthmân the raids and conquests continued in many directions but with diminishing amounts of booty despite the increasing number of immigrating tribesmen. The main conquests were in the Iranian highlands. After a pause, the Sâsânian home province, Fârs, was occupied by 650, and then the armies moved on into the great northeast province, Khurâsân, more or less brought to terms by 651. Westward, after it became clear that the Byzantines were not to be dislodged from Anatolia by land expeditions alone, under Mu'âwiyah's leadership the Arabs also took to the sea. A successful raid on Cyprus in 649 encouraged further efforts. With the aid of Syrian and Egyptian naval skills, Cyprus was occupied and the Byzantine fleet—stripped of its Syrian section—was shattered by 655. But such operations yielded less immediate plunder than those of a decade before. They were suspended by a movement of revolt against the caliph by the discontented Arabs themselves.

'Uthmân had continued 'Umar's policies but with less skill. Under 'Uthmân the principles emerged of what may be called the 'Umayyad' caliphate (because all the effective representatives of it, starting with 'Uthmân, were of the Umayyad family). The soldier-tribesmen (*muqâtilah*) of the garrison towns, under 'Umar quartered there on a war basis, were to remain there permanently even though warfare became only episodic, living as Arabs set off from a non-Arab population. They were to be governed by the merchant families of Quraysh and its allies of Thaqîf (of Ṭâ'if), most notably men of the Umayyad family, who would uphold the central power against tribalism and localism—a situation seemingly transient under 'Umar, which now became regular policy. And both the soldier-tribesmen and the governors were to be held in check by a sentiment for a common Islam, as that which made one a true Arab.

'Uthmân could not avoid, as had 'Umar, allowing the richest Meccan families to go to the provinces, especially the Iraq, and make business ventures there—to the annoyance of the less well-advantaged local Arabs. But he did manage to reverse a tendency to allow private estates in the Sawâd, the rich irrigation land of the Iraq. He forced those who had begun to form such to transfer their investment to the Ḥijâz; there the irrigation resources of the several oases, consequently, were worked to the full for a time. This at once reduced the threat of a simple merging of Arab culture into that of the Fertile Crescent, and strengthened the central power physically. But it did not make 'Uthmân popular with the Meccans.

After some years, complaints began to mount up. A riot had to be punished with Arab blood in Kûfah. Especially after the Iranian campaigns were more or less completed, some garrison towns became discontented. After a time, most Baṣrans were satisfied under 'Uthmân's governor Ibn-'Âmir, a good general who made money in peacetime but encouraged others to do so too. The Syrians were content with Mu'âwiyah. But at Fusṭâṭ and Kûfah nothing 'Uthmân could do would satisfy. A governor's drunkenness was an obvious crime, though no worse than what 'Umar had had to tolerate. Some complained of his minor regulations of the cult, which by now was assuming fixed time-honoured forms. Essential to the role of Islam as a pledge of Arab unity was his insistence on the use in all garrison towns of a single standardized collection of the Qur'ânic revelations. He caused all deviant editions to be burned. This was accepted in most places ('Uthmân's version is the present form of the Qur'ân), but it aroused resentment among the Qur'ân-reciters (especially the revered Ibn-Mas'ûd at Kûfah), many of whom had had their own versions, varying in minor details. The Kûfans long refused to comply.

Many began to complain of 'Uthmân's tendency to nepotism, seeing in a clique of his relatives the cause of their other grievances. Though himself one of the first converts, 'Uthmân was of the Banû Umayyah family (the Umayyads), most of whom, like their leader Abû-Sufyân, had opposed Muḥammad till almost the last minute. 'Umar had made extensive use of the experience and skill of members of that family, but 'Uthmân gave them and their associates almost a monopoly of top posts, often letting himself be dominated by them. This made him unpopular with the Anṣâr families of Medina.

Finally, some in the garrison towns complained of the financial system itself, which 'Umar had set up but which under 'Uthmân displayed its weak points. They disliked seeing the revenues of their districts controlled, as fay', state property, from Medina (not without some traces of nepotism again) rather than reserved directly for themselves. Some seem to have suggested that the conquered lands, like the booty in battles, ought to have been distributed outright among the soldiers. In any case, no part of the revenue was to be sent to Medina. There is some indication that 'Alî b. Abî-Ṭâlib, Muḥammad's young cousin (and also son-in-law) who had grown up in his household, had already opposed 'Umar's policies and opposed 'Uthmân's still more. He was known as a mighty warrior and was felt to be a spokesman for the malcontents. He now became a symbol of the party of protest.[5]

In 656 the discontent culminated. The Medinese had encouraged the provincial garrisons in resistance—notably at Kûfah, where 'Uthmân's governor was finally refused outright. A group of Arab soldiers, come back from Egypt to claim what they felt were their rights, seem to have been cozened by 'Uthmân's associates into returning home with false assurances of redress; when they discovered their leaders were to be executed instead, they returned mutinously. After a period of general negotiation and counterplotting, in which

[5] A case for an early active role of protest on the part of 'Alî has been made by Laura Veccia-Vaglieri in 'Sulla origine della denominazione "Sunniti"' *Studi Orientalistici in onore di Giorgio Levi della Vida*, 2 (Rome, 1956), 473–85, an article relevant also to the subsequent Marwânî times. All of Veccia-Vaglieri's several writings on this period are worth reading.

the non-Umayyad leading families at Medina seem to have been largely neutral, the mutineers broke into 'Uthmân's house and murdered him. (His power like that of Abû-Bakr and 'Umar had rested on pious prestige alone; he did not even have a private bodyguard.)

Thereupon, two dozen years after Muḥammad's death, began a five-year period of *fitnah*, literally 'temptation' or 'trials', a time of civil war for the control of the Muslim community and of its vast conquered territories. 'Uthmân had had many opponents among Muḥammad's associates at Medina, who had done little to control the mutinous soldiery. They now divided over the spoils.[6] The mutineers, and most Medinese too, acclaimed, as new caliph, 'Alî, who accepted after a brief delay. Muḥammad's favourite wife, 'Â'ishah, with two of his most eminent associates among the Meccan Muhâjirûn, thereupon called for revenge for 'Uthmân and attacked 'Alî for not punishing as murderers the mutineers, now his most ardent supporters. The mutineers maintained that 'Uthmân had been justly killed, for acting treacherously and for not governing according to the Qur'ân; hence no vengeance was to be invoked. 'Alî had to accept this argument. He withdrew to Kûfah, where he had partisans, and his opponents to Baṣrah; for all military strength was in the provinces. Victorious in the resulting struggle, 'Alî made his capital at Kûfah. He was able to appoint his partisans governors in most provinces; but his chief strength lay in the Iraq. Kûfah was the chief Muslim post in the Sawâd, that part of the Mesopotamian alluvial plain where investment in irrigation had reached its peak, and where the revenues had been reserved by the Sâsânians for state purposes directly. The Sawâd formed perhaps the single most lucrative part of the fay', therefore. 'Alî did distribute what was in the treasury to the soldiers, but did not get round to dividing up the Sawâd, if he ever intended to.

'Alî had not been recognized in Syria, however, and Mu'âwiyah b. Abî-Sufyân, as governor there, in turn took up the call for revenge for 'Uthmân, his cousin. 'Alî marched toward Syria, but extensive skirmishing and negotiating in 657 at Ṣiffîn, on the upper Euphrates, was inconclusive till Mu'âwiyah's men (who, according to the Iraqis, were finally threatened with defeat) put Qur'âns on the ends of their lances and called for arbitration according to God's word. Many of 'Alî's followers approved this way of ending fighting between Muslims and forced him to accept it. A good number of Muhammad's leading associates were 'neutrals', refusing to take sides in quarrels among Muslims. 'Alî was forced now to choose as his representative one of these,

[6] The 'associates' of Muḥammad, those Muslims who came into contact with him personally, formed, especially in later Muslim eyes, a special body of men and women, many of whose names are known. The Arabic term is *ṣaḥâbah*, for which I use the term 'associates' where most writers say 'companions'. The term 'companion' implies too close a familiarity to include, as the expression must, those who associated with Muḥammad only briefly or even transiently. With a proper warning, such as scholars usually give somewhere, the word 'companion' is doubtless harmless, but 'associate' seems less misleading, being more impersonal.

Abû-Mûsà al-Ash'arî, whom the Kûfans had made their governor in defiance of 'Uthmân but who was no special friend of 'Alî.

Meanwhile, however, some of 'Alî's soldiers repented of having left up to arbitration by neutrals a question—the guilt of 'Uthmân—which they felt

Events of the First Fitnah, 656–661

656	Caliph 'Uthmân is killed at Medina (siege of 'Uthmân's house) by mutineers from Egypt vs. defenders, of Umayyad family	
	Party of 'Alî (cousin and son-in-law of Muḥammad) raises him to caliphate—	Opposed by party appealing to vengeance for 'Uthmân,
	supported by the mutineers, Medina Anṣâr, and Kûfans	led by 'Â'ishah (favourite wife of Muḥammed) and Zubayr and Ṭalḥah (close associates of Muḥammad)
	—'Alî victorious at 'Battle of ('Â'ishah's) Camel' near Basrah—	
	Party of 'Alî, caliph at Kûfah, recognized in most provinces	—resisted still by party of Mu'âwiyah (Umayyad governor of Syria) appealing for vengeance for 'Uthmân
657	—Stalemate at battles of Ṣiffîn on the Euphrates—	
	('Alî's commander: al-Malik al-Ashtar)	
	—leading to—	
658	—fruitless arbitration (both 'Alî and Mu'âwiyah rejected) at Adhruḥ in Syrian desert—	
	('Alî's mediator: Abû-Mûsà al-Ash'arî, governor of Kûfah).	(Mu'âwiyah's mediator: 'Amr b. al-'Âṣ, conqueror of Egypt).
	'Alî's partisans split: Khârijî party (opposed to arbitration) vs. party of 'Alî (the Shî'ah). Khârijî party defeated at the Nahrawân canal in the Iraq	Meanwhile, Mu'âwiyah gains Egypt; 'Amr b. al-'Âṣ, governor there.
660		Mu'âwiyah proclaimed caliph in Jerusalem
661	'Alî murdered by Ibn-Muljam, a Khârijî	
	—Ḥasan b. 'Alî sells his rights as caliph to Mu'âwiyah—	

already had been settled by Qur'ânic standards. When 'Alî refused to join them and held to the agreement to arbitrate, they left him to form their own camp, first at Ḥarûrâ', near Kûfah. These included some of his most pious followers, notably many Qur'ân-reciters; they accused 'Alî of compromising with the supporters of injustice and so betraying his trust, which was to right the wrongs committed by 'Uthmân. These extremists, the *Shurât*, more commonly (though less accurately) called *Khârijîs* ('seceders' or 'rebels'), elected their own commander, independent of the other Muslims. Most of the first group who seceded were wiped out by 'Alî's forces, but their movement spread, inheriting the more uncompromising claims for egalitarian justice which had arisen among the opponents of 'Uthmân.

When the arbitration did take place, in 658, the position of the mutineers was condemned, and hence implicitly 'Alî as well. 'Alî rejected the decision (but without repenting of having awaited it, and so without reconciling the Khârijîs, who now saw him as acting purely for personal power) and tried to march again against Syria. But his severities against the Khârijîs seem to have discredited him even at Kûfah, where he often could raise no army at all to fight. Thereafter, in years of often desultory fighting, Mu'âwiyah made steady headway, first taking over Egypt. Many Arabs remained neutral and 'Alî gradually lost much of his following. A second arbitration, in which most leading Muslims but not 'Alî took part, tried in vain to agree on another candidate for the caliphate; for Mu'âwiyah's followers were by now insisting that the caliph be he, and most others were not yet ready to accept this. The arbitrations had had little success except to discredit 'Alî's claims to the caliphate. But Mu'âwiyah's forces proved able to defeat local resistance in Arabia. In 661, 'Alî was murdered by a Khârijî; his son, Ḥasan, was elevated by his still loyal following at Kûfah, but came to an accommodation with Mu'âwiyah whereby he retired in wealth to Medina. Mu'âwiyah, who was a brother-in-law of the Prophet, was then accepted in all the provinces as caliph.

During the civil strife, the Arabs had been driven out of the province of Khurâsân by upholders of Sâsânian power and had made no advances elsewhere; these setbacks were soon recovered. But enduring party strife had arisen. The handful of surviving Khârijîs had established a pattern: at Baṣrah and Kûfah, already under Mu'âwiyah's caliphate, more than once zealous groups of men set themselves off against the bulk of the Arabs in little war bands, summoning the Muslims to higher standards and meanwhile living by pillage and tribute. They believed themselves the only true Muslim community, the only genuine supporters of divine justice. They conceived that the way of true Islam implied making war on all self-styled Muslims who did not accept the Khârijîs' own rigorous standards; and, leaving the garrison towns, the more activist of them proceeded to do this whenever practicable. More immediately important, the Arabs of the Iraq and those of Syria had become enduringly embittered against each other. The Iraqîs were quiescent for the time, but in Kûfah 'Alî and his family continued to be regarded as symbols of local power against the Syrians. And potentially 'Alî was even more than this. He had ceased to stand, as he may have at first, for an abstract principle; this the Khârijîs had made impossible. But his fate took on all the more meaning on a symbolic level. He could be seen as a great and serious man (and he was certainly intensely loved by those who did adhere to him at all costs), caught by the ignoble logic of events and abandoned and dragged down to a defeat which he may have deserved on the level of practical politics, but which his personal stature could make seem intolerable. His figure was an appropriate one henceforth round which to rally those who would protest against the logic of events, as well as against the injustices of a centralizing government. Very early his story came to be written as that of the noble man ruined by the inconstancy of his friends as much as the malice of his enemies and finally by that power of brute force which we must inexplicably confront.

On the other hand, there were many Muslims everywhere for whom the fitnah wars had been a lesson in the importance of Muslim unity. For them, the *jamâ'ah*, the whole Muslim community taken collectively, took on a special spiritual importance as being under divine protection. But it was the neutrals, whose allegiance to Mu'âwiyah had been reluctant, for whom the principle of the jamâ'ah remained primary. They did not merge with Mu'âwiyah's own Syrian partisans. They regarded the Syrian power as a stopgap, and if they had been dissatisfied with 'Alî, they remained ready to condemn Mu'âwiyah also if he failed their high expectations. Mu'âwiyah could re-establish 'Uthmân's policies, but he could not regain 'Uthmân's prestige. Even those who rejected the incipient Shî'ism of the time, in favour of loyalty to the whole community in its actual historical fate, had become potentially oppositional in spirit. On 'Uthmân's murder, the centre of power had been irretrievably withdrawn from the ideally neutral Medina, lying in the shadow of Muḥammad's prestige, to the provincial garrison towns where lay military might. Henceforth the Muslims were not to be held together without calling into play the might of one faction or another.

In launching the venture of Islam, the events of the first generation after Muḥammad were almost as formative as those of Muḥammad's own time. It is not accidental that later Muslims have identified themselves in terms of these events and of the factions that grew out of them. They have interpreted the whole of history in symbolism derived from them, and have made the interpretation of those events and of the leading personalities in them the very test of religious allegiance. This has confused the factual historical picture. But at the same time it has highlighted the points at which we must see the events of the time as crucial in the development of Muslim religious awareness.

The reign of Mu'âwiyah and the second fitnah

Mu'âwiyah (661-680) restored unity to the Arab ruling community. In fundamentals, he restored the system that 'Umar had created and that under 'Uthmân had been adapted into a continuing political tradition, though Mu'âwiyah (Umayyad though he was) depended less on the Umayyad family as the central support of his policy. But he restored unity no longer on the basis of the prestige of Muḥammad's city and the consensus of Muḥammad's old associates there. It was rather on the basis of a more generalized awareness of common interests—together with the military force of Mu'âwiyah's own loyal Syrian troops. The Arabs, aware of their precarious position in the conquered provinces and touched by a widespread horror of dissidence within Islam, were mostly happy to accept an arrangement which settled their mutual rivalries on a basis of reasonably generous agreements, even though one party, that of the Syrians, was somewhat advantaged. Mu'âwiyah did not depend, therefore, as had 'Umar and 'Uthmân, on the inherent sanctity of the fact that he also, like them, had had close relations with Muḥammad (if only at the last minute); his Syrian Arab troops honoured him personally, and were ready to use force even against other Muslims. It was this strength that helped persuade most Muslims to judge him the man most likely to be able to enforce unity among Muslims and, accordingly, to give him their allegiance as Islamic leader.

The caliphal state stood now as a more mundane imperial power, no longer based directly on Islam. Rather it was supported internally as well as externally by a particular complex of military and physical power which was partially supported in turn by Islamic faith. Militarily, Mu'âwiyah could depend, in a crisis, on the Syrian Arabs—including Christians as well as Muslims among them—whose relatively strong discipline allowed them pre-eminence (if not yet dominance) among all the other Arabs. The other Arab troops, however, still formed the major part of the force of the state, and were at his disposal so long as he controlled Syria. Fiscally, Mu'âwiyah could likewise depend in a crisis only on the revenues of Syria; but here, too, other revenues were greater. Mu'âwiyah took measures to make the central control of revenue more effective than 'Umar had made it. Already under 'Umar, the direct tax intervention necessary in the Sawâd of the Iraq had been leading to similar tax patterns in Syria and elsewhere. There the original treaties were adjusted to a standard level—and the poll tax of city people was graduated rather than left as a lump sum on a per capita basis. The state was becoming more centralized.

During the fitnah wars, many Muslims had reserved the right to refuse their allegiance to any given claimant, insisting that as Arabs and as Muslims they could not be governed without their personal consent. When Ḥujr b. 'Adî in Kûfah, an ardent partisan of 'Alî, made this refusal now and on the basis of it insulted Mu'âwiyah's governor, threatening to rouse rebellion, Mu'âwiyah captured him, haled him to Syria and, on his continued refusal, had him killed. Rightly, the Kûfans saw in this act an infringement of the free dignity of a tribesman and perhaps of the direct responsibility of a Muslim individually to God. Mu'âwiyah saw it, also quite correctly, as a step essential to maintaining intact the Islamic community.

Nevertheless, Mu'âwiyah respected the freedom and dignity of Muslims once they admitted his rule. And Islam was a cornerstone of his policy. He had to curb equally those who would disrupt the community through asserting local authority and those who would insist on central authority but without the religious purpose that such authority was founded on. Mu'âwiyah represented, in fact, the Muslim community as a whole, the jamâ'ah. As had been true from Muḥammad's time on, Muslim community policy as formed by the ruler, though not directed by the Qur'ân, was still given effective support by it. Mu'âwiyah was no autocrat, but remained more the Arab chief, first among equals. Though, like 'Uthmân, he was of the Banû Umayyah (Umayyads), he gave them no special precedence. Though he depended on his Syrians, they received only a minimum of special privilege. His first appeal—which was in fact what had given him victory in the fitnah—was to unity in Islam.

Mu'âwiyah's reign saw the reconquest of most of Khurâsân, and its permanent settlement with garrison towns; many further eastern Iranian lands were systematically subdued, including part of the middle Oxus valley. Much of Anatolia was garrisoned for brief periods, naval supremacy was maintained in the eastern Mediterranean, and Constantinople besieged; but little permanent advance was achieved in Byzantine territories except for the subjection of the Armenian highlands. Westward from Egypt, there was a first occupation of the eastern Berber lands in the Maghrib as far as the present Algeria. As was appropriate to the restorer of the caliphal state, the conquering force of Islam was renewed; but the expansive power was no longer so overwhelming. A new political balance had had time to develop in such lands as had not been overwhelmed at first, and henceforth further conquests were due as much to the resources of an established major empire still in full vigour, as to the pressure of the mass enthusiasms which seemed almost to carry themselves forward in the time of 'Umar and 'Uthmân.

In his lifetime, Mu'âwiyah insisted that the Muslims recognize his son Yazîd as his successor. (Yazîd was probably the only man whom the Syrians were ready to accept, for a man of any other family would bring in his own family and clan ties, which would upset the delicate balance of forces Mu'âwiyah had fostered.) Yazîd continued Mu'âwiyah's policies for four turbulent years (680–683) but was less fortunate in his governance. In northeastern Iran his lieutenants continued to advance; but against the Byzantines he was on the defensive. Just before Mu'âwiyah's death, a four-year siege of Constantinople had had to be abandoned with great loss. Even within Syria, some Christian mountaineers were carrying out raids with Byzantine support. Yazîd had to begin his reign by fortifying the Byzantine frontier. And his appointee in the Maghrib provoked a successful revolt of the Berbers.

Yazîd was soon preoccupied with the beginnings of a second round of fitnah wars at home. The old Muslim families of Medina refused to recognize him and encouraged resistance to him. 'Alî's second son and (through his mother, Fâṭimah) Muḥammad's grandson, Ḥusayn, was invited to raise a rebellion in Kûfah; but then the Kûfans were cowed by the Syrian governor before he arrived. Ḥusayn and his tiny force refused to surrender; they were isolated in the desert at nearby Karbalâ' and killed (680). Then the Ḥijâz itself rose in revolt; the most prominent figure in this movement was 'Abd-Allâh Ibn-al-Zubayr, son of one of the major associates of Muḥammad who had opposed 'Alî after the death of 'Uthmân.

Events of the Second Fitnah, 680–692

Syria	Hijâz	The Iraq
680 Yazîd I succeeds Mu'âwiyah as caliph		**680** Ḥusayn b. 'Alî attempts to raise Kûfah, is killed at Karbalâ
	681 Ibn-al-Zubayr raises revolt in Mecca and Medina	
683 Yazîd dies, leaving a small son (Mu'âwiyah II), who dies	**683** Marwânî forces take Medina (under Muslim b. 'Uqbah, at Battle of the Ḥarrah), besiege Mecca	
	Siege of Mecca lifted; Ibn-al-Zubayr generally recognized as caliph	
684 At Marj Râhiṭ, Kalb and Umayyad party victorious over Qays and Zubayrid party, establish Marwân in most of Syria; from which he then takes Egypt	**684** Khârijîs rebel in Najd, under Najdah b. 'Âmir	**684** Azraqî Khârijîs, largely from Baṣrah, rise in the Iraq and Iran; are opposed by general Muhallab b. Abî-Ṣufrah (who at last defeats them in 699)
		684 The Tawwâbûn Shî'îs of Kûfah attack Syrians in revenge for Ḥusayn
685 'Abd-al-Malik succeeds his father, Marwân, in Syria		**685** Mukhtâr asserts rule of 'Alî's son Ibn-al-Ḥanafiyyah at Kûfah
	687–691 Khârijîs prevail in much of Arabia	**687** Muṣ'ab b. al-Zubayr (brother of the caliph), governor at Baṣrah, puts down Mukhtâr
		691 Muṣ'ab defeated by Syrians
	692 Ibn-al-Zubayr defeated and killed by Syrians (under Ḥajjâj) at Mecca	

This revolt had been almost crushed when Yazîd died, leaving no suitable successor in his family. His death delivered the support of most Muslims to the most eminent of the candidates for the caliphate, Ibn-al-Zubayr, who now appointed governors to the provinces from his capital at Mecca. But tribal rivalries in some provinces and religious partisanship in others undermined his authority. The local powers that acknowledged Ibn-al-Zubayr proceeded effectively on their own, each chiefly for itself. In Syria, the Arab tribes were divided into the Qays, relatively new immigrants, and the Kalb, relatively long established in the land, and with whom Mu'âwiyah had cultivated close ties. The Kalb upheld against Ibn-al-Zubayr an Umayyad cousin of Mu'âwiyah's, Marwân (who had been 'Uthmân's chief adviser) and, defeating the Qays, succeeded in imposing his rule in that province as a counter-caliph.[7]

Elsewhere, the party of protest which had been associated with 'Alî became active; but it too was split into factions. Though for a time some Khârijîs were willing to support Ibn-al-Zubayr, soon, in Iran and in Arabia, bands of Khârijîs set up two separate régimes; that in Arabia controlled for a time the greater part of the peninsula. Egalitarianism and puritanism were carried so far among them that the ruler of the moment was subject to deposition at any time for any moral error that the group chose to condemn. In principle, the Khârijîs made no distinction between Arab and non-Arab: what mattered was that a man be Muslim; but those in Iran (called Azraqîs) condemned as apostates all those professing Muslims that did not accept their position; and literally put them under the death sentence.

From the viewpoint of the non-Muslim population at large, the Khârijî

[7] In this case, as in some others, the historical categories used in this work differ from the usual. Marwân is usually regarded as the legitimate caliph and Ibn-al-Zubayr as an 'anti-caliph' because in the end the Marwânids won. At the time, however, there was no question of legitimacy, and Ibn-al-Zubayr was in fact the nearest to an effective successor to Yazîd's power, or at least to his status. Ignoring this fact has caused some authors to misevaluate the meaning of 'Abd-al-Malik's victory, which can appear merely as suppression of rebellion. The error results from projecting backward, without warrant, an alien notion of dynastic legitimacy.

This has been done not only in the case of Marwân, but throughout the early period: writers have marked off the periods of the caliphate according to extraneous criteria. Following later Sunnî Muslims, they make the reign of 'Alî (with that of Ḥasan) a fourth Medina (or 'Orthodox') caliphate, set off from the reign of Mu'âwiyah, who (with his son) is lumped—as an Umayyad—with the Marwânids, though 'Uthmân is not (despite his pro-Umayyad nepotism). For the older Muslim historians, the distinction between 'Orthodox' and 'Umayyad' caliphs had a symbolic value. When 'Alî came to be lumped with the three Medina caliphs (quite late), Mu'âwiyah was correspondingly lumped with the Marwânids. This allowed the Muslims to split the work of establishing the caliphal structure into two parts: into the 'good' side of that work (including whatever was approved, of the work of subsequent caliphs), which was ascribed to 'Umar; and into the 'bad' side (including much of what 'Umar did), symbolized in the setting up of 'kingship', which was ascribed to Mu'âwiyah and the 'Umayyads'. For this purpose, 'Uthmân was 'Orthodox' and not 'Umayyad'. But such considerations need not bind the modern historian. They are of the same order as the inclination to see as 'heretical' any forms of Islam which were not later received by the majority (or rather by certain widely respected later Muslim authors).

form of Islam may have seemed the ideal form of Muslim rule: the Khârijîs remained separate from the dhimmî populace and in maintaining the purity of Muslim life ensured clear control over the Muslims in the lands, who did not become rivals to the local establishment. They were lined up against the garrison towns and, at least in the following decade or so, received a degree of support (at least in the Jazîrah) from the rural population. At any rate, they were able to carry on in the Jazîrah and in Iran what amounted to guerilla warfare. During the second fitnah, it was the Khârijîs who succeeded in controlling the largest extent of territory, though they did not control any of the important garrison towns. But a more or less passive support by the peasantry could not make up for lack of support among the organized Muslims (except among the Arabian tribes themselves, who, however, were not inclined to allow the Khârijîs an overruling power, to escape which some of them may have supported the Khârijîs against the city Muslims). The troops of Baṣrah, with some support from elsewhere, made steady progress against them.

In Kûfah, a quite different party of protest prevailed: that of ʿAlid loyalism. It proved less conscientious than the Khârijîs and also less intolerant. Repentance for the failure to support Ḥusayn at Karbalâʾ, whose death was all the more horrible because of his descent from the Prophet, moved many to attempt some form of expiation. Those who were actively loyal to the cause of ʿAlî's family came to be called the *Shîʿah* (party) of ʿAlî. A number set off to avenge Ḥusayn's death against the Syrians, without positive results. This sentiment soon was channelled into an attempt to set up another of ʿAlî's sons, Ibn-al-Ḥanafiyyah, as caliph. This Shîʿî revolt was led by Mukhtâr b. Abî-ʿUbayd, who attempted an egalitarianism more moderate than that of the Khârijîs.[8] He gave the non-Arab converts to Islam, called *Mawâlî*, equal status as to booty. But this so enraged the old Kûfan families that they turned against him. Even so, he was put down (687) only with difficulty by Ibn-al-Zubayr's governor at Baṣrah, who diverted Baṣran energies for the moment away from the Khârijî campaigns, to this end.

Each of the major claimants to the caliphate hoped to control the whole of the Muslim territory, no one province being conceived as capable of standing alone. Of all the conflicting forces, the Umayyad house in Syria proved the strongest. As we have seen, those who were keeping the Khârijîs at bay in the Iraq accepted the Zubayrid leadership and under it overcame the Shîʿîs in the Iraq; but Ibn-al-Zubayr, head of his party, remained isolated in the Ḥijâz, partly because of Khârijî control of so much territory in Arabia. Meanwhile, those who counted in Syria proved more able to unite than did the Iraqis; Egypt had quickly fallen to Marwân and his son, who thus succeeded to the

[8] The form *Shîʿî* as derivative of *Shîʿah* is awkward to pronounce in English and sometimes even those who usually use the *-î* ending, instead of the older *-ite*, will say 'Shîʿite'. In India, a Shîʿî is commonly miscalled 'a Shîʿah', but properly a Shîʿah is a *party*, not an individual; if one says 'the Shîʿahs did' such and such, this should mean that the several Shîʿî parties did so—the 'Twelver' Shîʿah, the 'Zaydî' Shîʿah, etc.—not the Shîʿîs as individuals.

home provinces of the Syrian caliphate. In the subsequent contest between Syria and the Iraq, Syria won. The forces of the garrison towns then continued their struggle against the Khârijîs as readily under vigorous Marwânî leadership as under the loose authority of Ibn-al-Zubayr. (I use the general term 'Marwânî' for the men associated with Marwân and with his descendants, the 'Banû Marwân' or Marwânids.) Thus eventually the Marwânî forces disposed of all their rivals; they took Mecca in 692 and put an end to Ibn-al-Zubayr himself. (In the process, the Ka'bah was wrecked and had to be rebuilt.)

The Marwânî state

It was Marwân's son 'Abd-al-Malik (692-705) who thus became the third great caliph in Islam, after 'Umar and Mu'âwiyah. The fitnah had not been brought to a conclusion by an accommodation, this time; it had been fought out to the end. Accordingly, 'Abd-al-Malik had to establish the state unambiguously on the basis first of all of force, with religious allegiance brought into play only when force had first decided who was to be master. Supreme personal power was made hereditary in Marwân's family (succession by designation of the previous ruler, in effect), as can be seen in the chart of the Umayyad family. 'Abd-al-Malik's lieutenant, al-Ḥajjâj b. Yûsuf (d. 714), who had reduced Mecca to obedience (it was he who had bombarded the Ka'bah), ruled single-handed the eastern half of the empire—what had been the Sâsânian dominions. A former school-teacher of the Thaqîf tribe (of Ṭâ'if), he had risen by his ruthless efficiency. He added to the revenues by administrative vigour which regularized and increased investment in the agriculture of the Sawâd of the Iraq, and he controlled the Iraqi Muslims by frank terror directed against the disaffected. After further Iraqi revolt, he built a new provincial capital, al-Wâsiṭ, between Kûfah and Baṣrah, handy to either centre of opposition, and garrisoned it with loyal Syrian Muslims; these were kept jealously separate from the Iraqi Muslims. In the western (ex-Roman and Arabian) territories 'Abd-al-Malik (and his brother, 'Abd-al-'Azîz, in Egypt) ruled with policies equally firm, though terror was less needed. (In such territorial arrangements we may see the last traces of the Meccan system as Muḥammad had reconstituted it. The lands from Syria to the Yemen were still the core of the empire, though now ruled one-sidedly from Syria; while the former Sâsânian territories were ruled as a huge appendage thereto.) 'Abd-al-Malik was succeeded without question by his son al-Walîd in 705, and then by other members of his family (the Marwânids), for almost half a century.

The Marwânî state was, however, thoroughly Islamic as Islam was then understood. In the first generations, Islamic religion was, by later standards, still rudimentary in the consciousness of the faithful: it was above all a badge of united Arabism, the code and discipline of a conquering élite. On this basis, 'Abd-al-Malik and his family upheld the ideal of jamâ'ah, of the solidarity of the Muslim community over against the factionalism of the Arab tribal or

The Umayyad Caliphs

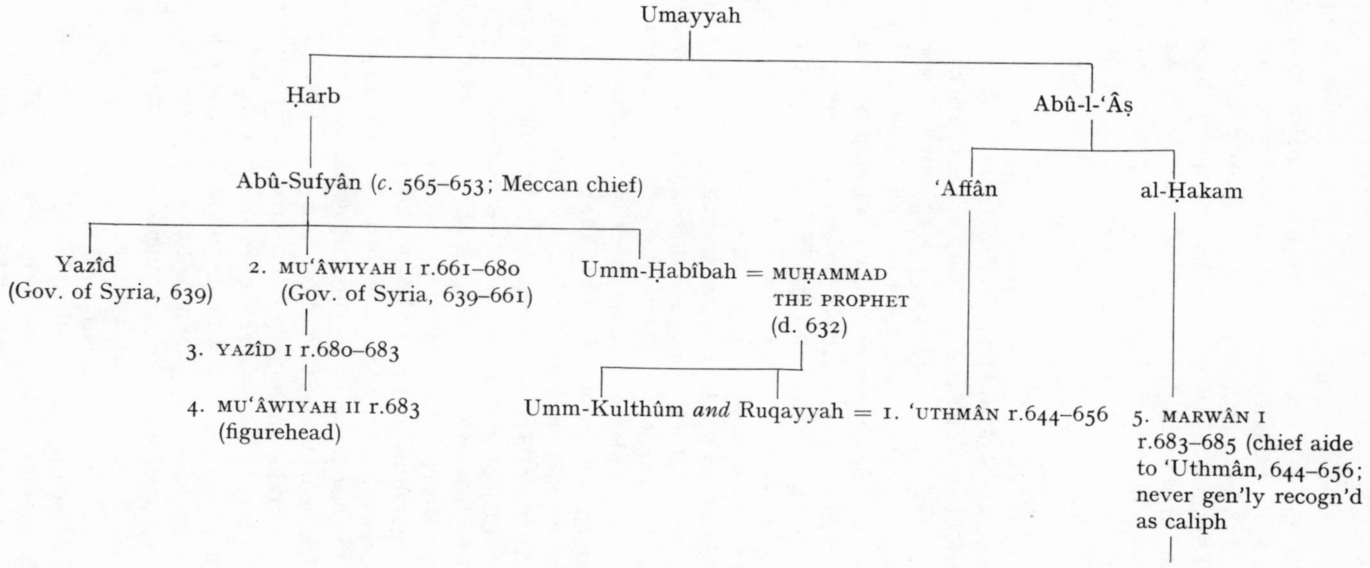

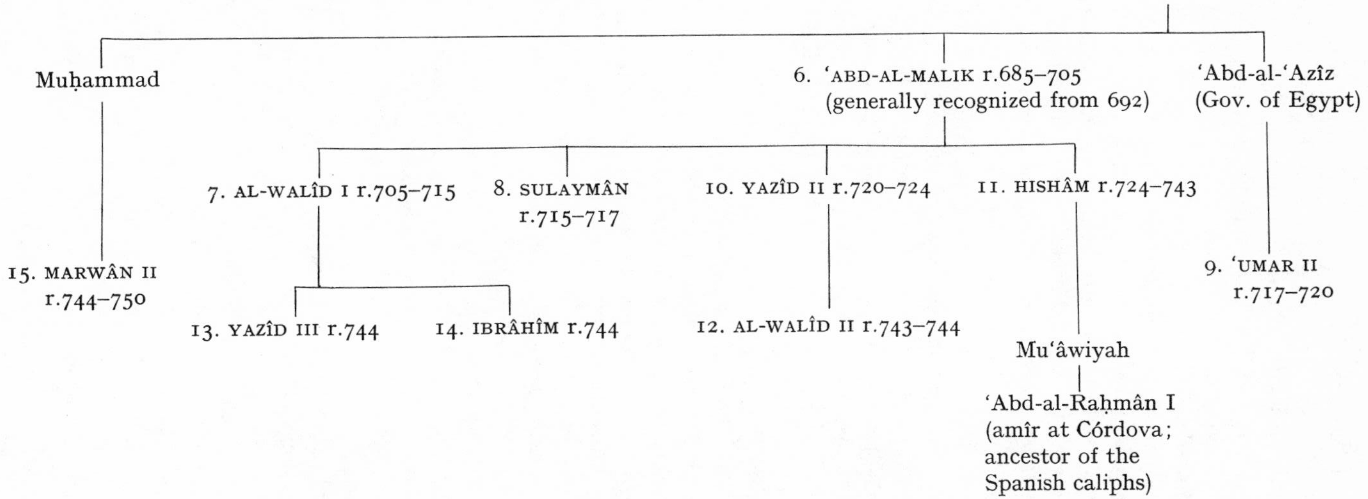

NOTE: Caliphs or claimants to the caliphate are in capitals, numbered in sequence (note that most Muslim historians would not include ʻUthmân among the Umayyad caliphs, for religious reasons).

Reigns are dated from the year of claim rather than of effective power over Islam.

regional groupings. ʿAbd-al-Malik and his lieutenant al-Ḥajjâj were concerned to maintain the supremacy of Islam when they substituted for the coinage of the old infidel empires new coins with Islamic inscriptions, and intervened to assure fidelity in the reciting of the Qur'ân by encouraging more exact ways of writing it down than an imperfect script had hitherto allowed. Alongside the governors, they appointed special judges in the camp towns, called *qâḍîs*, who were to settle disputes among the Muslims on an Islamic basis. They did not encourage, and even discouraged, conversions to Islam from the subject populations; but this was in conformity with the most common view of Islam among Muslims. Islam, among the several revealed religious allegiances, was the one that should guide those in command among men, and these should be the Arabs, to whom Islam was properly given.

The Arab realm made its last major advance under ʿAbd-al-Malik and al-Walîd (705–715). The losses suffered during the second fitnah were recovered, notably in the Oxus valley and among the eastern Berbers. The Berbers, the bulk of the inland population in the Maghrib (North Africa), were rather like the Arabs themselves in having been marginal to citied civilization, though their mountain nomadism was less unsettled; they had little confessional religion and were converted en masse to Islam. Once they had had to admit the superior power of the Arabs, they joined them in the further conquests. The more westerly Berbers were relatively easily swept up into the movement. Thus a secondary centre of Muslim conquest was established in the west Mediterranean, in some respects relatively independent of the main centre. By 711 a raid was launched into the Spanish peninsula, with the aid of newly converted Berber troops, and that kingdom (like some other Christian lands subject to a fiercely persecuting church) was quickly and definitively conquered with local Maghribî resources and little help from the east Mediterranean.

Expeditions from Syria against the heart of the Byzantine empire led again to a great siege of Constantinople, but when that failed no part of Anatolia beyond the Taurus mountains could be held. (The Byzantine cities in the Maghrib, however, were occupied when the Berber tribes were converted in their hinterland.) Eastward, the lower Indus valley, Sind, was conquered partly by land and partly by sea. The local Buddhists, who were evidently in part mercantile in orientation, seem to have preferred the Muslims to the Hindu ruling classes.

More important was the occupation, from Khurâsân, of the Oxus and Zarafshân basin to the northeast under the able lead of the general Qutaybah b. Muslim. There, mercantile city-states tried to play off, for a time, Chinese against Muslim influence, but in the end were forced to accept Muslim control. The frontier between Muslims and Chinese was finally settled in the high mountains just halfway between the capitals of the two imperial powers.[9] The

[9] The best introduction to the nature of Muslim conquest, after the very first thrusts, is H. A. R. Gibb, *The Arab Conquests in Central Asia* (London, 1923); it brings out the

Muslim conquests, like any conquests, had their shameful episodes. The story goes that when Baykand (near Bukhârâ) was occupied by Qutaybah's men, the captain in charge took possession of the two beautiful daughters of one of the citizens, and ignored the man's complaint that he should be so singled out; whereupon the man stabbed the captain. In any case, the rest of the region being as yet unoccupied, when the main part of the Arab forces had withdrawn southwards, the town rose against the Arab garrison and drove it out, presumably regarding the Arab incursion beyond the old Sâsânian territories as a transitory event. But the town was immediately reoccupied and made an example. The captured men were all killed and the women and children enslaved, and the city itself was levelled. (Yet this ferocity was mitigated—and the mitigation is doubtless as indicative as the ferocity. For, as it happened, a large part of the merchants of the city—the main body of its inhabitants—had been away on the trade caravan eastward; when they returned in due course, they were allowed to ransom their wives and children, and eventually they rebuilt their town.)

Under the later Marwânids some of these acquisitions were further entrenched (notably in the face of a rebellion in the Zarafshân valley [a northern near-tributary of the Oxus] which threatened Muslim holdings in the whole region, crushed in 737). Some lesser bases were acquired, for instance in southern Gaul. But on the whole, conquest came to a stop. The whole of the Sâsânian and half the Roman empires had been conquered, together with several lands which had been in the cultural orbit of one or the other empire but had not recently been under their sway.

The Arab tribesmen had established themselves in the occupied territories as rulers and as ultimate dispensers of the revenues of the land (that is, according to ways dating from the time when cities were first established, whatever produce could be taken from the actual producers without incapacitating them). They had left the internal life of the conquered Christian, Jewish, Mazdean, and Buddhist communities to proceed on its own, provided the supremacy was left to the Arabs. For the time being the prevailing culture continued to be Hellenistic, Sâsânian, or whatever existed locally, while the Muslim Arabs themselves carried with them as much of the old Arabian culture as could survive transplanting.

This Arabian culture possessed, in fact, considerable vigour. It was carried and reinforced by a reconstituted tribal system, based on the garrison towns (and not very influential among those who had remained Bedouin in Arabia). On the imperial scale, the smaller tribal units had lost their importance and tribal groups tended to coalesce into larger alliances. In each garrison town or occupied country, two or three main tribal blocs were formed, which in turn recognized allies in corresponding blocs elsewhere. In a general way, they

---

complications introduced by a local setting and by long-distance connections, and the special role played by Islam as such. It also shows how the evidence can be used to cut through legend to actuality. Though it is limited to one area, it is suggestive for all.

The Tribal Blocs of the Garrison Towns, by Alleged Genealogy

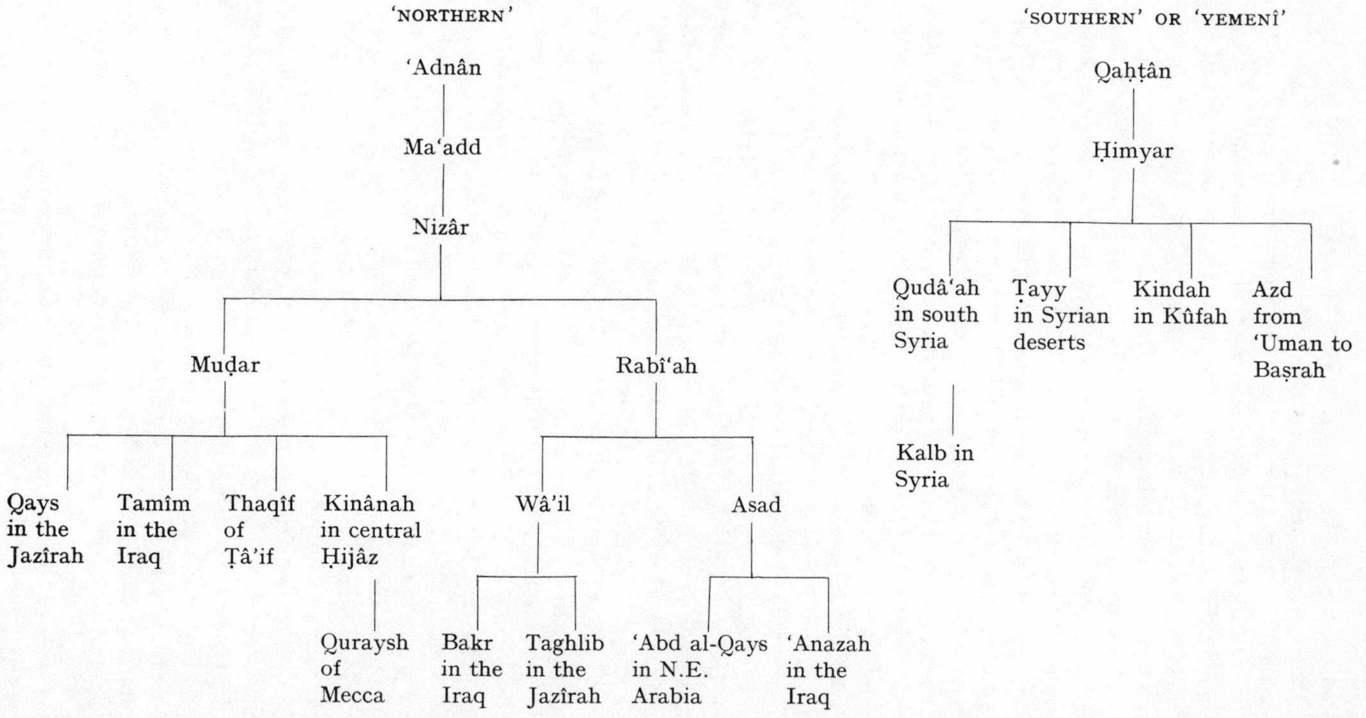

identified themselves (from the time of the struggle between the Qays and the Kalb in Syria) as the 'northern' (Nizâr) Arabs, represented by the Qays, against the 'southern' (Yemeni or Qaḥṭân) Arabs, identified with the Kalb. (This was an ancient division, having long ceased to have much geographical significance, which was given a largely artificial genealogical form.) At least as important was a division within the 'northern' bloc between 'Muḍar' tribes and 'Rabî'ah' tribes. Tribes affiliated together as Rabî'ah and as Qaḥṭân tended to be those which had long been associated with the settled populations in Syria and the Iraq; many of them had been Christian. Rabî'ah and Qaḥṭân found themselves allied together more often than did Rabî'ah and Muḍar. While some important non-Arab groups were associated with Muḍar tribes, especially with Tamîm, it was eventually with movements more or less associated with Qaḥṭân and Rabî'ah that the ordinary non-Arab Muslims threw in their lot.

It was in terms of this neo-tribalism that power struggles within the Muslim group took place: they were carried on in factional fighting among the Arab tribal blocs. It was also on the basis of this neo-tribalism that elements of the old Arabian culture were carried over into the conquered lands. Without the all-Arabian, Bedouin-based common patterns, even the force of Islam could probably not have forestalled a renewed Aramaism or Hellenism such as had absorbed earlier Arab conquerors in the Fertile Crescent.

These Arabian traditions had relatively little inherent connection with Islam itself. Islam possessed, indeed, enormous dynamic force as a cultural tradition. But it could offer little, at first, toward the settlement of day-to-day social questions. Here a common body of cultural patterns which the conquerors shared as Arabs served better. In the new garrison towns, being an Arab was as important, therefore, as being a Muslim. Christian Arab tribes which had joined in the conquest were regarded first of all as Arabs, and not classified with the conquered dhimmî Christians. It was in no way anomalous that one of the greatest poets of the court at Damascus was al-Akhṭal (*c.* 640–710), a Christian Arab, panegyrist of 'Abd-al-Malik. The Marwânids, as had Mu'âwiyah, continued to see their power as based on agreement among the Arab tribes, rather than on individuals. Hence to be a Muslim in the full political sense, a convert had to become associated, as client (*mawlà*, pl. *mawâlî*), with one or other of the Muslim Arab tribes; as such, he and his descendants were socially inferior to the original members of the tribe, but shared its allegiances. Hence even the new converts expressed their interests through the Arab factional fighting. In this way, a base was maintained for the expression of the old Bedouin ideals, passed on even to the new recruits to Islam.

When the society of the garrison towns was well established, the classical Arabic poetry of Muḥammad's time was vigorously transplanted to the new setting; there, as in the Bedouin society, it was in the service of tribal pride or ambition. (Bedouin poetry continued to be composed within the Bedouin setting itself, of course, but it rested no longer on financing from the old rival empires, and henceforth its cultural importance there was less dynamic.) Much poetry served to express memorably the new, large-scale tribal loyalties of the garrison towns. Poetry was adapted to a newer type of loyalty also, religious loyalties; some of the best poets were zealous Khârijîs and Shî'îs. The two greatest poets after al-Akhṭal were al-Farazdaq (d. 728), a Shî'î, and Jarîr (d. 728); their rivalry was celebrated throughout Islamdom and involved all the Arabs in partisanships that crossed tribal lines (for both were of the same tribe). As before Muḥammad, the poetry was expressed in the standard Bedouin tongue (to which the Qur'ân also approximated). This became the regular language in which Muslim religious reports, legal decisions, and the like were recorded, to the exclusion not only of any particular tribal dialects (even Quraysh) but also of the uninflected dialect associated with the 'settled Arabs', which rapidly came to be more commonly spoken in the camp towns.[10] Thus the best in the pagan Arabian tradition was preserved, with its language, and adapted to the new urban and Islamic conditions. It was thus assured a share in the new culture to be created.

Under the Marwânids, what had been a collection of occupied territories was gradually transformed into a relatively unified empire, the whole apparatus of the rule of which was taken over by the Arabs and run in Arabic. At the same time, conversions to Islam from among Aramaeans and Persians were becoming ever commoner, even while much of the administering personnel continued to be non-Muslim. On the other hand, the Arabs were learning how to live like eastern Mediterranean or Iranian landlords to some degree. Distinctions inherited from older political conditions, such as the autonomy of the formerly Sâsânian areas as a body, tended to disappear; governors were appointed to every province directly from the capital. The Arabs ceased to be occupying troops and became the ruling stratum among the rest of the population, which was gradually being assimilated to them as they in turn adapted themselves to its expectations. A new civilization, common to all in the region, then began to take form.

[10] J. Blau, 'The Importance of Middle Arabic Dialects for the History of Arabic', *Studies in Islamic History and Civilization*, ed. Uriel Heyd (Hebrew University, 1961), pp. 206–28, points out how early sedentary Arabic was, as a non-inflected language. It has been speculated that even the pre-Islamic Quraysh used a non-inflected language such as some Syrian Arabs may well have used, but this seems highly improbable. The psychological gap between an inflected and a non-inflected language is greater than some students of the problem seem to suppose, masking the reality for themselves by using the word 'colloquial' where they mean 'vernacular'. The point of departure in these studies is Johann Fück, *Arabiya: Untersuchungen zur arabischen Sprach- und Stilgeschichte* (Berlin, 1950), which collects information on the fate of the classical Arabic from the time of the conquests to that of the Seljuqs. Cf. also Chaim Rabin, *Ancient West Arabian* (London, 1951), for dialect study.

BOOK TWO

The Classical Civilization of the High Caliphate

Thereafter [the Tin Woodman] walked very carefully, with his eyes on the road, and when he saw a tiny ant toiling by he would step over it, so as not to harm it. . . . 'You people with hearts,' he said, 'have something to guide you, and need never do wrong; but I have no heart, and so I must be very careful . . .'.

—*L. Frank Baum*

PROLOGUE TO BOOK TWO

With the caliphal state established as an enduring political structure within whose framework the high-cultural life of the region was to be carried on, we come to the time when the Islamic impulse began to have at least a conditioning and limiting, at best a positively formative effect on all aspects of the Irano-Semitic cultural life. We enter the time of Islamicate civilization.

The refonting of traditions

From about 692, the caliphal state was a well-established agrarian-based empire and it continued so till about 945, when the caliphal government became subordinated to other powers. We may call this the 'High Caliphate' in distinction from the more primitive caliphate from Abû-Bakr to Mu'âwiyah, when the character of the state and its durability were still in question; and in distinction from the latter-day 'Abbâsî caliphal state after 945, which was sometimes only a form carrying a figurehead, and was at best a local power with special prestige—as well as in distinction from other, less universally recognized governments claiming caliphal status. (This implies a periodization at variance with that which has been conventionally used. The chart on comparative periodization will show how the two systems mesh.)

The period was one of great prosperity. It is not clear how far this was the case throughout the Afro-Eurasian Oikoumene, but at least in China at that time what may be called a 'commercial revolution' was taking place. Under the strong government of the T'ang dynasty, which had reunited the whole Chinese agrarian region and maintained internal peace there and power abroad till near the end of our period, commerce became much more extensive and more highly organized. The intensity of commerce within China and of the accompanying urbanization greatly exceeded the preceding peak, reached in the immediate post-Axial centuries, when it was on a level with that of the contemporary Hellenistic Mediterranean. The Chinese economic activity was directly reflected in the trade in the Southern Seas (the Indian Ocean and seas eastward), where Chinese ports became an important terminus for Muslim vessels. More generally, at this time began a long period of limited but unmistakable Chinese cultural ascendancy in the Oikoumene as a whole—replacing the recent ascendancy of Indic impulses and the still earlier ascendancy of Hellenism. In art and technology, new ideas came with more persistence from China than from any other one source; and the image of a well-governed Chinese empire became well-rooted abroad, at least in the Muslim literature.

It can be surmised that the commercial life of the lands of Muslim rule was given a positive impetus by the great activity in China, especially considering its important connections with China both via the Southern Seas and overland

Comparative Periodization of the Caliphate to 1258

Periodization in This Work: Broader	Periodization in This Work: More Specific	Events and Dates (Hijrî dates in parentheses)		Conventional Periodization
		570	Birth of Muḥammad	Meccan period of Muḥammad
Period of genesis of the civilization		622(1)	Hijrah	Medina period of Muḥammad
		632(11)	Death of Muḥammed	
	Medina caliphate			
		656(35)	Death of ʻUthmân	Orthodox caliphate
	Primitive caliphate	661(41)	Reign of Mu'âwiyah	
		692(73)	Death of Ibn-al-Zubayr	
	Marwânî caliphate			Umayyad caliphate
		750(132)	Death of Marwân II	
High Caliphal Period (High Caliphate)		847(232)	Death of al-Mutawakkil	
	High ʻAbbâsid caliphate			
		945(334)	Baghdad occupied	ʻAbbâsid caliphate
Earlier Middle Period	Later ʻAbbâsid caliphate			
		1258(656)	Baghdad taken by Mongols	

through central Eurasia. In any case, commerce also enjoyed the great benefits of an extended peace which the caliphate was able to ensure within its own domains. In contrast to the disastrous warfare between Byzantium and the Sâsânians which had destroyed cities and ruined agriculture again and again here and there in the Fertile Crescent, that central area was seriously ravaged only toward the end of our period. Even when the west Mediterranean lands of Islamdom became independent, as they soon did, fighting between them and other Muslims was minimal. Muslim navies dominated the whole Mediterranean. The caliphate limited its military endeavours to annual expeditions against the Byzantine empire and minor operations along the other northern frontiers, where its power was enough concentrated, effectively to overawe any threats. Internally, disturbances were relatively infrequent and generally localized. The scourge of warfare was kept in check in most places most of the time during almost the whole of the High Caliphal Period.

Under the Marwânid caliphs and especially under the ʿAbbâsids who succeeded them, the barriers gradually fell away that had kept the evolution of the cultural life of the several conquered nations separated from each other and from the internal development of the Muslim ruling class. The leading social strata of the empire, of whatever background—even that minority that was not yet becoming Muslim—lived in a single vast society. Their common cultural patterns formed what can be called High Caliphal civilization.

These cultural patterns continued to be expressed, till almost the end of the period, in terms of a variety of linguistic and religious backgrounds. Syriac and Pahlavî continued to be major vehicles of high culture along with the newer Arabic. The revivifying of the Hellenic intellectual tradition, a most striking feature of the period, was marked by Greek translations into Syriac as well as into Arabic; Christians, Mazdeans, Jews, and even a group of Hellenistic pagans (at Ḥarrân in the Jazîrah) alongside Muslims, shared in many of the concerns of the time either within their own religious traditions or across religious lines, often in co-operation with each other.

Nevertheless, it was under the common administration and protection of the Muslim caliphate that the society prospered and the civilization flowered. What brought all the traditions together increasingly was the presence of Islam. Mazdean polemics, the ecclesiastical organization of the several Christian communities, Jewish commercial activity, all reflected the effects of the caliphal power and sometimes even the challenge of the Islamic sense of the divine. Not only was the common government, which all communities had learned to respect, Muslim. 'Muḍarî' Arabic, which the early Muslim community had used, was the one generally recognized language; it rapidly became the common language of administration and (in a form more or less touched with sedentary dialects) of longer-range commerce; accordingly, all men of wide ambition had to learn it. Those who became members of the Arabic-using, and still more of the Islam-professing, group found themselves in an advantaged position, not only politically and socially but intellectually.

This position became steadily stronger as the various cultural traditions, even in many cases religious traditions and still more so those traditions less directly associated with religion, were rendered into Arabic by translation of texts and by other transmission of skills and of lore. Eventually, he who had access to what was in Arabic had access to all the regional heritages. And once the traditions were carried in Arabic and their carriers became Muslims, the Islamic impulse began to penetrate them and to inform them with its spirit.

By the end of the period, the many older Semitic and Iranian communities had given way to a single comprehensive Muslim community. The representatives of a strictly Mazdean or Syriac Christian culture had become few and those who remained were ceasing to be culturally productive. The living traditions had been largely brought together and transformed under the auspices of Islam. What had been lost in the process—especially on the level of religious doctrine or of literary forms and ideals—was supplied from the older Arabian heritage as it had been reconstituted in the early Muslim community, and most especially from the norms and expectations which had been developed by Islam itself both in the time of Muḥammad and in the following centuries as it took up and continued the old monotheistic traditions of the region. The significant cultural life of the region was flowing within the framework of the Arabic language and the Islamic faith, among Muslims and such adherents of other religious traditions as had been assimilated culturally to Muslims.

On continuity and cultural florescence

The process of Islamicizing the traditions had done more than integrate and reform them. It had released tremendous creative energies. The High Caliphal Period was one of great cultural florescence.

Before quite Modern times, in civilized societies, a sense of continuity and repetition of established patterns moulded overwhelmingly the channels within which historical life flowed. The dialogue through which traditions were developed moved cautiously and did not readily introduce radical changes. Wholly new traditions were few. Always people were confronting new situations and inventing new ways; initiative and originality were always praised, if they were on a high level and in good taste. But 'good taste' was felt, usually, to exclude overly drastic innovations.

Continuity is easily explained. There was in fact a limit, under agrarianate conditions, to the amount of innovation that could effectively be absorbed. There was a limit, for instance, to the amount of capital available for investment; the amount was tied closely, ultimately, to the agricultural surplus. Any innovation that required great capital outlay was normally ruled out in advance, and this limitation alone was very far-reaching. People could not afford to tear everything down, retrain all the social cadres, and build anew. But apart from such considerations, there was an inherent tendency in style which militated against radical innovation. As particular forms of cultural expression developed richly, individuals found they could rise to more subtle and more refined levels if they worked out more fully the possibilities of an already well-developed tradition, than if they struck off crudely on their own. Where patterns of cultivated awareness already existed, they were rarely sacrificed to private experiment.

Hence great cultural florescences were fairly rare: that is, times of general cultural creativity and innovation, when relatively independent literary, artistic, social, and religious traditions were launched afresh over the whole range of culture. Even periods in which major creativity was dominating some but not other aspects of culture were less common (even in the core regions) than periods with only relatively secondary sorts of innovation, within established traditions. When overall florescences did occur, of course, they marked the course of world history. The 'Axial Age' had seen such major creativity in all the major core regions. India had evidently known another such period in the early centuries of our era; by the time of the advent of Islam, the results of this latter Indic creativity were being felt very widely across the hemisphere in art, science, and religion, as well as in more trivial ways. In the Islamic period, T'ang (618–907) and Sung (960–1279) China saw such a florescence. Western Europe was to go through times of florescence somewhat later—florescence which, in fact, was ultimately to lead into the Modern world-wide cultural transformations. The High Caliphal cultural ferment too formed such a florescence and its outcome largely dominated world history for centuries after. To be sure, even these outstanding periods of creativity built upon elements of received knowledge and expectations, if only by way of revolt. Even lines of the most radical innovation presupposed the primacy of continuity.

A conflict and contrast of traditions within a single social group naturally offers opportunities for creative ventures into new forms not fully grounded in any one tradition; certainly the existence of such contrasts was one of the several circumstances which made possible a florescence in early Islamic times. We cannot look on it as a full explanation of the florescence; for cultural creativity may arise with a minimum of conflict of cultures, being set in motion rather by internal impasses when all old ways seem to break down, or by internal openings when old limitations become irrelevant; whereas sometimes a conflict among traditions has no creative outcome at all. Yet the High Caliphal culture took creative form, as it happened, very much in terms of the conflict and mutual accommodation of cultural elements of diverse origins. It was here in large measure that the creative opportunities lay which people then realized.

Before Islam, the various sorts of tradition had had each its stronghold in its own sphere—not only in this or that phase of culture, in art or government, etc.; but also, to some extent, within the lines of this or that religious community. With the coming of Islam, the older balance among types of traditions was upset and new elements were juxtaposed. Islam itself had set going new traditions, relatively independent of any older heritage, with which people had to come to terms. With the inclusion of areas in the empire which had not originally belonged to the Sâsânians, their local traditions were brought into the melée. Perhaps above all, all traditions had to be refonted within the loyalties and symbols of a single community: a major change in the life of the region. Insofar as each major tradition of thought and expectation was potentially applicable throughout all of life, the several traditions came into conflict once the old compromises that had delimited spheres of action among them were broken down. Here lay the necessity and opportunity for basic innovation. In High Caliphal times a new balance was worked out, in which again each of the various orientations, transformed, had its own sphere of primacy.

Rival cultural orientations under the High Caliphate

Certain fields of thought and practice came to be dominated by piety-minded representatives of the Islamic hope for a godly personal and social order—a hope inherited from the Jewish and Christian priests and monks and rabbis and their flocks. Muslims learned something from these latter, but proved very independent in giving the hope an integrally Islamic form. Every individual's life should be directly under the guidance of God's laws, and anything in society not clearly necessary to His service was to be frowned upon. Among both Sunnî and Shî'î Muslims, a host of pious men and women who came to be called the *'ulamâ'*, the 'learnèd', worked out what we may call the 'Sharî'ah-minded' programme for private and public living centered on the Sharî'ah law. As might be expected, these 'ulamâ' scholars dominated Muslim public worship. They exercised a wide sway, but not exclusive control, in Muslim speculative and theological thought. They exercised an effective—but never decisive—pressure in the realms of public order and government, and controlled the theoretical development of Muslim law. The fields of Arabic grammar, of some sorts of history, and even sometimes of Arabic literary criticism were largely under their influence. But many aspects of culture escaped their zealous supervision—including much of the Islamic piety of the time. It was probably only among the merchant classes that their ideals came close to overall fulfillment. Their work, however, gave a certain dignity to the whole social edifice. As a whole, that edifice reflected the aspirations of the 'ulamâ', and the intellectual and social patterns that followed therefrom, more than it reflected any other one set of ideals.

Two other religious orientations then found less widespread expression in Islam. The ascetic and monastic tradition within Christianity (and probably Buddhism) found its counterparts among Muslims, called ṣûfîs, who learned as much from their predecessors as did the Sharî'ah-minded, but had a rather less comprehensive programme for other than contemplative aspects of life. A second movement, that of the Bâṭiniyyah, with more immediate political implications, appealed to a tradition of esoteric love which may also have had pre-Islamic roots. It proved potent at moments of social protest.

Set over against the ideals especially of the Sharî'ah-minded Muslims was what may be summed up under the heading *adab*, the worldly culture of the polite classes. While the Muslim courtier, administrator, or intelligent landowner paid due honour to the aspirations of the professional Muslims, most of their efforts were devoted to living out a very different pattern from what the latter approved. Their etiquette, their conversation and fine arts and literature, their ways of using poetry and music and even religion, and their whole social pattern of position and privilege, with its economic and political institutions and its politics, formed a distinct set of genteel standards, prevailing among Muslims and non-Muslims of wealth and position. These standards, this adab, spread from one end of the Islamic domains to the other; fashions would most commonly be created in Baghdad, the most important seat of government, and would be eagerly adopted everywhere else. In this adab culture ancient pagan Arabian ideals had their place, a poetry inspired thereby was the highest gift, and the Arabic language was supreme; but a greater place on the whole, even in literature, was reserved for the Iranian imperial tradition of Sâsânian times. Both elements were consciously adapted to Islam.

Independent, both of the prophetic-monotheistic and of the imperial traditions, was the highly self-conscious tradition of *Falsafah*. This was an inclusive term for the natural and philosophical learning of the Greek masters. Some other elements from the Greek traditions had a place in the developing Islamicate culture, but it was only in this intellectual sphere that Greek tradition was supreme. Already before Islamic times, science had been the Hellenic stronghold in the Fertile Crescent and Iran. Several sciences which depended exclusively on natural reason for their development, including speculative philosophy, were carried over in a body from the Greek-Syriac tradition. Writers such as Plato, Aristotle, and Galen were the acknowledged masters. When the main classical works had been translated into Arabic they became a primary part of the intellectual equipment of a class of students (Muslim, Christian, and Ḥarrânî pagan) who, while never fully accepted by the Sharî'ah-minded Muslims, were nevertheless respected by society at large. They flourished especially in their role as practitioners of medicine or of astrology, two of the most popular sciences. In principle, however, they too had more comprehensive claims on life, which rivalled both the Sharî'ah-mindedness of the 'ulamâ' and the adab culture of polite society.

A caveat on our use of periodization

When we are studying a total civilization, we can no longer follow a single chain of events from key point to key point, as is possible when we are tracing the origin of particular components in a culture. We must see how the society developed simultaneously in many parallel and interconnected spheres. We must take whole chunks of time at once, that is, presenting first one sort of activity, then another, in the given period. But since the culture constantly changes, to relate the art or the religious thought, say, of any particular time span to other events in that time span means to see that art or that thought in a special way. We must stress what most stands out in that particular time span. For instance, when the unit for comparing different facets of culture is the two and a half centuries from 700 to 950, such continuing movements as the Islamic religious partisanships of the first decades loom much larger than the relatively transitory Arab tribal feuds of the same decades, though the latter filled the chronicles. Accordingly, our choice of periodization will help determine the weight we give to various events and hence the sort of picture we get of the civilization as a whole.

The selection of time spans must be anyway somewhat arbitrary—even more so than the setting of demarcation lines between one region and the next. In some respects, the shorter the intervals chosen, the more precise can be our understanding of developments. But in a detailed study by decades or by generations one may not see the forest for the trees. The autonomous internal development of the various traditions that make up a culture comes clearer if we take as our periods one, two, or even perhaps three centuries together. In Book Two we will concentrate on those social pressures, those currents of thought, those lines of tradition, that were of relatively continuing significance throughout the High Caliphal Period. Some of these, for instance natural science, we will treat mostly as a single development for the period as a whole. Yet even the movement of natural science was dependent on other movements and affected them in turn. Within the longer period, we will interrupt the various separate movements so far as feasible—and not only the political ones—so as to trace the interactions that took place among them within much shorter time spans as general cultural conditions evolved. More than in any other period before Modern times, intellectual, religious, social, and political developments were then closely correlated within fairly short time limits.

I

The Islamic Opposition, 692–750

From the time of the Riddah wars, at least, the Muslim community, or its leaders, had undertaken major political responsibilities as an essential consequence of their faith. Under the conditions of Marwânî rule, those who were most serious about Islam were also most serious about the political responsibilities which an acceptance of Islam entailed. Inevitably, a sensitive conscience found that much was lacking. It was almost a corollary of the political responsibility called for by Islam that the tradition of faith proved to be developed most actively in an atmosphere of political opposition to the ruling forms.

Meanwhile, the Muslim rulers were governing not only the Muslim group—piously conscientious or not—but also the general population of the conquered regions. These too had their ideals; and among them a most potent ideal was the longing for a strong central authority which would suppress warfare and defend the rights of the weak. It was such demands the caliphs found easiest and most expedient to move toward satisfying. Gradually, the ideal of a benevolent absolutism attached itself to the caliph's court, confronting the ideal of an Islamic egalitarianism in the opposition. Even in Marwânî times the contrast became increasingly noticeable.

The caliphal state approximates an absolute monarchy

From the point of view of leading classes among the conquered peoples, the rule of the Arabs had been acceptable as approaching, even more closely than the older states, the principles of justice represented in the great Irano-Semitic imperial tradition. In that tradition, the absolute monarch was expected to rise above all more limited interest groups and privileged classes and maintain some balance among them, so that the stronger should not freely override the weaker. In the first instance, the Arabs won support in Roman territories and probably in the Iraq and even parts of Iran by curbing a persecuting ecclesiastical rule and imposing equality among the sects. 'Umar's organization of the empire had been designed to maintain the unity and purity of the Muslim Arabs, but at the same time it confirmed the subjects' hopes in considerable measure. This may best be illustrated in the crucial matter of taxes.[1] Arrangements about taxes varied from locality to locality, depending upon the mode of conquest and on the local traditions. Some municipalities were permitted to handle their own tax collecting, handing on a fixed sum to the Arabs. But in most of the richest lands, the Arabs had maintained a rough supervision of the taxation. This had been necessary from the start in the Sawâd of the Iraq, so dependent on central administration, and experience there had been generalized. This system proved efficient (under shrewd men of the Quraysh), tending to bypass superfluous middlemen, and was informed by an intention of equal justice which 'Umar regarded as inseparable from Islam and which was often a boon to the weaker subjects.

In the old empires, or at least in the Roman, with time more and more privileged families and institutions had acquired preferences and exemptions in tax matters, leaving a disproportionate burden on such as had won fewer or no privileges. It was precisely the privileged great families who held power in their hands, and the central government was so far committed to them politically that its efforts to rectify the imbalances were ineffective. In the Roman empire the point had seemed to be coming (a point of no return for any state of the Agrarian Age) when the imperial resources were so compromised by such internal commitments that they were no longer sufficient to allow a reforming ruler to overcome his privileged subjects in case of contest. In this situation, only an overthrow of the privileged class generally, from within or from without, could redress the imbalance. This the Arabs performed. Beholden to no local elements, they could exercise their own central authority freely. Where the tax structure was the least fair, they insisted that it be set in balance; for (and here justice and interest coincided) a balanced taxation yielded a larger proportion of the revenue to the central authorities.

What had happened found special expression in the new incidence of the poll tax, the tax to be paid by an individual as such, rather than as holder of lands. In both the Sâsânian and the Roman empires a poll tax had been collected; in each case, the privileged elements had been exempted from it. (In the Roman empire, the exemption seems to have been extended even to the city mobs, who probably had more political leverage than their opposite numbers in the more agrarian-oriented Sâsânian state; thus it fell chiefly on the mass of peasants.) The Arabs now continued much the same system. But the 'privileged', who were to be exempt from poll tax, were to be only Arabs. Those who had been privileged under the old empires had to pay the poll tax —unless, indeed, they converted to Islam and joined the ruling Arab community (as some did, precisely to maintain their privileged dignity). All the non-Arab non-Muslim population was classified together under one rubric, dhimmî, as recipients of Muslim protection provided they submitted to

[1] Early Muslim taxation and especially the poll tax have been illuminated by Daniel C. Dennett, Jr., *Conversion and the Poll Tax in Early Islam* (Harvard University Press, 1950), a keen study which is, however, unfair to Wellhausen in its broader generalizing.

Muslim rule—however much that dhimmî population differed internally in degree of social privilege.

The new privileged class was not indeed subject to the caliph in the same arbitrary manner as had become a monarchical ideal in many minds. Yet at first its situation provided equivalent assurances. It was kept apart from the bulk of the population and under a special discipline. Hence at first it must have weighed relatively little, in day-to-day matters, upon the masses. The older class structure persisted in ordinary life except that its very top level was gone in many areas; but at least symbolically (and increasingly in fact) the remaining privileged groups were levelled before the conquerors, to whose collective justice appeal could be made. Indeed, all were not contented. By the time of ʿAbd-al-Malik, an increasingly close supervision of taxation to maximize the yield was producing peasant discontent in some places, renewing the perennial agrarian tension between the producers and their exploiters. But in the central parts of the empire, where the new régime ruled most directly, and whence it derived its major strength for controlling more outlying areas, the major urban classes of the subject communities seem to have been glad to support the government.

However, with the gradual breakdown of the isolation of the ruling Arabs from the general population, the special situation ceased to hold. Hence there arose pressure on the government to control more closely the new privileged class. As the relation of privileged and subjects came to have traits more normal for an agrarian society and as the need for absolute monarchy came, correspondingly, to be more strongly felt, the Marwânî caliphate came steadily closer to the ideal of the absolute monarchy.

Already by the time of ʿAbd-al-Malik, the social intermingling had gone far. On the one hand, many of the conquering Arabs had themselves bought lands (or been granted former crown lands by the caliph), and become landlords. The distribution of the revenues was no longer purely a matter of ʿUmar's army dîwân; many Arabs now began to have personal, private contact with the sources of revenue. On the other hand, non-Arabs had begun to settle in ʿUmar's military garrison towns; so that even these towns, for instance Kûfah and Baṣrah in the Iraq, were becoming ordinary cities such as Damascus had always been, closely linked with the surrounding countryside. Officials and grandees became Muslims to maintain their status. Merchants found markets, landless peasants found work in the Muslim towns; they learned Arabic, often became Muslims, and settled down alongside the children of the conquerors.

The result was that the administration of the conquered lands and the governance of the Arab ruling class could no longer be readily separated. It was no longer possible to deal with the Arabs in one way, as an occupying military force, and with the conquered populations in another way, as an occupied territory administered on its own principles, of no direct concern to the Arabs. Either the Arabs must be gradually submerged into the population at large, their business increasingly carried on in the languages and according

Chronology of the Marwânî Umayyads, 692–750

692–744	The Marwânî Umayyads: The empire continues to expand till about 740, and internal peace is broken only by Khârijî revolts (increasingly extensive) and occasional scares raised by Shî'îs ('Alid partisans); the administration is consolidated and regularized; a 'pious opposition' to Umayyad rule, of many shades of opinion, centres at Medina and is increasingly inclined to support the 'Alid claims raised at Kûfah; specific events are:
692–705	'Abd-al-Malik undisputed caliph, Arabizes the administration (696, Arabic coinage); Ḥajjâj b. Yûsuf at Wâsiṭ (694–714), as his lieutenant in the former Sâsânian provinces, bloodily suppresses dissenting Arab movements, encourages economic development
705–715	Walîd I, caliph, conquest of Spain and Sind, and first conquest of Transoxania. Succeeded by Sulaymân (715–717), who fails to take Constantinople (717) and permits the 'southern' Arabs (Kalb and allies) to triumph over the 'northern' Arabs (Qays and allies, among them Ḥajjâj's men), intensifying feuds among the Arab soldiery
717–720	'Umar II b. 'Abd-al-'Azîz, caliph, whose piety, of the new Medina type, conciliates even Shî'îs and Khârijîs; he encourages admission to the ruling class by conversion, and attempts an 'Islamic' solution to the problem of taxation on converts' land. Succeeded by Yazîd II, 720–724
724–743	Hishâm, last great Syrian Umayyad caliph, organizes the administration for efficiency; Transoxania is subdued, but the Shî'îs become restless in the Iraq, the Khârijîs everywhere. (Zayd, an 'Alid, revolts at Kûfah, 743). Succeeded by Walîd II, 743–744. John of Damascus (d. *c.* 760), major Greek Christian theologian, associated with the Umayyad court
744–750	The third fitnah civil wars: a dissident Umayyad force led by Marwân II, destroys Syrian Umayyad power and suppresses three other rebellions representing groups of the 'pious opposition' till it is overthrown by a fourth, the 'Abbâsî, which reunites the empire
	For comparison in eastern Europe:
717–741	Leo the Isaurian reorganizes the Byzantine empire to resist the Arabs
	For comparison in western Europe:
714–741	Charles Martel restores strength to Frankish kingdom and defeats an Arab force in northern Gaul

to the principles of the conquered lands, or the administration of the conquered lands must be made a part of the internal government of the Arab ruling class.

Supported by the social resources of the Arab garrison towns, ʻAbd-al-Malik and his lieutenant in the east, al-Ḥajjâj b. Yûsuf, were able to avoid the former alternative. First, the military decision which had restored the jamâʻah, the united community, was followed up with a determined power policy designed to maintain central authority in detail over all tendencies to tribal autonomy. This policy was incarnated in al-Ḥajjâj. Al-Ḥajjâj began his rule in the Iraq (694) with terrifying violence, designed to reaffirm ʻAbd-al-Malik's control in the garrisons themselves. His first task thereafter was to crush the rebellious Khârijîs of the Iraq and Iran; this was accomplished within six years. The Khârijî pattern may have afforded some satisfaction to the dhimmî non-Muslim population, possibly especially to the peasantry, because it might seem to offer a return to the clarity of the Muslim policy of non-involvement of ʻUmar's time; but in the long run it was not so satisfactory as an absolute monarchy would seem to be. The non-Muslim city populations seem to have readily accepted ʻAbd-al-Malik.

But by 701, al-Ḥajjâj's high-handedness had pushed the Iraqî army—led by a chief from the Qaḥṭân tribal faction in Kûfah, Ibn-al-Ashʻath—into a rebellion in which Baṣrah and Kûfah joined together. When it was put down, his building of Wâsiṭ as new capital, with a Syrian garrison, confirmed the outcome. Henceforth the Iraqis in Kûfah and Baṣrah were little trusted either as citizens or even as soldiers for frontier expeditions. This outcome in the Iraq meant, speaking more generally, that the Arab ruling class there were ceasing to be rulers as such and were becoming part of the subject population; and something analogous was happening, if less rapidly, in many other provinces, where the line between Arab and non-Arab was becoming ever more a matter of social privileges rather than of political function. Yet with centralization, Arabism was preserved in a new form.

It was appropriate to the new role of the Arabs that, from this point on, al-Ḥajjâj dedicated himself, till his death in 714, to restoring, to the profit of the treasury, the irrigation works of the Mesopotamian plain. Though the costly irrigation of the Syrian hinterland (which the Roman empire, with its interest in Christian holy places as well as in Syrian products for the colder Anatolian highlands, had patronized) was kept up under the Marwânids, more effort was put in on irrigation in the Iraqî Sawâd and also in the Jazîrah. (This latter area had been neglected, it seems, when it marked a frontier between Roman and Sâsânian empires.) The irrigation of the Mesopotamian basin gave larger returns on investment than the irrigation of Syria. Thus even while the political role of the Iraq was being reduced, its economic role was being magnified. We may say that ʻAbd-al-Malik had restored the Ḥijâz-Syria axis which Muʻâwiyah had depended on, and which was an intelligible outgrowth of Muḥammad's enlarged reconstitution of the Meccan mercantile system in the

Ḥijâz. But henceforth the former Sâsânian lands became increasingly important, and with them the agrarian basis of the empire and the pressure for the empire to be assimilated more firmly to the old Irano-Semitic imperial tradition: a tendency which was finally consummated after two generations in the shift of the capital back to the vicinity of the Sâsânian capital.[2]

On the basis of ʿAbd-al-Malik's policy of centralizing power, the central authority could build its direct bureaucracy. It soon imposed the Arabic language on the administration, replacing Greek and Pahlavî; the coinage was minted and the tax books kept henceforth in Arabic. The official classes, at least on the upper level, were made to learn Arabic, and promotion came to depend on a man's skill in Arab ways. Thus was assured the supremacy in civilian life, as in military life, of Arabic-speaking cadres. But this supremacy implied, at the same time, integrating into a single process both general administration and the governance of the Arab class; and this whole process was dominated by the indigenous administrative tradition, not by Arabism.

Though he was not fully an absolute monarch, ʿAbd-al-Malik went far toward establishing, in the course of fighting for power and of confirming it, the unbounded authority of his own office over the Arab community. This policy, forged by political necessity, fitted in perfectly with the monarchical expectations of the conquered subjects. In his relations with the Arabs, ʿAbd-al-Malik stood for the principle of the jamâʿah, the moral and political unity of all Arabs under the aegis of Islam; a unity which was to be enforced, if necessary, by military power. But the same principle of unity served as a basis for making the financial and agrarian administration of the whole empire more unified; an endeavour which in turn increased the role of the caliph as master of an increasingly entrenched central bureaucracy, through which the interests even of Muslims could be governed.

The new status of Islam and of the Muslim government was given symbolic form in the visual arts. The new coinage in Arabic was doubtless in part a gesture directed against Byzantium, whose gold *denarius* coins (in Arabic, *dînâr*) had formed the dominant monetary standard in Syria and the Ḥijâz; it was an assertion that Muslim rule was permanent and fully independent, whatever temporary tribute-money the governor of Syria had had to deliver during the fitnah wars, and that it could perform all the functions which the older imperial governments performed. The symbols on the coins appropriately pointed to Muslim power. An experiment was made with a portrait of the caliph, an absolutist gesture for which the Muslims were not yet ripe; but the successful symbolism was more abstract and referred to Islam directly. Some coins showed a *miḥrâb* (niche indicating the direction of Mecca), symbolic of the common worship of all Muslims, and the Prophet's lance; but finally (perhaps in response to a Byzantine substitution of the figure of Christ for that of the

[2] Oleg Grabar has touched on the importance of such economic shifts and how all fields of history, such as art and economics, are interrelated. See for example, his 'Islamic Art and Byzantium', *Dumbarton Oaks Papers*, 18 (1964), 67–88.

emperor) the word of God itself was used—in Qur'ânic phrases which presaged the might of God and of the Muslims.

The use of writing as the only imagery on coins was a daring innovation, which the population nevertheless accepted, showing their confidence in the new power; more than that, it was an iconographic stroke of genius, taking advantage of the strong clear lines of the squared-off *kûfic* form of the Arabic script to produce a design at once highly abstract and very immediately symbolic. In other public places, a comparable symbolism of Muslim power was displayed: at the Dome of the Rock, now built in Jerusalem to assert the continuity of Islam with the pre-Christian prophetic tradition, such symbols of power as crowns and pictures of holy buildings were used. In line with an iconophobic tendency already prevalent among Jews and among those Christians most opposed to Byzantium, and adopted by at least some Muslims, figural images were avoided in public places. (This tendency was later to become important in Islamicate art generally.)[3]

'Abd-al-Malik built well. After thirteen years, in 705, he left a well-established power to his son, al-Walîd I. With al-Walîd, a hereditary principle of succession was accepted for the first time without demur; or, more exactly, the principle that the monarch could dispose of the succession at will within his family, without more than formal intervention on the part of the Arab notables—for 'Abd-al-Malik's settlement provided that power should go to his several sons in turn. It was under al-Walîd that the last of the outlying conquests occurred, in Spain and Sind. Al-Walîd ruled uncontested and ably for another ten years, continuing his father's policies, till 715, and left the power, again without contest, to his brother Sulaymân. As the Arabs became accustomed to such power, the caliphal state was more and more moulded after the image of a true absolute monarchy, maintained by a centralized civilian officialdom.[4]

Discontent with the Marwânids, and the Piety-minded opposition to them

'Abd-al-Malik was able to win considerable favour at Medina—perhaps even more than had Mu'âwiyah—despite the great unpopularity of his régime in the Iraq. Since 'Uthmân's time, there had grown up at Medina a new generation of men who saw themselves, as heirs of the traditions of Muḥammad's own city, the special custodians of the ideals of Islam, if no longer of its power. 'Abd-al-Malik took a special interest in the religious questions that were interesting them, and showed his respect for their opinions. If 'Abd-al-Malik

[3] In addition to the work by Oleg Grabar cited in note 2 above, see his 'The Umayyad Dome of the Rock in Jerusalem', *Ars Orientalis*, 3 (1959), 33–62. We shall deal later with the iconophobic tendency, already visible here, to avoid figural images.

[4] Martin Sprengling, 'From Persian to Arabic', *Amer. Journal of Semitic Languages*, 56 (1939), 175–224, 325–36, is a very valuable study of early Muslim administration, largely on the basis of the later kâtib literature. (The latter part of the article, on the term *wazîr*, has been largely superseded.)

carried on the political side of Muḥammad's heritage, most especially in his insistence on the jamâ'ah principle of Muslim unity, he could also claim that the Qur'ân, as represented in its most ardent spokesmen at its home city, still played the supportive role toward his policies it had played since Muḥammad. But gradually under the Marwânids the political and the ideal sides of Muḥammad's heritage came not only to be represented by different sets of people, but these largely found themselves in tacit or even active mutual opposition. The civil wars had in fact seriously undermined the balance that Muḥammad had established. The defeat of the attempt of the Ḥijâz Muslims to regain leadership under Ibn-al-Zubayr and the suppression of the Shî'î and Khârijî movements necessarily still rankled.

As the new generation—and not only at Medina—began exploring what Islam could mean to them personally now that its political triumph was assured, their thinking was deeply coloured by the experiences of the civil wars. The notion of the jamâ'ah, the unity of the community, did not suffice as a comprehensive Islamic ideal, even when it was accepted on the specific point of who should be caliph. Many came to feel (as the Khârijîs had early insisted in their own way) that the Qur'ân should play a more active role in the life of the community. Thus many of those who had been associated with the defeated parties, not only in the Iraq but even in the Ḥijâz, came to constitute a semi-political, semi-cultural body of opposition to the ruling trends among the Arabs. In their view, the community at large which gave allegiance to Islam seemed mostly devoted in fact to enjoying the fruits of conquest under the leadership of men whose position in power had resulted largely from force and from tribal alliances. Given such a mood, it was natural that, among those relatively few who were taking a special interest in Islamic ideals, an oppositional standpoint, in greater or lesser degree, became common. It was in this spirit that they began to develop a more intimate and more universal conception of Islam. These men envisaged a society which should embody justice on earth, led by the most pious among the Muslims.

They had before them the example of a few men who, by their own intense sense of the divine challenge in their personal lives, reminded all Muslims of what the Qur'ânic challenge could mean to them simply as human beings. From the very first generation, there had been individual Muslims, like Abû-Dharr (d. *c.* 652), who took their piety sufficiently seriously to undertake the rebuke of the early caliphs when they seemed too worldly. But now such figures were no longer just eccentric purists.

The model Muslim of Marwânî times was Ḥasan al-Baṣrî (d. 728), popular preacher (and for a time qâḍî, judge) at Baṣrah. He was brought up in Medina, the son of a freedman, in circles close to Muḥammad's family. He meditated on the spirit of the Qur'ân intensely and showed its fruits in his upright, fearless conduct as well as his overwhelming sermons at Baṣrah. He won the respect of all parties, of al-Ḥajjâj the governor and of those who most hated al-Ḥajjâj. Ḥasan accepted the Marwânî rule, but he criticized the Marwânids when he thought them wrong. When 'Abd-al-Malik was punishing men in Syria for raising religious discussions that carried implications of criticism of the régime, and in particular for suggesting theological positions he disapproved of, it came to his attention that the well-known Ḥasan at Baṣrah was teaching just such positions (in this case, that God, being necessarily just, would necessarily leave human beings free to choose to do right if they wished). 'Abd-al-Malik asked for clarification from Ḥasan, evidently expecting a prudent disavowal. But Ḥasan, who felt it necessary to emphasize people's freedom to do right, so as to bring home their moral responsibility, responded with a forthright justification of his position; and 'Abd-al-Malik let him be.[5]

Often those inspired by Ḥasan's example and teaching, even if they did not directly oppose Marwânî rule, encouraged an anti-government spirit. Gradually these and others developed a generalized critique of the Marwânid caliphs and of their policies, as well as of the Arab life they represented. In the course of such discussions, Islamic religion itself in the full sense, as a comprehensive aspect of human culture, began to take form. As long as they were isolated, however, these pious dreamers remained politically irrelevant.

But such men found allies among others who were less religiously minded. The ordinary Muslim Arab supported the Marwânid rulers in Syria as religious leaders, inasmuch as, by maintaining Islam, they guaranteed the moral unity of the Arab community—the unity of a ruling class that had to maintain its position in a subjugated land of non-Arabs. But there were many groups that had material objections to the policies of the Marwânî régime, despite its strong moral position. Built on the power of Syrian Arab troops as it was, it favoured the Syrian over the other Arabs, over the rival Arabs of the Iraq, and above all over the wealthy old families associated with Muḥammad and centred on Medina. The bloody severities of al-Ḥajjâj against the proud independence of the great families were never forgotten. These politically less favoured Arabs would have liked to gain more political leverage or even to change the locus of power to some point nearer themselves, in this case preferably setting up as rulers one of the old Medina families which would depend on support from the Ḥijâz and the Iraq. Such discontents were complicated and reinforced when, after the time of al-Walîd, the Marwânids themselves seemed to take sides in the Arab tribal factional quarrels.

In the long run more important than these discontented Arabs was a class of men whom the society of the garrison towns was creating but whose interests were in conflict with that society. A rising number of non-Arabs had aligned themselves with the Arabs and joined generally in the life of the Muslim Arab centres. They had become duly affiliated as 'clients' to an Arab tribe (and hence were called *Mawâlî*, 'affiliates' or 'freedmen') and had learned to speak Arabic; and many had embraced Islam, as essential to full identification with the Arab community. Yet even when they became Muslims, neither they nor

[5] On Ḥasan Baṣrî it is worthwhile comparing the studies in *Der Islam* by H. Ritter (21 [1933], 1–83) and H. Schaeder (14 [1924], 1–66).

their descendants were treated as full partners in the Arab privileges; indeed, they could hardly be so treated without breaking down the social order formed by the garrison towns, which presupposed a reasonably small élite tied together by common traditions and experiences. The Muslim Mawâlî, however, could take little comfort in this; they had every reason to wish for a government and a society which would distribute its favours on the basis of acceptance of Islam rather than on the basis of Arab descent. Thus large groups of Muslims, non-Arabs as well as Arabs, wished for some change and might, if any weakness should appear in the Marwânî régime, prove receptive to projects of revolt; always provided they could hope that an overturn of the accepted order would be in their favour.

But no rivals to the Marwânîs could present a plausible case unless the moral position of the Marwânîs, based on the jamâ'ah ideal of unity, could be undermined. It was here that the oppositionally inclined among the Piety-minded could play a role and at the same time escape their political isolation. Such men and women, for whom Islamic piety took precedence over any other interest, were found among both the disaffected Arabs and the Muslim Mawâlî, and even among the Syrian Arabs themselves. As they took leisure, now that the great excitements of the days of first conquest were over, to consider more closely what 'Islam' ought really to mean, they realized it must reach beyond simply being the envied badge of a favoured ruling class. The grievances of their fellows made them see more keenly what was wanted. But such a viewpoint led them to discover the points of moral weakness in the régime; in doing so they became rallying points for all the elements of potential opposition. The outcome was that at last they gathered it into an all-Islamic tendency, rather than merely a series of local rebelliousnesses that might have broken up the community and so, probably, done away with Islam altogether. But they would not have had their great influence had there not been other motives for opposition present among large numbers.

I refer here to the 'Piety-minded' element as a general term to cover all the shifting groups opposed to Marwânî rule, or at least critical of current Muslim life, so far as their opposition embodied itself in idealistic religious attitudes. I am speaking, of course, primarily of the religious specialists, later called *'ulamâ'*, who provided much of the leadership. At the same time, the more pious of their followers are to be included, for there was no sharp line, at first, between 'ulamâ' scholars and others. Only gradually did the social element that we designate as the 'Piety-minded' resolve itself later into sharply differentiated Sunnî and Shî'î 'ulama', followed with lesser or greater sectarian devotion by partisan groups in the wider population.

The position of the Piety-minded opened the way to very extensive cultural implications, as we shall see. The Piety-minded rarely objected to the fact of Islam's being the badge of a ruling class; they were content to leave the Christians and Jews peacefully in their state of subjection. But at least within the Muslim class they wanted Islam to be more than merely such a badge, as it often was in Marwânî times; to be more than a minimum standard of public conformity in point of key beliefs, standard ritual, and elementary morality. Without formulating this in any abstract way, they expected Islam to carry with it its own law, its own learning, its own etiquette, its own principles of private life and of public order: to be self-sufficient without any reference (in principle) to pre-Islamic ways as such. At that time, they made no specially radical demands on any aspect of Muslim life: grievances were relatively few and could be pinpointed. Yet the tenor of their thought was that the new society should be freed of the corruptions of the old.

This outlook had historical roots deeper than merely the play of interests that followed the civil wars. The very origin of Islam gave the Piety-minded a point of leverage for associating their ideals with the interests of the disaffected. The Islamic tradition already under Muḥammad had developed political implications, and this commitment was confirmed in the Riddah wars. Hence it already carried a responsible and egalitarian social commitment. In Marwânî times, this commitment could be turned against the Marwânî power on the basis of Islam itself, interpreted to justify the opposition to Syrian Marwânî power. The concerned could count on the non-Syrian Arabs' harking back to a pre-Marwânî Islamic age supposed to have been more legitimate and just. At first, this memory referred generally to the early Muslim society from Muḥammad on, and notably to the time of 'Umar; there they had the concrete example of a pious society, the details of which were not yet forgotten. Gradually, at least among Shî'îs, the ideal period was limited to that of Muḥammad himself, except possibly for 'Alî's own reign. In either case, the concerned could rally to such a memory all the political strength of the various oppositional elements.

The Marwânids were by and large neither more nor less pious than most of the followers of these Piety-minded men who opposed them. But their strength was based on a sense of the power and unity of the Arab ruling community at large and on the special position of the Syrian Arabs; they were not in a position to espouse a minority's impractical programme. They perforce made some use of the administrative machinery, the economic order, the legal standards, the arts, and the learnèd heritage of the peoples in whose midst they found themselves. Their palaces were decorated in the usual Hellenistic fashion, the taxes they raised were essentially the same taxes as those raised by the governments before them, and if their records were—after a time—kept in Arabic instead of in Greek or Pahlavî, it was nonetheless after the Greek or Pahlavî manner. What else could they do? There did not exist even a pagan Arabian pattern for doing these things, let alone a purely Islamic one. Nevertheless, because of their un-Islamic 'innovations', they were labelled impious by the opposition and sometimes accused of betraying Islam itself; the task of working out the social implications of Islam was to be carried out as much as possible without them.

The programme of the Piety-minded

The proposals that the Piety-minded offered in response to the discontents present in the social and historical situation were summed up as government according to 'Qur'ân and *sunnah*' (custom). But what could this mean in particular? What was the Qur'ân was clear enough, but in itself it did not provide for day-to-day cases. The crux lay in defining the sunnah, which as a word merely meant the 'established practice'. What was objected to as contrary to sunnah was the seemingly arbitrary departure from what Muslim Arabs had expected—or hoped for. The restrictions and indignities for the privileged Arab families which were inseparable from the development of a centralized monarchy were seen as innovations, called *bid'ah*; and the seemingly more liberal days of earlier rulers—especially of the Medina caliphs and of Muḥammad himself—were recalled as models of what all could agree ought to be: as sunnah (the word had been used for approved customary practice by the Arabs before Islam). At the same time, it was recognized that the bid'ah, the deplored innovation, was not entirely a matter of the rulers; their power and arbitrariness were partly the consequence of the moral laxity and luxurious habits of the Muslims themselves—for it was in these terms that moralizers naturally saw the assimilation of the Arab ruling class into the cultural and social life of the occupied lands. Accordingly, abiding by the sunnah would mean restoration, for both rulers and Muslims at large, of the norms of the primitive caliphate and (or, among many Shî'îs, only) of Muḥammad's time; what did not go back to such times was bid'ah and ought to be eliminated from Muslim life.

This programme (if so generalized a demand can be called that) rested on the assumption that the Muslims as a class were to retain a distinctive character, keeping separate from the subjected peoples and all their diverse ways so far as possible. If a member of the subjected peoples embraced Islam—which as a human being he had the privilege of doing—he should assimilate to this Muslim character. But the distinctive character of the Muslims could not be simply their Arabism. They already felt themselves Arabs, and any distinction of worse or better Arab was expressed in divisive tribal rivalries. The distinctive character of the Muslims must be their Islam. Proper sunnah practice, then, should not be primarily Arab sunnah but Islamic sunnah. What was to be looked for in the times of the primitive caliphate was its representation not of Arab norms but of Islamic norms.

This meant a reversal of the place of Islam in the Arab society in the conquered lands. From being a society of Arabs who happened to be bound together by Islam, it must become a society of Muslims who happened to use the Arabic tongue and respect parts of the Arab heritage. This meant, ultimately, that Islam was not to be an Ishmaelism, analogous to the Israelism of the Jews, in which converts could enter fully into the community only as they were assimilated into a stock all of which, in principle, descended from

Abraham. Despite the obvious possibilities in exalting the Arabs as being of the line of Ishmael and producing an ethnically-bound community, the comprehensiveness of the Islamic vision prevailed, in conjunction with its sense of political mission, to mould Islamic idealism in a more universalistic direction.

This did not always mean a radical reversal; much that was old-Arabian had been sanctified as Islamic by being accepted in primitive Islamic times. In some points there was convergence: for instance, the sense of the inviolability of the Arab tribesman was undermined, indeed, by his subjection to Islamic penal sanctions; but it was otherwise reinforced by the fact that a Muslim had an individual dignity as such that no other Muslim could be justified in abridging: all Muslims were to be as one tribe. The Piety-minded tended, therefore, to support what was otherwise a tribal demand: that every free Muslim should be accorded that personal liberty and dignity which was expected by the Arabian tribesman—being bound to obey no man without his own assent. Consistent with this anti-state attitude was a general distrust of the more elaborate forms of urban luxury and social distinction. The old Arabs, far from the centres of wealth concentration, had had little in the way of visual arts, for instance. Men like ʿUmar had freely enjoyed the art objects that they had inherited by conquest; but now some of the Piety-minded raised religious scruples against such things. Probably encouraged by a distrust of luxury already present in the populistic monotheisms, they likened the use of precious carved and figured objects to idolatry and condemned it as innovation.

A most important consequence of the new attitude, which gradually became clearer, was that all free Muslims ought to be treated on an essentially equal basis. Not that the great families of Medina, descended from Muḥammad's closest associates, should not be accorded social priority; but that in point of public policy all should be on a level. Here a logical consequence of the Piety-minded viewpoint accorded with the widespread demand, put forth by most of the discontented, that there be no arbitrary distinctions of rank or class within the Muslim class; neither distinctions based on tribal allegiance (which led to the disruptive factional feuds), nor distinctions based on military power blocs such as that of Syria on which Marwânî power rested. The demand was that at least all the Arab Muslims, of whatever bloc, should share equally in the fruits of conquest (at least so far as they had participated in it) —in the booty and the pensions based on revenue from the conquered lands. Nor (added some) should Muslims recruited from the subject populations be discriminated against: they and their descendants should have the same rights, obligations, and liberties as those descended from the conquering families. (This latter was a corollary only slowly accepted by a great many of the Arabs, and never without reservations. Various minor privileges for Arabs found their way into the Sharîʿah law.) This popular demand, in its various aspects, struck sharply at the bases of Marwânî rule and even at the requirements of their everyday administration. But obnoxious as was this demand to the principles of empire, it fitted in very well with the aspirations of the opposition; and it was required, moreover, to assure the homogeneity of Muslim life-ways which the demands of the Piety-minded looked to. In particular, assimilation of converts could not be complete without it.

But the Piety-minded could not rest content with a few general principles. The expectations of the Piety-minded called for settling, in explicit detail, what ways should be associated with Islam. Though the full scope of the task only gradually became apparent, it was launched in Marwânî times. It was the work of several types of specialists—the intellectuals of the early Muslim community. The earliest tradition of such specialization was that of the Qur'ân-reciters, dating from the life of the Prophet himself; they had been prominent in the early Muslim disputes. Now the Qur'ân-reciters began to develop a complex intellectual discipline, in which there came to be many schools each with its own set of minor variant readings; eventually they made of declaiming the Qur'ân an elaborate fine art. It was apparently in connection with Qur'ân-recitation that the analysis of Arabic grammar began in the Iraq, so as to ensure correct parsing.

Perhaps less central than preserving the Qur'ân itself, but in the long run more fruitful of varied cultural implications, was the collection of lore about the prophets and especially about Muḥammad. People would share anecdotes about what he had been seen to do or say, called 'news', *ḥadîth,* and gradually an increasing number of such ḥadîth reports came into general circulation: reports about what the Prophet and his associates had said or done that would be relevant to modelling the pious life.[6] Probably some of the associates of Muḥammad had already in their day been more or less well known as reporters of his doings; they would have found an audience in the pious, the patriotic, or simply the curious. In the following generations, ḥadîth-reporters came to share with Qur'ân-reciters the repute of authority in matters religious.

Among such men were some who systematized these reports sometimes into full-scale narratives. A school which traced itself to Muḥammad's cousin, 'Abdallâh Ibn-'Abbâs, attempted to find and transmit the occasion for as many as possible of the passages in the Qur'ân and to explain, more generally, what was meant by the various passages. Others collected narratives of Muḥammad's campaigns or other events. Muḥammad Ibn-Isḥâq of the Mawâlî of Medina (d. 767) composed a detailed life (*sîrah*) of the Prophet, which included a history of monotheism in Arabia and of the Quraysh before Muḥammad's time, and full reports on the Muslims of his time. A major theme of the history was the honour of the Anṣâr, Muḥammad's Medinese associates, over

[6] It has been common usage to translate *ḥadîth* by the word 'tradition', but a more mischievous case of mistranslation would be hard to find. In many contexts, and often in crucial ones, *ḥadîth* means just the opposite of what is implied in the English word 'tradition'. The ḥadîth report was documented, not anonymous; it was explicit and written, not oral, immemorial, and imprecise; it was very often just contrary to custom as practiced. Compare the discussion in the section on usage in Islamics studies in the Introduction.

against those Meccans who had remained hostile till the last minute. The implication was that (despite the principle that acceptance of Islam wipes out the past) the later Medinese, descendants of the Anṣâr, had more right to leadership among the Muslims than had the Umayyad Marwânids whose ancestors had opposed Muḥammad at Mecca. (Ibn-Isḥâq's own preferred candidates for office seem to have been the 'Alids.) Ibn-Isḥâq was part of an incipient Islamic school of history which was not limited to the prophets but extended to the Arab conquests and to all the events of the early community, preserved anecdotally in the form of ḥadîth reports. Thus the Muslims maintained a sense of historical identity which was coloured by opposition to the dynasty in the name of Islam.

But still more immediately relevant to social purposes than the specialists in Qur'ân-recitation and in ḥadîth-reporting were the men who specialized in the attempt to state, in precise legal terms, what the Islamic way of doing things should be. In Baṣrah and Kûfah, in Medina, in Damascus, they took current practice in the Muslim courts as a starting point and refined it. The Muslim courts, designed chiefly to settle disputes among the occupying soldiery, were still relatively unsophisticated, lacking an established body of technique and limited in the range of their cases; they afforded an excellent opportunity for developing new ideas.

This attempt to determine the proper answer to questions of legal (and personal) practice was called *fiqh,* 'understanding'. Qur'ânic passages would be applied when they were clear, of course; but by and large the men of fiqh had to work on less explicit bases. Sometimes they appealed to a general sense of equity or of social utility; sometimes to local precedent—the decisions of respected earlier Muslims in their own centres. Gradually it became the custom to trace the local tradition (sunnah) back to associates of the Prophet who had settled locally, so tying it to the sources of Islam. Sometimes the anecdotes of ḥadîth-reporters—about the Prophet himself or about his associates, including the first caliphs—would prove relevant to legal questions; well-known reports of the sort would be used by the men of fiqh. Some of the men of legal fiqh were practicing qâḍîs (judges). Others remained private experts, like Abû-Ḥanîfah (699–767), a well-to-do merchant of the Mawâlî of Kûfah (his grandfather had been an Iranian war captive who was freed and became a merchant). Abû-Ḥanîfah stood out as a teacher, sharpening the legal reasoning of his predecessors and attempting to present a consistent total system of law. Through the work of Abû-Ḥanîfah, the legal fiqh tradition of the Iraq became a model of Muslim legal acumen for the time.

All these fields of inquiry, and especially memorized retention of Qur'ân and ḥadîth, constituted *'ilm,* 'knowledge'—that is, knowledge of what was right. Collecting, elaborating, and transmitting such 'ilm was a primary activity of the Piety-minded. In 'Abbâsî times, these lines of inquiry developed into an elaborate intellectual culture among the Sharî'ah-minded 'ulamâ' scholars. But though many of the Piety-minded were content to work privately, educating disciples in their views, private 'ilm by itself was not enough; it needed to be agreed on by the community and put into practice. This had political consequences. The unwillingness or inability of the Marwânids to take the lead here intensified the feeling of discontent with them as rulers. In a military ruling class, reform was above all public reform and power was military power. Hence there was always a presumption anyway that serious change would come by an armed replacement of the top command. There were no autonomous establishments to reform, short of the state power itself; and insubordination at that level meant revolt.

On this, many could agree. But revolt required a candidate to replace the Marwânids; and the candidate himself ought to be a suitable expression of Islamic piety. At this point the Piety-minded disagreed among themselves.

The problem of authority: 'ilm and imâmate

It was against this background that the disputes proceeded among the Piety-minded as to what sort of authority, when such was needed, should take the place which had been held by Muḥammad and his immediate successors. Such authority was needed particularly for practical command of the community, in assigning tasks such as those of defence or of maintaining public order. But at least as important, someone was needed who could settle disputes about 'ilm if, for instance, what was claimed as ḥadith should vary. The Marwânî power, based on the jamâ'ah, had at its disposal Syrian troops; what sort of authority would be able to replace it with power based, as the more militant of the opposition agreed it should be, on 'Qur'ân and sunnah'?

In Muḥammad's lifetime, the authoritative commander, later called the *imâm*, leader (for his first duty was to lead in the worship), had without question been Muḥammad himself. Upon his death, authority had lain, in a general way, with those closest to him, who knew his ways the best (and hence knew God's will the best), and were accepted as worthy by the community at large on the basis of personal acquaintance. The Piety-minded wanted the imâm to be of this sort: in their terms, this meant that he who is the admittedly most pious and most knowledgeable of God's will ought to have the command, to be imâm of the community; as to whom this implied in practice, they differed.

Perhaps the earliest group to pose this problem in its essentials—already in the days of Mu'âwiyah—were the Khârijîs. They broke off from 'Alî's party when he appeared to be willing to compromise with Mu'âwiyah, and for generations they fought almost every Muslim government that appeared. Their solution was an extreme one: it was up to each believer to decide who was the most pious, or at least an adequately pious commander; to join with others who acknowledged that man's command; and to separate from any self-styled Muslims who irresponsibly accepted as imâm an unworthy man. The man who showed by his sinning that he was no true Muslim was unworthy of rule over Muslims, and any who accepted that rule showed themselves traitors

The Main Khârijî* (Shurât) Movements through the Time of the Third Fitnah

Primitive Khârijîs (Muḥakkimah or Ḥarûriyyah) Rebels *vs.* 'Alî and *vs.* Mu'âwiyah, from Kûfah and especially Baṣrah				
Not necessarily in overt rebellion			Insisting on overt rebellion	
Ibâḍîs	Ṣufrîs	Shaybânîs	Najadât	Azraqîs
(chief teacher Ibn-Ibâḍ, fl. 684); quiescent till they rebel overtly in the third fitnah under 'Abd-Allâh b. Yaḥyà and Ṭâlib al-Ḥaqq; center at Nazwâ in 'Umân; groups in most provinces, especially the Maghrib The most enduring of the groups; accepted taqiyyah (concealment of views)	Quiescent till groups rise in the Maghrib, early 740s; they were later (*c.* 758) displaced in Qayrawân by Ibâḍîs	Several raids along Tigris in time of al-Ḥajjâj and after; great rising in the Iraq and Jazîrah in third fitnah under Daḥḥâq b. Qays	Followers of Najdah b. 'Âmir in Arabia during second fitnah	(named for Nafi' b. Azraq, extremist theorist and leader); the most drastic of the Khârijîs; accepted isti'râd (killing of all, including nominal Muslims); rise in the Iraq and in Iran in second fitnah; finally defeated by al-Muhallab in 699

* The term Khârijî (seceder, rebel) causes no confusion in an English context; in an Arabic context, however, it can be considered uncomplimentary, and it may not always be specific to the Shurât (which means "those who sell [themselves to God]")

to the Islamic ideal and hence no true Muslims either. In effect, the Khârijîs—or the more extreme of them—claimed that their own purist war bands were the only adherents of true Islam. The rebelling Khârijî groups were small enough and dedicated enough to reproduce and indeed exaggerate the devoted homogeneity of Medina. The command depended very directly on the assent of all the faithful to the piety and knowledgeability of the commander, who could be and was deposed for the slightest of sins. So long as the majority of the population—being dhimmî non-Muslims anyway—were neutral, the Khârijîs treated them favourably, attacking only rival Muslims.

The Khârijî solution had the merit of consistency. But, as we have suggested, the main body of the Piety-minded opposition sought a solution along very different lines, for they could not afford to abandon the greater part of Marwânî society. Yet, while the Khârijî party was eventually isolated from the main body of Muslims, for some time many who sympathized with the Khârijî war bands continued to reside in places like Baṣrah and taught Khârijî doctrines on a modified basis. These men participated actively in the development of the thinking of the Piety-minded as a group.

The old families at Medina had at first their own solution, supporting for the imâmate one of the families close to Muḥammad on the basis of public recognition in Medina itself. They demanded that the rest of the Muslims, by supporting such a candidate, renew their allegiance to the descendants of the mother community in Medina. But after the failure of the attempt of Ibn-al-Zubayr to retain the caliphate in the Ḥijâz after the death of Mu'âwiyah, this approach lost ground. Many might have preferred the family of 'Umar, whose son had great repute at Medina in matters of 'ilm knowledge; many of the Piety-minded there traced their teachings to him. These tended to accept the Marwânids in the name of jamâ'ah unity—and their religious teachings were received also in Syria. There were those who looked to a reform of the Marwânî régime itself, and in the caliph 'Umar II (717–720) these even saw their man on the throne for a time. But some of the old families of Medina came to give their support to one strand in another movement, which in its various forms became most prominent among the oppositional Piety-minded: the Shî'î movement.

The party of 'Alî, which was the nucleus of the Shî'ah, had in Mu'âwiyah's day been a fairly small group centred at Kûfah in the Iraq. They clung to the candidature of 'Alî and of his family for leadership after most of the Muslims had united in support of Mu'âwiyah as restorer of Muslim unity and power. 'Alî's family soon became for the Kûfans representative of the time when Kûfah was near to being the capital of Islamdom, much as the family of 'Abd-al-'Azîz b. Marwân—governor of Egypt under 'Abd-al-Malik—came to represent Egyptian autonomy and were looked to for leadership by later Egyptians. But Kûfah was, with Baṣrah, the most important political, economic, and intellectual centre not only for the Iraq but for the whole eastern, formerly Sâsânian portion of the empire; its cause could easily become the cause of all the Muslims east of Syria. (Indeed, it was at the natural centre of gravity for any agrarian empire in the whole region.) To the extent that 'Alî had stood for 'soldiers' rights' and justice against the central authorities, Kûfah's loyalties to his house could readily be given a broader interpretation which deepened their claims in Kûfah itself beyond a merely political slogan; and by the same token, the natural sympathy for their cause elsewhere could be reinforced with broader moral considerations.

From small beginnings, the Shî'îs gradually gained widespread importance, not only in a town like Qum, an Arab garrison town in the west Iranian highlands of 'Irâq 'Ajamî, but also in places not normally dependent on Kûfan leadership. The party grew partly through the zeal which 'Alî's devotees displayed, perhaps, and certainly by taking advantage of the historical accident that not only was 'Alî a member of Muḥammad's family, the house of Hâshim, but the senior lines of 'Alî's descendants were also the sole progeny of Muḥammad, through his daughter Fâṭimah. (Descent through a female was regarded as secondary, among the Arabs, but was not ignored.) At any rate, an 'Alid candidature came to be accepted by many, by the last Marwânî decades, even in Medina, which had decisively rejected it at the time of the second fitnah.

There were numerous 'Alid and related candidates and the claims they made with regard to solving the problem of authority for the godly community were various. Shî'ism in this period meant support of 'Alid candidates (or candidates of lines closely related to 'Alî's) for the command; in itself it implied no particular religious doctrines. The claims amounted sometimes to little more than a variation of the old Medina belief that the command of members of the Medina families associated with Muḥammad, sanctioned by the present generation at Medina, would assure a maintenance of Muḥammad's practice and a restoration of the primitive Medina purity. This was the normal approach among those Medinese who, preferring, on the whole, the 'ilm knowledge of the tradition of Ibn-'Abbâs (the Prophet's cousin) to that of Ibn-'Umar, also were inclined to wish for an 'Alid candidacy, even, if necessary, at the expense of the jamâ'ah unity principle of the Marwânids.

But even in the case of a simple Medina candidate, support for the 'Alids came also from a wider circle. In this wider circle of followers of the 'Alids there were greater expectations than these mild Medinese hopes. Most commonly it was expected that in some way the 'ilm, the knowledge of the ways of Muḥammad, and hence of God's will, was retained more fully and uncorruptedly in 'Alî's family, or in some branches of it, than elsewhere. This might be the case merely through close family association with the Prophet, or perhaps by a more explicit divine intervention. At any rate it was supposed that with the purer 'ilm of the 'Alids would come a greater right to command; a right which was only partly the function of the inherited 'ilm, and was more crucially a divinely sanctioned authority to decide any question of 'ilm which was disputed. Hence Muslims could look to an era of justice based on true Islamic 'ilm if 'Alids came to power.

With the stress on knowledge of the Prophet as basis for true Islamic life, the close association of ʿAlî with Muḥammad became more important; and as this came largely of their family connection, such connection took on new religious aura. The ʿAlids—especially those descending from Fâṭimah—came to be called *Ahl al-Bayt*, 'people of the house' (an old tribal term referring to the family from whom chiefs were chosen, often the custodians of the tribe's sacred objects); here designating Muḥammad's more intimate family, which included ʿAlî. But it was recognized also that all the house of Hâshim, the Hâshimids, were especially close in relationship to Muḥammad; these included the descendants of all Muḥammad's uncles; not only the Ṭâlibids, descendants of ʿAlî and his brothers, but also the ʿAbbâsids, descendants of ʿAbbâs, who had failed to accept Islam till long after the Hijrah. All these family lines could be beneficiaries of ʿAlid loyalism (a term I use for loyalty to the ʿAlid family in particular but more generally for the whole complex of attitudes associated with that loyalty).

By the last Marwânî decades there had developed a radical form of the ʿAlid-loyalist notion: some people thought that the all-essential ʿilm, and more generally the inherent authority to decide points of conscience and bear command over the community, was retained in just one or another particular line of ʿAlids alone. In such a line there would always be one ʿAlid who was inherently the sole legitimate ruler, the legitimate imâm, appointed explicitly (by *naṣṣ*) by his predecessor. Thus there was always in existence a true imâm, whether or not he was at the moment ruling or even making an attempt to gain rule. It was the responsibility of every Muslim to find him and abide by his rulings. The pious person might, then, endure the unjust government of the Marwânî caliphs for the time being; for in guiding his own life, at least, he could refer to the ʿilm of the true imâm, which was available here and now. Such a notion of the imâmate made possible a continuing dissident body of people attached to a continuing line of imâms regardless of the fate of particular political movements. It also encouraged a systematic development of special religious ideas which could gain acceptance among such dissident bodies without competing for the attention of all Muslims generally. Here we have the roots of a sectarian Shîʿism, which later gained major importance.

By the middle of the eighth century there were two such lines of imâms recognized by different groups of Shîʿîs, each tracing its imâmate back uninterruptedly to ʿAlî. (The chart showing the candidates of the primitive Shîʿah shows how this type of imâmate became more important with time.) One line was represented by Jaʿfar al-Ṣâdiq (d. 765), great-grandson of ʿAlî's son Ḥusayn; his imâmate was to become the basis for most subsequent Shîʿism. Jaʿfar's father, Muḥammad al-Bâqir (d. *c.* 737), may already have accepted followers who regarded him as sole legitimate imâm of the time, appointed by naṣṣ designation; at least he seems to have been a reporter of ḥadîth. Jaʿfar was certainly regarded as such an imâm; but he taught ḥadîth, and probably legal fiqh too, not only to his own 'shîʿah', his special followers, but to others

The Candidates of the Primitive Shî'ah

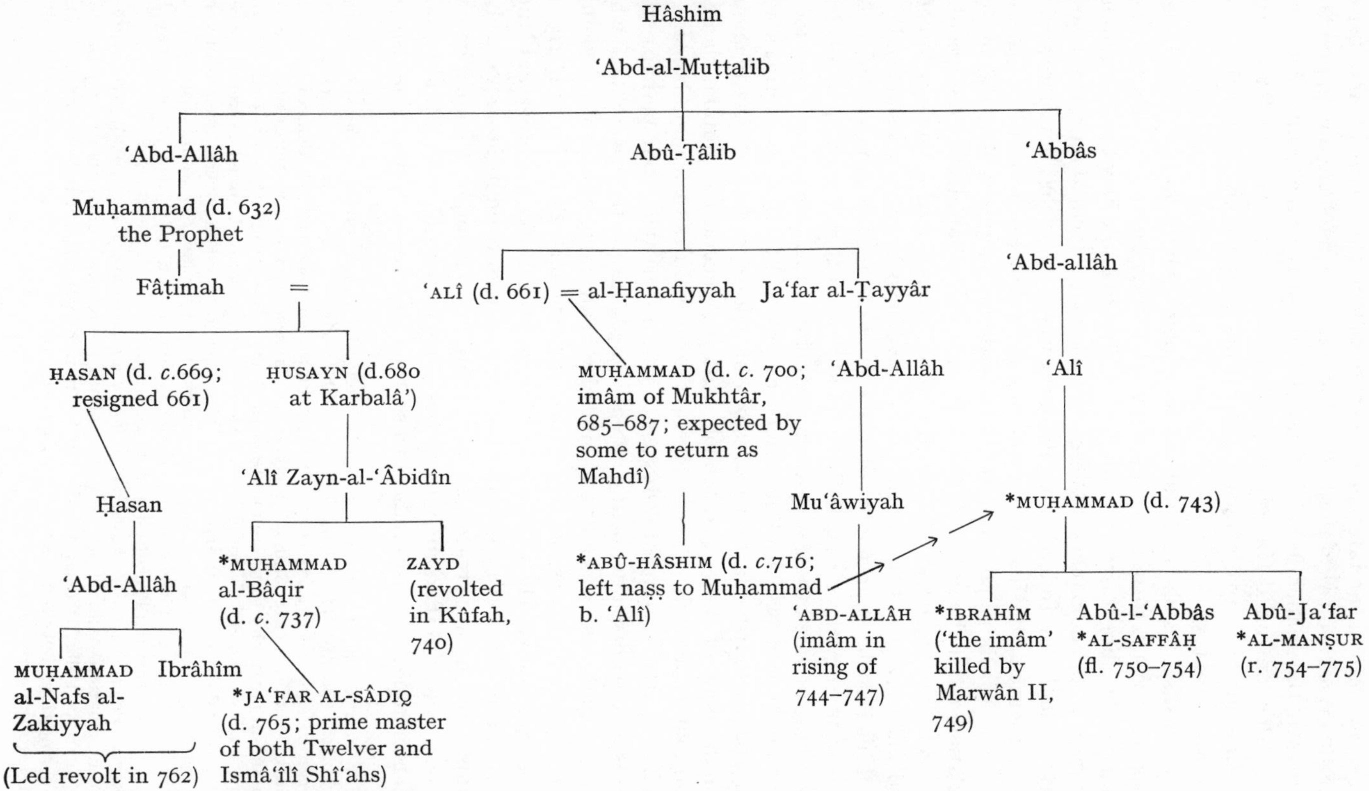

Capitals indicate men regarded as imâms in their own lifetime.

*These candidates' position received, in their lifetime, at least some of its force from the doctrine of naṣṣ, i.e., that the imâm was appointed by his predecessor and has sole legitimacy, whether he is an active claimant or not. Possibly 'Abd-Allâh b. Mu'âwiyah should also be included among these.

who became prominent later as authorities among the Sunnîs. A number of the most active theological thinkers of the time were associated with him and with his son, the imâm Mûsà al-Kâẓim. The authority of the second ʿAlid line, that of ʿAlî's son Ibn-al-Ḥanafiyyah, seems to have been claimed for at least three different men, two of whom led revolts at the time of the fall of the Syrian Marwânids.[7]

All these disputes about the imâmate among Khârijîs and Shîʿîs and their rivals gave occasion to, or at least sharpened, further questions in the realm of ʿilm knowledge. For it must be a matter of ʿilm, to know how the commander of the faithful should be chosen; to recognize who it was could represent Islam, who it was had ʿilm. Indeed, not only in the case of the ruler, but more generally as concerned any Muslim, it was of first importance to know what it meant to be a true Muslim, a person faithful to the divine summons. And this meant speculation about the nature of the soul, of faith, of ʿilm itself. This speculation was in part enshrined in ḥadîth reports, transmitted by men who convinced themselves that this or that must have been Muḥammad's attitude or that of his associates; in part it took the form of independent argument. As can be seen from the chart of Piety-minded groups in Marwânî times, the Piety-minded tended to be divided in each chief town into two or more local schools of thought, which often figured as political factions (sometimes answering partly to tribal factions), each of which developed distinctive religious teachings; none of these local schools achieved general recognition, though several found some adherents in several centres besides their main home.[8]

Perhaps partly inspired by discussions with Christians, but perhaps still more inspired by disputes about who was a good Muslim, there were those who discovered that there was a logical difficulty in affirming at once God's omnipotence and humans' responsibility for their own acts. Put a bit vulgarly: if God can do whatever He wills, how can humans deserve either praise or blame for acts that it is in God's power to force them to do or to omit? More precisely: if God is truly the sole creator, as the Qur'ân seems to imply, He must be not only more powerful than anyone else but alone responsible for all that is; but if God is omnipotent in this radical sense, then He must be responsible also for

[7] For an analysis of the development of religious and sectarian dimensions in the early Shîʿah, see my 'How Did the Early Shîʿa Become Sectarian?' *Journal of the American Oriental Society*, 75 (1955), 1–13, which also discusses the ideas of the early speculative thinkers, the Ghulât. That article traces the rising fortunes of the early Shîʿah and in particular of the imâmate of the line of Jaʿfar, but it does not adequately account for how the Shîʿah could have become so important. It must be remembered that the early dating, in that article, of certain ideas rests on the overall weight of very scanty evidence rather than on any sure ground point by point. I would suspect, now, that the disciplining of the notions of the Ghulât begun by Jaʿfar came chiefly in response to the anti-Shîʿî reaction under al-Manṣûr.

[8] Charles Pellat, *Le milieu baṣrien et la formation de Gâḥiẓ* (Paris, 1953), gives a great deal of information—among other things—about the religious currents in early Baṣrah. Unfortunately, Pellat is disappointing in his notions of religion, notably in assuming naïve correlations between doctrine and morals, and in retrojecting later notions like 'Sunnî' into the early period.

Piety-Minded Groups in Marwânî Times

KÛFAH

Shîʻah: looking to ʻAlid and related houses for imâm (and rejecting ʻUthmân):
Moderate (i.e., not recognizing imâmate by naṣṣ designation)—often concentrated on collecting ḥadîth reports (and some were later accepted by the Ḥadîth folk)
Radical (recognizing one or another line of imâms designated by naṣṣ—and rejecting the Medina caliphs as illegitimate)—among these appeared the speculations of the Ghulât about soul and inspiration and imâmate; had Mawâlî connections
Murji'ah: willing to accept Marwânid as imâms, but reserving right of criticism; among these arose the chief school of Kûfan fiqh (Abû-Ḥanîfah, etc.); often looked to Ibn-ʻAbbâs in Qur'ân interpretation (*tafsîr*)
Khârijîs (Ibâḍîs): a very few survived in Kûfah

BAṢRAH

ʻUthmâniyyah: rejecting ʻAlî in favor of ʻUthmân, but willing to accept the Marwânids only for the sake of jamâʻah. These overlapped with the school of Ḥasan al-Baṣrî, who accepted the Marwânids but asserted the duty to criticize and oppose them when they were wrong, and who taught the justice of God, human freedom to do right, and that great sinners lacked true faith
Muʻtazilah: refusing to judge between ʻAlî and ʻUthmân; took off from Ḥasan al-Baṣrî, adding emphasis on unity of God in the sense of a rejection of any anthropomorphism; their viewpoint was spread widely in the caliphate by the end of Marwânî times; had own fiqh
Khârijîs: rejecting both ʻAlî and ʻUthmân and looking to a righteous imâm chosen by a righteous remnant of Muslims: taught that great sinners not merely lacked true faith but were legally infidels; their doctrines were spread widely by their guerrilla bands, but the less activist (Ibâdiyyah) centered in Baṣrah

MEDINA (followed by MECCA)

School of Ibn-ʻUmar: accepted Marwânids for sake of jamâʻah, but critically; often concentrated on collecting ḥadîth reports, emphasized the determination even of human acts by God; had beginnings of own fiqh
School of Ibn-ʻAbbâs: inclined to prefer ʻAlids to Marwânids (in fiqh were independent of the moderate Shîʻah of Kûfah); concentrated on interpretation of Qur'ân (strong in Mecca)

SYRIA (DAMASCUS and ALEPPO)

ʻAdliyyah or Qadariyyah: accepted Marwânids critically; taught the justice of God and human freedom to do right, in part following Ḥasan of Baṣrah; especially among the Kalb tribal faction, around Damascus
Jamâʻîs: accepting Marwânids uncritically, were close to the school of Ibn-ʻUmar of Medina; had own fiqh

EGYPT

Same schools as Medina

KHURÂSÂN

Jamâʻîs: as in Syria
Shîʻah: as in Kûfah
Jahmiyyah: highly critical of Marwânids; taught the determination of human acts by God, and rejected anthropomorphism; perhaps related to *Murji'ah,* who in Khurâsân had Mawâlî connections

human acts, since they form part of God's creation; therefore He alone must have decreed them, and the human actors can have had no power over their destiny. Passages in the Qur'ân about how God leads further astray those who have once neglected Him seemed to lend themselves to such a notion.[9] Some Muslims, especially at Medina, drew the conclusion that human freewill was illusive. In reaction, others analyzed the meaning of the term for the decrees of God, *qadar*, and tried to show that God need not necessarily determine all human acts; these men were called, by their opponents, *Qadarîs*. (The most famous man to take this position was Ḥasan al-Baṣrî, who, as we have seen, opposed indignantly the deterministic interpretation of the Qur'ân that had become popular in Medina.)[10]

The Qadarîs began a reform-minded religious party especially among the Kalb tribal bloc in Syria, which was increasingly alienated from the later Marwânids. On the test case provided by the fitnah wars, which—as for Khârijîs and Shî'îs—became the model in terms of which a party's attitude to the imâmate was formulated, they supported Mu'âwiyah against 'Alî, and hence the principle of the jamâ'ah; but they reserved the right to criticize the Marwânid rulers in the name of enlightened religious concern.

In other, related debates, set going especially by the Khârijîs, men discussed the meaning of human submission to God—and hence the meaning of the relevant Qur'ânic terms, *muslim, islâm* (submitter, submission) and *mu'min, îmân* (faithful, faith): the Khârijîs (convinced of the invalidity of rule by bad Muslims) insisted that islâm and imâm must carry an observable moral consequence, by which people could judge both ruler and ruled. Men who were impressed with Khârijî arguments but were willing to allow professing Muslims, including rulers, the benefit of a doubt insisted that what counted was the inner conscience, which only God could judge; they were called *Murji'îs*. (The most famous of these was Abû-Ḥanîfah, the Kûfan legist.)[11] On the problem of

[9] Though the discussion of Muslims' positions (including an alleged early Islamic dogma of predestination) ascribed to John of Damascus in the Marwânî time is clearly apocryphal—see A. Abel, 'Le chapitre CI du Livre des Hérésies de Jean Damascène: son inauthenticité', *Studia Islamica*, 19 (1963), 5–26—yet since such problems were mooted among Christians, and since Muslims and Christians did argue, it seems likely that such arguments formed a theological stimulus; but they would surely have arisen independently anyway.

[10] Cf. Julian Obermann, 'Political Theology in Early Islam: Ḥasan al-Baṣrî's Treatise on Qadar', *Journal of the American Oriental Society*, 55 (1935), 138–62. There it might appear that the first to take a position on 'qadar' were men of power justifying their sins by predestination; this is unlikely.

[11] The development of Khârijî thinking and its interpenetration with other tendencies has been traced by W. Montgomery Watt in 'Khârijite Thought in the Umayyad Period', *Der Islam*, 36 (1961), 215–31, and more summarily in chapters 2 and 4 of his *Islamic Philosophy and Theology* (Edinburgh University Press, 1962)—a book which is a very quick survey dealing chiefly with the early period, and more satisfactory at those points that he knows personally than elsewhere. Wm. Thomson 'The Character of Early Islamic sects', *Ignace Goldziher Memorial Volume*, part I, ed. S. Löwinger and J. Somogyi (Budapest, 1948), pp. 89–116, brings out the relation between Khârijîs and Murji'ah. In several places, Watt has developed an improbable thesis that Shî'ism can be

the fitnah wars, in particular, they held that judgment on both ʿAlî and Muʿâwiyah was to be suspended; neither should be condemned. Accordingly, the subsequent Marwânî imâmate likewise could not be condemned in advance, though the rulers must be called to account for particular acts. The Murji'îs formed a reform-minded party especially at Kûfah (and Baṣrah), but the name was sometimes extended to any who supported the Umayyads in the name of the jamâʿah principle of unity.

But the most far-ranging speculation was carried out among the more radical Shîʿîs (those recognizing imâmate by naṣṣ designation); this was apparently favoured by the development of relatively closed groups of followers of particular lines of naṣṣ imâms. Those most active in this speculation were called retrospectively, by later Shîʿîs, the *Ghulât*, the 'exaggerators', at a time when many of the positions they had held were regarded as unsophisticated exaggeration of what came to be regarded as proper Shîʿî views. These Ghulât theorists tried to work out, above all, the religious implications of a historical situation in which truth and justice seemed to be represented by a defeated minority, the Shîʿah, overridden by an arrogant majority in the name of Islam itself.

The notion of the imâm, with his special divine ʿilm and his destiny of bringing true Islamic justice to the oppressed, seized the imaginations of many, especially of the Muslim Mawâlî. Among the radical Shîʿîs, not only ʿUthmân and the other Umayyads were regarded as cursed usurpers, but even Abû-Bakr and ʿUmar, who should have yielded to ʿAlî. ʿAlî and his family, on the other hand, became almost superhuman heroes. A messianic role was expected of several of them—first Ibn-al-Ḥanafiyyah and then others were, by this or that faction, thought not to have died but to have departed, awaiting the moment of return, when they should carry all before them and 'fill this world with justice as it is now filled with injustice'. The title *Mahdî*, the 'Guided' (as used by Mukhtâr for Ibn-al-Ḥanafiyyah in his rebellion against Ibn-al-Zubayr), at first merely a designation for the correct Islamic ruler, sometimes took on eschatological tones. Even before the coming of the imâm who would be Mahdî, moreover, the current imâm by naṣṣ was felt by many to have a special relation to God—at least, to receive immediate divine guidance rather as had Muḥammad himself. Without rejecting the unity of the Muslim Ummah, something of the expectation of continuing prophetic revelation or at least guidance, such as had been suppressed in the Riddah wars, seems to have been revived. Only through continuing contact with the original source of ʿilm could the continued purity of the ʿilm be guaranteed. Then such notions became the starting point for speculations about the status not only of the

traced to 'south' Arab tribes harking back to Yemeni kingship and desiring a charismatic *ruler*, while Khârijism represents 'north' Arab tribes desiring a tribally charismatic *community;* whereas actually a present charismatic individual proved more crucial for Khârijîs than for Shîʿîs. He seems to have accepted certain misconceptions about the cultural role of ancestry (as well as about its factuality). (On the Murji'ah, compare also my article on the Ghassâniyyah in the second edition of the *Encyclopaedia of Islam.*)

imâm but also of the minoritarian faithful themselves. Already in Mukhtâr's time at Kûfah during the second fitnah, recourse had been had to special divination. Later, with more sophistication, several teachers seem to have stressed the ability of the ordinary soul, if selected out from the crude world by its loyalty to the cause, to come angelically into touch with God; and correspondingly, to have stressed a present spiritual, and not merely a future corporeal, resurrection from the dead—in the light of which worldly defeat could seem less overwhelming, the cause of justice more enduring, and future supernatural success more promising.

In such perspectives, the role of the developing Sharîʿah law, emphasized by most of the Piety-minded, became less important for some of the Ghulât theorists (though not for all). What mattered was loyalty to the cause and to its representative, the imâm; preoccupation with legal minutiae was at best futile in the presence of massive injustice, and at worst might be distracting. Some taught that the apparent wording of the Qur'ân, wherever it dealt with external minutiae, had a symbolic meaning of a more spiritual import—or perhaps a hidden reference to the ʿAlid loyalist cause itself: behind the *ẓâhir*, 'externals', of the revelation which the superficial majority knew and took literally, lay a *bâṭin*, 'inward meaning', which the majority were blind to and which only those loyal to the imâms could know. In this way, side by side with the germs of a future Sharîʿah-minded interpretation of Islam were sprouting the germs of an equally potent future inwardly-turned interpretation of Islam, which was to come to fruition especially within the mystical movement called Ṣûfism. And just as among the legists and those close to them many elements were broadly modelled on the traditions of earlier religious communities, so among some of the Ghulât theorists notions entered in that had been long current, especially in heretical minority groups.[12]

All of the more adventurous of these early thinkers among the Muslims tended to be under suspicion as disruptive of Muslim unity and introducers of bidʿah (innovation); the more so, as they tended to represent the most active of the Piety-minded in formulating the general principles of opposition to the dynasty. Several were executed on the grounds of holding a Qadarî position (that is, maintaining an oppositional mood within Syria itself), others for too ardent and obviously subversive an advocacy of Ghulât principles about the Shîʿî candidates. (Murji'îs and more moderate Shîʿîs might be oppositional too, but compared to their rivals, in the Iraq, they were less frightening to the dynasty.) Later, after the revolutions which overthrew the Marwânîs and in the post-revolutionary reaction, the positions they had held, or at least the names given to those positions, were widely discredited; Qadarîs, Murji'îs, and Ghulât alike, along with most other schools of thought of the time mentioned on the chart, were supposed to have been heretical (and the more revered

[12] Cf. my article on the Ghulât in the second edition of the *Encyclopaedia of Islam*, in which will also be found an evaluation of the evidence presented by some (not all) of the Muslim historians of dogma.

figures, like Ḥasan al-Baṣrî and Abû-Ḥanîfah, were gradually dissociated from such labels). Nevertheless, their thinking formed the point of departure for Islamic thinking thenceforth.[13]

The Marwânî dynasty loses its mandate

Mu'âwiyah had still been able to represent for most Muslims the unity of Islam, despite much hostility toward him personally. 'Abd-al-Malik gained much personal approval at Medina, but he and especially al-Walîd faced a rising hostility from the Piety-minded, above all in the Ḥijâz. Al-Walîd's governor at Mecca, Khâlid al-Qaṣrî, took great pains to honour the holy city and to maintain a certain religious gravity there, despite the mood of song and dance which, with the advent of the wealth from the conquest, had made Mecca the most renowned centre for singing girls and love lyrics. He insisted, for instance, that men and women must be separated in performing the rite of running in a circle round the Ka'bah, to prevent inappropriate jostlings. Yet when he built, at al-Walîd's command, an aqueduct to bring abundant sweet water to the town, the Piety-minded party made it an occasion of complaint. The brackish well of Zamzam, which had a part in the ḥajj as the most important well in Mecca, had taken on a holy aura for Muslims (as presumably it had earlier for the pagans); it was regarded as the work of Abraham and as the well which Muḥammad had used. Al-Walîd's aqueduct would now rival Zamzam; it proved how impious was the reigning dynasty.

Al-Walîd's successor, his brother Sulaymân (715–717), was still more readily despised by the pious; he was notoriously pleasure-loving. (He also had a streak of cruelty; for instance, he enjoyed watching captives being hacked to death with dull swords. Hereafter this sort of taste began to recur among hereditary rulers.) Perhaps worse for the state, he allowed party spirit to compromise his position as representing Arab unity. In the great strife between the tribal blocs, he allowed his governor of the Iraq and Khurâsân to favour the Qaḥṭân Arab faction, exercising special cruelty against the family of al-Ḥajjâj, who had been of the Qays faction. Henceforth, in the eastern provinces, governors found themselves driven almost irresistibly to depend on one or another tribal bloc for support during their term of office—and in consequence to incur the opposition of the other bloc. Nevertheless, in 716 the

[13] I owe much of this discussion of early schools of thought to Wilferd Madelung, who has supplemented orally his discussions in *Der Imam al-Qāsim ibn Ibrāhīm und die Glaubenslehre der Zaiditen* (Berlin, 1965). (But he is not responsible for my interpretations.) It is a rich, sound, thorough book which yields more than its title suggests. On Jamâ'îs, Murji'îs, Qadarîs, and Jahmîs, see his masterly appendices, indispensable to an understanding of early Muslim factions. The Murji'îs are especially clearly analyzed; but it seems rather mechanical to suppose, as Madelung does, that any participation in rebellion on their part was necessarily contrary to their principles. His identification of the Ḥadîth folk of 'Abbâsî times, from al-Rashîd on, with the pro-Umayyad jamâ'ah party may be oversimplified.

Arabs were able to force the submission of the Iranian princes in Ṭabaristân, the rainy lands at the southern end of the Caspian.

But under Sulaymân, the wars with Byzantium led to a point of crisis. Successful as were Arab arms under ʿAbd-al-Malik and al-Walîd in Spain (and even, a bit later, in Gaul up to a point), in Sind, and in the Syr-and-Oxus basin, the most important enemy was always the Byzantine empire, whose heartland was the nearby Anatolian highlands. No further attacks were launched against Abyssinia, relatively distant, poor, and inaccessible; but the capture of Constantinople remained a primary goal of the Muslims; to have seized the Sâsânian empire and yet let the main parts of the Roman empire escape seemed only half a victory. As soon as ʿAbd-al-Malik found himself free of internal enemies, he broke off the truce he had made with the Byzantines, defeated them soundly (692), and launched yearly attacks into Anatolia. These carried the Arabs steadily further until in 717 (under Sulaymân) they were ready again to besiege Constantinople. The Syrian army and a large part of the ready resources of the empire were committed to the effort; it failed, and the Marwânî power was seriously weakened for the moment; it was the last attempt on Constantinople by the caliphal state.[14]

Whatever his inadequacies, Sulaymân was very devout; he respected greatly one of the Piety-minded preachers resident at Damascus, who persuaded him, in his last illness, to alter the succession established by ʿAbd-al-Malik. After a reign of but three years, therefore, he left the caliphate to a pious and upright cousin, ʿUmar b. ʿAbd-al-ʿAzîz (717–720). ʿUmar II (as he is called) had been closely associated with the Piety-minded groups at Medina, and tried to carry out the spirit of their policies. He was able to win the support of all elements of the incipient Piety-minded party, even Khârijîs and some Shîʿîs; at the same time, he retained the respect of his own family, the Marwânids and the house of Umayyah;—he was looked to as a model, in some degree, by his successor. His brief reign offers a glimpse of the lines along which the Islamic vision of the time might have been more fully embodied in practice.

He tried to model himself on ʿUmar b. al-Khaṭṭâb, though not blindly (for sometimes he reversed even what had been acts of ʿUmar himself which he regarded as injustices).[15] In the first place, he scrupulously accorded the old

[14] H. A. R. Gibb, 'Arab-Byzantine Relations under the Umayyad Caliphate', *Dumbarton Oaks Papers*, no. 12 (1958), pp. 219–33, and reprinted in his *Studies on the Civilization of Islam* (Boston, 1962), points out that from this defeat on, the caliphal policy—economic and administrative—was directed toward things that would make their state a successor to the Sâsânian, rather than to the Byzantine; or, as I would put it, more toward internal agrarian centralization than toward an expansive Mediterranean foreign policy.

[15] Muslim historians have generally given ʿUmar II high honours, but for a time Western historians thought him a pious fool; the evidence for his practical sagacity is gathered by Julius Wellhausen in the chapter on ʿUmar II in *Das arabische Reich und sein Sturz* (Berlin, 1902). For a recent confirmation of ʿUmar II's combination of piety and good sense, see H. A. R. Gibb, 'A Fiscal Rescript of ʿUmar II', *Arabica*, 2 (1955), 1–16.

Medina families the special status 'Umar had granted them; in particular he admitted their legal claims to certain properties which they had forfeited as the caliphal state was being consolidated. He ended the condemnation of 'Alî from the pulpits, which the victorious Mu'âwiyah had instituted to reinforce unity but which now had the reverse effect. Indeed, whoever could show that his rights by the original settlements of the conquest had been later abridged, or that he suffered other unjust settlements, could obtain redress. A Berber tribute in children was abolished; some Christian groups had their tribute dues reduced; church lands in Egypt were freed of certain taxes; other illegal taxes in Iran were remitted; some excess taxes already paid were restored. He managed to find effective governors who yet ruled without brutality to the persons of the Muslims and who abstained from building up private fortunes.

Perhaps his most important policy was one of quietly treating all provinces alike. In particular, he removed from the Iraq the more obvious evidences of Syrian dominion, perhaps even many Syrian troops; he gave some remoter provinces more local control of their revenues. The central budget was reduced (despite a programme of charities which extended to all provinces, not just chiefly Syria as had previous Marwânids' charities), partly by eliminating jihâd wars on most of the frontiers, which in many cases had become glorified plundering expeditions without permanent results. (On the Byzantine frontier, however, a policy of peace was dictated by sheer prudence.) The chief agitator of tribal rivalry under Sulaymân was jailed.

But perhaps 'Umar II's most heartfelt concern was to encourage general conversion to Islam. Already under 'Umar there had been a clear desire that all Arabs be Muslims; and other pastoralist groups, notably the Berbers, had been assimilated to the Arabs in this respect and had joined them in their conquering expeditions. Occasional Muslims had encouraged or forced dhimmîs (non-Arab non-Muslim subjects) to convert, especially in the case of individuals or families whom it was important to attach to the Arab cause. Now conversion became a government policy extended to all the non-Arabs. It was required that village heads in Egypt be chosen from among Muslims. Even while scrupulous justice was extended to them, within the terms set by the Arab conquest, Christians were made to feel inferior and to know 'their place'. It is likely that some of the humiliating sumptuary laws that later were sometimes imposed on the wealthier dhimmî non-Muslims (and fictively ascribed to the first 'Umar) were sanctioned by 'Umar II: that Christians and Jews should not ride horses, for instance, but at most mules, or even that they should wear certain marks of their religion in their costume when among Muslims. 'Umar II has passed in Christian tradition for a persecutor. Though he disparaged jihâd for plunder, 'Umar II was eager to persuade frontier princes to become Muslims, if necessary by the lures of interest. Sometimes because dhimmîs assessed the taxes, and latterly because governors like al-Ḥajjâj had been unwilling to admit Muslim converts, especially of the lower class (whom he wanted to stay on the land as labourers to boost agriculture), many upper-class dhimmîs had continued to be free of poll tax while many less powerful Muslims continued to pay it. 'Umar II insisted that all dhimmîs and no Muslims pay the poll tax (to which the term *jizyah* was eventually restricted).

A complaint of the converts and their descendants, the Muslim Mawâlî, was that though some of them had fought in the Muslim armies, helping in the conquests, they had not been included in the army dîwân so as to draw a share of the revenues. In Kûfah in the second fitnah, the Shî'î Mukhtâr had bound them to him by so including them—and had enraged the Arab Kûfans. 'Umar II did not include the descendants of the Kûfan Mawâlî, but he did allow Mawâlî who had personally participated in the fighting a (limited) share in the booty from the most recent conquests, for instance those from Khurâsân.

In his land tax policy, 'Umar II's concern for conversion was reinforced by another concern—to avoid the growth of an unduly privileged sector within the Muslim ruling class. Landowning Muslim Arabs within Arabia paid a land tax in the form (more or less) of a tenth of the produce—a tithe (*'ushr*). (This was in addition to the zakât tax paid by Muslims on property other than land.) But most land tax derived from the conquered lands, which normally paid much more than a tenth. The tax on such lands was called *kharâj*, in contrast to the tithe, and went in principle to the Muslims who had conquered them and to their heirs, according to the army dîwân. It was naturally felt that only dhimmîs, not Muslims, should pay the kharâj—Muslims, who formed the soldiery on which the caliphal state relied, should be on the receiving end. As gradually more and more Muslims acquired kharâj-paying lands—and as, alternatively, kharâj-paying dhimmî landowners became Muslims—what happened to the taxes varied from place to place and from occasion to occasion. Al-Ḥajjâj had gone to an extreme in defending the state revenues by insisting that all land once kharâj land should pay kharâj whoever owned it; otherwise, the revenues coming to all the Muslims as a body, and divided among them, would be gradually reduced, to the profit of those few Muslims who happened to acquire the formerly kharâj-paying land and need pay only the tithe on it.

Al-Ḥajjâj's measure had been bitterly resented by the more privileged Muslims and had therefore added to his ill-repute at Medina. But 'Umar II recognized that the problem was real. He rejected al-Ḥajjâj's measure as reducing Muslim and dhimmî to one level, but he was equally unwilling to let the wealthier Muslims monopolize the fruits of the conquest. He allowed lands already acquired to continue paying only the tithe. But from the principle of 'Umar I, that the Muslims generally should receive the revenues as a lump sum rather than divide the lands among themselves, he derived a new rule that Muslims henceforth (after the year 100 of the Hijrah) should cease acquiring kharâj land. As for converts, he evidently provided that in relevant cases they should give up the kharâj land they personally held—as belonging to all the Muslims—though they might still work it, paying through their village the amount of the kharâj, not as kharâj but as rent. Converts to Islam at that date commonly were not landowners primarily, but went to the new Muslim towns to reside; accordingly, this measure was a fairly realistic adaptation to the time of 'Umar II of the conception of 'Umar I that the Muslim Arabs should form a separate privileged community, benefiting from taxes paid by the dhimmî countryside as a mass. Now, however, with non-Arabs freely admitted, the emphasis was more clearly on the Islamic allegiance as such.

With warfare almost eliminated, there being neither revolts nor frontier raids, 'Umar II's treasury stood up well under the considerable demands he made on it by his generous measures. But after less than four years, at the age of thirty-nine, he died. Some of his measures seem to have been maintained in principle, but they were not well enforced. Power reverted to Sulaymân's brother Yazîd II (720–724), given to women and song. A revolt at Baṣrah greeted him, which was not only carried on in the name of Islamic justice, but was sufficiently influenced by the scruples of pious theorists (referred to as being Murji'îs) to be hampered in its tactical operations. (They insisted on not assaulting fellow-Muslims without discussion first.) But it was primarily a movement of the Qaḥṭân tribal faction, and its defeat was followed by a partisan rule favouring the opposed Qays faction throughout the eastern provinces.

Under the devout Hishâm (724–743), who restored a strong hand to the helm, relations between the dynasty and its miscellaneous opposition did not mend. For meanwhile, the underlying development of an integrated agrarian-based society, calling for a strong central rule, continued to make for just the sort of monarchy the Piety-minded objected to. Even the reign of 'Umar II, with its tendency to equalize Arabs and Muslim Mawâlî on the basis of a common Islam, further contributed to the integration of the Arab rulers into the regional life, despite some of his intentions. By the time of Hishâm, and partly through Hishâm's own labours, an impressive amount of bureaucratic organization was directly in Muslim hands and centrally controlled from the caliph's capital. Hishâm was surrounded by high officials who stood between him and the commons, Muslim or not. The early 'Abbâsid caliphs, masters in absolutism, subsequently acknowledged him as an administrative model.

The absolute temper of his rule was illustrated in an institution (the *muṣâdarah*) which had been used as early as 'Abd-al-Malik but was more usual and perhaps more essential in Hishâm's time. The governors and heads of financial bureaus were under temptation to enrich themselves at the expense of the treasury. It became an established practice that an official who incurred the special displeasure of the caliph might be discharged and arrested in a moment, subjected to a more or less arbitrary scrutiny to determine the amount he might be supposed to have embezzled, and fined a corresponding sum; it became common to use torture either to discover the amounts embezzled or, especially later, to force the official to disclose the places where or the merchants with whom he had deposited his wealth, so as to collect the fine by confiscating it. Such personal degradation of a high-placed Muslim would have appalled 'Umar or Mu'âwiyah. It was inconsistent not only with the Islamic standards of the Piety-minded opposition but with the personal ideals of free

Arab tribesmen. But those who wished no limits to be imposed on monarchical authority regarded such a threat as a salutary curb on those overly advantaged in society.

Hishâm did not alter 'Umar II's fiscal principles as such. But in carrying forward the process of administrative and fiscal consolidation, he proved both tight-fisted and greedy. His tighter fiscal measures provoked numerous revolts, which in some areas (notably among the Berbers) took a Khârijî form.

The results of the absolutist tendency were exacerbated by the empire's being based eccentrically in Syria: unless controlled by a masterly chief like 'Umar II, it came to imply increasing control by that one province over the others, and by the time of Hishâm everywhere it was garrisons of Syrian troops that counted militarily. The Iraq witnessed the rising of several Khârijî bands protesting public religious laxity, but it was especially alive with threats of Shî'î revolt centred on Kûfah. Khâlid al-Qaṣrî, who as governor of Mecca had been unable to please the zealous, now as governor of the Iraq faced active anti-Syrian plotting based on the new ideas of 'ilm and imâmate; in 737 he seized two such leaders, with a handful of followers, and burned them. He was unable, however, to get at perhaps the most dangerous Shî'î organization, that which placed the imâmate in the line of Ibn-al-Ḥanafiyyah and by Hishâm's time acknowledged the leadership of the 'Abbâsid family. Such organized Shî'ism was not yet predominant, but it seems to have sapped the strength of more moderate Shî'î movements, notably that of Zayd b. 'Alî. A chief of one of the 'Alid families in Medina, in 740 Zayd led in Kûfah a futile insurrection which, however, had wide support elsewhere also.

The 'Abbâsî compromise

Hishâm's nephew and successor by Yazîd II's arrangement, al-Walîd II (743–744) was not a strong ruler; moreover, he was notoriously careless of religion. Perhaps worse, like Yazîd II he was partisan to the Qays faction and offended the Kalb tribesmen sufficiently to evoke a rising against him in Syria itself. He was killed and another Marwânid (Yazîd III) made caliph instead with the support of the Kalb tribal faction and of some of the Piety-minded; but the untimely death of the new reforming caliph soon followed. His brother, who took his place, was less able.

Meanwhile, a Marwânid general of a side branch of the family, Marwân b. Muḥammad (744–750, styled Marwân II out of respect to his ancestor Marwân), rose to avenge Walîd II in the name of Qays sentiment; for his military power was based largely on Qays tribal alignments in the northern frontier areas. He was the most important of the commanders against the Byzantines and hence the strongest single military chief. But he stood for faction rather than for Muslim unity. The field was wide open for whatever movement could seize the initiative, especially if it could be identified with the anti-Qays factions. Two Khârijî movements, one in southern Arabia and the other in the upper Mesopotamian plain (the latter, as ever, identified with the Rabî'ah tribal faction) gained large numbers of supporters, and each for a time seemed destined to triumph. Marwân II proved able to out-general them. He had done much to improve the Arab military organization in his frontier wars, concentrating his men in solid drill units. With his experienced troops, first he suppressed the latest Syrian Marwânid candidate (and eventually wiped out the Syrian power altogether); then he turned to his rival movements of revolt and crushed them one by one.

Along with the two Khârijî attempts failed also one important Shî'î attempt. Its imâm, 'Abd-Allâh Ibn-Mu'âwiyah, was a descendant of Abû-Ṭâlib, 'Alî's father, and hence a member of Muḥammad's house of Hâshim. (Some are said to have supposed he would give the rule to an 'Alid when he had won.) He made Kûfah his first centre of revolt and gained general Qaḥṭân tribal support; when hard-pressed there, he retired to the Iranian highlands and staved off full defeat for some time, gaining the support of representatives from almost all elements of the Piety-minded opposition. But Marwân's disciplined Qays troops proved too much for his ill-assorted malcontents.

Meanwhile a second Shî'î revolt was replacing his (also with Qaḥṭân support). Ibn-Mu'âwiyah may have claimed the blessing, in his endeavour, of Abû-Hâshim, the deceased head of the partisans of 'Alî's son Ibn-al-Ḥanafiyyah; but it seems likely that Abû-Hâshim had actually bequeathed his authority, which carried with it organized support, to another family of the house of Hâshim, the 'Abbâsids, descendants of Muḥammad's cousin 'Abd-Allâh b. 'Abbâs. The 'Abbâsids, at any rate, were carrying on a very effective propaganda against the Marwânids on a largely Shî'î basis.

Tribal-bloc jealousies had been peculiarly strong in Khurâsân, the highlands northeast of the central Iranian deserts. There the Qaḥṭân faction was actively discontented. The Mawâlî formed an important and active element among the Muslims of that distant frontier province and were jealous of the privileged position the central Marwânî régime still tried to accord the old-Arab element, despite 'Umar II's decree of equality. A local revolt in the name of Qur'ân and sunnah began in 734, not to be put down till 746 (one of its leaders, Jahm b. Ṣafwân, was a Piety-minded thinker). The able Marwânî governor, Naṣr b. Sayyâr, could barely keep order. Into this ferment came agents of Abû-Hâshim's partisans, under 'Abbâsî direction, secretly pleading the cause of the house of Muḥammad. The chief of these, Khidâsh, is said to have preached radical ideas in the manner of the Ghulât and to have been disowned by the 'Abbâsids; he was executed in 736. But the propaganda continued till a freed slave of the 'Abbâsid imâm Ibrâhîm, Abû-Muslim, was sent (*c.* 745) to arouse active revolt among an already substantial group of partisans.[16]

[16] I use the term *'Abbâsid* for the Banû 'Abbâs, the descendants of 'Abbâs, Muḥammad's uncle; and the more general term *'Abbâsî* for the adherents of the dynasty and for their ways. I make a corresponding distinction for later dynasties also.

Abû-Muslim seems to have stressed revenge for the deaths of various members of the house of Muḥammad (the Hâshimids) at the hands of the Umayyad house, starting with Ḥusayn at Karbalâ' and including most recently the rebel Zayd and his sons; the latter had been pursued into Khurâsân and killed. (Yet Abû-Muslim himself was said to be responsible for the death of the defeated Ibn-Mu'âwiyah when that rival Hâshimid fled to Khurâsân.) The black banners which he raised, as had some earlier rebels, as an eschatological symbol seem to have been felt to symbolize mourning for these deaths—and indirectly, therefore, for all the injustices that either old-line Arabs or insulted Mawâlî felt they had received at the hands of the ruling Arab factions—personified in the Umayyad house. By 747, he was ready to emerge from secret agitation and take the field. Even then, canvassing support in the name of the house of Muḥammad generally, he named no candidate to the caliphate, seemingly leaving that to be settled on victory. Marwân II discovered, however, the connection of the 'Abbâsid Ibrâhîm with the revolt and had him put out of the way. Abû-Muslim added him to the list of Hâshimid martyrs. With the defeat of the other anti-Marwânî movements, Abû-Muslim's was the only opposition movement still in the field by 748 and attracted wide support.

Against Abû-Muslim's Khurâsânîs, Marwân's military reorganization and good generalship proved not enough. Abû-Muslim proved a talented statesman, able to mobilize excellent generals. In any case, Marwân II was too busy suppressing other movements to deal adequately with so distant a danger, despite his governor's urgent pleas for help. By the time he could turn his full attention to it, it was overwhelming and swept all before it. Abû-Muslim moved through western Iran with little opposition; at the Euphrates, a major Marwânî army was defeated. Abû-Muslim's men now brought the 'Abbâsids into the open as claimants, proclaiming Abû-l-'Abbâs, Ibrâhîm's brother, as caliph (with the byname of al-Saffâḥ) in the heart of Shî'î territory at Kûfah. Muḥammad's house of Hâshim was to rule at last (749). Marwân's whole power was defeated near the Tigris (750); he was unable to raise new forces among the Syrians, whom he had himself crushed; at last he was trapped and killed in Egypt. Gaining an almost unquestioned domination as far as Egypt, the 'Abbâsî movement thus ended the series of revolutions that the Syrians themselves had begun.[17]

All but one of these movements—all, that is, but Marwân II's—were coloured by the demands of the Piety-minded for a new and more adequately Islamic social order. That of the 'Abbasîs was keyed to Shî'î expectations. Their imâm had been supposed to have authority by virtue of his connections with 'Alî by bequest and with Muḥammad's house by nature (for his ancestor 'Abd-Allâh b. 'Abbâs was, like 'Alî, Muḥammad's cousin); he was said to have foretold, through the 'ilm knowledge so acquired, many detailed events of the

[17] Claude Cahen, 'Points de vue sur la revolution "abbaside" ', *Revue historique*, 230 (1963), 295–338, has the most careful recent study of the 'Abbâsid cause and its leadership of the Shî'î movement.

time of the revolutions. But when the 'Abbâsids had seized power they turned their backs on their more strictly Shî'î supporters, for the most part, and made relatively little of their role as imâms endowed with 'ilm. Nor did they make a serious effort to rule according to the ideal religious attitudes cultivated by the pious among the opposition. Instead, they based their power on the force of their Khurâsânî supporters; and above all on their ability to provide a much desired peace after all the revolutions, on the basis of acceptance of the chief practical demands of the main ethnic elements of the opposition to the Marwânîs. They showed from the very first that their rule, far from embodying ideals of egalitarian personal responsibility, was to be one of bloodshed. Almost their first care was to massacre all accessible members of the scapegoat Umayyad house. But these were soon not the only ones to suffer. Whatever else their rule might do, it would brook no opposition to itself.

The 'Abbâsids took the power away from the Syrian Arabs and distributed it more widely; though they favoured the Khurâsânîs, they placed their capital in the Iraq (building for that purpose the city of Baghdad), and made it clear that no region, unless perhaps Syria itself, was to be discriminated against. At the same time, they made no effective distinction between the old Arab families and the new Muslims, the 'Mawâlî', who had come up from the conquered population (and many of whom no longer even had any affiliation with an Arab tribe). In this way they satisfied some of the most pressing demands of the opposition. On a more idealistic level, they were content to offer to the Piety-minded groups a de jure recognition of the legal programme they were working out, and were willing to honour and occasionally pay attention to the representatives of ḥadîth reporting and Islamic 'ilm. In this latter point they differed from later Marwânids like Hishâm, among whom representatives of the Medina piety were by no means despised. But the 'Abbâsids were willing to accord formal and exclusive status to the representatives of the former Piety-minded opposition. They tried to appoint as qâḍîs, for instance, men whom the pious would recognize as representative of the new ideas about the sunnah, and some (but not all) such men were willing to accept the appointments. At any rate, the qâḍî courts were to be bound by the legal fiqh of the Piety-minded. In those several ways, the old historical constellation under which the Piety-minded opposition had developed was broken up. The support the Piety-minded groups had derived from ethnic complaints disappeared, and they were themselves divided. The old Piety-minded opposition could no longer expect to institute their demands on the basis of the general sentiment of the Muslims.

The Shî'îs, and the Piety-minded opposition generally, were disappointed. Sensing or anticipating this disappointment, indeed, the 'Abbâsids soon did away with their leading Shî'î supporters, paralyzing immediate resistance to their policies. The head of the Shî'î group in the Iraq (Abû-Salamah) had evidently hoped, on the triumph of the 'Abbâsî armies, to proclaim one of the chief 'Alids caliph; he accepted the 'Abbâsî chief only with reluctance when no 'Alid proved ready or adroit enough. Not surprisingly, ground was soon found to have him killed. More disquieting was the death of Abû-Muslim himself. He was on bad terms personally with al-Manṣûr, who became caliph in 754, soon after the victory. He distrusted the new caliph but was lured by promises of reconciliation into the caliph's presence alone without his devoted soldiers, and was murdered; the unprepared soldiers were made to accept the fait accompli.

The 'Alid loyalists further from the seat of the new government tried to pull themselves together for a new effort. One of the most prominent of the 'Alid candidates, Muḥammad 'al-Nafs al-Zakiyyah' ('the pure soul'), staged a revolt in the Ḥijâz. He claimed the title *Mahdî*, '(divinely) guided'—the title implying a religious mission, already used by Mukhtâr for his candidate Ibn-al-Ḥanafiyyah—and he seems to have had the sympathy of Piety-minded groups everywhere apart from the Khârijîs and the particular band of Shî'îs that personally supported the 'Abbâsids; even Baṣrah revolted and was bloodily reduced. But this revolt, which in the Ḥijâz, at least, was so pietistic that it tried to imitate, against 'Abbâsî might, techniques Muḥammad had used against Arab tribesmen, finally failed miserably.

The Piety-minded groups, accordingly, were presented with two alternatives: to continue their overt opposition but on some new historical basis; or to accept the settlement offered by the 'Abbâsids as a half-loaf. Gradually the majority accepted the 'Abbâsî settlement and adopted the black robes which, like the black flags, were the emblem of the dynasty. In effect, they clung to the jamâ'ah, recognizing the validity of the general community experience however imperfect the community might sometimes be. Those Piety-minded who had made a point of not breaking with the majority of the Muslim community had long referred to themselves as adherents of the jamâ'ah, the community as a body. But till now, the various Piety-minded factions had been relatively local, and their rejection or acceptance of the ruling dynasty had varied in many degrees. There had been no overall schism in the community. Now the 'Abbâsid house gradually won a position, among most of the heirs of the Piety-minded groups everywhere, as sole legitimate rulers, whatever their faults; while those who anywhere still remained unreconciled found themselves frankly in a minority position. The Muslims' allegiance was to be polarized throughout the empire, pro or con.

The two sides in this schism have subsequently been labelled, conventionally, 'Sunnîs' and 'Shî'îs'. Each side adopted a historical position in justification of its present attitude. The Shî'îs came to reject the religious authority of those, even among Muḥammad's associates, who had not recognized 'Alî's sole right to the caliphate (a position hitherto held only by radical Shî'îs). Correspondingly, it gradually became characteristic for their opponents to accept the religious authority of all Muḥammad's associates without distinction, despite the quarrels that had taken place among them.

The term *Sunnî* is short for 'Men of the Sunnah and the Jamâ'ah'. This name

Events of the Third Fitnah, 744–750

ʻUmân (and the Ḥijâz and the Maghrib)	Syria	The Jazîrah	The Iraq (and western Iran)	Khurâsân (and Oxus basin)
	744 Walîd II deposed and killed by Yazîd III, Marwânid reformer supported by Qadarîs	**744** Marwân II, Marwânid frontier commander, revolts, becomes caliph at Damascus	**744** Shîʻî leader ʻAbd-Allâh b. Muʻâwiyah rises at Kûfah, retires to west Iran	
	744 Yazîd III succeeded by brother, Ibrâhîm			
	745 Syrians rebel against Marwân		**745** Shaybânî Khârijîs, under Ḍaḥḥâq, take Kûfah and much of the Jazîrah	**745** Al-Ḥârith b. Surayj, ʻMurjiʼiʼ, again revolts **745** Abû-Muslim comes to Khurâsân to lead ʻAbbâsî movement
c. **746** Ibâḍî Khârijîs, rising in ʻUmân under Ṭâlib al-Ḥaqq, sweep west and north	**746** Syrian rebellion crushed	**746** Shaybânî Khârijîs crushed in the Jazîrah		**746** Al-Ḥârith b. Surayj put down by gov. Naṣr b. Sayyâr
			747 Shaybânî Khârijîs defeated in the Iraq	**747** Abû-Muslim openly rebels; (747/8) takes Marv
			747 ʻAbd-Allâh b. Muʻâwiyah defeated by Marwânîs in west Iran	
748 Ibâḍî Khârijîs take Medina and are defeated by Marwânîs	**748** Ibrâhîm, ʻAbbâsid imâm, dies at hands of Marwân II			**748** ʻAbd-Allâh b. Muʻâwiyah dies at hands of Abû-Muslim
			749 ʻAbbâsî forces occupy Kûfah after battle of Lesser Zâb; al-Saffâḥ acclaimed caliph; Abû-Salamah, Shîʻî leader at Kûfah, executed	
750 Ṣufrî and Ibâḍî Khârijîs temporarily defeated in the Maghrib, but Ibâḍîs renew revolt in ʻUmân	**750** Marwân fails to raise new forces; is killed in Egypt		**750** Battle of the Greater Zâb, ʻAbbâsî forces defeat Marwân II	**750–751** Shîʻî revolt in Bukhârâ suppressed by ʻAbbâsîs

was first adopted by only one faction among those who accepted the 'Abbâsids—a faction which stressed continuity with the Marwânî past (and was not especially friendly to the 'Abbâsids as such) and combined this with a special interest in the sunnah practice as expressed in ḥadîth reports about the Prophet. But since that faction eventually was specially recognized as representing the jamâ'ah position, the term has come to refer not necessarily to all that faction's complex of teachings, but simply to the acceptance of the jamâ'ah principle in contrast to the 'Men of the Shî'ah', the 'Alid-loyalist party.

We do need a term for those who rejected the Shî'î (and Khârijî) positions in favour of the continuing jamâ'ah; but for this, the term *Sunnî* is inappropriate. At best, the term *Sunnî* is confusing, for it has been used, from the beginning, in special ways by those who wanted to use it exclusively for their own brand of orthodoxy. Some used it for those devoted purely to the use of ḥadîth reports (*sunnah*), without speculative discussion (*kalâm*). It was used later, among those who were willing to accept kalâm discussion at all, for the Ash'arî or Mâturîdî schools of kalâm as against the Mu'tazilî; it was used by Sharî'ah-minded zealots to distinguish Sharî'ah-minded people from the Ṣûfî mystics; and generally as the equivalent of English 'orthodox'. (A special disadvantage of the term *Sunnî* is that, unfortunately, laymen commonly make the mistake of supposing that the Shî'îs, because they are contrasted to Sunnîs, do not accept ḥadîth and sunnah.) A far more accurate term would have been *Jamâ'î*, for the point at issue was the acceptance of the historical jamâ'ah unity, whereas all parties accepted the sunnah practice in relatively similar forms. However, the term *Sunnî* has become so well established in the sense of accepting the jamâ'ah, among Muslims and non-Muslims, that one can hardly displace it at this point. In this work it is not used in the various more specific ways, but only in the minimal sense, as contrasted to *Shî'î*. To stress this usage, I shall use by preference (though rather unhappily) the hyphenated phrase *Jamâ'î-Sunnî*, except in contexts where no confusion can arise.[18]

The Jamâ'î-Sunnî 'ulamâ' scholars, in this general sense, did not all adopt a common doctrine; they varied even as to the degree of respect they accorded the 'Abbâsî régime; but they agreed sufficiently under 'Abbâsî leadership to establish eventually a common modus vivendi, and to this day the great majority of Muslims accept a Jamâ'î-Sunnî position. Those of the 'Alid loyalists who refused became the Shî'îs in the modern sectarian sense, gradually distributing themselves into a number of oppositional sects which have also persisted to the present. (Many persons more or less loyal to the 'Alids

[18] We may summarize three ways in which the term *Sunnî* has been most used, as follows: to mean *Jamâ'î* as vs. *Shî'î*; to mean *Ḥadîthî* as vs. *Kalâmî* (including Mu'tazilîs and Ash'arîs); to mean *Shar'î* as vs. *Ṣûfî*. Then it has been extended to those 'Alid-loyalists, kalâm men, and Ṣûfîs who accepted key positions of their respective opponents. Once one no longer assumes the old stereotypes which these usages embodied, they serve merely to confuse the issues.

accepted nonetheless a Jamâ'î position.) The Khârijî groups—tending to splinter into mutually hostile bands—likewise continued their opposition, of course, but it became steadily less effective as the bulk of the population turned Muslim.[19]

[19] Leonard Binder and L. Carl Brown have been kind enough to help me clarify a draft of these early chapters.

II

The Absolutism in Flower, 750–813

From the viewpoint of the Piety-minded, the ʿAbbâsî régime represented at best a compromise with their pious ideals for Muslim society—and some aspects of ʿAbbâsî rule, notably its arbitrariness, presented an extreme corruption of, or even a rude and alien intrusion into, the proper Islamic social order. The Piety-minded ʿulamâʾ scholars proceeded to develop, in the form of Sharîʿah law and of Sharîʿah-minded disciplines harking back to Muḥammad and to the Irano-Semitic monotheistic tradition generally, a programme of Islamic culture which allowed the ʿAbbâsî caliphate at best a secondary role. But from a viewpoint far more popular in court circles and among a great many of the ordinary population, both non-Muslims and also, now, Muslims, the ʿAbbâsî régime represented a reasonably close approximation to a social ideal. This alternative set of norms cultivated in courtly circles stemmed back likewise to the early Muslim community, as it had developed under the caliphs as conquerors, and to the older Irano-Semitic traditions of culture, especially those of the Sâsânian empire. Just as the Piety-minded ʿulamâʾ were developing a comprehensive cultural pattern, so also did the society surrounding the caliphal court develop a comprehensive cultural pattern, in which the incipient culture of the Piety-minded could have, at best, only marginal relevance. This pattern—in contrast to that associated with the Sharîʿah—was more aristocratic than populistic; it was based in large measure on agrarian traditions such as those which had been kept alive from Sâsânian times among the landed gentry of the Iranian highlands, including Khurâsân.

The caliphal absolutism

Seen from within this tradition, the caliph was to be a major figure, successor to the Great King of the Iranian empire close to whose capital Baghdad was built. He even ought to have a certain religious aura, foreign to the spirit of the Sharîʿah as envisaged by the Piety-minded, but close to that of the old Sâsânians. When the caliph was addressed—as he was—as 'the shadow of God on earth', the ʿulamâʾ scholars could only be profoundly shocked. The Sâsânian monarch, standing at the summit of the divinely ordained aristocratic society of the Mazdean tradition, had been held to be a special instrument of the divine will. He had been invested with the sacred divine glory, a mystic aura which represented the authority and power of God. Shar'î Islam, with its egalitarian insistence that all men were on the same level before God, could ill tolerate such a figure. Yet the courtly circles were willing to ascribe a very similar position to the caliph, only limiting themselves to language which did not go so far as to ascribe to him any part of actual divinity.

In our day, when representative democracy is regarded as the only proper principle of national government, the monarchical ideal is easily misunderstood. Too readily we speak with a certain scorn of 'Oriental despotism'. We are sometimes surprised to find that most wise men, in both Christendom and Islamdom, in all ages down to recent centuries regarded monarchy as unquestionably the most excellent form of government.

In fact, before the advent of Modern technical conditions, a strong monarchy was by and large the most satisfactory form of supra-local government in any agrarianistic society. In very small states—where all that was involved was a city and its immediate environs, and most people could meet face to face—in many parts of the world there have existed a variety of viable forms of municipal governments: rule by one man or by committee, by oligarchic or by popular assemblies. But once a state gained a certain size, except in those rare cases where an enduring free federation of municipalities could be created, monarchy seemed the only suitable alternative to a rapacious armed oligarchy. Monarchy became everywhere the acknowledged political ideal; hence even when, as often happened, the central monarchic authority was actually too weak to fulfill its functions, nevertheless the forms of monarchy were retained as window-dressing by the oligarchy which shared rule in its own narrow interest.[1]

The principle of monarchy was to give one man in the community the disinterestedness of unchallenged supremacy—to make him so highly privileged

[1] The most recent attempt to revive the concept of 'Oriental despotism', Karl A. Wittfogel, *Oriental Despotism: A Comparative Study of Total Power* (Yale University Press, 1957), is a brilliant and monumental anti-Soviet tract, but so over-schematized as to be very little use for making intelligible the political institutions of the Arid Zone (or probably anywhere else.) The previously cited study by Robert Adams, *Land behind Baghdad* (University of Chicago Press, 1965), shows how rare, and how limited as a political model, was the 'hydraulic' type of government based on irrigation to which a large bureaucratic administration was necessary. In the mid-Arid Zone, some such pattern was fully effective, probably, only under Nûshîrvân and his immediate successors.

Even Wittfogel notes that if any such entity as 'Oriental despotism' can be distinguished at all, it is to be found in many other places than the traditional 'Orient' and is not universal within that 'Orient'; that is, even he sees that he is discussing not a culture trait of a particular segment of the world but a phenomenon which may arise anywhere under the right conditions. But closer examination will carry one further still. Distinctions between absolutisms in Western Europe and absolutisms in other parts of the world may possibly be of a certain moral importance; but they are of no greater degree, in regard to manner of political functioning, than distinctions between absolutisms in, say, China and absolutisms elsewhere. To divide all absolutisms into only two sorts, speaking of 'Oriental despotism' as contrasted (at least in pre-Modern times) to 'Occidental monarchy', is to make a false dichotomy.

that no one could hope to be his rival, so that his interests were no longer pitted against those of other individuals but became merged with those of the community as a whole, of whose general prosperity he was invariably the beneficiary whatever the fate of individuals. His authority must be absolute, one before which the rich and the well-born were as vulnerable as the little man. He must be able to settle, without hope of appeal, the dangerous quarrels of the great; and must have no reason to turn a deaf ear to those who would plead the case of the poor. Chinese and Arabs, Indians and Occidentals alike delighted to tell of the petitioner's drum, or bell, outside an olden king's palace, at the sound of which the king immediately emerged to do justice. Actuality, of course, was less romantic, but not wholly beside the mark. Such a monarch might amount merely to a court of final arbitrament; but the monarchy would be the more effective, the more the whole administrative activity of the state could be centred in the hands of his immediate subordinates, his creatures, dependent on him for all their power. Monarchy was perfected by bureaucracy. Ideally, such a power could be looked to as the ultimate guarantee of equality and justice for the ordinary subjects—the sole recourse for counterbalancing the natural tendency in society to inequality and privilege.

Long before Sâsânian times, at least since the times of the Achaemenid dynasty of Darius and Xerxes, the Semitic and Iranian peoples had been evolving their tradition of the absolute monarchy, which became a basic pillar of the social order of the Sâsânian empire. The Sâsânian society had maintained itself more than four centuries in relative prosperity and with relative human dignity under a single line of kings. Those who cherished the monarchical ideal looked back to that society as the embodiment of social order and stability and even of justice for the individual. Its principles were taken as political axioms. First, the monarchy must be universal—at least it must embrace all the civilized lands in its part of the world, in which a rival power might spring up; for only with such universality could peace be assured among the various cities and peoples. Second, the monarch must be personally unassailable, exempt from anyone's admonition or criticism (lèse majesté); bound by the ancestral laws, to be sure, but otherwise by the opinions of no one subject or clique of subjects. Only so could he wield his mercy and his wrath disinterestedly upon all those who, in his presence, were equally as nothing. Finally, the monarch must be surrounded by an aristocratic professional staff—heading the bureaucracy—who (though themselves subject to the arbitrary will of their master) in turn also were in sufficiently exalted position in society at large to be able to govern in a relatively detached spirit of noblesse oblige. The ideal Sâsânian monarch was seen in the figure of Nûshîrvân, who personally embodied both justice and a graciousness toward the humble which marked off all the more his exalted status. And Nûshîrvân was seconded by that wisest of ministers, aristocratic head of the bureaucracy, Buzurgmihr, who became the model of wisdom for all grand viziers.

But if this kingly personal position was to be assured, as well as that of the great courtiers, it must be reinforced by a pattern of behaviour which set the monarch off from all his subjects across a great psychological gulf, as well as the royal court from ordinary life. Everyone knew well enough that in fact the king was a mere man among others. In himself he was a mere six feet of flesh, with passions like any other man, by no means unassailable; and likewise his courtiers. Accordingly, the Sâsânian monarch had been shielded from the ready access of his fellow creatures and surrounded with the pomp of majesty. Now the same was done with the caliph, who from a simple commander among equal believers was raised to a magnificent figure, remote in a world of awesome luxury, walled off by an elaborate courtly etiquette, whose casual word was obeyed like divine law. The court etiquette of Baghdad was consciously modelled on that of the Sâsânians and the social implications of it were essentially the same.

Only the most privileged could normally speak with the ʿAbbâsid caliph at all. He could be approached only through a chain of officials and in accordance with an elaborately formal ritual, which included kissing the ground before him. It was especially the etiquette of obvious personal submission before the caliph that roused the ire of the ʿulamâʾ and of the pious generally. Only God should receive anything smacking of worship. The caliph, being a man, should be addressed in just the same simple manner as that which the Sharîʿah prescribed for anyone else. As ḥadîth reports were found to prove, the Prophet himself had been so addressed, and who was a mere caliph?

Finally, as symbol of his power, there stood beside him the executioner, ready to kill the most exalted personage at a word. From the point of view of the Sharîʿah, with its insistence on personal dignity and a carefully safeguarded trial according to God's rules, the caliph's summary executions were an abomination. From the point of view of the absolutists, they were an essential means of cutting the Gordian knot of privilege. As with the muṣâdarah (the fining of dismissed officials and their torture to force payment), the misuse of summary executions commonly hit only those who voluntarily frequented the court, had enjoyed its luxury, and had at the same time deliberately risked its dangers. The ultimate sanction afforded by such executions was thought to guarantee an effective peace to the wider public.

Such a temper was obviously inconsistent with the personal ideals of the free Arab tribesmen as much as with the hopes of the Piety-minded. Earlier manifestations of it had contributed to undermining the support of the privileged Arabs for the Marwânî dynasty even while the new converts and their descendants hated the dynasty for its Arabism. Yet even in the midst of the third fitnah, Marwân II, in such parts of the empire as he controlled, had tightened still further the bureaucratic organization and with it the caliphal absolutism. When the ʿAbbâsî cause came out victorious, the power of privileged Arabism had already been greatly weakened. Pious ideals notwithstanding, the way had become open for a still more forthright reconstitution of the state in terms of the long-standing absolutist civic ideals of the region.

The first 'Abbâsids were completing the work which had already been carried some distance by 'Abd-al-Malik and Hishâm. In al-Manṣûr, the whole society could recognize its direct ruler; the Arab families formed but one privileged element among the rest, the caliphs being as far exalted above them as above any others.

The foundations of al-Manṣûr's power

The first 'Abbâsî caliph, al-Saffâḥ, who happened to be the head of the 'Abbâsid family at the moment when the 'Abbâsî movement seized power in 750, set the 'Abbâsî pattern chiefly in the sense that he slaughtered indiscriminately, treacherously, and, according to the accounts, with gross brutality as many members of the Umayyad family as he could lay hands on. He ordered that even the dead be desecrated. Among other tales is this: at one point he pretended to relent in his bloody search for Umayyad scions and invited all that remained to a banquet in token of forgiveness. Sitting at the meal, they were cut down by attendants; a carpet was spread over their dead and dying bodies and the banquet continued in the same room to the sound of their groans. The story is scarcely credible but illustrates what people thought of the 'Abbâsid dynasty.

To the end, the Syrian Umayyads had been careful of their personal and tribal relations with the other great Arab families; there had often been feuds and murders and executions, such as that of the Kûfan recusant, Ḥujr; but everyone felt and behaved as if the killing of any of the more prominent Arabs was not to be taken lightly. Al-Saffâḥ, on the contrary, was sweeping in his violence. His power rested less on either Iraqi or Syrian garrison town Arabs, with their tribal jealousies and personal dignities, than on the Khurâsânî mixed Arab and Persian gentry and their peasant troops, many of whom presumably wanted him to play the absolute ruler as had the Iranian kings of old. His unconstrained use of power announced unmistakably that his régime would meet such requirements.

Al-Saffâḥ died (754) a few years after his accession. His brother, al-Manṣûr (754–775), succeeded him as head of the 'Abbâsid family and hence as caliph. Al-Manṣûr proceeded to round out the 'Abbâsî absolutist imperial structure. When by murder he rid himself of the most prominent Shî'îs, he was by the same act ridding himself of men who had figured prominently in bringing his family to power and therefore were in a position of relative independence toward it, quite apart from ideals. When he put down the Shî'î rebellion of al-Nafs al-Zakiyyah at Mecca and forced the 'ulamâ' to choose either hopeless opposition or accommodation, he was at the same time asserting the freedom of the monarchy from limitations on the part of any subordinate group—that is, of any sector of the privileged elements in the population.

Even so, he was unable to restore so full an absolutism as had prevailed among the Sâsânians. A gifted administrator of his, Ibn-al-Muqaffa' (a convert from Mazdeism), presented him with a programme that would have restored a fuller measure of their agrarian-based absolutism. Ibn-al-Muqaffaʿ urged him to supplement the direct military basis of his power by rallying the agrarian classes—in particular, conciliating those families that were still oriented to the Marwânî régime and its values; and by tying the religious specialists to the state—making the Piety-minded ʿulamâʾ scholars into an officially established order parallel to the old Mazdean priesthood, and capping such a priestly structure by asserting a final caliphal authority in questions of fiqh law. Such

The Early ʿAbbâsid Caliphs

- Al-ʿAbbâs ibn ʿAbd al-Muṭṭalib, uncle of the Prophet
  - Muḥammad (d. 743)
    - Ibrâhîm ('the Imâm') (d. 749)
    - Abû-l-ʿAbbâs AL-SAFFÂḤ (750–754)
    - Abû Jaʿfar AL-MANṢÛR (754–775)
      - Muḥammad AL-MAHDÎ (775–785)
        - Muḥammad AL-HÂDÎ (785–786)
        - Hârûn AL-RASHÎD (786–809)
          - Muḥammad AL-AMÎN (809–813)
          - ʿAbd Allâh AL-MAʾMÛN (813–833)
          - Abû Isḥâq AL-MUʿTAṢIM (833–842)
            - Later ʿAbbâsid Caliphs

a course was made difficult, however, by the very conditions of ʿAbbâsî victory: its dependence on the Khurâsânî animus against the Syrians, and its betrayal of the ʿAlid cause, popular among many of the Piety-minded. These conditions, in turn, were the effect of Arab tribal prejudices and the independence of the ʿulamâʾ; it was as champions of individual dignities and foes of central power that the ʿAlids were desired, so that even an ʿAlid could probably have done no more than al-Manṣûr toward effectively stable absolutism. The power of Arab prejudices and pious individualism to play so key a role, finally, was surely, in part, the effect of weak solidarity among the agrarian classes. Eventually Ibn-al-Muqaffaʿ was executed on suspicion of heresy. But al-Manṣûr did his best.

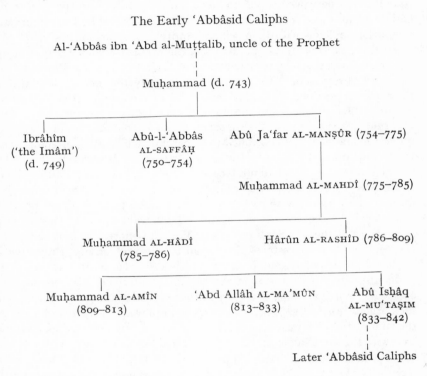

Al-Manṣûr was concerned to control his newly-won empire through a bureaucracy capable of minute supervision over every province. He found an unscrupulous but highly talented secretary (*kâtib*, scribe) to organize the whole financial structure; his work was sufficiently specialized that a single head of finances such as he was seemed thenceforth usually indispensable, and the position eventually evolved into that of the all-powerful minister, the *vizier*. (Al-Manṣûr was noted for watching the finances closely—he was ridiculed as 'the penny pincher'; at his death he left a full treasury.) He also was careful to build up a network of spies to keep down any future conspiracies such as had raised his own family to power, as well as to control by their information the various officials with their widely ramifying responsibilities.

All this governmental apparatus was maintained financially from a carefully calculated revenue, primarily agricultural. As under the Marwânids, the agricultural resources of the Fertile Crescent played a major role; but not in the same proportions. The inner hinterland of the Syrian cities, an arid belt east of the Orontes and the Jordan, had been highly developed under Christian rule as part of an east Mediterranean nexus of commerce (and pilgrimage); under the Marwânids it continued to be carefully cultivated, often directly in the form of dynastic holdings. But already under the Marwânids, the Jazîrah, which as a frontier area had not received much large-scale agricultural investment, was being developed more fully; and likewise the Sawâd of the Iraq, formerly the basis of Nûshîrvân's strength. After a time of neglect under the Medina caliphs, when many of the canals remained almost in disuse after the disruptions of the last Sâsânian years, Marwânî efforts, such as those of al-Ḥajjâj, seem to have restored the Sawâd to full productivity. But under the 'Abbâsids, the Sawâd came to play almost as central a role in state finances as under the later Sâsânians. The Syrian inner hinterland, disproportionately expensive to irrigate (and probably at the point of diminishing returns when such other areas as the Jazîrah were opened up) was largely abandoned upon the ruin of the Umayyad family. Yet the Sawâd was not used as a political base with the same single-mindedness as it had been, evidently, under Nûshîrvân. Its direct value to the government seems to have begun declining, in fact, soon after the 'Abbâsid accession, as ever more individuals intercepted the revenues. (But this very lack of intensive state exploitation may account for its having been maintained—despite alternative resources in the Jazîrah—economically at something near the top Sâsânian levels and for a longer time: till the mid-ninth century, when investment in the Sawâd seems to have begun to decrease decisively.)[2]

[2] Cf. Adams, *Land behind Baghdad*; and the work of Jean Sauvaget on the Syrian back country, e.g., *L'enceinte primitive d'Alep* (Beirut, 1929). There is an unhappy tendency for global comparisons to be made of economic conditions under the Romans and under the Arabs on the basis of spotty data. Starting, in fact, from the relative desolation of the start of the nineteenth century, when Ottoman realms, occupied by Arabs and ruled by Turks, seemed to show the disastrous consequences of Islam, Western observers used to note that in 'antiquity' (a period of over a thousand years,

At the same time, the role of merchants and even of craft production was not irrelevant to the state finances. Merchants paid zakât 'alms' tax (in principle, only once a year) on their goods as they transported them through government checkpoints; perhaps at least as important, they maintained a network of consumer channels and credit facilities which made possible central control of monetary taxation on an imperial scale stretching from the Maghrib and the Yemen to the Oxus basin. Considerations of commercial accessibility, as well as imperial precedent, seem to have determined the site of the new capital which al-Manṣûr proceeded to build, Baghdad, safely away from Shî'î Kûfah and appropriately near the site of the Sâsânian capital, Ctesiphon.

Muslims had built cities before. The garrison towns the Arabs had often built at the first conquests soon became full-scale cities; these were organized in terms of the tribal contingents that had first settled there. Baghdad was built on a different plan (anticipated only in part by a new city Hishâm had built). Its location was not (as in the case of towns like Baṣrah and Kûfah) on the edge of the desert, of easy military access for a camel-borne people. Like Ctesiphon, Baghdad was built on the Tigris at a location carefully chosen as an economic centre for the whole population of the region. It was chosen partly to command the agriculture of the Sawâd, and partly as a crossroads of bulk and luxury trade; trade by water—along the Tigris and Euphrates rivers from the Persian Gulf and the east Mediterranean Sea—as well as by land from across the Iranian mountains. Moreover, Baghdad was not built as the sum of several independent and equal quarters housing various Arab tribes, but was focused on the enormous caliphal palace. Its most important part was the 'round city', the administrative complex in which the caliph lived and around him the other members of the 'Abbâsid family and the various courtiers, each in vast establishments which sheltered large numbers of dependents. At the outskirts sprang up the bazaars and housing for the rest of the servicing population. The site was so well chosen that though later caliphs tried to escape its popular pressures as had al-Manṣûr those of Kûfah, it remained unrivalled as a cultural and economic centre throughout the High Caliphal Period.

The first 'Abbâsid caliph had adopted a surname of eschatological over-

---

within which they tended to make no distinctions) areas now desert had flourished grandly, as the ruins of waterworks and of cities proved. In this context, the scholarly question arose: at what point did the presence of the Arabs commence its supposedly ruinous work; and it was a major discovery when it was shown that, at least in Syria, the land most open to investigation, this was not immediately upon the Arab conquest. But we are still in want of sufficiently detailed studies according to place and time. When such are in hand, it will be more easily remembered that the ruin of one area need not indicate a general decay of the whole region from Nile to Oxus; not only in social and historical terms broadly, but even specifically in economic terms, a decreasing investment level in one area may be more than compensated for by an increasing investment elsewhere. The undeniable economic decline which the region as a whole suffered at some point between the eighth and the eighteenth centuries must be assessed with subtler techniques.

The Flowering of the High Caliphate, 750–813

750–775	The caliphate of the brothers of the imâm Ibrâhîm, al-Saffâḥ and al-Manṣûr
	THE GENERATION OF THE THIRD FITNAH
723–759	Ibn-al-Muqaffaʿ launches adab prose with translations from Pahlavî
765	Death of Jaʿfar al-Ṣâdiq, imâm of those Shîʿîs who held to a Fâṭimid line; from his death date their divisions
767	Death of Ibn-Isḥâq, biographer of Muḥammad
700–767	Abû-Ḥanîfah, great imâm of the Iraqi school of fiqh, refuses to serve under ʿAbbâsids
786	Death of al-Khalîl, first systematic grammarian, prosodist, and lexicographer
756–929	Spain independent under an Umayyad dynasty of amîrs (929–1031; they are styled caliphs); rivalry of various Arab tribes and of locally converted Muslims maintains turmoil there
762–763	Foundation of Baghdad, which becomes commercial and cultural capital of all Muslim territories
775–785	Caliphate of al-Mahdî; establishment, gradually, of pattern of ʿAbbâsî relation to Sunnî ʿulamâʾ—acknowledgement of their type of piety; henceforth, the former Piety-minded Opposition either come to terms with the ʿAbbâsîs, as Jamâʿî Sunnîs, or (a minority) eventually go into oppositional Shîʿî sects; persecution of Manicheans, especially as attracting courtiers
	THE GENERATION OF THE FIRST ʿABBÂSIDS
715–795	Mâlik b. Anas, imâm of the fiqh of the Ḥijâz
793	Death of Sîbawayhi, Baṣran systematizer of Arabic grammar
798	Death of Abû-Yûsuf, major successor in fiqh of Abû-Ḥanîfah, along with Muḥammad al-Shaybânî (d. 805)
801	Death of Râbiʿah al-ʿAdawiyyah, of Baṣrah, ex-slave-woman ecstatic in God's love
786–809	Caliphate of Hârûn al-Rashîd; Sâsânian court tradition brought to its height under Barmakid viziers (fall of Barmakids al-Faḍl and Jaʿfar, 803)
	THE GENERATION OF AL-RASHÎD'S TIME
813	Death of Maʿrûf al-Karkhî who brought Ṣûfism to Baghdad
816 (?)	Death of Abû-Nuwâs, dissolute representative of the 'new' Arabic poetry in contrast to the pre-Islamic and Marwânî type
767–820	Al-Shâfiʿî, at Baghdad and in Egypt, consolidates doctrine of Muḥammad's legal authority and founds, as imâm, a personal school of fiqh distinguished from those of the Iraq, the Ḥijâz, and Syria
823	Death of al-Wâqidî, pioneer historian of the early Muslims, a major inspiration of the historian al-Ṭabarî
c. 828	Death of Abû-l-ʿAtâhiyah, poet of philosophic renunciation
809–813	On death of al-Rashîd, partition of empire between his two sons; civil war; the empire is forcibly reunited when al-Maʾmûn, with Khurâsânî troop support, defeats al-Amîn at Baghdad

tones, al-Saffâḥ, which in itself implied at once nobility and bloody ruthlessness in exacting divine vengeance. The name al-Manṣûr was likewise such a surname, implying that the caliph was singled out for divine help in his victories. The Marwânî rulers to the end had been known by their simple given names; al-Manṣûr made exalted surnames customary in his line by giving one officially to the son whom he made his heir. He called him al-Mahdî, a title which the Shî'îs had used for the expected restorer of Islamic justice. In this way he may have implied that the son would make up for the bloody ways in which the father had established his power, but certainly in effect gave notice that in any case 'Abbâsî absolutism was to be the definitive outcome of the hopes and plans of the Piety-minded.

The Manichean temptation

Al-Manṣûr passed on a relatively subdued and peaceful empire to al-Mahdî (775–785). He had failed to take over only Spain, where an escaping Umayyad set up a somewhat precarious independent amîrate, and the western parts of the Maghrib, where Hishâm had not succeeded in subduing Berber rebellions. Al-Mahdî made no great attempt to recover those distant provinces. In the main he continued his father's policies but with less than the paternal parsimony.

His reign furthered the rapprochement between the court and the disappointed Piety-minded factions through both words and deeds, though in a way which contrasted sharply with that of 'Umar II. The proclamations of the Marwânids, justifying their own rule in the name of Muslim unity, had commonly breathed a positive self-confidence in the active political destinies of Islam as it stood; 'Umar II also had expressed this confidence in his work. The discourses ascribed to al-Mahdî seem to reflect, more than those even of al-Manṣûr, a new and less buoyant attitude of the Jamâ'î-Sunnî 'ulamâ': that the days of the first caliphs had been a time apart which the present could not hope to rival. And al-Mahdî made no attempt to soften a growing absolutism that seemed unavoidable.

Al-Mahdî's piety went beyond words, however. It was expressed in a rigorous communal spirit, championing the exclusive claims to truth of the true community. He did not fail to push (without great result) the raids on the frontiers against the Byzantine empire; but he waged perhaps as vigorous a campaign internally in a religious persecution of the Manicheans. These presented, in fact, an attractive alternative both to the Muslim communal spirit and to the sort of piety represented by the 'ulamâ'.

Among the subjected communities, Manicheanism (a sect of the Gnostic type founded in the third century under the first Sâsânians) had never received the protection accorded the more established religious allegiances. Throughout the Roman and Sâsânian empires it had been bitterly persecuted under both Christian and Mazdean rulers, wherever it had spread. The same attitude of execration was taken up by the Muslim 'ulamâ' as soon as they became aware of the Manicheans' existence. They refused to admit that Mânî, the founder, who had lived two centuries after Christ, was one of the true prophets; his followers, therefore, were not to be tolerated as were those of Moses, Jesus, and even Zoroaster. Though for a time Manicheanism was able to convert even kings in central Eurasia, in the end it succumbed to the unanimous enmity of the world's rulers. It is a unique example of a major 'world religion' which has left no living traces.

Manicheanism was not a people's religion; it was not enshrined in the peasant's heart. It represented a particular style of piety which long appealed to spiritual seekers, including many of an intellectual bent (one of these was Augustine). In the eighth century this sort of piety seems to have appealed strongly to a great many Muslims; the tradition which carried it was not limited to an endogamous group, as were the other non-Muslim traditions, but played an active role in the course of events. It seems to have won many secret followers at court among persons who were officially Muslims. The danger it posed was at such a level that the earliest Muslim theology seems to have been developed partly for the sake of opposing the Manicheans intellectually.

Manicheans saw the universe as being sharply divided between spirit and matter. Spirit was free, creative, beautiful, true, and in general good; matter was cold, destructive, evil, in general just the reverse of spirit. The human soul was captive in a dark material body and could escape to the true Light of Spirit only by rejecting that material body so far as in it lay, allying itself with the positive forces of Spirit as they broke through into one's life. The extremest asceticism was to be prized above all; if one could not be highly ascetic oneself, one could at least associate oneself with those who were, for in them Spirit was overcoming Matter. The Manicheans reckoned some of their number as having achieved the spiritual goal of renunciation. These were honoured and served by the rest, while ordinary individuals tried to carry out at least a minimal curbing of the flesh.

Such an orientation fostered at once gentleness and aloofness. Manicheans were known as being unwilling to kill even animals and as being ever ready with acts of charity. On the other hand, they viewed the rest of mankind as lost in ignorant darkness. They did not, indeed, push their search for moral purity to the point of rejecting all imaginative culture, as have some puritans. They had their own system of all-inclusive natural science, on which they prided themselves. Even their enemies admired their school of magnificent painting. But the sustaining base of their faith was its transcendentally ascetic mood. They rejected the world of material existence loved by the mass of people (including aristocrats), in favour of a truth into which could enter only a pure élite (an élite of the spirit, of course, where earthly distinctions did not matter).

For some time, apparently, a good many well-placed persons, intellectually inclined, found in Manicheanism a spiritual counterbalance to the polished life that emanated from the court, to the clever brilliance of the littérateurs and men of manners, the *adîbs*. Its faith was more serious than the usual courtly ideals; yet it seemed to go deeper than the legalistic system being developed by the Piety-minded 'ulamâ', with their matter-of-fact populistic spirit. The populistic tendencies of Manicheanism, with its recognition that a person of any social status could join the élite, were tempered by its strong sense of an esoteric truth not accessible to the uninitiated. Tending to exalt detachment from mundane affairs, it no doubt appealed to world-weary courtiers. But its very appeal to sophisticated Muslims earned it the hatred of the 'ulamâ'. In refusing to grant Manicheans dhimmî status along with other religious communities, they condemned them, in effect, to a mass choice between conversion and extermination; and the 'ulamâ' were yet more indignant at what may be called 'Manichean Muslims', who formally professed Islam but adopted the Manichean world view. Al-Mahdî manifested his support of Islamic purity in a practical way at the expense of this sect by killing any courtier who would not or could not free himself of its taint.

In the ninth or tenth centuries, Manicheanism lost ground in Islamdom and everywhere. The Arabic name for it, *Zandaqah*, became a word for every sort of socially abhorred heresy; anyone suspected of cloaking an esoteric faith beneath his profession of Islam was called a *Zindîq*. The original application of these terms came to be forgotten.

By the end of al-Mahdî's reign, the bulk of the 'ulamâ' seem to have been reconciled to the 'Abbâsî compromise, and the absolute monarchy had gained the minimum institutional religious support that it needed. Even most supporters of either Khârijism or Shî'ism were at least willing to acknowledge the de facto success of the 'Abbâsî régime for the time being. In the latter part of al-Mahdî's reign, the Egyptians made a bid for independence under a descendant of 'Abd-al-'Azîz, the Umayyad governor whose family had long had prime prestige in Egypt; but the hard core of his supporters turned out to be Khârijîs, and when he failed fully to accept their doctrine, the movement fell apart.[3] When upon al-Mahdî's death the 'Alid party again revolted in the Ḥijâz, it was easily suppressed.

Hârûn al-Rashîd: the caliph and his court as patrons of culture

Al-Mahdî's son Hârûn al-Rashîd (786–809), after a brief reign by al-Rashîd's brother al-Hâdî, enjoyed the position of caliph at the peak of its splendour

[3] Abû-'Umar Muḥammad al-Kindî (d. 961), who reports this movement in his *Kitâb umarâ' al-Miṣr*, ed. Rhuvon Guest (Leiden, 1912), pp. 124–30, represents the careful gathering of data—especially on a local basis (in this case, Cairo)—which is the foundation of most of our knowledge of Islamicate history. Typically, al-Kindî is not free from occasional legend, and he fails to see the wider issues which his details illuminate for us, but his painstaking listing of names and remembered acts and qualities seems reasonably objective and in any case allows for extensive correlation and verification with other sources of data. But his work would not be readily accessible to us without the painstaking modern editing of men like Guest.

and luxury. For a brief generation there was relatively unbroken peace and prosperity in the caliphal empire. The occasional rebellions and foreign wars were important only locally. Al-Rashîd was recalled fondly as the ideal great monarch in the stories of the *Thousand and One Nights*. His reign typifies, indeed, the society of classical Baghdad at its height.

Under the caliph, the government was now largely delegated to administrators, a vizier as financial chief and generally head of government, and his secretaries in their many bureaus (*dîwâns*). The caliph was not expected necessarily to take a personal role in government, but rather to be a court of ultimate appeal. An energetic caliph, or a lazy caliph in an energetic mood, might indeed make his own decisions; but commonly enough even matters of general policy were left to the vizier. When this system was fully developed, a caliph would change the line of policy not directly but by choosing a new vizier. Al-Rashîd tended to intervene chiefly in matters of his personal concern or special interest, such as charities.

It was hoped, however, that a caliph would nevertheless perform two ceremonial obligations of great weight. He should lead the Friday ṣalât worship in the capital on special occasions at least. In this connection the caliphs made a point of acting as the heirs of Muḥammad; they acquired a cloak the Prophet had allegedly worn and other personal items of Muḥammad's, in which they could deck themselves at appropriate moments. (Al-Rashîd and most who followed him usually preferred, however, to leave the actual leadership to a representative, themselves simply forming a part of the body of worshippers, though safely apart in a specially partitioned area in the mosque, the *maqṣûrah*). The caliph should also lead the armies on the great jihâd raids into Byzantine territory, even though he left actual military decisions to generals. (Al-Rashîd preferred to alternate between leading the caravan of the ḥajj to Mecca one year and the jihâd army the next.) For it was not forgotten that the caliph remained in principle the *amîr al-mu'minîn*, commander of the faithful; managing finances and even dispensing justice he might leave to others, but not the common Muslim undertakings, the public worship and the war against the Tyrant—as the Byzantine emperor was called.

This conception of the caliph's role reinforced a concept of government already common enough in agrarianate times. That the ruler should be above all the commanders in war had answered, as late as Marwânî times, to a certain individualism on the part of Arab tribesmen, jealous of their freedom. Over against the wider population of the Nile-to-Oxus region it now implied an attitude of social laissez-faire. Al-Rashîd's son, who took the duties of governing very seriously, summed up those duties under three heads: maintenance of justice in the courts, of security in streets and highways, and of defence on the frontiers. That is, the government had no concern with positive social ordering, with actively creating conditions for the good life (this was left to family tradition or to the efforts of the 'ulamâ', according to taste); it was simply to guarantee security: security against fraud, against force by in-

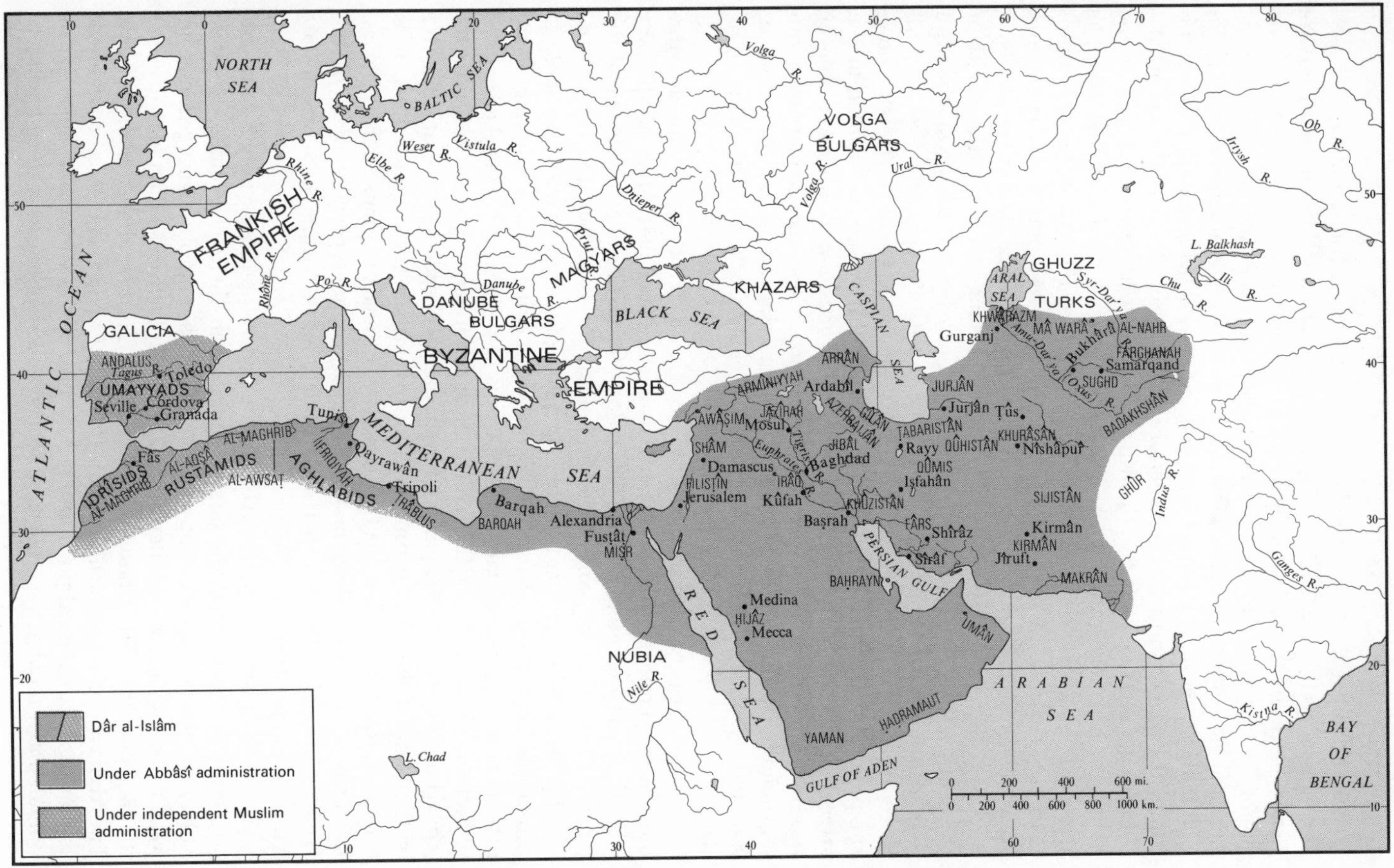

Muslim lands at the time of Harun al-Rashid, 786–809

dividuals, and against force by alien groups. If the central resources were used for digging wells or even for building cities, this was looked on as private benevolences by the caliph or the vizier; benevolences incumbent on them, no doubt, but as rich men rather than as officials. The Arab and the Islamic heritage encouraged people to conceive absolute government in its most individualistic sense, the role of common endeavour being reduced to a minimum, the role of individuals (generally, privileged individuals) maximized.

However restricted his daily political role, in the affairs of high society the caliph was actively leader of all. The caliphal family itself took first place, as in receiving, so in disbursing wealth as patrons of the arts of luxury and of learning. Ibrâhîm al-Mawṣilî (d. 804), the most celebrated musician, and Abû-Nuwâs (d. *c.* 803), the most celebrated poet of the time, both of whose lives were identified with wine and the gaiety of song, lived from the wealth of the court, as was to be expected. A cleverly turned poem could win a bag full of gold, a horse from the caliph's stables, a beautiful singing slave girl—or all three at once. On every occasion of courtly joy, largesse was scattered among the populace, rich and poor—in the form of coins tossed in abandon in the streets, of food served to all comers, or of robes of honour of luxurious silks or brocades passed out among favoured courtiers. A less spectacular but more dependable way of rewarding talent or expressing favour was to grant an individual the revenue for life from a given village, or to give him lands outright from the government's holdings.

Along with poetry and song, the courtly life was felt to be incomplete without a large component of more sober learning and even piety. Learnèd literary culture was represented in al-Kisâ'î (d. 805), for instance, who was one of the most eminent grammarians of the day and at the same time the tutor of the royal princes. Some eminent 'ulamâ', indeed, refused to be found too close to the caliphal court; but al-Rashîd—between his bouts of wine-drinking—paid attention to their exposition of the religious law. There are several anecdotes of how Abû-Yûsuf, chief qâḍî and the most prominent legist of the Iraq after Abû-Ḥanîfah, solved legal puzzles for the caliph in such a way that the letter of the Sharî'ah law was maintained; and whatever their genuineness, it is certain al-Rashîd and his court honoured the authority of pious Shar'î scholars, favouring those specialized in ḥadîth reports, and especially those of the Ḥijâz. Al-Rashîd tolerated their independent spirit within the limits of outward public propriety.

Al-Rashîd's whole clan, the 'Abbâsids in general, but especially his immediate family concentrated the largest spending in their own hands. His wife Zubaydah made herself famous for her charities, notably causing numerous wells to be dug along the pilgrim trail from the Iraq to Medina for the use of the ḥajj pilgrims. Other families close to him might be almost as munificent. The 'dynasty of viziers', the Persian Barmakid family, showered out almost as many gifts as the caliph himself. As a group, the various big spenders of Baghdad attracted artists, poets, scholars, philosophers, as well as tricksters and sheer career men from every part of the empire; whoever could please one or another great man had his fortune made—provided he could avoid a sudden disgrace and execution, such as befell the Barmakid favourite one day.

The Barmakid family had been Buddhist priests at Balkh (near the Oxus) before their conversion to Islam. Already under al-Saffâḥ and al-Manṣûr, Khâlid al-Barmakî had become a top-ranking kâtib, secretary, and trusted adviser of the caliph. Al-Mahdî had placed Khâlid's son Yaḥyà in charge of al-Rashîd's affairs when, as a youth, he was a titular provincial governor; al-Rashîd had grown up close friends with Yaḥyà's son Ja'far, whom he retained as chief courtier and companion of his leisure hours, making his brother al-Faḍl b. Yaḥyà head of affairs during most of his reign. By 803 al-Rashîd had grown jealous of the enormous power of the Barmakids, to whom suitors for favours naturally turned even more readily than to the caliph himself. One night, without notice, he had Ja'far beheaded. (The head was publicly displayed next day as usual, to prove to his partisans that he was dead and beyond help from any coup.) Ja'far's brother, al-Faḍl, and their father were imprisoned and died not long after.

Luxury was most brilliant at the capital—and probably most insecure there. But the well-to-do could lead a very comfortable life even in the provinces. Nîshâpûr, for instance, the capital city of Khurâsân (founded under the Sâsânians—though presumably some such city had been in the vicinity still earlier) was noted for its wealth and healthfulness. It was watered by streams from the hills to the northward in the wet season (winter) and there were famous garden districts around it bearing all kinds of fruits; the Nîshâpûrîs took a special interest in techniques of fruit tree breeding and cultivation. In the Arid Zone, the use of water was highly developed. Long underground water channels (*qanâṭs*), sometimes hewn through rock, carried water from mountain sources far out over plateau or desert. Such means were used at Nîshâpûr not only for irrigating gardens and fields but also to provide water for the city: every well-to-do household (and with it not only the master family but all the dependents) had its own underground water source and its cistern for the dry season. The water then ran out below to irrigate the fields. Travellers were awed by its magnificent Friday mosque (the one most heard of was built by the Ṣaffârî power subsequent to al-Rashîd's time), which both rich and poor enjoyed, and by the diversity on display in its markets as well as its manufactures.

Cities were not alike. In contrast to the healthfulness of Nîshâpûr, we hear of the filth of Gurganj in Khwârazm, in the delta of the Oxus (as contrasted to the Khurâsân plateau): travellers complained that though the city was wealthy, yet there the offal was left in the streets so that even the mosque (generally kept fairly clean by removal of shoes at the gate) was dirtied by the feet of those who entered without having worn shoes outside. Gurganj may not always have been so filthy, but it did not have the drainage system of

Nîshâpûr. However, in any wealthy home there would be many amenities: rugs and pillows to sit on, elegant book stands, carved chests and handsome jars for storage and good looks alike; low cushioned daïses and pools in courtyards, often with at least a miniature waterfall; braziers for warmth in winter and water evaporation for cooling in summer. Perhaps such luxuries as ice in summer could be obtained more readily at Baghdad than in most provincial towns, but the privileged classes of the empire lived a life comfortable and delightful; and if they were subject to the vagaries of natural calamities, disease, and occasional riot, they were relatively free of the threat of war.

Letters and learning

The point of greatest splendour in the caliphal court was its patronage of letters. These were, above all, Arabic letters: ever since the administration had been put into Arabic, the traditions of a cultivated bureaucracy were being built up in terms of that language. Formal Arabic prose received its first great impulse with the translation into elegant Muḍarî Arabic of several Pahlavî works. (Later, at least, certain forms—such as lives of saints—seem to have been based on Syriac traditions also.) Among translations from Pahlavî, most notable was a collection of tales (*Kalîlah wa-Dimnah*, anecdotes of two jackals as advisers to the lion-king) ultimately taken from the Sanskrit (allegedly in Nûshîrvân's time). The translator was Ibn-al-Muqaffa', the ex-Mazdean administrator who had urged al-Manṣûr to a more systematic absolutism. This prose was limpid, entertaining, and edifying; for some time such remained the norm of the Arabic prose honoured by the kâtib class, the courtiers and bureaucrats who supported the absolutism. They delighted in literature which was worldly-wise and informative and could add to the polish and brilliance of their sophisticated conversation—and of their official correspondence. The adab, the polite cultivation of that class, gave a large place to verbal brilliance and hence to literature.

But at least as important as prose, for the adîb and for the kâtibs generally, was poetry. But poetry is essentially untranslatable; in this sphere, though the tradition of Sâsânian administrative culture may have established the literary status of poetry, its substance at any rate came from the old-Arabian tradition, to which the kâtib class was early and enthusiastically committed. Here too, however, a certain effort at mental translation was required. For whether in its pre-Islamic Bedouin form or in the form it took when revived in the Arab garrison towns of Marwânî times, that tradition was alien not just to the family heritage of most of the Muslims of 'Abbâsî times, nor even to the daily language, which was (if Arabic at all) an eroded, 'settled' Arabic, and the old inflected Muḍarî of the Bedouin. More important, the Arabic poetic tradition was alien also to the deeply urban patterns of the bureaucracy and of the other elements in the population which now turned to honouring it. Hence among literary scholars (like al-Kisâ'î) arose a school of collectors and editors of the old poetry, dedicated as much to its philological niceties as to its aesthetic delights; while the more poetically gifted, rebelling against the limits which interpreters of the tradition had thought to lay down for it, took up the sense of Arabic rhythm and image and the straightforward spirit with which the tradition confronted them and transmuted all that into a form and a mood more appropriate to the courtier, the kâtib, and even the merchant. This process had indeed begun under the Marwânids, but was now fulfilled.

Abû-Nuwâs of Baṣrah (and of Persian stock) was personally a libertine and dedicated his verse to love and wine. He had studied philology at Kûfah and was said even (as was the custom for students of the language) to have spent some time in the desert with the Bedouin; he glorified licentiousness with an echo of such old-Arabian models as the love-prologue that initiated a Bedouin formal ode (*qaṣîdah*); but he rejected the heroic grandeur that had gone with the qaṣîdah in favour of a more intimate, even a pert and playful, relaxation. Abû-Nuwâs dedicated much of his erotic verse to the love of youths, thus setting a fashion that was later to become fixed in some Islamicate circles even if the poet had no personal homosexual interests. Abû-l-'Atâhiyah (d. 826), though of Arab stock, went even further in transforming the poetic tradition: ascetic and of a speculative turn of mind—yet a loyal Muslim of Shî'î sentiments—he dedicated his verse to a philosophic melancholy which proved more popular in the market place than at court; his lines formed a mine of soberly pious quotations for future popular writers.

Along with the cultivation of literature went a reflection on the mechanics of that literature. A major achievement of the time was the systematization of Muḍarî Arabic grammar (which subsequently became the model for grammatical analysis in other Semitic languages). Such analysis had already begun in Marwânî times. After the experience of two generations, Sîbawayhi of Baṣrah (d. 793), representing a tradition more faithful to the vagaries of actual usage than were some Kûfan grammarians, produced the standard book of grammar (afterwards called simply *The Book*)—though naturally he left many minor problems to be worked out by later generations. The task, of course, was to sort out the ways in which various particles, word orders, verbal or nominal patterns, etc., could be used without causing confusion through conflict with other usages. It was not conceived in just this functional manner, indeed; grammarians saw themselves as identifying a complete set of the natural distinctions among types of word and of sentence pattern, and then discovering, from ancient poetry, from surviving Bedouin usage, and from Qur'ân and ḥadîth, how each type had in fact been used among respectable Arabs of Muḥammad's time. But living speech within a given generation does, in fact, ordinarily present mutually consistent usages. At any rate, the result was to establish standards which effectively safeguarded essential intelligibility, however specialized the jargon became, however complex the sentence—or however alien to the old Arabic by birth was the person undertaking to compose in it. No other Islamicate language was ever so minutely examined and disciplined.

Already under al-Manṣûr, the caliphal court had come to patronize, beyond Arabic belles-lettres and the work of Sharîʻah-minded piety, learning of the most varied sorts. In contrast to Kûfah and Baṣrah, which long remained important centres of the Arabic and Sharʻî studies, Baghdad thus became a centre not only of these studies but of natural science and metaphysics. The most famous works of medicine, mathematics, and astronomy, especially, were translated: probably first from Pahlavî and Syriac but then also from Sanskrit and Greek. Whereas the Arabic and the Sharʻî studies were pursued chiefly by men born or converted to Islam, those who pursued natural science tended to retain their older religious allegiances as dhimmîs, even when doing their work into Arabic. If their work found favour at court, it was not so much as direct expression of the cultural ideals of the kâtibs but rather as having practical personal use or else as fulfilling individual speculative curiosity. Al-Rashîd's son, al-Ma'mûn, was to prove personally much interested in the science and even the philosophy of the Hellenistic tradition; by his subsidies and encouragements he gave a great fillip to the developing movement of translating from Greek and Syriac into Arabic the classic works of medicine, astronomy, mathematics, and natural philosophy generally. Al-Ma'mûn endowed (in 830) a fine research library, the Bayt al-Ḥikmah, 'House of Wisdom'. He went so far as to seek for manuscripts in Constantinople, where the Greek tradition was naturally highly cultivated. From his time on, the quality of the translations improved greatly.

But the most important centres where students could gather such learning were older cities within the empire. It was from the great medical school founded in Sâsânian times at Jundaysâbûr in Khûzistân that the Islamicate medical tradition was to get its greatest impulse. Already al-Manṣûr had brought from there to Baghdad a prominent Nestorian physician (Bakht-Îshûʻ), who founded a line of physicians in the capital. The town Ḥarrân, in the Jazîrah, had become perhaps a still more important centre. It had to some degree succeeded Alexandria and even Antioch as an active centre of learning. In Ḥarrân, even Christianity had not greatly penetrated and older Pagan cults had been perpetuated; in Islamic times the Ḥarrânîs called themselves *Ṣâbi'ans*, a term found in the Qur'ân to designate an otherwise obscure group of tolerated monotheists, and so managed to pass as possessing a legitimate form of prophetic religion; the neo-Platonic (or neo-Pythagorean) faith of their educated class, indeed, justified this. Ṣâbi'ans, Christians, and Mazdeans increasingly taught Muslim students and used the Arabic language. With the patronage of al-Ma'mûn, Baghdad soon became the greatest centre of such science and philosophy in the empire, as it had become that of Arabic belles-lettres and of Sharʻî Islam.

The war of succession to al-Rashîd

Wealth and power from the eastern Maghrib to Sind and the Oxus basin were concentrated almost uprecedentedly in the splendid families at the heart of the 'Abbâsî state in Baghdad, which Shar'î 'ulamâ', Arab tribesmen, Persian landlords, cosmopolitan merchants, and (more passively) peasants of every land were united in regarding as at once the symbol of Islamic unity and of civil order and powerful justice. The acquiescence of the Muslim idealists and the relative satisfaction of traditional Irano-Semitic political expectations seemed to assure the 'Abbâsîs a solid power. The former Iraqi centres, Kûfah and Baṣrah, where law and grammar had developed, increasingly yielded their sons and their students to the attractions of the capital, where all viewpoints mingled.

Al-Rashîd himself made a move which turned out to illustrate how unsure this caliphal state power was as compared, say, with that of the Sâsânians of yore. He decreed (and duly caused the Muslim notables to agree) that the control of the empire was to be divided on his death: the Fertile Crescent and the western provinces were to go to his son al-Amîn (with the dignity of caliph) while Khurâsân and the eastern provinces were to go to another son, al-Ma'mûn, with an army and full autonomy (and the right of subsequent succession), though al-Ma'mûn also was bound to obey al-Amîn in ultimate matters. Al-Rashîd posted his decree in the Ka'bah to give it sacred authority. There was no one social element in the state strong enough to gainsay this dismemberment of the hard-built political structure for a personal whim.

This social fact was reflected in the legal situation. There was no basis for theoretical protest by the Jamâ'î-Sunnî 'ulamâ', who did acknowledge the legality of the 'Abbâsid caliphate. In accepting the 'Abbâsid dynasty for the sake of Muslim unity, they had grudgingly accepted, for want of a more principled norm, the dynastic rule already in use among the Marwânids: designation by the predecessor, confirmed by public acceptance among the notables of the chief cities. But the 'ulamâ', refusing to recognize the absolutist state and wanting to deal even with public duties as personal responsibilities, before God, of those who happened to be charged with them, interpreted that designation and its acceptance as purely personal convenants, not as autonomous state institutions; hence the designating caliph could attach to his designation such conditions as he chose—including a subsequent succession—and once these conditions had been accepted and sworn to by the designees and the notables of the Muslim community, the only Shar'î legal principle that applied was that of fidelity to covenants. But if the 'ulamâ' had no basis for protest, neither had the kâtibs themselves, for all their direct interest in the monarchy. To supplement the Sharî'ah, there was no generally recognized dynastic or monarchic body of law, based on the nature of the office as such, to override such conditions: no rule of primogeniture, for instance, nor any definition of the rights of an office as such, which would have a prior claim on men's consciences and allow them to brand al-Rashîd's covenant as illegal even apart from Shar'î principles.

For some years after al-Rashîd's death (809—in the course of an expedition against Khârijîs in Khurâsân) the empire was in fact divided. The division did not then last, however—a civil war soon ensued. The warring lasted for over two years (811–813) and a number of factions participated, each aligned against all the others. Yet the struggle took on a very different air from the Second or the Third Fitnah wars, when diverse viewpoints, each appealing to all Muslims, brought forward their candidates for the caliphate. The main struggle was between al-Rashîd's two sons, each of whom (or his advisers) desired to be supreme in the whole empire and believed this possible—though the immediate occasion was the question whether al-Amîn could set aside al-Ma'mûn, who was to succeed him if al-Amîn died first, in favour of al-Amîn's own son. The choice was partly one of personality: al-Amîn (favoured by his well-born mother, al-Rashîd's wife Zubaydah) had the reputation of being debauched and hence manipulable by his ministers, while al-Ma'mûn (son of a Persian slave-girl who had not survived to have even such influence as slave-mothers could have) was intelligent and more likely to be independent. However, al-Amîn's incompetence and the victories of al-Ma'mûn's generals soon won some even of al-Amîn's ministers, who could have expected to control their ward, over to al-Ma'mûn. Yet Baghdad held out against al-Ma'mûn's besieging general Ṭâhir for over a year despite fire and famine and lack of support from the provinces. Al-Amîn had the support of the great families and of the populace in the capital, who evidently feared the Khurâsânî orientation of al-Ma'mûn; for al-Ma'mûn kept his headquarters at Marv in Khurâsân and had Persians as generals (such as Ṭâhir) and as ministers. Al-Rashîd already had preferred Raqqah on the Euphrates to Baghdad as his headquarters and possibly the Baghdadis feared for the status of their city, in which al-Amîn had spent the imperial revenues profusely. In any case, no Islamic principle seems to have been at stake.

Even outside Baghdad, the accompanying struggles tended to be of local scope. During al-Rashîd's reign an 'Alid rebel had held his own for a time in the sub-Caspian mountains in the Shî'î cause, and Khârijîs had led a major rising in the Jazîrah, which was put down; and Khârijîs were again active in Khurâsân during the war of succession. Shortly after al-Ma'mûn's victory, the Shî'îs of the Iraq made a potent bid for power. But during the war of succession itself, neither Shî'îs nor Khârijîs played a major role. In Syria, Damascus made a bid to regain the caliphate, but factional fighting between the Kalb and the Qays tribal blocs there ruined the chances of their candidate. In Egypt, opposing local factions took advantage of the central government's weakness to attempt each to master the other, but the theoretical supremacy of the 'Abbâsid caliphs was not questioned.

At last when Baghdad was crushed, a single ruler was recognized again throughout most of the empire of al-Manṣûr and al-Rashîd. Al-Ma'mûn was to face many rebellions, but he was the undoubted master of most of the empire most of the time. For a season the wondrous prosperity of the great monarchy was prolonged. On the basis of this prosperity, the new Islamicate culture was being created.

Economic expansion and the popularization of Islam

Islam became a mass people's religion on a wave of economic expansiveness; which, indeed, carried the whole range of cultural innovation of which Islam was a part. As the commercial activity along the interregional trade routes of the hemisphere increased, the tendency to intensive urbanization in the region from Nile to Oxus increased. Baghdad, a major trade centre even when the caliphs fled from it, became larger than had been Seleucia and Ctesiphon, its Hellenistic and Sâsânian predecessors. This urban economic expansiveness, so far as it was a product of hemisphere-wide economic activity, contributed to making possible the power of the caliphal state; but it was in turn accelerated, at least, by the absolutism itself.

As generally happens, economic expansiveness tended to be self-perpetuating. The surging urban prosperity allowed fortunes to be made by large numbers and encouraged a social mobility rapid even for the Nile-to-Oxus region. Under the broad peace established by the empire, commerce flourished freely and markets, and hence possibilities for new investment, were expanding. Merchants, buying cheap and selling dear, found it profitable to carry exotic goods long distances with less danger of interruption and consequent increase of price than in politically more troubled times; hence luxuries were available not only at Baghdad but in many other places in unusual abundance. Such trade stimulated further local production. Of the wealth so released, at least a part went to encourage still further economic activity. To supply the needs of far-flung merchant houses, a regular banking business grew up, which evidently had developed, as often in agrarianate times, out of money-changing business. Bankers accepted draughts drawn in one place on funds deposited far distant. The government naturally made use of these bankers in expediting its tax collecting and in other operations of its bureaucracy; as we have noted, without the commercial network the effective bureaucratic centralization could hardly have functioned. But conversely, without the dependability provided by the bureaucracy the commercial network would not have been able to function in such large-scale units as it often did.

Though money still often went into land, the most dependable source of income in the Agrarian Age, funds available for investment were very commonly put into trade. Transport of luxury goods was most spectacularly profitable, but less consistently so than transport of more mundane goods like grain, which was also important. Commercial arrangements always tend to be relatively flexible, but this was a time of unusual diversity and inventiveness. Almost all forms of mercantile life tended to be carried on in partnerships;

these varied almost indefinitely as to the terms of co-operation between the partners and as to the number of partners engaged in a single endeavour. Muslims and non-Muslims were sometimes partners together; this could be convenient: for instance, in a partnership between a Muslim and a Jew, the Jew would take off on the Sabbath and the Muslim on Friday. To maintain the far-flung contacts which long-distance trade required—a merchant stationed in Gujarat (in India) might have a relative travelling in Spain or be planning a commercial venture to the Oxus basin or the Volga valley—there were regular postal services, arranged by private individuals, over the most important sea and land routes; usually these were slow, but some seem to have been express services; perhaps, as in the official messenger services (*barîd*) for central government use, messengers could carry missives very rapidly by changing horses at pre-arranged servicing stations.[4] The merchants themselves travelled with their goods in ships—normally owned by private individuals, whether on seas or on rivers—or in privately managed land convoys of camel transport, the caravans.

Trade was the usual investment, but some funds were invested in hand industries. A number of new industries spread in the region under the High Caliphate: paper-making, learned from China via the Oxus basin, replaced the processing of papyrus leaves for writing material. The use of cotton came in from India. Paper and sugar mills sometimes employed large numbers of workers—as did government enterprises such as the workshops in which were made the robes of honour which the caliphs dispensed. Nevertheless, the ideal of craftsmen was to work as independent masters at their trade, perhaps hiring one or two other workers as assistants; or to work in apprenticeship, if they could not afford to set up shop on their own. Both merchants and craftsmen found ways of associating to protect their common interests against outside competition; among dhimmîs, this could be done through the community organization of the local dhimmî group itself. But at least in some places—like Cairo—individuals tended very often to be almost on their own. For instance, though commonly tradesmen of the same calling were located in a common market area, sometimes individuals took space elsewhere; and though

[4] Cf. S. D. Goitein, 'The Commercial Mail Service in Medieval Islam', *Journal American Oriental Society*, 84 (1964), 118–23, which reports on those mail services that led to Cairo. The Arabic word *barîd* meant 'official messenger service'. For 'postal service', maintained privately for private use, there were quite different terms (e.g., *fayj*). Unfortunately, a mistranslation has occurred which has occasioned a fair amount of wasted ink. The French term 'courrier' has been quite legitimately used for the word *barîd*, in one of the several meanings of 'courrier'. But since 'courrier' can also mean 'postal service' as well as 'official messenger', readers have tended to be misled and have had to be warned that the barîd did not carry private letters. In English the confusion is quite inexcusable; the use of 'post' for 'courier' is quite archaic. But unfortunately early scholars wrote as if translating not the Arabic *barîd* but the French 'courrier', and mistranslated it; so that the barîd is commonly miscalled 'postal service', with which it had little in common; then every time the reader must be warned at length that it was not, in fact, a postal service. The French confusion has entered the modern Arabic, in which *barîd* does in fact, mean 'postal service'.

the tradesmen of a given trade were often referred to collectively on a family basis, individuals could frequently take up a new trade which their families had not pursued. The principle of free contract ruled in a wide range of city life, allowing for much fluidity such as an expanding economy required.[5]

In this expanding prosperity and its concomitant social mobility, Islam and the Muslims' institutions played a key role. To a degree, the monarchical discipline and broad extent of the caliphal state—under strong caliphs, at least—had its effect in assuring tranquillity and a favourable atmosphere for trade. With order came prosperity. To a degree, of course, it was just the prosperity which made possible the strong rulers. But once the monarchy arose, it had a further autonomous effect. In particular, the extensive power of the monarchy had its own direct influence in producing a ferment in high culture. Even after the caliphal monarchy had been destroyed, the new questions raised and the new traditions launched bore fruit in a vigorous continued cultural dialogue.

The court was the focal point of the prosperity of the times, and the example and influence of the court spread throughout the empire because of the attractive power of wealth. Whatever of the revenue—that is, of the taxes—could be gotten away from the provinces came to Baghdad, there to be redistributed through the channels of a fashionable life of luxury; thither came likewise, accordingly, the most ambitious young men from everywhere. From the capital poured back into the provinces not only governors, but merchants, landowners endowed from the caliphal bounty, and all sorts of men who had occasion to taste temporarily of the splendour of Baghdad. The fashions set at the court in administration, in social life, and in literary and artistic taste were thereupon spread to all the provincial centres, while the court itself was a melting pot in which all cultural traditions confronted each other.

A key trait of the new common culture so formed, one which helped in turn to make that culture possible, was a high degree of social mobility: not merely the social mobility in economic life presupposed by economic expansion, but a specifically cultural openness—based on the possibility that a man of spirit or of special gifts could rise in the social scale without the advantages of family or of communal connections, or could move among circles formed by other communities despite the advantages which local ties gave him in his own. The Muslims were aware of the vitality which could come from 'new men'. We read of a debate between two scholars, one of whom came from

[5] The articles of Professor Goitein about the manuscripts in the Cairo Geniza, in his *Studies in Islamic History and Institutions* (Leiden, 1966), have thrown much light on conditions of trade, especially among a minority group in Cairo. His work also includes a good bibliography on Islamicate commerce generally. We cannot be sure that equal liberty of trade prevailed in smaller towns, but it is clear that even there no hard and fast guild structure inhibited initiative; cf. Ira Lapidus, *Muslim Cities in the Later Middle Ages* (Harvard University Press, 1967), on Syrian towns in the (later) Mamlûk period.

Kûfah and despised the other for coming from a little-known small town; said the other, You degrade your city, while I bring lustre to mine. A man's illustrious genealogy should begin with himself rather than end with himself. Men of arts and letters were constantly on the move, rarely residing in the town of their birth, and usually able to report visits to many widely distant cities.

The caliphal court itself soon took the lead in encouraging social mobility. The courtiers clung to some elements of hereditary position, which had been very important in Sâsânian times. Sometimes they wrote as if this were essential to adab, to polite cultivation. The landed gentry continued to look to noble descent—especially from royal heroes of ancient Iranian times—as the criterion of social eminence. The descendants of the old Arabian tribes still prided themselves on the purity of their line; and particularly the 'Alids were generally looked up to, and the 'Abbâsids themselves. (There were special governmental bureaus to register the generations of these families, so that genuine descent could be guaranteed, and to regulate the considerable properties and privileges accruing to the two families as such.) But such aristocratic tendencies were at a disadvantage. Already in the time of Nûshîrvân, the Sâsânian nobility had lost some of its power. The Piety-minded among the Muslims had further helped to lower the pride both of the Arab tribesmen, with their pagan ancestors, and of the formerly infidel gentry. The 'Abbâsî programme was largely based on the principle of equality among the Muslim faithful, even apart from the other sort of equality that prevailed among subjects of an absolute king. At Baghdad under the 'Abbâsî absolutism a man of talent could make a fortune or reach the highest positions with little regard for his birth. What mattered even at court was his personal adab, especially his literary cultivation.

But it was not merely the economic and political role of the Muslim court that made for a new common regional pattern of culture. Other social pressures favoured by economic expansiveness expressed themselves directly through Islamic religion. Its spread altered the social relations holding among the several traditions of high culture from what had obtained in Marwânî times. By now Muslims no longer formed merely a small ruling class, but were becoming a substantial part of the population at large, in some places a majority. Consequently, there were no longer simply many religious communities divided from each other in geography, in language, and in lettered traditions—a situation which even the Mazdeans, linked to a specifically Iranian ethnic sense, had not transcended. There was now available a community which fit into and even fulfilled many of the expectations of the Irano-Semitic tradition, but which also combined a neutral appeal, not linked to any of the major agrarian ethnic groups of the region, with political power which united all the lands of Iranian and Semitic heritage on a territorial scale which the Sâsânians had never matched. Even those who did not adopt the religion tended to use the language of the new community; but the community won its position above all through the large number who entered into its religious tradition.

Since the time of 'Umar II, conversion to Islam had been officially fostered. Under Hishâm, for instance, an application of 'Umar II's principles in Khurâsân and the Oxus basin had encouraged widespread conversion, undermining the position of the old-line local rulers and contributing to the political ferment which led to the 'Abbâsî triumph. With the advent of 'Abbâsî rule, conversion seems to have become very general. After several generations, the majority of the town populations and even many peasants in the greater part of the empire seem to have become Muslims.

To be Muslim carried with it great prestige and no doubt merchants found it a special advantage. Certain trades seem to have become largely Muslim, while others remained largely Christian or Jewish. Above all, immigration of country population into the growing towns (whereby the town populations, never self-reproducing, were recruited) was probably often accompanied by conversion to the dominant religious tradition there; the peasant who must learn a new, urban, way of life anyway may as well learn a new religious pattern too. Once the number of Muslims became considerable, the mosque became the most lively, and certainly the most cosmopolitan, centre of all activities. Popular story-tellers (*quṣṣâṣ*) held forth there upon the wonders of the prophets and other Biblical and Talmudic tales, all conceived within an Islamic framework. A popular Islam thus arose, complete with its own history, ethics, and eschatology, drawing on the most striking notions found in all the earlier religious traditions. When the towns had thus become primarily Muslim, their innumerable links with the dependent village populations assured the gradual conversion of the villages also.

Under the 'Abbâsîs, the new converts no longer had to be identified with any Arab tribe, for such tribes themselves gradually were losing their privileges. Islam became a badge, not of a ruling class, but of a cosmopolitan, urban-oriented mass; it became a symbol of the newly intensified social mobility. Of course, it was not only within Islam that social mobility showed its effects. With accentuated urbanization came accentuated social mobility generally. Many Jews who had been agriculturists in the Iraq turned to commerce and became great merchants. But it was especially as Muslims that persons took up more profitable careers or moved from one area to another.

The piety of the dhimmî peoples

As the more active population, urban and urban-oriented, turned to Islam, the social and cultural role of the older traditions shifted. Their people were becoming minorities in the empire as a whole. But for a long time the rites and folkways of these minorities—which locally might still be majorities—played a part in the life of the whole community which was not necessarily creative but which maintained a continuity with the soil and with the past on the level of daily and seasonal life patterns, which Muslims as such, with their urban orientation, tended to lack.

At the time of the Arab conquest, the several religious groups which were to form protected, dhimmî, communities gained equality of status among themselves and protection against each other's interference; for instance, against proselytism from one dhimmî community to another, which the Muslims discouraged. Jews found a much more favourable position than they had had under the Byzantines, at least; it was not only economic but political openness which permitted an increase in their commercial activity. Even the position of the relatively favoured Nestorian Christians temporarily improved over against the Zoroastrian aristocracy, at least until the aristocrats turned Muslim. The Monophysite Christian establishments of Egypt, Syria, and Armenia profited immediately and immensely from the withdrawal of the privileged Greeks. Quite apart from a general championing of piety as understood in the Abrahamic tradition, the Muslims seem to have favoured the viewpoint of the Monophysites on particular issues—notably the relative repugnance to be found among Monophysites to religious statues and to figural art, which perhaps sprang partly from their more general hostility to the richer churches which could better afford such attractions. Already in Marwânî times, the Muslims began to frown on figural art in any religious connection, to the delight of some Christians.

But by 'Abbâsî times, the dhimmî communities were becoming isolated, as communities, and as distinctive spiritual traditions, from the spiritual life of the majority, at least on the level of high culture. They were becoming identified with individual ethnic groups. When we speak of ethnic groups, we mean not nationalities as such, of course, but any groups with a common cultural affiliation into which individuals are born, and in particular those smaller, more cohesive groups that have a common language or dialect and a sense of common loyalty as against outsiders, though they may not be living in a single homogeneous area. Religious communities between Nile and Oxus had long tended to be identified with such ethnic groups, and now the identification became more rigorous. Almost every ethnic group that did not adopt Islam came to be identified by its own special religious allegiance even more than by its language. Thus Armenians, though they possessed a distinctive language, were more certainly identified by their own church, which remained independent not only in the Armenian mountains, where Armenians were most numerous, but in Syria or Egypt (despite the similarity of the Armenian theology to the Monophysite theology received there) or in the Iraq or Iran. An Armenian who spoke Arabic was still an Armenian if he held to the church; while an Armenian who abandoned the church (normally for Islam) soon found himself a member of a completely different community. (Within Islam, of course, old ethnic lines persisted on the basis of language or dialect, or of locality or economic function, and new ones eventually arose, often associated with new Islamic sects; though generally such ethnic groups were not quite so rigidly defined as were the dhimmî groups.)

The piety of each of the dhimmî religious bodies naturally retained its distinctive character. Christians looked to the Redeemer who had suffered in his love of human beings and had triumphed over death. Jews maintained the sacred covenant, looking to the ultimate restoration of God's faithful people and the purification of the world. Mazdeans strove to serve the triumph of Light and Truth in a world where darkness seemed very strong. Such continued development in the forms of piety as took place in the several groups was limited, however, to the internal life of a given group. It seems to have had little effect on the relation of the various groups to Islam or to each other.

On the contrary, the piety developed in Islam may have had a noticeable effect on that of some of the dhimmî bodies. There is some evidence that the leaders of the Mazdeans, in the eighth and ninth centuries, were partly reformulating some expressions of their tradition in response to the Muslim impact. At any rate, the court Mazdeism of the Sâsânians, which had allowed a great deal of leeway in worshipping godlings alongside the Good god Ahura Mazdâh, seems to have quite disappeared. The priests now saw to it that Ahura Mazdâh became the centre of all devotion and a proper analogue to the Allâh of the Muslims. They bolstered this approach, of course, with theological metaphysics and possibly even with reinterpretations of scripture. Whatever reformulation took place, however, seems not to have hindered the rapid numerical decline of Mazdeans relative to Muslims.

The older religious traditions made their contribution to the spirituality which now took form within Islam, individual by individual and village by village rather than as established communities. But throughout the High Caliphal Period, this contribution was very important. We have noted that in law and ethics and popular lore, which concerned everyone, both the 'ulamâ' and the story-tellers of the mosque drew on the dhimmî background for their spirit and often for their materials; the like happened in more special cases, also: in the techniques of the ascetic and the mystical life, which only a few concerned themselves with, and in the invention or perpetuation of local cults. Indeed, as long as the dhimmîs remained sufficiently numerous, they remained the custodians of whatever rites were publicly acknowledged, in the folk traditions of every day, for relating human beings to the round of the seasons and to the local landscape. This happened all the more readily because the Islamic lunar calendar—designed by soldiers and travelling merchants—disregarded the solar seasons altogether; so that religious festivals on the calendar appeared in every natural season in the course of thirty-three years, and all festivals associated with nature had to be held by non-Islamic calendars, inevitably associated with the older cults. Its cultic calendar branded Islam as radically urban, detached from any given locality with its local rounds of climate; the whole cycle of nature was abandoned to the older traditions.

Even in the cities, a great many persons were not Muslims; but the great non-Muslim strength was among the peasants. Except among the Arabian (and Berber) tribes, to a large degree the people of the countryside at first retained allegiance to their old traditions; and these country people were of course far more numerous than the city people. Of the chief non-Muslim protected communities—the Christian, Jewish, and Mazdean—Christianity and Mazdeism rapidly lost their position of social leadership as the landlords and merchants turned to the ruling community. These two traditions particularly became typical of the backward masses, especially but not exclusively of the peasants, who were socially passive except in the case of the popular revolts.

From the Muslim point of view, at least, the most prominent feature of their piety was its peasant emphasis on sacred shrines and on seasonal holy days and festivals. In Syria and Egypt the whole population, Muslim and Christian alike, celebrated the return of spring with the Easter holiday, when the Christians had their processions while the Muslims looked on. In the same way other saints' days marked the whole round of the agricultural year. At the shrines dedicated to Christian saints, the peasants' hopes and fears expressed themselves in ways often directly traceable back to local pagan shrines that had served the agriculturists of generations before. Eventually, many of these shrines, and even the seasonal festivals occasionally, were to find a place within Islam. For the time being they remained Christian; the Muslims had to content themselves with a more or less vicarious participation in the age-old piety of the peasant, with its superstitions on the one hand and its grand drama of the returning year on the other.

In the Iranian plateau it was the old Iranian seasonal festivals, hallowed by Mazdeism, that correspondingly persisted. They were celebrated on the Sâsânian solar calendar and, while they gradually lost their association with the older religion, they could never be strictly Islamized.

West Mediterranean Islamdom

Already in High 'Abbâsî times, the areas remoter from the centre of the caliphal government were evolving a distinct historical pattern—extending even to local relations between Muslims and dhimmîs. This was especially true in the largest distant region—the Muslim lands of the western Mediterranean basin.

Most Muslim provinces of the west Mediterranean had never been subjected to 'Abbâsî rule at all. There the Berber population, converted en masse as tribes and assimilated juridically to the Arabs from the start, had played the part that Arabs had played elsewhere in Islamdom; but with acceptance of Arab cultural leadership. The Maghrib, islanded between Mediterranean and Sahara, was to the Berbers what Arabia, of a like extent (though mostly less well-watered), was to the Arabs; but among the Berbers in their mountains, pastoralism was more closely joined with agriculture. The Romans had played a larger part in the cities of its northern coast than had the Sâsânians in eastern and southern Arabia. Yet these cities, at least once the power of the Roman empire was withdrawn, had little power over a hinterland which had not been reduced, for the most part, to peasant status except in the immediate vicinity of the cities; there was no network of secondary market towns in the Maghrib to form a base for extensive citied agrarian domination. Within the Maghrib, Islam seems to have become largely a matter of slogans under which relations with outsiders could be regularized. The Berbers had crossed into Spain in much the same spirit as that in which the Arabs had come into the Fertile Crescent.

In Spain the Berbers who had come over were an unruly governing class alongside a still more limited number of Arab families. Their feuding had been held under a minimum of control by the caliphal governors. When the Syrian caliphate foundered, a young member of the ruling Umayyad family, ʻAbd-al-Raḥmân, escaped the massacre of his cousins and after numerous adventures arrived in Spain, where he was able to persuade the diverse groups among the ruling Muslims to accept him as arbiter under the title of *amîr*, commander, instead of a governor sent by the upstart ʻAbbâsid. He and his successors managed to maintain a precarious supremacy for over a century and a half, supported sometimes by a new bloc of Arab families from Syria who set themselves off both from the Berbers and from earlier Arabs who had come via the Egyptian Maghribî advances. (In the tenth century one of ʻAbd-al-Raḥmân's scions transformed this Umayyad amîrate into an absolute rule as a caliphate modelled on that of the ʻAbbâsîs.)

Spain's Latinized population, remote from the main centres of civilization, had been ruled before the conquest by an aloof Germanic aristocracy and a rigid church hierarchy which combined to repress any intellectual or civic stirrings. Most of the cities were readily at the disposal of the new, more liberal, rulers, who had allowed the desperately persecuted Jews their freedom and left the Christian population to their local Roman institutions. But neither Berbers nor Arabs were then able to offer stable political or cultural principles. Renewed prosperity and Muslim prestige rested largely on contacts with the expansive economy further east; it was from the ʻAbbâsî domains that cultural fashions were set in Spain.

But these cultural fashions were so much more attractive than what the Spaniards had been used to, that they were readily adopted by all the population. The leading Christian elements in the Muslim-ruled area tended to share Islamicate culture, learning Arabic more than Latin. But they did not lose the consciousness of belonging to a wider Christendom. Their church continued its ties to Rome.

While in the dominions of the caliphs the area under Muslim rule was slowly being enlarged, in the amîrate the area brought under Muslim control by the first conquests, which had included almost all Spain and much of southern Gaul, was steadily eroded away. The Frankish dynasty of northern Gaul, and most notably Charlemagne, easily drove the Muslims out of Gaul and made contact with the remaining pockets of unconquered Spaniards along the mountainous northern border of the peninsula, an area rather answering to lands south of the Caspian which the caliphal state was then incorporating. These Christians in turn, under petty kings in several little states, soon advanced at the expense of the Muslim power, whose main centres were in the more fertile and populous south. Before long, Spain was divided between a prosperous Muslim-ruled south (centred on Córdova and the Guadelquivir basin) in regular contact with the east Mediterranean Muslims, and a smaller zone of Christian-ruled kingdoms in the north. Between the two zones were the Muslim marches, northward from Saragossa in the northeast, from Toledo in the centre, and from Mérida in the west, normally (but often insecurely) under Muslim control but organized on a war footing; and between the Muslims and the Christian states war was normal.

In the Maghrib itself, the Berbers were left to themselves with very little Arab immigration to provide alternative leadership to that of the dominant tribal groupings. But Islam had yet posed a new basis for the recurrent tribal combinations. Other religious allegiances, except the Jewish, soon disappeared. (Or the practices associated with them were overlain and reduced to subordinate elements in the religious life.) In the far west of the Maghrib (Morocco), another refugee from the ʿAbbâsids, Idrîs b. ʿAbd-Allâh, an ʿAlid who had taken part in a Shîʿî rising (786) at Mecca after al-Mahdî's death, persuaded a number of tribes to accept his lead as a descendant of Muḥammad. He himself lived only long enough to provide a tomb which became a shrine for all the area (Mawlâ'î Idrîs), but his son, Idrîs II, established a dynasty which retained, from its urban centres, and in several rival branches, the allegiance of a diminishing area through the High Caliphal Period. Idrîs II (in 808) founded (or refounded) the inland city of Fâs (Fez), which became a centre of international commerce and culture. More important than any political role, the Idrîsid presence became the starting point for extensive missionary work among the population, especially by immigrant ʿAlids and their progeny, who could count on the tribesmen's respect on account of their descent. So, the Berbers learned to identify themselves with traditions stemming from a wider world.

In the more central and eastern Maghrib, where fertile land did not extend so far inland from the sea, the pressure of the caliphal power and of Arab settlers had been stronger and Berber resistance from the time of Hishâm accepted the leadership of Khârijî theorists, some of whom had come from the Iraq or Arabia. An ʿAbbâsî governor was able to establish himself at Qayrawân (Kairouan), dominating the eastern Maghrib (by 761), but under ʿAbd-al-Raḥmân Ibn-Rustam (by 778) Ibâḍî Khârijî leadership was able to establish a state in the central Maghrib (now Algeria) centred at Tâhart (Tiaret). This state flourished under a series of imâms, successors to, but not necessarily descendants of, Ibn-Rustam, who were held more or less respon-

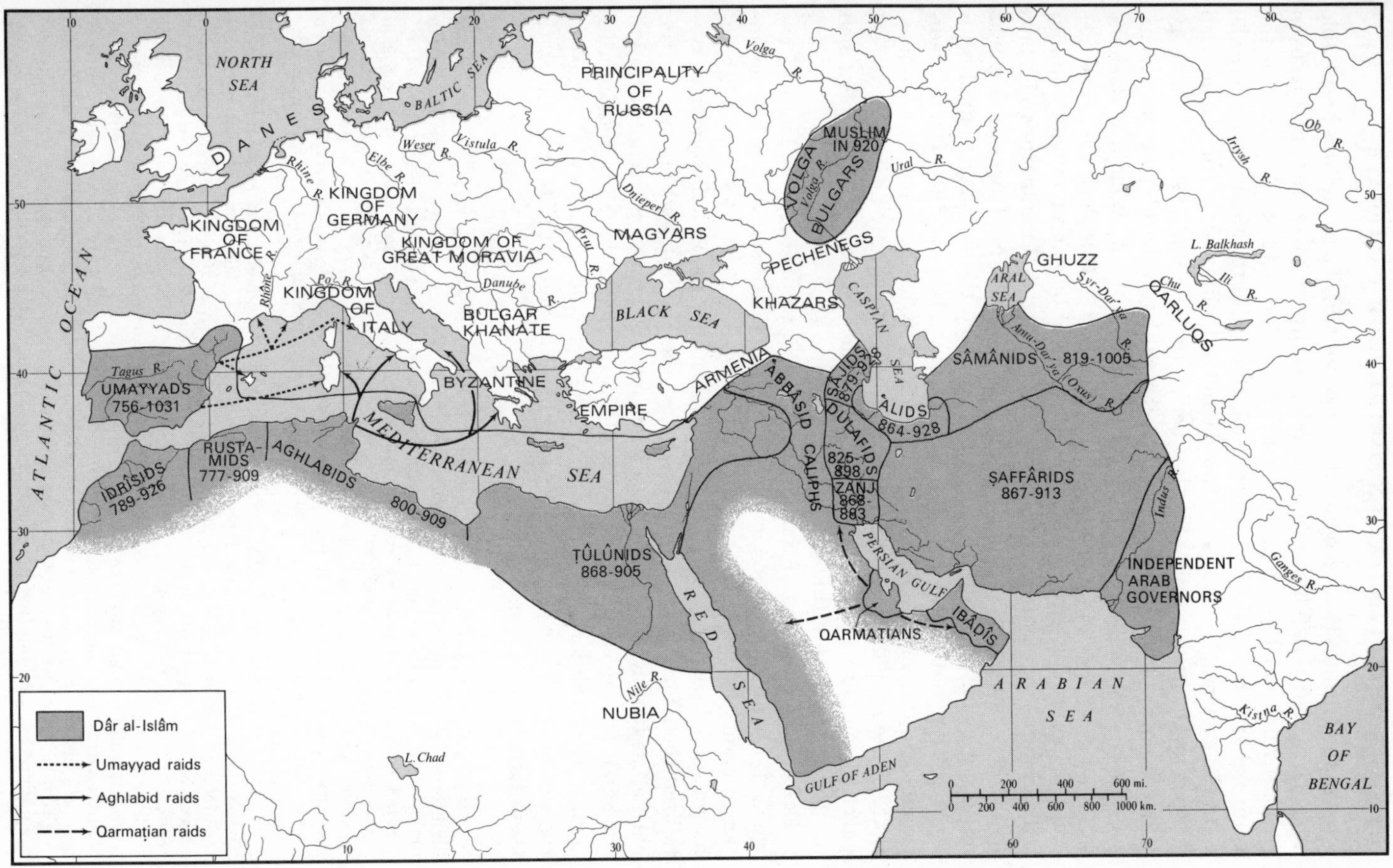

Muslim lands, ninth and tenth centuries

sible to the Muslims that recognized their command. This state was hospitable to Khârijî and non-Khârijî Muslim refugees from elsewhere, notably from ʿAbbâsî rule, and proved prosperous; its merchants took advantage of the trans-Saharan trade which was increasing along with the Mediterranean trade.

In the eastern Maghrib (now Tunisia and Tripolitania), there was no need to open up the area to contact with wider currents; from the time of Carthage it had been a commercial centre. Here, it was the ʿAbbâsid governors themselves who became independent, in the line of Ibrâhîm b. Aghlab, al-Rashîd's governor who had put down the Khârijîs there (800). Al-Rashîd had exempted the province from control by the central bureaurcracy and required only a lump-sum payment from its revenue; under al-Maʾmûn, the Aghlabids made their own policies with little reference to the caliph. It was probably as much a growing commercial prosperity, in which the shipping from Muslim lands predominated and gave Muslims an advantage, as the by now traditional expectations of Arabs and Berbers for new lands to loot and conquer, that led the Aghlabids during the ninth century to occupy Sicily and several parts of southern Italy taking over from the Byzantines; Sicily remained mostly under Muslim rule for about two centuries.

Despite the close ties of the eastern Maghrib to the east, the lands of the whole Berber-associated region, both the Maghrib itself and Spain, maintained close contact among themselves. Ultimately, they developed in common a special pattern of Islamicate life. When the ʿulamâʾ subsequently crystallized their Sharʿî law into rival schools, the Maghrib and Spain were the chief areas that accepted Mâlikî law when most of Islamdom accepted Ḥanafî or Shâfiʿî. They even developed a special form of the Arabic alphabet, differing slightly from the form used elsewhere. The dynasties that grew strongest in the west Mediterranean were likely to extend throughout that area, and with them fashions of art and education.[6]

[6] Writers concerned only with European history often set off Islam in the western Mediterranean countries, as 'Western Islam', from Islam in the eastern Mediterranean and beyond, which they lump together as 'Eastern Islam'. In terms of European history, where the Latin-German West is set off from the Greek-Slavic East, this twofold division makes some sense. As applied to Islamicate history, to call everything east of Tunisia 'eastern' is absurd. Even Mecca is west of centre. The usage may derive a specious warrant from the fact that the modern *Arabs* can usefully be divided in this way into western and eastern. But in Islamic history as a whole, such a division has yielded only a number of confusions.

It is true that Spanish and Maghribî Islamicate culture had a history of its own, distinct from that in the central lands from Nile to Oxus. This warrants some special terminology. But it does not, except when one is explicitly writing from a Maghribî viewpoint, justify lumping all the rest into a single complementary category, 'eastern'. The lands to the north, to the south, and to the east of the central area also had their distinct traditions. One can—at some risk—distinguish, i.a., between far western Islamdom and *central* Islamdom. But to make a twofold division in which everything except the west Mediterranean lands appears as 'eastern' is to reinforce the Europocentric illusion that Spanish, Sicilian, and Maghribî Islamdom formed something like half the whole. It has helped falsify, for instance, the history of Islamicate science and philosophy by facilitating the notion that these shifted from 'east' to 'west' and then died out with Spanish Islam;

Alternatives to the caliphate

In the main body of Islamdom, most lands remained longer in close association with the caliphal state. Even here, however, there were movements that sought to dispense with the central absolutism; but it was only locally—where they were most remote from the Fertile Crescent and Iran—that they had any great success.

Under the early 'Abbâsî régime, as under most agrarian régimes, there were revolts from time to time by peasants who resisted providing the raw material for all the splendour of the cities. The possibility of such revolts did set a certain limit to what the city classes could hope to squeeze from the peasants. But the revolts played no major role in the life of the time. Occasionally, likewise, factional struggles—for instance, warfare in Syria which took the form of the old fighting between Qays and Qaḥṭân Arabs—led to local resistance against the central power. From time to time Khârijî bands still gave trouble and desperate 'Alids appealed to the loyalty of the Shî'ah against a dynasty that was betraying Islamic idealism. Eventually the Khârijîs and Shî'îs were able to build permanent footholds in several parts of Arabia and of the Maghrib. But none of these quarrels proved a major threat to the absolutism, within the region from Nile to Oxus, before the end of the ninth century.

The most serious rebellions there were a series of efforts by Iranians, more or less Islamized or frankly Mazdean, to shake off at least locally the Arab dominance. The earliest of these, already in the time of al-Manṣûr, seems to have set the keynote for a number of less active movements, by setting out to avenge Abû-Muslim, the chief general of the 'Abbâsî revolution in Khurâsân, making him posthumously a defender of the Iranian tradition against Arabism. For a time most of Khurâsân fell into the hands of al-Muqanna', the 'veiled prophet', an associate of Abû-Muslim, finally obliterated in 780. Some of these movements seem to have combined elements of Shî'î millennialism with sectarian forms of Mazdeism.[7]

It was under the 'Abbâsids that the last independent princes of the lands south of the Caspian were finally reduced; but many of them continued to wield their hereditary powers under Muslim control. It was in those lands that

---

a notion itself resulting from the habit of lending significance to Islamicate thought only to the degree that it was translated into Western languages, in which process Spain (and Sicily) naturally were prominent. A more banal example: the *Encyclopaedia of Islam* article on armies has a primary section referring chiefly to the central areas (called the 'Muslim east'), and noting exceptions for the 'Muslim west' (Maghrib and Spain), but not for the south or the north, where conditions were just as divergent; nor, of course, for the truly eastern lands. Then there is a long special section on the 'west', but none on north, south, or east. This is one of the many cases where Muslim history has been dealt with from a purely European viewpoint—as a parameter, if not a function, of Occidental history. In general, the categories 'West and East', like 'Orient' or 'Asia', are relevant at best only to European history and must be avoided in other fields.

[7] G. H. Sadighi, *Mouvements religieux iraniens* (Paris, 1938), gives a not altogether balanced but yet very useful survey of these movements.

the old Sâsânian tradition was kept most vividly alive. The last and most nearly successful of the Iranian movements, however, was that of Bâbak, who established his independence in Azerbaijan early in al-Ma'mûn's reign. It seems that Bâbak inherited the following of those who claimed the spirit of Abû-Muslim, and based his movement on special religious teachings, probably chiliastic, with both Mazdean and Shî'î Muslim elements. But he gained the support of some from the respectable landed classes. He had allies in the sub-Caspian provinces, won some support from the Byzantines, who treated his state as an independent power, and held out for two decades (to 837). For centuries after, there were small groups in the Iranian countryside who traced their chiliastic hopes to Bâbak.

In Arabia, as in the more distant Maghrib, the caliphal absolutism was avoided locally while the prosperity it stood for helped maintain relatively sophisticated social conditions. But any independence there was achieved on a far more limited scale. At Nazwâ in the 'Umân, in the later eighth century the Ibâḍî (or moderate) Khârijîs made themselves independent, maintaining ties with Tâhart. Only in the later ninth century was a Zaydi (or moderate) Shî'î state at Ṣa'dah in the Yemen able to establish itself—at about the same time as a more transitory small Zaydî state arose in the sub-Caspian mountains. Like the lands of the Maghrib on the routes to the Sudan and western Europe, the more fertile of the lands of Arabia seem to have flourished largely through the trade routes which linked the caliphal lands with the coastlands of the Southern Seas.

By the time of al-Rashîd's son al-Ma'mûn, in the early ninth century, the most active parts of the population of most of the caliphal state were becoming Muslim, and the caliphate had been reaffirmed as an absolute monarchy answering to the expectations of the mass of its population. No alternative had proved viable within the primary region of caliphal power, the historic lands from Nile to Oxus. Correspondingly, the culture of that region was coming to be carried on in Arabic, and all the major dialogues of the high culture of the following centuries were well launched in their new Arabic forms: the courtly tradition, centred on a literary adab and on Hellenistic learning, and the Shar'î tradition of the Piety-minded 'ulamâ' among the bourgeois. It was within the Islamic tradition, likewise, that the more active forms of religious concern and personal piety were developing. The social concern and factional disputes of the Piety-minded were yielding to a broad range of religious activity answering to the broader spectrum of the population that were now Muslims.

III

The Shar'î Islamic Vision, c. 750–945

The first task of the Piety-minded after the 'Abbâsî triumph—still more than before it, when they still had some political hopes—was to elaborate a Sharî'ah religious law that would be admitted as binding on all Muslims. Many of the 'ulamâ' were judges under the 'Abbâsids, like Abû-Yûsuf. Most theorists, perhaps, were not. But at this period they did their work with the practical problems of actual government in mind. Their thought set off from the situation as they knew it from Marwânî and early 'Abbâsî times and they did not lose sight of the masses, their disciples. At the same time, much of the impelling emotional force was provided by their need to bring their whole lives into ever tighter accord with the divine will as found in Qur'ân and ḥadîth.

The Islamic aspirations: universalistic, populistic spirituality

In all the confessional religious traditions there was a tendency to wish to reform all social patterns in accordance with demands set up by religion, without adulteration from earlier, secular ideals. In China, to take one extreme, any such wishes developing in the more markedly confessional traditions failed almost totally. The occasional triumphs of Buddhist or Taoist religionists against Confucian philosophy, in the centuries just before Muḥammad, did not prevent the Confucian élite from regaining a dominating position in Chinese social life—though not without introducing into Confucianism itself a cosmic orientation coloured by the confessional religious outlooks. In Europe, on the contrary, the Christians did succeed in eliminating the social power of the Platonist and Stoic philosophers, though their triumph was not completely unchallenged till the sixth century, shortly before Muḥammad's time.

But even in Europe, the Christian triumph was limited. The same Justinian who closed the Platonist Academy of Athens promulgated the greatest of Roman law codes. This has perpetuated throughout Christian Europe the legal thought of the great Pagan lawyers of Greco-Roman antiquity in substantially its original form despite its Christianized tone. And, though the Academy was closed, Plato's works as well as the whole dramatic, epic, and historical corpus of Pagan Greece (or Rome) continued to inform the higher education of Greeks and of Christian Europeans generally. The head of the state was the old Roman *imperator*, unmistakable even when converted to a new faith.

In the Sâsânian lands, on the contrary, Christian bishops built their own codes for their flocks, codes which can be called Christian; but even here the challenging standard of the Sermon on the Mount relegated to more or less stopgap status all replacements of the Jewish law that were less exacting than the Sermon itself. Even in the lands from Nile to Oxus, the monks represented the true conscience of the Christian world, protesting against a life conformed to a semi-Pagan society; though they might accept the existing conditions for Christians generally, for themselves they wished to build quite new and specifically religious institutions. In monastic communities, the laws of daily life, social order, and (to cite the Benedictine example) even labour were alike created afresh. The godly life was their explicit purpose. But they formed a minority community apart, dependent on the ungodly society of the world. The Christian spirit did not favour building all society on a monastic model.

Among the Jews and the Mazdeans, on the contrary, there was an explicit effort to build a code of personal and social life which should spring in every detail from the received principles of religion. All adherents should equally be subject to the all-embracing religious requirements, while being married and carrying on the ordinary work of the world. The Piety-minded Muslim attitude to the demands of religion upon life turned out, when fully formed, to resemble the corresponding attitudes among the Jews and Mazdeans more than it did anything among Christians. But it differed from each of these in significant ways.

The Mazdeans developed a detailed code of personal and social behaviour based on concepts of ritual purity and impurity and on a sanctified social stratification, in which the priests of Ahura Mazdâh reserved to themselves a prominent position. The role of the king under the blessing of Ahura Mazdâh was to maintain the divinely ordained social order, on the basis of an elect aristocracy in an imperial nation. The Sâsânian empire thus represented a serious attempt to order all society in terms of religious insight. It rejected the pattern of Buddhism and Christianity, of restricting such a total religious demand to monastic communities.

Rabbinical Judaism, as it is reflected in the Talmudic writings of the Iraq and Palestine, likewise created for its elect people a general code of personal and social life on the basis of explicit religious legislation, and likewise rejected the monastic alternative. But unlike Mazdeism, after the fall of Jerusalem it no longer effectively had any real priesthood, but in its place had a class of learned men, rabbis. The rabbis interpreted the law but otherwise were not differentiated, in point of relationship to the divinity, from any other Jews. In the same spirit, there should be no other aristocratic class. All Jews were essentially equal.

By the time of Muḥammad, Judaism was very important numerically between Nile and Oxus, particularly in the towns of the Iraq, where its most widely recognized chiefs came to reside. It is clear that a significant part of the population that accepted Islam in its formative centuries was composed of Jews, whose narrative traditions, called *Isrâ'îliyyât,* dominated the popular legendry of early Islam. It would appear that much of the spirit that formed Muslim expectations of what a religion should be was inspired by Jewish example. Political accidents from the time of the Riddah wars on through the rise of the Piety-minded opposition to Marwânî rule had assured a key position to socially-minded Muslims: more particularly to those Muslims who saw Islam as imposing political responsibility, and yet saw this responsibility as shared on an equal basis among the Muslims—not being left to the rulers or to any official organized body. Such Piety-minded Muslims, by the time of 'Abbâsî rule, had been conceded at least a veto power over what was to be considered legitimately Islamic. This strategic position was confirmed in the following centuries, as the wider population became Muslim, by those circumstances which had already been at work to develop a populistic spirit in the Irano-Semitic monotheisms: a spirit hitherto most fully respresented in Judaism.

Like the Jews and Mazdeans, those Muslims recognized as most authoritative, when the Islamic tradition was fully formed, came to take very seriously the aspiration of religion to form all ordinary life in its own mould. Most forms of Muslim piety rejected monasticism as withdrawal from the social obligations laid upon men by religion itself. Particularly among some sections of the Piety-minded, the supposed example of Muḥammad was to be followed throughout ordinary life, in matters small and great, from brushing the teeth to deciding life and death. The Islamic Sharî'ah (adj. *Shar'î*), or sacred law, was at least as universal in scope as the Jewish law, the Halakha. In a remarkable number of details, the practice finally espoused by Muslims in their Sharî'ah law was parallel to that inculcated by the rabbis. Like the Jewish, moreover, the Muslim ideal allowed of no aristocratic class order such as the Mazdean. All Muslims were to be equal.

But (after the establishment of the Piety-minded ideals) the Muslims, unlike the Jews, did not regard their own community as a unique and (in principle) hereditary body selected out from a world left otherwise without direct divine guidance. The Muslim community was thought of as one among many divinely guided communities such as the Jewish or the Christian, all (at their origin) equally blessed. Thus far, Islam took explicitly the form that various Christian and Jewish bodies had implicitly been assuming under the confessional empires—an autonomous social organism with its own law for its own members. The difference between Islam and the other communities was that Islam was first to rule over and then to supersede all others. Islam was to bring the true and uncorrupted divine guidance to all mankind, creating a world-wide society in which the true revelation would be the everyday norm of all the nations. It must not merely guide an autonomous community like the Jewish; it must guide the practical policies of a cosmopolitan world.

Thus Islam was formed in terms of the expectations which had been fostered by the great monotheistic religious traditions, in particular as they had been understood in the Fertile Crescent and Iran. It chose the social attitude of Judaism and Mazdeism in particular, in the egalitarian form of Judaism. But it introduced its own conception of universality, which gave it a radically fresh approach. We subsume the most central of these aspirations, as they were embodied in concrete norms of life in the High Caliphal Period, under the name of 'Sharîʿah-mindedness'. For it was in the development and exposition of the Sharîʿah law, and in insisting on its central position in the culture, that these aspirations most effectively expressed themselves.[1]

The Sharʿî image of the pristine Medina

From Abû-Ḥanîfah (d. 767) at Kûfah, and Mâlik (d. 795) at Medina, who developed a criticism of Muslim law as it prevailed under the Marwânids, through al-Shâfiʿî (d. 820) and his successors, who established a comprehensive legal theory based upon that criticism, the practical growth of Sharîʿah law was complex. But pervading this growth was a persistent common tendency which received ever more adequate expression as the Sharîʿah was developed. Though each particular step in the formation of the Sharîʿah had its immediate rationale, there were inevitably many potential alternatives. That the major choices prevailed as they did was surely due to their enabling Muslims to come closer to fulfilling the overall ideals of the Sharîʿah-minded. These ideals they did not present in the abstract manner required by the historian, who measures them against the corresponding ideals of other eras. We must state in our own modern terms, and against the background of the ages that had preceded, what it was that those early Muslims were taking for granted; what it was that they were acting upon without articulating. But we may hope to come to a formulation which, while they would not have made it, they would not have repudiated once they understood it. Once we have seen the overall tendencies that went into making the Sharîʿah of High Caliphal times, we can study more clearly the detailed process by which it was realized.

Central to the Qur'ânic challenge and a keynote of Islamic faith, distinguishing it to a lesser or greater degree from that of most of the other religious traditions, was an emphasis on direct and universal human responsibility before God. The Sharîʿah-minded carried to their furthest implications the populistic and moralistic tendencies already important among their predecessors. For them, this meant first that every person, as such, with no exceptions, was summoned in his own person to obey the commands of God: there could be no intermediary, no group responsibility, no evasion of any sort from direct confrontation with the divine will; and, moreover, that a person was sum-

[1] Basic problems in the role of Islamic faith in the historical life of the Muslim peoples are studied by W. Montgomery Watt, *Islam and the Integration of Society* (London, 1960).

moned to nothing else; anything not in accordance with the divine commands was frivolous if not worse. The demands of the faith were personal and total—or at least so the pious saw them, who tried to work out a social order on such a basis.

The Masters of Fiqh

SYRIAN LEGISTS
Influenced by Syrian and Umayyad governmental practices

al-Awzâ'î
(d. 774)

MEDINAN LEGISTS
Claimed closer memory of Prophet's Sunnah, and less taint of innovations

Mâlik b. Anas
(715–795)
'Mâlikî school'

IRAQI LEGISTS
Used analogy but also preferred equity; influenced by Iraqi and 'Abbâsid governmental practices

Abû-Ḥanîfah
(d. 767)
'Ḥanifî school'

al-Shaybânî
(d. 805)

Abû-Yûsuf
(d. 798)

al-Shâfi'î
(d. 820)
'Shâfi'î school'
Rigorous care to verify ḥadîths, especially of Prophet's Sunnah; use of analogy

Ibn-Ḥanbal
(d. 855)
'Ḥanbalî school'
Emphasis upon using carefully chosen ḥadîths; preference for 'a weak ḥadîth over a strong analogy'

Dâwûd b. Khalaf
(d. 883)
'Zâhirî school'
Emphasis upon and restriction to literalist use of Qur'ân and ḥadîths of the Prophet's Sunnah

There could then be no question of a church, ministering God's grace to humans, nor of priests whose ritual acts mediated between a group of worshippers and God. It was symbolically correct that in public worship the leader, the imâm (who might be any one of the faithful) performed the same acts as anyone else, only standing in front of the others, who made their gestures in time with his. With the rejection of Arabism as the basis of Islam, there could not even be a chosen people. Though Muslims were set off from others, it was only in that they had chosen personally to obey God, a duty incumbent upon everyone else as well.

But so far as Islam was to govern social life as a whole, such attitudes had consequences beyond the sphere of how the cult itself was to be organized. The Sharî'ah law could recognize no hereditary social class structure, for all Muslims must be on the same footing before God, the only legitimate distinction being a person's degree of piety. Nor could it recognize a territorial distinction, such as we Moderns are used to, of nationality, whereby a political boundary line determines an individual's rights and duties: his only rights and duties were those laid down by God, and these were the same everywhere. Indeed, it could not even recognize a state, properly speaking an organization responsible as an organization for seeing to public concerns. For any public concern was either a matter of fulfilling God's will, or it was illegitimate frivolity; but if it was a matter of fulfilling God's will it was a matter incumbent upon every individual, at least in principle. There could be no corporate limited liability through which the individual could evade his duty. In short, no man, no institution, no human structure of any sort could legitimately be vested with any responsibility which could relieve the individual Muslim of his direct and all-embracing responsibility before God.

And yet Islam could not be a community of hermits with no common institutions: on the contrary, part of God's command was precisely that persons should live in community, should worship together, should marry and bring up children, and even should see to it that right and justice prevailed in the earth among all human beings. The substance of human beings' obligation to God was to be God's vicegerents on earth, ordering all things aright. One of the basic duties of any Muslim, which had been recognized from the time of the Piety-minded opposition, was to 'command the right and forbid the wrong'—which meant not only mutual exhortation to right action among the faithful, but universal responsibility for public good order. The Sharî'ah law could not ignore social duties, even if it refused to legitimize any formal organization for carrying them out. Some sort of pattern, then, must be found, on the basis of which humans could, in principle, without abandoning their individual responsibility, actively order their community and indeed the whole world according to the divine norms. The pattern found was both ingenious and daring.

The heirs of the Piety-minded opposition naturally found the answer in the community which Muḥammad had established in Medina, and which his close associates had maintained with Medina as their capital. But now it was no longer, as in Marwânî times, a matter of providing a political norm, primarily, with social patterns supplementary. Rather, it was the social pattern that was to form the essential, and any political implications were derivative. The rejection of bid'ah, innovation, was erected into a system of law.

It was especially among the legists of Medina, naturally enough, that this ideal was worked out in its purest form. The legists of each province at first identified their own local traditions with original Islam. Al-Awzâ'î (d. 774), the foremost legist of Syria, regarded the original tradition as unbroken up till 744, the beginning of the third fitnah, and frankly decided questions on the basis of Marwânî practice. Those of the opposition could not be at ease in such an approach. Yet the legists of Kûfah, disciples of Abû-Ḥanîfah and his peers, continued to identify Kûfan practice with original Islam. At Medina several legists, of whom the most judicious, or at least the most influential, was Mâlik b. Anas (d. 795), in insisting that it was *their* local tradition that perpetuated original Islam, introduced the new concept most clearly. Mâlik worked on the explicit assumption that the ways recognized by the pious elders of the Anṣâr of the Prophet's city were uncorrupted either by the indifference of the tardily converted Umayyads or by the tribal ways of the garrison towns; hence the ways of Medina went back not just to early Muslims but to Muḥammad himself. Mâlik composed a comprehensive collection of rules, the *Muwaṭṭa'*, designed to preserve this old Medinese lore, which became the foundation document for a whole school of legists—active even in his day as far as Spain.

A somewhat idealized picture of Medina emerged for this purpose. The Shar'î theorists interpreted that community in terms of the religious attitudes of which I have just given a modern and oversimplified formulation; and, so interpreted, the Medina community served well as pattern. In the pristine Medina there had in fact been neither church and priest, nor state and law, in any ordinary sense. There was instead Muḥammad, who demonstrated empirically in his own actions the commands of God; for it must be assumed that he would not act except in accordance with them. Accordingly, the first principle which the pristine Medina provided to the later theorists was a new basis for law. This was neither legislation by a human assembly nor deduction from a set of human principles but, rather, empirical observation of individual actions which God had approved. For Mâlik, what mattered was still the typical action, that which Medina had acknowledged; later even rare or almost unobserved actions could become normative. These might be either the actions of Muḥammad himself or those of others to which he did not object; the essential was not the man who had acted but the act that was approved.[2]

[2] Too often, modern writers tend to assume current Western patterns as normal and to account for Muslim deviations from them on the basis of the accidents of Muḥammad's life and Arab circumstances of his time. The present discussion may seem to encourage such analyses. Of course, Islam did not '*unite* church and state' at all (as often stated) but rather—never having had such an institution as a church—it did not invent or adopt for itself the distinction between the two (though it did adopt some other distinctions which the Occident in turn did not make). But even this different evolution had its own historical reasons: while the shape of Islam in Medina reflected local conditions there where no state or church had been, yet one cannot say that the later Muslims failed to legitimize a distinct state (or church) '*because* Muḥammad had lived in Mecca and Medina'. There

A second principle was also provided by the pattern of Medina: the basis for organization within the community—that is, for the distribution of tasks. For duties that not everyone could or need fulfill, Muḥammad had appointed individuals who were personally responsible for carrying them out; and if they did so, others were not given the burden. Accordingly, theorists divided all duties into *farḍ'ayn,* which everyone was obligated to whether others performed the duty or not, such as worship or keeping one's contracts; and *farḍ kifâyah,* which were inherently incumbent upon all in the community, but which could be left aside by others if some one person performed them satisfactorily. Thus if some saw to it that the mosque was kept in repair or the weights used in the market were true, others were relieved of the responsibility; but they were relieved only provisionally and on the assumption that the one responsible fulfilled his task. Nor could the man responsible be content to leave a matter to subordinates, for the duty was not one of an office, but a personal one. A story was told of how 'Umar, the caliph, personally delivered food to a needy widow who had been overlooked by his lieutenants; for he knew he could not assert, as defence on Judgment Day, that his responsibility was fulfilled by appointing the best possible state functionary. On the basis of this principle there need be no constitution and no separate public law; what might be called public duties were to be handled legally on almost the same basis as private ones.

A third principle formed the basis of the relation of the community to non-adherents. It was the mission of the community to bring God's true ways into all the world; hence the *rule* of the Muslim community should be extended over all infidels. As in Medina, however, these latter (if they were adherents of a former revealed religion, which had merely been corrupted, such as Jews and Christians) were allowed to continue in their own religious allegiance, as dhimmîs, 'protected subjects', so long as their worship was not too blatantly inconsistent with the public recognition of God's unity, and so long as they submitted to Muslim control of general affairs. Thus only those who had personally undertaken the obligations of Islam were expected to live the Muslim way, but only they were allowed to bear responsibility for society at large.

Implications of the Medina ideal for High Caliphal times

All the religious communities have been accused of a certain dissociation between the explicit grounds adduced for their tenets and any analyzable historical actuality. Thus the main body of later Roman law, which made no religious claims, adduced as its basis precedents going back to a *jus gentium,* common practice among Mediterranean peoples, interpreted in the light of Stoic philosophical principles; and in fact, historically, this was substantially

---

was no Sharî'ah at Medina either. Rather, because of Muḥammad's experience Islam was able to serve as a good vehicle for the Irano-Semitic communal tendencies, which took advantage of the Medina example to enforce an ideal valid for more general reasons.

its formation. But so soon as religion enters in, this frankness tends to disappear. We are confronted with dogmas—statements it is held immoral to disbelieve; hence explanations which may be rational enough in themselves must be put in such a form that the dogmas are kept intact. Thus in the case of Roman ritual, when once it was ascribed to Numa, the Romans no longer dared explain its importance rationally in terms of social solidarity and of dramatizing the moral and the sacred. They had to explain it in terms of Numa's ancestral wisdom—which came to the same thing in a roundabout way.

The Shar'î doctrines of social order undeviatingly maintained such a dissociation, in the form they finally took, perhaps in part because of the apparent rationality and clarity of the few dogmas involved. We must for the moment go behind the way in which the early Muslims formulated the ideal, so as to analyze in our own way the Medina ideal as it applied to High Caliphal society. That society differed doubly from that of the pristine Medina. Under the Marwânids, to begin with, the Muslims had been a ruling minority in a vast rich empire, rather than a small compact rural community. Later yet, the bulk of the population of that empire was becoming Muslim. How could the old social pattern be applied to the new situations? Let us review in this perspective what had been happening already in Marwânî times among the Piety-minded.

The community in Medina presented three distinctive features which all the legal principles traceable to Medina presupposed. Above all, it presented an ideal orientation: Muḥammad's whole aim was to build a godly life, and the community responded to him in this aim. Second, it presented a personal relationship within the group—each person knew everyone else and, being treated as a responsible servant of God, did not behave, and was not behaved to, in the impersonal manner of an official functionary. Third, it presented a cultural homogeneity within the group; and it was this homogeneity—one of common Arab custom as modified by the group allegiance to Muḥammad—that made possible the other two features: the immediacy of the ideal orientation, as well as the immediacy of the personal relations among the faithful. The problem posed, then, was to reproduce in the caliphal society, spread out over thousands of miles, the ideal-oriented, personalized, cultural homogeneity that had prevailed in pristine Medina. Such questions as that of authority, on which the various factions of the Piety-minded differed, were given their urgency by the terms of this problem. When we consider in its light the various solutions proposed to such questions, each solution is seen to have reasonable grounds, whatever the bizarreness of the terms in which it is formulated.

Islam had to prove capable of forming the whole basis of a society. To this end, it was necessary for Muslims to find what, in the pristine Medina, would form the basis for an Islamic society as such; and what, in the circumstances first of Marwânî and then of 'Abbâsî times, would answer to the relevant elements of the pristine Medina, so that the Islamic society could be reproduced.

It was this cultural homogeneity that was referred to in the demand for sunnah practice as a standard of Islamic life. In the Muslim empire the homogeneity of the pristine Medina was represented by continuing elements in the actual life. The Piety-minded took advantage of these in their effort to recapture the ideal. Most generally, the cultural homogeneity of Medina was represented at first by the common traditions of the Arab ruling class, which retained the old Arab sunnah, customary practice, as modified by Muḥammad's reforms. What they had in common was the old and indeed largely pre-Islamic Arab ways; what they had taken over from the life of the several conquered provinces was not included except so far as it had been generalized by the Marwânî administration. In recognition of the importance of this Muslim Arab homogeneity, the Piety-minded had established the principle of adherence to tradition (at first, to local tradition), which later finally crystallized as the doctrine of *ijmâ'*, that whatever had been accepted generally by the community was to be regarded as sanctioned by God. It was on this basis that the use of circumcision (male and female) was imposed, for instance, though it had no special sanction beyond Arab custom, and the more careful legists could not regard it as fully binding. The prohibition against bid'ah, innovation in practice, corresponded to the assertion of ijmâ'; its tendency likewise was to preserve homogeneity. This prohibition was aimed against every sort of deviation, inherently immoral or not, though the legists sometimes relented in favour of obviously helpful innovations.

More particularly, the legists could depend on the existence of inherited knowledge about the pristine Medina itself. Though the immediate example was no longer present, ways could be found of recapturing it for the wider community. This was the intention of the legist Mâlik in recording, for all to read, the practice in Medina in Marwânî times, as it was known to the oldest and best-informed inhabitants. But others were not sure that the later Medina could be relied on to afford the ideal standard desired. Despite Medinese pride, the practice of every Muslim centre seemed to go back just as clearly to the first Muslims. What came increasingly to substitute for the immediate experiencing of the pristine Medina was the collecting of eyewitness reports, ḥadîth, about thousands of details of its life, transmitted by men and women whose concern for preserving the record of that life could be depended on.

This method had the added advantage (though it was not usually noted as such) that mingled with these reports was the collective wisdom of two or three generations of Muslims gained in a variety of experiences throughout the Muslim empire.[3] This wider experience was expressed both in sifting and in inventing ḥadîth reports. On both counts the ḥadîth corpus in its classical form must be ascribed as much to Marwânî times and later as to Muḥammad's

[3] For the process whereby Marwânî legal practice was transformed into the ideal Sharî'ah, see Joseph Schacht, *The Origins of Muhammadan Jurisprudence* (Oxford University Press, 1950), especially part III, chap. I. Perhaps he gives too much credit to al-Shâfi'î.

own generation. Nevertheless, a unity of spirit was maintained through insisting on showing that the reporter's central concern was with the life and ideals of Muḥammad's community—that, as it was put, the reporter was sound in faith and the report was consistent with the Qur'ân. Forgery did little harm if the common spirit was adhered to, and might even foster homogeneity in points otherwise left in doubt.[4] (The legists themselves, to be sure, rarely forged a ḥadîth report; they made use of what they found available.)

The 'ilm knowledge embodied in this ḥadîth came to be considered by the Piety-minded as the highest knowledge and in fact the only really legitimate knowledge; learning it was incumbent upon every Muslim so far as he was able. It was no longer possible, as it had been in Medina, for a man to take these things as 'common knowledge', merely asking a respected neighbour if for some reason he needed to know a particular point; the personal contact of Medina life was missing. But, as in the case of cultural homogeneity, a certain approximation to this condition of personal interrelationship was possible. In Marwânî times, not all Muslims knew each other personally; but the prominent Muslims (whether in politics, poetry, or any other line) in each of the relatively few communities in which the Muslim class lived could be and were known, as personalities, to informed Muslims elsewhere. It was, therefore, still possible for Muslims at large to have an opinion of the piety and the dependability of individuals active as transmitters of ḥadîth reports or as representatives of 'ilm knowledge generally. By travelling from centre to centre, a concerned young man could learn personally from all the more active men of his day; in 'Abbâsî times such travelling became very common. Hence the search for 'ilm on the part of the pious youth could conceivably be carried out on the basis of a personal relationship between the older and younger generations in the community as a whole, without institutionalization or theoretical abstraction.

In Marwânî times, then, the garrison-town society, with its Arabism, provided an effective context in which to develop the principles of an Islamism which was to reform it. Personal interrelationships such as the Medina community had known could be maintained, within the circle of concerned pious persons at least, by travel among Muslim centres, and the solidarity of the society was further reinforced by many details of the Islamic code as that was built up. The cultural homogeneity needed to make these details effective was valiantly striven for through the cultivation of hallowed practice, sunnah, and the opposition to bid'ah, innovation. As to the ideal orientation of the Medina community, that was provided with enthusiasm—even if only on a minority basis—by the Piety-minded themselves, strengthened by the ever-present Qur'ân. In this way the model of Medina became relevant to later Muslim society.

[4] Compare on the rise of the ḥadîth reports especially Ignaz Goldziher, *Muhammedanische Studien*, vol. 2 (Halle, 1890). Joseph Schacht has added precisions to our understanding of the legal ḥadîth in particular, in *The Origins of Muhammadan Jurisprudence*, cited above, especially part II, 'The Growth of Legal Traditions'. Various other subsequent studies have not yet made Goldziher out of date.

Under ʿAbbâsî conditions, when Muslims were numbered in the millions, such concerns and principles had to be reduced to a complexly technical system. It was no longer true that every important Muslim could be known in a significant way to all the well-informed, nor could cultural homogeneity based on essentially Arab family traditions be maintained. Accordingly, the system adumbrated in Marwânî times had to be institutionalized in such a way as to retain as much as possible of its original virtue. Where the face-to-face relations at Medina had been replaced by relations based on general repute within a ruling class, these now had to be formalized into a relatively impersonal relationship of colleagues in a common specialty. The pious specialists became themselves a distinct class, as ʿulamâʾ scholars; and principles that had earlier included in their scope the wider Muslim community in an informal way, now often applied to this religious class alone. Moreover, their application no longer depended on informal attitudes but followed a strictly codified set of rules. The custom, the local ijmâʿ, of the garrison towns had to be replaced altogether—in principle—by the use of reports about early Medina; reports which were circulated as text and were often explicitly contrasted to local tradition. (In fact, of course, such reports did embody what was essential of the Arab garrison-town tradition.) But all this further transformation had already been prepared for in the less formal conditions of Marwânî times. The adaptation maintained close continuity with the ways of the older Piety-minded groups: for they had made the essential leap in substituting Islam for Arabism as the norm of the community.

Sharʿî theory and al-Shâfiʿî: ḥadîth from the Prophet

Both the Shîʿî and the Jamâʿî-Sunnî ʿulamâʾ scholars worked out systems of Sharîʿah law in response to the developing need. Here we shall describe, rather summarily, the Sharîʿah as worked out by the Sunnî ʿulamâʾ. The radical Shîʿîs, at least, differed on the theory they used—they accorded also to ḥadîth from the imâms the dignity Sunnîs ascribed to ḥadîth from the Prophet alone, for instance, and rejected as transmitters of it those who they felt had betrayed Islam. Yet in their concrete results, the Shîʿî forms of the Sharîʿah were not very distinctive except on points specially relevant to Shîʿî piety. Dealing with the same questions, all the systems found comparable or even identical answers. The Shîʿî systems seem to have received their rigorous discipline after al-Shâfiʿî had disciplined the Sunnî systems, and probably their principles, like those of other Sunnî systems, were set forth in response to those of al-Shâfiʿî. It was the Jamâʿî-Sunnî systems that took actual effect, for the most part, so far as the Sharîʿah was then embodied at all in civil practice.

The ḥadîth had been, at first, any reports of primitive Muslim practice (sunnah). Ḥadîth reports were cited on the authority of diverse prominent early Muslims; when they were authenticated with a chain of guarantors, an *isnâd*, this chain led back only so far as the figure regarded as authoritative for the point in question—who might or might not have been an immediate associate of the Prophet. Under al-Mahdî (775–785) and al-Rashîd (785–809), it had become increasingly accepted that ḥadîth reports traced back to Muḥammad himself had precedence over reports traced merely to his associates or to the first caliphs; and such reports were being, in fact, increasingly traced to Muḥammad. (Thus an early position of the Shî'îs was being accepted, that decisions of the first caliphs, as such, were not binding.)

It was the legist Muḥammad b. Idrîs al-Shâfi'î (d. 820) who took the most decisive steps. Born in Syria of Hâshimid family, he grew up an impoverished orphan in Mecca, then studied as a young man with the legist Mâlik in Medina. As an official in the Yemen, he joined in a moderate Shî'î rebellion and was taken prisoner under the caliph al-Rashîd; thereupon he came into contact with the legists of Baghdad. It was evidently safer for him, however, to launch his own ideas in Egypt, where he did most of his subsequent teaching.

Taking advantage of the growing number of reports claiming to go back to Muḥammad, he abandoned definitively reliance on the local tradition of any one centre, even Medina, in favour of relying on reports about the Prophet. This was to carry the Medina ideal to its logical conclusion and at the same time to liberate legal thinking from traditional limitations, giving full play to the ideals developed among the Piety-minded—in whose circles it was, that reports about the Prophet had been proliferating. But this consequential, if somewhat risky, position was reinforced by al-Shâfi'î's rigorous legal thinking. In detailed legal argument he much refined Abû-Ḥanîfah's pioneering legal thinking. At the same time, he attempted to create a logically self-contained legal whole which should derive every detail of law from incontrovertible Islamic principles; and he was successful (given his assumptions, particularly about the validity of those reports that were accepted among the Piety-minded).

Al-Shâfi'î proposed to show, in the introduction to his main law book, *Kitâb al-Umm*, that it was possible to derive the whole Sharî'ah from the Qur'ân (and hence from the immediate human-divine confrontation which had taken place historically and which the Muslim community was founded on). This was an unpromising task; as we have seen, the Qur'ân is, on the surface, very inappropriate as a legal text. If it does make rules, it makes them for the occasions of a developing community, and commonly softens in the next phrase what it has fulminated just before. Yet al-Shâfi'î started with the Qur'ân and showed, by an incisive critique of its language (in which he brought out all the diverse ways it called for interpretation), that that Book presupposed Muḥammad not only as its deliverer but as its interpreter.

This gave Muḥammad and his sunnah practice a theological status more exact and far more determinative than they had had before: Muḥammad was to have more than the generalized prestige of having been the vehicle of revelation and the first commander of the Ummah community. He was also the divinely certified exemplar, whose practice itself had a revelatory status: it was through his personal words and acts, and only his, that the commands of the Qur'ân could be legitimately interpreted. In comparison, the practice of even the closest of his early associates had at best merely a presumptive value in the absence of direct evidence as to what the Prophet himself had done in a given contingency. But Muḥammad's sunnah practice, in turn, was to be known not by tradition, in which the individual had to follow blindly what he could not test, but by the text of ḥadîth reports, which the individual could learn personally just as he learned the Qur'ân, and which he could (if qualified) personally evaluate. It was hard for a pious Muslim to resist the idea that, if the Sharî'ah could in fact be built on such principles, this must be accepted as the ideal to strive for by all suitable means.

The doctrine al-Shâfi'î espoused was the most rigorous form of the new preference for Prophetic ḥadîth: that reports from the Prophet not only had precedence but were alone authoritative. Moreover, the Prophetic origin of a report must not be left implicit nor be merely asserted without proof; it must be shown by the isnâd of the particular report, the list of persons through whom it had reached the current speaker, which must be unbroken all the way from Muḥammad. Al-Shâfi'î hoped that such a test would eliminate innovations introduced after the corruption of the Medina community. For in principle the practice (sunnah) of the Prophet himself, so attested, must be unquestionable. In practice, the results were more subtle.

The isnâd, to which little attention had been paid anyway in the early use of ḥadîth reports, had rarely if ever originally led back explicitly to Muḥammad, even if the report happened to be about Muḥammad. At best one of his associates might be mentioned. When an explicit isnâd leading to Muḥammad came to be required, this was often supplied to reports already current—whether they were explicitly about Muḥammad, or merely offered an opinion which must now be supposed to go back to him. Presumably, the more honest analyzed the probabilities of the case and supplied a full isnâd to any given report on the basis of what they knew of its provenance and of the sources from which their own teachers had been in a position to draw. On the other hand, some of the pious had little hesitancy at simply inventing isnâds—and in fact the ḥadîth reports themselves as well—in a good cause; for they assumed (quite explicitly) that whatever was true and of value for Muḥammad's community must have been said by Muḥammad, as an agent of Providence, whether it was actually recalled by anyone or not—or even whether it had actually passed from his lips. (We have ḥadîth reports ascribed to Muḥammad making Muḥammad assert just this!) Accordingly, a considerable body of ḥadîth was soon available with the required isnâd documentation going back to Muḥammad.

But this body of ḥadîth reports was not a mere conglomeration of anyone's forgeries. For in the generations following al-Shâfi'î, this potential source of invalidation in his system was remedied: the wholesale acceptance of newly invented reports was limited by 'isnâd criticism'. By analyzing the isnâd chains of guarantors, the 'ulamâ' scholars were in fact able to assure a selection of ḥadîth with characteristics appropriate to their needs. Both in the substance of the report and in the selection of the chain of transmitters to father it on, the attitudes of the person who had put the ḥadîth into circulation were manifested. Potential transmitters were known; men with reputations for improper doctrine could be ruled out.

At this stage, isnâd criticism amounted to selecting those reports that were circulated by persons who respected the same sorts of authorities as did the critic, and who showed this respect by using them in the isnâd. This did not make for historical accuracy, as to what Muḥammad himself had said; but it did make for an effective religious homogeneity. The method was of course a bit unsure; what was more dependable was that, for the future, it would be relatively easy to sort out ḥadîth reports which had not yet been accepted by the community at the time when the standards for the isnâd documentation became formulated: roughly about the time of al-Shâfi'î himself. To be sure, even in this respect isnâd-forging was not impossible. The determination of the validity of ḥadîth reports on the basis of the isnâd never fully overcame the inherent difficulties in the method. Yet in at least a rough way it served effectively to formulate, and then to preserve, a self-consistent body of doctrine and practice recognizable by and acceptable to the Jamâ'î-Sunnî 'ulamâ' as a body. Moreover, as demanded by the individualist spirit of the Piety-minded, this recognition and acceptance took place without recourse to either hierarchical authority or councils or any other human instrument that would come between the individual human critic and his conscience.

Al-Shâfi'î's system of uṣûl al-fiqh

Al-Shâfi'î's system had to make some allowance for traditional custom and even for the individual legist's judgment. But the scope of these was rigorously delimited; they were made to derive from his Qur'ânic system. Once this body of ḥadîth reports with their isnâds going back to the Prophet had been developed as expressing the community insight—or rather, the insight of those held to represent most closely the 'Qur'ân and the sunnah of Muḥammad'—it was possible seriously to reduce the arbitrary element remaining in particular legal decisions.

This element was labelled *ra'y*, personal judgment. It could not be eliminated completely from the theoretical justification of the legal positions that came to be held; even ḥadîth reports could not be expected to cover all possible contingencies. But a law dependent on the initiative of every new lawyer was obviously intolerable. Various principles had been suggested for limiting the arbitrariness of ra'y. Some who distrusted the reliability of ḥadîth reports preferred to appeal to *'aql*, reasoning, when the reports were not decisive; hoping that sound reasoning would lead to universal results, and so avoid arbitrariness. Some suggested that a decision must be in accord with equity or else with the public interest. For those who were devoted to ḥadîth, however, the most effective way proved to be to subordinate an individual's judgment to ḥadîth, in that unprecedented decisions should be made at least on the analogy of decisions found in ḥadîth or Qur'ân. This process of drawing an analogy was called *qiyâs*, and al-Shâfi'î adopted it as a major adjunct to the use of ḥadîth, for it multiplied greatly the effective force of individual reports.

One more principle was needed to cap the system. The custom of a given centre had been recognized as authoritative when it could claim consensus among the weighty men there—ijmâ'. Such ijmâ', consensus, had played a basic role in the legal thinking of the Piety-minded. In addition to being conservatively practical, it represented, in maximally concrete form, the ideal requirement of cultural homogeneity, without which it seemed impossible to create a society in which each man was immediately responsible before God for everything. Now al-Shâfi'î insisted that the only ijmâ' that carried authority was that of the whole Ummah community of Muḥammad: on the grounds, in effect, that so wide a consensus must have originated with at least the tacit approval of Muḥammad himself. But even this he was able to justify more concretely by discovering a ḥadîth report assuring that Muḥammad's community would never be agreed on an error. Hence what they all agreed on must be sound; if an explicit report was wanting on a given point to illustrate Muḥammad's sunnah practice, the agreement of the Muslims would bear witness equally well to what that sunnah must have been. (Certainly it was the surest guide available for reconstructing it.) In principle, the Muslim community in this sense meant the whole body of the faithful, or of the weighty among them; but for more technical purposes it eventually came to mean the 'ulamâ' as they expressed themselves in their recorded *fatwàs*, that is, decisions in points of law or conscience. If all recognized 'ulamâ' were on record as accepting a position, it was to be considered binding.

Al-Shâfi'î's method was intensely factualistic, allowing almost no leeway for private fancy. He based his method on quite concrete events: the coming of certain words to certain people under certain conditions; and the meaning of these events must depend on the exact meaning of those words to those people under those conditions. (He noted, incidentally, how important it was to have an exhaustive knowledge of the nuances of the Muḍarî Arabic grammar of Muḥammad's time.) Thus he gave full recognition to the intensely historical nature of the revelation that had launched Islam; though not, except unconsciously, to the continuingly historical nature of the reception of that revelation in the community committed to it.

The method was also legally effective. By rejecting the authority of precedent, of custom, he gave the pious more leeway in building a law to their taste. But by the precision of his method, he reintroduced, once the new norms were accepted, more determinacy and predictability into the law than had existed on the old basis. Above all, he went far toward ruling out all arbitrary decision, ra'y, by the judge purely on the basis of a personal sense of justice: the judge must show some foundation for his decision in what the Piety-minded had accepted as sound; and he had to prove that foundation by rigorous criteria, linguistic and logical.

Al-Shâfi'î established a basis for a law that should be at once founded on ideals and also (most important in any legal system) uniform and predictable. He did so at a price. In their very lack of system, the earlier legists were capable of a practical realism which, after al-Shâfi'î, could sometimes appear only backhandedly and in despite of the ideal. More important, al-Shâfi'î's system was necessarily, if unwittingly, founded on a pious fiction.

Al-Shâfi'î himself clearly believed he was founding it on the *man* Muḥammad, as he lived at Medina. In fact, since he accepted the existing body of ḥadîth as representing Muḥammad, he was founding it on the *figure* of Muḥammad, as this had been built up in pious circles; and therefore on the community as a whole so far as it was committed to Muḥammad's vision. Clearly some, at least, of the later collectors of ḥadîth were aware that it was the figure that mattered; that the figure was a legitimate and necessary enlargement of the man. This is implied in one of the ḥadîth reports that justified accepting dubiously historical reports: it makes Muḥammad say that, in judging the validity of reports about him, the Muslims were to accept any report that was consistent with the Qur'ân: that is, of course, consistent with what meant most to Muḥammad—at least, as this was understood by the Piety-minded. This was to throw the authority back to that section of the Ummah on whose good judgment, in fact, al-Shâfi'î was relying. From a historian's viewpoint, so to include within the act of revelation itself the tradition that sprang from it may seem only reasonable, and not misrepresentation at all. But to a less sophisticated mind, such a procedure, if detected, would look like direct fraud. To al-Shâfi'î (could he have recognized what he was doing without first imbibing a modern historical viewpoint), to have to admit that he was ascribing later judgments to Muḥammad himself would have invalidated his whole system.

Al-Shâfi'î was an eminently good legal thinker and his suggestions had, moreover, an obvious appeal. His requirement with regard to ḥadîth was soon quite generally accepted. But with this requirement came a great stress on criticism of the isnâd documentation, which meant criticism of the various reporters through whom the report had been transmitted. Everyone knew that many ḥadîth reports said to go back to the Prophet were forged. In time, the transmitters were less generally known; offhand ways of sorting reports became insufficient. The 'ulamâ' naturally looked for surer ways of eliminating false ones. A special discipline grew up devoted to testing the isnâds of all reports in circulation. Critics of the isnâd were to trace the recorded character of each transmitter and reject those whose virtue, memory, or judgment—or doctrine—were suspect. If there were only sound transmitters in the isnâd, this should prove that the report actually went back as far as it claimed and had not been invented by the unscrupulous or mixed up by the forgetful.

There resulted eventually a vast body of specialist literature, dealing both with personalities and with standards to be maintained in judging them and their reports. The personal contact of acquaintances in the primitive Medina was thus replaced by the learnèd analysis of the ḥadîth literature and its authors. The evaluation of the worthiness of each man as a source of authority and knowledge was no longer a matter of common assent among neighbours, nor even a matter of notoriety among a group of limited communities as in Marwânî times. It was henceforth a technical task, to fulfill which an elaborate special study was developed with its own rules, the *'ilm al-rijâl*, 'knowledge of the men'. This 'ilm al-rijâl was used both in sorting out ḥadîth reports and in deciding whose judgment was to be included in settling points of ijmâ'.

The corpus of ḥadîth continued to grow and the added reports were even utilized in law. But pious Muslims learned (in effect) to discriminate between the earlier, 'sound', ḥadîth and later reports which might be useful but were not so dependable. Six major collections of reports were accepted eventually among Jamâ'î-Sunnîs as canonical (even though some legal positions were still based on ḥadîth not there included). Two of these, the collections of Bukhârî and of Muslim, came to be revered as especially holy because it was felt the reports they contained were sifted by the most careful tests of genuineness; the other four allowed 'weaker' reports the benefit of the doubt so as to afford a somewhat wider basis for legal decision. (Shî'îs had their own collections.)

The ḥadîth corpus, however, was never merely a source for law. It had its own autonomous character even in point of doctrine. Inconvenient individual ḥadîth reports sometimes became so well entrenched that they had to be explained away (thus some of the 'Alid-loyalist reports about 'Alî could not be denied by Jamâ'î-Sunnîs and had to be emasculated by exegesis). The overall weight of ḥadîth sometimes went directly counter to the positions ultimately taken in Sharî'ah law. The ḥadîth corpus became a reservoir of pious opinion that sometimes could be used even against the Sharî'ah-minded.[5]

Legal fiqh

After al-Shâfi'î's time, some legists, especially among the devotees of ḥadîth—representing a form of piety to which this line of thought was congenial—tried to push al-Shâfi'î's system even further. As the body of ḥadîth reports

[5] Even the ḥadîth corpus, as distinguished from legal use of ḥadîth, is not properly regarded as 'tradition' (save in the sense that, once launched, it formed a cultural tradition of its own). R. Brunschvig, in particular, has shown how greatly the positions upheld in the ḥadîth corpus could differ from received attitudes; see his 'Considérations sociologiques sur le droit musulman ancien', *Studia Islamica*, 3 (1955), 61–73.

became gradually larger, it became convenient to base directly on ḥadîth decisions which had originally been accepted on other grounds. Even qiyâs, analogy, was eventually rejected by some uncritical extremists in favour of ḥadîth pure and simple. Ijmâ' was suspect among some—perhaps as being based on tradition rather than on explicit text—and they allowed that authoritative status only to the consensus of the first generation of Muḥammad's associates, as shown in ḥadîth reports.

But by and large, al-Shâfi'î's system became normative. A systematic science of law and ethics and cult was recognized, the fiqh, jurisprudence, through which the Sharî'ah law was determined in detail. Fiqh necessarily dealt with every case of conscience, not only in ritual but in private interpersonal relations. In this latter realm, such questions were discussed as when a Muslim should or should not tell the explicit truth. (Christian moralists have condemned Muslims for allowing lying on occasion; but the Muslims were discussing cases where every society has in fact condoned or even required lying, and were attempting to introduce restraint: notably cases assimilable to warfare and cases in the area of courteous speech, where evasion can take the form of misstatement without real deception.) But in the most intimate questions, such as this, the decision of qâḍîs was rarely invoked. Moreover, other sources of ethical judgment (sometimes more demanding) intervened to guide the social conformists or the philosophically emancipated or even the specially pious. Hence the greater part of the efforts of men of fiqh went into settling ritual or the less intimate interpersonal activities: what may be called expressly legal fiqh.

The fiqh was based on four 'roots' (*uṣûl al-fiqh*): the Qur'ân, the ḥadîth, ijmâ', and qiyâs; among them these four 'sources' were supposed to be exhaustive. Each of the 'sources' had been referred to in Marwânî times; but they were now linked systematically and comprehensively. Even those who opposed the system accepted its terms of debate. Ḥanafîs defended the use of what others called ra'y, personal judgment, by their early masters, on the basis of appeal to a supplementary principle, 'preferability', similar to supplementary principles that even al-Shâfi'î had to introduce to guide qiyâs.[6]

The legal precedents and rules provided by Qur'ân and sunnah, even thus elaborated, naturally did not provide a full law, however. They were the sources of fiqh, but fiqh had to operate on them by an elaborate system of rules before they could become a fully developed and processed Sharî'ah, a

[6] Later Jamâ'î-Sunnîs interpreted the relations among the four *madhhabs* which they accepted, in such a way as to make their common existence intelligible and their continuity from Muḥammad authoritative despite their differences. They presented each one atemporally as the work of a single founder with a given attitude to fixed 'sources' of law; and pointed out that each tolerated the others as Muslims, even though as erring ones. Such a picture has been taken up by some modern writers, but it is, of course, anachronistic. The early legists had no need to assert ra'y, for instance, as one of the formal uṣûl al-fiqh, but at most only as common sense against a few ḥadîth-minded extremists. Originally, all the schools of legists, and not merely the Ḥanafîs (as later) were accused by the Hadîth folk of using *ra'y*, which was practically synonymous with *fiqh*, 'inquiry.'

legal system.[7] First of all must be decided the relevance and degree of applicability of any given rule or precedent. For instance, some prescriptions followed in Muḥammad's time had been temporary and superseded by more permanent ones, as turning toward Jerusalem in worship had been superseded by turning toward the Ka'bah in Mecca. As much as possible should be known of the occasions for the revelation of particular Qur'ân verses and of the chronology of events in Muḥammad's life of which ḥadîth reports might be transmitted, so as to know what had been superseded by what. Likewise, it must be determined of any given report whether it presented a duty incumbent on Muḥammad alone (such as proclaiming a new divine message) or relevant only to a particular occasion (such as the behaviour of certain Muslims when 'Â'ishah was accused of infidelity), or whether it had a more general bearing. The most important distinction of this sort that had to be made in fiqh was as to the degree of legal weight borne by a particular rule: whether a given practice was obligatory or merely recommended; whether, if it were obligatory, it was to be enforced by penalties in the courts or left only to the rewards and penalties of the other world; and indeed (to complete the picture), whether a given act might be subject neither to an obligatory rule, pro or con, nor even to a recommendation, but be indifferent and so permitted at discretion.[8]

But at least as important was a set of considerations only barely adumbrated in sacred texts. However complete the body of legal rules might be, it could not be used with precision without an equally complete body of legal definitions. What is a sale, what is a gift? What is property? To a degree the answer to such questions, also, could be cast in the form of ḥadîth; but for the most part it must depend on careful reasoning. It was in this realm that the masters of fiqh showed their finesse. It was especially in this sort of question that the Roman law (and doubtless other law less well known to us) seems to have been a source of the Muslim fiqh. Roman concepts may have entered especially by way of the law applied by Christian bishops; and the Jewish example was naturally also strong.[9]

[7] It will be seen that there is no single appropriate rendering of *Sharî'ah* into English. 'Law' by itself answers to only one aspect of it unless one has clearly in mind the 'Law' of Moses. Moreover, a great deal of actual Muslim law was never taken up in the Sharî'ah and even remained contrary to it, but was applied in Muslim courts. 'Sacred law' scarcely extends the meaning of 'law' without the same special reference to Moses, though it does remind one that not all law was Sharî'ah. 'Canon law' carries some analogies but also some wrong ecclesiastical associations. A word like 'code' might suggest the scope of the Sharî'ah, but the Sharî'ah was never codified in the strict sense.

[8] Frédéric Peltrier pointed out that the collection of ḥadîth by Bukhârî, in contrast to that by the earlier Mâlik, allows very expressly for distinguishing when an act, however uncommendable, has full legal effects and when it is legally void: such distinctions being essential in practical law courts, though unimportant when the 'ulamâ' were still concerned primarily with cases in conscience. See his *Le Livre des ventes du Mouwaṭṭâ de Mâlik ben Anas, traduction avec éclaircissements* (Algiers, 1911), Preface.

[9] S. G. Vesey-Fitzgerald, 'The Alleged Debt of Islamic to Roman Law', *Law Quarterly Review*, 67 (1951), 81–102, grants only the possibility of some influence. Elsewhere he points out Jewish influence: 'Nature and Sources of the Shari'a', *Law in the Middle East*, vol. 1, ed. M. Khadduri and H. Liebesny (Washington, 1955), pp. 85–112.

Thus fiqh had become a highly technical process, based on debate throughout the Muslim community. The traditions of fiqh which had grown up in each main provincial capital now were crystallized into schools, consciously disputing with each other about both the method and the detailed rules of fiqh. They came to be called after the most revered master of each. Abû-Ḥanîfah, the master of Abû-Yûsuf, was the great imâm (here a generalized term for teacher of 'ilm knowledge) in the Iraq; the fiqh which remained faithful to the Iraqi tradition was called 'Ḥanafî'. Al-Awzâ'î was the great imâm in Syria. Those who clung to the example of Mâlik b. Anas, in the Ḥijâz and elsewhere, were called 'Mâlikîs'.

Each school of fiqh was called a *madhhab*, a 'chosen way'. As the fiqh became more technical, new madhhab schools arose, tied to an ideological position rather than to a geographical area. Al-Shâfi'î himself founded a new madhhab school which he finally went to Egypt to teach, which spread widely. Another madhhab school was associated with Aḥmad b. Ḥanbal, whom we will meet as the proponent of the populistic Ḥadîth-folk piety; he compiled an important collection of ḥadîth and his followers tried to use ḥadîth (and Qur'ân) as exclusively as possible. Still later, Dâ'ûd al-Ẓâhirî (the 'literalist') believed that ḥadîth reports were abundant enough to allow him to construct a complete system of fiqh with no use of qiyâs analogy at all; it was he who insisted that the ḥadîth must be taken literally and no implications introduced by the initiative of the *faqîh*, jurisprudent; critics feel that he too used inference without admitting it.[10] Schools of Shî'î fiqh were growing up at the same time, appealing to the privileged 'ilm of the imâms. The Shî'î imâm Ja'far al-Ṣâdiq was made the leading authority by both Twelvers and Ismâ'îlîs among the later Shî'î sects; the various Zaydî Shî'î imâms developed two chief systems of their own. A separate madhhab was worked out among those Khârijîs who were most active in 'Abbâsî times (Ibâḍîs in particular, the group who had controlled much of Arabia during the third fitnah and had created a state in the Maghrib).

Each Muslim had to choose which madhhab school he would follow unless he were a great enough scholar to work out his own way (as did the historian al-Ṭabarî); normally, Muslims naturally accepted the madhhab prevalent in their regions. In effect, most Muslims, except for Shî'îs, ultimately became Ḥanafîs or Shâfi'îs, while in the Maghrib and Spain the Mâlikîs prevailed. For whatever matters could be settled privately—personal ritual and ethics, of course, and matters like inheritance or fulfillment of contract—a person need only consult a *muftî*, 'jurisconsultant', of his madhhab. If a matter was carried to the point of litigation in a court, the qâḍî appointed by the governor ruled according to his own madhhab.

[10] Something of the subtlety of the Ẓâhirî position appears in R. B. Brunschvig, 'Sur la doctrine du Mahdî Ibn-Tûmart', *Arabica*, vol. 2 (1955), pp. 137–79, as that position was taught much later. For fuller treatment, see Ignaz Goldziher, *Die Ẓâhiriten, ihr Lehrsystem und ihre Geschichte* (Leipzig, 1884).

The spirit of the law: public order, individual rights

Thus was built in ʿAbbâsî times a solid structure of fiqh, not exactly 'case law' but law case by case, which could govern the whole field of ethics, cult, and private and even public law in a manner clearly derived from, and to a considerable degree actually consistent with, the ideal of individual responsibility before God's will as expressed in the Prophetic mission. In all madhhab schools, however much they had at first varied in their stress on this or that element in deriving the law, the spirit of the law was much the same, and the same spirit pervaded all its branches.

At least within its range, the system was comprehensive and rigorous. There was as yet, indeed, no attempt actually to reason out all elements of social law and practice on a Sharʿî basis. Once the position of caliph was recognized by the Sharîʿah, large discretion was left to him in practice to decide many matters of public policy without explicit reference to Sharʿî principles. The Sharîʿah covered, in the first place, matters in which the Arab soldiery had a direct interest, and then also those in which the merchants were interested—family and commercial law, above all; other matters were globally covered under the principle that actions not expressly prohibited in the Sharîʿah were to be tolerated. Such limitations in scope were confirmed in ʿAbbâsî times, at least so long as the caliphate remained powerful, by a further shift in social outlook among the ʿulamâʾ scholars. As the identification of Islam with old Arab families receded; as the popular Islam of the lower-class urban story-tellers became numerically more important—that popular Islam which was largely a retelling of Christian and Jewish tales from a Muslim viewpoint—the outlook of the pious leadership, Jamâʿî-Sunnî or Shîʿî, also changed. Building for an audience which could hope for little political role (under pre-Modern agrarianate conditions) save possibly the essentially negative intervention of street mobs on behalf of one or another ruling faction, the ʿulamâʾ scholars turned their interests ever more to questions of private life or perhaps of factional dogma.

Yet even so, this private life was seen largely from the viewpoint of public order: public order in worship, public order in the market place, or on the highway or the frontier. Those responsible for enforcing the law were to take cognizance only of what appeared in public—that is, to the scandal of the Muslims. Though minute prescriptions were worked out covering the most private acts, the qâḍî was given jurisdiction only over what was brought to his attention without prying (unless the rights of an innocent party were being infringed). The Sharîʿah was above all the norm of the Muslim community as a community.[11] However (as already in Marwânî times), this was a public order

[11] There have been some to see in the Sharʿî approach to law and community life—as in much else where Islam does not make the distinctions Europeans have made—a 'primitiveness' which they ascribe to its being developed among Bedouins (which, of course, it was not) or at least among 'unsophisticated' Arabs. But to be at once comprehensive and simple is not primitive; indeed, it is just the reverse. That kind of simplicity has histori-

in which individual rights, as we shall see, often took precedence over collective interests.

The first concern of the law was, of course, with acts of worship, the public ceremonies of the regular ṣalât and of the ḥajj pilgrimage, as well as of other special occasions. These were regulated down to the minutest detail. But there was no precise line between public ceremonies and individual, private ritual. In the public ceremonies the effect depended chiefly on punctilious participation by every individual, for there was no priest; the imâm served chiefly as model for the rest. The legists required the same precision on the part of individuals in all their ritual acts, whether they were being performed publicly in a group or privately with none observing. These acts of worship were the homage mankind paid to God and even in the most private detail formed, in a sense, part of a common universal obligation.

The ritual obligations of the individual were therefore minutely described on the basis of ḥadîth; the disputes among madhhab schools (often virulent and even violent enough) usually took the overt form of disputes about ritual details (based on contrasting ḥadîth reports) such as how a person should hold his hands in one or another stage of performing the ṣalât. In performing divine worship, however, almost as much weight was put on ceremonial purity as on precise propriety in execution. First, plain bodily cleanliness was required (and the manner of washing was described in detail) but, in addition, purely ritual ablutions were required after a variety of contacts not very tangibly polluting; some conditions invalidated the ṣalât altogether—thus a menstruating woman must not perform it. This concern with externals in the formal homage human beings paid to God, however, was not allowed to become formalism in the strictest sense, for God was held to judge by the intention, even in matters of ritual, rather than by the actual event. But one could not justify allowing a sloppy performance to slip by on the ground that one had intended better, if by taking pains one could have done better.

Such minute prescriptions were worked out, above all, for the five main ritual acts to which every Muslim was in principle obligated (sometimes called the 'five pillars of Islam'): the formal declaration that there is no divinity but God and Muḥammad is God's messenger (called the *shahâdah*), the ṣalât worship, the zakât (legal alms), the ḥajj pilgrimage to Mecca, and the fast in the

---

cally been very hard to attain. For law to be subsumed under ethics, in particular, is not necessarily the same as primitive undifferentiatedness, if all the main features of law do exist: distinction between what bears sanctions and what does not, specialist terminology and knowledge, written authorities, emphasis on predictability, and so forth. These were all present. But the spirit was directed toward trying to find a transcendent norm, rather than leaving a human decision as absolute precisely qua human decision. Hence for Shar'î law, precedent holds only so far as it is ethically correct; for Anglo-Saxon law, precedent holds qua precedent (for the sake of predictability). Nor is a law oriented to public life reducible to a 'primitive' identification of morality only with the expectations of a tribe. It may, rather, spring from a healthy respect at once for individual privacy and for the need to smooth the ways of public intercourse, such as cosmopolitan merchants are bound to appreciate.

month Ramaḍân. But there were also minute treatments, supported by ḥadîth reports, on such matters as the potency of this or that form of words as prayer, or what historical persons are to be cursed (as public enemies) or blessed (as divinely favoured) and in what form.

The Derivation of a Shar'î Legal Decision

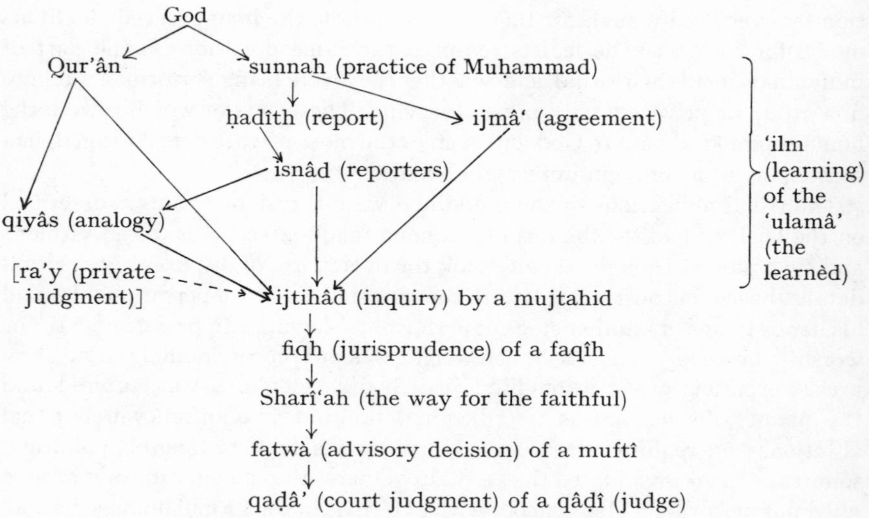

For instance: Muḥammad used a toothpick after meals (sunnah); there is a report to that effect (ḥadîth) transmitted through a chain of reporters (isnâd); the mujtahid studies this report (ijtihâd) and decides that the use is recommended not only for the Prophet but for the ordinary believer (fiqh); it is therefore to be included in the Sharî'ah, the established way of life; and a muftî may deliver a fatwà to an inquirer, telling him he should do it; but as it is merely recommended, the qâḍî will assess no penalty if he does not.

The law of the market place was almost equally a public concern with the law of the mosque; here especially, good public order was required. But again it was not so much collective interests as individual justice that was the chief concern of public order. In the law of contracts, the Sharî'ah insisted more on substance than on form. A contract was not binding unless it involved some sort of real equivalence in an exchange, for instance. On the whole it was expected that most human relations, outside of close friendship and family ties, would tend to take the form of contract relations rather than be determined in advance by status; yet many provisions attempted to guarantee those who were weak in one way or another against the strong taking great advantage of them. Perhaps rather naïvely, for instance, contracts that called for taking interest were banned: a position that was becoming stronger in the monotheistic traditions, and that the Muslim legists now tried to make absolute by interpreting a certain Qur'ânic word as covering any money payment for money.

It was more or less tacitly expected that contracts, deeds, and the like would be in writing, but the personal guarantee of an honourable man was required in any case as providing living assurance which sheer paper could not. Here, as in some other cases, the heritage of the Arab garrison towns can be seen: though the Qur'ân had encouraged the written contract, the public word of a tribesman was trusted more than a written word which might be that of a hired scribe and in any case could be verified only by the literate, who were likely to be the rich. The qâḍî, judge, of a town maintained lists of honourable citizens who could serve satisfactorily as witnesses; some of these were simply professional notaries, but it became an important honour to be included in the list.

The contract law was thus tied fairly closely to ideals of honour, generosity, and mutual aid among the faithful, at once congenial to the feeling of the Arab tribesmen and to the old populistic spirit of monotheism. For more 'businesslike' affairs, some of its explicit provisions were impractical. Certain useful types of ground rent were ruled out, for instance; and interest, banned in principle, has always been a major resource for investment. Already by the end of Marwânî times, legists like Abû-Ḥanîfah were working out ways of carrying out more 'businesslike' proceedings when appropriate, without setting aside the more idealistic provisions of the law as basic norms. One should, indeed, not make of a loan to someone in need the occasion of profiting from his distress; but if two businessmen were agreed, then it might be legitimate for the one who was to profit by the consequences of a present deal with the other to be bound to share his profit in a complementary future deal. The 'tricks' (*ḥiyal*) which the legists worked out to this end were at first, at least, a means of safeguarding the spirit of the law. In time, they amounted to a vast treasury of subterfuges whereby practices that could not practically be disallowed were given legal status; the most pious, naturally, came to frown on their use.

From a pre-Modern point of view, the Shar'î criminal law was so mild that most pre-Modern Muslim rulers felt bound to save their subjects from the results of applying it intact. It required quick procedure—'the law's delays' were anathema to the 'ulamâ'— and safeguarded the accused in ways that in the Agrarian Age, devoted to the use of torture and of *Schrecklichkeit*, seemed dangerously soft on criminals. Penalties ran to public humiliation, corporal beatings, and monetary compensations. Mutilation of various sorts was very commonly used in pre-Modern times and was countenanced in the Sharî'ah also in certain cases. Money fines, which bear far more heavily on the poor than the rich, were not common. A handful of penalties happened to be prescribed in the Qur'ân and were given a prescriptive status. Among these was cutting off the hand of a thief; but the legists limited this, as far as possible, as to amount and circumstances of the theft. A great many deviations from the ideal were, of course, not penalized on this earth at all.

Family law: pressure toward equality in personal status

Muḥammad had been especially concerned with family law and it retained a major place in the Sharîʿah. A proper regulation of each person's civil status was the very foundation of public order, and that status was not left to the free play of contract between individuals. Only a limited range of provisions in the marriage contract was allowed, for instance, or of inheritance or of other family relations. No one was free to arrange whatever relations suited him best: these relations were a concern of the community as a whole. In part, of course, the regulations were a means of protecting the weaker against the stronger; but in part they were an enforcement of common norms of public propriety.

In discussing family law, it is convenient to consider the rights of women, children, and other dependents as against the male head of the family, who by nature, if law makes no contrary provision, is in the most advantaged position (being not only, on the average, stronger than a woman but more independent, since he is free of pregnancy and the immediate care of children). Family law largely consists of restrictions upon his presumed freedom. In the context of the Nile-to-Oxus region as a whole, the Islamic family law, even when it perpetuated rules laid down by Muḥammad, naturally meant something rather different from what it had in Muḥammad's time.

The Islamic marital rules had encouraged individual responsibility in Medina by strengthening the nuclear family. Against the background of a formerly Christian and Mazdean population, where the nuclear family was already strong, the rules encouraged that egalitarianism and social mobility, especially among males, which Islam favoured in other ways also. Wealthy men, at least in ages of sharp social stratification, have commonly maintained more than one woman as sex partner; in the Christian Occident for instance, until fairly recently, it was common for men of quality to have one or more mistresses in addition to a wife. (Most men of ordinary means have naturally had to be content with a single mate in all societies, if only because of the biological sex ratio.)[12] Among the Christians and Mazdeans (as in most socie-

[12] In older writings, 'monogamy' and 'polygamy' were usually distinguished as the two contrasting normal forms of marriage—Christians practicing the one and most other peoples the other. (As 'monogamy' had prestige value, too often writers intending to justify various non-Christian social systems tried to show they were in fact monogamous, sometimes even by taking note that polygamy was practiced 'only by a minority'—overlooking the fact that this is no special merit, for it is usually guaranteed by the laws of nature.) This conventional dichotomy unfortunately obscures artificially many of the most important questions. Not only does it make too sharp a distinction between systems that differ much less in practice (given the custom of keeping mistresses); it cloaks the points of real difference. Thus the presence of a slave-based 'harem' system, even with only one wife, may be socially more decisive than the presence of two unsecluded wives.

ties), such wealthy men as maintained more than one woman had to accord special privileges to a primary mate and to her children. Among the Mazdeans, the secondary mates received some legal protection and their children might under some circumstances inherit. Among the Christians, the secondary mates had in principle no rights whatever and their children were stigmatized as mere bastards (though in practice such 'natural sons', in contrast to the offspring of casual unions, sometimes might maintain a high position, just as in the Medieval Occident the bar sinister sometimes inherited not only good breeding and wealth, but even lands and sometimes title). The effect of the Shar'î rules on marriage was to accord to up to four mates absolutely equal rights, which their children also shared in; the kept mistress or the free-born concubine disappeared, in effect, from among the ordinary privileged classes. Moreover, though the male was permitted to take his slave girls to bed (as normally happened wherever slavery itself was allowed), girls who became pregnant by him were granted privileges and their children, if recognized, had rights exactly equal to those of children of regular wives.

Among wealthy circles (and the fashion of the wealthy tends to become the norm of those lower on the social scale) the tendency of such a regulation was the exact opposite of that of the Christian exclusivism. Especially in Mediterranean Europe, where women tended to be secluded and domineered in both communities, the Christian marital pattern and the Muslim could look very much alike in the ordinary case; yet in special cases the two legal constructions had sufficiently different consequences to set, cumulatively, a different tone. The Christian system sanctified—and under favourable circumstances surely fostered—a solidarity of interest in a couple committed to a single marital union despite the temptations of wealth. The Muslim system sacrificed the primacy of conjugal unity in favour of equality of rights on the part of all concerned.

There being no privileged mistress of the household, privileges often associated with her were also missing; and among ordinary families, with a single wife, this fact was more important. Here the male prerogative, as the one who was required to support the household, was protected by the Sharî'ah, and the wife was protected primarily by her family. For a woman to divorce a man would mean to unsettle her husband's economic investment—and to exact financial support from her own kin. It was not only prejudice against women's mental capacities but sound agrarianate economics that insisted on one-sided divorce privileges. According to all madhhab schools, a husband could divorce a wife almost at will, if he did not fear retaliation from her family; but a wife who wished to leave her husband had to show good reason. The chief legal check upon the man in divorce was essentially financial and a matter of contract between equal parties: it became customary that, of the

---

And where there are secondary partners, their status may determine family patterns as decisively as that of the primary partner, who alone tends to be taken into account in discussing 'monogamy'.

mahr, bridal gift, which the man settled upon his wife, only a part was paid at the time of marriage; if he divorced her without special reason, he had to pay her the rest of the mahr, which might by contract be substantial; if she obtained a divorce from him, she forfeited what mahr he had paid. (In the Shâfi'î system, the wife might get a legal separation more easily than a divorce.)

But the equality of the wives among themselves (and inheritance by daughters and widows) carried with it an important financial independence for the women. Whereas in the closely tied Christian household what the woman had was the husband's, the Muslim woman's property could not legitimately be touched by her husband, who, however, had to support her from his own funds. This potential feminine independence had to be curbed primarily by keeping marriages, as far as possible, within the extended family—for instance, by the marriage of first cousins, so that family property would not leave the family through women marrying out.

A well-born woman thus had a personal status which might allow her to go into business on her own (as sometimes happened especially in widowhood), but she lacked the entrenched dignity of a materfamilias, with a marital and maternal status assured for life. At the same time, the mingling of all classes among the males, encouraged by Muslim disregard of inherited rank, threw all levels together on intimate terms; if men and women had mingled freely, this could have tended to eliminate any remaining aura of exclusive respect for well-born wives. If the wives might have been content to take the consequences of a free and relatively contractual position, the men were not willing to have it so. It early became a mark of a woman of quality that she was secluded from all men but her own—in private apartments at home, behind a veil if she walked abroad.

This had been a common custom on the higher levels, it would seem, in both the Byzantine and Iranian traditions; the egalitarianism of Islam paradoxically spread it throughout urban life. With all wives on a level, it became the practice for any woman with pretensions to high quality to take the veil; the upper classes were followed by the middle classes; in the end only poor women who had to labour in the open were left unsecluded in the towns (in the countryside and among the Bedouin, naturally, the custom was not carried very far). Thus arose a marked segregation within the society, with men (and singing girls) maintaining one social circle, in which primary political and social decisions were made, and respectable women maintaining a separate circle, very much secondary in the public life of society, but ruling each man's private home life. (The situation somewhat resembled that in classical Athens.) Under such conditions, the other marital practices of the upper classes became relatively generalized; while of necessity most men had but one wife at a time, divorce became relatively common even in lower-class circles, and sometimes even a poor man might have more than one wife at a time.

All these ramifications were not explicit in the Sharî'ah. The earlier-formed madhhab schools, notably the Ḥanafîs, tended to give the male an extensive prerogative (though short of that of the old Latin paterfamilias in many ways), which other madhhabs somewhat cut away. But all the madhhabs presupposed a considerable social role for women. The Qur'ânic injunctions to propriety were stretched, by way of ḥadîth, to cover the fashionable latter-day seclusion (and special precautions Muḥammad had been allowed to take for his own women were—perhaps somewhat impudently—adopted by ordinary Muslims who would not think of imitating his privilege as to the *number* of permitted wives). But even so, segregation was not made explicit: the veil was still presented simply in terms of personal modesty, the female apartments in terms of family privacy. Women were not required to share in the Muslim public rites, except the ḥajj (where the veil, as suggesting social distinction, was not permitted); but they were held for the daily ṣalât and they were acknowledged as transmitters of ḥadîth and as teachers. The debilitation of upper-class women which followed upon rigorous segregation was unforeseen.

Children were under ward of their parents or of a legally established guardian. Muḥammad had been especially concerned about orphans (having been one himself) and the Sharî'ah reflected this in attempts to avoid illegitimate wastage of the orphan's property by a guardian. Children could be married off very young, normally to mates expected to be of their parents' choice; some legists even allowed a girl to be married without her consent if still under age, but then allowed her to repudiate the marriage when she came of age. In any case, a girl could not be required (or allowed) to marry beneath her. But at maturity, sons, and to a much more limited degree daughters, gained legal independence of their parents as free Muslims, largely on their own. The father could not even threaten them very effectively with disinheritance. There was no primogeniture: one son was not privileged over another; indeed, though descendants necessarily inherited, they might receive only a fraction of the estate: under the influence both of the Qur'ân and of the tribal-minded Arab garrison towns, inheritance was obligatorily shared, sometimes even by cousins. In principle any large accumulations of family estates must therefore be broken up each generation.

Most wealthy households had other dependent members: slaves (that is, persons bound to labour at the will of their master, and the rights to whose labour could be bought and sold) and freedmen. The slave condition was inherited, unless a master acknowledged a slave woman's child as his, but Muslims were encouraged to manumit their slaves, and penance for numerous misdeeds included freeing slaves, at least those who had turned Muslim. Sources of new enslavement were limited. A Muslim could not legally be enslaved, nor a dhimmî non-Muslim living under Muslim rule. Since there was a constant tendency to free existing slaves, the supply of slaves came largely from beyond the Dâr al-Islâm, either by purchase or through capture in warlike expeditions. (Slaves came especially from northern Europe, where the export of slaves was a major trade, eastern Africa, and central Eurasia.) Slaves were to be given considerable rights by their masters, but as a master's abuse of his position entailed few penalties, a slave's life was in fact largely at his master's mercy. Correspondingly, a slave had fewer responsibilities; legal penalties for misdeeds were halved in his case. A slave might set himself up in a trade and purchase his freedom by contract, which the owner could not break once he had granted it. Freedmen had the same rights as the freeborn, though in practice they commonly remained associated with the former master even to the point of inheritance.

Limitations on collective authority

The overall effect of the Sharîʿah was to stress the rights of the individual as such. Equality was the basic principle, above all among free adult males. Corporate bodies, apart from the Muslim Ummah itself, had no standing, and an individual derived few Sharʿî rights from membership in any particular group. The insistence on individual interests over collective is illustrated in the rules about the public right-of-way. The Sharîʿah ruled that town streets should have a certain minimum width at least—and when towns were founded, streets were commonly much wider than that. But it also allowed the individual householder to build out upon the right-of-way so long as the passage rights of individual passers-by were not obstructed. This second right was given precedence over the first rule: that is, the balance between the rights of one individual and those of another was more carefully maintained than that between an individual's rights and the common interest, which was not immediately felt in any one case though it was cumulatively felt by all. In this way the law itself was in part responsible for the Islamicate towns having rapidly lost the free open circulation their founders usually intended for them and being broken up into tiny crooked passageways and culs-de-sac.

An individualistic egalitarianism can favour the strong and the bold over the modest and the honest. The Sharîʿah tempered its equality partly through special provisions to protect the weak, but perhaps still more fundamentally through a strong bias toward public propriety and uniformity. Its heritage of respect for the cultural homogeneity of Medina and then of the Marwânî Arabs now became a pressure for all Muslims to conform to a bourgeois pattern of life, a pattern necessarily adapted to the average man. Sharʿî Islam demanded no 'religious athletes' and discouraged any other special callings. The bold experimenter was required to show, at least externally, the face of mediocre propriety. The ʿulamâʾ declared Islam to be the religion of moderation, the natural way of life: every child was held to be born a Muslim till his parents corrupted him into another faith.

In this way, God's will was to be established, the members of the community were to be organized to carry it out, and the community's mission to bring justice to all was to be assured, yet a purely individual responsibility would be maintained throughout. Indeed, an imâm or caliph was still needed to fill a role Muḥammad had played at Medina in presiding over the application of God's will in detailed instances, in particular in assigning to each his task in the public sphere. Not, of course, that anyone might replace the responsibility of each individual before God; but someone must fulfill the particular social obligation, which only one at a time could fulfill, of exercising command in public matters. But such a figure became less practically crucial. He was required, on many occasions, more as an authoritative guarantor of the validity of the agreed-on 'ilm than as personally active intervener in disputes. Even where his personal interventions and his appointments made a difference, the Sharî'ah and the opinion of the Muslims in support of it could be expected to keep his appointees within bounds.

The Jamâ'î-Sunnîs now were willing to settle for whomever the bulk of the community, the jamâ'ah, found it politic to accept as ruler, hoping that the weakness of one man or another would be less harmful to the community as a whole than would the dissensions any other principle must occasion. The Shî'îs were theoretically less casual about the person of the imâm. Their imâm must be the authoritative possessor of 'ilm. Those called 'Zaydîs', indeed (rather like the Khârijîs), still held out for an imâm of the house of the Prophet who would be at once a master of 'ilm and a successful rebel-statesman. But most Shî'îs were willing to acknowledge an imâm whose actual position was solely a matter of his possession of authoritative 'ilm, whether he happened to hold political power currently or not; which meant acknowledging the power of the de facto caliph in practice, but not granting him even a moral authority as guarantor of the Sharî'ah.

It was a universal problem among the religious communities, to carry the demands of religion through in the whole of life. The peculiar Islamic formulation of this problem had called for a solution on the basis at once of a radical equality of the faithful and of an effective governance of the world's affairs. The principles we have just sketched present an attempted solution of the problem. But it must be borne in mind that the development of these principles was not purely in response to a highly sophisticated intellectual and spiritual challenge, though it clearly was this in part. In part it was a more general moral protest against the sophisticated ways of corrupt society, in part it was an expression of escapism and even of a primitive ignorance of the nuances of complex social processes. Such ambiguities are present in any major social endeavour. Yet what is most notable, surely, is the drastic and far-reaching attempt that was in fact made to remould society from its very first principles.

The Islamic Ummah under the 'Abbâsîs: the two orders of justice

As envisaged by the 'ulamâ' scholars, the Ummah, the community, was to be organized as a political body in terms quite as uncompromisingly religious as those of any other provisions in the Sharî'ah law. The 'Abbâsids professed to acknowledge the Sharîʻah as the rules of life which formed the basis for the Muslim community, the Muslim Ummah. Yet in the face of ʻAbbâsî arbitrary rule, the real hopes of the ʻulamâʼ could not be put in effect in the political order. But, though the Sharîʻah was never allowed to mould the whole social order, it was always given more than lip service. It is not only a theoretical triumph of the human mind, but has always had a significant practical role to play; and this role has often been reflected in turn in the theoretical structure itself.

What the ʻAbbâsids did concretely was to require that the qâḍî courts follow the Sharîʻah as it was being developed by the Piety-minded theorists, a move which they attempted to implement by persuading those theorists themselves to serve as qâḍîs. On the one hand, this forced the ideal Sharîʻah into practical forms so far as the qâḍîs' jurisdiction extended. At the same time, the move imposed limits on the qâḍî courts which stemmed from the Sharîʻah itself. It went far toward crystallizing the role of the Sharîʻah in Muslim society as ruling in practice only certain sectors of it, even while retaining its ultimate primacy in the whole.

The Sharîʻah, originating in the military courts of the garrison towns, had been military and had had more than a touch of aristocratic colouring: the dignity of the Arab tribesman was a major touchstone in it. This was especially true as to its formalistic procedure: everything was done to respect the personal dignity of the accused—which meant that conviction was difficult unless there were honourable eyewitnesses, for otherwise the defendant could clear himself by an oath, and the chief penalty was his shame. This suited an egalitarian army very well, though it might not suit the army's commanders. But it was never aristocratic in the agrarian sense—it was not suited to a landed gentry, among whom particularistic ancient precedent was at least as important as personal honour. On the contrary, apart from the army, it lent itself fairly readily to modification which adapted it to the mercantile classes: for merchants, also, who had always to defend their inviolability against both masses and aristocrats, personal dignity was a very serviceable principle. The rules of procedure were tacitly modified by the use of honourable witnesses as notaries in advance—and it was precisely in commercial questions that it was possible to provide for possible future disputes by way of notarization. As to any substantive rules that the dignity of a military fraternity had introduced into the Sharîʻah which might conflict with mercantile activities, these were almost from the beginning modified by ḥiyal rules, whereby the form of awkward prohibitions was observed while its substance was evaded. (These rules were adopted first in what became the Ḥanafî legal school and then in the Shâfiʻî school; they were not adopted in the third great legal school, the Mâlikî, but there their place was taken by the introduction of a series of new categories which produced the same effect and which were ultimately formalized by a rule of accepting judicial precedent, not so much needed in the other two schools.)

Acclimated thus to mercantile life, the Sharî'ah did preside over all the lesser institutions of the city. The market inspector and supervisor of public morals generally, called the *muḥtasib*, was the officer whom the small tradesman, the housewife, the craftsman looked to for daily regulation of city intercourse. He got his law from the qâḍî judge, and the more developed was the Sharî'ah, the more his activities reflected it (though in routine matters he was not bound to Shar'î procedure). His force was provided by the caliph or his governor, whose captain and his men (the *shurṭah* force) were to see that the muḥtasib's orders were complied with. Accordingly, the Sharî'ah became the basic mould in which the social order flowed at its lower urban levels, at least; the more this was true, the more difficult was it for the highest levels of the polity altogether to escape its influence.

But the more the qâḍî courts, in particular, became governed by the Sharî'ah in the strictest Piety-minded sense, the more their limitations forced the rise of other courts supplementing them. However suitable Shar'î procedure was for an independent-minded soldiery, it was hardly appropriate to the sort of army that an absolutist caliphate increasingly was turning to: a standing body of troops subject to transfer or dismissal and in general personally dependent on the caliph. More important yet, however much it suited the commerical activity of a mercantile class, it was less appropriate to other elements in urban life, and to other aspects thereof. For many purposes, the personal dignity which Sharî'ah procedure protected seemed less important than effective prosecution of defendants, which it often hampered. Supplementary courts not tied to Sharî'ah procedure (even if they attempted to adhere to Shar'î substantive standards) were called for, then, by the very nature of the Sharî'ah. But they were called for also by the nature of the caliphal absolutism.

For the spirit of the absolutism remained profoundly contrary to that of the Sharî'ah. By the side of the great monarch stood his executioner, to behead a man at a word from the caliph. Here was no question of muftî and qâḍî or of the sunnah of Muḥammad. If the will of God was involved at all it was, as the courtier might in awe repeat, because the caliph was the shadow of God on earth, as had been the Sâsânian monarch before him. The caliph must maintain justice, and against a great man sometimes only the most summary justice could prevail, lest the man use his resources and influence to raise a rebellion and perhaps force his own terms on the caliph.

But it was not only against the great who frequented the caliph's court that the direct caliphal justice prevailed. As essential part of a monarch's function, the caliph or his vizier was expected to hold regular sessions to redress the wrongs of whatever petitioners should appear: initially, wrongs committed by those in authority, in the course of their administration. The jurisdiction of such a court was, of course, readily extended. Hence alongside the regular qâḍî's court was held the ruler's own court for redress of wrongs, *maẓâlim*. In the courts of maẓâlim, the vizier or the judge who represented him could take any measures that seemed necessary in equity without regard to the rules of

Shar‘î judicial due process. The Sharî‘ah was indeed to be followed so far as possible in substance, but not if proved a hindrance. Thus obscure cases could be settled by the weight of probability; powerful defendants could not overawe by their respectable position; above all, the torture and the severe punishments that all post-Axial societies, at least outside China, thought indispensable for good order (at least on the level of the masses) could be applied at will. While commercial and family questions remained the province of the qâḍî, criminal accusations especially were brought to the courts more directly dependent on the caliph; and more than one sort of court was specialized off from the overall court of maẓâlim wrongs to handle such cases.

Hence the very legal order—at the heart of the Shar‘î realm—was divided into two sectors legitimized in mutually exclusive ways. On the local urban level, legal decisions were recognized as acceptable so far as they answered to the Shar‘î norms, expressing the populistic culture of the market. But on the level of overall territorial government, legal decisions, in their ultimate sanctions, rested on norms which answered rather to the aristocratic culture of the court and of an agrarian gentry; and though the city merchants might prefer to support the court in any possible struggle with an aristocracy, the culture of the court remained alien to them.

The legitimation of the caliphal state

A landed aristocracy in the mid-Arid Zone, however, now proved too weak to dominate the society of the vigorously mercantile cities. This fact is almost symbolically expressed in the remarkable feature of Islamicate history: that the third natural locus of high culture, the temple, which under the Sâsânians had supported the monarchy and had been closely related to the court culture and its agrarian background, had been captured by the culture of the market. The mosque was dominated by the Sharî‘ah-minded. This meant that the local, Shar‘î legal sector—and all aspects of culture associated with it—alone was fully legitimized on a basis that the whole society could honour. The courtly culture remained essentially illegitimate.

In the immediate situation, such a want of legitimation made little difference, perhaps. In fact, each cultural tradition carried its own commitment on the part of the groups dedicated to applying it. The general expectation in a given group has its way in all those routine cases where personal interest pulls as readily in one direction as another; and such cases establish the patterns of society. Yet these cultural traditions and their dialogues were not ultimately separable one from the other. Whenever a crisis occurred in the courtly order, and new ideas were needed to maintain the absolutism under the particular current conditions, the very right of the absolutism to exist was put in question by the presence of the more highly sanctioned alternative tradition of norms.

In the end, though there was some continuity in the absolutist legal tradition, it was only as it approximated to and could be justified by Shar'î norms that this continuity could be depended on. The Sharî'ah enforced itself by the respect that even its violators perforce paid it; the violations never abrogated the principle, which stood ready to come back in force at the next proper legal decision. No other legal system could rise above the level of an ad hoc equity which each individual could apply and develop at discretion, and which accordingly had little binding force in the public expectation. If the very court of laws in which the vizier passed judgment was not fully legitimate, then if the next vizier disregarded the precedents of the last, he was in any case no worse than any other vizier. On this basis, the culture of the court required a legitimation in Shar'î terms if it was to endure past the crises that would shatter any ad hoc arrangement.

The 'ulamâ' gradually made a theoretical place for the court. But it was grudging and tardy, and did not really afford the court true legitimation in its actuality—in the spirit it necessarily had to express to fulfill the demands of the absolutist ideal. Even at that, the theory received full elaboration only after the caliphal state had in practice collapsed.

After the disappointment the Piety-minded opposition suffered in the 'Abbâsid triumph, neither Shî'î nor Sunnî 'ulamâ' scholars were inclined to allow much of a role to the ruling caliph. Even though they recognized his position, the Sunnîs remained as autonomous as the Shî'îs; so far as possible, they vested legal authority in all the possessors of knowledge, 'ilm, literally the *'ulamâ'*; who were in turn distinguished as more or less sound by the autonomous working of a process of mutual recognition within any present generation analogous to the process governing isnâd-criticism as to the past. The 'ulamâ' were the true 'heirs of the Prophet' and law was to be established by fatwà issued by a private learnèd man, rather than by the decree of the caliph or his agents. But it was only legal judgment that was, as far as possible, to be retained in the hands of this 'clerical class'; administration had to be provided for by a 'political class' even at best. Eventually, the Sharî'ah law came to recognize this. The clerical class led the prayer in the mosque, decided cases of law in the market, and declared the Muslim's duty on the frontier; the political class—the police, the tax-collectors, and all the various kâtibs, secretaries—saw to keeping the mosque in good condition, preserved order in the market, and commanded the defence of the frontier. It was here that the caliph was to have his role.

(It is important to note that this division of labour, as it was eventually conceived in the Sharî'ah, is not a distinction between religious and secular fields of action. In practice, however, the 'clerical class' certainly represented an Islamic 'religious institution' which was much less total in its operations than the Sharî'ah theoretically might require, and which answered in large measure to specifically religious institutions in other societies.)

As we have noted, the political class, to operate, stood in need of individual men of authority—the caliphs; hence the Jamâ'î-Sunnî forms of the Sharî'ah, which were applied in practice, finally gave to the caliph a considerable administrative role. But in limiting this assignment sharply to administration, the 'ulamâ' were denying to the caliph—and to any to whom he might delegate his authority—any truly political role: that is, the independent decision of ultimate policy which had characterized alike Muḥammad and the early caliphs, and which had launched Islam as a power in the world. If the Islamic vision was to be preserved, it must be at the expense of its dynamic political motor force.

For such an unpolitical role, Jamâ'î-Sunnîs came to agree that any of several processes could theoretically serve for the caliph's selection, provided the community at large acquiesced; and that he need not be the wisest or the most pious but must simply be sufficiently qualified to carry out an administrative task: be possessed of his faculties, have sound and effective judgment—and come from the generally honoured stock of the Meccan Quraysh. Such minimal criteria were enough to legitimize the way in which the caliph was chosen in practice—by designation of the predecessor, within the caliphal family. But one primary ideal requirement was still insisted on. That there should be only one man in supreme authority within the Dâr al-Islâm, the territory within which Muslims ruled and where the Sharî'ah was the law of the land, was yet maintained, for the sake of unity and peace among Muslims. Hence as provinces fell away from practical control by the caliph at Baghdad in later 'Abbâsî times, they were constrained by Jamâ'î-Sunnî feeling to acknowledge at least the caliph's theoretical authority. Finally, recognition for the caliph came to be a central point in the Sunnî Shar'î demands in the face of increasing political fragmentation of the Ummah community.

Intellectual patterns associated with Shar'î Islam: the study of history

The Sharî'ah in itself, of course, was far from sufficient to define a whole Islamic culture. Both the Shî'î and the Jamâ'î-Sunnî 'ulamâ' carried their concern beyond the law and even the ethics embodied in it to wider reaches of intellectual life. They built especially on the kind of studies that had interested the Piety-minded in Marwânî times—exact and elegant recitation of the Qur'ân, elaboration of Arabic grammar and lexicography, and history not only of the Prophet but of his community. To these they added the newer disciplines that had arisen in connection with the fiqh jurisprudence itself, such as the 'ilm al-rijâl. All these studies combined to develop a general sense of life and of what mattered most in it which, since it centred in the Sharî'ah, I call 'Sharî'ah-mindedness'.

Islamicists have often applied the term 'Orthodoxy' to that kind of Islam—whether Sunnî or Shî'î—which accepts the Sharî'ah, the all-embracing sacred ritual law, as fundamental to the religious life. Such a term cannot be applied in this sense (if in any at all) to the earliest Muslims, for whom the Sharî'ah in its developed form did not yet exist; but after the processes we have been describing, in which the Sharî'ah was perfected and exalted, the notion has a certain relevance. But because the word 'orthodoxy' can be and has been seriously misleading when applied to the particular approach to Islam here indicated, I prefer to use explicitly a phrase referring to the Sharî'ah and to its central role in the outlook. Then I can reserve the term 'orthodox' for any case where a given position may be regarded as established, either officially or socially—and such a usage will by no means always coincide with 'Sharî'ah-mindedness'.

Yet the common use of 'orthodoxy' for what I call 'Sharî'ah-mindedness'—provided one recalls always that it can have either a Sunnî or Shî'î (or a Khârijî) form—does point to a central role Sharî'ah-mindedness has won for itself among Muslims.[13] There came to be, indeed, many groups of Muslims who in one way or another depreciated the Sharî'ah in its literal sense; but always the majority feeling placed these outside—possibly sometimes above—the accepted Islamic norms. The supremacy, or at least the crucial importance, of the Sharî'ah has been accepted not only in most Islamic currents, but even by most sorts of opinion within each current—whether mystic or literalist. This has been true even when respect for the Sharî'ah, while present in a group, has not been the only or even the most important element in their religious life. Indeed, even those who rejected its literal application for themselves have usually regarded it as binding on most other Muslims. Hence the Shar'î system has been something of a constant throughout subsequent Muslim history.

The practical social order of the Muslim Ummah community was central to the Sharî'ah-minded conception of life. But the intellectual labour required to elucidate this social order and to guarantee its spiritual validity was granted its due: for instance, the historical scholarship presupposed in the isnâd-criticism by which the acceptability of ḥadîth was assured, and the analytical reasoning necessary in developing a body of ḥadîth-based law. And just as the legal and social side of the system was held together in a common spirit, so was its distinctive thinking. In all the fields of intellectual endeavour cultivated by the Sharî'ah-minded, a set of intellectual patterns arose which shared many techniques in common but also, more significantly, bore the impress of a common spirit: a spirit populistic and factualistic, with a persistent sense of the moral importance of historical events.

We can see this spirit especially in the realm of historical inquiry; for here

13 The adjective from 'Sharî'ah' is 'Shar'î'. This refers to the Sharî'ah law itself, whereas my term Sharî'ah-minded' refers to a whole complex of attitudes characterizing those Muslims for whom the Sharî'ah has had an unrivalled primacy in religion and in life. (The use of the term 'Orthodoxy' has serious disadvantages. For one thing, it is often identified with Jamâ'î-Sunnism, or with a certain sort of theology—whereas for a long time most of the Sharî'ah-minded rejected all logically formulated theology at all. Still worse, the uncautious reader—and too many scholars—can get trapped into an identification of other forms of Islam not only as 'unorthodox' but as somehow more or less 'un-Islamic'—an attitude we have no right to import into the materials.)

the technique of historical reconstruction by ḥadîth report and supporting isnâd was quite at home. The same method of criticism of authorities as used for law or dogma could be used in general history—in a form much less intense than for legal purposes of course. The chain of reporters might be wholly oral or one link might be formed by a written text; but the isnâd treated both cases alike, for what mattered was the personal continuity of witness that guaranteed, from teacher to pupil, even a written text.

The subject matter of history was also often determined by the Sharîʻah-minded world outlook. For such men an understanding of history was necessary if only because the divine revelation had itself been historical—through prophets sent to given peoples at given times—and the Islamic community, in which the godly life was to be lived, was a historical community. The historical inquiry of the ʻulamâʼ had begun with two indispensable themes: the life of Muḥammad, the all-important model; and the evaluation of the transmitters of reports about him, which had come to replace the original direct homogeneity of the Medina community. Their interests soon widened. But when in ʻAbbâsî times a great Jamâʻî-Sunnî legist, such as Ibn-Jarîr al-Ṭabarî (d. 923), wrote a universal history, he was still concerned with tracing the success and failure of the various communities that had been summoned to follow God's will, and particularly the triumphs and backslidings of the Muslim community. Moreover, he was, as befitted a Sharʻî scholar, concerned above all with the responsible behaviour of individuals, not with the working of institutions as such or even, primarily, with the splendour of kings. He produced a record of the personal decisions of Muslim souls in the series of choices which had faced the Muslim community.

From Ṭabaristân, the south coastland of the Caspian Sea, Ṭabarî came to Baghdad just too late to study with the man he most hoped to see, Ibn-Ḥanbal (founder of the populistic madhhab school of fiqh law). He then travelled widely in the Fertile Crescent and elsewhere seeking religious ʻilm knowledge before returning to Baghdad to teach as a scholar. His primary interest lay in building a more perfect system of fiqh; in the course of this, he created the most substantial of all Qur'ân commentaries, in which he collected the chief interpretations of every discussable verse, and gave his own point of view so soberly that it came to be very widely accepted. His history was part of the same overall effort.

Far from embodying sophisticated historical principles, Ṭabarî's historical method can seem, at first sight, to rule out any interpretive intent at all—to consist merely in the driest chronicling of data. Ṭabarî rarely speaks in his own voice, except in jejune frame or transition passages. What he has to say is told purely by judicious selection, arrangement, and documentation of verbatim reports which he has received.

As compared with a historian who modifies the wording of the reports he receives to fit his selection and arrangement of the facts, and who adds his own deductions and comments, the verbatim method suffers severe limitations. Stylistically, the resultant picture tends to seem a bit confused, especially to the reader who does not already know (as Ṭabarî's audience would) the main outlines. The same detail may be often repeated, as it recurs in this or that separate report. In Ṭabarî's description of the death of 'Uthmân, for instance, numerous reports (primarily telling of some detail early in the story) go on summarily to report the death itself in such a way that the report would lose vividness and sometimes point if the portion about the death were excised; hence 'Uthmân dies in the narrative many times before the actual death is recounted in detail. On a more fundamental plane, Ṭabarî cannot make his own conclusions explicit; he is like the detective who would give in immaculate detail every piece of evidence which he has found relevant to his own private conclusions about a case, but in the end would fail to set forth his reconstruction of it, leaving you to draw your own conclusions from the evidence he has set in order before you. Unless you have something of the mind of a detective yourself, you are likely to miss the point.

For a conscientious writer, the verbatim method has its advantages too. With strict documentation of each report by its isnâd, it allows an accuracy of detail which a conscientious modern historian must envy on occasion. Moreover, if the evidence is misleading, at least the historian has provided the reader with every opportunity he himself had to evaluate it; while if the evidence is sound, it comes honourably by way of the integral human witness, demanded also in the Shar'î law courts. An incidental advantage, in the case of Ṭabarî's material, is the preservation of the vivacity of style which seems to have been cultivated in such reports and which a judicious legal mind such as Ṭabarî's would probably not have been able to duplicate on its own: despite its ponderous length and detail, Ṭabarî's story does not become boring, for almost every report is humanly vivid.

But perhaps a decisive advantage of the verbatim method for Ṭabarî is that it allows a writer to avoid committing himself too publicly on any given issue; indeed, to suggest two contradictory conclusions at once to two different sorts of people. Most readers (even when a work is quite explicit) see in what they read only what they have expected to see, or at least what does not depart far from the categories they are used to thinking in; if bare evidence is presented them, most readers will readily deduce whatever fits most readily into the patterns they are already familiar with. If they are not prepared to face certain problems, the writer is not forcing them to do so; but if they are prepared, the writer gives them the leads they require; thus every reader is satisfied at his own level. It was important for Ṭabarî to try to please a wide audience. Teaching his own system of fiqh in Baghdad, he was fully in the public eye. His viewpoints were sufficiently free that the zealously ḥadîth-minded faction then dominant in the city distrusted his loyalty to what they regarded as proper Sunnî doctrine, and at one time he barely missed lynching. Ṭabarî turned the method of ḥadîth reports to masterly account on occasion.

Ṭabarî on the death of 'Uthmân: the great divide for the Sharî'ah-minded

The events at the death of 'Uthmân present a singularly revealing problem for the pious Jamâ'î-Sunnî historian, even as they present a prima facie vindication for the Shî'îs. The Muslim community as an ongoing Ummah experienced then its first flagrant breach of unity. Not only was unity broken in a political sense, which might allow the event to be handled as a repetition of the Riddah wars. Unity was broken within the Medina community, with close associates of the Prophet lined up against one another and the Prophet's successor murdered as the outcome. The foundations of the Muslim Ummah were called in question. Historically, all later breaches derived from this one. For the Sunnîs, it was a test case: if the whole body of the associates of Muḥammad was to be relied on as transmitters of ḥadîth reports and, more generally, as exemplars of the Ummah at its historical best; and if the Ummah was indeed to be regarded as specially blessed by God (as implied at the least in the doctrine of ijmâ' consensus), how is such a calamity to be interpreted? It was indeed the first fitnah, the first trial or temptation, not only for the original participants, but above all for the later historians, who so named it.

Ṭabarî's presentation of the death of 'Uthmân confronts the dilemma squarely, in its own way. But this becomes clear only if one understands the genre form within which he wrote, and examines what he did with it there. One must attend closely to his sequences. Ṭabarî tells at length of the events that led many Arabs to be discontented with 'Uthmân. Then he announces that he will recount the first public insults hurled at 'Uthmân, and what led up to his killing. He begins, however, with what seems like a redundant reminder of the causes of people's discontent with 'Uthmân's weakness: 'Uthmân gives some camels, sent in as zakât, to certain members of his own Umayyad family; on hearing this, 'Abd-al-Raḥmân b. 'Awf, a leading associate of Muḥammad, has them brought back and distributed among the ordinary people—and 'Uthmân stays at home doing nothing. But then Ṭabarî does go on to describe, as he said he would, the first public insults.

From this point, he builds up the crisis. Through a patchwork of anecdotes, he tells how a delegation came to Medina from the mutinying Egyptians, how 'Uthmân used conciliatory words with them, and how they found themselves being dealt with treacherously (presumably by Marwân, who was 'Uthmân's chief aide); then how they returned and demanded 'Uthmân's abdication, how the leading figures in Medina gave 'Uthmân little support (or found their efforts at urging peaceful acquiescence to the Egyptians' claims frustrated), how the Egyptians besieged 'Uthmân in his house, how 'Uthmân sent for military support from the provinces, how when this became known the Egyptians broke down the door by violence and burst in murderously upon 'Uthmân.

To this point, the tissue of reports from various sources has been essentially consistent, very vivid, and quite credible as a human document making the actions of all those concerned intelligible. But before actually going into details upon the act of killing, at this dramatic point Ṭabarî interrupts his patchwork narrative with a new account which starts over almost from the beginning, all derived from one reporter, Sayf b. 'Umar. Sayf's account presents the mutineers as rabble, inspired by a converted Jew with weirdly heretical ideas, animated by base personal feelings; whereas it presents all the leading associates of Muḥammad at Medina as actively supporting 'Uthmân ('Alî, for instance, orders his sons to stand guard at 'Uthmân's house)—even Muḥammad b. Abû-Bakr, son of the first caliph and rabid opponent of 'Uthmân, is made to repent of his opposition (in direct contradiction of a report given earlier, in which on the same occasion he is merely relatively moderate). This account explains the absence of effective resistance by any save 'Uthmân's special family and partisans by saying that to avoid fighting among Muslims, 'Uthmân piously sent his other defenders away; and it presents the actual killing as full of gross impiety. In contrast to the vividness of what has preceded, Sayf's account is not only incredible in the various motivations it implies, but is even relatively schematic in some of the detail of its narrative.

When this account is completed, Ṭabarî resumes his patchwork of less well concerted reports from the point where it had left off, telling of the actual killing. He concludes by pairing, in retrospect (and hence out of time sequence), two well-turned speeches: one is by 'Uthmân defending himself against accusations of major crime, reasserting his right to rule, and warning that if he is killed the community will never again be graced with a genuine united allegiance; the other speech is by the mutineers, arguing lucidly that whether 'Uthmân is personally guilty or merely too weak to control his aides, for justice' sake he must either resign or be deposed, i.e., killed. Between them the two speeches present a clear dilemma—the dilemma of how political power can at once be held within the limits of justice and yet retain sufficient supremacy and independence to be genuine power.

This whole section can be read in at least two ways. A loyal, but somewhat naïve, Jamâ'î-Sunnî will accept the central and most obviously coherent account, that of Sayf, for it solves the historical dilemma for him very nicely: all of Muḥammad's associates were really at one with 'Uthmân; it was a combination of 'Uthmân's excessive piety with the confusion caused by alien troublemakers that did all the damage—and the breach in the community was all a mistake, in which none of the guarantors of the ḥadîth of the jamâ'ah was really at fault. Such a Sunnî can dismiss the other accounts as alternative reports which cancel themselves out by their very confusedness. The section was often so read.

In contrast, a subtler reader will know that Sayf had a bad reputation as a ḥadîth reporter and will look elsewhere. He may not fully trust al-Wâqidî, whose narrative he will find to be the core of the chief alternative interpretation; indeed, in this very passage Ṭabarî puts him on guard against al-Wâqidî's detail: after a romantic incident which al-Wâqidî gives, Ṭabarî interrupts to give from elsewhere a shorter version of the same incident, which omits the central detail of al-Wâqidî's version, a detail which if genuine no eyewitness could have omitted; thus providing effective commentary on al-Wâqidî's credibility without a word of comment. Yet the subtler reader will find al-Wâqidî's version thrust at him by Ṭabarî's arrangement. While the woodenness of Sayf's version—and hence of the conventional Sunnî interpretation of 'Uthmân—is made to stand out by the very position it takes, interrupting the flow of the passage at its most dramatic moment, al-Wâqidî's version is highlighted by its arrangement; for to it belong the anecdote at the beginning and the two speeches at the end, both of which occur out of sequence, and which together offer food for thought.

The dilemma of how to have power at once practically effective and morally responsible, presented in the last pair of speeches, is also developed in some detail in al-Wâqidî's anecdotal material, but the speeches bring out especially one point: that 'Uthmân and his opponents disagree on what is the *law* in his case, and both appeal to the Qur'ân indecisively. Neither speech, on the other hand, recognizes an alternative to either accepting the injustice that results from 'Uthmân's inadequacy, or deposing 'Uthmân and disuniting the community. Yet just such an alternative in the dilemma was acted out by 'Abd-al-Raḥmân in that first anecdote—the anecdote which attracts attention by its failure to recount what Ṭabarî says he is about to recount; for, by taking personal initiative, 'Abd-al-Raḥmân caused justice to be done in the case of the camels without questioning 'Uthmân's position as caliph.

The initial anecdote and the final passage are complementary. In the initial anecdote, we find foreshadowed the sophisticated Jamâ'î-Sunnî response to the dilemma: the principle that every Muslim has the duty of 'commanding the good and forbidding the evil', so far as he can do so effectively, if no one else is fulfilling the duty—so that, in principle, the community should not be entirely dependent on the caliph for justice. Then in the paired speeches we are reminded of what has to be done before such a principle can be socially effective in practice—for obviously Ṭabarî is not inviting every Muslim to behave with the freedom of 'Abd-al-Raḥmân. The law must be worked out so that everyone will know what it is: what will make up for the inadequacies of the caliphs will be the independently developed Sharî'ah, upheld by a responsible Muslim population.

Ṭabarî does not even pretend to give here an exact reconstruction of events. All his main sources had weaknesses of which he was himself aware, and perhaps he could not hope to sort out the actuality in detail. Yet at Ṭabarî's hands the death of 'Uthmân, supreme occasion for fitnah, trial, in the Muslim community, becomes a perfect occasion for showing the naïveté of a conventional response and suggesting, instead, what the true Shar'î response must be.[14]

[14] Many scholars have underestimated Ṭabarî's own work, looking on him only as a remarkably useful source of earlier material. His history has been accused of being ill arranged as compared with his commentary on the Qur'ân, and he has been blamed for

The historical work of Ṭabarî is not, indeed, typical; it is the work of a master. What it demonstrates is the sort of intellectual subtlety that the Sharî'ah-minded methods made possible at their best. Other historians—whether as annalists or as collectors of biographies—used the same technical forms, but their isnâds were more simply documentary, their selection reflected more frankly their generally more partisan and less sophisticated viewpoints. Even among them, however, the technique of isnâd documentation as well as the overall sense of proportion in judging what was important to the Ummah of Muḥammad assured a notable sobriety, factuality, and dignity to the historical work of this school.[15]

The same attitudes prevailed in the study of grammar and literary criticism. These formed, in effect, a single activity, the purpose of which was to maintain high and pure standards in the use of the Arabic language, which was the language of Qur'ân and ḥadîth. The discipline originated among circles whose concern was the precise understanding of old Arabic words found in ḥadîth and not readily understood by later generations. As in the development of the Sharî'ah law proper, it was hoped to avoid bid'ah, innovation, and to preserve a pristine simplicity and homogeneity of attitude. However, the peculiar importance assumed by this branch of studies resulted from other currents in the society—from ways of life associated with the 'Abbâsî court rather than with the pious 'ulamâ'.

More tenuously, the Sharî'ah-minded attitudes penetrated even to the realm of abstract thought—of theology and philosophic analysis generally.

---

popularizing Sayf's legends, notably in his account of the conquests—where Sayf thoroughly confused the chronology. As prime source for subsequent chroniclers, Ṭabarî played a role somewhat comparable, in setting attitudes to early events, to the role of al-Shâfi'î in law. Like al-Shâfi'î's, Ṭabarî's work achieved ideological clarity at the expense of historical openness. Yet Ṭabarî's voluminous narrative, though often not comprehensive, is always illuminating, never dry. Surely it was not for nothing that he pointed out to his students that he was selecting only one-tenth of the reports he could have included (the common notion that he actually wrote a longer version of which this history is but an abridgement is not supported by the original wording). A word to the wise should have been sufficient to put them on their guard. It is no accident that it is only since the discovery of Ṭabarî's work (as Gibb pointed out) that modern historians have begun to be able to reconstruct the periods he dealt with. Ṭabarî meant it that way.

[15] The study of Islamicate historical writing has only begun. Bertold Spuler has shown, in 'Islamische und abendländische Geschichtsschreibung', *Saeculum*, 6 (1955), 125–37, that pre-Modern Muslims did not have so potentially universal an outlook as Modern Westerners, and has listed much bibliography; but his article is marred by several false stereotypes and oversights. Franz Rosenthal has written *A History of Muslim Historiography* (Leiden, 1952), chiefly focusing on a few Arab chroniclers, especially of Mamlûk times; it is philosophically obtuse, and not very illuminating; see also his study 'Die arabische Autobiographie', *Analecta Orientalia*, 14 (Rome, 1937), 1–40. D. S. Margoliouth, *Lectures on Arabic Historians* (Calcutta, 1902), is a more interesting but still superficial review. Most useful, though still slight, is H. A. R. Gibb on 'Ta'rîkh' in the *Encyclopaedia of Islam* supplementary volume, reprinted in *Studies on the Civilization of Islam* (Boston, 1962). History of dogma has been studied by Helmuth Ritter and others, but chiefly only from the viewpoint of the interrelation of sources, a task Claude Cahen, in *La Syrie du Nord* (Paris, 1940), has undertaken for certain chroniclers of the Middle Periods.

(We will devote special attention to this later.) Here the concern of the Shar'î 'ulamâ' scholars was to defend—with appropriate means—the doctrinal positions the holding of which had been established as legally correct in the fiqh. Here several mutually hostile factions were engaged, from their differing points of view. It could, indeed, be legally shown, by the example of Muḥammad, that God approved the holding of certain opinions, and for many of the pious this in itself was sufficient. Nevertheless, a great many of the 'ulamâ' felt it incumbent on them to show that the positions sanctioned by the Qur'ân and by ḥadîth reports were reasonable; the effort to do this led them into the whole world of abstract thought.

Finally, the Sharî'ah-minded attitudes had a reflexive effect in the very field from which they had received a major component of their original impulse: in personal devotion and piety. Muslims' sense of cosmic self-orientation and their ways of responding to divine challenge were deeply coloured by the Shar'î spirit, however much they varied otherwise.

IV

Muslim Personal Piety: Confrontations with History and with Selfhood, c. 750–945

In the courtly society, the surface of life was brilliant and decorative. We have seen how it fostered the ideal of adab, of polished personal refinement. A cultivated discipline of the externals of living—grandly proportioning the buildings one lived in, using delicate colour and form in one's utensils and in one's clothing, above all skilfully refining the words one used and the ideas one presented—all this could establish a pattern in the daily round which at best could glow with true beauty. The magnificent court sifted out the loveliest from the offerings of a world of competitors, and in the protection of that court's might, and in the prosperity it fostered, such a culture proliferated. Throughout the empire, whoever could afford such things was inclined to follow the lead of the court. But set over against this tasteful surface was the deeper and more tumultuous realm of spiritual responsiveness, expressed in personal piety. For within almost every man or woman, even among the privileged, was a rebellious spirit inclined to smash all this elegance in the name of ultimate reality.

The glitter of the court and its refinement were founded at last upon pride and greed, upon torture and murder, upon innumerable falsehoods of word and deed. Nor could any privileged circles in Islamdom fully escape a like indictment. There were those who longed to break through the everyday round of life, however beautiful, to confront the realities of the universe in the deepest realities of their own beings, to confront its awesomeness with their own immensity of hope, and find a radical commitment which should claim the stakes of life and death. Some individuals devoted their whole lives to such an effort; many others, happy to cultivate the surface as best they could, nonetheless supported the more committed ones sufficiently to make them a force in the world. Thus personal spiritual concern became one of the most active forces in the high culture of the Muslim cities.

The splendour and power of the Muslim state could seem to be the splendour and power of Islam, and all that a loyal Muslim could reasonably hope to see in this world; but it was perhaps especially Muslims, aroused by the fresh Islamic challenge, that felt the thrust of cosmic discontent. Yet they were not willing to go back to the old parochial systems of piety, nor even to Manicheanism; for it was just in Islam that they found the greatest impulse to their seeking. Amidst the wealth and in the varieties of opportunity provided by the great monarchy, these seekers of cosmic commitment also, like the seekers of learning or of beauty, found wide scope for inventive initiative. The great venture of Muḥammad and of the early Muslims still had implications that had not been worked out, a constant stimulus to those for whom the Qur'ân had become a sacred text. Its latent challenges roused many to try to win through to their aims.

We are speaking here not of religion generally but of personal piety—that is, a person's spiritual devotion: his manner of response to the divine, to what he finds to transcend the order of nature, to a felt cosmic dimension of life giving it ultimate meaningfulness. 'Religion', as we have noted, includes all the diverse ramifications of those traditions that are focused on such responses. Religious communities commonly possess not only ultimate responses but organizations, members of which may have very little spiritual piety even when they are very loyal to the organization; or they may possess art forms, or roles in the social structure, or cosmological doctrines. These may reflect the orientation of the personal piety, but they also reflect other social and intellectual traditions. Nor can piety be reduced to ethics, though it may issue in special standards of behaviour toward one's fellows. Piety cannot even be identified with zealous acceptance of myth and ritual, which may occur without real spiritual feeling, and at best may be only partial or occasional expressions of it.

Personal piety is in some ways but a small part of religion. Yet it is the core of it. For it is in personal devotion (whether by way of the usual rituals, or otherwise) that the cosmic dimension is entered upon which makes religion religious; and hence that the whole structure of a religious community ultimately justifies itself. Accordingly, what we call personal piety or devotion plays a key role in civilization as a whole, at least wherever religious traditions are of major importance. Changes in culture generally and changes in moods and styles of piety are closely interdependent. Styles of piety are even more elusive to study than styles of art, but may be a good deal more important.

In some individuals, personal piety is a quiet background to ordinary cares and pleasures; in others it can be an existential experience and a driving force. In either case, it has consequences of its own, to be distinguished from the social consequences of allegiance to a particular religious community. Similar devotional attitudes may arise within two different religious traditions, or the like may occur independently of any particular religious tradition. By the time of al-Rashîd and al-Ma'mûn there had arisen within the Islamic tradition several sharply contrasting styles of personal piety and devotion. No one of these styles of piety can be identified simply with 'Islam', though the adherents of each claimed it presented the only true Islam.

The various forms of devotional response of the time, especially within the Muslim community, jostled and enriched each other. As they interacted with various social interests and pressures of other sorts, they gave decisive twists to the fate of the great monarchy and of the proud social and intellectual life which it fostered. But the various forms of piety that arose at that time require especially close attention because they entered pervasively into the whole fabric of Muslim life from that time on; elements of them often persisted long after the particular tradition that developed them had been eclipsed or dissipated.

The relation of style of piety to religious allegiance

Devotional response is inevitably a highly personal thing. As in the case of aesthetic appreciation, every individual has his own bent. The piety of some types of personality runs to luxuriant expression of a sense of divine grandeur; in others, a daily walking in the divine Light issues chiefly in a gentleness of touch in personal relations. Whatever the religious allegiance, all the various types of devotional expression tend to reappear in those personalities to whom they are congenial. Devotional response, if it be genuine, varies infinitely as persons do.

Nevertheless, the forms of devotional response do vary also from religious tradition to religious tradition and from culture to culture and even from class to class. It is not simply ritual and creed that vary, but the style of personal devotion itself. A parallel is to be found in the case of art. Despite all personal differences, the art of the Italian Renaissance, for instance, shows a distinct style. No doubt the personal bent of many artists was hampered by the standards of expectation then fashionable, and their potential genius was left undeveloped. At the same time, a considerable range of temperament was expressed even within the broad lines given by the style. So also in piety and devotion. Presumably, some spirits are relatively cramped in one tradition or one period, and relatively encouraged to express themselves fully in another, even though within each style of piety the range of personal variation is considerable. Islam, for instance, like Protestantism, has discouraged the celibate monastic life. In both traditions, individuals who as Catholics or Buddhists would surely have become monks have found other forms for expressing their devotion; but these forms are likely to be relatively unsatisfying to them and in any case strongly coloured by the prevailing anti-monastic piety.

Not only overall religious traditions, but the various subtraditions within them have developed distinctive styles of piety, within which personal differences must find expression. These styles remain within the broad lines set by the tradition as a whole, yet may vary drastically among themselves even so. Thus Christian piety has always been founded upon and coloured by the experience of personal redemption. But this has taken very different forms in the Catholic rite of the mass on the one hand and in evangelical Protestantism on the other; and within Protestantism, the rigorous and intellectual preaching of sixteenth-century Puritans was very different from the later 'enthusiasm' of the American frontier revival movements. The same sorts of diversity within certain broad lines have occurred in Islam.

Not only different social levels and different historical circumstances may occasion such different styles; the play of dialogue in a tradition will ensure that different temperaments receive expression even within a single milieu. Generally a given cultural tradition, and more especially a religious tradition, tends to be first established among people of a more or less common temperamental cast. But if the tradition retains the loyalty of a broad sector of a population, then in the second or third generation, as all temperaments reappear among its heirs, the tradition is likely to be reinterpreted in all the directions that the full range of human temperament might suggest. The same formula, which holds the loyalty of all, will come to carry quite contrary meanings in different quarters. The integrality of the tradition puts limits to such a process, so that not all temperaments ever become equally at home in any given tradition, but the process normally allows for sufficient differences to develop, to strain the unity of any group that attempts a rigorous internal discipline. The differences in styles of piety that developed among Muslims in the High Caliphal society reflected in part different social levels and relationships to power. But even more they reflected different temperaments, and the major groups that formed can be described as reflecting different ways of seeing life which recur in almost any society.

Piety among Muslims in High Caliphal times was highly diverse; nevertheless, certain movements stand out as formative in the course of events. Such a movement as the Manichean crossed confessional lines; but the most active movements flowered within the framework of Islam. Among Muslims it was a time of ferment, in which new patterns were being created—a fact not surprising, since Islam itself, as a religious allegiance, was adding numbers so rapidly in this time, drawing upon peoples of many different backgrounds. Like many times of ferment, it perhaps favoured fresh creativity more than it did profundity. But we may distinguish two main types of piety within Islam, despite the diversity. One type was the mystical, not yet dominant at that time. The other was kerygmatic, focused on history. Even more than usually in the Irano-Semitic traditions, Islamic piety reflected a strong historical consciousness; a kind of consciousness that was becoming rare then in the non-Muslim traditions, which had been abandoned in favour of Islam by the most historically active classes.

We have defined the term 'religious' (in the Prologue) as applying, in the first instance (i.e., as core of the heterogeneous phenomena by extension called 'religion'), to any *life-orientational* experience or behaviour in the degree to which it is focused on the role of a *person in an environment felt as cosmos*; a focus which has normally entailed some experience of the numinous and/or some notion of cosmic transcendence, and efforts to respond thereto. One must add that the devotional or 'religious' response, in this central sense, can occur in at least three modes—each of which has played a role in Islamic piety. For we may distinguish three components in devotional religious experience and behaviour; these components are not mutually exclusive—indeed, they presuppose each other—but they mark different moments of spiritual experience. Each of these components may be determinative in a devotional tradition, or even in an individual devotional life, and the other two subordinate to it; and to the extent that it is so, that component determines the overall mode of the devotional experience and behaviour.

We may refer to the *paradigm-tracing* component in personal piety, when ultimacy is sought in enduring cosmic patterns, in recurrent *nature* (including social nature): through myth and ritual as symbolic or interresonant paradigms, the persisting natural (and cultural) environment may be articulated as cosmos. For instance, as the worshipper faces Mecca in the mosque and bows, he sets himself symbolically in the right relation to God—submission; and to the other Muslims—all facing the same way; and so ever again restores some cosmic harmony to his life. (Some writers speak as if this were religion par excellence.)[1]

Secondly, we may refer to the *kerygmatic* component, when ultimacy is sought in irrevocable datable events, in *history* with its positive moral commitments. In response to a revelatory moment, the environment, particularly historical society as it is and is about to be, may be seen as radically other than what it appears, and the individual is challenged to find fresh ways to respond to its reality. For instance, as the worshipper recites the Qur'ân he may realize that the great of this world are about to die and be judged and are not deserving of all the reverence they receive; and that he himself must find a way to change his cringing ways to them and be bounden to God alone. This

[1] This is the mode primarily discussed by Mircea Eliade in *Le Sacré et le Profane* (Paris, 1965), translated into English from the German as *The Sacred and the Profane* (New York, 1959). The illuminating study of religion by Clifford Geertz, 'Religion as a Cultural System', *Anthropological Approaches to the Study of Religion*, ed. Michael Banton (New York, 1966) likewise defines actually only the 'paradigm-tracing' mode—interpreting the other components in terms of the 'paradigm-tracing'. Incidentally, it also includes implicitly a wider range of phenomena than what we have called 'religion'; for what he says applies to the whole of what I have called the 'life-orientational'—for instance, it would apply with little or no modification to the 'paradigm-tracing' dimension of Soviet Communism (including 'socialist realism', etc.). If one is looking for a purely formally identifiable cultural 'perspective', as he is, this is proper; and what we have called the 'religious' represents only a matter of degree within what he has shown to be the formally more exact category of the life-orientational. This is the case, it may be added, whether the religious is in the paradigm-tracing, the kerygmatic, or the mystical mode: something corresponding to each mode can occur in non-religious life-orientational behaviour, that which puts little emphasis on the role of the person in a cosmos. (We may perhaps refer to 'self-penetrational' behaviour—which can include, for instance, certain types of psychotherapy—as the broader category within which mystical behaviour is the religious form.)

kerygmatic component has been crucial to the prophetic monotheistic traditions (and hence some theologians have even set them off as transcending mere 'religion' taken in its paradigm-tracing mode).

Finally, we may refer to the *mystical* component in personal piety, when objective ultimacy is sought in subjective inward awarenesses, in maturing *selfhood:* exploring or controlling his consciousness, the person may penetrate into or through his self to find ever more comprehensive meanings in the environment. For instance, as the worshipper meditates on God's creative power and his own pettiness, he may come to feel his body as but a speck floating among specks; his aims that had mattered so seem silly, and just doing what God may require seems obvious and easy.

Among most Muslims, to whom religion was of secondary interest, devotional behaviour was commonly in the paradigm-tracing mode; that is, the latter two components tended to be subordinated to the paradigm-tracing component: to the extent that the person recognized a challenge in the Qur'ân, or underwent a transformed awareness of himself, this served chiefly to reinforce the paradigm-tracing experience as such, especially as it came to be embodied in the Sharî'ah as universal model. But the great traditions of Islamic piety were created and developed mostly in either a kerygmatic or a mystical mode—they expressed response most characteristically either to a kerygmatic sense of history or to a mystical sense of selfhood. The formative figures in Muslim spiritual life, that is, most often worked in one of those two modes; and to the extent that ordinary individuals deepened their spiritual consciousness, they also tended to one or the other of the two modes.

A. KERYGMATIC ORIENTATIONS

In the High Caliphal Period, the most prominent traditions of personal piety were marked by a kerygmatic orientation: their positive commitment to moral challenges revealed in datable events was decisive for the structure of their religious consciousness and behaviour. This does not mean that paradigm-tracing components and even some mystical elements were absent from these traditions; indeed, the paradigm-tracing component was sometimes of first importance. But in all these traditions, the kerygmatic element played a role disproportionately large, at least as compared with most religious life of the Agrarian Age.

The piety of the Piety-minded factions: its exclusivity

Already among the Piety-minded opposition to the Marwânids, many points of view had been expressed in matters religious. From early 'Abbâsî times the names of multifarious schools of thought have come down to us, or at least of partisans of one or another leading tenet; it is hard sometimes to sort out which names reflect real differences in basic devotional mood.[2] Yet they had in common an intense sense of the historical challenge of Islam as this was embodied in the Qur'ân. Often even the differences in devotional style among Muslims were directly related to the common background of factional traditions which grew out of the Piety-minded factions of Marwânî times; the differences reflected their common stress on the social and historical dimension of human life. They all saw the divine power as being expressed in the fate of human communities generation by generation, but saw it differently. Thus a political disagreement about the imâmate could be explored and yield profound consequences on the most personal level.

This social and historical orientation continued to colour the piety of all the movements derived from the Piety-minded factions. Often it gave it an austere temper, demanding a rigorous standard of public decency free of luxurious display or of other concessions to aristocratic culture that might be regarded, from an egalitarian viewpoint, as degenerate social corruption. In general, it made Islam an excellent vehicle for the social concerns of the continuing monotheistic tradition.

While some older traditions were being attenuated—or enriched—into primarily peasant cults with a tendency to centre on nature myth, the old search for the combination of a pure personal life with a just social polity was being taken up above all among the Muslims. Among them, accordingly, the Irano-Semitic populism, with its personal moralism, came to a singularly consistent flowering.[3] One side of this populism was expressed in an extraordinarily intensive sense of the moral exclusivity of the true community, which had accepted allegiance to the true creative moment—to the true moment of revelation and to what it revealed. Only in that community was there truth and validity; but whoever shared in its allegiance was by that fact not only socially but cosmically on a plane above those who refused allegiance, on a plane where the only true difference among the faithful was in degree of piety. The Muslims felt themselves the defenders of the faith of Abraham in the midst of re-paganized dhimmî communities.

This exclusivity was mirrored in the shahâdah declaration, made up of two equally important statements: there is no deity but God, and Muḥammad is the messenger of God. In principle these phrases could be—and on rare occasions were—interpreted as on different levels: the first phrase as universal, the second as a special case; then any other prophet's name could be substituted equally well in the second phrase without invalidating the phrase as a testimony to the essentials of divine truth. The status of the other prophets

[2] All too often every possible shade of grouping, from an isolated opinion to a substantial school of thought or even an organized religious body, is called by the scholars a 'sect' without any distinction of kind or degree or grouping. This can lead to absurd confusions. (Compare the Appendix on Usage.)

[3] I have attempted to develop this consideration in detail in 'Islâm and Image', *History of Religions*, 3 (1964), 220–60; the sense of development over time is largely wanting there, however.

could not be denied. But in practice, pious Muslims could not acknowledge that the traditions derived from the moments of revelation granted to those other prophets had more than a limited legal validity as compared with the tradition arising from the revelation to Muḥammad. The others were all quite hopelessly corrupted. Hence the second phrase carried a force not fully indicated in its bare words: it was not just *messengership*, of which Muḥammad was the present instance, but *Muḥammad's* messengership that was the second eternal verity to put on a line with God's unity. The messengership of former prophets was but a pale corollary of Muḥammad's, inasmuch as he acknowledged them. There was a sternness and uncompromising dignity in the position of the Muslim as such, which every Muslim could share in: he alone, in contrast to all the infidels, had undertaken the trust, had undertaken to be God's representative in the earth; the others were not really even fully human. If the Muslim was not in this period the actual political ruler, yet he was equal member in a community that did rule, and cosmically he shared its status.

The same exclusivity was expressed in the overwhelmingly central role played by the Qur'ân in Muslim piety—by that Qur'ân which was in some measure, at least, on everyone's lips, and which no educated or specially trained élite could really monopolize. The whole of pre-Islamic monotheistic experience and lore was drawn on to build Islam, which thus could be defined as Irano-Semitic monotheism in its most populistic form; yet nothing was allowed to derogate from the place of the Qur'ân as the point of commitment in the tradition. Qur'ânic passages could, indeed, be interpreted away, and non-Qur'ânic viewpoints could be read into the Qur'ân. For instance, for one who read the Qur'ân without preconceptions, there could be found in it little objection to the painter or sculptor but much to the poet; and yet by High 'Abbâsî times Muslim piety had generally reversed this judgment—to the point that the very words which in the Qur'ân had designated merely special symbolic stones were being transferred to the sculptor's art, so that later generations saw their latter-day prejudices retrospectively embodied in the Qur'ân itself. Yet for all that, the central challenges of the Qur'ân were strongly felt and the Irano-Semitic heritage was closely canalized through that document. Islam as felt by the more pious, then, could also be defined as response and loyalty to the Qur'ân and its message.

The potency of the Qur'ân

The Qur'ân's appeal proved to wear well. What had challenged the old Arabs of Mecca and Medina carried perhaps as potent a challenge to the city merchants and craftsmen of the settled lands from Nile to Oxus. As has happened in many religious traditions, the relative lack of intellectual sophistication of Muḥammad's environment, which was evident throughout the Qur'ân, lent itself to highlighting the elemental realities of human living. The homely situations, the everyday analogies could be understood directly even by the illiterate. Perhaps more important, there was no preoccupation with the subtler niceties of either aesthetic or moral awareness as cultivated in a learnèd élite, to disguise either the savagery or the nobility that men have in common. For chopping off the hand of a thief, the Qur'ân offered neither subtle apologies nor (as were its commentators to do) niceties of legal circumstance; the cruel punishment stood forth as a judgment, within the terms of awareness of ordinary people, both on the thief and on whoever would allow either his pity to blind him to responsibility, or his wrath to yield to an arbitrary vengeance. Even those who feel they have found a better way than was available to the Medinese to respond to the demand for justice so presented must pause to consider whether their response is truly as soberly balanced as that, or whether perhaps it is tainted with sentimentality or even self-righteousness.

For the Qur'ân continued, as in Mecca and Medina, to be a monumental challenge. In its form, it continued, even after the ending of active revelation with Muḥammad's life, to be an event, an act, rather than merely a statement of facts or of norms. It was never designed to be read for information or even for inspiration, but to be recited as an act of commitment in worship; nor did it become a mere sacred source of authority as the founding of Islam receded into time. It continued its active role among all who accepted Islam and took it seriously. What one did with the Qur'ân was not to peruse it but to worship by means of it; not to passively receive it but, in reciting it, to reaffirm it for oneself: the event of revelation was renewed every time one of the faithful, in the act of worship, relived the Qur'ânic affirmations.

Accordingly, the worshipper reaffirmed for himself through the Qur'ân, in whatever passage of the Qur'ân he was uttering, its single massive challenge: the challenge best summed up in the word *tawḥîd*—the assertion of God's unity. He certified anew that the authority of the Creator-god and His demands on human consciences confront us without any lesser rival, any intermediate source of norms, any slighter duty; thus he undertook to live up to a standing claim which every individual faced anew in the Qur'ân each time he renewed his recitation of it; a demand to which he rededicated himself in every act of worship. Every verse of the Qur'ân presented and illuminated in its own fashion this challenge, applied to numerous details of common life or envisaged through the lessons of nature and of history.[4]

[4] There is pressing need for a study of the Qur'ân from a modern scholarly viewpoint that can provide a way of reading the Qur'ân alternative to that traditional in the West. Even if we get a better translation than yet exists in English, we will need an extensive 'comp anion to the Qur'ân' that will show the reader what to look for. At present, what is available to the general public is typified by W. T. de Bary, ed., *Approaches to the Oriental Classics* (Columbia University Press, 1959), devoted to ways of introducing exotic classics into Western general education. There, Arthur Jeffery, a philological authority on the Qur'ânic text, says that what commends the Qur'ân to general study is solely its enormous prestige among Muslims; he concedes it neither religious nor literary value. Its prestige he tries to explain as resulting from its unique theological status, but he does not say that that status itself must be explained—that the Qur'ân must have won considerable prestige on internal grounds before serious persons would be willing to assign it so unique a theological status.

The unique potency of the Qur'ân, calling for a person's undivided attention to its single and total challenge, brought a purely religious component to the growing movement of iconophobia in the Irano-Semitic traditions; a movement which typified their piety and how that piety was fulfilled in Islam. The use of images could be felt to be inappropriate to a prophetic religion of the moral God because of its association with the nature gods; but in the presence of the Qur'ân they became directly distracting and divisive, quite apart from any such associations. For the Qur'ân itself can serve as a sensible, almost tangible symbol of the One whose challenge it presents.

That challenge is single-mindedly a moral one. If, in the Qur'ân, we are directed to the glories of nature, it is not that we may praise God's beauty or stand in awe of His wisdom, but that we may be warned of His power to enforce His ordinances. In the spiritually more sensitive individual, the exclusive focusing of his thoughts on the Qur'ân could generate an overwhelming moral force that might mould his whole personality. Hence to juxtapose any other symbols in worship alongside the Qur'ân, however honestly they might point to other aspects of divinity, must necessarily, in the nature of the power of symbols in human beings, share in, channel away, and finally dissipate the concentrated devotional energies. Such alternative releases of the emotions were not alternative means of coming before the One; rather, they divided and weakened the devotion to the One expressed in the Qur'ân, and to its moral demands. It may be said that the doctrine of the unity of God, which has been so central to developed Islam, is largely the theological expression of the unity of the act of worship at its best, its undivided dedication to realizing the moral lordship of God over the worshipper.

Accordingly, the central presence of the Qur'ân excluded such symbolic expression of more limited distinct aspects of the divine-human relation as in Christianity was given in the sacraments; and with the sacraments, it excluded the priest-craft which the sacraments presupposed. Necessarily it excluded those other symbolic expressions of spiritual awareness represented in the arts; much as later happened in a somewhat similar movement in Protestant Christianity. But the feeling of the pious went beyond the service of worship and the place where the worship was held. All life should be informed with the religious spirit; nowhere should be tolerated anything that could rival the Qur'ân in evoking the deeper responses of the spirit. The whole imaginative life was suspect: science and fiction, music and painting. So far as any art that is true to itself is not, in fact, a mere pleasing of the senses but evokes the whole spirit, all art was potentially a rival to the Qur'ân, a subtle form of idolatry. Nor is science merely an objective satisfaction of curiosity: it calls for its own morally single-minded devotion. The pious, therefore, could well fear all the arts and sciences wherever they appeared, and indeed all aspects of high culture that did not clearly subtend the moral purposes to which the Qur'ân summoned.

Finally, the unity of the cult centred on the Qur'ân issued in the exclusivity of the religious community itself: if within Islam no rival form of cult could be tolerated, however monotheistic, then still less could be admitted the legitimacy of any religious communities rival to the one which maintained the Qur'ânic cult. The one God implied the one medium of worship and the one worshipping community.

Shar'ism as an expression of Qur'ânic piety

Among the very seriously concerned, this spiritual experience was doubtless the strongest motive to the exclusivity of Islam; its exclusion of all cult images, more generally its exclusion of all symbolism rival to the Qur'ân and of all rival communities. Yet these few concerned could not, by themselves, have enforced even a small measure of exclusivity. Their sentiment could not have been effective if it had not coincided with the more general tendencies of populism as fostered in a mercantile milieu: the distrust of the aristocratic, the luxurious, the exceptional, which must include all true science and art; and the substitution, for these splendours of high culture in high society, of the pre-eminence of the sacred community in which the most ordinary man found his dignity in the daily moral relationships of his life. Hence it was only where the sentiment of populism at large reinforced the sense of worship of the most pious, that their spiritual convictions took effect. Accordingly, the most luxurious form of art, requiring the greatest aristocratic or priestly taste and resources, sculpture, was almost entirely banned; while that art which every class could indulge in, poetry, was almost never condemned. Yet perhaps the populist impulse itself could not have had so much success, had it not been supported by the spiritual insights of the exceptionally sensitive; certainly it was only in the mosque itself, where such men had special prestige, that the sentiments of exclusivity were fully effective.

In any case, it was precisely what was universal in the vision of Islam, its hope of equal justice and of a human responsibility under transcendent norms, that issued in the exclusivity of Islam. The very response to the vision which allowed that vision to be embodied in a living tradition, and the responsible commitment which then carried it forward in actual society, were what closed Islam off from rival values and rival traditions. The Qur'ân, to whose words Islamic symbolism came near to being restricted, became the one great concrete image in Islam.

Despite the immediate potency of the Qur'ân, the text by itself would still, presumably, not have been enough to focus the tradition so forcefully without being tied in concretely with the ongoing community life. In Muḥammad's time it had answered to the current sequence of events, illuminating and guiding them. Later Muslims had to find the equivalent for their own generations. One solution, embodying the challenge in daily life, was to work out rules of practical morality which would be consistent with the Qur'ânic cult. Thus arose the Sharî'ah, the autonomous body of law being spelled out for increasingly detailed cases. In this process (which never really ceased), the Qur'ân played a central role and so entered actively into the community life.

The Sharî'ah was given further emotional force because it embodied loyalty to the Muslim community, whose idealized ways it described. The exclusivity latent in the Qur'ân was early complemented by an exclusivity grounded in the historical Muslim community. In the reaction that followed the third fitnah and the 'Abbâsî triumph, this *communal* orientation of this Shar'î spirit was explicitly emphasized: that is, loyalty to the community of Muslim allegiance, even at the expense of any other value. It was readily combined with the new Shar'î spirit; since for the Piety-minded, who had rejected the Marwânî leadership and did not love the 'Abbâsî, identification with the community could only mean acceptance of the Sharî'ah.

In Shî'î circles, this spirit helped to discipline even the Ghulât theorists. The imâm Ja'far al-Ṣâdiq, soon after the advent of the 'Abbâsids, found it wise to disown a prominent follower, one of the Ghulât, Abû-l-Khaṭṭâb, for going too far in neglecting the growing Shar'î spirit; he was more concerned with inner symbolisms than with legal applications. (Not long after, Abû-l-Khaṭṭâb was executed by al-Manṣûr for heresy.) In general, the thinking of the Ghulât theorists was curbed about this time, at least verbally, so as not to offend the Sharî'ah-minded. Thus the later theorists among all the Ja'farî Shî'ahs could exalt their imâms as 'proofs' (*ḥujjah*) of God or carriers of a divine light—both of which notions could have broad metaphysical implications in the Irano-Semitic tradition; but (in contrast to the practice of the first Ghulât) in deference to the common legal supremacy of the Prophet par excellence, the imâms were never thenceforth called even very minor 'prophets' (*nabî*) despite the lesser implications of such a term.

A related communalistic mood appeared among the legists themselves. Abû-Yûsuf, disciple of Abû-Ḥanîfah, stressed in Baghdad the legal norms of the old times under the Marwânîs almost as much as did al-Awzâ'î, leader of the Syrian school, who was naturally nostalgic for the time of Syrian primacy. Through such men, something of the older Arabism survived in the Piety-minded Sharî'ah itself.

But even so, this Shar'ism was not sufficient in itself to establish a living involvement with the Qur'ân, and so to form the whole content of a vital mode of piety. Some sort of Sharî'ah-mindedness was almost universal among the Islamic movements stemming from the Piety-minded factions. But each of them added its own further ingredients.

We shall discuss here first the sorts of piety that arose among those who refused accommodation to the established Muslim order—Khârijîs and especially Shî'îs: Zaydî Shî'îs in their persistent politically-minded insurgency, and the chief radical Shî'î groups, Twelvers in their chiliastic longing and Ismâ'îlîs in their esoteric and conspiratorial intellectualism. Then we shall return to those who accepted the jamâ'ah as established, notably the moralistic Mu'tazilîs and their rivals the populistic and loyalistic Ḥadîth folk, chief heirs of the older Piety-minded groupings; and especially the Ṣûfîs, whose mysticism formed a primary basis for most Muslim devotional life in later centuries. I shall necessarily present here what I do see fairly clearly in these several traditions, and omit what I do not see; hence what I say will look better informed than it is. But it is only with closer studies of the piety both of individual leaders and of more typical individuals in each tradition that we can hope for an adequate understanding of what is now, all too often, a field for conjecture.

We have seen how by early ʿAbbâsî times a distinction was forming between the Shîʿah, the partisans of ʿAlî, looking to a repurification of Islam, and the Jamâʿah, the partisans of community solidarity, looking to maintain what had been achieved; the two positions appealed respectively to persons more inclined to risk all for an ideal, and to those more inclined to estimate that no better could be had than was had. Within each of these broad allegiances appeared further distinctions—reflecting again (within each group) a relatively idealistic demand for perfection, or a relatively practicalistic demand for conservation; or reflecting, further, a distinction between those more inclined to public, exoteric truth accessible to all, and those inclined to an esoteric truth accessible only to an élite. Out of diverse combinations among these and yet other tendencies arose several strong movements with a distinctive style of piety, some of which played major historical roles.

Two early movements, which persisted long into ʿAbbâsî times, especially represented the spirit of austerity present among the Piety-minded dissidents. They demanded a turn to higher standards than generally prevailed, and demanded this of the Muslim public at large, with little condescension to human weakness. They gradually became less prominent during High Caliphal times, and later persisted only in isolated places; but as long as a strong central empire still presented a relatively simple political challenge to the rigorous reformer, they offered cogent answers for certain temperaments.

The movement most notorious for its social austerity, that of the Khârijîs, had rejected even the Shîʿah as a vehicle of reform. We have noted them as working out a consistent attempt to maintain the absolute equality and responsibility of believers within a homogeneous community, often at the expense of abandoning the Muslim community at large and retiring into self-righteous war bands. They were intensely concerned with Sharʿî questions, but insisted, above all, on effectively righteous public order. Sometimes they explicitly tolerated behaviour that other Piety-minded groups banned in theory, so as to make their theory really applicable in practice. But on the whole their temper was puritanical and exceedingly militant. The Ibâḍî Khârijîs were able to establish, among considerable populations in out-of-the-way Muslim-majority areas (notably ʿUmân in eastern Arabia), a public norm at least superficially proper. After the eighth century, however, they gradually ceased to be important except in these limited areas.

Within the Shîʿî movement, a very like position was represented by the

Zaydiyyah. The Zaydîs insisted, from the time of al-Qâsim al-Rassî (d. 860), their great theorist, that the true imâm must be that 'Alid (descended from Fâṭimah, that is) who combined mastery of legal and religious teaching with the political initiative and acumen to carry out armed rebellion against the authorities. The imâm might be of the line either of Ḥasan or of Ḥusayn, and need not be the son of an imâm; nor need there always be an imâm at all, if none appeared who was truly qualified. The result was a series of highly competent imâms—ruling in out-of-the-way places, especially in the Yemen.

Shî'ism, the piety of protest

After the great disappointment to pious expectations at the time of the 'Abbâsî revolution, Shî'ism developed more and more in its own course apart and cultivated its own forms of piety. The Shî'îs gradually developed their own sense of the Sharî'ah and their own variants of it. But to it they added a strong 'Alid loyalism of an intensely religious quality. (I use the term *'Alid loyalism* for the varied complex of special religious attitudes associated with loyalty to the 'Alids—not only reverence for the 'Alids themselves, but certain exalted ideas about Muḥammad's person and the supposition of a secret teaching he transmitted specially to 'Alî, and so on—whether these attitudes appear among Jamâ'î-Sunnîs or among those who, by explicitly rejecting the jamâ'ah, identified themselves as Shî'îs in the proper sense.) For the Shî'îs, it was not sufficient for the law to be an autonomous corps of authoritative norms which the community as a whole would maintain against any given ruler. Its continuity must be ensured, as in Muḥammad's time, through the presence of an authoritative spokesman for the divine will—a true imâm. 'Alid loyalism offered just that.

The more intense Shî'îs had from an early date felt that 'Alî was not merely one caliph among others, but that he had had a special authority to lead the community of Muḥammad. As they explored the implications of his early leadership and of their moral commitment to him, they became sure that he alone had acquired, through his closeness to his cousin and father-in-law, the Prophet, the full 'ilm necessary to guide the consciences and the lives of true Muslims—the knowledge of what was lawful and just, and perhaps of many other things as well. In abandoning him, they felt the Muslims at large had abandoned the truth; since that time the true adherents of Muḥammad had been the few who remained loyal to 'Alî and his family, in which the sacred 'ilm continued from generation to generation.[5]

Such a point of departure necessarily launched an active and highly varied dialogue among those who felt themselves to be the élite remnant, whose

[5] Something of the mood of this 'Alid loyalism emerges in Louis Massignon, 'Salman Pâk et les prémices spirituelles de l'Islam iranien', *Soc. études iraniennes*, no. 7, 1934. Highly valuable studies by Massignon on Shî'ism and Shî'ism and Ṣûfism are listed in the 'Bibliographie' in vol. 1 of *Mélanges Louis Massignon* (Damascus, 1956), itself a rich collection of articles on Islamic religion and other Islamicate matters.

Islam must be distinguished from that of the common herd of renegades. Though a certain generalized 'Alid loyalism persisted among the population at large, who commonly felt that any 'Alid claimant to the caliphate at least deserved a hearing, those who had assumed a commitment to the 'Alid cause could not leave it at that. The Zaydîs, indeed, developed (as we have noted) a full-fledged 'Alid loyalism which was sectarian but hardly esoteric.

In contrast to the Zaydî position, which offered just a more purified version of the ordinary Muslim outlook, the position of the more radical Shî'îs, those committed to a designated imâmate of naṣṣ as a basis for sectarian continuity, became widely influential even beyond the circles of those who explicitly adopted the position. For it presented a distinctive style of piety which appealed to a widespread human temperament, and which loomed especially important within the structure presented by any monotheistic tradition. First, it was an esoteric position: the radical Shî'îs looked to a privileged truth inherently inaccessible to the unworthy masses, and into which those who were worthy had to be specially initiated. The notion of a secret, hidden wisdom, which only an élite were worthy of, was an almost inescapable corollary of the position that only a few were privileged to perceive the true destiny of Muslims and hold to the true leaders of Islam. Hence the sectarian Shî'îs focused their interests on the special 'ilm of the imâms which only Shî'îs could appreciate. But the appeal of the esoteric was not enough alone. Other forms of esotericism were available, in Islam, that proved compatible with a Jamâ'î-Sunnî position; notably an esoteric approach to the inward personal experience of mysticism, into which a disciple could be initiated only by an experienced master. What was distinctive in esoteric Shî'ism was that it presented a privileged vision of history. It was a 'kerygmatic' esotericism.

On the everyday side of common doctrine, urged indiscriminately upon everyone and hence (from an esoteric viewpoint) exoteric, the notion that history began and was to end decisively and once for all was fundamental to the moral position of monotheism. The traditions had all early developed an eschatology, a doctrine of what was to happen at the end of time when all humans would be duly rewarded or punished. (This was implicit in their kerygmatic mode of piety, as this was expressed in monotheistic terms.) But this exoteric eschatology need not amount to more than a personal destiny, in which adherence to the one true historical community will have been important, but which was not really a part of history, for it took effect only when history was over. Alongside this milder approach there was always a more radical strain within the eschatological thinking of the traditions: chiliasm. Not merely a final Judgment was expected after history, but history itself was to be completed with a blissful millennium, a culminating age when the world as we have known it will be put right within the terms of history. Chiliasm expressed radical social protest. Very shortly, the wicked great of this world would be humbled or destroyed, and the lowly, or those of them who had proved capable of maintaining the true faith and the true loyalty, would be exalted to share the good things of this world free from oppressors. The world would be 'filled with justice as it is now filled with injustice', in the Shî'î phrase.

Such an expectation meant not merely a hope for the future, but a re-evaluation of present social and historical life. In the light of what was to happen—and every generation found reason to suppose that it was likely to happen in their own time—present social and political arrangements were temporary and even highly precarious. It was always possible that the foreordained leader (the Mahdî) might appear and test the faithful by summoning them, just as they were, to launch the great social transformation themselves under his command, with the promise of divine succour when it would be needed. But even before he appeared, the social role of the various elements in the population took on a changed air for those who knew what was to happen. Every mundane historical event might presage or prepare the Mahdî's coming. The faithful were always on the alert, ready to take their part in the final acts. In this way, a chiliastic vision dramatized all history, in the present as well as the future. But the more seriously a chiliastic vision was received, the more it necessarily contradicted received social viewpoints. Both socially and intellectually, a chiliastic vision had to take esoteric form, if only in self-defence.

Once its partisans ceased to attempt immediate and direct political action, the Shî'ah became the chief vehicle among Muslims of chiliastic hopes, perpetuated in terms of esoteric lore. For Shî'îs, the Qur'ân had a secret interpretation which made it speak of the imâms and their historic fate; and independent books of predictions, circulated in the name of an imâm, commonly Ja'far al-Ṣâdiq, darkly foretold events to come in such a way that every new generation could see its trials and hopes mirrored there. Many Shî'îs were also interested in other esoteric lore—notably the occult sciences, such as chemistry in the form of alchemy. But an esoteric historical vision was of the essence of radical Shî'ism. Even when chiliastic expectations spread into Jamâ'î-Sunnî milieus, it was largely in 'Alid-loyalist forms that it did so.

This Shî'î esoteric thinking built largely on the work of the early Ghulât theorists. Their speculations had exalted the role of the imâm as saviour of the ordinary human being, and often introduced esoteric notions from pre-Islamic heresies. Faith tended to be conceived in terms of a personal devotion to a divinely guided hero, and a heady enthusiasm sometimes resulted. The more zealous enthusiasts, however, had rarely been long separated from less visionary persons, concerned above all with the true imâm as a decider of points of sacred law and restraining their curiosity for anything more strongly esoteric. From this varied milieu grew both the Twelver and the Ismâ'îlî sects, the Ja'farî Shî'ahs.

The Twelver Shî'ah

Of the radical Shî'î groups, that which was centred, at the time of the 'Abbâsî revolution, on 'Alî's great-great-grandson Ja'far al-Ṣâdiq, was the only one to

The Ja'farî and Zaydî Shî'ahs

Ja'far al-Ṣâdiq (d. 765)
(buried at Medina)

—ISMÂ'ÎLÎS—

Ismâ'îl (d. before his father)

Muḥammad

(allegedly three imâms in hiding)

'Abd-Allâh al-Mahdî al-Fâṭimî r. 909–934 in Maghrib as caliph

al-Qâ'im (d. 945) maintained position vs. Khârijîs

al-Manṣûr (d. 952)

al-Mu'izz (d. 975) established the Fâṭimids in Egypt, 969

'Abd-Allâh (first accepted by majority as imâm; died without sons)

—TWELVERS (ITHNÂ'ASHARÎS)—

Mûsà al-Kâẓim (d. 799) imprisoned by 'Abbâsids at Baghdad; buried at Kâẓimayn

'Alî al-Riḍà (d. 818) made heir apparent by al-Ma'mun; buried at Mashhad-Ṭûs

Muḥammad {al Taqî / al-Jawâd} (succeeded as a child)

'Alî {al-Naqî / al-Hâdî} (succeeded as a child)

Hasan al-'Askarî (d. 873 at Sâmarrâ without any known son) — Ja'far (some accepted as successor)

(allegedly)

Muḥammad al-Munṭazar: in hiding, to return as Mahdî

Represented by 4 wakîls—the fourth, 'Alî b. Md. al-Sâmarrî, d. 940, refusing to name a successor; ending the 'Little Absence' and beginning the 'Great Absence' (Ghaybah)

—ZAYDÎS—

Some other 'Alid revolts during this period (as at Mecca, Qumm, etc.) are omitted

Ḥusayn b. 'Alî (Ḥasanid) at al-Fakhkh, near Mecca, 786

Idrîs in west Maghrib (fleeing from al-Fakhkh), 789

Yaḥyà (Ḥasanid) in Daylam, d. 792

Muḥammad, revolted in the Ḥijâz, 815, simultaneously with Abû-l-Sarâyâ, general of two imâms at Kûfah, 814–815

Muḥammad b. al-Qâsim (Ḥusaynid) in sub-Caspian highlands, 834

(al-Qâsim al-Rassî, d. 860, chief Zaydî theorist: no effective revolt)

Ḥasan b. Zayd (d. 884) in Ṭabaristân, 864; (successful: dynasty lasted till 928)

Yaḥyà b. 'Umar b. Ḥusayn b. Zayd, at Kûfah, 864 (after this, Kûfah loses importance)

Yaḥyà al-Hâdî ilâ-l-Ḥaqq, in Yemen, 901 (successful; d. 911) have a great future: partly because the movement harking back to Ibn-al-Ḥanafiyyah had aborted in the ʿAbbâsî cause; partly because of the Fâṭimid ancestry of Jaʿfar's line; partly, no doubt, because of its intellectual and political disciplining at the time of Jaʿfar. One of the chief sects to issue from this group traced six more imâms beyond Jaʿfar. Each time an imâm died and a successor was to be recognized, issues were raised about the nature of the imâmate (was the proposed successor qualified?), and consequently of the group and of its faith, and were resolved through the choice of the next imâm, which was almost never unanimous. Except in the case of the Ismâʿîlîs, however, the bulk of this group, the Twelver Shîʿîs, eventually settled on a single course and dissidents died out.

Jaʿfar himself had been acknowledged as his father's successor almost without dissent; he was personally learnèd and respected, and the sectarian view of the imâmate was still barely formed anyway. But at his death questions arose. At one time he had duly designated his son Ismâʿîl as successor; by the rule of naṣṣ, succession by designation, this should have settled the matter; but Ismâʿîl died before his father. Was the imâm fallible in so crucial a matter as the designation? If not, had he been dissimulating in foreknowledge of the event, so as to protect the true heir from the eyes of the authorities—who looked on any Shîʿî imâm with understandable suspicion; or was the designation merely contingent, as in other human affairs, to be superseded by a new designation at need? Without necessarily agreeing on the answer, most of the Shîʿîs turned to the eldest surviving son, ʿAbd-Allâh, who seems to have claimed a second designation by Jaʿfar. Some objected to him, however, claiming that, on being questioned, his ʿilm knowledge did not show itself sufficient. Was this a sound test on the part of ordinary human beings? Within a few weeks, ʿAbd-Allâh's death without heirs seemed to confirm the doubt about him. The majority turned to another son, Mûsà al-Kâẓim, but without all agreeing whether he was ʿAbd-Allâh's successor or had been the true successor to Jaʿfar all along; for this question hinged on how one was to interpret the imâm's ʿilm. Many, however, clung to the designation of Ismâʿîl and proclaimed Ismâʿîl's son; these were the Ismâʿîlîs. Still others seemed to have maintained that Jaʿfar himself, dead or alive, was still the only true imâm.

Mûsà spent most of his time in an ʿAbbâsî jail and was spared much questioning by the faithful. On his death, his son ʿAlî al-Riḍà was accepted, though not unanimously. But ʿAlî's son at his death was only a young lad, and his son in turn was still younger, too young to have received instruction from his father in the family lore, at least in the ordinary way. In what sense were such orphans to be looked on as still possessing the private ʿilm which Muḥammad had confided to ʿAlî? Those who accepted them—and not all did—were forced to acknowledge not merely a divine designation of the given leader as authoritative, in the sense that a constitutional high court is authoritative whatever its decision; they had to acknowledge a more active divine intervention: at the very least, to protect the imâm from false learning as he grew up; and preferably in more positive ways: by way of a magic book containing all knowledge, which remained in the imâm's possession alone, or, more simply, by way of divine inspiration; or even by way of the imâm's metaphysical substance, that special divine Light which was infused in him and caused him to know truth by his very nature.

At last Ja'far's great-great-great grandson, Ḥasan al-'Askarî, died with no known son at all (873). Most found his brother, who had been at odds with him and now claimed the position, unacceptable. But by this time it proved feasible and necessary to suppose that Ḥasan must have had a son and that that son must have disappeared; presumably being hidden to save him from 'Abbâsî persecution. Diverse accounts sprang up to fill in the details; but what mattered was that a son for whom such total precautions were taken must be a very special imâm. It was he, then, who was to be the Mahdî, Muḥammad al-Muntaẓar, 'Muḥammad the awaited'. Reckoning without 'Abd-Allâh, he was the twelfth imâm, and innumerable prophecies were now found to foretell the greatness of the twelfth of the line. (Hence his adherents were called 'Twelvers', in Arabic, 'Ithnâ'asharîs', as recognizing just twelve imâms; but they generally preferred to call themselves 'Imâmîs'.) He was held to be waiting in hiding, undying, till at the end of the world he should return and finally bring victory to his loyal partisans, and truth and justice to prevail in the world.

The custom had arisen for each imâm to communicate with his followers—for instance, for the purpose of receiving the alms paid in to him as imâm, and of disbursing them for pious purposes—through a *wakîl* or *safîr*, a personal representative. (The imâm did not always wish to expose himself personally to his followers' zealous expectations, and in any case was usually either in Medina, far from Kûfah, or else was imprisoned as politically suspect—if he was not a child, requiring adult guardianship.) On the disappearance of the twelfth imâm, a succession of four wakîls, each naming his successor, continued this role on a provisional basis, so maintaining the continuity of the organization and its financial structure. But in 940 the last of these died, refusing to name a successor. Thereafter there was no central organization. The sect maintained itself nevertheless; the time of the four wakîls was called the 'lesser absence (of the imâm)', the lesser *Ghaybah;* thereafter the Twelvers found themselves in the 'greater absence', the greater Ghaybah. But by then the High Caliphal state itself was at an end.

The imâms, then, came to be invested with cosmic worth, and their lives reflected the sad vicissitudes of the divine cause among ungrateful mankind. As 'Alî had been abandoned by the Muslims and finally murdered, so the Twelvers came to feel that each of the imâms that had followed him had been persecuted and finally executed or at least secretly poisoned by the wicked and worldly Muslims in power, both Umayyads and 'Abbâsids. Muḥammad himself was depicted as suffering silently the incomprehension and infidelity of those who seemed to support him most, and anticipating the sufferings of his descendants and their followers; his daughter Fâṭimah, mother of ʻAlî's sons, wept over the wrongs she and her children suffered at the hands of the violent ʻUmar; and ʻAlî, too just for this world, received a martyr's death. All these wrongs the pious Shîʻîs wept for, but above all for the murder of ʻAlî's son, and Muḥammad's grandson, Ḥusayn, betrayed by his own supporters to be tormented with thirst in the desert and slaughtered by his enemies at Karbalâ'.

Set as a minority against a too-triumphant world, the Shîʻîs wept on the anniversaries of their wrongs and at the tombs of their heroes, and believed that their love for the suffering imâms would win them forgiveness for their own sins and a share in the victory of the righteous in the end. The resemblance at many points to Christian piety has often been noted, but no historical link has yet been traced.

As to doctrines of law and social order, the Shîʻîs differed but little from others of the Piety-minded. They had their own Shîʻî Sharîʻah (in points like inheritance, it clung more literally to the Qur'ân than did the Jamâʻî-Sunnî schools); and their own Sharîʻah-mindedness in general, from which various groups tended to deviate less or more. Like the Jamâʻî-Sunnîs, they depended on ḥadîth reports for validating their tenets; but they looked to ḥadîth reported from the imâms, and vouched for in the isnâd by known Shîʻîs, in contrast to the kinds of isnâds preferred by Sunnîs. Yet except as regards the special role of ʻAlî and the imâms, their ḥadîth were often almost identical with those of the Sunnîs. What gave them their vitality was a special mood of devotion superadded to the common Sharʻism.

This Twelver Shîʻî piety proved highly attractive. With its exaltation of both ʻAlî and Muḥammad as superhuman heroes, it has, from ʻAbbâsî times on, affected the outlook of Jamâʻî-Sunnîs as well. For a time, in the tenth and eleventh centuries, the Fertile Crescent and much of Iran were under Shîʻî rulers. Shîʻî days of triumph (the recognition by Muḥammad of ʻAlî as imâm on the day of Ghadîr Khumm) and of mourning (especially the month Muḥarram, when Ḥusayn was killed) were publicly solemnized. Many of the leading figures then in the arts and sciences were Shîʻîs. Yet throughout the period, Shîʻîs remained a minority and could not control the overall social life. Sunnîs could not be persuaded to adopt a minoritarian mood of self-pity and self-blame, such as Shîʻism sometimes tended to become. They did, however, respond to the glorification of the main figures. ʻAlî became a major hero and Muḥammad was given metaphysical status, while Ḥusayn has been bewailed by many Sunnîs almost as much as by Shîʻîs.

Ismâʻîlî piety: esotericism and hierarchy

Quite a different turn was taken by others of the followers of Jaʻfar al-Ṣâdiq. Recognizing the line of his son Ismâʻîl as the true imâms, they created a dynamic social and intellectual movement which fostered numerous rebellions and finally seized power in Egypt in the tenth century, on the decline of 'Abbâsî power. Esoteric Shî'ism played a more far-reaching role among the Ismâ'îlîs (adherents of Ja'far's son Ismâ'îl) than among most Twelvers.

Indeed, they may be regarded as the most successful section of a movement which we may call the *Bâṭiniyyah*, those who gave primacy to an 'inner meaning', a *bâṭin*, in all religious words and formulations. (Some sections of the Bâṭiniyyah owned the Twelver imâms, however.) Growing out of the Ghulât theorists, such groups seem all to have been Shî'î in tendency. Their piety was built on a sense of the esoteric hiddenness of truth and holiness. These were concealed from the masses, who were held capable only of the husks of faith, not its inner kernel. It was to 'Alî alone, the family confidant of Muḥammad, that the inward, secret meaning of the Qur'ân had been confided; and only those spiritually alert enough to recognize 'Alî's position were vouchsafed such truths, for which they alone were ready.[6]

There is something in the Bâṭinî mood that resembles that of the Manicheans; in fact, it is probable that some of the same sort of men who at the beginning of the 'Abbâsî régime secretly adopted Manicheanism, a century later were adopting Bâṭinism and especially Ismâ'îlism (with equal secrecy). Both Manicheanism and Ismâ'îlism proposed to give their initiates a wisdom and a cosmic dignity which the coarse minds of ordinary mortals could scarcely aspire to; outsiders were scarcely granted full human status. Like Manicheanism, Ismâ'îlism cultivated its own comprehensive body of science; this was based on that of the followers of Hellenic philosophy, but was modified in terms of an esoteric vision of the cosmos as a symbolic whole.

Ismâ'îlism contrasted with Manicheanism, however (and herein showed its Muslim character) in being oriented strongly to the practical development of the world's social order, to the movements of human history. Significantly, most Ismâ'îlîs, like the other Piety-minded groups, recognized the binding force of the Sharî'ah—regarded as the prime overt work of Muḥammad. Its

[6] In studying the Bâṭinî movement, more even than in most other religious studies, we need to make use of what Massignon calls the psychosociological 'science of compassion'. The scholarly observer must render the mental and practical behaviour of a group into terms available in his own mental resources, which should remain personally felt even while informed with a breadth of reference which will allow other educated persons to make sense of them. But this must not be to substitute his own and his readers' conventions for the original, but to broaden his own perspective so that it can make a place for the other. Concretely, he must never be satisfied to cease asking 'but why?' until he has driven his understanding to the point where he has an immediate human grasp of what a given position meant, such that every nuance in the data is accounted for and withal, given the total of presuppositions and circumstances, he could feel himself doing the same. Such a grasp is to be checked, of course; for instance, by testing whether circumstances which must be presumed, so as to account for an attitude, can then be attested independently. Yet however risky the method is, it is less risky than any more external method. Massignon refers to the work of Wilhelm Dilthey and of Carl Jung to illumine his point of view. Cf. Louis Massignon, 'Les Nuṣayris', in *L'Elaboration de l'Islam*, ed. Claude Cahen (Presses universitaires de France, 1961), pp. 109–14.

high position was symbolized in the primacy of Muḥammad himself in the Ismâ'îlîs' symbolic historical hierarchy—whereas some other Bâṭinîs went so far as to exalt 'Alî and his secret knowledge above Muḥammad. Yet the Isma'îlîs' Shar'ism was not merely reinforced by, but to a degree transcended by, their 'Alid loyalism, interpreted as the basis for esoteric truth.

The purpose of the believer was to fulfill himself through the fulfillment of God's self-realization in the world—that is, of God's fulfillment here of His own rational cosmic possibilities. The world was no mere indiscriminate testing ground into which souls were placed to see how well they would do their duty; still less was it a work of blind evil; it presented, in all its details, a complex and beautiful divine plan. The Ismâ'îlîs—in a tradition which went back at least to the Pythagoreans—loved to present their sense of an invisible underlying cosmic order in terms of numerical parallelisms: the seven openings in the human head answered to the seven visible planets, for instance, and to the seven days in each quarter of a lunar cycle, and to the seven intervals of a musical octave. This interest in numbers, though it sometimes took the subtler form of an interest in proportions, had in common with modern physical science only a very general trait, the expectation that rational, non-sensory uniformities were to be discovered, in whose light the most diverse phenomena would prove to have a common nature and a common meaning. The overriding interest was in finding a physical and moral unity in the cosmos and in its history, which would invest all details of an individual's life with cosmic meaning. The natural test of a religious system, then, was the degree to which it reflected the cosmic harmonies, even in its details, and allowed its adepts to reflect them through participating in it.

The cosmos itself was conceived in the traditional Irano-Semitic lore in which the Greek philosophical tradition played a large role, as hierarchically structured; the Creator was at the peak, working through the diverse circular motions of the heavenly spheres to evoke all the complex movements of our sublunar earthly sphere. Corresponding to this natural hierarchy of Creator and angelic heavens and ordinary mundane life was, for Ismâ'îlîs, a religious hierarchy. The Prophet was at its head, of course; and the hierarchy was formed by delegation of authority from him. His single representative in each generation was the imâm of the time, designated by naṣṣ in the family of 'Alî; in him was invested the sacred 'ilm which knew the divine plan and could be unfolded to those who were worthy. But delegation did not end with the imâm. Indeed during most of High 'Abbâsî times, in contrast to the group that was to become the Twelvers, the Ismâ'îlîs had no accessible imâm. Their imâm was 'hidden' since Ismâ'îl's death—his son Muḥammad had travelled off, it seemed, not even the initiates knew where. Instead of a single spokesman, the Ismâ'îlîs acknowledged twelve chiefs, each with his own territory, to represent him; and the faithful under their command were further ranked in various increasingly numerous levels of hierarchy from the *dâ'îs*, summoners or missionaries, down to the simple converts.[7] Those of higher ranks taught those of lower ranks as much as they were ready to learn of the imâm's secret 'ilm.

This hierarchical organization was protected by an extreme use of an old principle. First those of the Khârijîs who did not actually go out in military bands, and then many of the Shî'îs who also had to accommodate themselves to authority which they could not in conscience accept, had developed the notion of *taqiyyah*, pious dissimulation of one's true opinions. It was not only to protect oneself but also to protect the community of which one was a member that a Shî'î was urged to practice taqiyyah dissimulation over against Sunnî majorities or Sunnî governments: at the least, not to press on their attention the Shî'î belief that the established Islam and the established government were illegitimate and should, in principle, be overthrown in the name of the imâm. Taqiyyah came readily to include not making public among enemies those of the group's doctrines that would be most subject to misunderstanding. Among the Ismâ'îlîs, now, it took on a more extensive implication: it became the protecting of the sacred lore from profane ears—even from the less fully initiated of the adherents; eventually, it was still maintained even under an Ismâ'îlî government. Taqiyyah dissimulation became the internal discipline which supported the hierarchy: the lore was protected at every level from those not yet ready for it.

Ismâ'îlî cyclicism

But the Ismâ'îlî hierarchical discipline was designed not only to guarantee the soundness of the secret lore; it was appropriate also to conspiratorial political purposes. For the Ismâ'îlîs expected, far more actively than the Twelvers with their quiescent imâms, a new dispensation for the world as a whole. A dramatic element was restored to the Muslim sense of history among the Ismâ'îlîs, not however, in the sense of a nature cycle but on a strictly moral level.

A cyclical sense of history is very natural once the historical process (under conditions of literacy and urban life) is moving fast and steadily enough for the individual to be aware of it as a long-term process of change. If an infinity of space and time are assumed, but a finite range of formal possibilities, then a certain reflection, applied to the 'old man's sense of time' (the feeling that 'the younger generation is going to the dogs', extrapolated to include the implication that ever since some idealized starting point each generation has gotten, on the whole, worse), leads directly to an expectation of cycles in which renewal is followed by a steady decline. A somewhat different cyclicism can result from the same supposition of infinity applied to the 'young man's sense of time' (that the older generation are 'old fogies'), as we see in the

[7] On the hidden, '*mastur*', imâm see the basic studies by Wilferd Madelung, 'Fâṭimiden und Baḥrainqarmaṭen' and 'Das Imamat in der frühen ismailitischen Lehre', *Der Islam*, 36 (190), 34–88, and 37 (1961), 43–135.

presuppositions of many modern clichés, which assume patterns of progress that would recur not only in other societies but even in future species if ours should destroy itself, or on other planets until some final cooling down. The fidelity of the religious traditions of Irano-Semitic heritage to the sense of a once-for-all linearity, which is strong even in Ismâ'îlism, bears witness to the high prestige among them of the moral insight that particular actions are absolutely decisive and not to be reversed or written off as mere incidents in a recurrent pattern.

The Ismâ'îlî cyclicism, like its esotericism, represented a revival of viewpoints which had generally accompanied in the Irano-Semitic traditions—perhaps as inevitable logical complement—the doctrine of a single irreversible historical sequence, with beginning and end, which tended to dominate those traditions. Elaborately as the world reflected, in some Ismâ'îlî thinking at least, a divine pattern, it was not free of corruption. As in all the systems of Irano-Semitic monotheism, there had been a point of initial error and sin. The Ismâ'îlîs (in the manner of the Gnostics) interpreted the rebellion of Iblîs (Satan), laconically sketched in the Qur'ân, as a cosmic turning point, necessitating an elaborate procedure of restoration, which constituted human history. (In some Ismâ'îlî philosophy, this initial aberration was identified with the false sense of independence from overriding cosmic rationality, which the vital will can be tempted to indulge in.) The greatest of the prophets (Adam, Noah, Abraham, Moses, Jesus, and Muḥammad made up the usual list) each had an 'executor' who taught the secret meaning of the prophets' outward revelation and initiated a sequence of imâms who in turn remained unrecognized except by the élite. These missions were to culminate in that of the Mahdî to come, who would form a seventh in the line and bring in the purifying Resurrection.[8] (Sometimes this was distinguished from the individual resurrection of each of the faithful, which was made an essentially spiritual matter based on transformation of the personality through the truth, while the great historical resurrection was to include the political establishment of truth and justice in the world.)

The sort of cyclicism worked out by the Ismâ'îlîs can be traced in much of the later esoteric Islam. However, the cyclicism of early Ismâ'îlî thinking can be exaggerated. For the most part, the periodicity of the seven great public figures (*nâṭiqs*), and of the seven imâms for each, was emotionally and logically subordinate to the linearity of moral progression from the initial cosmic aberration to the restoration of cosmic harmony. Their readiness to adopt a political role demonstrates the history-mindedness of the Ismâ'îlîs, who were as convinced as any other Muslims of the special mission of Islam. Later, as the Ismâ'îlî doctrine became more highly developed, its philosophers interpreted

[8] Henry Corbin, in 'Le temps cyclique . . .', *Eranos Jahrbuch*, 20 (1951), 149–217, and elsewhere, is the latest to stress the importance of cyclicism in Ismâ'îlî thinking. The work on cyclicism by Mircea Eliade is also relevant here, notably 'Mythologies of Memory and Forgetting', *History of Religions*, 2 (1963), 329–44.

it by way of neo-Platonism and thus imposed on it an atemporal quality little in keeping with its historical role. Moreover, as it became involved in public political events without the expected final consummation, the historical theory became steadily more refined and complex, incorporating explanations for all the contingencies which in fact had arisen; in this process, also, its cyclicism was sometimes carried to the point of overshadowing its sense of linearity. (This happened at least in the much later Nizârî Ismâʿîlî thinking.) But the Ismâʿîlî core was chiliastic.

Counting from Ḥasan (for ʿAlî was not a mere imâm but the Prophet's executor), the seventh imâm was Muḥammad b. Ismâʿîl; as seventh, many expected him to be the Mahdî; he was to take power as soon as the effective organization of his followers was sufficient. The hierarchical authority and the esoteric secrecy thus served the individual not only in his personal spiritual development but at the same time through his participation in an ongoing historical cause; this social programme was as essential to the divine self-realization as was the personal development of the élite. (In the tenth century, in fact, an imâm did appear publicly—but only as a descendant of Muḥammad b. Ismâʿîl—and launched a campaign which first rallied the Ismâʿîlî movement to the imâm and then hoped to win the whole of the Dâr al-Islâm.)[9]

During High ʿAbbâsî times, Ismâʿîlism came to be the chief vehicle of the more esoteric of the chiliastic hopes that had gathered around Shîʿism, though there continued other esoterically oriented Bâṭinî groups (notably that which separated from the Twelvers only at the end of the tenth century to become the Nuṣayrîs, of whom a body still survives in a peasant area in northern Syria). Ismâʿîlism offered much to many. To the speculatively inclined, it offered a remarkably well worked-out picture of the cosmos; in particular, the rich mythical symbolism which had found a place in the earlier parts of the Qurʾân, but which the moralistic temper of many of the ʿulamâʾ scholars tended to reduce to rationalized prosaic irrelevance, was allowed its own vitality. To the intellectual, the shelter of its esotericism provided a worthy place within an Islamic framework for many interests which in the ordinary courtly order could well be dabbled in by Muslims, but scarcely *as* Muslims: philosophy and even natural science. It was under Bâṭinî, and probably Ismâʿîlî, patronage that the most popular of the earlier compendia of Hellenic-type

[9] Bernard Lewis, *The Origins of Ismâʿîlism* (Cambridge, 1940) is still the standard account of the rise of an Ismâʿîlî imâm to power. He may be over-enthusiastic in tracing the movement to a fairly explicit economic class orientation. His picture of the wider Ismâʿîlî movement of the time is to be corrected by the studies by Wilferd Madelung mentioned above; and by articles of S. M. Stern, ʿIsmāʿīlīs and Qarmatiansʾ, in *L'Elaboration de l'Islam*, ed. Claude Cahen (Paris, 1961), pp. 99–108; supported by ʿHeterodox Ismāʿī-lism at the time of al-Muʿizzʾ, *Bulletin of the School of Oriental and African Studies*, 17 (1955), 10–33; and ʿAbu'l-Qāsim al-Bustī and His Refutation of Ismāʿīlismʾ, *Journal of the Royal Asiatic Society*, 1961, pp. 14–35. These writers have used the Ismâʿîlî materials to get past not only the tendentious image of the Ismâʿîlîs presented by their enemies, which used to be reproduced by scholars, but also the ex post facto image of earlier Ismâʿîlism presented by the later Ismâʿîlîs themselves.

lore and science, the *Epistles of the Pure Brethren* (Ikhwân al-Ṣafâʼ), was composed (of which more later); and the chemical work of Jâbir b. Ḥayyân—foundation of the major corpus of early Islamicate chemical studies—likewise breathes this spirit. Finally, to the concerned man in the busy cities, trying to get a fairer share of prosperity, it offered hope of social justice and a sense of active participation in the struggle for this under the blessing of God. Wherever Shîʻism was found, and sometimes elsewhere too, Ismâʻîlism was potentially influential in favourable circumstances. Nevertheless, the Ismâʻîlîs, like the Manicheans, seem nowhere to have established their allegiance as commanding the daily faith of a whole population or even of a normal cross-section of it. Ismâʻîlism remained the faith of an élite.

Jamâʻism: the piety of solidarity

While many Shîʻîs cultivated a sense of isolation and suffering in a blind and wicked world from which they awaited a foreordained historical deliverance, certain of the Jamâʻî-Sunnîs were developing an ethos more appropriate to a historically successful majority. While the Shîʻîs stressed the historic mission of the Muslim community and bewailed its betrayal, these Jamâʻî-Sunnîs stressed its great heritage and cultivated a pride in identifying themselves with it.

In the Jamâʻî fold, as in the Shîʻî, several sorts of piety were in rivalry. Of the several factions of the Piety-minded opposition which then accepted the ʻAbbâsids, the Muʻtazilîs survived the longest as an independent school, while most others were gradually absorbed in what we shall call the Ḥadîth folk. They were as active at Baghdad and elsewhere as at Baṣrah where they had originated. In Marwânî times, the Muʻtazilî scholars had sometimes attempted to find irenic positions, on which all the opposition factions might agree: they refused to judge between ʻAlî and his opponents, and in the disputes as to the status of a sinner, they chose simply to use the Qurʼânic term for 'sinner'. But then they pursued their chosen positions with logical rigour; thus they refused to allow the sinner any other status than what was implied in that Qurʼânic term—hence he was neither faithful nor infidel. Under the ʻAbbâsids, they were relatively content with the orientation of Islam as it was or had been, and did not care for either emotional involvement or esoteric lore; their interest was in moral and especially doctrinal purity.

The Muʻtazilîs were noted for the rigour of their personal lives; but still more for their doctrinal speculation—if they allowed themselves a religious delight, it seems often to have lain in the charms of logical analysis. They commonly took a great interest in law, but they supplemented it with a strongly intellectual concern with ultimate questions. Here they insisted especially on sound monotheistic propriety. They stressed the responsibility of free men before a just God: humans' evil deeds must not be ascribed to God, but to the human beings themselves, who will be justly punished for them. It was equally important that no weakness proper to creatures be ascribed to God—any Qur'ânic references to physical or personal traits in God must be understood metaphorically. Withal, they were sufficiently concerned with the practical moral commitment to which the Ummah was bound, so that among the five headings into which they divided their general treatises of doctrine, along with God's unity, God's justice, sin, and the state of the sinner, came the duty of 'commanding the right and forbidding the wrong' by tongue, hand, and sword.[10]

The Mu'tazilîs were among the first Muslims to push strongly a point of view which was already represented in the Qur'ân, though it did not have so exclusive a place there: that *belief*, in the sense of acknowledgement of certain propositions, was crucial to salvation. The monotheistic conception of faith implies, initially, an act of will more than one of intellect: at once trusting God and being faithful to what He requires of one. But in all the monotheistic traditions, the notion of *trusting* God—not a convenient basis for identifying adherents—has tended to be replaced with the notion of *believing* that God is trustworthy; the notion of being faithful to His commands has been replaced with that of believing that one should be faithful. The notion of *belief* allowed a reasonably objective criterion of community allegiance. Hence the very words that conveyed the more voluntary notion of 'faith' have come to be understood as meaning 'belief'. (Such a rendering of the words makes nonsense of many passages in the Qur'ân, though it fits some fairly well.) The Mu'tazilîs emphasized works as well as belief, but it was insistence on intellectual belief that led them to develop their elaborate systems of doctrine, defining and defending the proper belief. This point of view was never lost among Muslims afterwards.

In defending their moralistic logical theses, the Mu'tazilîs became the chief early exponents of apologetic theology, kalâm; most later Islamic religious analysis goes back to them, and we will meet with them further under that head. They appealed little to the masses, though they stressed the responsible equality of believers and usually had little patience with aristocratic luxuries. Their outlook, in fact, seems to have been better suited to a small ruling élite whose members could be required to stand on their dignity in the face of a rabble of whom a high faith could not be expected. This the Islam of the ninth century CE no longer was, if it ever might have been.

The Mu'tazilîs were activists. Many of them actively supported the 'Abbâsî dynasty after it came to power. Some of these evidently hoped to use their influence with the 'Abbâsid caliphs to enforce their rigorous outlook on Muslims generally: first against the Manicheans; later, against those Muslim 'ulamâ' whose beliefs, they held, failed to maintain, clearly enough, human responsibility before God—especially, as it turned out, the Ḥadîth folk, the representatives of that form of piety which ultimately came to be specially

[10] The combination of intellectualism and moralism in the Mu'tazilîs is nicely set forth by Ismâ'îl R. al-Fârûqî, 'The Self in Mu'tazilah Thought', *International Philosophical Quarterly*, 6 (1966), 366–88.

associated with the Sharî'ah-minded Jamâ'î-Sunnî position. Before the end of the High Caliphate, Jamâ'î-Sunnî Mu'tazilism went into decline in most places, pursued by the hatred of its triumphing adversaries. (Its intellectual principles, however, were maintained and elaborated by other groups of a somewhat different cast of piety, and eventually, in a modified form, came to prevail generally.)

On the other hand, many Mu'tazilîs proved pro-'Alid, continuing the posture of the Piety-minded opposition. Some of them won disciples in the militant faction among the Shî'îs which eventually formed into the Zaydî sect. Without the Mu'tazilî name, much of the Mu'tazilî piety thus prevailed in Zaydî Shî'ism (and much of its doctrines in other Shî'î groups as well). Otherwise, Mu'tazilism as a Jamâ'î piety gradually faded away.

The Ḥadîth folk

Far the most influential form of Jamâ'î piety, by the end of High Caliphal times, was that associated with the *Ḥadîth folk*, the *Ahl al-Ḥadîth*, a group for whom ḥadîth reports about the Prophet formed the chief source of religious authority. (They are sometimes regarded as the 'orthodox' par excellence.) They combined with a keen concern for conservation of what had been achieved a moral rigorism more emotional than intellectual, which led them into an opposition to the actual current conditions among Muslims, in the name of an ideal past. Their triumphant yet populistic piety won them a large popular following, notably at Baghdad.

This tradition of piety seems to have grown up in circles that were looking back to the jamâ'ah solidarity of Marwânî times—either, as at Wâsiṭ (the Syrian capital in the Iraq), because they had never approved the intervening revolutions, or because they shared in the feelings of reaction against them that were already having an effect under al-Manṣûr. The Ḥadîth folk made a point of revering Mu'âwiyah as an associate of Muḥammad, and at first were inclined to depreciate 'Alî; they adopted the term *jamâ'ah* as a favourite designation for themselves, along with *sunnah* and *ḥadîth*. They respected especially the school of Ibn-'Umar of Medina (which had been acceptable among the Marwânîs), but rallied to themselves many of the heirs of certain other schools also—many disciples of Ḥasan al-Baṣrî and of the moderate 'Alid-loyalist ḥadîth transmitters of Kûfah (on this account, the worth of 'Alî was recognized, eventually in a compromise formula: as the fourth in dignity of the caliphs—according to their temporal order—thus still coming after 'Uthmân but having decisive precedence over Mu'âwiyah). Thus they amalgamated several traditions into a new dialogue in which everyone gave or took a little. This new tradition became increasingly the typical vehicle of piety among the Jamâ'î-Sunnî 'ulamâ' scholars, and gained great popular respect.

Its tendencies toward anti-revolutionary reaction had extensive effects.

The whole movement of the Piety-minded opposition to the Marwânîs had a certain disrepute among the Ḥadîth folk, and it was they who blackened the names of most factions in it (even when they respected individuals who had supported those factions). One of the principles that tended to be sacrificed in the new 'Abbâsî circumstances was that of the duty of individuals to 'command the right and forbid the wrong'. The Ḥadîth folk did not deny this duty, especially as among private individuals, but they did not insist on it in public matters, they recognized the established Muslim ruler on principle. Nevertheless, in their own way they were oppositional enough, and certainly not socially passive. It was in their circles that the work of formulating a Shar'î Islamic order proceeded most effectively: they had won the allegiance, not at first of the Ḥanafîs at Kûfah to be sure (who had been Murji'îs), but of the circles around Mâlik in Medina, and al-Shâfi'î. The Ḥadîth folk organized themselves informally in Baghdad, with honoured leaders whose word was law to their disciples. When al-Rashîd came to the throne (786), the Mu'tazilîs lost favour and the Ḥadîth folk were encouraged by the régime. Thereupon they used their growing popularity in Baghdad to launch a social persecution of dissidents; and on occasion the government even imprisoned some of their opponents.

The Shar'ism in the piety of the Ḥadîth folk was based on broad community loyalism which expressed itself in devotion to ḥadith reports as transmitted by (or in the name of) all Muḥammad's associates—as embodying the wisdom and glory of the community as a whole. They declared that all the associates of Muḥammad were to be revered on a common basis, and that the explanation of the disputes and enmities which had divided them was to be left to God. The conquering community of Muḥammad carried in itself and in its unity a special blessing from God, which should not be disturbed by over-nice questioning. The Twelver Shî'îs had come to see truth and justice forever a losing cause, to see the righteous persecuted and coming to God only through oppression and suffering in this world. In contrast, the Ḥadîth folk saw the truth as normally dominant among mankind, and indeed found a test of truth in the common opinion of the ruling community, in ijmâ'; when the truth was, on occasion, persecuted (as for a time, later, by the Mu'tazilîs), this was an anomalous, temporary storm to be ridden out defiantly. They were not given to weeping but to a sober sense of responsibility for a world at their feet. Their piety served as focus for a broad Sharî'ah-minded programme of social order looking back to the homogeneity of the primitive Muslim community.

This piety, however, was more than community consciousness or a broadly-based legalism. Their concern with the detail of revealed law had a dimension of highly personal and immediate devotion, as emotional and imaginative in its own way as the mourning of the Twelver Shî'îs. Their assumption, in trying to develop the Sharî'ah law on the basis of the historical community as a whole, was that the Qur'ân and the sunnah practice were alone enough to allow a community of human beings to achieve a life of unmediated responsibility to God. This could be felt to be so only if God could be found truly unmediatedly in the Law itself. Hence when the doctrine arose that the Qur'ân was God's eternal speech—not merely His creature as were human beings and other things—the idea was eagerly seized on.

Such an idea glorified the textualist tendencies which these men necessarily were led to in basing their system on the ḥadîth texts rather than on either community tradition—as the older legists had done—or on private reasoning, as the Mu'tazilîs tended to do. Against either traditionalism or rationalism or indeed the personal loyalism of the Shî'îs, the Ḥadîth folk glorified the explicit words (*naṣṣ*) of texts held to be sacred—above all, of course, the Qur'ân. Accordingly, the piety of the Ḥadîth folk was given its supreme expression in the doctrine (expressed in ḥadîth) that the Qur'ân which they recited was, as word of God, not merely another of God's creations but somehow an eternal cosmic entity, something of God Himself; the more ardent of them were willing to die rather than say that the Qur'ân was merely created. These men admitted no images to cloud for them the face of God; they admitted no heady incense or sacred music, no kindly saints, and no graciously redeeming Saviour. But they did want God to be palpable—they wanted to see God when they died, and right now they wanted to hear Him directly. Their imaginations were set afire by the presence of God Himself, Whose speech, which was not other than Himself, was on their very tongues when they recited the Qur'ân, in their very hands when they held it reverently.

Such doctrines were as alien to the primitive Medina piety as was the Shî'î hero worship. The Mu'tazilîs, shocked, accused the Ḥadîth folk of derogating from the unity of God and from his transcendent majesty by their over-familiar attitudes. The Mu'tazilîs felt that to make the Qur'ân, as word of God, 'not Creator but not created either' (in the phrase of the Ḥadîth folk) was to set it up to be worshipped beside Him. This was obviously contrary to the whole spirit of the Qur'ân, which the Mu'tazilîs were dedicated to defending. With the support of the caliphal authority from al-Ma'mûn's time on, they tested the orthodoxy of the Ḥadîth folk by requiring them to admit that the Qur'ân, like everything else, had merely been created by God. The Ḥadîth folk could not grant this: such an admission would strike at the heart of their sense of the immediate presence, in the Qur'ân, of God Himself challenging the human soul.

Nevertheless, they had their own way of dwelling on God's overwhelming greatness, which was as necessary to their piety as to that of the Mu'tazilîs. They pushed further a position which had already been suggested at Marwânî Medina (and at which Ḥasan al-Baṣrî had been shocked). In their emphasis on the supremacy of God over all things, they insisted that it was He alone who created human acts, even a person's evil acts. God was above any human criteria of good or evil, of just or unjust; all things sprang from Him, and if an act was to be regarded as unjust it was because He so labelled it, not from any inherent nature in it which God was bound to respect. God could not be bound! The Ḥadîth folk in turn, therefore, accused the Mu'tazilîs themselves of dishonouring God. The Mu'tazilîs, in their attempt to rationalize their faith, asserted the freedom of the human will which would be rewarded necessarily by God's justice. The Ḥadîth folk felt that this was to insult God's power doubly: by assuming that God was powerless to be author of acts labelled by us as evil, that He was forced to be what we human beings call just; and by ascribing to human beings alone their evil deeds, as if human creatures could create, like God, deeds or anything else. They cited the Qur'ânic verses which spoke of the need to submit to God or else find oneself willy-nilly in sin, and condemned as un-Qur'ânic a doctrine which seemed to make human beings their own masters. No, God was the only true actor in the universe and human beings were merely his momentary creatures, unfit to judge Him just or unjust, reasonable or unreasonable. When His Word came to them they dare not treat it as a mere created thing to be disputed about; they must simply tremble, obey, and be grateful.

The spiritual temptation which faced the Ḥadîth folk was to try to seize the creative moment, the Qur'ânic point of contact with Transcendence, and to try to hold onto it—by turning it into something which can be held onto, and which therefore inevitably must lose the dimension of transcendence. This the Mu'tazilîs could see, and accused the Ḥadîth folk of *shirk,* of idolatrously associating something else with God. But the Ḥadîth folk were surely right in retorting that the Mu'tazilîs, in their intellectualism, were in danger of putting reason in the place of God—that is, of reducing the divine mystery to an abstract formula of belief.

Ibn-Ḥanbal and Ḥadîthî populism

This textualist piety did not achieve its success without some heroes of its own to revere: notably the great ḥadîth-reporter and legist, Aḥmad Ibn-Ḥanbal (780–855). Ibn-Ḥanbal from his youth dedicated himself to Islamic learning, listening to all possible ḥadîth-reporters and memorizing prodigious numbers of reports. He long lived in abject poverty, which was further complicated by scruples against admitting any personal practice which he could not base on Muḥammad's example as transmitted in ḥadîth. His powerful memory, his piety and generosity (he later forgave his chief persecutor), and his good judgment and eloquence made him a pre-eminent teacher of ḥadîth.

Under al-Ma'mûn (813–833), the Mu'tazilîs were restored to favour, and under him and his successors they were allowed to persecute, in a sort of inquisition called the *miḥnah,* the leaders of the Ḥadîth folk (who had been intolerant enough themselves under al-Rashîd). Al-Ma'mûn selected Ibn-Ḥanbal to make an example of if he would not recant the notion of an uncreated Qur'ân, threatening him with death. His steadfast refusal gave heart to the others. His life was saved by al-Ma'mûn's own timely death, but he underwent a long imprisonment and was hailed as a martyr to the cause.[11]

Ibn-Ḥanbal seems to have been a man of humble background and the piety which he represented appealed to the simpler folk of the cities, especially of Baghdad. For by now the different sorts of piety often seem to have reflected social class divisions even more than local history as under the Marwânids. In particular, the difference between Jamâʻî-Sunnî and Shîʻî, which may initially have answered partly to temperamental differences, had, as it became hereditary, fallen into socially significant patterns: in certain groups, a particular allegiance was reinforced, even among those initially neutral, by appeals of interest. In the countryside many of the landed gentry, as they became Muslim, adopted the Jamâʻî-Sunnî position which was official at court. In the cities many of the wealthy merchants and bankers were Shîʻîs; the merchant quarter of Baghdad, al-Karkh, was the Shîʻî stronghold there. Many of these must have been of old Mawâlî families whose traditions went back to Marwânî times.

Conceivably the Shîʻism of this class represented the greater persistence of such merchants in holding out for more purely Islamic and egalitarian social ideals against the ʻAbbâsî compromise, which cannot have seemed any great blow to the aristocratic gentry. From this class were drawn many of the kâtibs and high administrators of the caliphal state, who were accordingly very often Shîʻîs even though serving the ʻAbbâsids. To the extent that general culture would flourish best among the upper bourgeoisie, it is probably also no coincidence that a disproportionately large number of the writers, philosophers, and other leaders in the Islamicate culture of the High Caliphate were Shîʻîs. There were other elements in Islamdom (for instance, certain cities like Kûfah and Qum) which had adopted Shîʻism, but the bourgeoisie played a major role in it.

The lower classes in the city in turn, the artisans and servants and also the common soldiery, seem to have been largely Jamâʻî-Sunnî; perhaps the common people saw little practical possibility of an egalitarian political order wide enough to include the lower strata in any effective way, and preferred (especially in the capital) to identify themselves with the Islamic community as a whole, membership in which set them above the dhimmîs and the unconverted peasants. They would also have had no objection to contradicting the wealthier bourgeois; the Sunnî-Shîʻî riots in Baghdad, during which the Karkh

[11] Walter M. Patton, *Aḥmed ibn Ḥanbal and the Miḥna: A Biography of the Imâm including an Account of the Moḥammedan Inquisition Called the Miḥna, 218–234 A.H.* (Leiden, 1897), is a useful English compilation of the data about Ibn-Ḥanbal. Unfortunately, it presupposes without examination some assumptions of the time when it was written—that the Muʻtazilîs were 'rationalists' and probably licentious and that the Ḥadîth folk were 'traditionalists' in the sense of holding to unaltered community tradition. The consequence is that the book misses all the problems. (In it occur some examples of the obscurity that can result when the word 'tradition' is used for a ḥadîth report as well as in the ordinary English sense, and it is not made clear which is which.)

quarter was sometimes pillaged, cannot have been motivated exclusively by theological disagreements. The majority of the population, of upper and lower class, were willing to accept the 'Abbâsid family as caliphs, prosperity having, in effect, vindicated their claims, however dubious at the beginning; hence Shî'ism depended on specific situations of discontent and did not become generalized among the great body of new Muslims after its first major defeats. As the population of the caliphal state became Muslims, they became Jamâ'î-Sunnî Muslims.

At any rate, the Ḥadîth folk found a vigorous response among many of the poorer classes of Baghdad. In the rest of the empire, in turn, religious expectations tended to be moulded by what was received in the capital; though in some provinces—such as Khûzistân and Khwârazm—it was the Mu'tazilî scholars who were able to set the public tone of religion. The viewpoint of the Ḥadîth folk was launched toward general success with its victory in Baghdad.

In no other movement did the traits of populism appear more strongly developed than in that of the Ḥadîth folk. The Ḥadîth folk were often at odds, indeed, with the quṣṣâṣ, the pious story-tellers who carried forward the popular legendry from pre-Islamic times (especially Christian and Jewish lore), or derived new legends by a lively imagination from the imagery of the Qur'ân. But it was among the Ḥadîth folk that at least the more reasonable of such tales found a responsible defence. For however much the Ḥadîth folk might in principle reject such things, anthropomorphism in tales of God, presenting Him in the image of a human being, and the legendry of spectacular deeds which prophets could achieve at God's hands, served to support a sense of personal contact with the divine presence in revelation. The Qur'ân teemed with anthropomorphic images and prophetic wonder tales which the Ḥadîth folk found no reason to tone down so long as they served to exalt the glory of God and the honour of His prophets.

Whatever could get itself embodied in ḥadîth reports received a hearing, then, however much it pictured God anthropomorphically. Some years after Ibn-Ḥanbal a riot was caused when the scholar Ṭabarî objected to a preacher in this tradition who dubiously interpreted a Qur'ânic verse to mean that Muḥammad would sit on the Throne with God (like Jesus for the Christians). The mob wanted to lynch the sceptical scholar. The cosmic figures in the Qur'ân received some recognition, too, if less explicitly than among the Ghulât theorists: Ibn-Ḥanbal himself made a point of citing such verses in support of the cosmic status of the Qur'ân. The movement was so closely identified with the common people that their opponents commonly called the Ḥadîth folk 'populists', Ḥashwiyyah.[12]

[12] A. S. Halkin in 'The Ḥashwiyya', *JAOS*, 54 (1934), 1–28, has made clear the identification of the Ḥashwiyyah as the Ḥadîth folk, but derives the name from the notion of 'redundant speech' rather than 'vulgar populace', both notions being carried by the word *ḥashw*. But the pseudo-Nawbakhtî's 'ahl ul-ḥashwi wa-l-jamhûr', which he imper-

Nevertheless, populism was not carried to the point of sheer concession of all popular notions; it remained limited by what the ʿulamâʾ scholars could feel was proper for the people. Accordingly, the Ḥadîth folk were careful to reject any outright anthropomorphism, which they recognized was inconsistent with the Qurʾânic notion of divine transcendence. Borrowing a formula originally used in legal thinking, they noted that phrases in Qurʾân and ḥadîth that seemed to sanction anthropomorphism in God or other unacceptable notions should be, indeed, accepted literally—but with the reservation 'without asking how'. Thus God might indeed, as the text had it, step down from his throne; this was not to be allegorized away as the Muʿtazilîs would; but at the same time it must be recognized that humans could not know what it meant—in any case, it could not be assimilated to a man's stepping down from a throne. Taken seriously, such an attitude took back any concessions which seemed to have been made to the imagination.

Eventually, when the successors of the Ḥadîth folk and of the Muʿtazilîs had fully merged into a common Jamâʿî-Sunnî tradition, this attitude became the basis for a general adoption among the ʿulamâʾ scholars of a drily rational spirit already foreshadowed by the Muʿtazilîs, which turned all the luxuriant cosmic imagery of Qurʾân and ḥadîth into common-sense prose. But by then the popular imaginative piety was already flowing in other channels.

After the reign of al-Mutawakkil, later in the ninth century, the more extreme representatives of this approach, who called themselves Ḥanbalîs, after Ibn-Ḥanbal, tended to have it their own way in the streets of Baghdad and to a lesser degree elsewhere. Those whom they suspected of a different approach were sometimes subjected to great abuse and even mob attack. The sort of piety represented by the Ḥanbalîs never succeeded in swaying the whole community. Throughout classical ʿAbbâsî times there were a number of rival schools. Yet in the end that sort of piety enforced its key dogmas and much of its temper upon almost all Jamâʿî-Sunnîs. Before this could happen, however, quite a different sort of Islamic piety had come to rival it, a piety which was to overshadow the piety of the old Ḥadîth folk in the following centuries: Ṣûfism.

B. MYSTICAL ORIENTATION

Twelver Shîʿîs, Ismâʿîlîs, Muʿtazilîs, and Ḥadîth folk all developed out of the Piety-minded opposition to the Marwânids and represented, in one form or

fectly cites, clearly means 'men of the people, of the majority': they are not verbose, a secondary notion, but populistic. In the course of a generally excellent study he suggests that the Ḥadîth folk took the 'easy' way of being 'uncommitted'; but they were 'uncommitted' only where texts in the ḥadîth corpus were mutually contradictory or where such contradiction might be implied (when Muḥammad's associates fought among themselves). The point of such neutrality was neither to take an easy way out nor, as Halkin also suggests, to express a quiescent fideist wisdom; it was to lay the basis for a positive programme, to which the Ḥadîth folk were fully committed even to the point of opposing the régime.

other, a kerygmatic orientation in which the historical development of the Islamic Ummah played a major role. From the beginning, other Muslims were attracted to a more individualistic piety, concerning themselves with more personal problems, which a pious man met when he tried to deepen and purify his inward worship. As this sort of piety matured, it became frankly mystical: it was inspired, above all, by subjective inward awarenesses emerging as the selfhood matured, and the historical, the political role of the Muslim Ummah came to play a minimal role in it. This less historically-oriented Muslim movement was called *Ṣûfism* at Kûfah, and this name came to prevail elsewhere also for many centuries. To some degree, Ṣûfism shared the traits of Christian mystical movement and developed it further; but, like the other main forms of Muslim piety, it was unmistakably Islamic. At least occasionally, men who might otherwise have become Christian monks were converted to Islam in its Ṣûfî form when they felt the call to a more reflective life. In creativity, Ṣûfism soon left contemporary local Christian movements far behind.

Spiritual athleticism within Islam: the aspirations of the Ṣûfîs

The early Ṣûfîs looked to disparate early founders, but soon formed a single movement, which was closely associated with the Ḥadîth folk. (Ṣûfîs seem to have found the intellectualistic Mu'tazilîs uncongenial.) In some cases it is hard to draw a line between what was Ṣûfî mystical self-examination and what was Ḥadîthî moralism. Several Ṣûfî masters also concerned themselves closely with ḥadîth; and most Ṣûfîs were Jamâ'î-Sunnîs, at any rate. On the other hand, not all the early Muslim mystics were clearly identifiable with an explicitly Ṣûfî movement. An important Jamâ'î-Sunnî group, the Karrâmîs, who converted and taught independently in Khurâsân, seem equally close to both Ṣûfîs and Ḥadîth folk, with whom they quarrelled. They were much preoccupied with law and ḥadîth reports and even speculative dogma, contributing to later kalâm thinking, but at the same time their founder (Ibn-Karrâm, d. 869) contributed significantly to later Ṣûfî analysis of inward experience. But, by and large, the Ṣûfîs formed a reasonably homogeneous group who kept in mutual contact despite being distributed throughout Islamdom.

In some ways, but not all, the Ṣûfîs represented in a Jamâ'î-Sunnî milieu what Bâṭinî piety represented in a Shî'î milieu. Mysticism, difficult by its inner-personal nature to share or explain publicly, naturally tends to become esoteric and to lend itself to all forms of esoteric interests. The esoteric side of Shî'ism was more prominent among Ismâ'îlîs than among Twelvers, but no Ja'farî Shî'î group was without it. Among Jamâ'î-Sunnîs, however, a historical esotericism of that sort would have been out of place. But Ṣûfism did provide an esoteric form of piety among them, which allowed those of them who were so inclined to explore hidden meanings and personal resonances not allowed for by the soberly public Sharî'ah. Just as the Bâṭiniyyah stressed the more personal and esoteric aspects of 'Alid loyalism, the Ṣûfîs stressed the more inward and esoteric aspects of the imaginative piety associated with the ḥadîth movement, till it overshadowed, though it did not replace, concern with the Sharî'ah law itself. Even more than among the Bâṭiniyyah, the Ṣûfîs' starting point was ever the Qur'ân, whose inward meanings they explored, attempting to get behind the surface of the words. Their technique was less allegorical or symbolical than that of the Bâṭinîs and focused instead on the personal experience that the words seemed to crystallize; even so, there were points of contact between the two ways of more deeply reading the Qur'ân.[13]

The Ṣûfî tradition was later, in a developed form, to dominate the whole inner life of Islam, Sunnî and even to a degree Shî'î; but in the high 'Abbâsî period it was a minority movement. From the first generations of Islam there had been those who tended to emphasize personal purity and freedom from the temptations and taints of living in the world. While the Islamic tradition set its head against monastic celibacy, there were many Muslims noted for their *zuhd*, a pious zeal which practically amounted to asceticism. This tendency was important among the circles of the Piety-minded; like other movements, notably Mu'tazilism, it claimed a source in Ḥasan al-Baṣrî (d. 728), the austere saint of Baṣrah in Marwânî times.

But with 'Abbâsî times such tendencies ceased to be merely ascetic. Much was learned by the mystically-inclined from Christian monks, and no doubt from other sources too, of the inward life of the soul that would detach itself from the world and love God only. Islam under the 'Abbâsids came to include a general cross-section of society and no longer merely a ruling minority; concurrently, the mysticism which had long been a part of life between Nile and Oxus, particularly among Christians, began to flower among Muslims. Great ecstatic saints arose around whom circles of devoted admirers gathered, to record their words and their exalted experiences and to try to imitate their abandonment of all things worldly.

The Ṣûfîs honoured the Qur'ân as enshrining God's message to Muḥammad; but rather than devote themselves to the letter of its words, they hoped in some measure to repeat in their own lives something of the experiences which presumably Muḥammad must have gone through in receiving the various portions of the words of God. They normally accepted the Shar'î approach in its Jamâ'î-Sunnî forms as valid in its own realm. But they tended to call the Sharî'ah law merely external, a matter of mere outward actions only incidentally relevant to the soul. The Sharî'ah and all related notions were

[13] Niyazi Berkes, in 'Ethics and Social Practice in Islam', *Philosophy East and West*, 9 (1959), 60–62, provides an excellently subtle statement of the several ethical tendencies in the Qur'ân and within Ṣûfism. He shows that in both Ṣûfism and Falsafah there was a degree of reaction against ways in which fiqh jurisprudence and kalâm disputation had departed from the spirit of the Qur'ân.

subordinated to an inward life. By searching the inner meaning of the meaning behind the words of the Qur'ân, they aimed to relive the spiritual states out of which the words had been formed. Their methods were retirement and meditation, meditation especially of the Qur'ân and of the very name of God; their results were very often an intense single-mindedness, a very pure ethic, and a total spiritual orientation of their lives which caused those about them to prize, as more precious than life, even fragments of their saintly existence.

In Islamicate civilization as a whole, three movements can be singled out as of especially pervasive formative effect: the militarizing of agrarian-based political authority; the assertion of Shar'î legal and social relations; and the rise of Ṣûfî experience and teaching. Nothing in literature or art, in the sciences, or in economic development so ramifyingly marked the civilization in its distinctiveness. We must take special pains to understand Ṣûfism here.

The history of religious experience and awareness has been singularly difficult to trace. It is clearly not reducible to the history of cult or of dogma or even of religious and sectarian allegiance. We must try to study the sort of expectations the most advanced people have been able to have at any given times as to what levels of spiritual perceptiveness could be attained, and what kinds of moral or numinal responsibility or responsiveness could be reasonably looked for. Almost certainly the rhythms of development of these underlying levels of spiritual life have been slower than those of the more visible levels; perhaps more on the order of the rhythms of technological development in pre-Modern times, and correspondingly hard to perceive even at best.

In the development of mystical traditions in particular, the deeper level is especially difficult to trace because of the notoriously ineffable character of mystical experience. Mystical experience is as incommunicable to those insensitive to it as is musical experience to those deaf from birth. But, since a mystical experience is almost always personal to a single individual, even among those who are in some degree sensitive to it, discussion of particular instances is at least as difficult as discussion of a musical piece with one who has not heard the music nor even seen the score. At most such discussion is not logically analytic, but impressionistic and evocative.

Yet it seems clear that, in the centuries of the High Caliphate and after, a new dimension was being added to the expectations mystics had of what mystical experience could lead to. In Christian Byzantium (and, at least a bit later, in Hindu India) as well as from Nile to Oxus we find in this period a new sort of literary expression of a high love-mysticism which seems to amount to more than just literary style. Though no older forms of religious experience were dropped, it seems that certain postures of the soul, which had doubtless been reached occasionally before and in combination with other things, were now being widely expected among relatively ordinary mystics; and ways were being found to cultivate what was expected. In Islamdom, this development of a high love mysticism was associated with the consolidation of Islam in its Ṣûfî form.[14]

Mystical life as personal discipline

'Mysticism' and 'mystical', in their technical sense, refer, in the first instance, to inward personal experience, more or less transitory as an event but enduring in relevance, which is felt to express or to lead to a special authoritative and normative relation between individual and cosmos; then the words refer also to the practices and behaviour that accompany or express such experience, and finally to the statements used to describe or explain it. The noun 'mystic' is applied to an adept of the mystical life. (But the adjective 'mystic' is commonly used—in contrast to 'mystical'—in a quite different sense, for anything occult or symbolic or simply romantic.) There may be a mystical dimension in most serious devotional religious experience; but we do not usually speak of 'mysticism' except where the inward personal experience is itself the focus of devotional attention.

It is usual to think of the mystical as simply an extraordinary occasion in consciousness. The most spectacular of the mystical experiences are marked, overwhelming states of consciousness, which are usually exceedingly transient and are as emphatic as an access of rage or as acute infatuation or as drunken hallucinations; indeed, the classic instances are held to be yet more overpowering and intense than moments of apoplectic anger or of climactic orgasm, yet at the same time much calmer and deeper. These can be referred to as 'ecstatic' experiences, in that the individual feels as if he were somehow beyond himself. But mystical experience has a wider range than ecstatic experience alone. The more striking events, at least as they appear in the classical Ṣûfî tradition, are but the peaks of a very widespread type of awareness. Mystics have almost always described a lengthy mystical 'way', leading by innumerable small steps from the first glimmerings of devout repentance in the sinner up to the most ecstatic moments of the saint. Most mystical writers have spent far more time speaking of the everyday virtues of patience, courage, and unselfishness, as they appear in the mystical perspective, than of ecstasies or even of the cosmic unity these ecstasies seem to bear witness to. We may refer to this wider range of inward experience and behaviour, in which ecstasies appear as special cases, as 'everyday' mysticism.

Freud popularized the term 'oceanic consciousness' for an undifferentiated, more or less ecstatic condition often described, by witnesses who have felt it, as a sense of oneness with the universe, that is, with the total environment. Freud suggested at least one way of accounting for the possibility of such a

[14] The work of Gustave von Grunebaum drew my attention to this as to so many other fundamental thrusts in Islamicate history. My treatment of mysticism here has been helped, I hope, by the drastic reactions of Alex Morin (whose comments throughout the manuscript have been provocative); and by Eugene Gendlin's sympathetic clarifications.

condition developing organically: the psychical groundwork for it may lie in the infant consciousness, which does not distinguish between self and environment. A recapturing or reconstituting of that undivided consciousness in adulthood—by any of several means—could be the vehicle for new sorts of awareness.[15]

Such analyses are essential. However independent a meaning one attaches to moral and religious phenomena, one must, so far as possible, identify the organic processes involved. Only when we understand such processes well can we speak with critical precision about the meaning and value of any human phenomena. Thus our increasing understanding of what is happening in human love and hate has helped us to distinguish degrees of validity in different kinds of loving. But we still know remarkably little about what goes on in aesthetic and in mystical consciousness. Unfortunately, this notion of 'oceanic consciousness', though suggestive, may emphasize too much one kind of subjective state, which is not the whole of mystical experience and practice and may not even be essential to it.[16]

Without leaving Freud, indeed, we may bring out some other aspects of the experience by noting how objects and events can evoke unconscious associations which can lend them overwhelming power. This mechanism surely underlies part of the experience of the numinous, as analyzed by Rudolph Otto; and nowhere is the numinous more evident than in most forms of mystical experience. That experience may be seen as a heightening and internalizing of the daunted awe and enchanted fascination with which any religiously sensitive person may respond to those moments that carry the numinous for him. Such experiences, though part of an inward transformation of consciousness, need not carry 'oceanic' implications.

But for purposes of understanding the role of mysticism in developing a civilization, one must see the more ecstatic mystical moments as part of a *moral process* which occurs almost universally. In this perspective, a more fruitful vantage point for making sense of the whole range of mystical experience,

[15] This is not exactly the way Freud put it. Freud sometimes spoke as if such an experience, if it did no harm clinically, could at will be reduced to 'nothing but' what lay organically at its origin, though he was cautious in his own formulations. But that a complex phenomenon can be interpreted in terms of its components and its preconditions need not reduce it to that level and deprive it of its own meaning on its own level. Such reduction is indeed a temptation. If one wishes to distinguish, in such phenomena, between their organic origin or mechanism and their moral meaning, one must speak with a special care which was perhaps irrelevant in the clinic.

[16] The most popular treatise in English on the phenomena of mysticism is Evelyn Underhill's *Mysticism* (London, 1911), which restricts itself largely to the West Christian tradition (which is not entirely typical). William James, *The Varieties of Religious Experience* (London, 1903) (which R. C. Zaehner's work cited in note 17 below, among others, will help to correct) is not yet out of date. But there have been several important studies of mystical phenomena recently, which are bringing the whole subject to a level where neither the old smugness of the mystics as an élite among the uncomprehending mass, nor the old disdain of the 'tough-minded' for the aberrations of gullible enthusiasts will hold up.

both ecstatic and everyday, is the commonplace experience of arriving at relative personal clarity: the clarity that comes when the elements of a problem finally fit together, or when one has shaken away the haziness after waking suddenly, or, perhaps most especially, when a surge of anger has died down and one can look at the situation realistically and with a measure of generosity. All these are first approximations to a fuller, but still relatively commonplace, experience of clarity that can come at moments of retirement and recollection: moments when one can look on one's own current resentments or ambitions with some objectivity, and even gain perspective on and some control over one's life-passions generally; when, for the time being, what one might call one's neurotic compulsions cease to be compelling. At best, in such moments (as many have discovered), one can face the loss of anything one has most desired, and even recognize one's own worst traits, without either anxiety or self-pity, and can find the courage to try to be the best one can imagine being.

In such moments one may experience, for the time being, much of what the Ṣûfîs described when they told of the states to which the soul attains along the mystical Way. Thus when one has oneself under control, one can, for the moment, cease needing to worry what anyone else will think of one's acts, if they be right in themselves. An accomplished Ṣûfî was expected to be enduringly emancipated in this way from desire for people's approval. It was said of the saint Bâyazîd (Abû-Yazîd) Bisṭâmî (d. 874) that, as he was on his way back from the ḥajj pilgrimage, the crowds at Rayy met him with excessive adulation. It was the fasting month Ramaḍân, and he deliberately took out some bread and ate it in public. Since he was on a trip, this was legal for him; but the crowds saw only the fast-breaking and abandoned him. Again, one can for a moment freely and honestly feel generous and compassionate impulses for those who most stand in one's way or behave most hatefully. Such an experience helps make intelligible the more enduring and ingrained compassion Ṣûfîs ascribed to Jesus (pictured as the ideal Ṣûfî) when they told how, as he passed along a road, people insulted him and he responded with blessings and helpfulness; and when asked why, he answered: a man can bring forth only what is within him.

Again, a person may find, at a moment of recollection, that he can depend on some healthy sense of fitness to guide his judgment among the different possible courses that present themselves, so that for the moment he seems free of the confusing effects of self-importance or of wilful preconceptions. Such an experience anticipates one aspect of what the Ṣûfîs meant by reliance on God. Among the Ṣûfîs it was a decisive achievement to reach a level of consciousness where one could let one's whole life be guided by the immediate will of God, and put one's trust in nothing lesser; so that one made no binding plans but depended on each moment to provide for its own needs. This meant, among other things, being willing to pass up any seeming opportunities that did not bear the marks of divine blessing, however dire the consequences might be. The tale is told of a wandering mystic who fell into a pit along a desert route. He started to call out to his companions for help, but felt a stop in his mind—he must be patient till God should help him. His companions went off into the distance and he was left alone. At length came a couple of other men, but again he was not free to call out; even when they saw the pit and covered it over, he had to remain quiet. It grew dark; then in the dark something reached into the side of the pit. Now at last he found himself free to grab hold and be pulled out, and when he reached the surface he found that what he had hold of was a lion's paw. That mystic was far along the Way, and had been called upon, correspondingly, to show extraordinary trust and fearlessness. The moral is not, as it might seem, that the mystic should depend exclusively on miracles: no mystic taught this. The tale was told partly, no doubt, to suggest that true servants of God are such great beings that even lions serve them. But it describes faithfully, at the same time, what dependence on God meant: not waiting for God in person to pull one out of a pit, but waiting till such means as happened to offer themselves proved compatible with one's sense of God's presence. Such an approach shares, on an advanced level, a like spirit with the more everyday experience of clear judgment during a moment of recollection.

The experience felt in such moments of retirement and recollection can have a further dimension which anticipates another side of mystical thinking. In such moments, as inhibiting fears fall away and one no longer feels the need to put up pretences and defences against any sort of truth—as one's personal ambitions suddenly appear petty, and one can find the resources to face any fact about oneself and to love any being capable of needing love—it is possible, even among fairly ordinary persons, for a more universal perspective on life at large to be felt. At such moments one's standpoint is least self-centred; that is, most nearly the standpoint that some cosmically objective being might have who could feel totally all human life and yet act in perfect detachment from any particular one of life's pressures. And this is just the moral standpoint that emerges (where any does) more intensely from the more striking mystical experiences.

From everyday moments of recollection, with such selflessness as they bring, the mystic may rise to ever more intense levels of awareness, which can take ecstatic forms. Ecstasy, carrying with it both intense euphoria and a sense of total clarity about reality, can occur in very diverse contexts. But so far as it has played a role in historical mystical traditions, it has done so as part of a total self-assessment and self-discipline. It is in such a context that an ecstatic experience ('oceanic' or otherwise) is most likely to carry with it the moral standpoint of universality. Always the ground of mystical life, in this historical sense, is a striving for clarity and sincerity; whatever the level they have reached, mystics, both Ṣûfîs and others, have spoken most persistently in metaphors of Light and Truth. To this sort of clarity, the touchstone of relevance to everyday life will apply. A primary criterion that mystics have used to test the 'genuineness' of an ecstatic mystical experience—that is, whether it is from God or from the Devil (or possibly consists merely in a similar, perhaps organically related but abortive, subjective event)—is its enduring relevance to all dimensions of a person's life, including the everyday. Hujwîrî (d. *c.* 1077), in his description of the true Ṣûfîs of his time (whom he distinguished from the many deluded or even fraudulent claimants to the Way), says of one of them, 'I found him to be like a flash of love'.[17]

Mystical practice begins in any case, with some sort of retirement and self-recollection: meditation upon the implications of some important truth; prayer, setting oneself in dependence before some being of a wider level of vision; adoration, acknowledging one's pettiness before the greatness of something that transcends one's own nature. For the Ṣûfîs, the focus of meditation was of course the Qur'ân; the object of adoration was the unique Deity to which the Qur'ân summoned.

Meditation then led to a certain amount of withdrawal, for the mystical way required the concentration of a person's energies. Ridding oneself of any dependence on satisfying one's desires or one's disgusts could even require severe ascetic exercises. To accustom himself to not caring whether he was physically comfortable or not, one man had himself hung by the heels for hours at a time; to accustom himself to not caring whether he felt hungry or not, another would eat but a few grains a day. But Ṣûfî teachers usually warned against pursuing asceticism for itself—for instance, we would say, being ascetic out of neurotic guilt feelings. All forms of withdrawal, like the disciplines of athletes, should serve to establish more complete self-control.

With withdrawal came temptations. Ascetic rigours, combined with moral liberation, could produce heady delights: ocular visions, auditions, and other abnormal psychic phenomena; all of which, and even the moments of sheer exquisite ecstasy, one's teachers warned one to discount, lest they become simply another pleasure one was attached to. As a good Muslim, the Ṣûfî must return and fulfill his social duties according to the Sharîʿah; hopefully with increased objectivity and sincerity. But he repeatedly renewed his meditation, seeking nearness to God—to discarding concern with all secondary

[17] R. C. Zaehner, in *Mysticism Sacred and Profane* (Oxford, 1957), has distinguished (much too schematically) 'nature mysticism', relatively commonplace experience of *identity with the environment*—attainable also in drug-poisoning and in schizophrenia; monistic mysticism, in which the experience is more disciplined and leads to the *isolation of the individual consciousness* in seeming transcendence of the natural environment; and theistic mysticism, in which the experience is likewise disciplined, but develops as a *loving response to a Transcendent* presence before which nature and the individual alike are as nothing; and suggests (unconvincingly) that what sets off the 'theistic' or, as he calls it, 'supernatural', mysticism from other kinds is its ethical consequences. G. C. Anamati and Louis Gardet, in *La mystique musulmane* (Paris, 1961), have likewise made the distinction between supernatural and natural (monist) mysticism, which they develop more subtly than Zaehner, but also with less comprehensive a sweep.

Such divisions falsify the integrity of the individual experience, but they do make us realize that each experience can have a definable structure and that, in the sort of experiences that become historically relevant, that structure has consequences.

preoccupations and to being impelled only by larger and deeper rhythms; or rather, as they preferred to put it, to seeing and loving only Him.

Mystical life as personal freedom

The results of all this in the individual's life varied, of course, as much as did the mystical process itself, from person to person. Certain main lines were common. The mystic tended to have a 'spiritual' orientation; that is, at a certain point he felt no routine to be binding, no law to be sacred, simply because it was a routine or a law; if he did follow the routine, it was out of conviction that it suited his place in the whole cosmos at the moment; but ever new possibilities of meaning might lead him beyond any customary, beyond even customary Ṣûfî, ways of looking at things. The favourite Ṣûfî word for God came to be *Ḥaqq*, simply 'Right' or 'Truth'. The later Persian poet Jalâluddîn Rûmî puts this beautifully (Mas̄navî, II, 3766 ff.) in the image of the duck that was hatched and raised by a mother chicken. The duck longs to go out into the water to swim—the water, especially the ocean, symbolizing the uncharted Infinite of God. The mother, which is Mother Nature, is frightened of this water, alien to her, and urges the duckling to stay on land. Each soul must decide, like the duckling, whether to stay on the safe land of routine predictabilities, of custom and Sharî'ah law, as our Mother and all our friends plead with us to do; or whether to answer the call of our true inner nature and launch out into the deep.

With some Ṣûfîs, this came to mean that all external rules, notably the whole Sharî'ah, were no longer binding on him who had come to live in the spirit behind the rules. Most Ṣûfîs felt that the Sharî'ah was binding on them as on all other Muslims, if only lest their liberty become a stumbling-block to weaker brethren. If one loved God, one would eagerly obey His commandments. For Ṣûfîs, the formal ṣalât worship often became the occasion of intense devotional fervour. But many agreed that the outer rules were valid only through their inward, spiritual meaning and purpose.

Hence Ṣûfîs increasingly tended to minimize differences among religious beliefs. In contrast to the communalist exclusivity of most of the Piety-minded, they readily tended toward a universalistic viewpoint, looking less to a person's religious allegiance than to his spiritual and moral qualities in whatever guise they appeared. Eventually, after the High Caliphal Period, it became almost commonplace for Ṣûfîs to argue that even idolaters, who fell down and worshipped stones, were really worshipping the true God: for they were worshipping the best approximation they could find to the Truth that is at the heart of all reality, including stones. Such a viewpoint was initiated early. One Ṣûfî sometimes made his disciples recast the Muslim phrase of witness as 'There is no deity but God and Jesus is His messenger'—a statement technically valid but psychologically upsetting to anyone bound to a specifically Muslim allegiance.

Indeed, many Ṣûfîs allotted a specially holy place to Jesus as the prophet of the inward life, of the gospel of Love. For among Ṣûfîs, as among other mystics, Love of God, and hence tenderness to all His creatures, came to be seen as the heart of the inward life, just as reverence for God and justice to all His creatures was the heart of the outward life, of the Sharîʿah. There remained no doubt, of course, in most Ṣûfîs' minds that the revelation to Muḥammad was the greatest and the purest of the revelations. Sometimes it was put thus: that Moses revealed the majesty of God, and the Law which we must obey out of respect to Him; Jesus revealed the beauty of God, and the Love which we must bear Him when we catch a glimpse of His Reality; but Muḥammad came with both Law and Love together, revealing both His majesty and His beauty.

With their spiritual and universalistic orientation, the Ṣûfîs naturally tended to develop a demandingly 'pure' ethic: that is, highly disinterested principles of interpersonal action. One of the favourite saints of the Ṣûfîs was Râbiʿah of Baṣrah, who had died in 801. She was said to have taken a jug of water in one hand and a fiery torch in the other and run through the streets; when asked her purpose, she said she was going to Hell to put out its flames and to Paradise to burn up its gardens so that henceforth people should no longer worship God from fear of Hell or desire for Paradise, but only from love of God Himself. The apocryphal tale is told that one day the saint Ḥasan al-Baṣrî saw her at a distance on a desert hill, surrounded by gazelles and other wild beasts, tame in her presence. As he came closer to her, the animals fled away. He asked her what it was she had that he did not have. She asked him what he had eaten that day. 'Only a bit of onion.' What was it cooked in? 'A bit of animal fat.' There he had his answer.

The spiritual temptation of the Ṣûfîs was complementary to that of those of the Ḥadîth folk who resisted going along the Ṣûfî path. For the Ḥadîth folk, the danger came from the attempt to capture the unformulable in a formula, to hold on to God Himself within the words of the Qur'ân. In such an attempt, they risked forgoing the spontaneous responsiveness which never ceases seeking beyond what it has already found, in favour of a disciplined responsibility to truth already known: responsibility such as had caused people to receive and live by the Qur'ânic challenge when it was first delivered. Such responsibility was always necessary to preserve the continuity of commitment in the tradition of any group. But, held to too narrow an exclusivity, such responsibility could impose a conformity which would preclude any new understanding, smother the creative dialogue which was equally necessary for any cultural tradition, and devitalize the very tradition it was meant to serve. The more venturesome Ṣûfîs, on the contrary, were devoted precisely to inward, spontaneous responsiveness: responsiveness to new truth, to new human possibilities, wherever found, such as had made possible the coming of the Qur'ân in the first place, and which kept alive the continuing dialogue necessary to the vitality of the tradition which it had launched. But this responsiveness, if given too free a rein in undiscriminating universalism, risked undermining respect for and commitment to the already formulated rules which in daily practice made possible the ongoing cultural patterns necessary to human life in a given community.

This form of the dilemma that can arise between responsibility and responsiveness became a determining thread in Muslim history for many centuries. As seems generally the case, an innocuous 'middle way', hoping to combine a free responsiveness with sober responsibility, would have been at least as likely to sacrifice the values on each side, in practice, as to combine them. To be wholehearted and effective, persons had generally to choose one path or the other; and in choosing the path, they committed themselves to preoccupation with its concerns—and to overlooking, misunderstanding, and despising other matters of concern. A relatively uninvolved—and impotent—historian may feel that the inward-minded Ṣûfîs and the Sharîʿah-minded Ḥadîth folk were complementary in Islamic spiritual life. In Baghdad and in the provinces, in the last century of the High Caliphate, such a viewpoint was rare. As the several forms of Islamic piety became more clearly articulated, the more Sharîʿah-minded came actively to distrust the Ṣûfîs and were inclined to persecute the less cautious of them for heresy; and the Ṣûfîs, though respectful of the Sharîʿah and of the ḥadîth-minded circles from which their movement had arisen, often privately looked down on the more Sharîʿah-minded 'ulamâ' scholars as concerned more with the husks than with the kernel of truth.

On reading mystical texts

The Ṣûfîs could not dispense with a verbal presentation and even an intellectual analysis of their experience. The awareness come to through mystical processes cannot properly be put in words any more than can, say, the awareness of music. One may well draw moral lessons from at least the first levels of deepening clarity. But the content of the more intense levels, especially at the point of ecstasy, is strictly ineffable. Nevertheless, if there is to be discipline of the endeavour, there must be some sort of communication about it so that the sagacity to be drawn from varying experience can be shared. It is perhaps improper for the person of small or no mystical experience to read such texts at all. They were certainly never meant for the general public. In modern times, however, nothing human retains its sacred inviolability; we feel that for better or worse all barriers must come down and even the amateur must taste so far as he can whatever has proved or seemed important to human beings, so as to have maximum opportunity to appreciate what life may be about. Hence with hands often profane we peruse the old, secret texts. If we do so, however, it behoves us to use proper respect and caution.

In particular, I must note that in discussions such as these, I necessarily make those points on which I am reasonably confident, and I cannot steadily keep in perspective the areas that have not become clear to me. Yet the whole realm of the mystical life is peculiarly resistant to so tidy a treatment as I may seem to be trying to give it.

In reading mystical texts we must keep distinct three components in the report of any given experience, which the texts themselves do not normally distinguish, for among devotees this would have been pointless. We must distinguish the event itself, the process which the given human organism went through—for instance, a moment of ecstasy or a visual image. This must have an organic character, latent in the human structure; it cannot happen to an ape for instance. Many of the classical events have been more or less reproduced by drugs; in fact, some of the later Ṣûfîs, particularly in the Later Middle Period, themselves made use of drugs as shortcuts, with some recognition of the implications of such a procedure. Second, we must distinguish the formulated meaning which the ecstatic or the visionary assigns to the event, or which he deduces from it. This is a matter of words in which the event is tied to a wider life context. In different contexts, the same event may have different meanings; we must see what context it had for the Ṣûfî. Then finally we must try to sense the experiential content behind the formulated meaning, what the non-verbal referent of the words was in the total experience of the Ṣûfî; only then can we begin to know truly the meaning of what he was speaking about.

One may compare to the mystical event an event such as a fright in which a person thinks he sees his whole life passing before him, and after which finds strength to be and do what he somehow had never been able to before. The event itself is certainly not actually a case of total recall, though it is indeed a severe trauma. The image the sufferer gives of the event helps us to see what role the trauma played for him; but if he says that fear of death and of Hell moved him to reform, we must still interpret such phrases, which refer to things no one has personally experienced. Only as we see the event in terms of its deeper implications for his sense of guilt and of responsibility can we see what really happened at that moment to have such far-reaching consequences. Or we can compare someone listening to a Beethoven sonata. There is the physical-mathematical sonic event; there is the critics' formulation of what has happened; but we shall not begin to understand until we have a feeling for the music itself as music.

In a narration recorded by a visitor, Bâyazîd (Abû-Yazîd) Bisṭâmî (d. 874) —whose aversion to public adulation at Rayy we have already mentioned— described one of his most intense experiences: 'I gazed upon Him with the eye of truth, and said to Him: "Who is this?" He said: "This is neither I nor other than I. There is no god but I." Then He changed me out of my identity into His Selfhood . . . Then I . . . communed with Him with the tongue of His Grace, saying: "How fares it with me with Thee?" He said: "I am thine through thee; there is no god but Thou".' This presents a famous state of consciousness which a number of Ṣûfîs found themselves in, the 'reversal of roles': the worshipper plays the part of God and God that of the worshipper. It is that which, later, al-Ḥallâj is said to have proclaimed succinctly by declaring: '*Anâ 'l-ḥaqq*', 'I am the Truth', that is, God. Bisṭâmî analyzes it more intricately in the passage from which I have quoted. In each case, the ground of the statement is a peculiar sort of experience, one in which the personal identity is put in question and yet at the same time consciousness is extraordinarily intense.[18]

Bisṭâmî's formulation of the experience shows that it had a far different implication for his life than just any psychic dissociation, or a confused dream —such he may also have had and disregarded. The phrases form an episode in a longer narrative of an inner experience which seemed to him to epitomize what he was coming to in his whole life: a narrative that also paralleled, in purely psychological terms, the description in ḥadîth of Muḥammad's heavenly ascent, alluded to in the Qur'ân. Bisṭâmî had been pursuing a long process of discipline, in which he had been forcing himself to peel off one self-centred preoccupation after another. This reduction of concern with his own wants was identified with an increasingly pure and intense concern with the Islamic figure of the Creator-god, Who alone defined the valid response to created things that might be wanted. It was like a concern with the beloved in a love affair: for it was to please God that he must cease pleasing himself. With the impetus of ascetic tensions, but in this moral context, God seemed increasingly vivid; he found himself confronting Him as if nothing existed but his self and God. At length, the confrontation became overwhelmingly intense, while the meaning he still attached to the self was vanishingly attenuated. This point was symbolized in a conversation in which—though there is indeed still conversation, confrontation—there is only one party to converse, the other having lost all identity of its own.

As to the ultimate meaning of the experience in its totality, apart from any symbolic formulations of it, each reader can respond only as his own experience has prepared him. Doubtless there was some neurosis present; some might say that Bisṭâmî was trying to press one line of consequences at the expense of all else that goes to make up a balanced organic life; that this forced him to a logical dilemma which—given his intense preoccupation—

[18] The translation here is taken from A. J. Arberry in the *Bulletin of the John Rylands Library*, 29 (1956), 36–37. However, the selection there printed is misleading because of its arbitrary omissions. R. C. Zaehner has made a more exact as well as a fuller translation in his book, *Hindu and Muslim Mysticism* (London, 1960), in the course of an attempt to show (again) that Bisṭâmî's ideas were monistic and derived directly from the Indic tradition of Vedanta; and were in turn the source of later 'monism' within Ṣûfism. Many have taken up this problem. (Bisṭâmî's notion of *fanâ'*—the disappearance of the individual in God—is often, dubiously, identified with the Indic *nirvâna*.) Indeed, Indic mysticism is likely to have had influence in the Irano-Mediterranean regions in some earlier periods; it would be surprising if there were no contact in the time of the High Caliphate. Yet there is no dependable evidence in Bisṭâmî's case. The last word seems still to rest with Massignon in his *Origines du lexique technique de la mystique musulmane*, rev. ed. (Paris, 1954), who denies both monism and Indic influence in Bisṭâmî.

became a psychological dilemma too, which expressed itself in a nightmare hallucination.

Another person may feel that what matters is what was done with the neurosis; that the line of consequences Bisṭâmî was following had a fundamental human relevance; and that whether the point it drove him to was nightmarish or liberating, it is a point whose potentialities all must come to terms with. Always to ask, Is this that I am bothered about what I really want? is to invite ever again the answer: No, I seem to want this only because I really want that other beyond it; till one's ultimate reference, what one really wants or lives for, becomes keenly focused. The bundle of reactions of every day that one started with as a self becomes paradoxically irrelevant.

But Bisṭâmî's experience cannot be reduced even to that (if that were all, he could have put it in so many words); for Bisṭâmî was describing a process and not just a result. The exact meaning for human beings of the 'reversal of roles' was debated for many centuries among Ṣûfîs, with many varying answers given; some made it the highest, some a relatively low stage in the mystical Way; some even regarded it as a false temptation, to be feared and shunned.

The Ṣûfî analysis of the unconscious

However these things may be interpreted, we are dealing with the sort of awareness that emerges out of the unconscious levels of personality. The Ṣûfîs were aware of this, and sought to pin down as closely as possible what they called the inner 'secret' of the heart. Already in the classical 'Abbâsî period, Ṣûfîs attempted systematic description and analysis of what they had found, especially from al-Muḥâsibî (781–857) on, who introduced (despite his devotion to the spirit of the Ḥadîth folk) the intellectual methods of the Mu'tazilîs.

The central and classical analysis took the form of a description of the stages of intensification of mystical consciousness. Two series of levels in consciousness were described. The *maqâm* was the level one had achieved in one's training and personal growth: patience, for instance, or faith or certainty. These levels were commonly ordered in a set sequence, one achievement laying the groundwork for the next; different analysts differed in describing the sequence. The *ḥâl* was the transitory affective condition experienced from time to time, regarded as a special grace from God.[19] At the upper reaches, discussion was likely to be especially complex, as 'unity with God' was approached, spirally, like a moth circling closer into the flame that must consume it.

All this helped one to recognize his own true condition, especially by re-

[19] The classical treatment of these is to be found in the *Risâlah* of al-Qushayrî, analyzed by R. Hartmann, *Al Kuschairis Darstellung des Ṣûfîtums* (Berlin, 1914), where some of the vast and frequently overlapping technical vocabulary of Ṣûfî analysis is set forth.

vealing weaknesses—as well as strengths—one might not have been aware of. For the Ṣûfîs were seeking to ferret out the secret sin as well as to evoke the secret love (for God) latent in each person. This was the aim, in practice, of the Ṣûfî master (*pîr*) as well as his disciples. Younger Ṣûfîs commonly learned the Way through a personal relation to an older Ṣûfî as pîr, master, who served as examiner and director of conscience; the disciple was expected to be wholly devoted to the pîr and to express to him fears and hopes which had been unconscious. (Ṣûfîs paid much attention to the imaged symbolism of fantasies and dreams; but their notions of interpreting dreams mostly strike us as ill-founded or even absurdly naïve.) Only later came a more private discipline based on ascesis and self-examination. The analyses which Ṣûfîs made of what they came up with were, then, analyses of the contents of the unconscious mind. It was an early Ṣûfî maxim that he who truly knows himself knows his Lord.

The Ṣûfî analysis, however, must not be confused with several sorts of more or less comparable analysis to be found in modern times. The Ṣûfî was not attempting a general scientific study of personality, though he might find partly relevant such attempts at it as were made in his time. Further, unlike the modern novelists, he was not primarily concerned with the complex individual personality, but with universal human potentialities in which individual variations were likely to prove a mere hindrance. Nor was the Ṣûfî even concerned with therapy for ill personalities, despite analogies to modern psychotherapy since Freud. Elementary therapy might help a person blocked in his self-exploration by repressive fears, but the moral and emotional discipline of the Ṣûfîs was primarily intended to develop normal personalities to abnormal levels. The analysis, then, was intended as an aid to understanding the psychical states of those upon the Way, and also, incidentally, to making sense of the human place in the universe. The starting point was naturally that document through which the challenge had come, to which the whole effort was a response: the Qur'ân; it was, then, in terms largely derived from the Qur'ân that the analysis was made.

The residue of that Ṣûfî activity of which the historian can take cognizance is its discipline, the symbolism which it evoked, and the analyses made of those symbols. A few Ṣûfîs—and among them, perhaps, Bisṭâmî, who wrote nothing and whose disciples did not form a disciplined body till a century or more after his death—seem to be notable above all for the effective symbolism which they produced. But the public greatness of a Ṣûfî did not lie in the intensity of his experience but in the skill with which he turned it into public channels either by organizing the discipline of his disciples, or by working out, in verbal composition, a symbolic presentation of life and its meaning or (most especially) an analysis of particular moral and psychical states as a guide to pîrs as directors of consciences.

The most important of the public Ṣûfîs, in this sense, was Junayd of Baghdad (d. 910). As can be seen from the chart of the Ṣûfî pîr masters, he learned

The Earlier Ṣûfî Masters

728	Death of al-Ḥasan al-Baṣrî, ḥadîth scholar and ascetic who preached fear of God
776	Death of Ibrâhîm b. Adham, figure of later importance to some Ṣûfîs (as first mystic)
801	Death of Râbi'ah, woman mystic exemplifying love of God
857	Death of al-Muhâsibî, familiar with Mu'tazilî positions, representative of transition of non-worldly piety from asceticism to full mysticism; wrote on moral purification through self-perfection; influential on al-Ghazâlî
861	Death of Dhu'l-Nûn al-Miṣrî, associated with Coptic neo-Platonism, systematically described the mystical states and stages, also interested in alchemy
874	Death of Abû-Yazîd al-Bisṭâmî, first of the 'drunken' Ṣûfîs
898	Death of al-Ḥakîm al-Tirmidhî, biographer of early Ṣûfîs, wrote on themes usually associated with Ghulât and Hellenistic circles; influential on Ibn-'Arabî
910	Death of al-Junayd, pupil of al-Muhâsibî, who developed a comprehensive system
922	Death of al-Ḥallâj, pupil of al-Junayd, 'drunken' Ṣûfî executed for heresy; became martyr for later Ṣûfîs

from most of the more prominent masters who had preceded him; in turn, most of the later masters traced their discipline in the Way, at least in part, back to his disciples. Junayd had a strong sense of the potential integrity of a human being as a perfectible whole, envisaged by God from the first. He studied with care the several particular states of consciousness and what they revealed; at the same time, he went beyond detail. He saw the whole process of the mystical life comprehensively as a return, on a new level, to that presence with the Creator which a person had had in a nuclear way when he was being created. The primal day when (according to the Qur'ân) God drew all persons forth from Adam's loins and, giving them separate existence, confronted them with His challenge was the beginning of sorrow—sorrow which became deeper as one realized more fully one's separation from Him. But to seek to escape the sorrow in superficial delights would be a false solution. The sorrow must be allowed to be deepened in longing for God. Then, in mystical consciousness, the individual would fulfill the original purpose of his creation, which had been veiled in the complexities and temptations of common living.

Junayd approved of the expressions of Bisṭâmî; but he felt that Bisṭâmî had not gone quite far enough to fulfill his experience. Bisṭâmî's ecstatic utterances, in which he seemed to identify himself with God, had marked him as the type of the 'drunken' Ṣûfî, who counted it the highest state to be swept off one's feet through one's sense of one's own nothingness and God's allness, and so to utter one knew scarcely what. Junayd maintained that this was a passing phase: the perfected saint would go beyond it to a state of sobriety in which his awareness of God would make him a more complete human being in complete self-possession.

Aware of the horror which all such talk of awareness of God aroused in the Sharî'ah-minded, who wanted no emotive extravagance to intervene between a man and his daily duties, Junayd took great pains to avoid any scandal in his private conversations with and letters to the like-minded. One of his disciples, al-Ḥallâj, lost patience with such caution. Convinced that all people could and should open themselves up to the love of God, he wandered about the lands of Islamdom preaching among the common people the ideal of an immediate loving responsiveness to God's presence as being better than any amount of ritual or other external proprieties. His teaching about human nature and divine love was subtle as well as poetic—and he put it in poetry—but it was, above all, rash. Like Bisṭâmî, he seemed to justify the 'drunken' state of responsiveness over the 'sober' state of responsibility. When he began making disciples in high places in Baghdad, the authorities found reason to imprison him as a heretic. Eventually he was tried, condemned as having taught that a symbolic and spiritual fulfillment of the law was as good as the actual rites, crucified with his hands and feet cut off, quartered, and burned (922). It is said that in his agony he expressed his delight that he was suffering so for God's sake, but acknowledged that his judges were as right to condemn him, so as to safeguard the community life, as he was right to express paradoxes so as to proclaim the love of God.[20]

[20] The student of Ṣûfism using Western languages has three sorts of resources. For a description of Ṣûfî activities and organization in a given modern area, see Octave Depont and Xavier Coppolani, *Les confréries religieuses musulmanes* (Algiers, 1897), chiefly on the Maghrib; John Subhan, *Sûfism* (Lucknow, 1938), on India (uncritical); and the central chapters of John P. Brown, *The Darvishes or Oriental Spiritualism* (London, 1867), on the Ottoman lands, the many errors of which are only partially corrected by H. A. Rose's edition of it (Oxford, 1927), but which is only limitedly replaced by John K. Birge, *The Bektashi Order of Dervishes* (London, 1937), excellent; Joseph McPherson *The Moulids of Egypt* (Cairo, 1941) is a smugly ignorant eyewitness. On the classical Ṣûfî works, we may cite the writings of Reynold A. Nicholson, careful and important studies; of Margaret Smith, sound on the earliest period; of Louis Massignon, whose *Lexique technique de la mystique musulmane* (see note 18 above) traces with keen documentation the spiritual development of the early period, and whose *Passion d'al-Ḥallâj, martyre mystique de l'Islam* (Paris, 1922) is a masterpiece which also includes much on the later period, and all of whose studies present a profound spiritual perception of what was going on, which, however, must be checked as to detail; of Louis Gardet, with reasonable Catholic views; of R. C. Zaehner, overschematic but not negligible; of Henry Corbin, hard to follow and pre-committed, but profound and essential; of A. J. Arberry, useful chiefly for the long translated portions he uses. Of Ṣûfî writers in translation, Kharrâz is systematic, dealing with moral progression; Kalâbâdhî has many anecdotes but is defensive in point of Shar'î propriety; Hujwîrî is systematic, covering all disputed issues of practice in a Sharî'ah-minded sense; Shabistarî presents unitive metaphysics; Jâmî's *Lavâ'iḥ* briefly discusses metaphysical issues; 'Abdulqâdir, *Futûḥ*, is moral and mystical sermons; Junayd's epistles, on mystical experience and discipline, are paraphrased very misleadingly in the English; Ibn-al-'Arabî, *Fuṣûṣ*, on metaphysics, is abridged even in the French. Muḥammad Ghazâlî gives intellectual defences; al-Qushayrî is systematic on spiritual states. We need more translations of Makkî and Junayd, fundamental guides to Ṣûfî, and of Ibn-al-'Arabî and Yaḥyâ Suhravardî, on metaphysics and visional life. Poets much translated are Rûmî and 'Aṭṭâr, eminently expressive.

V

Speculation: Flasafah and Kalâm

c. 750–945

The way of life and thought of the Sharî'ah-minded grew directly out of those Irano-Semitic cultural traditions which stemmed from and further developed the prophetic summons of Axial times. These traditions were expressly transformed with the advent of Islam and recrystallized in new common patterns. They were sustained by the high seriousness represented in the various forms of Muslim piety and in turn came to form the most dependable basis for the legitimation of the social order. The intellectual disciplines cultivated by the Sharî'ah-minded came to be thought of, among ordinary Muslims, as the pre-eminently Muslim disciplines par excellence, and as essential mainstays both of social order and justice and of personal dignity and purity.

But Irano-Semitic culture had also shown another face from Cuneiform times on: one in which not the moral judgments of history but the rational harmonies of nature were the source of inspiration. This tradition had its own high seriousness in life, as alien to courtly elegance or frivolity as was that of the monotheistic tradition. But Islam as such initially was no part of the dialogue of this rationalistic tradition and indeed seemed quite alien to it; at first, it continued its way side by side with Islam, little affected by it.

The independence of the two dialogues was partly reflected in a linguistic difference. The Abrahamic monotheistic traditions were associated largely with various forms of Aramaic (Syriac) and with other confessional languages. But, as we have noticed, one of the results of the Hellenizing of some sectors of society from Nile to Oxus after Alexander was that the rationalistic tradition of mathematical science and associated philosophical thought came to be pursued in Greek and associated with the Hellenic tradition. In both the Sâsânian and the Roman provinces at the time of the Arab conquests, this was still largely the case. Scientific works were being increasingly translated into Syriac and to a lesser degree Pahlavî, but even in Syriac the tradition was still associated with the Greek masters.

Both the Abrahamic prophetic tradition and the Hellenizing philosophic and scientific tradition had, in their origins, dealt with comprehensive life-orientational problems. Even the mathematical and scientific traditions of Cuneiform times were instrumental to larger religious visions. The transition into the Greek language had at the same time been a transition into a new religious framework: that of the Socratic tradition of Philosophia, to which the particular scientific traditions were more or less ancillary. Socrates and Plato, by the definitions of religion we have been using, were as much religious figures as Amos and the Isaiahs; geometry or astronomy were almost as subordinate to the total cosmic vision which adherents of the several Socratic traditions were working out as was Hebrew historiography to the spiritual vision of the adherents of the Abrahamic tradition. But in contrast to the Abrahamic, the Socratic traditions had appealed, from the first, only to an intellectual élite; they made no effort at forming their own popular religious patterns. Everyday cult and popular religious ideas were left to the established priesthoods and to the folk traditions; at most, the Philosophers suggested limited reforms or reformulations. With the rise of the monotheistic traditions, especially Christianity, these took the place of popular paganism in the Philosophic outlook, being accepted in much the same spirit as the former religion.

However, the advent of the monotheisms made a difference: the exponents of the monotheistic traditions were more comprehensive in their demands and jealous of any alternative life-orientational outlook. Philosophia could not afford to appear in an explicitly religious role, even for an élite. Hence the exponents of the Socratic or Philosophic tradition tended to emphasize the autonomous validity of the several specialized elements in their tradition, as independent scientific traditions in which a person could participate regardless of his religious allegiance or even his personal spiritual outlook. Not only their mathematics and astronomy and logic were so treated, but even their metaphysics was sometimes regarded as an autonomous discipline, whose axioms implied no spiritual pre-commitments and which could be pursued as a sheer intellectual exercise—a notion that would have been as repugnant to Plato, for partly different reasons, as to modern existentialists or linguistic analysts.

This accentuation of the autonomy of the several scientific disciplines, insofar as they could claim to be independently demonstrative, opened their dialogues to wider participation, in principle, at the same time that it tended to limit the sorts of questions that could be pursued within those dialogues. It also resulted in an ambiguity as to the place of the more life-orientational, the more religious aspects of the tradition, which had to present itself simply as 'philosophic' human wisdom, and which came to seem, even to some of its adepts, to be merely uncommitted rational understanding. Nonetheless, in practice, the Philosophic tradition as a whole continued a common dialogue in which those who pursued the several specialized disciplines generally took part, and which continued to presuppose a more or less common world view, common spiritual commitments, and even, in large measure, a common manner of joining the Philosophic spiritual commitments with those of prevailing popular religion.

The adherents of the Socratic Philosophic traditions readily formed a world of their own aloof from any society in which they found themselves. By High Caliphal times, the tradition had become associated in a practical way with Christianity, since this was the communal allegiance of most Syriac-speakers. Christianity itself had been profoundly touched by it: Christian thinkers had had to confront the Hellenic metaphysical and logical traditions, and the formulation of the problems of Christian theology—problems concerning the nature and power of God and the freedom of human beings—reflected this. At the same time, the Hellenic intellectual traditions persisted independently of Christianity and were pursued by Christians and non-Christians alike. And in the Mesopotamian town of Ḥarrân, the community of Hellenistic pagans still cultivated the Hellenic tradition as an all-sufficient spiritual and cultural whole.

The practical disciplining of the natural-science heritage

Whereas the objective studies proper to the Sharî'ah-minded, that could be pursued in relative autonomy from an Islamic commitment, were especially historical studies, from the collection of ḥadîth reports to the elaborate compositions of Ṭabarî, the Philosophic tradition expressed itself most objectively in nature studies, particularly those based on mathematics. Without an intensive culture in positive sciences, a rationalistic philosophic approach to life could be as vacuous as one that attempted to found itself in the prophetic spirit without a solid historical sense. Moreover, such positive sciences could be eminently useful. When the learning of regional rationalistic traditions was being rendered into Arabic, it was naturally first technical texts in medicine and astronomy that were most translated. Only later could serious metaphysical work be carried on in Arabic.

From the time of al-Ma'mûn through the ninth and well into the tenth century, translation of older texts, primarily Greek or in the Greek tradition (Syriac or Pahlavî), but also some from Sanskrit, was the most important sort of scientific activity. The Christian Ḥunayn b. Isḥâq founded a school of translators who were themselves of high scholarly standing and were able to improve greatly on the first translations that had been made as well to enlarge the range of the translations. They took pains to gather as many manuscripts of a given work as possible and to collate the texts, so as to have a sound basis for translation to begin with: a major achievement in days before printing could avoid the errors of uninterested hired transcribers, and essential if the texts were to serve as more than bare hints to subsequent investigators. Thus, gradually, the full Greek philosophic and scientific heritage became far more freely and accurately available in Arabic than it had been in any Sâsânian language. The results showed themselves in a steady enrichment of Arabic scientific writing with old Greek materials.

Perhaps almost as respectable an achievement was to work out both a technical vocabulary and a pattern of syntax which would allow scientific work to be carried on fluently in Arabic. Every human language is potentially adaptable to every linguistic use, but when it has not yet been used for abstract discursive purposes, every language presents its own obstacles when such use is attempted. Arabic was not rich in means of subordinating one phrase to the next, for instance, but the translators established patterns which served all purposes effectively. With this work, the labour begun by prose-writers such as Ibn al-Muqaffaʿ was completed, and Arabic became a written language sufficient to carry the whole range of pre-Modern culture.[1]

Within the same period, Arabic was being used for important scientific advances, largely the work of Muslims. Some of the most notable advances came only in a later age, but in the last century and a half of the High Caliphate more discoveries were made than in many centuries previously either from Nile to Oxus or in the Mediterranean lands. Some of these were due to the confrontation of the Greek tradition with part of the Sanskrit tradition—a process which had begun in Sâsânian times after the flowering of Indic science had come to Sâsânian attention. Much of the advance was due to a practical orientation which was brought to scientific studies—as often happens—when circles take them up who have cut themselves loose from the older context of those studies and hence from the symbolic overtones which had come to surround them; or who have never even been acquainted with that older context.

Perhaps the most generally appealing of these studies was astronomy. The earliest of the nature studies to be highly developed almost anywhere, it yielded dramatic and imaginatively satisfying results to the application of elementary but precise observation. But the results could be rather too satisfying. For the Greek tradition, the temptation was great to find in astronomy just the perfection which their vision of pure reason called for, in the shape of the universe as a whole.

Aristotle had projected a system in which the seeming movements of the stars and planets about the earth were reduced to exactly circular movements in concentric spheres, movements which, moreover, were accounted for through physical laws. Ptolemy had developed a mathematically more accurate astronomy designed to account for actually observed positions of the planets in complete detail. He continued to use circular paths in charting the geometry of the movements; such circles not only fulfilled the general

[1] Every language tends to have its own particular genius, of course, even apart from the way it happens to develop when cultivated in literature and scholarship. The spiritual genius of Arabic has been studied imaginatively—if not always persuasively—by Louis Massignon in several articles. Nevertheless, the common remark—that one thing the Arabs 'contributed' to Islamicate civilization was their 'amazingly adaptable' language, which, though hitherto used only by crude Bedouin, was found suitable to the highest needs of science—bears little weight. There is nothing special in such a feat. The much-praised Semitic system of vowel-pattern changes for forming verbs and nouns may be more rhythmically suggestive than a system of prefixes and suffixes; but it is, if anything, less flexible and less precise.

assumption that bodies not subject to outside interference must naturally so move, but also proved easiest to handle in point of mathematical geometry, which called for regular movements if any calculation of them was to be made at all. But his were circles within circles, unaccountably complex; and indeed he renounced any effort to show how the movements were actually produced, being concerned only to trace planetary paths which would answer to actual observations, and so to allow maximally exact prediction of planetary conjunctions and so on. By the time of the Arab conquest, Aristotle's observationally less satisfying system was still preferred in some circles because it formed part of a larger system of physics in which, apart from such details, everything was beautifully accounted for.

As late as the time of the astronomer Muḥammad b. Mûsà al-Khwârizmî (d. 844 or later)—from whose name we derive the term *algorism*, on account of his arithmetical studies—it was the Aristotelian system that was rendered into Arabic. But under Muslim rule well-equipped observatories were built and observations were refined still further than in earlier times. (Al-Ma'mûn took great pains to see that a degree of terrestrial latitude be accurately measured.) By the time of the Jewish astronomer Rabban al-Ṭabarî, the practical advantages of the Ptolemaic system had become obvious; from that point on, Islamicate astronomy built upon Ptolemy, as did later the Occidental astronomy dependent on it.[2]

Mathematics, though important in other connections also, was especially the handmaiden of astronomy. Hence it claimed special attention in the form of geometry; Arabic-writing mathematicians turned to developing, especially, spherical trigonometry. But in late Hellenistic and Roman times, the new mathematical openings were in the realm of algebra. Though we know little of what happened, it seems clear that the algebraic outlook was inherited from the later Cuneiform mathematics, whose tradition now came to the fore as more efficient than a strictly geometrical approach. In any case, under Muslim rule, algebra was pushed very far along with a revival of other useful traits of the Cuneiform tradition. The solution of equations of higher degrees was a fascinating puzzle pieced out bit by bit.

Muḥammad al-Khwârazmî brought together much of the Hellenic and Sanskritic traditions, as they had been present in the Sâsânian schools, including elements of the Cuneiform tradition which have survived otherwise neither in Greek nor in Sanskrit, in a synthesis which established the import-

[2] O. Neugebauer, 'The History of Ancient Astronomy: Problems and Methods', *Journal of Near Eastern Studies*, 4 (1945), 1–38, in a general review of the state of studies in ancient science at that time, brings out well how older views could survive alongside newer ones in an age when scientific communication was largely a matter of chance (and how isolated discoveries of importance could disappear without a trace—especially, one can add, if they were bound up with outdated techniques, such as the complex geometry used by many Greeks in the place of simpler algebraic methods). It was probably not only Islam and Arabic but the use of paper that increased scientific communication somewhat at this time.

ance of the field and defined its most important initial methods. From the name of his chief book, which, however, was as much a practical handbook of reckoning as a theoretical exposition, Western languages have derived the term 'algebra'. In mathematics, one of the most useful techniques, which he helped to popularize, was the system of place-value numerals with a zero (instead of the usual alphabetical systems which were nothing but short notations of the numbers' names). A system of place-value numerals had been used in the Cuneiform. The Muslim scholars found the system with zero in the Sanskrit tradition and gradually generalized its use—sometimes on a sexagesimal base of sixty as well as a decimal base of ten, following ancient Cuneiform precedent.

Apart from astronomy, mathematics was important in the physical studies, such as optics and music, the theory of which, already partly developed in Greek, was eventually given a great impetus in Arabic. The study of musical proportions was thought of not only as the study of sound (mathematizable in the form of distinct musical tones in the octave) but as an introduction to proportion generally: in particular, as a tangible model of the 'music of the spheres', the system of proportions expected to prevail in the motions of the heavenly bodies. Music received the attention of the most prominent scholars.

With medicine, we move into a different circle of nature studies, the biological, where the use of mathematics was attempted with much less success. The centre of attention here was human anatomy and its pathology. Building on the work of the Greeks, the Islamicate physicians maintained their high traditions (including the Hippocratic oath) and, like the latter-day Greek and Syriac physicians, tended to be tied to the classical books. However, many of them were acute clinical observers. The most famous physician of High Caliphal times, Ibn-Zakariyyâ', al-Râzî (d. 925 or 934), pinpointed the distinction between measles and smallpox as well as solving other less dramatic cases. The caliphal administration attempted to maintain high standards in the public hospitals and provided for the examination of physicians, attempting to suppress quacks through the muḥtasib officer, at least in the capital.[3] But medicine, with its very practical use, was a privileged case; biology at large was not very seriously pursued (indeed nowhere had it been so). The practical study of plant and animal breeding and agriculture generally, in which much advance was made in Muslim times (for instance, in the development of hybrid citrus fruits still in use) and to which many manuals were devoted, was kept largely separate from the general body of natural science.

[3] Joseph Schacht and Max Meyerhof, 'The Medico-Philosophical Controversy between Ibn-Buṭlân of Baghdad and Ibn-Riḍwân of Cairo', Egyptian University, Faculty of Arts, Publication 13 (Cairo, 1937), a badly written paper, nevertheless gives one a feel of the scientific life of the time, for instance the broad sense in which a concept like 'heat' was understood for medical purposes, almost analogous to our 'energy'.

Alchemy

Because of the usefulness of its results to the pharmacopoeia, however, some contact was maintained between medicine and chemistry, which in fact dealt largely with organic materials. Al-Râzî, in particular, is known for having developed, from the chemistry of the time, several effective medical preparations. While astronomy may best symbolize, among the old sciences, the sheer grandeur of the power of the human mind to comprehend what at first seem mighty and mysterious forces incommensurate with human life (its chief application was in astrology, whereby people sought to understand fate), chemistry may best symbolize the human drive to control such forces and bend them to human ends; a drive almost equally early, if less pervasive (before recent times) in forming the scientific tradition. At the heart of chemical studies in both Greek and Muslim times was the practical application that we call *alchemy*, the search for ways of transmuting one substance into another and, in particular, less valuable metals into silver and gold.

The alchemical tradition seems to have originated in Greek times in the use, for producing special effects, of recipes developed by ordinary craftsmen in their work. Scholars were aware of the Aristotelian theory of the two sorts of quality—fluidity and temperature—which were differentiated as the four elementary qualities: moist, dry, hot, and cold; which in turn accounted for the four simple elemental substances of which all compounds were composed in different proportions: air (hot, moist), fire (hot, dry), water (cold, moist), earth (cold, dry). On this basis, all ordinary substances were regarded as compounds which could presumably be taken apart and put together again differently. Combined with the practical experience that could be had with the craftsmen's recipes, such a theory led to a conception of the metals as condensed vapours which in vaporous form could be recombined and reconstituted. With an ever-increasing battery of furnaces and stills, the chemists set about producing what new combinations they could.

The more philosophical-minded among them seem to have been chiefly interested in the theoretical implications of their studies. They expected to learn not merely about the recombination of the elements into various metals and other substances, but about the analogical processes which they supposed went on in the universe at large and in the human soul, which could be illustrated from alchemical experience insofar as all existence is built on the same principles. The human being was regarded quite literally as the microcosm, the world in miniature, within which all the cosmic processes repeat themselves in the organism. A great goal of the alchemist was to purify the various substances to the highest degree possible, in the thought that in its truly pure state a substance was incorruptible: the incorruptibility of gold showed its peculiar chemical purity. But for the philosopher, what really mattered was what one could learn from all this about the purification of the human soul. The more philosophically inclined alchemists were discussing, in highly developed symbolisms, basic psychological principles quite as much as they were discussing material chemical ones. Thus the mutual attraction of man and woman was held to answer the chemical fusion of contrasting elements. (In consequence, they were sometimes rather careless in exactly assaying the merely material substances they produced.)

It is doubtless on this account that it was under the auspices of Ismâʿîlî, or at least Bâṭinî, piety that arose the most important corpus of chemical literature in High Caliphal times: the writings associated with the name of Jâbir (Lat. Geber) b. Ḥayyân. Jâbir was a historical personage, a disciple of the Shîʿî imâm Jaʿfar al-Ṣâdiq (d. 765), but most of the works ascribed to him—which contain many different sorts of doctrine—are of later dates.

Yet it is in the Jâbir corpus that reappears, in the Muslim period, a tendency which had been less prominent in late Roman times: a strong interest in the practical as against the symbolical side of the study. The material theory was further developed: for instance, all metals were held to be reducible to two primary ones, ideal sulphur (an embodiment of the hot and the dry) and ideal mercury (an embodiment of the moist and the cold) from which if they could be gotten in their really pure forms, all other metals could be developed, including gold. An attempt was even made to work out the mathematical ratios that would assure purity. Such theoretical development answered to an increased production, in practice, of elixirs of all sorts (that is, artificial chemicals used to produce further chemical reactions); some had explicit medical uses and some, it is said, were used commercially to make surrogates or, less honourably, unavowed substitutes for various wares—especially for drugs. Some of the practitioners, doubtless, dishonestly made the most of a dubious skill, but others certainly believed that they were producing somewhat impure forms of the genuine article: if their gold, for instance, tarnished, it was not that it was not gold but that it was not yet quite pure.

The alchemists, naturally nonconformist souls and readily suspected by the masses of magic and commerce with the devil or of subversion or at least of counterfeiting, when not regarded as sheer imposters, naturally had to do their work as secretly as possible.and often in intellectual isolation. In the mass of often highly conjectural theory and practice which they developed, sometimes means were used, such as the numerical relations in 'magic squares' or even in alphabetic symbolism, where the proportions resulting are purely specious to the eye and can have no deeper grounding, either theoretical or empirical. And doubtless sheer magic did occasionally sift in: the use of means whose efficacy is thought to presuppose not intelligible natural processes, however recondite, but the intervention of special occult forces, often personal to the practitioner or else thought of as non-human beings subject to his control by special techniques. But scholars recognized the radical difference, in principle, between chemical processes and magic. Whether or not they thought that the alchemists could in fact succeed in transmuting substances (or whether, as some did, they maintained that only magic could achieve this), they recognized that the processes they were primarily operating with were a genuine part of nature. Chemistry formed a recognized part, though a part much less honoured than astronomy or mathematics, of the total body of positive science on which a Philosophic view of the world could be founded.[4]

The Faylasûfs and society: medicine and astrology

As in earlier times, so also in Arabic and among carriers for the most part Muslim, Philosophic tradition maintained its overall unity, which led its scholars far beyond a mere academic occupation with the several positive sciences. One who participated intellectually in the tradition by his studies and researches was called a 'Faylasûf' (the Greek *philosophos*); the tradition as a whole was called 'Falsafah', *philosophia*. The word is originally identical with our 'philosophy', but it implied not just the study of metaphysics and logic, nor even these disciplines plus the positive sciences, but, more fundamentally, the Philosophic approach to living, of which interest in such studies was an expression.

The Faylasûf ('Philosopher') was dedicated to governing himself by his reason. Reason, such as we find impurely expressed in our human selves, was thought to underlie the cosmos as a whole. All aspects of nature were studied in the spirit of seeking always the uniform logical, rational, principles behind the apparent diversity of manifestations. This study included the human being itself, both as body (to be understood in the science of medicine) and as rational being, to be guided by the science of ethics and politics. Given this rational knowledge of the first principles of nature and of himself, everything else followed for the Philosopher, both his personal manner of life and his conception of how society as a whole should be ordered. The more nearly a person could approach to such rationality, the more nearly he could fulfill his own purpose in existence and be at harmony with all life. For the Faylasûf, the ideal man was a sage 'philosopher'—a man who fully lived up to the demands of the tradition of Philosophia. (When referring to 'philosophy' and 'philosophers' in this idealized sense, I shall sometimes put them into *quotation marks* to set them off from any special subject matter; and I shall *capitalize* references to the actual historical tradition as a whole.)

[4] The most useful introduction to Islamicate chemistry is the first half of E. J. Holmyard, *Alchemy* (Baltimore, 1957), which stresses the physically chemical side of the tradition at the expense of the psychologically philosophical side. Holmyard's historical sense is conventional at best, and very uncritical, but he writes clearly and carefully.

The Faylasûfs stood in conscious contrast to the mental world of the Shar'î 'ulamâ' scholars, though they often regarded themselves as good Muslims; at the same time, they rather looked down upon the sort of society represented by the luxurious and despotic court. It cannot be said that the Faylasûf scholars actually represented a total social programme, in the way that both the 'ulamâ' and even the men of courtly culture, the adîbs, tended to do so; yet their thought embraced all aspects of living. Some of them even seem to have had serious hopes of seeing society remodelled according to their own conceptions. In any case, their attitudes had considerable influence not only among the adîbs but eventually among the 'ulamâ' themselves. As had already begun to be the case in the Sâsânian empire, Falsafah in High 'Abbâsî times came to play a prominent, though marginal, role in cultural life. But in order to do this, its carriers, the Faylasûfs, had to find for themselves a niche where, despite the contrast between their tradition and the dominant ones, they could win social recognition.

Hence the adepts of Falsafah, like the 'ulamâ' and the adîbs, tended to follow certain professions. Most typically they became physicians and astrologers, practicing the two most widely recognized lines of 'applied science' of the day. (It was probably as apprentices to physicians and astrologers that many Faylasûfs gained access to the tradition as a whole.) These two professions had certain characteristics in common which made them peculiarly appropriate to the Faylasûf scholar. Both medicine and astrology required considerable scientific training, in anatomy and astronomy respectively; both involved in addition a set of speciously logical theories which to us appear crudely fallacious but which appealed strongly to the expectation that nature must form a total intelligible system; both involved at least as much the tact and personal insight of a wise man as they did the practice of impersonally applicable techniques.

Agrarian Age medicine based its diagnosis and prognosis on a large fund of experience, embodied above all in the writings of the great physicians. Of these the most honoured west of Indus was Galen, along with other men who had written in Greek. (To the short list of classic physicians were subsequently added, even in Latin Europe, such Arabic-writers as al-Râzî.) Though it was often socially impossible to do desirable dissecting on the human body, these men maintained a tradition of careful clinical observation which became the foundation of later medical developments.

The treatment of diseases diagnosed, on the other hand, was as always less sure. A large pharmacopoeia of drugs was known, specifics for various ailments. Considerable surgery was used—without anaesthetics, of course. General rules of healthful living and of care in convalescence were urged on the patients, with the usual results. But much medical analysis and even some treatment was based on theories which sprang rather from abstract reasoning than from actual experiment.

The most famous of these was the theory of the four humours, four types of liquid (blood was the most obvious of them) which kept the body functioning. The four humours were held to answer to the combinations among the four physical qualities which theory made basic to all physical things (hot and cold, moist and dry); it was held that much disease resulted from an imbalance in the four physical qualities in the body, which led to an imbalance of the humours. A common application of this theory was the use of bleeding in cases of fever (to diminish the hot blood) where we would less dangerously use aspirin.

Most diseases cure themselves; on the other hand, sooner or later for every mortal, however skillful the physician, some disease must prove fatal. It was never easy to tell in practice what was and what was not effective. There were no good grounds to reject theory that seemed to fit into the general scheme of the natural order, so far as it could be known (and the Faylasûf scholars hoped that human reason could know it fairly well). Accordingly, medicine was based partly on a great deal of factual knowledge of anatomy generally and of medical resources in particular; partly on general systematic considerations based on suppositions about the rationality of the cosmos; and partly on the personal skill of the physician, his sensitivity to the physical situation and, perhaps still more, his ability to reach the patient psychologically.

The case in astrology was similar. The physician was called upon to give advice in a dangerous medical situation; the astrologer was called on to give advice (as to timing, or even as to choice of moves, as well as in more symbolical ways) whenever any practical situation was critical and the outcome seemed to depend more on luck than on any calculable moves by the individual involved. This sense of dependence on fortune emerged especially in major enterprises such as military campaigns, but also at marriages or at births. In each case, the ordinary person did not know how to help himself or at least he had no way of controlling an unfathomable future. If he took the specialist's advice and things turned out well, that was all to the good; if things turned out ill, it was at least no worse than would probably have happened anyway.

The ordinary person—be he peasant or king—believed equally in medicine and in astrology. Some of the 'ulamâ' rejected both, as not provided for in the example of Muḥammad (except for a minimum of 'Prophetic' medicine, mentioned in ḥadîth, such as the eating of honey as a panacea). Most of the 'ulamâ' scholars rejected astrology as diabolical (though perhaps quite effective), but were more tolerant of medicine. Many of the Faylasûf scholars made a sharper distinction, rejecting the attempt to predict outcomes by astrology not as diabolical though true, but as actually a bogus practice. (It was more widely admitted that heavenly movements did have effects on human life than that humans could discern those effects.) However, even some who personally denied the usefulness of astrology, like the great mathematician Bîrûnî (d. *c.* 1050), were willing to write on it and to practice it to satisfy their clients' demands.

Astrology was based on the doctrine that changes in the heavenly bodies were to be correlated with changes of fortune on the earth. Yearly changes in the course of the sun had obvious effects on human life, and changes in the moon affected both tides and lovers. When the ancient Babylonians had accumulated enough data about the courses of all the visible planets to enable astronomers to begin predicting their track in the sky, including such events as eclipses, it came to be thought that the complicated cycles so discovered in the heavens must lie back of the otherwise inexplicable course of earthly life—that is, of human life (for what else was so important?). On the basis of inherited myth and perhaps some case histories, and of reasoning by analogy, a basic set of correlations was set up; for instance, the movements of the planet Venus—associated with the amorous goddess—must have something to do with love. Once these basic assumptions were accepted, sheer logic could elaborate an interpretation of every combination of planetary positions (in particular, the planetary situation at a given moment as it bore on the planetary situation that had presided over a given man's birth). The required calculations were so delicate and subject to human error that it was hard to disprove or to prove the system in practice. It became so popular that it spread far from Babylonia as the most important element in all the lore of divination which humans seemed to require as insistently as they needed medicine. Along with the mathematics and astronomy with which it was associated it became part of the Hellenic tradition from Nile to Oxus (and in Europe), and hence a typical ingredient of Falsafah in Islamic times.

The theory of astrology was based on assumptions about the solidarity of cosmic events with human events, assumptions that easily recommended themselves to people who expected the universe to present an intelligible rational structure. Its practice, moreover, depended on that exact knowledge of astronomy which was in any case part of the rational information which the Faylasûf cultivated. Hence the Faylasûfs could hardly avoid studying astrology on almost the same basis as medicine. Finally, the practice of astrological divination required the same sober temperament as did medicine. It was demanded by clients in crises, much as was medicine, and depended even more than medicine on the personal sensitivity of the astrologer and on his psychological skill.

In consequence, the same man was often both physician and astrologer and sometimes he became famous for his effectiveness in crises calling for both types of skill. Prominent Faylasûf scholars could thus gain access to powerful men, who protected them from the ignorant fears of people at large (who tended to distrust them generally, and not only the alchemists, as wizards or dealers in black arts). At the same time they were able to gain the funds necessary to build up good libraries on scientific and philosophical subjects, despite the relatively small number of those interested. In this way, Falsafah played an important role in Islamicate society despite the disapproval of most of the 'ulamâ' and the relative indifference of most of the adîbs, absorbed in genteel living and the elegant niceties of language.

Philosophy as a vision of the world

The Faylasûf, we have said, was dedicated to philosophic reason, to following its conclusions, without yielding to preconceptions, wherever it might lead. But 'reason' had for the Faylasûfs a more exacting implication than mere 'reasoning' as a general activity. True rationality was not merely to manipulate things cleverly in given particular instances (it is discussed how far even apes can exercise such 'Yankee ingenuity'). Rationality involved bringing all experience and all values under a logically consistent total conception of reality. Falsafah proved to have its own special world view, its cosmology, to which its adherents were implicitly committed. This began with a special concept of rationality itself.

The Philosophic version of rationality required, to begin with, the acquisition of a good deal of specialized information. But the Faylasûf scholar was not interested just in gathering facts; he studied mathematics and astronomy, chemistry, biology, and medicine, as rational, universal sciences. Such knowledge, it was supposed, depended on grasping basic ruling principles—such as the circular motion of cosmic objects, or the fourfold nature of the sublunar elements; then all particulars, so far as they were essential to the subject under investigation, could be logically understood. Empirical observation (including occasional deliberate experiment) was given weight only insofar as it promised to lead to universal principles: it was assumed that, on the basis of a minimal (and hence practicable) amount of observation, the essential principles would emerge, from which everything could be deduced if clear logic were held to. Even as examples of universals, indeed, particular observations were distrusted. It was recognized (correctly, in the conditions of the time) that in any given case too much chance entered in for it to be a pure instance of universal rules; hence no one experience—experimental or accidental—could be decisive on the level of rational principles. The true number of teeth in the human mouth could not be learned, for instance, just by examining an actual mouth: few people have all their teeth, and one may always have happened on a freak. Empirical observation, though important, could not substitute for more systematic reasoning.

In any case, a true 'philosopher' ought not to be interested in the particular for its own sake, as a mouth surgeon might be, studying the formation of one man's teeth so as best to fit in an artificial one. This was of interest to craftsmen only, skilled in an applied art, not in science fit for gentlemen. Any concern with the time-bound, the accidental, the whole realm of the historical, as such, was despised as unworthy, irrelevant to genuine self-cultivation. What was wanted was an adequate understanding of the unchanging whole; any particular instance was at best only one more repetitive exemplification, and acquaintance with it could be of only transient relevance, meeting needs of the moment. Some have seen a relative increase in interest in field observation and experiment among Muslim scientists as compared with the ancient Greeks—perhaps, with accumulating information and technique, this became more feasible (we know too little yet to judge well); but at best, the increase did not go far enough to alter the pervasive ethos.

The model sciences of the Greeks had fitted this principle. In geometry a whole range of propositions could be deduced from a few axioms. It was the true triangle, which never occurs in nature, and not actual more-or-less three-cornered objects, that could be known and was worth knowing; neglect of the rest was what made possible geometrical calculations that were effective even on the practical level. In astronomy, if one observed essential regularities in a few heavenly bodies, the course of conjunctions and eclipses could be predicted to the end of time. Ideally, all truth should be reducible to this level of exact statement, incontestably demonstrative and timelessly applicable (at least by approximation) to anyone anywhere. But the effort to carry this task through required a far-reaching set of presuppositions, which the Faylasûfs had to be prepared to take as given.

A systematic admission of ignorance about crucial matters is an intellectual luxury which non-literate peoples have rarely been able to enjoy: consequently the best guesses available have been made and worked out to full consequences even though no real evidence was available to support (or deny) them. Out of this circumstance have risen the less critical conceptions of the world, such as that which fills it with Power answering to what we feel within ourselves, and accounting effectively for whatever may happen: if one does not know any explanation, but dare not admit, and act deliberately upon, ignorance, nothing makes more sense than conceptions of *mana*, of spells, of exorcisms, of evil eye, of charms, of all the apparatus of animism and magic. These are merely an extrapolation of what is most familiar. Among the privileged classes of urban society on the agrarianate level, some were allowed a certain intellectual leisure, that is, were in a position to devote themselves to speculation with little thought to practical consequences. Among them, a systematic admission of ignorance became more feasible, and indeed essential as a prerequisite to fundamental inquiry. Falsafah presupposed just this, and Faylasûfs took pride in their emancipated views which the masses could not afford to share.

Apart from lapses that might occur on occasion, especially in such fields as alchemy, Faylasûfs did keep free of the grosser popular errors. But there must be a limit to one's admission of ignorance; inquiry requires not only an unknown to explore, but some field that is known for a starting point.

For the Faylasûf, the required basic assumption was that the universe is essentially rational—that is, rational in its essences, though perhaps more or less unknowable in the incidental forms which these take in the coming and going of actuality. This rationality, moreover, must be not simply an amenability to our minds à propos of this or that particular question, but an inherent ontological rationality, in principle independent of our minds.

But such an ontological rationality has further implications. In actual inquiry, questions on the nature of a given thing almost necessarily include questions on its value. If one's inquiry answered to cosmic reality at all, it would do so on the level of valuation also. Hence throughout pre-Modern cosmological speculation ran the expectation that different sorts of being, different substances as such, carried a greater or lesser inherent dignity or worth: this was not a function of one or another particular human purpose in terms of which this or that had an intelligible value; it was an ontological worth independent of any human consideration. A plant was higher in the scale than a stone, an animal than a plant, a man than other animals, an angel than a man. Such a conception seemed to be a natural consequence of the ontological rationality of the universe as a whole: if the rational interconnections of events are to be ontologically inherent in the structure of existence, then the values of given events, without which we cannot really think of them or reason about them, must be ontologically inherent likewise.

If, then, this ontological rationality and value-structuring of the universe be accepted (as that essential starting point for inquiry, beyond which a systematic admission of ignorance becomes self-defeating), a total world view can be built up in which everything has its place. Falsafah, as inherited from the Greek schools, had developed this viewpoint very consequentially. All knowledge, from the most special sciences to the most general synthesis, formed a single whole; in particular, theories in any one field derived their premises from the conclusions of other fields. Just as theories in medicine depended on the results of investigations in physics, so theories in physics, in turn, depended on metaphysical conclusions, as did the principles of ethics or of aesthetics. To attack the edifice at any one point was to attack the whole.

Being was composed of entities which might act on each other. Each entity was made of fixed substances, characterized by changeable accidents—as a piece of wood might be painted green or blue. What one sought to explain was not events or situations, but the distinct entities as such: the word answering to our word 'cause' meant not a cause of an *event*, but a constitutive principle of an *entity*—the material it was made of, the form it took, the purpose it served, and the agent (itself an entity) that occasioned it. (Hence, in contrast to systems presupposing flux or process in a continuum of fields and gestalts, movement and change were seen as something superimposed from without.) Each type of entity had its timelessly essential character, without which it would be something else, and which could be formulated in a categorical definition: wood was in the generic class of earthy solids, singled out specifically from other such solids by its fibrous character as the densest part of a growing plant. The human being was an animal, specifically a rational one. And to each species, each type of entity, could be attached an equally changeless inherent worth or dignity.

The entities, as studied by physics, were mostly made up of compound substances—compounded of the four elements, with characteristics derivable from the nature of their compounding (chemists attempted to find what reactions could produce what compounds). The purest compounds—that is, those coming closest to an ideally harmonious combination of the elements—were endowed with greatest dignity. The four elements, ideally, were located in concentric spheres, earth at the centre, then water above it, then air, and fire highest of all: their mixture was already impurity and occasioned all the motion they were constantly in, trying to regain their natural position. Astronomers claimed, however (though not all did so), that it was only the substances in and on the earth, in the sphere below the moon, that were compounds, and hence perishable, subject to coming into being and disintegrating, to generation and corruption. From the moon's sphere upward, the changelessly circular nature of the heavenly motions showed that they were of 'ethereal' stuff purer even than the four elements here below—which latter moved only when they had been displaced, and then linearly, and hence not indefinitely.

The Faylasûfs' notion of God

Given this conception of the material universe, it was natural to proceed to a systematic account of the cosmos as a whole. In Aristotle's system, metaphysics was merely what one could study once one had mastered the principles of physics; it was basically the same sort of study, with the same sort of consequences. It is especially clear in such inquiry, how far this sort of rationalistic analysis could go in discussing questions on the most complex human levels; and what its human implications were.

These presuppositions about being underlie the proof of the existence of God given (on the basis of earlier writers) by Ibn-Sînâ (Avicenna—d. 1037), the most famous of the Faylasûfs. For those to whom 'God' meant, in the first instance, not an experienced challenge but a cosmic entity, as such not directly experienced, its very existence had to be demonstrated. Ibn-Sînâ's proof assumed two features of the Philosophic world view. The world is made up of composite things, in which our minds must distinguish more than one component—not only compound entities, but even the simplest are composite, distinguishable at least into form and matter. Yet our reasoning looks ultimately to something not composite but truly simple—something that shall be irreducibly itself. We speak of a tree, a stone, water, air; but if we find these things can in turn be analyzed into component parts (bark, wood, pith; silicon, mica, quartz), we know we cannot rationally understand them till we take into account their components, reducing them to ever simpler elements till we can no longer subanalyze them. If, then, such rationality is conceived as not merely a function of the way our minds work, but as defining the ontological nature of existence, we will find that the simples will seem primary and the compounds derivative; likewise, what is at rest will seem primary and what is changing will seem derivative.

In this case, it makes sense to say that anything composite must not merely be accounted for in terms of our minds, but must be admitted to be caused by something, ontologically, and therefore to be contingent upon something outside itself. Whatever is contingent has a lower status, a lower dignity, than whatever is self-dependent, just as in a family the children depend upon the father's wishes and are ordered about by him and so have a lower dignity than the father, who does as he wills and is not controlled by, or dependent upon, the children. Only what is absolutely simple, then, will not be caused by something else and hence lower in dignity than it; what is absolutely simple will be a necessary being—that is, it comes into being through itself. Is there then such a 'necessary' being, in the sense of something simple and uncaused? It is tempting just to say that since such a being is 'necessary', it needs must be. But in this context what matters is ultimately that a rational hierarchy of entities requires one ultimate entity at the top of the hierarchy; a sequence of caused beings requires an uncaused being at the end to start the causes, lest we find ourselves in a rationally intolerable infinite regress.

In what sense is such a first cause of all being to be identified with what in the monotheist tradition was called *God?* A metaphysical first cause is not necessarily the same as a Creator-god. Yet the Faylasûfs' 'necessary being' will have the highest possible ontological attributes—be the most worthy and excellent of all beings; for it will be perfect (being self-sufficient, not dependent upon anything else). And if it is perfect it will not be lacking in any valuable quality; not only valuable in that we regard it so, but inherently valuable in the rationally ordered universe: hence it will know, if anything knows; it will be alive, if anything is alive; it will be most powerful if anything has any power—it will, then, be a most excellent and perfectly admirable being, worthy of worship and honour by any other, more than a strong king is honoured by his subjects or a good father by his children. The Faylasûf could feel that such a being was worthy—and alone worthy—of the status the monotheists ascribed to God.

In later Roman times, a group of Greek Philosophers (called neo-Platonists), led by Plotinus (d. 270), had developed some of Plato's insights into an elaborate cosmology relating this First-Cause God to human life in a way that made religious sense. The neo-Platonist cosmology rested on three bases: on Aristotle's astronomy and metaphysics, which pointed to a cosmic first cause in rather the way we have seen above; on some of the logical and mythological conceptions of Plato, who had been interested in the aspirations of material beings toward non-material norms beyond them; and on mystical experience. The neo-Platonist cosmology originally presupposed the pagan Hellenic religious notions, but could be adapted to Christian doctrines; it was generally accepted in the tradition of Philosophia by Islamic times. (We have already seen traces of it in the Ismâ'îlî system.)

As the Muslim Faylasûfs developed this cosmology, it was a timeless drama of the unfolding at once of logical and of material potentialities. The universe originates eternally, timelessly, from an absolutely transcendent One, the absolutely Simple, of which nothing positive can be properly predicated except what is necessary to define it as the First Cause. Just by the rational purity of its oneness, however, emanates from it eternally Absolute Reason, rationality as such—still a single thing, but carrying within it implicitly the multiplicity of harmonies and relations. From the confrontation of the Absolute Reason with the Absolute One can arise, then, all that goes with multiplicity—movement and change; and in particular, the Absolute Soul—the ultimate principle of self-motion. Soul produces motion (and so time) in its necessary response to Absolute Reason, its attempt to imitate the perfection of Reason; which it cannot achieve, precisely because its nature is derivative from Reason and not reason itself. From Absolute Reason and Absolute Soul proceed the concentric heavenly spheres of the Aristotelian and Ptolemaic astronomical systems, and their pure circular movements; each of these spheres, from that of the fixed stars through the several planetary spheres to that of the moon, has its own Reason and its own Soul, governing its motion. The interaction of all these circular movements, which become more complex as they descend toward us, accounts for the complexity of the sub-lunar sphere, the earth with its four elements and the diverse compounds thereof. (Over all this complexity presides the Active Reason of the lowest sphere.)

To this point, the theory merely accounts for the diversity and movement we find in the observed universe of entities; but its religious meaning emerges when it is seen that human reason is a reflection of that Active Reason that presides over our world. If we purify our own rationality, we can participate positively in the whole process, thus reversing in our own consciousnesses the descent from unity to multiplicity by reascending intellectually from multiplicity to ultimate unity. In this way, the whole Philosophic life is justified: the search for intellectual awareness, and in particular for understanding of the universal as against the mere transient instance; and the moral purification of the self which at once makes dispassionate rational inquiry possible, and is its outcome. The Philosophic search is the truest way of honouring and worshipping God; the cults and moral rules and doctrines of ordinary ignorant people are merely imperfect attempts at the true Philosophic way.

Such a religious vision could be harmonized, to its own satisfaction, with almost any popular religious cult. But the exponents of alternative visions might not be satisfied with the terms of the harmonization. The monotheists of the Irano-Semitic tradition, in particular, could doubt if the Philosophic One First Cause were God at all. The monotheists conceived their God as having rather different fundamental attributes, both as supreme Creator, creating by an act of arbitrary will, and as final moral Judge, intervening positively and personally in human life. The monotheists' notions of God had been built up precisely from observing and responding to those contingent and historical data which the Faylasûfs tended to disregard as not amenable to reason. The prophets' idea of God was more moral than ontological, more historical than timeless; God might want honour, but first of all He wanted obedience, and the honour would follow if He chose to exact it. It had long been evident that the Philosophic and the Prophetic traditions were not in ready harmony. In Islamic circumstances, as earlier, it was not easy for them to come to terms with each other.[5]

The Faylasûfs' 'God' remained a very different figure from the God of the prophets, as different as their sense of human destiny; and however much the difference was disguised by the use of common words, it showed up at crucial junctures. The Faylasûfs, above all, rejected any cosmic history with a beginning and end; hence they could not accept God as Creator, as Providence, or as Judge, in the Abrahamic sense. Instead, for them, the world was eternal; God (as ultimate Reason) could take cognizance only of abstract 'universal' intelligibles; and He certainly would not arbitrarily resurrect human bodies at some end of time. It was at such inescapable points that it became clear whether a person's first allegiance was to the Abrahamic or to the Philosophic tradition.

Falsafah and the Islamic revelation

The adepts of Philosophia saw it as a necessary consequence of pure reason, the same for any rational being of whatever nation or time. (Philosophia was felt to be simply *philosophy*, in the sense of true understanding and wisdom.) When, like all other cultural elements, Philosophia too was translated from older languages into Arabic, nothing new need have been anticipated from it. But, as we have already seen in the natural sciences,

[5] An excellent presentation of the assumptions and methods of basic inquiry and its pervasive moral implications, as the Faylasûfs saw it, is al-Fârâbî's *Philosophy of Plato and Aristotle*, translated and introduced by Muḥsin Mahdî (Glencoe, Ill., 1962). Note that though, as Mahdî points out, the neo-Platonist system of emanations from the One is not mentioned even in the first portion (which shows what any proper philosophy must do—the latter portions exemplify this in the two master cases—and presents very few other positive doctrines either), yet the emanations are clearly presupposed in more than one place, and the basis in method that leads to them is clearly stated, especially where the study of stars and of souls is made the double point of departure for studying the divine principles in metaphysics.

Islamicate Falsafah proved to be more than a mere continuation in Arabic of the Syriac tradition. The burgeoning society of the 'Abbâsî cities gave a strong impulse to rational inquiry; but the new intellectual constellation of Islamicate society also had an effect. The results were historically distinctive even in what we would call philosophy proper.

Despite its rejection of the historical and the traditional, despite its attempt to deduce everything from abstract and timeless rational principles Falsafah itself was, of course, a historical, cultural tradition. It had had its own charismatic founders—most notably Socrates, to whose memory and example Faylasûfs were loyal. And while Faylasûfs made a point of their independence toward earlier authorities, quoting Aristotle's point that he owed great friendship to Plato but greater yet to Truth, they inevitably studied such masters and had to come to terms with their thinking, even when they tried to improve on it. Under the new circumstances introduced by Islam, new questions and new opportunities arose and the Philosophic dialogue was quickened: Falsafa, too, was developed through the interplay of conscious individual decisions when the social contact raised new problems; and the outcome of those decisions affected the whole subsequent tradition of Falsafah, setting limits to what Faylasûfs could attempt to do for the future in relation to society, and hence to the kind of viewpoints they could relevantly develop.[6]

As we have seen, the Philosophers of the Greek tradition had gradually developed a certain degree of unity in their general approach, taking the logic and a good deal of the particular sciences from Aristotle, while the picture of the cosmos and the place of the individual in it went back largely to Plato or to Plotinus' interpretation of Plato's thought. Within this general orientation there was considerable variety in the schools in the emphasis put on Aristotle or on Plato; and indeed other strands of thought, notably the later Stoic, continued to command attention. But each student was expected to read a certain set of works with his masters and in almost a set order.

It was in this more or less standardized form that the Philosophic tradition appeared at the time when its most important works were translated into Arabic, and it was from this point of departure that the Muslim Faylasûfs began to speculate. However, when the classics of philosophy and science

[6] The contrast sketched in this chapter between the Prophetic and the Philosophic traditions has been standard in the literature for decades now. It has played somewhat comparable roles in Islamdom and Christendom. Often it is identified with a contrast of Semitic, or at least Hebraic, culture vs. Greek. The contrast is so neat that it is always in danger of being pushed too far. This danger is at the worst when it is made to look like a contrast in 'racial' temperaments. In interpreting it as a contrast between historical dialogues, each of which is (by the nature of dialogues) open to interinvolvement with the other, I have hoped to minimize the danger. In particular, it becomes clear that each dialogue has been an integral part of the total culture both in the Irano-Semitic complex and in the European, even though each dialogue has played a somewhat different role and even carried somewhat different elements in the two regional cultures.

were translated into Arabic, this tended to be done piecemeal for the benefit of individual laymen and scholars who could not trouble to learn Greek. In the process, the old system of a set curriculum was partially interrupted. Those who learned their Falsafah only or primarily in the Arabic translation were likely to come at it arbitrarily *ad libitum*. This in itself was enough to suggest new perspectives: when the problems were not reached in the standard order and explained by the standard commentators, new facets of them became obvious, and the Islamicate Faylasûfs were led to present the material in new, independent syntheses.

Thus Muḥammad b. Zakariyyâ' al-Râzî (d. 925 or 934), the physician, was moved, evidently having read a number of earlier philosophers not normally included in the Philosophic curriculum, and having become intensely aware of the gaps in intelligibility still left by the standard views, to reject a cosmic system in which there was just one eternal First Cause, 'unmoved mover' eternally setting in motion the otherwise unformed matter of the universe. Instead, he postulated five eternal first principles, co-existent and possessed of equal logical necessity. He could not see how time or space or matter could either be generated from another intelligible first principle (Reason or Soul), or be subsumed under any other category. His picture of the cosmos presupposed all the basic assumptions that Faylasûfs had to take for granted, and in this sense marked a relatively slight new departure in the tradition, which was as powerful in him who so severely criticized the old metaphysicians as in those who departed less noticeably from their solutions. But under the new circumstances brought by Islam (though he was at most but a nominal Muslim), al-Râzî was led to deduce from the general framework some quite novel conclusions.

But the most important consequence of the Islamic environment was the new confrontation with the monotheistic tradition which it enforced. Though some Faylasûfs clearly accepted no regular religion whatsoever, most Arabic-writing Faylasûfs were either Christians, Jews, or Muslims; they all acknowledged the pagan Greek sages, especially Plato and Aristotle, as their masters, but their doctrines on crucial points did vary according to the allegiance they held. Christians had worked out their solutions to the problem of reconciling Christianity and the Greek intellectual disciplines some time since. But Islam presented a more concentrated challenge. The Muslim solution was only in part parallel.

The first of the philosophically independent Faylasûfs of Muslim faith was Ya'qûb al-Kindî (d. after 870—by way of exception among Muslim scholars, he was of old-Arabian descent). He adapted to the Islamic doctrine with little change in spirit the Christian solution which his teachers had accepted, that revealed teachings about God and the soul were parables of Philosophic truths. He seems to have worked closely with Mu'tazilî thinkers in their attempt to eliminate anthropomorphisms from their faith, and to have believed that their solutions were not incompatible with rationalistic philosophical views. He was especially known for his collection of philosophical definitions and was perhaps more concerned with encouraging a general rationalistic viewpoint than with working out any particular system. But this approach could not remain satisfactory. The Socratic tradition could not rest content with being bound to limit its questioning within a framework which was imposed by a historical intervention such as Islam. Nor could the Qur'ânic tradition accept subordination fo its conclusions to the authority of private human speculation.

The alternatives of Socratic faith and Abrahamic faith

The dilemma is illustrated in conversations recorded by Abû-Ḥâtim al-Râzî, an Ismâʻîlî dâʻî preacher, as taking place publicly between himself and the Faylasûf Râzî, Ibn-Zakariyyâʼ.[7] Of all those who shared the Qur'ânic tradition, the Ismâʻîlîs were the most actively interested in the doctrines associated with Falsafah; their symbolism presupposed the old Hellenistic image of the world, and in the following centuries they were to adapt the old Philosophic cosmology to their own purposes. But the Ismâʻîlî was as shocked as any other adherent of a monotheistic revelation at what he regarded as the dangerous and arrogant rejection of historical revelation recognized by the community, in favour of the momentary speculation of an individual.

The Faylasûf Râzî began by objecting to reliance on revelation on the ground that, since more than one doctrine is supported by revelation and there is no way to decide between the conflicting claims, such an appeal can only lead to destructive conflict among mankind—which cannot be God's purpose. All humans alike being endowed with reason, this alone has any hope of settling disputes, and it must be God's intention that we use it for reaching truth. The Ismâʻîlî Râzî retorted that while we all have reason, we do not have it all alike; some persons are so much more intelligent than others that it is inevitable that some lead and that others follow. Hence there must be an ultimately authoritative leader if truth is to be found at all—as surely God desires it to be; this leader (to be identifiable by the less intelligent) must be a prophet bringing revelation.

But then he turned the Faylasûf's point against him, noting that in fact the proponents of individual reason differed among themselves just as did the proponents of revelation. He noted that the Faylasûf Râzî had himself condemned important conclusions of great earlier rationalistic Philosophers and asked if he, their disciple, thought himself wiser than they who had taught him—implying that even the wisest Philosophers make mistakes and

[7] Both were from Rayy, hence called Râzî. I summarize here from 'Munâẓarât bayn al-Râziyyayn' by Abû-Ḥâtim al-Râzî in Muḥammad b. Zakariyyâʼ al-Râzî, *Opera Philosophica*, ed. Paul Kraus, Fu'âd University Faculty of Letters, Publication no. 22 (Cairo, 1939), vol. 1, pp. 291–316.

have no way of coming to a final settlement. The Faylasûf declared that the later thinker, having the benefit of all that the earlier ones had done, could add his own inquiries and so improve on their work; on which the Ismâʿîlî pointed out that there would always be still later thinkers to improve further on al-Râzî's own improvements, so that al-Râzî had no assurance that he was right; and (since in fact the various opinions were all retained in the books side by side) the result was simply a multiplication of the number of diverse opinions about which people could dispute.

But at this point the Faylasûf turned to the heart of the matter. He was not immediately concerned with an indefinite progress in knowledge for the benefit of hypothetical future generations (when supposedly the range of diverse opinions might have been narrowed by exhaustive selection). Rather he was concerned with the pursuit of truth in any one generation. He maintained, then, that what counts is that each thinker be putting forth his own best effort; he will then be on the way to truth, even if he does not attain it, and it is being on the way that is desirable. For what is wanted is to purify the soul of its 'turbidness', of the confusion of mind induced by the sensory impressions and passions of living, so that it can judge and act objectively. And 'souls are not purified of the turbidness of this world or freed for that other world [the life of spirituality]' except through independent study and examination; 'when someone studies it [rationalistic Philosophy] and attains something of it, however little it be, he purifies his soul from this turbidness and renders it free. And if the common crowd who ruin their souls and are neglectful of study would devote but the slightest concern to it, this would liberate them from this turbidness . . .'

The Ismâʿîlî, however, convinced of human intellectual inequality, was less optimistic about the common crowd. He asked if a person who continued to believe in the doctrines of revelation could be purified by studying (rationalistic) Philosophy a little on the side; to which the Faylasûf responded that no one who persevered in submission to established opinion could become even a student of 'Philosophy' (thus indicating what he really was demanding when he asked for even a little bit of independent study). But the Ismâʿîlî pointed out that, in practice, those who went into rationalistic Philosophy less than very deeply (which would be most of the would-be rationalists) might indeed reject revelation, but only to submit to a different tradition—a different set of established opinions—those to be found in the books of the Philosophers, which the Faylasûf had admitted were not necessarily in themselves true. Such a person would lose the benefit of the historical revelation without achieving the purification the Faylasûf called for; none could be in a worse state than that.

Both the Faylasûf and the Ismâʿîlî were concerned with the moral dimensions of living, to which sheer knowledge was only an instrument. The Faylasûf Râzî looked to the process of inquiry to make a good man, and was (exceptionally among the Faylasûfs) ready to see a relatively large public join in this process—he wrote a book on treating the ailments of the soul, aimed partly at persuading the adîb to look beyond his polite and superficial culture. The Ismâʿîlî Râzî demanded, as a good Sharîʿah-conscious Muslim, that responsible living be based on something more objective than on an inner 'purity'; he looked for the most tangible possible assurance of a socially valid position—which meant turning to a historically accepted revelation, that of Muḥammad and the Qur'ân. Most Faylasûfs acknowledged that, as regards the common masses at least, the Ismâʿîlî had a point.

Al-Fârâbî: revelation as political truth

To the problem, how the rational potentialities of human beings are to be fulfilled without leading them into mazes of subjective and anti-social error, most Faylasûfs had long since found a solution on the practical level. To begin with, they minimized the differences in opinion among Philosophers. We have noted how, already in Greek and in Syriac, the standard Philosophic curriculum was based on both Plato and Aristotle, in different respects, despite the well-known contradictions between their views. Unlike al-Râzî, most Faylasûfs continued relatively close to the old syntheses. Though the differences among the old masters were not ignored, Philosophia was felt to offer a single orientation and purpose, and hence, at least potentially, a single doctrine. Explicit harmonization between the two greatest masters was furthered in two ways. Plato's logical method, for instance, was interpreted by way of Aristotle. This simply reflected a straightforward attempt to solve the intellectual problems both had left open. But some harmonization was in direct response to the need to justify Philosophia as not contradicting revealed religious dogma. Thus Aristotle's teachings that seemed inconsistent with immortality for the soul and with a temporal act of creation were interpreted by way of Plato, sometimes with the aid of a neo-Platonist booklet early translated into Arabic and mistitled 'the theology of Aristotle'. But this assurance that true Philosophers did come to the same conclusions in their independent inquiries was only part of the answer to the danger of vulgar confusion resulting from too free a use of individual reason. The Faylasûfs' more basic solution was to preserve rationalistic Philosophia for themselves alone, and to sacrifice any possible human universality of rationalism in cautious recognition of the inadequacies of ordinary people. This meant coming to terms with popular revealed religion.

The man who established the classical tradition of the Muslim Faylasûfs' attitude to revelation was Abu-Naṣr al-Fârâbî (d. 950). Al-Fârâbî, born on the Syr river in a Turkic military family, studied at Baghdad and lived there on private means until late in life he became court musician at Aleppo. Unlike Ibn-Zakariyyâ' al-Râzî, al-Fârâbî took Islam seriously. But he had studied under a school more uncompromisingly rationalistic, among the Hellenic Christian traditions, than did al-Kindî, as can be seen from the

Early Islamicate Philosophic Schools

By *c.* 500 CE	School of Alexandria: became classical; more Aristotelian, including late Stoicism; philosophy primes revelation (Christian)	School of Athens: more Platonic; more inclined to honor (pagan) revelations
By advent of Islam		Nestorians have adapted this school to Christianity
Ninth century	School of Baghdad (Ḥunayn the translator) is in this tradition	Al-Kindî, who accepted Mu'tazilî Kalâm, is of this school
c. 900 CE	Al-Fârâbî (d. 950) stems from this tradition, puts philosophy above revelation, which he interprets politically	Al-Râzî (Rhazes, d. 925 or 934), of unidentifiable background, rejects Islam; no major followers
		Ibn-Sînâ (Avicenna, d. 1037) and the Iranian school derive from Fârâbî with Platonic emphasis; Ibn-Sînâ interprets revelation psychologically as well as politically
	Ibn-Rushd (Averroës, d. 1198) and the Spanish-Maghribî school derive from Fârâbî with Aristotelian emphasis; reject compromise with Kalâm, stress Sharî'ah	

This chart is based largely on R. Walzer, 'Islamic Philosophy', in Sarvapelli Radhakrishnan, ed., *History of Philosophy Eastern and Western* (London, 1952), vol. 9, pp. 120–48.

chart of early Islamicate Philosophic schools. Then he added a powerful perceptivity of his own.[8]

Al-Fârâbî and his followers seem to have had a more developed concern with social or political questions—especially those where religion entered in—than Christian (or most ancient Pagan) Philosophers had had; the political orientation of Islam itself suggested this, but the general cultural fluidity of the times perhaps suggested, even apart from Islam itself, the revival of Plato's political hopes which he had expressed in Sicily and which his disciples had expressed somewhat more successfully in new Greek foundations. Al-Fârâbî, and no doubt others, perhaps felt that with the coming of Islam and its universally accepted godly ideals a new situation had appeared, which might be favourable to building a philosophically more ideal society. At any rate, al-Fârâbî and his successors spoke of gradual reform and put some of their best efforts into political philosophy.

The phenomenon of Islam was too massive, whatever a man's personal feelings toward it, to be ignored by one who would understand the universe and human life in it. Why did so many human beings adopt this interpretation of life and society? What was its meaning and its worth as a system of thought and action? Already Plato had suggested that a well-ordered society required doctrines which would be supposed by the population to be divinely revealed, doctrines which were not necessarily true in themselves but would lead the people to behave in the ways that were best for society and for themselves. Al-Fârâbî adapted this point of view to Islam.[9]

The inhabitants of a good society ought to believe that there is a single God—though they need not be expected to have a full rational—i.e., Philosophic—insight into that God's nature; and to believe that humans, as beings endowed with reason who should rise above material preoccupations, should, in respect before God, behave justly toward one another—though, again, they need not understand rationally the nature of either human beings or of justice. These basic beliefs could be put before the masses in the form of images, such as the depiction of Hell as a suggestion of the subhuman fate of the person preoccupied with material lusts. Ideally, perhaps, a good society should be ruled by a perfect 'philosopher', a sage in the Faylasûfs' sense, who would understand all its principles himself as well as know how to inculcate the needful ideas in others. But if this were impossible, various approximations would do; at least the laws should have been constructed

[8] Useful general articles on al-Râzî and al-Fârâbî, by Abdurrahman Badawi and Ibrahim Madkour, respectively, appear in M. M. Sharif, ed., *A History of Muslim Philosophy* (Wiesbaden, 1963)—a very uneven collection of disparate pieces.

[9] Leo Strauss, 'How Fârâbî Read Plato's Laws', *Mélanges Louis Massignon*, (Damascus, 1957), vol. 3, pp. 319–44, gives an instructive example of Strauss' way of reading the Faylasûfs to bring out this viewpoint; the method can seem unconvincing in one sample, but cumulatively it comes to impose itself. The alternative is to suppose that al-Fârâbî and all his admirers were fools. It must be added that Erwin Rosenthal, in his various writings, displays a consistent incomprehension of the Faylasûfs' political thinking.

in accordance with rational, philosophic requirements and presented in a form which would induce the unphilosophical people to observe them. The role of Muḥammad, then, was that of lawgiver: his great mission was to bring the Sharî'ah law and to surround it with sanctions which would cause it to be observed.

Popular religion, in this view, was more than an expedient fiction, though it was also not wisdom to be placed on a level with rational 'philosophy'.[10] Revelation was a natural process essential to the constitution of society, which could not exist without some form of imaginatively sanctioned law. The Prophet was bringing truth, in the form that he had the gift of bringing it in, even though it was not so high a truth as was open to the rational 'philosopher'. Its highest doctrines were statements of basic rational principles, but put in a simple or an imaged form which ordinary people could understand. The law which the Prophet promulgated was valid and genuinely incumbent on those human beings who happened to be within the community for whom he was legislating.

There might be little reason, in the abstract, for a rational 'philosopher' to prefer one popular religion over another. But the Faylasûf might feel that Shar'î Islam, with its emphasis precisely on law and on the social body and its relative freedom from such excessively fanciful dogma as that of the Trinity, met the rational requirements for a good popular religion with singular purity. Al-Fârâbî used language that suggested (at the Shî'î court of Aleppo), by stressing the importance of an imâm sound by nature as the continuing head of the community, that not just Islam but Shî'î Islam might be looked to to bring about a more satisfactory society. In any case, the rational 'philosopher' was philosophically bound to adhere to the popular religion of his own community, acknowledge its doctrines (however he might tacitly understand them), and support its practices. The religious learning formed an integral part of what a 'philosopher' ought to know—under the heading 'political philosophy'. In this limited sense, a Faylasûf in Islamdom not only could but should be a good and believing Muslim.

Yet the traditions of Falsafah were not only older than and independent of Islam; they presupposed a radical élitism, in which only those could share who disposed of the material as well as the intellectual leisure to devote themselves to pursuits that had little practical application. Even such utility as the Faylasûfs could in fact offer was restricted to the wealthy,

[10] Many scholars have supposed that al-Fârâbî was trying to reconcile 'religion and philosophy', 'faith and reason', as two independent sources of the same truth. He did want to show that nothing which the monotheistic tradition insisted on had to be rejected by rationalistic philosophy; but unlike al-Kindî, who might indeed have conceived the question in some such terms, al-Fârâbî and the later Faylasûfs restricted the spiritual role of popular religion very sharply and gave it very little intellectual credit in any case. R. Walzer, Leo Strauss, and Muḥsin Mahdî have been the most helpful scholars in pinpointing the Faylasûfs' attitude. I have learned a good deal from Mahdî orally, though I have not been willing to accept some of his viewpoints.

generally monarchs and courtiers, who could afford their expensive ministrations. Sharî'ah-minded Muslims always felt the Faylasûfs as alien. Their reaction was taken up by the man in the street, and Falsafah as a whole, together with the sciences which it specially fostered, was never fully accepted in High Caliphal society as an integral part of culture, in the way that both the prophetically-based Sharî'ah and even the absolutism were accepted. It remained a bit apart and foreign.

Earlier Translators, Philosophers, Scientists

fl. 770s	Jâbir ibn Hayyân, alchemist, eponym for Jâbir corpus of alchemical knowledge
c. 800	Teaching hospital established in Baghdad
813–848	Mu'tazilism flourishes, intellectual endeavor of all kinds heavily patronized by the court
c. 850	Death of al-Khwârazmî, 'father of algebra', mathematician (user of the 'Indian' numerals) and astronomer
c. 873	Death of al-Kindî, often called 'the first Faylasûf'; death of Ḥunayn ibn Isḥâq, important translator of Hellenistic works into Arabic
Early tenth century	'Jâbir corpus' of alchemical knowledge in circulation
925	Death of al-Râzî (Rhazes), Faylasûf, alchemist, physician
929	Death of al-Battânî, mathematician (trigonometry), astronomer
950	Death of al-Fârâbî, Faylasûf-metaphysician
c. 970	Collection of 'Epistles' (Rasâ'il) of the Ikhwân al-Ṣafâ', a comprehensive compilation of esoteric (Pythagorean-type) 'scientific' and metaphysical knowledge

Kalâm and Falsafah

The glory of the Faylasûfs was their cosmology, their rationalistic portrayal of the universe as a whole and of the place of the human soul in it. This was a standing challenge to the devotees of the monotheistic tradition to do as well. The Piety-minded had tended to develop, as part of their over-all intellectual structure, the rudiments of an argued theory of God and mankind. At first, this was done point by point at need; for instance, where the Islamic revelation was challenged by other monotheists: the absolute unity of God, the prophethood of Muḥammad, and generally the validity of Qur'ânic descriptions of God and of the Judgment. The first aim of the Mu'tazilîs, who first cultivated extensively this sort of apologia, was negative, to show that there was nothing in the Qur'ân which was repugnant to careful reasoning. But very soon, in the course of disputes with non-Muslims as well as with Muslims (such as the subtle anthropomorphist—and Shî'î—thinker Hishâm b. al-Ḥakam), they had to decide standards of what should be considered repugnant to reason; this ultimately meant establishing an overall cosmology which they could claim was rational and with which they could show the Qur'ân to be in harmony.

Such activity was called *kalâm*, 'discussion', that is, discussion of points of religious belief on the basis of rational criteria. The more exacting of the Sharî'ah-minded regarded this as bid'ah and denied that human minds should presume to 'prove' what was given by revelation, but the activity became widespread as Islam became the prevailing religious allegiance, and it gave rise to several competing theological schools.

The first great systematic thinker among the Mu'tazilîs, who gave that school of piety, already devoted to argumentation, the framework of a comprehensive dogmatic system was Abû-l-Hudhayl (d. 840). Among his followers, doctrines were worked out under five heads: (1) the unity of God, under which heading Manichean dualism, but also anything that smacked of anthropomorphism, was condemned—and in particular the cruder literalism with which the Ḥadîth folk took Qur'ânic images; (2) the justice of God, under which any ascriptions of injustice to God in His judgment of human beings was rejected—with the consequence that human beings were made alone responsible for all their acts, and so punishable for their bad ones; (3) the coming Judgment, under which the importance of righteousness was insisted on, as against mere Muslim allegiance—with a tendency to exalt the Qur'ân as the standard at the expense of ḥadîth; (4) the intermediate position of the Muslim sinner, neither faithful nor infidel; finally, (5) the obligation to command the good and forbid evil—to take initiatives toward godly social order. Within this framework, a wide range of differing opinions was to be found within the school as it developed.

It was under the heading of the unity of God that the Mu'tazilîs raised the most cosmological questions, for they had to find an understanding of God's creation and governance of the world: was there, for instance, anything that God could not do?—which most denied. Their terminology—substance, accident, existence, non-existence, etc.—seems to echo, though imprecisely, the Greek philosophical tradition; perhaps it reflects Christian theological discussions with which the Mu'tazilîs and other Muslims took issue. But their orientation was to the primacy of revelation.

Mu'tazilism was never the only school of Islamic speculative thought, but for long it was the most intellectually effective. However, with the rise of the piety of the Ḥadîth folk, it found itself increasingly out of step with the most popular currents of the time. The metaphysical unity and the rational justice of God could be defended out of the Qur'ân and were consistent enough with the relatively imprecise faith of the ordinary Muslims of early times. But on these as on almost all their main points the Mu'tazilîs were at odds with the Ḥadîthî movement, which tolerated seeming anthropomorphism, stressed the omnipotence of God more intensely than His justice, and accepted ḥadîth reports often at the expense of the Qur'ân. By the end of the ninth century several men, including some who identified themselves with the Ḥadîth folk, had begun making efforts to justify rationally, against the Mu'tazilîs, these more popular views—departing from the more common position of the Ḥadîth folk, of rejecting all kalâm disputation altogether. Two of the most prominent were Abû-l-Ḥasan al-Ash'arî (d. 935) and Abû-Manṣûr al-Mâturîdî (d. 944).

Such men attempted to limit kalâm and its cosmology more closely to a defence of the doctrines given in the accumulating ḥadîth, which now represented the more generally approved doctrines of the Sharî'ah-minded. But their concern was not simply with individual doctrines, but also with the temper of the whole intellectual movement. Sceptical of the powers of abstract reason, they tried to deduce as little as possible from the supposed requirements of reason as such, as the Mu'tazilîs had often done. To this extent, they backed away still further from the viewpoint of the Hellenic tradition even while retaining its categories.[11]

What positions were actually adopted by al-Ash'arî is not yet clear; as eponym of a school of thought, he has been ascribed all the basic positions taken later by the school; and not all the works bearing his name are genuine. But it was probably al-Ash'arî himself who developed the key formulations on some of the issues most mooted by the Mu'tazilîs. The Mu'tazilîs had insisted that to describe God as possessed of any distinct attributes at all, such as knowledge or power, was to run the danger, if not of anthropomorphism, then, worse yet, of asserting other eternal entities with God: for any knowledge or power attributed to him must be, as such, eternal. They insisted that God knows or is powerful not by a special knowledge or power but by His simple essence in each case. Doubtless unconsciously, they were here allowing the very notions of 'attributes' and 'essence', inherited from the Philosophers, to carry them along a path analogous to that already trodden by the neo-Platonists, toward asserting the utter simplicity of God. The Ḥadîth folk objected that this was to empty the notion of 'God' of all content—and was hardly better than denying God altogether. Al-Ash'arî seems to have insisted that God did have attributes, and to have met the Mu'tazilîs' point by saying, neatly, that they were not other than His essence. The logical categories were retained, but were not allowed to detract from the effectiveness of a God that could intervene in history.

He might have liked to avoid the Philosophers' categories altogether. We have noted how the notion of *îmân*, 'faith' in God and His message, was intellectualized into sheer 'belief', assent to propositions, especially among the Mu'tazilîs. The Ḥadîth folk, as conscious of needing to define the godly community as the Mu'tazilîs, agreed in principle; but they felt that faith must require a more personal involvement as well, citing Qur'ânic passages

[11] J. Schacht, 'New Sources for the History of Muhammadan Theology', *Studia Islamica*, I (1953), 23–42, has a variety of useful observations on the relation of the schools of kalâm to other Islamic currents. (Despite the title, it is not about a theology of Muḥammad or one derived directly from him personally, but is about Islamic theology in general.)

in which faith was said to increase in quantity—which sheer assent could hardly do. The expressive anecdotes of ḥadîth and the Sîrah, the life of the Prophet, best set forth what was required. But kalâm disputation required a concise general formulation. In this case, al-Ash'arî did not attempt a new sort of abstraction from the texts, nor even a nice logical distinction. He turned to formulations of 'faith' that had been extracted from the texts for legal (not doctrinal) purposes, for the sake of defining who is entitled to the rights of a mu'min, a man of îmân, faith, by his ḥadîth-minded friends. 'Faith', then, included assent and affirmation and action as well, though the assent was primary. In this way he introduced into systematic kalâm a formulation which made the essential point, yet compromised as little as possible the human quality of the texts.

By the latter part of the tenth century, several schools of kalâm disputation were actively combating each other, sometimes violently. Besides the still vigorous Mu'tazilîs and the Ṣûfî-inclined Karrâmîs, the two most important schools traced themselves to al-Ash'arî and to al-Mâturîdî, respectively. The Ash'arîs were associated with the Shâfi'î legists, the Mâturîdîs (and the Mu'tazilîs) with the Ḥanafîs. The Ash'arîs went the furthest toward a strict adherence to the positions of the Ḥadîth folk, and developed withal a highly sophisticated interpretation of cosmology which moved as far as logically possible from the positions of Falsafah.

The character of the cosmology of the Muslim Faylasûfs becomes especially clear when contrasted to the cosmology of the Ash'arî kalâm. The Faylasûfs were interested, since the days of Plato, in the unchanging, in the permanently valid. Thrust into the water, a stick appears bent; in the air, it appears straight. When one is angry, one's neighbour seems an object for violent assault; a few minutes later, he may seem an object for pity. If one is born in India, it seems of the utmost importance to burn one's father's corpse; if one is born in Arabia, one will bury it, and do one's best to prevent anyone's burning it. A year ago one's fields were rich with wheat and this year the same fields are almost barren. In such a world what can one be sure of? The rationalistic answer of the Philosophers was that though individual plants and even fields appear and disappear, we can know what wheat is, as such, and what a field is, and what is universally true of any wheat growing in any field; we can know what anger is, and what pity is, and what a human being is as such, apart from any particular feeling we may have for particular persons. Knowledge is therefore a matter of timeless concepts, essences, and natural laws, rather than of transient and changing details. We can be sure that there are 180 degrees in a triangle, that justice is more admirable in men than injustice, that oaks grow from acorns; we cannot be sure, but can only have a provisional opinion, that this three-cornered piece of wood is a triangle, that this man is just, that this acorn will actually grow into an oak.

The Ash'arîs, on the contrary, doubted that there were any inherently unchanging essences and natural laws. For them the most important facts were not abstractly universal but very concrete and historical. These were, first, that the individual man Muḥammad had brought to human beings supreme truth in a particular place at a particular time, and that this truth was carried by his community from generation to generation; and second, that every individual was faced with the supreme choice of deciding in his own case whether to accept this truth or not. One could know the individual man Muḥammad, or more exactly one could know by documented ḥadîth reports, various individual facts about him; it was much harder to say anything dependable about the universal essence of prophecy. The Ash'arîs granted that certain sequences of events tended to repeat themselves—God, as it were, has habitual ways of ordering nature. But they insisted that we have no evidence that events must necessarily always repeat themselves; all we can actually know is the concrete momentary fact.

The Faylasûfs, looking to unchanging essences and laws, thought of a world timelessly proceeding from self-sufficient Reason, each event in it being but an exemplification of logical possibilities. Mankind might change its condition from time to time, societies rise and fall and learn and unlearn; but there could be nothing inherently new. Such men as learned to fulfill the moral and intellectual demands of their truer natures might purify their intellectual spirits to the point that after death they were released into the realm of the changeless. The wise man was summoned to a virtuous contemplation and knowledge of existence, from the objects of the individual sciences up to the nature of Divine Reason itself.

The Faylasûfs saw a realm of natural order transcending the arbitrary power of isolated and unpredictable events, which power had formed the basis for the religious awe in which unthinking persons tended to hold everything that was out of the ordinary. But such a realm of nature seemed to allow meaning only to the type—even the human being, as an individual, could be meaningful only so far as he came to embody an abstractly rational nature. Monotheists of the prophetic tradition found themselves too deeply and individually challenged by personal moral demands to accept such a world. In God they saw a power that transcended in turn the order of nature —and thereby made possible meaningful human existence apart from mere fulfillment of natural types. The Ash'arîs wanted to safeguard recognition of that divine transcendence at every cost (even if it seemed incompatible with the notion of free will in a person, which in any case could be no more compromised than it was by the Faylasûfs' determining rule of cause and effect)—for only in God's presence could they feel that they possessed, on whatever terms, a personal responsibility.

Accordingly, the Ash'arîs, looking to revelatory events and authoritative ḥadîth reports, thought of a world produced as an act of will in time, as an event itself, by the Divine sovereignty; and within it, every particular event was in turn the immediate act of God. Mankind had had a beginning and was having an all-important history, in the course of which God gathered peoples to His obedience through His prophets. Such persons as obeyed God's commands would be rewarded at the end of history in Paradise, and the others punished in Hell. For the Faylasûfs, it was the wise and knowing élite, the few who could become objective scientists and philosophers, that were the only persons really fully human. For the Ash'arîs, on the contrary (sure that a little learning is a dangerous thing), the Divine blessing was upon the average individual whose overt acts conformed with the pattern laid down for the community of Muḥammad.

Kalâm as a system: the problem of divine power

On this basis, the Ash'arîs—by the end of the tenth century—developed a comprehensive system. A central problem with which they started was that of the relation of God's power to human actions. The Mu'tazilî solution had usually been too simplistic. Al-Ash'arî himself is said to have posed to his Mu'tazilî teacher (the great al-Jubbâ'î), who frankly asserted that God always rewarded humans as they deserved since humans could choose their actions at will, the question of the three brothers: One brother had a high post in Paradise, having lived long and done many good works, and the second brother, with a lower post, complained that he had died young and had not had the opportunity to do as much good as his brother; whereupon God explained that he had foreseen that the less-rewarded brother would have sinned had he been allowed to live longer, and would have been still worse off. At that, the third brother raised his voice from Hell, demanding why God had not cut him off early too.

Clearly, there was no way, within the bounds of ordinary logic, to declare God at once omnipotent and omnibenevolent. It was more realistic just to say that all was His will, without explanation or justification. Yet at the same time, it would not do simply to ascribe every movement that happened to God: one had to make some sort of distinction between the actions of a responsible human being and the motions of a stone as it falls. The solution to this problem advanced by the Ash'arîs was an attempt at simple description of the moral situation. First they pointed out that good and evil, indeed the laws of logic itself, are what God decrees them to be and it is presumptuous for human beings to attempt to judge God (or to justify Him!) on the basis of categories God has laid down only for human beings. In particular, what humans were to be held responsible for was God's arbitrary decision. Hence human responsibility was not, as some Mu'tazilîs had said, a function of the way that the action is produced—by choice as against inherent nature; rather, God alone creates all actions directly, but in some actions there is superadded a special quality of voluntary acquisition (*kasb*) which by God's will makes the individual a voluntary agent and responsible.

But a more theoretical solution of the problem, at the same time an expression of a fundamental monotheistic viewpoint on nature and history, lay in the theory of existence which the Ash'arîs worked out. The world was not made up of entities, enduring substances with their accidents, each with its own nature which accounted for its activities and its effects. This was to introduce secondary causes besides the immediate willing of God. Rather, the world was made up of atomic points, each at a given moment in space and time, among which the only continuity was the will of God, which created every atomic point anew every moment. If a given object seems to endure over a period of time, it is that God creates at every moment a new set of atomic points corresponding to what was there. Certain sequences and combinations of atomic points answer to God's customary ways; but none is necessary.

In such a world, of course, there can be no such thing as miracle: there can only be wonders, breaches in the normal custom of God, which, however, are in themselves just as 'natural' as any other event; or, rather, everything is a miracle, a special intervention of God's power. (Accordingly, the Ash'arîs could allow for any amount of miraculous accounts of the prophets, but at the same time avoided laying any great weight on such mere wonders; for evidentiary miracles, wonders which were to prove anything, they demanded a clear and declared connection with a divine message—so that it was, finally, the message which proved the miracle, rather than the reverse. This effectively put the emphasis, in recognizing a prophet, on the quality of his message rather than on any extraneous signs.) In such a world, also, human actions could not be ascribed any organic internal cause and effect; they were as much the creatures of God as any other. Yet God could give any human action whatever psychic quality He willed. Finally, in such a world, the only dependable knowledge was historical knowledge—and knowledge of the truth revealed in historical moments: in any case, knowledge of explicit individual events. All generalization, however useful it might be, was hazardous; and such generalization could never, in any case, lead to ultimate truths about the nature of life and the universe.

Such kalâm disputation was militantly (and, one might add, philosophically) anti-Philosophical. Nevertheless, kalâm of every school was long suspect in the eyes of many, perhaps even most, scholars of fiqh law, and of the more consistent of the Sharî'ah-minded generally. Till well after High Caliphal times, its position was at best secondary to that of the Sharî'ah in the eyes of most of the 'ulamâ'. If it was true that speculative generalization could in fact, as this atomistic analysis suggested, lead nowhere, then why speculate even so much?

VI

Adab: The Bloom of Arabic Literary Culture

c. 813–945

If the Sharî'ah-minded, and generally people of a pronounced Muslim piety, tended to be chary of associating with the court, and if even the Faylasûf scholars, who often depended personally on court patronage, commonly rather despised its ways, the court continued nevertheless to sit at the head of the Islamicate society as a whole. It was there that the most striking of the decisions were made which set the political, social, and even, largely, the economic context which all other currents of the high culture presupposed in practice. On the central government and its absolutism depended the peace and prosperity within which all the new cultural flowering was taking place.

But this absolutism depended not on sheer military might but on cultural expectations which could legitimize it. That is, it required habits of mind that would lead people to look to its restoration if it fell on hard times, rather than merely to enjoy or suffer its strength when it was strong and look to whatever seemed likely to take its place if it faltered. Only so could it have a chance to recover from serious temporary defeats. For maintaining such habits of mind, the absolutism could depend but little on the grudging recognition afforded it by the Shar'î 'ulamâ' It must depend heavily on the attitudes of a large class of officials and bureaucrats, together with wider strata of landowners and even rich merchants from whom the officials were drawn. Such men placed their greatest political hopes not in a problematic universal justice (through which they, indeed, might have been levelled down into the masses), but in a more realistic system which should assure the good order necessary for the security of those who were fortunately placed—and for the highly cultured living which for them constituted the good life.

The kâtibs, administrative clerks, seem to have come to differ, under the High Caliphate, from their earlier equivalents, even those of earlier Islamic times and presumably especially from those in Sâsânian times, in being drawn less exclusively from the old Iranian gentry, with their local roots in an agrarian order, and more freely from Arab families or nearly risen converts or from mercantile and other urban elements, which had little in common save their bureaucratic work and well-paid social standing. Such an administrative and cultural élite was not only city-based but cosmopolitan in outlook. They acknowledged the ideals of the 'ulamâ' scholars but did not take them too seriously, and they regarded the ideals of the Faylasûfs as an esoteric specialty for a few. Their culture can be summed up under the heading *adab*, the pattern of cultivated living which grew up around the court and in the provincial centres and was imitated yet more widely. It was in this culture that must be found those enduring patterns of expectation which could give solid support for the absolutist tradition, independent of the limitations imposed on it by Sharî'ah-mindedness.

The adab culture which centred on the court had its own serious triumphs, which gave it more than a transient dignity. It was at the court that the fashion was set, and the highest level of achievement displayed, in important intellectual and aesthetic dimensions of culture which Shar'î 'ulamâ' and Faylasûfs, as such, almost ignored. By the time of the caliph al-Ma'mûn at the start of the ninth century, these patterns too were being given a new classical form which was being accepted, as was the new religious allegiance, throughout the Muslim domains. All more limited older traditions of elegant living faded in its presence, even that which had prevailed at the Sâsânian court. This new cultural tradition bore a large part of the burden of assuring the prestige of the government and with it the stability of the whole society.

To this extent, the ultimate failure of the absolutism to maintain itself can be traced in the failure of the adab culture to establish a permanent basis for it. The prestige of the caliphate allowed a certain time of grace during which a basis might be built. But by al-Ma'mûn's reign, this time was beginning to run out. The adab culture laboured under several handicaps. First of all, the basis had to be built without serious reference to any cultural norm of any longer standing than the Muslim communal allegiance itself.

The breach with the older traditions

In Europe, in India, and in the Confucian Far East, the classical languages and the cultural ideals of the Axial Age continued to be studied directly and to influence fundamentally the regional high-cultural life down to modern times. But in the Nile-to-Oxus region there had been no single classical lettered tradition since Cuneiform times. Each confessional community had had its own; the Muslim community likewise had established its own tradition. This grew out of the older traditions but looked to its own creative moments which had been experienced in the new language and within the new religious allegiance. The central elements in the Islamicate cultural background remained (as in the other core areas) those of its own home ground—the Irano-Semitic lands; but the actual documents of the ancient Irano-Semitic cultures were no longer studied. Not merely were Cuneiform classics such as the Gilgamesh epic quite forgotten; even the masterpieces of the prophetic traditions were—if not forgotten—at least neglected. For the cultural achievements of even the Axial Age and since were for the most part retained only in a drastically Islamized dress.

The Earlier Classical Arabic Belles-Lettrists

Fifth and sixth centuries	Pre-Islamic Arabic poetry—the 'classical' qasîdah ('ode') style; the Arabian poets Imru'l-Qais, Ṭarafah, Zuhair, and others; important Sâsânian and Byzantine cultural eras also
Early eighth century	Umayyad poets Jarîr, al-Farazdaq, and al-Akhṭâl; rise of ghazal (love song, and generally lyric) style—'Umar b. 'Abî Rabî'ah, d. 719
c. 760	Death of Ibn-al-Muqaffa', translator of Persian works, caliphal adviser, and prose writer
c. 815	Death of Abû-Nuwâs, court poet of new styles, detractor of the old poetry
c. 828	Death of al-Aṣma'î, Arabic grammarian and lexicographer, collector of old Arabic poetry
c. 845	Death of Abû-Tammâm, collector of old Arabic poetry, poet in his own right who imitated the old style
869	Death of al-Jâḥiẓ, Mu'tazilî theologian, master of the Arabic prose essay
889	Death of Ibn-Qutaybah, grammarian, theological and literary critic, prose writer in the spirit of adab, moderate exponent of new forms
892	Death of al-Balâdhurî, collector of ḥadîths; wrote history of Arab conquests
923	Death of al-Ṭabarî, master exegete and ḥadîth-based historian of pre-Islamic and Islamic periods
951	Death of al-Iṣṭakhrî, geographer, who wrote a description of the world using work of al-Balkhî (d. 934)
956	Death of al-Mas'ûdî, well-travelled and erudite writer, 'philosophical' historian
965	Death of al-Mutanabbi', last great poet in older Arabic style, paragon of subtlety in poetic allusion

This breach in continuity made by Islam answered (on a more total scale) to such breaches made by all the lettered traditions between Nile and Oxus almost from the time when the Cuneiform tradition was abandoned: in its monotheistic exclusivity, each new religious community tended to reject the culture of outsiders as false. Perhaps among some Muslims there was a certain hostility to agrarian aristocratic tradition in the rejection of at least Pahlavî Sâsânian culture. But the Muslims were able to make a more effective overall breach in cultural continuity than had previous groups, ultimately because of the remarkable degree to which the more populistic and moralistic of the monotheistic religious aspirations were fulfilled in Islam, especially in its Sharîʿah-minded form. It was, initially, the effort to fulfill these religious aspirations that set off the Islamicate society from its past and, in effect, assured the distinct existence of an Islamicate civilization at all. Hence these aspirations had a key position in withholding or acknowledging legitimacy to any other tradition in the civilization as a whole, even though they may have done little more substantively than colour the content of that civilization. To such withholding of legitimacy, a lettered tradition was singularly vulnerable, being carried anyway by a minority and subject to the sway of opinion. It was a strong sense of the religious alienness of the Greek, Syriac, and Pahlavî traditions that prevented their classics from ever achieving a legitimate status as cultural authorities in the new community. It was just in fulfilling the communalistic ideals of the most active of the older traditions that Islam built up the exclusivity that found those traditions alien.

The most immediate victims of the Islamic exclusivity were the other Abrahamic religious traditions. Already Muḥammad had accused the Christians and Jews of having misinterpreted the messages sent to them. At the least, according to the Qur'ân, the Christians had of their own accord invented added obligations, notably monasticism, which God had never imposed on them; much worse, they (or many of them) had misinterpreted Jesus and Mary, making them objects of worship alongside God. The Jews had likewise brought upon themselves added burdens because of their chronic hard-heartedness, and those of Muḥammad's own time had furthermore suppressed scriptural evidence that would have supported Muḥammad's mission, out of jealousy that any but themselves should be divinely favoured. The Muslims were not to have fellowship with such secret enemies. Yet nothing in the Qur'ân required the total rejection of their books.

Among the early Piety-minded, however, these indications were developed into a comprehensive condemnation of the two peoples of the Bible generally, not merely their representatives in Muḥammad's Arabia. First, they had corrupted their own scriptures by suppressing some passages and distorting or interpolating others. Second, their learnèd men had nonetheless been able to know (from these same holy books) that Muḥammad was to come, and had recognized the signs of his coming, yet out of jealousy the Christians and Jews had refused to admit his prophethood. Consequently the peoples of the Bible, having wilfully rejected Muḥammad and the Qur'ân at that time, and having generation after generation persisted in their contumacy, were not merely ignorant but guilty in their refusal of Islam; if they were tolerated, it was not as fellow-worshippers who happened to be partly mistaken, but simply by command of God in His unfathomable mercy. Correspondingly, their books, far from being mines of information about the earlier prophets whom every Muslim was pledged to acknowledge, were to be shunned as worse than merely human books, for such true revelations as might be among them were mixed with impious falsehoods inspired by the Devil himself. Anything of value in their books would have been brought to Muslims by early converts, whose reports about Torah and Gospel, transmitted as ḥadîth, were alone to be trusted.

Zealous Shari'ah-minded Msulims elaborated gladly their code of symbolic restrictions on the dhimmî non-Muslims—they must wear certain humiliating garments and signs, they must not build new houses of worship, and so on—most of which was retroactively ascribed to 'Umar; later caliphs such as al-Mutawakkil made some effort at imposing it in practice. As the dhimmî communities dwindled, popular Muslim sentiment more and more readily insisted on stigmatizing the minorities. But one of the most fateful restrictions was that on the Muslims themselves: unlike the Christians, who could despise the Jews yet read the Hebrew Bible, the Muslims, more consistently communalistic, were debarred from the Bible altogether. In High Caliphal times, a certain number of intellectual Muslims, finding themselves in close contact with Christian colleagues, were able to develop a serious critique of Christian beliefs, reading parts of the New Testament in translation. But such efforts remained marginal and had little reflection in the overall development of Islam.

Accordingly, even so explicitly honoured a body of classics as the Bible—the corpus embodying the Hebrew prophetic tradition as well as its Christian development—was known to the Muslims chiefly in the form of corrupt and often legendary fragments. It exercised its influence more through the unconscious continuity of social patterns than through even an indirect literary tradition—let alone a direct confrontation of each new generation with the records of the original inspiration.

In fields where religion was less explicitly at stake, the discontinuity could be less drastic. But even the most important of those traditions never gained a universal standing. In the culture of the adîb, apart from Islam itself, four chief traditions played a conscious role. The adîb was fully conscious of a certain Arabism, associated with the nobility of the Muḍarî Arabic language and of the pure camel nomads, its titular carriers. With this was also associated, in theory, the old high culture of the Yemen; but in practice, nothing of that survived save by way of peripheral legends. The adîb was also aware of an Iranianism, associated with the glory of the Sâsânian court and of the wise emperor Nûshîrvân, in whose time Muḥammad was born. This awareness had a major impact. He rejected explicitly the cited Semitic tradition carried in the various Aramaic tongues and associated with underlings even in Sâsânian days—yet many of the Arabic lettered patterns, religious and otherwise, were tacitly taken over from Aramaic. Finally, he was ambivalent to the Hellenic tradition, associated with the sages of antiquity but also (since Christian days) with paganism.

Greek science and philosophy maintained (in translation) such universality, at least, as they had previously achieved between Nile and Oxus; the Muslim

Faylasûfs never entirely replaced the older writers as points of departure for the continuing tradition and its dialogue. But that tradition was not the overall Hellenic one and even in its truncated form it was less at home in Islam as a religious community than it had been even in some of the previous communities; it could never form the primary intellectual impulse in Islamicate culture.

The heart of the pre-Islamic heritage of Muslim Arab culture lay, in many respects, in the Semitic Aramaic traditions of the Fertile Crescent. But this was true especially of the several aspects of the religious tradition, since Islam was a development of the Abrahamic prophetic tradition; and it was just in the sphere of religion that direct reference to the older heritages was suppressed. The secular literature of the Aramaic languages, except so far as it embodied the tradition of Philosophia, may have been relatively unimportant as compared with the communally religious literature. It served as a model—how extensively, it is hard to judge on the basis of the surviving Aramaic and Syriac literature, largely religious; but it was despised by the privileged circles as the heritage of peasants. (Yet persistent tradition made it the language of Adam and the earlier prophets.)

Pahlavî, however, had been becoming a rich cultural language in all dimensions at the hands of the Sâsânian ruling classes. The communally religious books of the Mazdeans were despised and shunned even more readily than those of Christians and Jews (though even this condemnation was not made inevitable by the Qur'ân); they were felt to be obviously false and he who even looked at them was suspected of betraying Islam. But the works of history and of belles-lettres, as well as of natural science, could not be so readily condemned. Moreover, it was this secular Pahlavî tradition that had embodied the cultural support and legitimation for the absolutism of the past. In the name of the caliphal state itself, some Muslims had appealed to its cultural standards as socially indispensable as well as humanly insurpassable. Here the Muslim exclusivity worked more subtly.

A conscious movement, which did arise, to depreciate outright the Arabian elements in Muslim culture, had only limited success (at least at the capital); in fact, in the Fertile Crescent, as well as in the formerly non-Arabic southern fringes of Arabia and even in Egypt, large areas were on their way to adopting versions of Arabic as the popular family language; and with the Arabic language came a pride in the Arabian heritage coupled with scorn for those (generally more rural and backward) elements that retained the Aramaic tongue and were scornfully called 'Nabaṭaeans'. But elsewhere, the ordinary family language remained non-Arabic and the ordinary people, on becoming Muslims, could not closely identify themselves with the Arabs as such. There, cultural theory was less relevant, positively or negatively, than the reality of everyday life.

In the Iranian highlands, in particular, Iranian tongues were the rule and in the greater part of the plateau the various dialects were closely enough related to justify a single common Persian literary language accessible to all. This had been Pahlavî. But literary Pahlavî had been used especially by priests and clerks of the bureaucracy, the most important literate elements in the more agrarian, Iranian parts of the Sâsânian empire; and it had been written in an uncommonly clumsy manner, which laymen such as merchants must have found exasperating. Moreover, the expectation had grown up that each religious community, along with its own literary language, would use its own special script, hallowed as it was by association with the community's sacred writings. When Persian-speaking Muslims who had been trained not in Pahlavî but in Arabic turned to using the Arabic script rather than the Pahlavî for their own Persian, the idea rapidly caught on as both pious and convenient. By the end of the High Caliphate, when Persian was written by Muslims it was being written not as Pahlavî but in a new form, expressed in Arabic characters and, incidentally, reflecting such changes in pronunciation and grammar (not very extensive) as had supervened in the spoken tongue since the standardization of literary Pahlavî. Especially in Khurâsân, under a dynasty of governors of Persian origin (the Sâmânids), this new Persian was being erected into a literary tongue, especially for poetry.

But the result was that even among Persians the old Pahlavî came to require special training. Pahlavî literature continued to be read by some Persian Muslims throughout the High Caliphal period, but the difficulty of learning it raised complaints. And while a certain amount of Pahlavî was translated into not only Arabic but, later, the new Persian, yet the new Persian had its own traditions tinged with a Muslim atmosphere, into which the Pahlavî materials scarcely fitted without a certain amount of adaptation. Thus the Muslim Persians cut themselves off linguistically from the Pahlavî past and adopted literary standards more closely bound to those of Muslim Arabic than to those of pre-Muslim Persian.

The Pahlavî tradition, in contrast to the Greek, did inspire a large part of the Islamicate lettered traditions in fields which received general recognition, most specifically in courtly and literary adab; thus it substantially extended the range of populations under its influence. But it did so not in its own form but in new guises. No more than the Greek did the Pahlavî, in original or in translation, establish a strong enough position so that it would be assumed that a learnèd man would be acquainted with its classics; and unlike Greek, Pahlavî, even among the Persians (apart from a few adaptive translations), did not long survive the High Caliphate, except for religious purposes among the Mazdeans themselves.

The consequence of all this was that, in contrast to Europe, China, and even India (where such works as the Vedas and Upanishads do breathe a very different spirit from that of Shaivism and Vaishnavism), in Islamdom there came to be little direct contact with the great human works of the pre-confessional periods in the Axial Age. The humanistic insight available in a work such as the story of David in the Hebrew Books of Kings was excluded in favour of classics all of which presupposed the Muslim allegiance. Apart from the almost esoteric tradition of the Faylasûfs, there was no heritage of classics transcending that of the community and its revealed origin. (The pre-Islamic Arabian poetry, which was retained, could not seriously fulfill such a role any more than the Niebelungenlied could have done so for a Germanic culture which rejected Latin.) The communal tendency of populism in the region had come to full flower. This characteristic of the Islamicate civilization, unique in the Oikoumene, perhaps made for a relative spiritual impoverishment of it as compared with the major civilizations contemporary with it. But it could also make for a uniquely self-sufficient strength and cultural integrity—a strength which, in subsequent centuries, was to play its part in allowing Islamdom to expand all over the hemisphere without great danger either of losing local cultural roots or of destroying the solidarity among all members of a far-flung community.[1]

The cultivation of an adîb

Meanwhile, the cultural resources of Islamdom were brought together and focused in the adab culture of the court. The adîb, the possessor of adab, was the man of a varied and brilliant set of attainments which were the adornment of his society. With public order assured by a strong monarchy, the private good of the privileged who benefited thereby was a life of good taste.

If one can distinguish two poles between which range our criteria for judging the quality of human life, a pole at which moral relationships among people take precedence over all else, and a pole at which what matters is the excellence of learning and art and the fine use and appreciation of human resources, in however few out of a given population, then the Sharî'ah-minded stood at the moralistic pole and the adîbs very nearly at the other. For them the justification of a man's life was at least in part the degree to which it was cultivated and refined and could with beauty make use of wealth and leisure. A Muslim rarely said as much explicitly, but such a gentlemanly ideal had been implicit in Aristotle's ethics, and it was Aristotle's ethics, out of all the corpus of Falsafah, that gained the greatest vogue—in appropriate Arabic adaptations—among the adîbs. While the 'ulamâ'

[1] On the process of transition of the high culture from earlier languages into Arabic we have no adequate studies, largely for want of adequate knowledge of the state of the several traditions in Sâsânian times. We do have a number of studies on the transition from Greek (not limited to natural science and metaphysics), notably those by Becker, von Grunebaum, and Kraemer already noted in footnote 8 to the General Prologue. Rudi Paret has also written on this and is always worth consulting: *Der Islam und das griechische Bildungsgut* (Tübingen, 1950). (I might add that the most accessible study in English, De Lacy O'Leary, *How Greek Science Passed to the Arabs* [London, 1949], like others of O'Leary's works, is marred by errors of fact and of judgment, and does not add to the more standard authors on Arabic science.)

scholars looked to the moralistic and populistic strains in the Irano-Semitic background and refonted them, the adîbs looked to just the opposite sorts of strains in that background and produced a new culture in their spirit.

But the adab of caliphal times seems to have diverged from that of Sâsânian times not only in language but in spirit. It was evidently—to judge largely by the older fiction that has been preserved—less rooted in local legends than the Sâsânian, more city-based, more cosmopolitan. The idealists among the kâtibs, following older models, tried to link adab culture to birth and breeding, and taught each other to despise the upstart merchant. But this was to fly in the face of the realities of social mobility. Adab could no longer presuppose the homogeneity of the Sâsânian gentry. Nor did it produce a new homogeneity similarly rooted in the land and devoted to the caliphal power.

Adab was necessarily, to a certain extent, the way of a particular class, that of the administrators and officials who depended ultimately on the caliphal authority. The special professions of the adîb were those of secretary and clerk, of bureaucratic manager. But adab was cultivated eagerly by well-to-do merchants and by anyone who wished to be up with the times. Adab cultivation entailed, in principle, a comprehensive synthesis of all high culture. It made a certain place for the Sharî'ah-minded learning and its requirements, and gave a certain honour to the 'ulamâ'; in turn, some of the 'ulamâ' made a point of cultivating the social graces and even appeared at court. Some touch of knowledge of Falsafah was an asset to an adîb. But adab had its own unmistakable spirit.

A central position in adab was held by Arabic literature: especially the poetry and the rhymed prose, which held a position of honour not accorded to any other arts. The spoken word well put moved cultivated men as nothing else in life was permitted to, and its refinements were explored by a galaxy of remarkable verbalists. Above all, then, the adîb should have a skilled command of the standard Muḍarî Arabic language. Good speaking, as well as good writing, was the supreme mark of good breeding and of polished and enjoyable intercourse among men. This meant, in the first place, knowledge of the grammatical intricacies of Muḍarî Arabic—a desideratum not only for non-Arabs but for Arabs themselves, whose vernacular was already shifting away from the Arabic of the Qur'ân; second, command of its rich resources of vocabulary. For every sort of composition, and preferably also for conversation, a linguistic brilliance, in which the right thought was put in the cleverest possible way, was admired; it decorated the scene as much as did rich robes or flowered gardens. It is for this reason that the discipline of grammar, early developed among the Piety-minded in Kûfah and especially Baṣrah, took on such a great social importance as part of the equipment of a man of the world.

But in addition to a sheer command of language, the adîb should know a bit about everything of interest to the curious. The ideal state letter, however prosaic its content, should be an elegant production. Gradually standards became ever more fully developed, as the styles of certain individuals won admiration and became models to be imitated and then surpassed. Finally, it was taken for granted that every serious missive would be adorned with rhyming prose and resonant periods. Any composition of importance should be varied with poetic quotations and illustrated with references to obscure points of learning. Piety and sobriety of living were highly valued by most adîbs; yet an elegant style of life (rather in the sense used in 'styling' American automobiles) and especially an elegant style of verbal production were given great honour. Any man who could show himself capable of a rounded and high-level adab was assured of good opportunities in the court society.

What an adîb should know: history and geography

Ideally, all kinds of studies should nourish a rounded adab culture. But distinctions were made. Literary studies in Arabic and studies associated with the Sharî'ah law (including history) were called 'traditional', 'transmitted', studies, for they depended on historical information about events and conditions which would not recur (even Arabic grammar, for instance, was based on the speech of the Arabs of Muḥammad's time and no other); sometimes they were called 'Arabic' studies because of the special role knowledge of Arabic played in them all. They were contrasted to 'rational' or 'non-Arabic' studies, such as natural science, which could (in principle) be developed from scratch on the basis of experience available at any time; and which were in fact known to have been cultivated also in the earlier languages of culture. It was the 'Arabic' studies that naturally had the highest prestige among the adîbs, as much for literary as for religious reasons.

The pious adîb, then, should know as much as possible of the Shar'î fiqh as it was then being worked out. Knowledge of fiqh was practical both for a private individual and for a state clerk, for it was the officially recognized basis of social order; knowledge of it also implied piety. At the same time, he should have a wide acquaintance with history (and geography); and he should know the famous tales and sayings to which allusions might be made. Naturally, he should be familiar especially with courtly precedents. Finally, he should command something of the natural sciences. But always he should have a good knowledge of poetry. This should include both knowledge of the rules of poetic propriety that were being built up by the grammarians, and the memorizing of as many lines of verse as possible, to be produced on appropriate occasion. Anthologies, encyclopedic surveys of learning, and descriptive catalogues of available books helped the adîb keep abreast of it all.

The learning of the adîb, whatever the field, was never clearly distinguished from his concern with belles-lettres. When the adîb studied 'biology', for instance, he was not so much interested in learning the structure of organisms as in finding out all the strange things that could be said of them. A discourse on animals commonly reads more like Ripley's *Believe It or Not* than like a text in zoölogy. The aesthetic propriety of various ways of making literary references to the animals discussed was a major concern. All knowledge was a means of adorning and enriching literature.

Historical writing—from which could be drawn examples piquant or cogent to enliven every point—was popular in a range of forms which illustrate the several strands that entered the adîb's thinking. Adîbs read history in the several genres used by the 'ulamâ'. The most important of these was the annalistic chronicle—a form carried forward from Syriac models, which might be modified (as by Ṭabarî) with the addition of the isnâd documentation and an Islamic orientation. Perhaps less important for adîbs were forms serving special Shar'î needs: the biographical collections which ranged prominent Muslims according to the generations elapsing since that of Muḥammad's associates, or the histories of dogma which recorded formulations of doctrinal position. But other sorts of history, wherein the literary effect or the courtly orientation were more prominent, were more closely associated with adab. For instance, the stories of the battle days of the Arabs: commonly joined with bits of poetry referring to the event, they had been preserved in an oral tradition and (written down) entered into the mental world of the adîb as much in connection with poetry as with history proper. To the extent that this old Arabian history had any continuity, it was not, of course, in terms of the chronology of the community of Muḥammad, like the Sharî'ah-minded history, but in terms of tribal genealogies.

This anecdotal history, stemming from the old Arabian background, was of relatively minor importance. In an urban setting it was the history of kings that loomed most impressively. Greek history (geographically marginal to the area) seems to have been very little known except as it came deformed through late Christian sources. The Hebrew Biblical historical tradition remote in time, likewise was known chiefly by way of debased oral reports from such people as converted Jews. Much more imposing was the Sâsânian history, which was in large part transferred into the new court language, Arabic. It centred neither on the development of the community nor on tribal raids and battles, but rather on the reigns of hero-kings. These were presented as enormous figures embodying in themselves the whole social order, in accordance with the old Iranian conception of absolute monarchy. A good monarch produced a blessed age; a weak or evil monarch meant catastrophe. Along with other elements of Sâsânian prose, this historical tradition entered not only Arabic learning and literature but, through the Muslim Persian language, all later Islamicate literatures.

Sâsânian historical attitudes could pervade historical materials from other sources. The Sâsânian tradition of Iran and the Biblical tradition of the

Fertile Crescent were uneasily co-ordinated to form the main body of pre-Islamic history. The first Iranian man was identified with Adam, who could take on kingly traits in consequence; and Solomon (Sulaymân) became an emperor as great as those of the legendary Iran. But the Sâsânian viewpoint was only one among several elements in historical writing.

Out of these backgrounds developed a variety of Islamicate historical approaches suitable to the special needs of the adîb. Even in historical material in which a courtly approach predominated, the isnâd documentation favoured by the 'ulamâ' might appear. Several ways of studying history were represented in the careful work of al-Balâdhurî (d. *c.* 892), who studied Muslim history from a more secular viewpoint than his younger contemporary, Ṭabarî. He wrote a massive history of the Arab conquests, arranged as a series of monographs on each area conquered, and including a number of documents verbatim or abridged. In connection with the conquest, he brought in a good deal of local administrative information—especially appropriate, since the local tax and administrative status was often supposed to depend in part on capitulation terms made at the conquest. He also made a comprehensive study of the chief Muslim families—arranging it in genealogical form (like some others who specialized in genealogy), but giving the sort of extensive biographical information that others were arranging by generations from Muḥammad—and also including much general information, not neglecting central administrative detail, when he came to deal with individuals who served as caliphs. This arrangement by families was especially appropriate to those who set store on ancestry and looked to family tradition as a major spur to loyalty and high standards in the descendants.

'Alî al-Mas'ûdî (d. 956) represents more obviously the desire for bits of curious information from all over and combines with his historical tidbits, organized by reigns and chronologically, surveys of geography, astronomy, and all the rest of the world of unlimited remarkable facts on which the adîb could draw to ornament his conversation and his state letters. He represented not only literary spice, however; his works embodied a philosophical view of mankind which allowed him to transcend communal lines in his curiosity and in his appreciation, in both time and space.

Geography was frequently treated as an independent discipline. It was useful for administrative (and commercial) purposes. It was even important for the study of ḥadîth transmitters, whose varied and distant birthplaces had to be known. Above all, from a literary viewpoint, it could offer a treasure-trove of exotic curiosities.

The subject could be studied from two viewpoints. Following the old Greek and Sanskrit traditions, the globe was marked off in degrees of latitude and longitude (the latter started sometimes from the supposed Western Isles in the Atlantic, sometimes from Ujjain, site of a major observatory in central India). Seven 'climes' were charted according to latitude (and hence, in principle, climate) between the equator and the north pole—answering to our three 'zones'. The exact position of various cities was determined, as nearly as possible, astronomically. This school of geography (following the Greeks and still afflicted with their incapacity to measure longitude well, before the day of good watches) exaggerated the length of the Mediterranean and made it the equivalent of the Indian Ocean, which was closed in with an African coastline that kept on east, instead of turning south, from the Horn of Somalia (despite the occasional protests of seamen, which scholars barely acknowledged). Even so the geographers added greatly in detail to what the Greeks had been able to accomplish.

Despite failures of calculation, educated Muslims had a reasonably clear idea of the substantive dimensions of the Afro-Eurasian historical complex. This was expressed in the second viewpoint from which geography could be studied, one less congenial to the mathematical bent of the Faylasûfs but more practical for literary purposes and perhaps more realistic. Following the lead of a man of Balkh who wrote on geography some years earlier (evidently largely from literary sources), al-Istakhrî (d. 951) of Fârs put together a comprehensive description of the world (especially of the Muslim lands) based largely on his own extensive travels, as well as on studies of individual lands that were also being made. Cities were usefully located in terms of travel distances from town to town; and the lore of exotic things a tourist might expect to see—and much that he would only hear tell of, at best—added colour. His work was widely imitated and supplemented. Maps were crude, and not standardized by printing. The sensible custom grew of schematizing drastically the overall maps: e.g., the Mediterranean might be shown as an ellipse, or even a circle.

Following an old Iranian tradition, with modifications, these geographers divided the inhabited world (i.e., the Afro-Eurasian landmass) into a number of great realms, conventionally seven (answering to the 'continents'—three, in the Old World—still used as arbitrary units in Western geography.) To each of these realms they assigned distinctive traits. In the centre, to be sure, were the realm of the Arabs and that of the Persians, thought of as the most active of peoples and the earliest to embrace Islam. These were flanked by the realms of two great civilizations, those of the Europeans (Rûm, i.e., Romans, Byzantines) and of the Indians, both noted as ancient homes of philosophy. (The 'Franks' of western Europe were most commonly not separated off sharply from the Byzantines, whose cultural lead they long followed, just as no distinction was made within the vast Indic realm.) Also generally included in the varying lists of seven realms—or peoples—were the Turks of central Eurasia and the Negroes of sub-Saharan Africa, and finally the Chinese, who were known for their technical skills as artificers and artists. The Muslims exaggerated their own relative military might, learning, and general place among mankind, to be sure, but in the following centuries the reality was to approximate steadily more closely to their sense of importance. In any case, they possessed a more realistic image of the world than did any other civilized tradition.[2]

Shi'r poetry as the consummate skill

If literature was the crowning art for the Arabs, within literature it was poetry, or *shi'r*. This was a major legacy of the old-Arabian cultural tradition, which had imprinted its norms on the Muḍarî Arabic as literary vehicle. Whatever the position of Pahlavî verse may have been in Sâsânian culture, the central place of Arabic poetry in Islamicate culture helped to confirm the breach between the two.

Poetry was chanted or sung—to conventional tunes—in public; not (in principle) read in the study. We must keep this in mind when evaluating its impact. It was not a personal message from writer to reader, couching in bursting words what a direct prose statement would have been insufficient to express. It was a graceful and beautiful expression of sentiments that could be common to a gathered audience expecting an evening of tasteful entertainment. Hence the form must be exactly held to, so that the attention might be drawn to the detail of presentation without being distracted by an unfamiliar overall approach. And likewise the substance must be familiar enough to allow each listener to concentrate on noting how well the thought had been put, without being distracted by considering overmuch the implications of the thought itself. This was true even of didactic poetry, in which wise advice was given: the object was not to present a new idea, but an old and tried idea in a striking and memorable way.

Poetry is, in effect, intensive verbal composition within formal limits. We assign the term 'poetry' to whatever type of composition, within a given language-tradition, calls for the greatest intensity and formality. Such intensive composition is then appropriate for symbolically evocative statements such as we call 'poetic' in a looser sense. But this is partly because the listener's expectations have been aroused by the very form. Hence some continuity of form is a part of the communication itself: it is imposed not by unthinking custom but by the ways of human perceptivity. In modern English we have become accustomed to a considerable relaxation of the formal requirements of rhyme, of meter, and of appropriate subject matter. But some subtle requirements do stand at least as to rhythm and subject matter. In Arabic (as generally before modern times) the standards were more rigorous in most respects. In classical Arabic, what answered to our word 'poetry' was certainly *shi'r*; the formal limits of shi'r included not only rhyme and a fixed number of rhythmic patterns, but also certain set types of subject matter and of verbal usage.

[2] The Islamicate notions of geography, inadequate as they were, were less misleading than the Occidental notions of the time, which still plague modern scholarship. See the section on usage in world-historical studies in the Introduction.

Society accepted a number of conventional types of rhythmic pattern, meters, which every cultivated man and woman knew the flow of. Some of these were fairly rudimentary, others reasonably complex, like an interesting tune. (The meter was based on variation in length of syllables, as in Latin, rather than on stress, as in English.) The poet was expected to fit words into one of these meters with sufficient closeness to allow the basic pattern to emerge. The meter was not necessarily readily evident from only one or two lines of verse. (Among later Arabs, at any rate, the ordinary person found it a help to know which meter was being adopted, so as more quickly to know how to read the words to bring out their flow; hence the meter was often mentioned in citing verses.) What was important was that the words sing well when felt within a given meter. A good poet might be quite daring in varying the number of syllables or the secondary rhythm elements in such a way that the feeling of the meter was maintained. (This fact adds to the difficulty many Moderns find in appreciating the Arabic poetry as compared, for instance, with the—later—Persian poetry, of a firmer rhythm.)

Lesser lights needed rules to tell them how far they could deviate from set patterns without getting lost—and in 'Abbâsî times such rules were worked out in tiresome detail. They may give an impression of artificiality to what was in origin a realm of liberty. Certain poets were credited with inventing whole new meters, but this was not normally expected; if one was to introduce a new meter, the audience must be, as it were, specially trained to hear the poet's new work, a task disproportionate to any likely benefits. For the most part, poets stuck to a very few familiar meters even among those which were recognized.

Poetry, shi'r, was the one great art adopted from pre-Islamic Arabia (where it was almost the only major fine art). In pre-Islamic Arabia the genres for which shi'r was used were relatively few—chiefly the poem of praise or of boasting, exalting one's own tribe or oneself; the insult-poem, recited against an opposing tribe; or the lament for the dead, commonly produced by women. These genres were kept consciously separate: each genre was carried as a distinct tradition, having had its own moments of invention and improvement which any subsequent poet might take advantage of, once the public had learned to receive them. Though what genres are ultimately possible is limited only by the limits of human sensibility and of the media available, the Arabs, like other pre-Moderns, were so aware that a given public could assimilate only a restricted range of forms that they even tried to name the inventors of some genres, and even a very creative man was not ashamed to work in one of the forms so established.

The most respected genre in ancient Bedouin poetry was the qaṣîdah ode, a long poem with a fixed series of subjects. It began with regrets over a past love affair and the traces of the beloved's encampment in the desert; continued with a ride through trackless wastes, in which typically the things of the desert, as well as the poet's alleged mount, were described by similes; then, only, the main burden would emerge, often sheer self-praise. The qaṣîdah might end with praise of some patron from whom the poet expected a reward for his efforts. But many poetic pieces were not qaṣîdahs but less formally developed 'fragments', which went more directly to the point. In any case, a limited range of subject matter had called for a limited range of emotions and a limited vocabulary. Within these limits the effect was perhaps as remarkable as any combination of the given elements could produce. When a fine pattern was found it was held to.

The poetry had been transmitted orally by reciters (often themselves poets), who chanted it publicly as it came from a poet's lips and passed it from generation to generation. In 'Abbâsî times what had survived of the work of the great poets was set in writing by various reciters or even philologians and became something of a poetic canon; it was then that it was appreciated not as living commentary on current events or on the virtues and failings of the tribes, but as a model literature to be pondered for its subtlety and its richness as a body.

Critics acknowledged the pagan Imru'-al-qays as the greatest of Arab poets. In a ḥadîth report, Muḥammad himself was made to confirm this judgment—Imru'-al-qays was the greatest of the poets and their leader to Hell. A dissolute and venturesome grandson of the head of a great central Arabian tribal agglomeration controlled by the tribe Kindah at the end of the fifth century, the story of his life stirred the imagination: his father had inherited an important tribal chieftainship. after the Kindah imperium had broken up, and had been murdered; and Imru'-al-qays turned from his scandals with the maidens of Arabia to exact on a grand scale the required vengeance for his father. Tradition made him a mighty but reckless and unfortunate fighter, who was finally destroyed by the mistrusting Roman emperor himself, of whom he had asked aid—he was sent a cloak of honour, which proved venomously poisoned. His language was pure enough for a grammarian, but, perhaps at least as important, his life was romantic enough to carry a bureau-clerk's dreams far beyond the prosaic streets of Baghdad.

His *dîwân* (collected verse) was gathered and, so far as possible, verified by the court grammarian al-Asma'î (d. 831). Imru'-al-qays was (incorrectly) regarded as having invented the erotic prelude with which every regular qaṣîdah ode ought to begin; certainly he was especially admired for his erotic passages—of a frank directness which was at the same time fresh and unstrained in its images. Critics praised him as the master of simile and metaphor. The images of simile, indeed, became the treasure of Arabic poetry, what above all a poet hoped to excel in. His most famous poem was a qaṣîdah ode included in a famous collection of seven Mu'allaqât, pre-Islamic masterpieces claimed by legend to have been poems which won the prize in annual contests at a fair near Mecca; but edited in 'Abbâsî times. Imru'-al-qays' poem powerfully paints us his passion and his self-will.[3]

In the varied urban society of 'Abbâsî times this pagan tradition had been maintained as an ideal of chaste and integral poetic expression; it was the standard by which more modern poetry was judged—and usually condemned. For some, it represented the specifically Arab heritage—and even persons not of Arab ancestry might like to be 'more Arab than the Arabs' by cultivating it. But probably a more subtle appeal was an undeniable romance and fascination in the verse of men seemingly unbound by the sober second thoughts of proper city folk, and in particular by the horizons of Islam, and so expressing untrammelled human feelings.

In the circles of the adîbs new poetry continued to be composed. But it was at least as important to use verses—normally part of a memorized stock and as old as possible—effectively in the midst of conversation or of prose composition. Already in the Bedouin poetry, each line of verse had tended to be a self-sufficient unit expressing a quite generalizable sentiment. Now such units were used to adorn a letter, a document, or even a treatise (and frequently to impress the reader with one's erudition). *Yâ 'îdu, mâ la-ka min shawqin wa-îrâqi, wa marri ṭayfin 'alà ahwâli ṭarrâqi*—'You hardened [man], who is like you for longing and sleeplessness, and a spectre's coming amidst the terrors of a far-wanderer', the poet addresses himself. (I simply take the first line of a famous collection made for al-Manṣûr, the *Mufaḍḍaliyyât*.) The words in Arabic are concise and direct, but archaic (by 'Abbâsî times) and of a strange turn. They were attributed to a sixth-century Bedouin outlaw, an uninhibited brigand whose usual name, Ta'abbaṭa Sharran, means 'mischief under his armpits' (referring to his sword, carried there). There is no piety in them, but a frank expression at once of human toughness and of human need and loneliness. At the right spot, in some clerk's prose, such a line could bring echoes of another world, and (if the prose were strong enough to carry it) could lend it magic.

For these varied reasons, religious, literary, and social, the qaṣîdah form itself (and the manner of poetic line derivable from it) took on an air of unassailable authority as embodying the norms of Arabic language and adab culture. In doing so, it gave rise to a varied and influential school of literary criticism, dedicated to guarding the standards thus achieved.

Criticism: the old-Arabian classical norm and the new poetry

The ascendancy of the Arabic poetic tradition thus gave further opportunity to the Sharî'ah-minded opponents of the absolutist tradition to inject some-

[3] A. J. Arberry, *The Seven Odes* (London, 1957), discusses the history of the Mu'allaqât in detail and also their various translations into English. Before him, the most respected translator was Charles Lyall; Arberry's own translation is very good, but still, like the other translators, he cannot bring himself to restrict his translation to the concise directness of the original.

thing of their viewpoint into the heart of adab culture—and, incidentally, to confirm the breach with the Sâsânian past. The ancient Arabian poetry was necessarily regarded by the grammarians as the only contemporary and therefore fully reliable source for linguistic parallels to Qur'ân and ḥadîth, on the basis of which the meaning of words and phrases used in these latter could be understood. Thus, paradoxically, the 'ulamâ' scholars gave a peculiar blessing to the study of the pre-Islamic poetry, pagan though it might be and very typical of a boastful, fictive, heedless luxury which Muḥammad himself had condemned and which many 'ulamâ' did not find particularly commendable as practiced in their own time.

To be sure, the 'Abbâsî appreciation of the earlier poetry was not much influenced by such theological considerations; it extended, but only with somewhat less approval, to the (often rather impious) Muslim poets of the Marwânî period who had continued the old tradition but could not be regarded as sure to be lexically impeccable. What mattered to the adîb was the exemplification of elegant grammar—and the echo of an olden time of liberty. But the 'ulamâ' did matter, and their implicit attitude was surely felt in matters of propriety in verse.

The debate in poetry was part of a wider debate on the cultural relevance of the old-Arabian tradition. Many in the courtly circles objected to even the limited role which the old-Arabian tradition had come to play in the culture of the empire. They resisted the tendency of the Arabic philologians (and, behind them, the 'ulamâ') to undermine the prestige of the Iranian-based adab tradition of the kâtib clerks. They pointed out that a large old-Arabian role could not be justified in the name of Islam—which had been directed against just the pagan Arabian tradition which now was so greatly honoured. A whole literature arose praising the merits of other peoples at the expense of the Arabs and their tribal pride; the Arabian tradition was condemned (in Arabic) as uncivilized and lacking in good taste.

This literary movement, called the 'Shu'ûbiyyah', the championing of the (non-Arab) peoples, had a vogue so long as Arab pride still played a role in the caliphal state. The conscientious researches of philologians like Abû-'Ubaydah (of Persian Jewish origin—d. *c.* 825), who did more than anyone else to standardize the tradition about old-Arabian affairs, were made use of to show how petty and uncouth the tribal Arabs had often been. But such an attitude was hotly attacked by those who mistrusted the aristocratic narrowness of the adab of the clerkly tradition. In particular, Ibn-Qutaybah of Marv in Khurâsân (d. 889), living mostly at Baghdad, showed that a prejudice against things Arabian was unjustifiable. Profoundly ḥadîth-minded in his religious views, in adab he integrated old-Arabian and Iranian-derived materials into a single adab corpus. He studied all the topics of adab, including ḥadîth (from a philological viewpoint). Of most general literary interest was a collection of apt selections from ḥadîth and verse and historical report arranged to illustrate various sorts of topic—many later literary guides for the adîb were based on it as a model. Soon the chief arbiters[4] of literary taste decided that Arabian poetry had been the supreme poetry; that Arabian taste, if not to be imitated, was at least to be respected; and even that Arab descent was an honour, as indicating kinship with the Prophet. In effect, it was recognized that society could not be restored to its cultural patterns as of any given Sâsânian century; that the special culture of the Marwânî-age Arabs had become an element in the heritage of all the Muslims.

Meanwhile in the field of poetry, already by the time of al-Rashîd, the old-Arabian norm was being challenged at its heart. At the hands of such as Abû-Nuwâs, the significant poetry composed and enjoyed (except, doubtless, in the desert itself still!) was more luxuriant than the older norm. Though a restricted number of forms were still used—normally every poem must be rhymed, with a single rhyme being repeated throughout, for instance—poems might deal with every kind of sentiment so long as it did not become too biographical but remained generalized. Thus there might be poems of hunting or of love or of grief or of philosophic resignation or of shrewd wisdom or of drinking. The luxuriance was limited. The various genres tended to remain distinct, each within a well-defined tradition; and in any case, each sentiment must be perfectly generalizable. If a poet sang of old age, he could refer to white hairs and the scorn of young damsels, he could say that friends were dead or forgetful; but he could not introduce special episodes that might have happened to him but could not be considered typical of old age. This would be to forget the audience and abandon the pure impersonality of art in favour of merely private anecdote. Yet, as compared with desert poetry, the new city poetry expressed an enormous variety of interests and sentiments, and allowed considerable freedom of form and imagery.[5]

Since the time of Imru'-al-qays, the tradition that he had helped render great had thus developed, transplanted to a new habitat, very diversely. But eventually the earlier norms of the tradition, always necessarily still taken note of, were reinforced by the arbiters of taste in adab as the only norms worthy an erudite adîb. Whether a new turn in a tradition can be fully legitimized—in this case, by the literary critics, as a basis for courtly

[4] H. A. R. Gibb, 'The Social Significance of the Shu'ûbîya', reprinted as chapter four in his *Studies on the Civilization of Islam*, ed. Stanford Shaw and Wm. Polk (Boston, 1962), clarifies the sequence of the establishment of the prestige of Arabic traditions among the clerks, and many other points by the way. Gérard Lecomte, 'Le problème d'Abû 'Ubayd', *Arabica*, 12 (1965), 140–74, shows how grammatical and adab discussions, in the time of Ibn-Qutaybah, got tied in with theology. (Some of his conclusions are subject to reserve because of his assumption that there was an 'orthodoxy' at the time; he even suggests someone might have been a 'crypto'-Mu'tazilî in an age when Mu'tazilîs dominated the field of grammar as well as politics.)

[5] Gustave von Grunebaum, 'Growth and Structure of Arabic Poetry AD 500–1000', in *The Arab Heritage*, ed. A. Faris (Princeton University Press, 1944), brings out excellently the differences that supervened generation by generation (though it concentrates on the pre-Islamic).

prestige—depends not so much on how close it remains to the past (every new step in a tradition jars a bit) as on its relevance to the ultimate expectations of its public. The 'new' poetry was indeed well loved, but the only basis in that milieu for full legitimation of poetry was as much grammatical and historical continuity as transient current delight. Many 'Abbâsî critics insisted that only the type of language and the range of themes consecrated by Imru'-al-qays and his peers could be legitimate in genuine shi'r; the test of skill was to excel within such limits. They condemned the 'new' poets, like Abû-Nuwâs, who had presumed to introduce not only new motifs but vocabulary alien to the old Bedouin purity which the critics prized; in effect, they had refused to attempt the old game and had yet proposed to express themselves in poetic form, calling their results 'shi'r'.

Among the most respected critics was Ibn-Qutaybah, who strongly appreciated poetic values as part of adab culture generally. His work on lexicography, rules of prosody, and grammar strengthened the more conservative critics. He himself defended Ḥadîthî standards in literature, and criticized adversely so free a writer as al-Jâḥiẓ (whom we shall meet shortly), but he also made a point of recognizing that the newer poetry might sometimes be just as good as that by ancient pagans.

After Ibn-Qutaybah, other critics worked out more ample analyses of the use of simile and the like, which allowed greater room for the 'new' poets. The result of this contest of critics was, for a time, an active production of literary criticism alongside the poetry itself. One of the most adventurous of the critics was himself a poet. Ibn-al-Mu'tazz (d. 908), the son of the caliph, wrote up the saga of a later caliph's victories in an epic poem such as was found in the Persian tradition but not elsewhere in Arabic. He developed an elaborate critique of the various sorts of tropes and literary turns, favouring inventiveness. Another critic even made use of the Greek tradition of literary criticism.

After the death of Ibn-Qutaybah, however, a certain systematizing of critical standards set in, especially among his disciples, the 'school of Baghdad'. It was at this time that in fiqh men began to speak not of the Iraqis and the Ḥijâzîs, but of the Ḥanafîs and the Mâlikîs and the Shâfi'îs; and every earlier legist was somehow placed in reference to one or another recognized school. It was also at this time that retrospectively the grammatical schools of Kûfah and of Baṣrah were distinguished and their positions contrasted. Literary lines likewise began to be drawn.

Finally the doctrine of the pre-eminence of the older classics prevailed. So far as concerned poetry in the standard Muḍarî Arabic, which was, after all, not spoken, puristic literary standards were perhaps inevitable: an artificial medium called for artificial norms. That critics should impose some limits was necessary, given the definition of shi'r poetry in terms of imposed limitations. With the divorce between the spoken language of passion and the formal language of composition, they had a good opportunity to exalt a congenially narrow interpretation of those limits. Among adîbs who so often put poetry to purposes of decoration or even display, the critics' word was law. Generations of poets afterwards strove to reproduce the desert qaṣîdah ode in their more serious work so as to win the critics' acclaim.

Some poets were able to respond with considerable skill to the critics' demands. Abû-Tammâm (d. *c.* 845) both collected and edited the older poetry and also produced imitations himself of great merit. But work such as his, however admirable, could not be duplicated indefinitely. In any case, it could appear insipid. A living tradition could not simply mark time; it had to explore whatever openings there might be for working through all possible variations on its themes, even the grotesque. Hence in the course of subsequent generations, taste came to favour an ever more elaborate style both in verse and in prose. Within the forms which had been accepted, the only recourse for novelty (which was always demanded) was in the direction of more far-fetched similes, more obscure references to educated erudition, more subtle connections of fancy.

The peak of such a tendency was reached in the proud poet al-Mutanabbi', 'the would-be prophet' (915–965—nicknamed so for a youthful episode of religious propagandizing, in which his enemies said he claimed to be a prophet among the Bedouin), who travelled whenever he did not meet, where he was, with sufficient honour for his taste. He himself consciously exemplified, it is said, something of the independent spirit of the ancient poets. Though he lived by writing panegyrics, he long preferred, to Baghdad, the semi-Bedouin court of the Ḥamdânid Sayf-al-dawlah at Aleppo; and on his travels he died rather than belie his valiant verses, when Bedouin attacked the caravan and he defended himself rather than escape. His verse has been ranked as the best in Arabic on the ground that his play of words showed the widest range of ingenuity, his images held the tension between fantasy and actuality at the tautest possible without falling into absurdity.

After him, indeed, his heirs, bound to push yet further on the path, were often trapped in artificial straining for effect; and sometimes they appear simply absurd. In any case, poetry in literary Arabic after the High Caliphal Period soon became undistinguished. Poets strove to meet the critics' norms, but one of the critics' demands was naturally for novelty within the proper forms. But such novelty could be had only on the basis of over-elaboration. This the critics, disciplined by the high, simple standards of the old poetry, properly rejected too. Within the received style of shi'r, good further work was almost ruled out by the effectively high standards of the 'Abbâsî critics.[6]

[6] H. A. R. Gibb's masterly *Arabic Literature, an Introduction* (first ed., London, 1926; new edition, 1963), lists in its appendix a good many translations of Arabic literary works into Western languages. Several organizations have latterly been adding to the list, notably the Unesco 'East-West' project. Among anthologies, I shall mention Reynold A. Nicholson, *Translations of Eastern Poetry and Prose* ('Eastern' here means Arabic and Persian, and the prose is mostly historical) (Cambridge University Press, 1922)—elegant and by a master, but suffers from a preoccupation with making the

Prose and saj': entertainment and edification

Arabic prose, which had begun as a direct inheritance from the Pahlavî of the Sâsânian absolutism, did not maintain this tone. Possibly it played a role comparable to what prose may have played socially at the Sâsânian court, but certainly it did relatively little to focus the ideals of the adîb on the great monarch—whereas almost all the secular literature we have from the Pahlavî tends to centre on the monarchy. The interests of the adîb were eclectic and cosmopolitan. Prose was no more royalist than poetry.

Like verse, prose also, of course, is formal and relatively intensive verbal composition. It is not simply 'conversation written down'; its appropriate forms must be cultivated. Prose too has its genres and conventions. But we use the word for less formal and less intensive compositions than the type we call 'poetry', for it answers to the need for more flexible means of expression.

As we have noticed with regard to poetry, the purpose of literature generally was not, in the Agrarian Age, to enable a tormented spirit to pour forth its soul; nor was it even to set forth every sort of information which might arouse someone's curiosity. Even in our time there are some limits imposed not only by public censors but by a general, if tacit, sense of literary relevance. Such limits were always stricter in the Agrarian Age, though they varied in detail from society to society. Some types of literary expression were cultivated in ancient Greece, for instance, and not in Islamdom; notably the tragedy, which allowed for an expression of cosmic fate in poignantly human terms, but which Christianity had no place for and which Muslims had no cause to revive. (Islamicate literature, indeed, consistently avoided the personally poignant.) Other types of literature found in Islamdom were wanting in ancient Greece. But always only a relatively small range of themes was acknowledged as appropriate for literature; in particular, the more intimately personal themes, which have modernly become so fundamental among us in novel and autobiography, tended to be excluded, for the most part, as not fit for public display.

Verbal cultivation in Abbâsî times among the adîbs had two major functions. On the one hand, it was highly refined play; making a poem or telling a tale was judged on rather the same basis as playing a good game of chess; and both were perhaps taken more seriously as the occupations of a gentleman than they are in a modern business community. The elegance

renderings sound superficially like what nineteenth-century Britishers would recognize as poetry (a very common sort of difficulty); James Kritzek, *Anthology of Islamic Literature* (New York, 1963)—in majority Arabic, with much Persian and some Turkish, including prose as well as verse, with the advantage of variety not only in substance but in translators; Herbert Howarth and Ibrahim Shukrallah, *Images from the Arab World* (London 1944)—an impressionistic set of freely rendered fragments (including some from non-Arabs who happened to use Arabic), and especially A. J. Arberry, *Arabic Poetry, a Primer for Students* (Cambridge University Press, 1965)—literal but intelligible renderings facing the Arabic text, with a helpful preface on prosody and literary figures. There are several useful anthologies in French.

of one's home appointments and the elegance of one's epistles—especially if one were a man of position—went far toward setting off one's rank, or rather one's worthiness of that rank. On the other hand, literature had the function of edifying. It should give expressly useful information, either rules for a person's behaviour or facts of an exemplary sort which he might have occasion to learn from for the future. Even sheer curiosities were presented in the guise of material which will increase one's urbanity or lend colour to one's epistles. Despite the high rank allowed to poetry, both these functions were fulfilled for the most part in prose.

The adîb should, among other things, have a good command of proverbs, preferably those originating with the Bedouin; and know the favourite tales of fiction—such as those in the *Thousand and One Nights* collection, already available in primitive form then, and the tales of the absurd Juḥà, a clownish figure through whose antics sometimes a simple wisdom can shine. (Such tales were not so highly respected as the proverbs, however.) Ibn-al-Muqaffa''s translation from the Pahlavî of a book of moralizing stories (animal fables), under al-Manṣûr, became a standard of style for subsequent writers to imitate.

This prose was simple and direct and admirably calculated to retain the attention with a clever interplay of image and of idea. The tradition of simple, clear prose found its most prominent exponent in ʻAmr al-Jâḥiẓ (*c.* 767–868), who made conscious use of variety in pace and in level of thought in order to prevent boredom, as he said, and to make his work serve both for amusement and for edification. But whereas Ibn-al-Muqaffa''s work was at least set at the lion-king's royal court, al-Jâḥiẓ' work was relatively unconcerned with princes. By combining informativeness and literary grace, however, he met the social needs of the adîb perfectly.

Al-Jâḥiẓ was ugly: his eyeballs protruded (whence his name) and Arab society held against him his Negro ancestry. He was also bitter of temper and evidently did not fit easily into official jobs. His gift for the apt phrase and the telling anecdote, and the comprehensive information he could draw on to back up any point, made him inordinately famous even in his own day. But it is said that when the caliph al-Mutawakkil sent for him to be tutor to a son (a post usually reserved for the chief scholars of the time), al-Jâḥiẓ' looks so appalled him that he sent him away immediately with a handsome gift in recompense.

Al-Jâḥiẓ delighted in anecdotes; his *Book of Misers* lists every breed of that unpleasant but variously eccentric species, illustrating his points with appropriate tales, some hung on prominent personalities and all allegedly true. The genre presumably continued in Arabic a tradition going back to the Greek *Characters* of Theophrastos. Aesthetic distance, allowing the reader to appreciate the absurdities without having merely to relive them, was maintained by selecting only those traits in the personality that expressed or pointed up the 'character' of a miser as such. Yet al-Jâḥiẓ' descriptions are endlessly and subtly individualized. He can tell of a legendarily extreme miser, a wealthy man who explains that he cannot in conscience exchange coins, on which is inscribed the shahâdah declaration of Islam, for mere unhallowed goods without even the name of God upon them (this tale is climaxed when, on the miser's death, the son who receives the inheritance examines everything and then—discovers a way to economize still further and condemns his father for a spendthrift). But more appealing is the picture of a reasonably decent man (a personal friend of the author's, deceased) who just cannot bear to spend money on hospitality for his friends—serving one's guests large amounts to eat, of course, was the heart of Agrarian Age hospitality, when wealth meant food—and is wonderfully inventive in keeping them from eating much; and even manages to justify his ways as representing the truest hospitality.

Al-Jâḥiẓ wrote innumerable tracts attacking or defending almost every party or group with memorable effect. He thus wrote on the virtues of Turks and of Negroes but also defended the superiority of Arabs over other peoples; he defended the reputation of Jews as against the then more honoured Christians; he attacked Mazdeism, maintained the superiority of merchants over officials, and compared the excellences of lads with those of maidens. Most of these little essays were designed primarily for amusement (though it is claimed he sometimes wielded his pen against someone for money); yet al-Jâḥiẓ had serious claims. His curiosity led him to make little experiments to disprove various popular superstitions, his comments on the Qur'ân were likewise on the side of reasonableness, and he could undertake a balanced and even convincing defence of an unpopular position which he did not himself hold—thus his presentation of the Shî'ah picks out not the most absurd traits (as was common with Jamâ'î-Sunnîs) but the most defensible positions that a Shî'î might maintain, and outlines them with urbanity. He was an eager Mu'tazilî and is credited with sufficient theological acumen and influence to have established a special Mu'tazilî school of thought.

His longest surviving works, however, are serious in a different way. They display unbounded philological and literary erudition, providing a storehouse of the sort of information that a kâtib clerk would need so as to write elegantly, knowledgeably, and exactly. Even the telling of anecdotes seems subordinated to illustrating technical points of good style. But it was subordinated more specifically to an *Arabic* good style, replete with old-Arabian references. Jâḥiẓ' works were probably instrumental in winning the clerks to accepting the Arabian tradition as a prime resource of adab, and this may have been his conscious intention. It is such erudite works, at any rate, that were regarded as peculiarly valuable by the adîb. In contrast to al-Jâḥiẓ' lighter prose, such works could be far from simple to read.[7]

[7] Charles Pellat, *Le milieu basrien et la formation de Djâḥiẓ* (Paris, 1953), is an invaluable study of social, religious, and intellectual life. It is marred by projecting back

More honoured than the tradition of Ibn-al-Muqaffa' and al-Jâḥiẓ eventually, however, was a different prose tradition, that of *saj'*, rhymed prose. Here the sentences were, if possible, cadenced; in any case, every two or sometimes three phrases or clauses were made to rhyme. Recherché words were preferred. The Qur'ân already presented a model of such rhyming, but the literary effect of saj' was more formal and artificial than that of the Qur'ân. But it could be pleasing, and was used for sermons and state letters alike. Ibn-Durayd (d. 933) used rhymed prose for a compilation of anecdotes and reports characterizing Bedouin ways and Bedouin events—combining successfully a fashionable subject matter with a fashionable style.

Saj' prose was marked by a degree of formalized pattern and of care for verbal expressions and their sound that might in another culture have been included in the realm of poetry. In fact, however, shi'r, poetry, was in Arabic so strictly delimited as to permissible forms that there was no tendency to intergrade between shi'r and saj'. Rather, saj' remained associated with ordinary prose and very gradually came to influence even the writing of history and of private letters. It reached its fullest flower, however, only after the fall of the caliphal state.

The line between saj' and simpler prose was not sharp, in any case. Even al-Jâḥiẓ could use rhyme in his prose, and the delight in balancing one word against another at once in sound and in sense was endemic. The structure of the Arabic language lent itself to this. As in other Semitic languages, compound words were formed from simpler ones not so much by prefixes and endings as by internal transformations in the sound. Each word could be analyzed into a root of (usually) three consonants, which could appear in a large number of set patterns, varying as to vowels and supplementary consonants; each of which tended to carry semantic implications: thus from S–L–M could be formed *muSLiM*, an active participle, and *iSLâM*, a verbal noun—and many other related words and word forms, such as plurals and pasts. These patterns were strikingly consistent in their formation: thus *muLḤiD* (a heretic) is likewise an active participle, and *iLḤâD* (the act of being a heretic) is a verbal noun. Hence both rhythm and rhyme tended to point to syntactical and even semantic meaning. Such words can echo each other down a page in far more intricate resonances than any mere correspondence of endings can produce. This is a feature of Qur'ânic style that helps make it hard to translate, and was almost inescapable throughout Arabic writing. Parallelism of sense very readily produced parallelism of sound.

The identification of sound and sense which the naïve speaker of a single language always does feel was thus reinforced in Arabic. Even the philosophically-minded were sometimes tempted to see in Arabic words

too early a later 'Sunnism' which he posits as immemorially orthodox, and even by an error too frequently found, of assuming that a 'heretic' must also be a libertine, as accused.

more than arbitrary conventional signs; and the tendency of every society to objectify its symbols—from the signs of the zodiac and the hours of the day to the letters of the alphabet—was intensified among Muslims, who often saw Arabic as embodying a natural order even when they knew other languages than Arabic as well. This had occasional consequences in theology and philosophy which we shall take note of. But its most immediate and persistent consequences were in the field of literature itself. The grammarians elaborated these traits into a system, the many exceptions to which must be accounted for (in this way they incidentally made Arabic grammar seem far more difficult than it actually was). They left the impression that the language was a closed whole: only a limited range of sound patterns could be admitted in genuine Arabic—and even the lexicon itself seemed derivable by a set of grammatical rules, once the basic sense of each three-letter root was given. The high regard in which the language of the Qur'ân was held reinforced this impression. Thus the immutability of classical Muḍarî Arabic, and with it of the ancient poetic forms sanctioned by the critics (already intimated when that classical Arabic was retained for literary purposes although it was not the actual spoken language) was further confirmed. Even without this intervention of the grammarians, the nature of Arabic gave an irresistibly distinctive flavour to Arabic writing, which encouraged the manipulation of words for the sheer delight of it (and sometimes misled writers into verbal temptations). The closed system of the grammarians then added to this tendency a rigid verbalistic classicism which eventually discouraged the literary use of Arabic by any who had an alternative.

The arts of luxury

The verbal arts were regarded most highly, but an elegant décor required full exploitation of the visual arts too. At the caliphal court and also at some governors' courts, enormous resources were available for artistic creations, notably monumental building. Yet the visual arts, like the verbal, were more cosmopolitan than monumental. In contrast to the Sâsânian tradition, which had maintained an elaborate continuity of royal iconography not only in its great buildings and in its stone carving but even in its more luxurious silverware or textiles, under Islam the caliphal office was almost never the focus of artistic symbolism.

The artist was an artisan, working to the order of wealthy patrons. In the normal manner of agrarianate-level society, both the stock of patterns and the technical skill were handed down from generation to generation within specialized families. Selection of the craftsmen was not chiefly by artistic temperament but by birth. Learning the techniques, the firing or glazing of the pottery, the weaving of the cloth, etc., and learning the particular shapes and designs to be used formed a single process in training the young.

Hence there was little occasion for drastic individual innovation from an artistic point of view; each town had its particular hereditary designs for which it was known. There might seem little artistic reason for change in style or substance.

Nevertheless, the existence of a major state like the caliphate had the effect of bringing out and developing an artistically distinctive style-complex. Like any other tradition, that of artistic standards and fashions always did change constantly, if gradually. The maintenance or renewal of high standards in each new generation depended on the taste and the wealth of the leading families, who were the patrons. The prosperous court, as well as the wealthier private persons, such as merchants, could afford to pay for technical refinement in what they had about them, refinement that cost endless time on the part of the craftsmen. At the same time, their taste, to which the craftsmen must cater, was susceptible of developing with the fashion. The fashion might call for religious or heraldic symbolisms, or might avoid them. But whatever other interests art served, in any agrarianate-level society it always filled the need for giving a rich décor to wealthy establishments, public or private. If it was not monumental in the Sâsânian tradition, it could still find its own ways to a renovation of taste.

The art of the High Caliphate was an aristocratic rather than a bourgeois art, yet it was evidently inspired by little sense of family tradition but rather by love for a rich immediate setting for whoever might be able to enjoy it. This immediate accessibility was accentuated by religious scruples. Painting in Islamdom—in direct contrast to the case of Medieval Christendom—had as little as possible to do with formal religion. Inheriting a suspicious fear of idolatry from earlier Jews and Christians between Nile and Oxus, the ʿulamâʾ scholars, Jamâʿî-Sunnî and Shîʿî, barred the representation of animate figures in any religious connection. (We will go into this iconophobia and its consequences in more detail later, when we treat of the more fully developed periods of Islamicate art.) Above all, figural art must not be used for worship—which use, among most other peoples, has been a prime source of profound artistic inspiration. Consequently, painting was a worldly luxury of courtiers and rich merchants. In an age when the deeper searchings of the human imagination expressed themselves mostly in one or another sort of religious terms, this put a severe initial limitation on the possibility of any more deeply interpretive visual art arising than what might be expected from the irreducible personal élan of the craftsman-artist, and from the social traditions in which he worked.

In the High Caliphal Period, the graphic arts were often beautifully sustained, but do not seem to have developed such major creative forms as became possible later. The wall paintings at Sâmarrâ developed yet further the Late Roman and Sâsânian tendencies toward a stylized recasting of the old Greek naturalism. The colourful dancing girls, for instance, showed traces of the old Greek handling of drapery in their garments, but their simplified faces and abstract postures were intended not to invoke an illusion of life but rather to elicit from the dance those lines which would most gracefully symbolize it statically on what was frankly a decorated wall.

A most pregnant tendency was displayed in the art of movable objects. During Parthian and especially Sâsânian times, the ceramic arts had been little patronized by the wealthy, especially east of the Iraq. Even in villages, the pottery remained undistinguished as compared with that of earlier centuries. But under the 'Abbâsids porcelains imported from China (in its expansive T'ang period) inspired a revival of ceramic art. The porcelain could not be duplicated, but ways were found to imitate its whiteness. Then in ceramics as well as in the other craft arts, metal and wood work as well as work in cloth, the resources which had been being developed by designers throughout the region—from Coptic plaster-workers and weavers in Egypt to silversmiths in Iran—were brought together in a new art with its own traits.

Freed of many of the symbolic implications which seem to have bound artists in some of the earlier traditions, Islamicate artists—of all confessions, though working largely for Muslims—created a new decorative tradition. The motifs of the earlier arts with the greatest geometrical potentials were selected for development: for instance, the old motif of a 'tree of life', which was simplified into a doubled curving pattern which then lost all tree-like character and—with new branches growing out of its tips—unfolded into a repetitive pattern indefinitely reproducible in all directions. Motifs popular in the Mediterranean had long lost much of their illusionistic naturalism. Now what was left of that naturalism was scuttled, and with it the habit of confining all form within borders and medallions. An 'all-over' art was cultivated of potentially endlessly symmetrical interweaving patterns, which had the virtue of giving an integrally 'rich' effect.

In this art, varied as it was, the Arabic calligraphy introduced a thread of unity. Calligraphy itself was considered a major art—great calligraphers, who introduced new styles of forming the script, were more famous than great painters.[8] Calligraphy formed a unifying theme among the various sorts of art media, and even within the individual work itself. The Arabic writing, most of whose characters were made by one or two lines at most, often repeated, and some of them long or sweeping strokes, could readily be exaggerated or stylized without losing in intelligibility. Many of its characters were linked to each other, in forming words, in a smooth flow, which added to the sense of continuity of design which parallelism of form could already produce. A band of Arabic writing marching across a door or

[8] The conventional Western distinction between 'major' and 'minor' arts—sometimes still encountered in discussions of Islamicate art—has, of course, no relevance in other cultures: in each setting, some sorts of media may acquire special prestige and play a major overall role. The peculiar expressiveness of a creatively beautiful hand is hard for those to appreciate whose culture regards such accomplishments as mere detail.

circling around a platter could thus replace a border in creating the impression of an integrated unit but without putting an end to its sense of indefinite extendability. The splendour of the court was reflected in the richness of the art that surrounded it.

In the new capital of Sâmarrâ, built at the direction of al-Ma'mûn's successor, some traces of the monumental architecture of the age have survived.[9] The scale built on was tremendous—the pillared area of the great mosque was larger than that of St. Peter's at Rome (though it did not, to be sure, support a dome). The artistic style was strong and simple, with a sense of decorative line growing out of Aramaic and Sâsânian work. But building seems to have been almost uniformly hasty; the wealthy were building rather for themselves than for posterity, and demanded quick results. Brick—which can be manipulated fairly readily—was the universal medium, even in Egypt, where (unlike the Iraq) stone is all around. Decorations were often in plaster. The mighty, enduring stone constructions of Sâsânian times were not reproduced, and most building of the time has long since passed away.[10]

[9] Some writers speak of Islamicate architecture as becoming more Iranian under the 'Abbâsids; but this is to confuse architecture at the capital with the architecture of Islamdom generally. In Syria, the style remained the same under the 'Abbâsids as under the Marwânids; and we have no evidence on Marwânî-time architecture in the Iraq.

[10] K. A. C. Cresswell's masterly and painstaking analyses of the early Islamicate arts of building (e.g., *Early Muslim Architecture*, 2 vols. [Oxford, 1932–40]) have enabled us to understand in some detail what went on in an art only traces of which are left. Unfortunately, for all his exact measurements and sorting out of 'influences', he seems to have no sense of art as such, and in this respect we are still, accordingly, largely at a loss.

VII

The Dissipation of the Absolutist Tradition, 813–945

After generations of prosperity and with the integration of the city masses into the Muslim community, the old Arab impulses which had formed the empire had become little more than vestiges, visible chiefly in the pedigrees of some families and in the classical cast of Arabic poetry. The empire had to be perpetuated on a more permanent basis. Al-Ma'mûn (sole ruler, 813–833) and his successors were ruling at the height of the development of the Sharî'ah law: al-Shâfi'î, the legist, died in 820; al-Bukhârî, the ḥadîth-collector, died in 870. They were also ruling at the peak of the formation of Arabic literary culture. Both 'ulamâ' and adîbs, in their own ways, supported the caliphal state or at least the position of the caliph. Yet the 'ulamâ' legists were doing, in practice as much as possible to reduce its authority to a tolerable minimum; while the cosmopolitan literary culture of the adîbs, avoiding the monumental, and being reasonably pious, did little that would serve to legitimize a land-rooted agrarian absolutism as such. By the time of al-Ma'mûn the court had, in fact, worked out the broad lines of an absolutism which seemed to satisfy the taste of the adîbs. But this was at the expense of risking ultimate alienation from the 'ulamâ', whose standards the adîbs themselves acknowledged.

In an agrarian society in which legitimacy was conferred by Islam, five sorts of solution might be offered to the problem of creating an enduring government. The Khârijîs and the Zaydîs were proposing one sort of solution: to reconstruct the early Muslim creative source of the tradition in a face-to-face community, on the basis of a very personal responsibility of the caliph to the Muslims at large. The Zaydîs allowed for a more institutionalized form of this than did most Khârijîs, but in neither case does the solution seem to have been adequate to a large-scale international society; neither Zaydîs nor Khârijîs showed signs of ability to erect more than local states, and those in relatively isolated places. Secondly, the Ismâ'îlîs, by way of the bâṭin interpretation, hoped to derive from the basic monotheistic principles of the tradition a quite new political system, which might have been more adaptable than the Medina pattern to large-scale agrarian society. But they were not able to persuade most Muslims that their hierarchical system of legitimation was sufficiently true to the original Qur'ânic and Muḥammadan inspiration. Thirdly, the Faylasûfs proposed, in effect, that Islam should play the role of a political mythology to support a Philosophically-conceived state; but such a solution would actually have meant a reversal of the decisive position gained by the prophetic tradition with the victory of Islam, and never attracted many adherents. By far the most popular solutions were those of the adîbs, in their pro-absolutism, and of the Shar'î 'ulamâ', whether Jamâ'î-Sunnî or Twelver Shî'î (who rejected the activist policies of other Shî'îs).

The adîbs had generally no explicit policy for solving the relations between Islam and the state, but the tendency of their implicit policy is clear: left to themselves, they would have adapted Islamic terminology to old agrarian monarchical principles (thus they were willing to call the caliph 'Shadow of God' on earth, almost implying a mediatory role for him), and might have subordinated the religious specialists to the authority of the court and its bureaucracy. Whatever their prospects of success in this, however, they either would not or could not go so far as to erect an authoritarian religious hierarchy on the Mazdean model of Sâsânian times. The 'ulamâ', on the contrary, lauded any resistance that was offered to such tendencies—for instance, the staunch refusal of some 'ulamâ' to address the caliph in any more obsequious way than as a fellow Muslim; they developed those aspects of the overall Islamic tradition that depended on initiative in society at large, as against those that depended on political leadership, and would have reduced the caliph to an administrator of the Sharî'ah, first among essentially equal Muslims. In fact, of course, the caliph had become a figure radically alien to such principles, a figure whom they had to hem in but could not genuinely absorb.

The comprehensive demands that the 'ulamâ' were perfecting breathed a spirit almost directly opposed to that of the adîbs. For the adîbs, social rank and privilege were of primary importance, however fluid they might be; high culture was the end of social organization; the littérateur with his inventive gifts was the model of living. For the 'ulamâ', almost any sort of special privilege (save possibly that of the family of Muḥammad) was ruled out; justice among ordinary men and women was the end of social organization; the hero was the man who conformed most closely to a moderate pattern of productive common life. Though the standards of the adîbs were alone very effective on the level of day-to-day politics, those of the 'ulamâ', embodied in the Sharî'ah, alone received long-run respect, at least in their chosen sphere, even among the adîbs themselves; respect of a sort that would enable the Sharî'ah, even in crises, to maintain its prestige—that is, to enjoy a general expectation that people at large would remain faithful to it despite temporary setbacks.

Al-Ma'mûn: experiments in aligning the Sharî'ah and the court

Al-Ma'mûn was both intellectually curious and piously concerned with justice. Yet he fully satisfied neither adîbs nor 'ulamâ'. Having begun his reign in Khurâsân, he ruled through Khurâsânî officers and, indeed, long delayed coming to Baghdad at all. But in any case, he was not popular at Baghdad—despite the traditional patronage of the dynasty, more than one poet opposed him. Even apart from such explicit discontent, he was intensely aware of the precariousness of the empire's unity, and concerned to strengthen it. His reign had started in the midst of the uncertainty and civil war let loose by al-Rashîd's notion of dividing the empire. His victory had undone the immediate effects of al-Rashîd's attempted division, but the unsettling of minds, that had resulted, persisted and demonstrated the lack of any political consensus among the population, especially among the Muslims.

In Egypt, the violence which had broken out during the main struggle for Baghdad itself persisted for years, with rival factions quarrelling in practical independence of the central power. More important, for the first six years of al-Ma'mûn's reign his control of the Iraq remained insecure. A great Shî'î rebellion, led by an adventurer, Abû-l-Sarâyâ, at Kûfah and Baṣrah (814–815), gained the support of Mecca. (It was the only movement that gave serious indication of stirring an all-Muslim consciousness.) Months after that was suppressed, the hostility of Baghdad to Khurâsânî rule reasserted itself. Al-Ma'mûn's long stay in Khurâsân led the 'Abbâsî leadership at Baghdad to rebel (816–819) and even to try to set up another caliph (Ibrâhîm, 817–819) who would stay in Baghdad; but al-Ma'mûn's good generals and his control of most of the provinces enabled him to quash this step, though he did find it necessary to move to the recognized capital (819). Meanwhile, in addition to the Khârijî rebellion already going on in Khurâsân, popular movements among the Iranians of Azerbaijan, the Arabs of the Jazîrah, and the Copts of Egypt were expressing a widespread impatience with central control.

Subtler was another danger to the absolutism. After most of the overt revolts had been suppressed and Baghdad itself fully pacified, in the latter part of the reign, governors in the Maghrib (the Aghlabids) and even in Khurâsân (the Ṭâhirids), who had been suppressing still other local rebellions, found themselves able to behave within their provinces like local dynasts—and indeed founded hereditary dynasties which, however, maintained close ties with the caliphs. Several families had won such loyalty among the troops that their members were found to be appropriate as governors in widely scattered areas—as were, for instance, the Sâjid family. When this independent prestige was combined with a particular territorial base, it threatened the central power. The general Ṭâhir and his family, in particular, were forming almost a state within a state. Ṭâhir was military governor of Baghdad, the submission of which he had assured; but, with local alliances in Khurâsân, he remained at the same time ruler of Khurâsân and its vast dependencies; and his son succeeded him without any question. That is, the most important troops in the empire, the Khurâsânîs—more effective than the still important Arab troops—were controlled by a family that had its own local basis of power in a single province, a province at once

The Weakening of the High Caliphate, 813–945

THE GENERATION OF AL-MA'MÛN'S TIME

813–833	Caliphate of al-Ma'mûn: court favor to new translations of Falsafah works from Greek; attempt to suppress the new Ahl-al-Ḥadîth piety (belief in uncreated Qur'ân) with support of Mu'tazilî kalâm (theological discussion)
780–855	Aḥmad b. Ḥanbal, disciple of al-Shâfi'î, persecuted by al-Ma'mûn as symbol of Ahl-al-Ḥadîth resistance to Mu'tazilî orthodoxy; he became imâm of an intransigent school of fiqh
816–837	Revolt of Bâbak against large landlords and Arabs, centered in Azerbaijan
819–873	Ṭâhirids, as hereditary governors, autonomous in Iran and the east
833–842	Caliphate of al-Mu'taṣim: introduction of Turkish mercenaries as basis of caliphal power (capital moved to Sâmarrâ)

GENERATION OF THE SÂMARRÂ CALIPHS (836–892)

842–847	Caliphate of al-Wâthiq, last great 'Abbâsî ruler of a relatively unweakened empire
869	Death of Ibn-Karrâm, Muslim evangelist of Khurâsân
870	Death of al-Bukhârî, author of the greatest collection of canonical ḥadîth reports; paired with that of Muslim (d. 873)
847–861	Caliphate of al-Mutawakkil, who abandoned the caliphal attempt to prescribe theological orthodoxy through Mu'tazilism, and gave support to Ahl-al-Ḥadîth piety; persecuted the Shî'îs; first caliph to be murdered by his Turkish soldier corps
861–945	Breakup of 'Abbâsî power; province after province becomes essentially independent, till at the end the caliphal government loses all territorial power; economic and social prosperity persist or increase in most areas
861–869	Three caliphs in the hands of the Turkish soldiery; all but the central provinces break away from effective control
861–910	Saffârids (military family) ruling independently in eastern, and sometimes in most of, Iran
864–928	Zaydî Shî'î state in sub-Caspian lands
868–906	Ibn-Ṭûlûn, and sons, practically independent governors in Egypt
869–883	Revolt of Zanj (African) slaves in the lower Iraq
892	Death of Muḥammed al-Tirmidhî, collector of ḥadîths and systematizer of categories in isnâd criticism
869–892	al-Muwaffaq, executive brother of Caliph al-Mu'tamid, re-establishes caliphal authority between Syria and Khurâsân

GENERATION OF AL-MUWAFFAQ'S RESTORATION

875–998	Sâmânid (Persian) governors semi-independent, but usually in accord with caliphal policy, in Transoxania
873–940	The twelfth imâm of the Twelver Shî'îs having disappeared, he is represented by four wakîls, in the Lesser Ghaybah; after which, in the Greater Ghaybah, the Twelvers lose contact with their imâm
838–923	Ibn-Jarîr al-Ṭabarî, commentator on the Qur'ân; and historian (his history reaches to 913) using chronological sequence; in contrast to his great contemporary, Aḥmad al-Balâdhurî (d. 892)
890–906	Qarmaṭians, Arab bands of Ismâ'îlî Shî'îs, active in 'Irâqi and Syrian deserts; they mark the beginning of rise to power of various Shî'î groups, thus hastening the collapse of caliphal control
892–908	Al-Mu'taḍid (to 902), son of al-Muwaffaq; and then al-Muktafî; caliphal control stabilized from Egypt to western Iran, with Aghlabid governors in North Africa and Sâmânid governors in eastern Iran tributary but not under control

GENERATION OF THE QARMAṬIAN REVOLTS

894	Qarmaṭian Shî'î state in east Arabia founded
c. 900	Zaydî state in the Yemen founded
900	Sâmânids under Ismâ'îl (892–907) add Khurâsân to their rule, upon ousting the Ṣaffârids; soon become patrons of Persian language works
908–932	Caliphate of al-Muqtadir; caliphal authority again founders on misrule; Shî'î families in considerable power at capital
905–979	Arab Ḥamdânids autonomous, and sometimes independent, in Mosul (and later Aleppo); they support Shî'ism
909–972	Ismâ'îlîs establish Fâṭimid caliphate in Maghrib, replacing Aghlabids
929–1031	Umayyad rulers in Spain assume the caliphal title (912–961: caliph 'Abd-al-Raḥmân III re-establishes Muslim united power within Spain); Spanish Arab culture flourishes so as to attract local Christian participation
913–942	Arabic and Persian culture both favoured under Naṣr II, Sâmânid in Transoxania and Khurâsân (940, death of Rûdaqî, first classical Persian poet)
873–935	al-Ash'arî, reconciles the methods of Mu'tazilî kalâm with the dogmas of the Ahl-al-Ḥadîth
934–1055	Rulers of Persian Bûyid military family independent at separate centers in western Iran and the Iraq using Persian (Daylamî) and Turkish soldiers; favour Twelver Shî'ism
935–945	Diminishing remnants of caliphal power wielded by an amîr al-umarâ, military chief, till that office is taken over by Bûyids occupying Baghdad
937–969	Ikhshîdid governors independent in Egypt

remote from central control and of primary importance in the empire as a whole.

This answered to more fundamental social facts: whereas the Khurâsânî troops who put the 'Abbâsids in power originally had still felt themselves largely as Arab settlers, those who supported al-Ma'mûn were frankly Iranians.[1] But Baghdad and the Fertile Crescent were not prepared to submit to a Ṭâhirid and Khurâsânî domination—nor was al-Ma'mûn himself; nor was it clear that Khurâsân was willing to submit to domination by any Baghdad-based force either. Everywhere, relatively local loyalties were prevailing.

There was still a general sentiment among the Muslims for Muslim unity, despite the growing importance of relatively local interests. Thus the rival factions in Egypt had depended for psychological support, as well as in a more material way, upon the powers at Baghdad, whose active intervention during the war of succession was readily effective when it came. In the Iraq itself, naturally, there was an unceasing demand for a single caliph of all Islamdom; the fact that al-Ma'mûn won the allegiance of other provinces and especially of the holy cities in the Ḥijâz was a major advantage for him in his original struggle, with al-Amîn. But this sentiment for a united caliphal state was obviously not fully dependable.

Al-Ma'mûn was an able ruler; choosing effective generals, he was able to bring under control most of the risings that defied him. He maintained a persistent military struggle for mastery; but he also launched an effort to tighten the religious base of the empire. This could take the form only of some understanding with the Shar'î 'ulamâ' which would not compromise the power of the absolute monarchy.

Al-Ma'mûn was of a serious and inquiring turn of mind, which in his courtly patronage led him to the increased fostering of natural science and philosophy that we have noted earlier. On the political level, the same trait led him to religious policies that might have had the effect of shoring up the courtly imperial ideal with an officially recognized religious establishment in which as many Muslims as possible could unite. Whether he ever had in mind the example of the hierarchical Mazdean high priests, who balanced the Sâsânian monarchy in social authority and, by and large, gave it effective independent support and continuity, his efforts, if successful, could even have led toward some such result. But, even to secure Muslim unity, no section of the Shar'î 'ulamâ'—not even the Mu'tazilîs, whom he favoured—was prepared to abandon, in favour of caliphal power, the ideals of the old Piety-minded opposition, even had this been feasible.

[1] On the Arab and Khrâsâni troops under the early 'Abbâsids, see Claude Cahen, 'Djaysh', in 2nd ed. of *Encyclopaedia of Islam*. H. A. R. Gibb, in 'The Caliphate and the Arab States', in Kenneth M. Setton, ed., *A History of the Crusades* (University of Pennsylvania Press, 1955), vol. 1, pp. 81–98, points out the change in the troops' outlook. But the point of departure for al-Ma'mûn's reign remains the study by Francesco Gabrieli, *Al-Ma'mûn e gli 'Alidi* (Leipzig, 1929).

The Fourth Fitnah: al-Ma'mûn's Wars

809	Hârûn al-Rashîd dies, al-Amîn becomes caliph according to the 'Meccan documents', al-Ma'mûn establishes himself in Khurâsân
810	al-Amîn names son Mûsà in Friday prayers as successor, bringing up question of al-Ma'mûn's place in the succession order as established in the 'Meccan documents'
810	al-Ma'mûn refuses to yield, is declared a rebel when he refuses to come to Baghdad
811	al-Amîn sends army under 'Alî b. 'Isà against al-Ma'mûn's forces commanded by Ṭâhir b. Ḥusayn; 'Alî killed; Ṭâhir defeats a second army sent by al-Amîn; al-Jibâl province in hands of Ṭâhir's forces; Syria in disorder
812	al-Ḥusayn, son of 'Alî, briefly deposes al-Amîn and declares for al-Ma'mûn; al-Amîn restored but al-Ma'mûn's troops occupy Khûzistân; Baghdad invested by al-Ma'mûn's generals Ṭâhir and Harthamah b. A'yan
813	Ṭâhir's men kill caliph when Baghdad falls; Harthamah had promised him safe conduct
814–815	Abû-Sarâyâ and Muḥammad b. Ibrâhîm b. Ṭabâtabâ raise Shî'î revolt in Kûfah, put down by Harthamah
816	Harthamah killed by al-Ma'mûn's vizier al-Faḍl b. Sahl
817	Baghdadîs try to persuade Manṣûr, son of al-Mahdî, to declare himself a claimant; he refuses
817	al-Ma'mûn makes the Shî'î 'Alî al-Riḍâ ('eighth' imâm) his heir on the advice of his vizier Faḍl, but Baghdadîs and others in the Iraq revolt; so also one of al-Ma'mûn's generals
816–817	Bâbak raises a religio-social revolt
817	Baghdadîs recognize Ibrâhîm, another son of al-Mahdî; 'Alî al-Riḍâ warns al-Ma'mûn of the nature and gravity of the situation; al-Ma'mûn may have felt his vizier Faḍl had not faithfully so apprised him
818	'Alî al-Riḍâ dies; Faḍl killed, possibly by order of caliph; al-Ma'mûn moves westward toward Baghdad
819	al-Ma'mûn enters Baghdad; rival caliph submits; has then to face a Khârijî revolt, unrest in various provinces, and Bâbak's revolt; Ṭâhir too powerful to remove, becomes almost independent governor in Khurâsân, principal commander of al-Ma'mûn's troops

Soon after the Shî'î rebellion in the Iraq, al-Ma'mûn had tried to capture the Shî'î movement itself, naming as his own heir the imâm of one of its most popular sections, 'Alî al-Riḍà, grandson of Ja'far al-Ṣâdiq. In theory, this might have helped reconcile all Muslims; for Jamâ'î-Sunnîs, in principle, should accept as their own any successor designated by the received caliph. The Shî'îs proved capable of offering little real strength, however, and his Shî'î turn added to the resistance of Baghdad. 'Alî al-Riḍà conveniently died while al-Ma'mûn was on his way to pacify Baghdad by making it his capital, and the caliph made no further attempt to integrate Shî'î sentiment into the régime so directly, though he continued to insist on general respect for 'Alî.

He did take further measures, nevertheless, aimed at suppressing religious factionalism. Without sponsoring any one theological school as such, he rejected the more extreme formulations of the Ḥadîth folk, who, as their popularity at Baghdad increased, were becoming militant in their opposition to those who disagreed with them, including the Shî'îs. A sensitive Jamâ'î-Sunnî religious teacher like al-Muḥâsibî, condemned by the Ḥadîthî Ibn-Ḥanbal, scarcely dared teach publicly at the capital. Al-Ma'mûn required that all officials, qâḍîs, and (so far as possible) 'ulamâ' generally reject certain Ḥadîthî doctrines, condemned by the Mu'tazilîs (and by all other specialists in kalâm disputation at the time) and now also by the state, as un-Islamic. But this meant adopting official theological positions and enforcing conformity to them. To the extent that he succeeded, al-Ma'mûn not only countered religious factionalism and reduced the public power of the Ḥadîth folk; more generally, he prepared the way for an Islamic institution more amenable than had been most of the earlier 'ulamâ' to the religious demands of an absolute monarchy.

But this intervention was itself factional in effect. Of all the former sections of the Piety-minded opposition, the Mu'tazilîs had been the most zealous in defence of Islam against its various non-Muslim opponents and (perhaps partly for that reason) the readiest to rely on deductive reasoning for their doctrine rather than on the letter of ḥadîth reports. It was the Mu'tazilîs who had taken the lead in the campaign against the Manicheans. They continued their severity against any un-Islamic infiltrations in officialdom, but now turned their attention, with al-Ma'mûn's aid and led by the great qâḍî Aḥmad b. Abî-Du'âd, to what seemed to be un-Islamic tendencies within Shar'î Islam itself.

That section of the 'ulamâ' which specialized in gathering ḥadîth reports—whom we have called collectively the Ḥadîth folk—had never been comfortable in too close contact with the worldly 'Abbâsîs. In addition, their own special religious enthusiasm, one well adapted to private lives, went to confirm their emotional independence of the existing Muslim state. It simultaneously fired their zeal to impose their private factional norms wherever they could, without regard to public policy.

As we have seen, this enthusiasm expressed itself in a doctrine that identified the Qur'ân very closely with God Himself: the Qur'ânic words which were so often piously upon their tongues were 'uncreated', unlike everything else in the world. This conception, which stressed the immediate accessibility of the divine law to every believer, was very appropriate to the Sharî'ah-minded conceptions of social equality and individual dignity; but by the same token it was ill suited to the ideal of absolute monarchy. What the Mu'tazilî 'ulamâ' (and other men of kalâm) disliked about it was perhaps not so much the independent and factional spirit it fostered as the un-Qur'ânic illogic of a doctrine which seemed to idolize the Qur'ân as almost a second god, introducing a mystery into Islam contrary to the straightforward reasonableness of the faith. But for both intellectual and political reasons, al-Ma'mûn was readily persuaded to decree that any who adopted the doctrine that the Qur'ân was uncreated were not true Muslims.

Those 'ulamâ' who dissented were, at best, excluded from public positions, which tended to be filled with Mu'tazilîs (many of whom, however, declined to identify themselves with the régime even so). Thus the religious authority of the state was staked upon the outcome of the Mu'tazilîs' controversy with the Ḥadîth folk. But since the populace of the cities, especially Baghdad, was turning against the Mu'tazilîs, this meant basing the state religiously rather on some of the intellectual élite than on the masses. It made for disunity rather than unity.[2]

Al-Mu'taṣim: the dilemma of the personal army

Al-Ma'mûn left to his brother al-Mu'taṣim (833–842) the caliphate and his controversy with the Ḥadîth folk. Al-Mu'taṣim continued his policies by and large, though with less initiative and vigour. He made a notable departure however, in military policy. If it was important to unite the empire on a common basis for authority, one means to this seemed to be to give the central power, the caliph, his own immediate base of military strength. Unfortunately, this was achieved at the expense of weakening further such

[2] Dominique Sourdel, 'La politique religieuse du caliphe 'abbâside al-Ma'mûm', *Revue des Etudes Islamiques*, 30 (1962), 27–48, is a very good study of al-Ma'mûn's policies. Sourdel stresses the Shî'î tendencies of some of the Mu'tazilîs, and inclines to see in the early Shî'î policy and the later Mu'tazilî policy two forms of the same impulse, which he associates with a Faylasûf-Mu'tazilî-Shî'î party at court (to which he prudently gives no name) set off against a Ḥadîthî party; he suggests that under al-Rashîd, the Faylasûf-Mu'tazilî-Shî'î party had been favoured by the Barmakids, while the Ḥadîthîs had been favoured personally by al-Rashîd, and then by al-Amîn (and again by Ibrâhîm). I think that in his analysis of this supposed Faylasûf-Mu'tazilî-Shî'î party, however, he is misled by a premature retrojection of later sect lines back into these formative times. He calls the Ḥadîthî position then popular in Baghdad 'orthodoxy', and refers to its 'traditional' doctrines—confusing the two senses of the word—and hence misses its factionalist and innovative role; while he correspondingly assumes that those who were then called 'Zaydîs' held the full doctrine later elaborated by al-Rassî; and hence fails to bring out the ways in which al-Riḍà, against whom they would have no immediate theoretical objection, might still be unacceptable to them. Hence the point he does make, that al-Ma'mûn was hoping to reconcile the more moderate Jamâ'îs and the more moderate Shî'îs, is not sufficiently articulated. But it is far more important than the hint of a Faylasûf-Mu'tazilî-Shî'î coalition party—which may never really have existed: without any such party, the intellectualist interests of the Barmakids and of al-Ma'mûn would have had like consequences independently in the fostering of Falsafah and kalâm discussion, in the conciliation of Shî'îs, in the tolerance of dhimmî non-Muslims—and in checking the Ḥadîthî factionalism and communalism which threatened all these policies.

links as existed between the caliphal power and the general Muslim populace. The caliph's personal military guard, which had already included purchased slaves in its ranks, was now put under the command of the caliph's personal slaves rather than of free men of standing in the community. This move might give the caliph independence from factional quarrels among the Muslims and in particular from the dominance of the Khurâsânî troops (who might be more loyal to their semi-independent Ṭâhirid commanders than to the caliph). It also gave the military guard, now a wholly slave corps (and thousands strong), a high internal cohesion and a dangerous irresponsibility vis-à-vis the wider community. The slaves were neither Arabic nor Persian, but mostly Turks from the central Eurasian steppe (a fertile ground for slave-raiding), who felt no tie with the local population in the Iraq or any other province.

Their irresponsibly violent behaviour among the people of Baghdad seems to have contributed to impelling al-Mu'taṣim to a second move which reinforced his alienation from the body of Muslims. He caused a new city, Sâmarrâ, to be built (836) for governmental purposes along the Tigris a good distance north of Baghdad, to which latter city he left the control of commerce and scholarship. In Sâmarrâ, surrounded by his Turkic slave guard, the caliph was indeed an absolute monarch, but one increasingly out of touch with the socially dominant elements in the empire.

Al-Ma'mûn had died during a defensive campaign against the Byzantines. Al-Mu'taṣim was able to renew the offensives of al-Rashîd's time and carry out the most ambitious raids since Marwânî times. In Anatolia, Ankara was wrecked and Amorium captured; preparations were made for another siege of Constantinople, but when the Muslim fleet was destroyed in a tempest, the project could not be carried through. Anatolia was again abandoned. It was the last great foreign exploit of the caliphal state.

The project of creating a religious establishment tied to the government meanwhile made little further progress. Religious communal sentiment, indeed, had its way, and it even served to enforce cultural conformity. Bâbak's Iranianizing rebellion in Azerbaijan gave occasion for sentiment at the capital to harden against men who were sympathetic to the more explicitly Iranian traditions. Victor (837) over Bâbak was al-Âfshîn, who was hereditary Persian ruler of a district beyond the Oxus, but also a masterful general for the caliph. He had converted to Islam, but made little secret of his sympathy for the old Iranian culture; he refused to be circumcised, for instance, alleging fear for his health, and he loved the old Pahlavî books with their richly colourful illustrations. On this basis, his enemies at the capital were able to have him arraigned for treason, suggesting that he had been secretly in league with Bâbak against the Muslims and the Arab spirit Islam carried with it. In particular, they took note that in his hereditary district he allowed himself to be addressed by titles that seemed to imply divinity—a posture inconsistent with true Islam. He defended himself with dignity; as to his title, in particular, he pointed out that the continuity of his dynasty presupposed certain popular notions, which he could not set aside without undermining the basis of his own rule (which he had used, indeed, in loyal service to Islam). He himself laid no stock in any such notions. But such politic arguments could not move an aroused Muslim audience. His enemies had their way, and he was condemned to death (840); his body, in the custom of the time, was shamefully desecrated.

The rebellions persisting from al-Ma'mûn's time were finally crushed, and under al-Mu'taṣim's son and successor, al-Wâthiq (842–847), the authority of the caliphal government was not (in principle) seriously questioned in the provinces (save always at the western end of the Mediterranean). But the position of the Turkic slaves at the empire's heart became constantly stronger.

The deterioration of the Sawâd irrigation

Apart from any political decline in the resources of the caliphal state in human loyalties, after the reign of al-Ma'mûn Baghdad was losing an important economic basis on which its central political and cultural position had been built. In the long run, economic failure may have been at least as fateful for the absolutism, as the political failure with which it necessarily interacted.

The rich Mesopotamian agricultural region, the Sawâd, was returning less revenue, not only to the government but in absolute yield. At least in the Diyâlah basin (the area nearest Baghdad), this resulted in part from cumulative causes beyond governmental control. The land seems to have been rising in such a way that the Diyâlah river came to flow faster—and sometime or other this increased rate passed a critical point: instead of flooding periodically and depositing silt round about it, the river began to scour out its own bed and lower its level as compared with the land around. The high banks formed by the silt dropped nearest the river had presented a relatively slight engineering problem for those who wanted to divert its waters bit by bit for irrigation. But when the river bottom dug substantially below the level of the plain, more had to be done than keep a way clear through the high banks. For one thing, the engineers had to shift the canal courses into more expensive patterns (eventually they even tried to pave the river's bed to prevent further scouring). But for all the increased investment, less land was under cultivation.

But these geological changes (which were probably not limited to the Diyâlah) were not all. With the intensive irrigation that had been pushed at least since Nûshîrvân's time, almost certainly large areas in the Sawâd must have succumbed to salinization—poor drainage producing a chronic rising of the ground-water level to the point where its salty waters would kill plant roots. Only a long process of restoration could normally drain out

The ‘Abbâsid Caliphs, 833–945

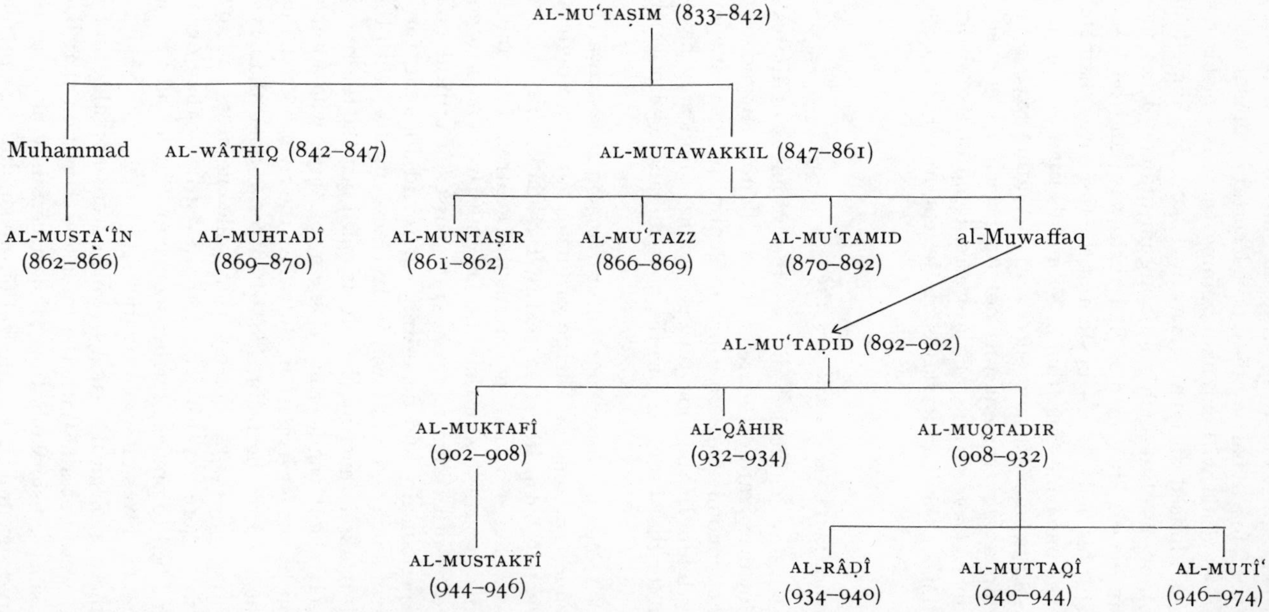

AL-MU‘TAṢIM (833–842)
Muḥammad
AL-WÂTHIQ (842–847)
AL-MUTAWAKKIL (847–861)
AL-MUSTA‘ÎN (862–866)
AL-MUHTADÎ (869–870)
AL-MUNTAṢIR (861–862)
AL-MU‘TAZZ (866–869)
AL-MU‘TAMID (870–892)
al-Muwaffaq
AL-MU‘TAḌID (892–902)
AL-MUKTAFÎ (902–908)
AL-QÂHIR (932–934)
AL-MUQTADIR (908–932)
AL-MUSTAKFÎ (944–946)
AL-RÂḌÎ (934–940)
AL-MUTTAQÎ (940–944)
AL-MUṬÎ‘ (946–974)

such lands again. In any case, by the early tenth century the Sawâd was yielding a much smaller revenue than even a generation earlier. A point had been reached at which the process of decline was self-accelerating. Military turbulence, itself resulting largely from the reduced resources of a government committed to high expenditures at court, contributed to hasten its own causes: when, in 937, the great Nahrawân canal was breached by soldiers in factional fighting between rival forces, it was not soon restored. Engineers were ceasing, in any case, to attempt to maintain the old agricultural level. Maintaining the Sawâd had reached the point of diminishing returns and no longer repaid the necessary investment.

In such circumstances, even civilian officials might give up the attempt to maintain administrative standards; and once demoralization set in, natural difficulties were accentuated by a tendency of officials to lower their levels of expectation as to what constituted acceptable bureaucratic behaviour. Corruption, always a danger, became worse.

But once the political and social structure of the Sawâd had become dependent on Baghdad and the other great cities, central intervention was necessary if the area was not to decline agriculturally even below the level which a more decentralized irrigation had maintained in pre-Sâsânian times. Local initiative was no longer in a position to restore a more moderate prosperity, for the land was controlled from the cities; or else it readily fell into the hands of pastoralists, who alone had the tribal social structure and the nomadic alternative resources which would enable them to hold out against pressure from the cities. In the following centuries, the Sawâd was eliminated as a primary source of centralized revenues in the region, giving the government that controlled it resources to outlast rebellions and other disruptions elsewhere in the empire. But there was no visible alternative financial basis of the same order for a centralized bureaucratic empire. To survive, the empire would have to find a more general economic basis for continuity in its authority. The problem of religious legitimacy was increasingly compounded by that of financial viability; and the political crisis of confidence, by interrupting and demoralizing central control, in turn hastened the economic troubles.[3]

The crisis of caliphal absolutism

The next caliph after al-Wâthiq, al-Mutawakkil (847–861), reversed the religious policy of al-Ma'mûn and al-Mu'taṣim, but was incapable of bringing the empire back to the non-committal but splendid strength of al-Rashîd's day. By his time, the Turkic troops were discovering that if they depended on the caliph alone, so did he on them. The caliphs tried to offset such a

[3] 'Abd-al-'Azîz al-Dûrî (all of whose work is important) has studied economic history at the end of the High Caliphal Period in *Ta'rîkh al-'Irâq al-iqtiṣâdî fi'l-qarn al-râbi'* (Baghdad, 1945).

consequence by introducing several different ethnic elements in the troops, whose rivalries would keep them all under control. Turks were set against Negro slaves and against troops derived from the more westerly provinces. But if, in fact, the soldierly forces were socially autonomous, then their collective power rested, in effect, with whichever group among them could gain the pre-eminence. Such a group could coerce the caliph without fear of outside interference, once it had cowed its military rivals. The caliph's efforts to divide and rule served his ends in the short run, but at any serious crisis they merely resulted in more uncontrollable and destructive factional fighting among the troops, making the commanders still less inclined to behave responsibly.

Al-Mutawakkil was set on the throne in the first place at the will of the Turkic guards. His personal life was taken up with trivial or vile extravagances, some of which, no doubt, gave encouragement to the arts—this was ideally one of the monarch's functions—but which in this case did so at the expense of kingly responsibility. (For one party he expressed the wish that all things should be yellow—guests must wear yellow clothes, girls must be blondes, the food must be of yellow colour on golden dishes, even the water flowing in a stream through the garden must be coloured yellow with saffron. Someone underestimated the amount of saffron that would be required before the caliph became too drunk to notice, so when the saffron ran out, precious dyed stuffs had to be soaked out in the water to keep its colour yellow.) His public policy was left to the most bigoted of the Ḥadîth folk, who celebrated, on the one hand, the end of the caliphal attempt to control the Jamâ'î-Sunnî 'ulamâ', while instituting, on the other hand, active persecution of their opponents. The Mu'tazilîs suffered disgrace, but little more. But Shî'î shrines were obliterated. In accordance with the doctrine that dhimmîs might not build new places of worship after the conquest, many such newly built churches and synagogues were torn down.

For fourteen years the government pursued no consistent imperial policy. Then the one power close to the throne that possessed sufficient solidarity to act effectively showed its hand: the Turkic slave soldiers murdered al-Mutawakkil and freely installed his son in his place, unhindered by any section of the public.

There followed a crisis in the state far more serious than that on al-Rashîd's death. At last the demand for Muslim unity, which had triumphed readily in the time of Mu'âwiyah and had persisted through every subsequent crisis, proved relatively impotent. For ten years (861–870), a series of four short-lived caliphs at Sâmarrâ tried vainly to evade the power of the Turkic soldiers who made and unmade them. The first (al-Mutawakkil's son, al-Muntaṣir) was branded as a parricide and was soon undone. One (al-Muhtadî) stood out for his exemplary frugality and honesty, by which he hoped to win religious awe and the support of the soberer of his subjects; he succeeded in staving off crises by sheer bravado for several months before he, too, succumbed. All were more or less creatures of one or another military faction and necessarily bowed to the general in power, who had to loot the treasury for his own troops and so prepare financially for his own fall. The provinces meanwhile were largely left to their own devices.

The next serious caliphal ruler, al-Muwaffaq (870–891), brother and lieutenant of the titular caliph al-Mu'tamid, succeeded in imposing his authority on the troops by political address and by good luck. Long favoured over other 'Abbâsids by Baghdad opinion, he had to win his way by patiently organizing military victories. He confronted rebellion and civil war in all directions. In the west al-Muwaffaq permitted the Turkic governor of Egypt, Aḥmad b. Ṭûlûn, to be practically independent in Egypt and even to annex Syria. (Ibn-Ṭûlûn then added to al-Muwaffaq's troubles by encouraging his brother, the titular caliph, to flee al-Muwaffaq's frugal tutelage to Ibn-Ṭûlûn's protection, and the de facto ruler had to take out time to suppress these intrigues. Still he preferred not to depose the disloyal brother but to maintain a show of caliphal legitimacy.) In the north he could not prevent the establishment of a Zaydî Shî'î state in Ṭabaristân, south of the Caspian.

In the east the governor of Sîstân, Ya'qûb b. al-Ṣaffâr, had risen from frontier fighting as a local popular hero. Ya'qûb had led local militia forces against the last of the Khârijî bands in eastern Iran, who had apparently degenerated into robber bands; they could no longer win the passive support of local populations, who were now turning Muslim themselves, in any case, and felt a stake in the Muslim order. Ya'qûb had risen rapidly to the governorship of his province during the disturbances following al-Mutawakkil's death, and gained the enthusiastic confidence of at least the city population. This was partly due to his personal gifts as a captain, no doubt (it is said that he first attracted public attention for his masterly management of a robber band himself), but also to his social policy. An artisan's son himself, he led forces the core of which seems to have been town-based and not at all aristocratic in their loyalties. He and his successors of his family were identified with the interests of the lesser townsmen as against the landed gentry. In the general uncertainty, Ya'qûb was persuaded to widen the sphere of his power; he led his men against the non-Muslim mountaineers eastwards, and (867) set about a conquest of all Iran, where the local populations proved not averse to his coming, especially as he seems to have kept his troops under strict discipline. The aristocratic Ṭâhirid régime could not withstand him. Al-Muwaffaq defeated Ya'qûb when he menaced the Iraq, but had to allow Ya'qûb and his brother, 'Amr, to retain an independent governorship in most of Iran.

Al-Muwaffaq's main efforts were concentrated on the financially crucial Iraq itself, which yielded less revenue than earlier but had not yet entered on its last, most ruinous, phase. In the south, the Negro slaves, called 'Zanj', many of whom were used for labour in the marshy areas at the mouth of the Tigris, had risen in 869 under a Khârijî leader and set up their own state, which tried to turn the tables on their former masters, enslaving the former slave-owners. Baṣrah itself was sacked, and for a time much of southern Iraq and Khûzistân was in their hands. They built themselves an almost impregnable marsh city, which required special techniques for al-Muwaffaq's soldiers to reach. It was only in 883 that the Zanj were finally reduced.

Despite these interruptions, al-Muwaffaq was able to restore a degree of strength and purpose to the caliphal state, though he did not overcome the basic weaknesses that had characterized the reign of al-Mutawakkil. In his hands and in the hands of his son al-Muʻtaḍid (891–902) and of his grandson al-Muktafî (902–908), his triumphs bore fruit. Egypt was reoccupied when Ibn-Ṭûlûn's sons proved incompetent. The resources that remained to the central power proved sufficient for it to control the key block of provinces extending from Egypt in the west to Fârs in the east, from ʻUmân in the south to Armenia in the north. Revolts were endemic but were somehow contained. More distant provinces in the west and south and east which had been included in al-Rashîd's empire retained full autonomy and contributed little to the caliph's finances, but mostly acknowledged the caliphal supremacy. A financial surplus was built up at Baghdad (which again became the capital in 892). Yet the soldiery continued to form a potentially independent element of power even at the centre, though for the moment subordinate to the civil administration.

The failure of the Qarmaṭian revolution

But the political initiative in Islamdom was shifting away from Baghdad—whether Baghdad was in the hands of the caliph and his civilian bureaucrats or of their military servants and occasional tyrants. Initiative lay increasingly with those who could command the allegiance of the dominant elements in the several provinces.

By the end of the ninth century, rebellions such as that of Bâbak, based on an older national tradition, lost importance; so likewise did the earlier type of general Khârijî or Shîʻî rebellion aimed at reforming the caliphal state from within the established Muslim ruling classes. Neither a common Muslim ruling class which felt itself set off as Muslim even if it included many social levels, nor an identifiable and potent stratum of pre-Islamic national leadership had retained political actuality: all major political elements, at all the more active levels of society, were Muslims in common. Instead of the earlier sorts of rebellion, the new movements which attacked or at least detracted from the caliphal power tended to be based on blocs of the population which could be assumed to be Muslim but whose political ideas were limited to less comprehensive and amorphous interests than those which now could concern the whole Muslim community.

The focus of attention came to be the province, such as Egypt or Syria or

Successor States and Principalities: The Weakening of Caliphal Control

	Spain and the Maghrib	Egypt and the Fertile Crescent	Iranian Highlands and Lands to the Northeast
756	Spain independent under an Umayyad prince		
788	Shî'î Idrîsids independent (to 974), build capital at Fez		
801	Aghlabids independent (to 909), capital at Qayrawân, launch attacks on Sicily, southern Italy; Islamization of Ifrîqiyah		
822			Ṭâhirids (to 873)
867			Ṣaffârids (to 908) take most of lands under Ṭâhirid rule
868		Ṭûlûnids (to 905) take power in Egypt, expand into Syria	
874			Sâmânids (to 999) for a while rule large area, develop important administrative practices; founder descendant of a Zoroastrian noble; patronized al-Râzi, Rûdaqî, Ibn-Sînâ
909	Shî'î Fâṭimids succeed Aghlabids in Ifrîqiyah		
929	Caliphate of Córdova declared	Shî'î Ḥamdânids in Mosul (to 991)	
934			Shî'î Bûyids take Shîrâz
935		Ikhshîdids (to 969) take power in Egypt; expand into Syria	
944		Ḥamdânids in Aleppo (to 1001), patronize al-Fârâbî, al-Iṣfahânî, al-Mutanabbi'	
945		Shî'î Bûyids take Baghdad	
c. 956 (?)			Seljuḳ Turks move into Bukhârâ area, adopt Islam

Fârs, rather than the empire as a whole. Whatever esprit de corps there was among the kâtib administrators of the caliphal state as a whole, it was not strong enough to keep the local kâtibs from joining with the bourgeois of their cities in their concern for the quality of the local governor and the effects of his administration on the cities of the immediate region. The sentiments of an older landed gentry—no longer the only military force of the empire, and increasingly disrupted anyway by a tendency for the administration to grant lands freely to new men—played at most a limited role. When Ibn-Ṭûlûn had been able to withhold taxes from Baghdad he kept them at home and spent them on public works in the cities of Egypt; this sort of change pleased the population and made them happy to see their governor independent. Under these circumstances, little resistance would be put up against either an appointed governor who threw off the caliph's yoke or even a military adventurer, leading local warlike elements (in the Fertile Crescent, for instance, Bedouin), who might take the governor's place.

The old-line Khârijî and Shî'î movements had by now been restricted to localized districts. Even the Ḥijâz took on the air, politically, of an isolated province. The efforts that persisted there to establish local 'Alid rule were eventually successful to a degree; but this had little meaning for any wider Shî'î movement; the Ḥijâz was no longer a focus of any general political movement. Yet Shî'ism had many adherents (notably among the Bedouin) in those more central areas where al-Muwaffaq's campaigns had maintained caliphal authority; discontent with an expensive caliphal government perhaps could express itself in rejection of the Jamâ'î-Sunnî 'ulamâ' who had compromised with it. But usually this was to mean only that some locally-based governors and their supporters would be Shî'î in religious sentiment, without carrying any distinctive Shî'î political programme.

One movement formed an exception, that of the Ismâ'îlî Shî'îs. It did presuppose an all-Islamic framework, but not on the basis of the generally recognized leaders of Muslim piety. It proposed to substitute at once a new political and a new religious élite, and based itself, to this end, on malcontents of any class. As the Ismâ'îlî faith was being spread by its often heroic dâ'î missionaries, the ground was being laid on which full-scale rebellion could flourish. Under the nickname 'Qarmaṭians', at the end of the ninth century, an Ismâ'îlî rebellion took place in the deserts between the Iraq and Syria.

The rebels had a certain amount of peasant support (we read of chiliastic peasant sects that identified their cause with the Qarmaṭians); and it must have depended heavily on Bedouin, whom the caliphal state had disillusioned long since. The leadership seems to have been urban and probably won some lower-class support from the towns. A large number of young men joined the Ismâ'îlî camps in the deserts; they felt that the old way of life was to be swept away, the privileged classes overthrown, and pure justice was to reign. Tremendous bitterness was generated on both sides, and the usual atrocities of civil war took place. We read of a pious mother who went out to the desert camps to reclaim her son, who had joined the rebels. She was horrified at the defiant atmosphere of the camps, egalitarian, consciously rejecting the proprieties of established society—and demanding rigid conformity to its revolutionary norms. The emancipated son made a point of his toughness and cruelty, showing no acknowledgement of a mother's dues; the mother disowned him and returned full of denunciations of the Qarmaṭians.

The movement continued for years to threaten 'Abbâsî rule in the Iraq itself. Any Shî'î might be accused of secret complicity in it, and jailed or killed. But it was eventually suppressed; the caliphal state was still strong enough to maintain control of the more central provinces. This was the empire's last major triumph.

Slightly further afield, the same name, 'Qarmaṭians', was applied to a group in mainland Baḥrayn, which had originally formed around a different Shî'î faction but was persuaded (at least for a time) to accept the Ismâ'îlî cause. After the failure of the movement in the Syrian desert, this group established its own republic in the east Arabian oasis towns. The government was oligarchic and the state interfered directly to maintain conditions of prosperity and equal economic opportunity in the towns; the forms of Shar'î Islam were neglected, though not suppressed. The peasantry, however, were not integrated into the new state but served merely, it would seem, as resources for the townsmen. For a time, these Qarmaṭians sent expeditions to distant points in Arabia and the Iraq (the most notorious such expedition took Mecca and carried off the sacred Black Stone from the Ka'bah—these Ismâ'îlîs regarded the reverence paid it as idolatrous; later it was returned). They renewed some of the ferment of the Qarmaṭian revolt. But after decades of quiescence, in the eleventh century, the Sharî'ah was restored in Baḥrayn and the republican forms were destroyed, probably in part with the help of the peasantry.

Fâṭimîs and Sâmânîs

While the 'Abbâsî caliphate did maintain a precarious hold on the inner provinces, the outer provinces were being organized as autonomous Muslim societies. There where there had been, at least since the death of al-Mutawakkil, no question of central interference, states could be constituted on bases less ambitious than the overall restoration of the caliphal state. Even the Ismâ'îlî movement served more provincial interests there.

The most effective Ismâ'îlî rebellion took place far from the centre, where the caliphal power had long ceased to be effective. The Qarmaṭian movement in the desert seems to have been associated with that section of the Ismâ'îlî leadership that made its headquarters in Syria. This leadership seems to have proclaimed its own candidate to the imâmate, who—whether the actual descendant of Ismâʿîlî or not—did not receive the allegiance of all Ismâʿîlî groups. Even the Qarmaṭians of the desert doubted him, and he had to look elsewhere. His dâʿîs prepared bases for him in both the Yemen and the Maghrib; when they had won the support of a major Berber tribal bloc (Ṣanhâjah) in the interior of what is now Algeria, he travelled thither (not without narrow escapes) and proclaimed himself true caliph under the eschatological name *al-Mahdî* in 909; so founding what was proud to be called the Fâṭimid dynasty, as descended from Muḥammad's daughter. Before enthusiasm waned, al-Mahdî succeeded in overthrowing both the Ibâḍî Khârijîs of Tâhart and the Aghlabid dynasty of governors in the eastern Maghrib.

The new caliph had to disown some of his followers who had been too sanguine in their eschatological expectations, and threw in his lot with the coastal merchant cities by moving the east Maghrib capital from Qayrawân, oriented to the land routes of the desert, to a new foundation, Mahdiyyah, a port. The change of atmosphere was signalized by the work of Qâḍî Nuʿmân, a former Mâlikî legist who opportunely converted to Ismâʿîlism and worked out a monumental system of Sharʿî law, based on the school claiming the authority of Jaʿfar al-Ṣâdiq, in time to provide the new dynasty with a working legal corpus of its own. It was explained that the eschatological work of the Mahdî in subduing the world would be shared among several rulers of his dynasty; meanwhile the state must function, on the whole, like any other Muslim state. Al-Mahdî and his son (also called by an eschatological title, *al-Qâʾim*, 934–945) had to resist a vigorous Khârijî Berber revolt, which cooped the Ismâʿîlîs up for a time in their new naval capital; but they had been able to win sufficient support in the cities to maintain their organization intact and break the Berber resistance. With loyal Berber troops, they conquered the whole of the Maghribî coast, subduing the last of the Idrîsid rulers in the Moroccan cities; but they did not cross over into Spain, which remained independent under its Umayyad amîrs. Inheriting the Aghlabî naval power, the Fâṭimids inherited also the Muslim position in Sicily, and Mahdiyyah became a major commercial capital of the Mediterranean.

At the same time that the former Aghlabî domains were being taken over by the Fâṭimid dynasty, the former Ṭâhirî domains were being reintegrated by governors of the Sâmânid family, the most loyal or at least respectful to the caliphate of all the new powers that were arising. Governors at Bukhârâ and Samarqand in the Zarafshân valley (north of the Oxus) since 875, in 903 (under Ismâʿîl b. Nasr) they had taken Khurasân away from the Ṣaffârid family. Ultimately, social power lay with those who could rally the agrarian forces, which the Ṣaffârids had alienated. The Ṣaffârids were soon driven back to their home base in Sîstân—where, however, they were able to maintain their authority locally for many generations subsequently. The Sâmânî state thus constituted in northeastern Iran and the Syr-Oxus basin was vast, but at least had in common a predominantly Persian population and common aristocratic and military traditions. The *dihqâns*, landed gentry, felt the state to be their own and defended it as giving national leadership against the nomadic Turkic tribes. The struggle with the nomads had coloured the whole aristocracy of the northeastern Iranians, exposed to nomadic attack not just at a single frontier line but spottily throughout a broad arid zone. This struggle was now identified with the defence at once of Iranianism and of Islam. Under Naṣr II (913–942), Sâmânî rule brought unquestioned peace and prosperity not only to the Oxus basin and Khurâsân but often to much of western Iran as well.

Within their realms, the Sâmânids maintained the structure of the caliphal bureaucracy almost intact, though modifying it somewhat according to local practices; they were enlightened patrons of literary culture both in Persian and in Arabic. Under their rule Arabic adab cultivation found a congenial home, almost as good as Baghdad. It was under them, also, that the new Muslim Persian, adopted by the petty dihqân gentry, became a regular literary language. Unlike the Ṣaffârids, who had been closely allied with less than aristocratic elements in Sîstân, the Sâmânids upheld the dignity and the privileges of the gentry; correspondingly, they received the praise of the lettered classes.

In the territories still effectively subject to the Baghdad caliphal government, on the contrary, sound government—so far as it existed—was still dependent on caliphal strength, and this was waning. At the succession to al-Muktafî (908), it is said, ambitious courtiers deliberately preferred to raise to the throne a boy who promised to be weak and manageable rather than a grown man with ideas of his own (the adult candidate was Ibn-al-Muʿtazz, the poet and critic). Al-Muqtadir, the boy, satisfied their short-sighted hopes, if this was the case, only too well. His caliphate (908–932) repeated the aimlessness of that of al-Mutawakkil, though on a somewhat reduced scale. But now the caliphal state could not afford a weak reign.

The breakup

This time there was no recovery for the state. Not only the army was socially rootless. Similarly, the state finances were commonly managed by wealthy entrepreneurs (often Shîʿîs) interested in making a private profit, rather than by an independent aristocracy or even by an entrenched self-perpetuating bureaucracy, with a vested interest in governmental stability. What was left of the old Sâsânian bureaucratic class was perhaps becoming more attached to local governors. Al-Muqtadir's court was wastefully extravagant; under these circumstances, the result was financial mismanagement, ending in chronic problems of fiscal supply and—when the soldiers' pay was consequently slow—of military indiscipline. By the end of al-Muqtadir's reign, the state was bankrupt. Simultaneously, the authority of Baghdad even in the nearer provinces was rapidly shrinking. On al-Muqtadir's death (at the unwilling hands of his best general, Mu'nis, driven to revolt for the sake of the caliphal state itself), what was left of the empire quickly fell apart.

Four caliphs ruled briefly between 932 and 945, each of them at the mercy of the military factions that had raised them to the throne. The most powerful general came to be given the title *amîr al-umarâ'*, commander-in-chief, and was granted an overruling power in the state; the caliph gave up any direct administrative role, retaining only ceremonial functions. But in any case the government at Baghdad, usurped as it was by the soldiery, soon ruled little more than the Iraq itself. The considerable territory which al-Muqtadir had inherited was being divided among military powers less responsible than those which now held the remoter western and eastern provinces. Here Shî'î forces were prevailing, less spectacular and also less ambitious than were the Ismâ'îlîs, but also, for a time, more prominent in imperial affairs.

Already by 897, Zaydî Shî'îs had established their rule in the Yemen. But this was a case apart, like the establishment of the Ismâ'îlîs in the Maghrib. Closer home, in 905 the Ḥamdânids, leaders of a Bedouin tribal bloc, had established themselves as governors of Mosul in the Jazîrah itself; before the end of al-Muqtadir's reign, they became effectively autonomous. They were Shî'îs, like many of the northern Bedouin at the time, evidently with Nuṣayrî leanings. But their main strength was their respected position as chieftains among pastoralists, whom they could not displease with impunity. From 944, a branch of the family was established at Aleppo. There they had to bear the main burden of the Muslim resistance to a renewed Byzantine military advance—almost the only non-Muslim attempt on the lands of the caliphate during this period of weakening in the central power. The Byzantines recovered Cilicia and much other territory just east of the Anatolian highlands, and were driving into Syria; *ghâzîs* volunteering for the sacred war came from afar to stave off disaster. Sayf-al-dawlah, the most famous of the Ḥamdânids, attracted poets and scholars to Aleppo: he patronized al-Mutanabbi' and al-Fârâbî. He was less successful in the war against Byzantium, in which he received little formal help from elsewhere, and could not save Antioch; but the poets praised his valour nonetheless, and for his place in their songs he received as much renown as if he had actually turned back the enemy.

By 928, in the lands southeast of the Caspian, the Ziyârids, military leaders, had become independent and were absorbing the governorships of 'Irâq 'Ajamî as well. Among their soldiers from Daylam, a small but rugged sub-Caspian highland territory, three brothers, of the Bûyid family (in Arabic, *Buwayhid*), rose to high captaincies and soon made themselves independent, with the help of Daylamî troops, at once of the Ziyârids and of the caliphs. By 934, they were in control of the greater part of western Iran though, like the Ḥamdânids, in ruling it they could not ignore the good pleasure of their men—professional soldiers, Daylamîs and latterly

Turks also. The Bûyids too were Shîʿîs, as were most Daylamîs (they had been converted largely by Shîʿî rebels using their mountains as base). The Bûyids were inclined to the Twelvers, though not exclusively; they gave official status in their territories to Shîʿî holy days.

Not having risen, like the Ṭâhirids or the Ṭûlûnids for instance, as regularly appointed governors but as condottieri who were filling a political vacuum, they had no special ties to the caliphs' government. Yet, like the Ḥamdânids, they made no attempt actually to replace the caliphs with other supreme figures: they merely nullified effectively their power and authority in whatever lands they could seize. They tried to carry on the caliphal administration however, though in a simplified form.

Egypt, retaken from the Ṭûlûnids in 906, was held for the central power through al-Muqtadir's reign, but in 937 the caliphal governor—a captain who had inherited from a state beyond Oxus the title 'Ikhshîd'—proved strong enough so that he could not be replaced. He proceeded to rule independently, controlling also much of Syria (and at first staving off the Byzantines with more success than later did Sayf-al-dawlah). His scions reigned fictively under the powerful protection of Kâfûr, originally a Negro slave-eunuch; only after his death could the Fâṭimids from Mahdiyyah realize their long-sought goal of occupying Egypt.

The partisans of the universal absolute monarchy had failed to build a viable power structure, having allowed the immense prestige of the caliphate to be frittered away generation by generation. Nor had the Sharʿîʿ 'ulamâ' been able to provide a stable political order, either in co-operation with the state under al-Ma'mûn and al-Muʿtaṣim or in the considerable independence of it which they enjoyed subsequently. But it was not merely the prestige of the caliphate that was dissipated, but that of a monarchical tradition which had begun long before Islam. It was the whole heritage of Irano-Semitic absolutism that was in question; it was neither effectively supported nor replaced.[4]

In 945, one of the Bûyid captains, whose brothers already controlled the western Iranian highlands above the Iraq, occupied Baghdad. Despite his Shîʿism, the Bûyid chief at Baghdad (Muʿizz-al-dawlah) took the title *amîr al-umarâ'*, commander-in-chief, and acknowledged the theoretical position of the 'Abbâsid caliphs, who maintained a local court with considerable local authority. But in fact the Iraq was now merely a province under the new Bûyid power. The caliphal state had ceased to exist as an actual independent empire.

[4] H. A. R. Gibb, in 'Government and Islam under the Early 'Abbasids: The Political Collapse of Islam', in *L'Elaboration de l'Islam* (Paris, 1961), pp. 115–27, suggests that the failure of the 'Abbâsî state to maintain itself so long as the Sâsânian was due to the lesser relative strength of the agrarian classes in the 'Abbâsî state, where the bureaucracy, army, and religious institution all developed in relative independence of the monarchy. I have rather followed this lead here. (The article also points to the remarkable prevalence of 'Alid-loyalist sentiment in this period.)

A Selective Bibliography for Further Reading

The following works are arranged by subject, corresponding in part, but not entirely, to the chapters in this work. I make no attempt at completeness, selecting largely according to where I have a comment to make. I have attempted only to point to works that form an effective starting point for those who would like to follow up a given field in more detail. For a number of more specialized topics, commented bibliography will be found at the appropriate place in the footnotes; this bibliography does not include all the works cited in the text. Readers should refer to the Sauvaget-Cahen bibliography (cited below) before beginning further reading.

Works of general reference

The Encyclopaedia of Islam, 2nd ed. (E. J. Brill, Leiden, 1954–66), of which the first two volumes and some following fascicles have appeared. Composed of articles contributed by leading Islamicists. *Each article includes a bibliography.* This is the basic work of reference on any subject connected with Islam or Islamicate civilization, especially in pre-Modern times. For articles dealing with religion and law in subjects not yet covered by the 2nd ed. see *The Shorter Encyclopaedia of Islam,* ed. Hamilton A. R. Gibb and J. H. Kramers (E. J. Brill, Leiden, 1953), which has brought up to date, especially in point of bibliography, selected articles from the first edition of the *Encyclopaedia of Islam* (Brill, 1913–38), in four volumes and a supplement, now largely out-dated but still to be referred to for articles not found in the second edition or in the *Shorter Encyclopaedia.*

Historical Atlas of the Muslim Peoples, ed. R. Roolvink (Harvard University Press, 1957). The only general historical atlas in the field; it has no index and practically no historical detail, and it wants revision and more maps of developments in the later pre-Modern periods. Harry W. Hazard, *Atlas of Islamic History* (Princeton University Press, 1951) is in fact primarily a study of the shifting power balance between Muslim and Christian powers in the general region of the Mediterranean, century by century; it does include some general information on political conditions in various areas in each century, but almost nothing east of Iran or in the farther north or south. A better atlas is promised in connection with the new edition of the *Encyclopaedia of Islam.* Useful maps may be found in G. LeStrange, *Lands of the Eastern Caliphate: Mesopotamia, Persia, and Central Asia from the Moslem Conquest to the Time of Timur* (Cambridge University Press, 1930), which also covers Anatolia; in the relevant articles in the *Encyclopaedia of Islam*; in E. de Zambaur, *Manuel de Généalogie et de Chronologie pour l'histoire de l'Islam* (H. Lafaire, Hanover, 1927, reprinted 1955), which contains exhaustive tables of rulers; and in some of the general secondary works noted below.

Clifford E. Bosworth, *The Islamic Dynasties: A Chronological and Genealogical Handbook* (Edinburgh University Press, 1967), 'Islamic Surveys, No. 5'. Contains brief notices of political events affecting the important Muslim dynasties from the western Mediterranean through the Indic region, and lists their rulers. Generally supersedes Stanley Lane-Poole, *The Mohammadan Dynasties* . . . (Constable, London, 1893; reprinted Paris, 1925), though the latter contains genealogical charts. E. de Zambaur, mentioned above, in spite of some needed corrections, remains primary.

Bibliographies

W. A. C. H. Dobson, ed., *A Select List of Books on the Civilizations of the Orient* (Oxford University Press, 1955). Useful for the general reader. The sections on Islamdom (and India) list the best books for English-speaking readers on most aspects of Islamicate civilization, including several translations.

Charles J. Adams, ed., *A Reader's Guide to the Great Religions* (The Free Press, New York, 1965). Very good chapter on Islam including recent developments.

Jean Sauvaget, *Introduction to the History of the Muslim East: A Bibliographical Guide*, revised by Claude Cahen (The University of California Press, 1965). Referred to as 'Sauvaget-Cahen'. The primary point of departure for the student of the subject, though it almost omits lands east of Persia, and in most cases gives more emphasis to political and social history. The French edition (Adrien-Maisonneuve, Paris, 1961), though not so recent, is yet useful.

J. D. Pearson, *Oriental and Asian Bibliography* (Crosby Lockwood, London, 1966). Not a bibliography in the usual sense, but usefully expands on some aspects of Sauvaget-Cahen.

Bernard Lewis, 'The Muslim World', in American Historical Association, *Guide to Historical Literature* (Macmillan, New York, 1961). Good introduction to pre-1450 period studies for the non-specialist historian. In the same volume, Roderic Davison, 'The Middle East since 1450', is weighted toward political interests. The pages on Islam under 'History of Religions' in the same volume are of little use.

D. Gustav Pfannmüler, *Handbuch der Islam-Literatur* (de Gruyter, Berlin, 1923). Though old, still useful on religious matters; gives contents and conclusions of the writers listed. To be consulted for the history of nineteenth and early twentieth century Western scholarship on any given point.

J. D. Pearson, *Index Islamicus*, 1906–1955 (Heffer, Cambridge, 1958). An exhaustive, uncommentated listing of articles in European languages on Islamic subjects in periodicals and other collective publications, by subject, with cross-references, for tracking down details. Supplementary volumes appear regularly.

Denis Sinor, *Introduction à l'étude de l'Eurasie centrale* (Harrassowitz, Wiesbaden, 1963). Detailed annotated bibliography, linguistic and historical, on the Altaic and Finno-Ugrian peoples, especially Turkic (but not on such major bodies, distant from the Steppe, as Ottomans and Hungarians).

Journals

FOR THE GENERAL READER

The Middle East Journal, published by the Middle East Institute, Washington, D.C. Concentrates on modern matters, *including a review of current events* from Morocco to Bengal; also has reviews and notices of books and periodical articles, and a *list of scholarly journals.*

The Muslim World, published by the Hartford Seminary Foundation, Hartford, Conn. Primarily designed to give Christian missionaries informed insight into Islam, but its range of interest is very wide; also has reviews and notices.

The Islamic Quarterly, published by the Islamic Cultural Centre, London. Edited by Muslim missionaries for English-speakers, it carries articles by Muslims and by non-Muslim Islamists, sometimes of high quality.

FOR CURRENT SCHOLARSHIP

Revue des études islamiques, including its *Abstracta Islamica* which reviews both books and articles, including those in non-Western languages.

Bulletin of the School of Oriental and African Studies (University of London), which has a very high proportion of important Islamicate historical material.

Studia Islamica, appearing irregularly with high-quality studies, in French and English.

Arabica, very good material in the field of Arabic studies.

For other excellent journals, see Sauvaget-Cahen, chapter 10.

On the historical development of the Islamicate lands generally:

Felix M. Pareja-Casañas, *Islamologia* (Orbis Catholicus, Rome, 1951; editions in Spanish and in Italian). A collection of information on most aspects of Islamicate history and culture, with extensive but unannotated bibliographies.

Bertold Spuler, *Geschichte der Islamischen Länder,* 3 vols. (Brill, Leiden, 1952–59; in the series *Handbuch der Orientalistik,* ed. Bertold Spuler). The first two volumes translated into English by Frank R. C. Bagley (and corrected) as *The Muslim World: A Historical Survey*, Parts I and II (E. J. Brill, Leiden, 1960). A summary of some political events with bibliography.

Carl Brockelmann, *Geschichte der Islamischen Völker und Staaten* (Munich, 1939). Translated into English by Joel Carmichael and Moshe Perlmann, *History of the Islamic Peoples* (Routledge and Kegan Paul, London, 1949). A densely written political narrative including some cultural history; largely on the Ottoman Empire; ignores the Islamicate peoples east of Persia.

Sydney N. Fisher, *The Middle East, a History* (Knopf, New York, 1959). Chiefly on the Ottoman Empire and its successor states; readable but not fully reliable.

V. V. Barthold, *Mussulman Culture* [1918], badly translated from Russian by Shahid Suhrawardy (The University of Calcutta, 1934). A brief and brilliant historical review from a Central Eurasian standpoint.

F. August Müller, *Der Islam im Morgen- und Abendland*, 2 vols. (Berlin, 1885–87). A narrative, carrying the story through the fifteenth century; it is now superseded by more recent studies, except that its description of ʻAbbâsid period developments is still useful.

On the Islamic religion generally:

Hamilton A. R. Gibb, *Mohammedanism, an Historical Survey* [1949], 2nd ed. (Oxford University Press, 1953). Outstanding brief study of the religion as it was formed in the earlier generations and evolved later.

Ignaz Goldziher, *Volesungen über den Islam* (Carl Winter, Heidelberg, 1910); French translation by Félix Arin as *Le Dogme et la loi de l'Islam* (Paul Geuthner, Paris, 1920). Equally brilliant with Gibb (and covering the same material), and more detailed, with useful notes; but somewhat out of date.

Kenneth Morgan, ed., *Islam—the Straight Path: Islam Interpreted by Muslims* (Ronald Press, New York, 1958). Prominent Muslim theologians and scholars acquainted with Western intellectual life interpret, for Westerners, Islam as they see it in their several parts of the world. Repetitive and often superficial.

Thomas Arnold, *The Preaching of Islam*, 2nd ed. (Constable, London, 1913); the edition of 1896 is much less full. Primarily a study of the methods used for spreading the Muslim faith, it is now rather out of date; but at least it chronicles the expansion of Islam from the beginning through the nineteenth century in all parts of the world.

Kenneth Cragg, *The Call of the Minaret* (Oxford University Press, 1956). The first half is a sensitive interpretation of the Muslim faith by a Christian missionary with true respect for Islam; the latter half discusses the task of the Christian mission among Muslims as he sees it.

General works on Islamicate culture under the High Caliphate:

Bernard Lewis, *The Arabs in History* [1950], 3rd ed. (Hutchinson's University Library, London, 1956). A brief and incisive historical survey of social and political history, especially before 1000 CE; since in this period Arabic and Islamic history largely coincided, in chapters 2–8 it covers Islamic society as a whole.

Philip K. Hitti, *History of the Arabs* [1937], 8th ed. (Macmillan, London and New York, 1964). Lengthier than Lewis, but undependable in its guiding conceptions and in its emphases. Far more fair-minded than Muir, cited below. The work may best be used for some detailed facts on pre-Islamic Arabia and on political developments up to about the year 750 CE.

Maurice Gaudefroy-Demombynes (and Sergei F. Platonov), *Le Monde musulman et byzantin jusqu'aux Croisades* (Boccard, Paris, 1931); in *Histoire du Monde*, ed. E. Cavaignac, vol. VIII. Depicts the changing political institutions more than the course of events, and is mostly superseded now by

Edouard Perroy, ed., *Le Moyen Age; l'expansion de l'orient et la naissance de la civilisation occidentale* (Presses universitaires de France, Paris, 1955); in *Histoire générale des civilisations*, ed. M. Crouzet, vol. III. Includes the early Ottoman period, and remarks some important social and economic changes.

Thomas Arnold and Alfred Guillaume, eds., *The Legacy of Islam* (Oxford University Press, 1931; and reprs.). Surveys aspects of Islamic cultural developments in the first four to five centuries, mainly from the point of view of their legacy to later European developments.

Gustave E. von Grunebaum, *Medieval Islam* [1946], 2nd ed. (University of Chicago Press, 1953). Traces the outcome, in the vicissitudes of history, of the world view initiated with Islam. Primarily on the High Caliphal period, but brings in some later material without special notice.

Gustave E. von Grunebaum, *Islam: Essays in the Nature and Growth of a Cultural Tradition* [1955], 2nd ed. (Routledge and Kegan Paul, London, 1961). A major supplement to the above.

Alfred von Kremer, *Culturgeschichte des Orients unter den Chalifen*, 2 vols. (W. Braunmüller, Vienna, 1875–77). Old but interesting. Partial translation by S. Khuda-Bukhsh as *The Orient under the Caliphs* (University of Calcutta, 1920).

Eric Schroeder, *Muhammad's People: A Tale by Anthology* (Bond Wheelwright Co., Portland, Maine, 1955). A beautiful sequence of translations from Arabic, pieced together to tell the story of the Muslims to about

1000 CE. A bit romanced and undifferentiated, it reflects traditional judgments (e.g. on Umayyads, Mu'tazilîs) subject to revision.

On some 'non-Arabic' pre-Islamic influences affecting Islam and Islamicate civilization:

Jörg Kraemer, *Das Problem der islamischen Kulturgeschichte* (Niemeyer, Tübingen, 1959). The booklet itself is a general essay, but its notes provide an introduction to the studies (mostly scattered in articles) on the transition from various pre-Islamic cultures into Islamicate culture, especially from Hellenistic.

Tor Andrae, *Der Ursprung des Islams und das Christentum* (Kyrkohistorisk årsskrift, Vols. 23–25, Uppsala and Stockholm, 1926). Later studies have cast doubt on such points as the relation of Christian sermons to the Qur'ânic sûrahs.

Richard Bell, *The Origin of Islam in Its Christian Environment* (Macmillan, London, 1926). On Christian influences on Muḥammad, stressing Muḥammad's independence.

Abraham Geiger, *Was hat Mohammed aus dem Judenthume aufgenommen?* [1833]; translated into English by F. M. Young, *Judaism and Islam* (U.D.C.S.P.C.K., Madras, 1898). Only partially superseded by

Abraham I. Katsh, *Judaism in Islam* (New York University Press, 1954). Studies of the Jewish origin of Qur'ânic material. Unfortunately, two curious studies of Jewish influence on Muḥammad are based on unwarranted assumptions: Charles C. Torrey, *The Jewish Foundation of Islam* (Jewish Institute of Religion, New York, 1933); and Hanna Zakarias, *De Moïse à Mohammed* (Minard, Paris, 1955).

On Muḥammad's life and times:

Frants P. W. Buhl, *Muhammeds Liv* [1903]; translated by Hans H. Schaeder, *Das Leben Muhammeds* (Quelle und Meher, Leipzig, 1930). Still a sound, full-scale narrative biography.

Tor Andrae, *Mohammed, sein Leben und sein Glaube* (Vandenhoeck und Ruprecht, Göttingen, 1932). English translation by Theophil Menzel, *Mohammed, the Man and His Faith* (George Allen and Unwin, London, 1936). Brief, masterly interpretation of the more inward side of Muḥammad's life.

William Montgomery Watt, *Muhammad at Mecca* and *Muhammad at Medina* (Oxford University Press, 1953 and 1956). A detailed study, bringing out the social and political implications of Muḥammad's work and statesmanship. Modifies Buhl's conclusions and complements Andrae.

Wm. M. Watt, *Muhammad: Prophet and Statesman* (Oxford University Press, 1961). A brief digest of the above.

Régis Blachère, *Le Problème de Mahomet, Essai de biographie critique du fondateur de l'Islam* (Presses universitaires de France, Paris, 1952). Stresses how much we still do not know.

ibn Isḥâq, *Life of Muḥammad*, translated by Alfred Guillaume (Oxford University Press, 1955); ibn Hishâm's additions have been placed awkwardly at the rear. The earliest extant biography, generally acknowledged by Muslims as authoritative.

Leone Caetani, *Annali dell'Islam*, 10 vols. in 12 (U. Hoepli, Milan and Rome, 1905–1926). The first forty years after the Hijrah are examined in detail but not always profoundly, with the chief sources translated. Caetani's evaluations are not always sound.

Translations of the Qur'ân into English:

The best translation for overall effect in continuous, careful reading is probably Arthur J. Arberry, *The Koran Interpreted*, 2 vols. (George Allen and Unwin, London, 1955). It makes use of archaic language which sometimes miscarries. Richard Bell, *The Qur'ân*, 2 vols. (T. and T. Clark, Edinburgh, 1937), is more exact but not designed for continuous reading and is sometimes marred by tendentious interpretations; the traditional order of verses is rearranged. N. J. Dawood, *The Koran* (Penguin Books, 1956) is perhaps the most readable translation but is very free and all too often arbitrary in its renderings. Mohammed M. Pickthall, *The Meaning of the Glorious Koran* [1930] (now in Mentor paperback) is best avoided because of its inept archaizing and its dubious modernizing interpretations.

Probably the best alternative to Arberry remains Edward H. Palmer, *The Koran* [1880] (now in World's Classics, Oxford University Press). It is less readable than Dawood but much more accurate. Still less readable than Dawood, but also more accurate, is John M. Rodwell, *The Koran* [1861] (now in Everyman's edition); like Bell's translation, Rodwell's has the verses rearranged. There are also several English translations by modern Indian Muslims, in which the slant of a particular brand of Islam is often visible. Abdullah Yusuf 'Ali, *The Holy Qur'ân* (Muhammad Ashraf, Lahore, 1938) is not easily disengaged from its modernizing commentary. Muhammad 'Ali, *The Holy Qur'ān*, 4th ed. (Aḥmadiyyah Press, Lahore, 1951) is unusually precise, and his Aḥmadî doctrine is chiefly, but not entirely, confined to the footnotes. Finally, the translation of George Sale (1734) (Wisdom of the East series) was for a century and a half the standard English version; it is a sound rendering, from the point of view of the Sunnî tradition, but heavy, and interwoven with the traditional Sunnî exegesis—which is an advantage if that is what one wants. Its footnotes summarize the most famous Sunnî commentaries.

Régis Blachère, *Le Coran; traduction selon un essai de reclassement des sourates*, 2 vols. (G. P. Maisonneuve, Paris, 1947–50) is a more comprehensive and judicious presentation of the Qur'ân as known to early Islam than anything in English; Vol. I (1947) is a historical introduction, a far sounder guide to the student than Richard Bell's *Introduction to the Qur'ân* (Edinburgh University Press, 1953), which is important but highly conjectural. Blachère's *Introduction au Coran* has been reworked for independent printing (1959) and his translation, *Le Coran*, has been reduced from two volumes to one, retaining the more essential notes (1957).

On the early Caliphate and through Marwânî times:

There is still no serious modern account of the early Arab conquests, in spite of one or two recently published works. For Syria, Egypt, and westward, see *The Cambridge Medieval History*, Vol. II, Chapters XI and XII, written by Carl H. Becker. For Transoxania, see Hamilton A. R. Gibb, *The Arab Conquests in Central Asia* (Royal Asiatic Socety, London, 1923).

Julius Wellhausen, *Prolegomena zur ältesten Geschichte des Islams*, in *Skizzen und Vorarbeiten*, VI (G. Reimer, Berlin, 1899), and *Das arabische Reich und sein Sturz* (G. Reimer, Berlin, 1902), the latter translated by Margaret Weir, *The Arab Kingdom and Its Fall* (University of Calcutta, 1927, and repr. Khayat's, Beirut, 1963). Still the standard account.

Leone Caetani, *Annali dell'Islam* (see above) is useful for the period before Mu'âwiyah.

Julius Wellhausen, *Die religiös-politischen Oppositionsparteien im alten Islam* (Weidmann, Berlin, 1901). Still basic on the political history of the early Shî'îs and Khârijîs.

Henri Lammens published a number of detailed studies of the Umayyad period; they are noted by Sauvaget-Cahen. Lammens sometimes reached too far, but his work is indispensable; that of Francesco Gabrieli (noted also in Sauvaget-Cahen) is surer but more pedestrian.

Wm. Muir, *The Caliphate, Its Rise, Decline, and Fall*, revised by T. H. Weir (J. Grant, Edinburgh, 1915). Follows the traditional Arab accounts, with revisions after Wellhausen and others; has a nineteenth-century Christian bias.

The studies of Hamilton A. R. Gibb on this as on other periods are important. Some are collected in *Studies on the Civilization of Islam*, Stanford J. Shaw and William R. Polk, eds. (Beacon Press, Boston, 1962).

Aḥmad al-Balâdhurî, *Kitâb futûḥ al-buldân*, translated as *The Origins of the Islamic State*, Vol. I by Philip K. Hitti (Columbia University, New York, 1916), Vol. II by Francis C. Murgotten (Columbia University, New York, 1924). The work deals with the campaigns of conquest and with the political and financial dispositions of each territory which came under Muslim rule. The translations are slightly abridged or expurgated.

On political and administrative developments under the High Caliphate:

William Muir, *The Caliphate*, revised by T. H. Weir (see above), is available for the earlier part of this period also.

Dominique Sourdel, *Le vizirat ʿabbâside de* 749 *à* 936, 2 vols. (Institut français de Damas, 1959–60). Sticks close to its subject, but illuminates the development of the administration. Extensive bibliography on the period and commentary on the sources.

Thomas Arnold, *The Caliphate* (Oxford University Press, 1924). Now no longer very useful, but readably made the point that the Caliphate was not a Muslim counterpart to the Papacy. On the Caliphate as an institution, see M. Khadduri and H. J. Liebesney, *Law in the Middle East*, Vol. I (Middle East Institute, Washington, D.C., 1955), Chapter 1, written by H. A. R. Gibb.

Emile Tyan, *Institutions du droit public musulman*, 2 vols. (Recueil Sirey, Paris, 1954–57). Describes the governmental institutions mainly theoretically; must be used with care.

Harold Bowen, *The Life and Times of ʿAli b. ʿIsa, the Good Vizier* (Cambridge University Press, 1928). A close study of the vizier's functions in the early tenth century CE.

Miskawayh and others [Portion of the 'Experiences of the Nations'], translated by H. S. Amedroz and D. S. Margoliouth as *The Eclipse of the Abbasid Caliphate* (B. Blackwell, Oxford, 1920–21). Volumes 4 to 7 give the translation of this and other Arabic historians of the tenth–eleventh centuries.

On general aspects of social and cultural life under the High Caliphate:

Adam Mez, *Die Renaissance des Islams* (C. Winter, Heidelberg, 1922); translated by S. Khuda-Bukhsh and D. S. Margoliouth, *The Renaissance of Islam* (Luzac, London, 1937). A bad translation of a work good for detail on tenth century Islamdom and for colour, but weak in its generalizations and in its proportions, and biased by nineteenth century prejudices.

Bertold Spuler, *Iran in früh-islamischer Zeit: Politik, Kultur, Verwaltung, und öffentliches Leben . . .* 633 *bis* 1055 (Franz Steiner, Wiesbaden, 1952). A great deal of information without deep insight.

Nabia Abbott, *Two Queens of Baghdâd: Mother and Wife of Hârûn al-Rashîd* (University of Chicago Press, 1946). A careful compendium.

H. G. Farmer, *A History of Arabian Music to the Thirteenth Century* (Luzac,

London, 1929). By 'Arabian' he means 'Arabic' and even 'Islamicate'. Largely on social and literary aspects.

E. Lévi-Provencal, *Histoire de l'Espagne Musulmane*, 3 vols. (Maisonneuve, Paris, 1950–53). The definitive study of political history and culture there to the eleventh century CE.

Antoine Fattal, *Le statut légal des non-musulmans en pays d'Islam* (Imprimerie catholique, Beirut, 1958). Comprehensive; based mainly on theoretical sources, though includes some historical fact, especially in the Arab countries; stops before the later Middle Ages.

Solomon D. Goitein, *Studies in Islamic History and Institutions* (E. J. Brill, Leiden, 1966). An uneven collection of articles, of which several survey some social and economic developments.

Solomon D. Goitein, *Jews and Arabs, Their Contacts through the Ages* (Schocken, New York, 1955). A popular review of their contacts throughout history.

Walter J. Fischel, *Jews in the Economic and Political Life of Mediaeval Islam* (Royal Asiatic Society, London, 1937). Studies five instances where Jews became prominent (three in the High Caliphal period), bringing out the social implications of their careers.

On classical Arabic literature:

Hamilton A. R. Gibb, *Arabic Literature: An Introduction* (Oxford University Press, 1926, 2nd ed., 1963). A masterly brief survey of the pre-Modern literature, noting good translations.

Reynold A. Nicholson, *A Literary History of the Arabs* (T. Fisher Unwin, London, 1907; Cambridge University Press, 1930 and later). An older but lengthier survey than Gibb's with short translations; mainly useful for the earlier centuries.

Gustav E. von Grunebaum, *Die Wirklichkeitweite der früarabischen Dichtung; eine literaturwissenschaftliche Untersuchung* (Vienna, 1937). Suggests the limits and consistency of the worldview of pre-Islamic Arabic poetry.

Charles J. Lyall, *Translations of Ancient Arabian Poetry* (Williams and Norgate, London, 1885; repr. 1930). Chiefly pre-Islamic poetry, with an excellent introduction and notes; his translations are at least as faithful as any others.

Arthur J. Arberry, *The Seven Odes: The First Chapter in Arabic Literature* (George Allen and Unwin, London, 1957). Modern, almost imagistic translations of the seven celebrated pre-Islamic 'odes'.

'Amr al-Jâḥiẓ (Gâḥiẓ), *Le livre des avares*, translated by Charles Pellat (G.P. Maisonneuve, Paris, 1951). A sample of the best work of this entertaining writer.

Gustave von Grunebaum, *A Tenth-Century Document of Arabic Literary Theory and Criticism: The Sections on Poetry of al-Bâqillânî's I'jâz al-Qur'ân* (University of Chicago Press, 1950). An influential theologian compares the Qur'ân and Imru'al-Qays in point of verbal beauty.

Ibn-Kutaibah, *Introduction au livre de la poésie et des poètes*, translated by Maurice Gaudefroy-Demombynes (Société . . . Les Belles Lettres, Paris, 1947). A ninth century CE Arab literary critic's remarks.

A number of anthologies exist. Valuable are Reynold A. Nicholson, *Translations of Eastern Poetry and Prose* (Cambridge University Press, 1922); representative writings in Arabic and also Persian. Arthur J. Arberry, *Aspects of Islamic Civilization as Depicted in the Original Texts* (George Allen and Unwin, London, 1964); also Persian as well as Arabic examples. Eric Schroeder, *Muhammad's People; a tale by anthology* (see above).

On the social outlook of Sharî'ah-minded Islam:

Noel J. Coulson, *A History of Islamic Law* (Edinburgh University Press, 1964), 'Islamic Surveys No. 2'. An excellent brief introduction to the Sharî'ah and to modern developments.

Joseph Schacht, *An Introduction to Islamic Law* (Oxford University Press, 1964). An alternative to the above.

Maurice Gaudefroy-Demombynes, *Muslim Institutions*, translated by John MacGregor (George Allen and Unwin, London, 1950). Suggests some social implications of Shar'î principles, and describes in its chapter on The Cult, the ṣalât, the Ḥajj, and other Muslim rites.

Duncan B. Macdonald, *Development of Muslim Theology, Jurisprudence, and Constitutional Theory* (Scribner's, New York, 1903; repr. Khayats', Beirut, 1965). Somewhat outdated but still illuminating.

Louis Gardet, *La cité musulmane, vie sociale et politique* (Vrin, Paris, 1954). The pre-Modern Sharî'ah-minded social ideal studied with insight; written from a Catholic viewpoint, with an eye to implications for modern Muslim peoples, especially the Arabs.

Alfred Guillaume, *The Traditions of Islam* (Oxford University Press, 1924). Not on the traditions, in the normal English sense, but on the ḥadîth reports and the system of their criticism; based on

Ignaz Goldziher, *Muhammedanische Studien*, Vol. II (Niemeyer, Halle, 1890); edited and translated by C. R. Barber and S. M. Stern as *Muslim Studies*, Vol. II (Aldine, Chicago, 1966). The classic study of the growth of the ḥadîth.

Joseph Schacht, *The Origins of Muhammadan Jurisprudence* (Oxford University Press, 1950). On the development of *fiqh* and of such ḥadîth as were used therein, showing the occasion for and the effects of the disputes over *ra'y*, *qiyâs*, etc.

Majid Khadduri and Herbert J. Liebesny, eds., *Law in the Middle East*, Vol. I, 'Origin and Development of Islamic Law' (Middle East Institute, Washington, 1955). The first four chapters are magnificent presentations of the formation of the Sharî'ah and of its basic theories; the remainder discusses the provisions of most aspects of the law that would come before the courts, with special reference to the Arab lands and the Ottoman empire.

Asaf A. A. Fyzee, *Outlines of Muhammadan Law* (Oxford University Press, 1949) gives more details of the law as applied in modern India.

'Alî al-Mâwardî, *Les statuts gouvernementaux*, translated by E. Fagnan (Jourdain, Algiers, 1915). Outlines the classical Shar'î tradition, modified with regard to the problems posed by the downfall of the caliph's power in the tenth century.

al-Bukhârî, *al-Ṣaḥîḥ'* translated by O. Houdas and William Marçais as *Les Traditions islamiques*, 4 vols. (Imprimerie nationale, Paris, 1903–14). The prime canonical collection of ḥadîth reports.

al-Muḥaqqiq al-Ḥillî, *Sharâ'i' al-Islâm*, translated by A. Querry as *Droit musulman*, 2 vols. (Imprimerie nationale, Paris, 1871–72). The favourite book of fiqh among Twelver Shî'î Muslims.

On devotional life in High Caliphal times and after:

Duncan B. Macdonald, *The Religious Attitude and Life in Islam* (University of Chicago Press, 1909; repr. Khayat's, Beirut, 1965). Still a good introduction.

Reynold A. Nicholson, *The Mystics of Islam* (George Bell, London, 1914; repr. by Routledge and Kegan Paul, London, 1963). The most elementary of his several good studies. A good introduction, alternatively with

Arthur J. Arberry, *Sufism, an Account of the Mystics of Islam* (George Allen and Unwin, London, 1950). Less perceptive than the above, but gives many translated excerpts.

G. C. Anawati and Louis Gardet, *Mystique musulmane: aspects et tendances, expériences et techniques* (Vrin, Paris, 1961). An insightful survey of earlier Ṣûfism, with an analysis of the classical practices from a Catholic viewpoint willing to see in them not only 'natural' but even 'supernatural' mysticism.

Louis Massignon, *Essai sur les origines du lexique technique de la mystique musulmane* [1922], 2nd ed. (Vrin, Paris, 1954). An intensive study of the development of Ṣûfî thought within the Muslim tradition.

Louis Massignon, *La passion d'al-Hosayn ibn Mansour al-Hallaj, martyr mystique de l'Islam* (P. Geuthner, Paris, 1922). Studies in detail the most famous case where Ṣûfism impinged on the public consciousness, and all the ramifications of it; a magnificently subtle study.

Margaret Smith, *Readings from the Mystics of Islam* (Luzac, London, 1950). Very brief selections translated. Her other, more extensive studies are also sound.

'Alî Ṭabarî, *The Book of Religion and Empire,* translated by A. Mingana (Manchester University Press, 1922). By a Christian convert to Islam, this work (patronized by a caliph) defends Islam against Christian attacks; presents Muslim piety on a relatively high level.

Dwight M. Donaldson, *The Shi'ite Religion, a History of Islam in Persia and Iraḳ* (Luzac, London, 1933). A quite uncritical presentation of later orthodox Imâmî views about the early Shî'ah, which does bring out much of the feeling in its legends and doctrines. It can be corrected in part by Marshall G. S. Hodgson, 'How Did the Early Shî'a Become Sectarian', *Journal of the American Oriental Society,* Vol. 75 (1955), pp. 1–13.

On philosophy, science, and theology in High Caliphal times and after:

Henri Corbin, *Histoire de la philosophie islamique,* Vol. I, with others to follow (Gallimard, Paris, 1964). The best brief introduction to the whole field; volume one ends with the twelfth century CE. The work may be usefully compared with

R. Walzer, chapter on 'Islamic Philosophy' in *History of Philosophy Eastern and Western,* ed. Sarvapelli Radhakrishnan, Vol. II, pp. 120–148 (George Allen and Unwin, London, 1953). Close-packed, judicious, illuminating introduction to selected aspects.

Muhsin Mahdi, ed. (with R. Lerner), *Medieval Political Philosophy* (Free Press, Glencoe, Ill., 1963). The selections from Muslim and Jewish philosophers are more enlightening on general philosophy than the title would suggest, but omit the later Middle Period philosophers. (The selection of Muslim writers does not fully correspond with that of Christian writers.)

Aldo Mieli, *La Science arabe et son role dans l'évolution scientifique mondiale* (E. J. Brill, Leiden, 1938). Concentrates on that portion which led into West-European Medieval science, but is quite comprehensive in scope; it is an alternate to the relevant sections in George Sarton's monumental multi-volume *Introduction to the History of Science.*

Paul Kraus, *Jâbir ibn Ḥayyân, Contribution à l'histoire des idées scientifiques dans l'Islam,* in *Mémoires de l'Institut d'Egypte* (Vol. XLIV, 1933, and XLV, 1942); a study of the most important early Islamicate chemical corpus.

Fazlur-Rahman, *Prophecy in Islam* (George Allen and Unwin, London, 1958). A keen analysis of the Faylasûfs' interpretation of Prophecy.

A. J. Wensinck, *The Muslim Creed, Its Genesis and Historical Development* (Cambridge University Press, 1932). A study of the development of Muslim theology through the earlier periods; to be read along with

W. Montgomery Watt, *Free Will and Predestination in Early Islam* (Luzac, London, 1948). Probes into the motive forces in Muslim theological development, but is not so comprehensive as Wensinck.

Louis Gardet and M.M. Anawati, *Introduction à la théologie musulmane, essai de théologie comparée* (Vrin, Paris, 1948). A profound Catholic analysis, restricted chiefly to the earlier period, and to some later Arabs.

W. Montgomery Watt, *Islamic Philosophy and Theology* (Edinburgh University Press, 1962), 'Islamic Surveys No. 1'. A brief introduction for the beginning student.

Richard J. McCarthy, *The Theology of al-Ash'arî* (Imprimerie Catholique, Beirut, 1953). Translations of two texts, notes, bibliographies; basic material on this crucial theologian.

On Islamicate intellectual attitudes in the Middle Periods (supplementing section on philosophy above):

Soheil M. Afnan, *Avicenna, His Life and Works* (George Allen and Unwin, London, 1958). A competent study, with bibliography of the many works which have made Avicenna much better known than other Faylasûfs; note especially the studies and translations of Miss A.-M. Goichon.

Juveynî, Imâm al-Ḥaramayn, *al-Irshâd* (*el-Irchad*), ed. and translated into French by J.-D. Luciani (Ernest Leroux, Paris, 1938), a complete and detailed treatise of kalâm by Ghazâli's master.

Wm. Montgomery Watt, *The Faith and Practice of al-Ghazâlî* (George Allen and Unwin, London, 1953), translation (with good short introduction) of two treatises by Ghazâli, the first being his so-called spiritual autobiography (*Munqidh min al-ḍalâl*), the second an introduction to the practices of the devout life.

G.-H. Bousquet, *Ghazâlî: Vivification des sciences de la foi* (*Iḥyâ 'ulûm al-dîn*) (M. Besson, Paris, 1955). A summary of Ghazâlî's great masterpiece.

A. J. Wensinck, *La Pensée de Ghazzālī* (Adrien-Maisonneuve, Paris, 1940), a study of Ghazâlî's spiritual position, with special emphasis on his Ṣûfism; perhaps it underestimates what was genuinely Muslim in the best of Ghazâlî.

Averroes [Ibn-Rushd], *Tahâfut al-tahâfut* (*The Incoherence of the Incoherence*), translated by Simon van den Bergh, 2 vols. (Luzac, London, 1954), an excellent translation of Ibn-Rushd's response to Ghazâlî, which also includes much of Ghazâlî's own work.

Henry Corbin, *Suhrawardî d'Alep* (*d.* 1191) *fondateur de la doctrine illuminative* (*ishrâqî*) (Publications de la Société des études iraniennes, No. 16, Maisonneuve, Paris, 1939), a pamphlet by the man who has done more than any other, in his subsequent work, to illuminate the later Ṣûfî thought of Iran; notably *l'Imagination créatice dans le soufisme d'Ibn-'Arabi* (Flammarion, Paris, 1958) and the most easily read *Terre céleste et corps de résurrection, de l'Iran Mazdéen a l'Iran Shî'îte* (Buchet/Chastel, Corrêa, 1960).

Muḥyi-d-dîn Ibn-'Arabî, *La Sagesse des Prophètes* (*Fuçuç al-Ḥikam*), translated by Titus Burckhardt (Albin Michel, Paris, 1955), an abridged translation of one of the two most important works of Ibn-al-'Arabî.

A. E. Affiffi, *The Mystical Philosophy of Muḥyid-Dîn-ibnul-'Arabî* (Cambridge University Press, 1939), a metaphysical study of Ibn-al-'Arabî.

Reynold Nicholson, *The Idea of Personality in Ṣûfism* (Cambridge University Press, 1923; repr. Muhammad Ashraf, Lahore, 1964). A careful study especially of later Ṣûfî thinkers on this point.

Abû-Bakr Ibn-Ṭufayl, *The History of Ḥayy ibn-Yaqẓân*, translated from Arabic by Simon Ockley and A. S. Fulton (Stokes, New York, 1929). A rendering of Ibn-Ṭufayl's main work, minus its important preface.

H. S. Nyberg, *Kleinere Schriften des Ibn-al-'Arabî* (E. J. Brill, Leyden, 1919), a masterpiece of scholarly elucidation.

Muhsin Mahdi, *Ibn Khaldun's Philosophy of History* (George Allen and Unwin, London, 1957). The best introduction to this important philosopher.

Glossary of Selected Terms and Names

Listings in the Glossary are technical terms frequently appearing in the text. Definitions and explanations given in the Introduction or elsewhere of other terms, including geographical designations, may be located by consulting the Index.

adab: the polite, literary culture of a cultivated individual; in modern Arabic, 'literature'. A cultivated individual is an *adîb* (pl. *udabâ'*).

Ahl al-Ḥadîth: *see* Ḥadîth folk.

ahl al-kitâb: people of the Book, the Bible; that is, Jews and Christians, though other groups sometimes were included.

'Alid: a descendant of 'Alî, cousin and son-in-law of the Prophet; the Shî'îs believed certain 'Alids should be *imâms* (q.v.). 'Alî's first wife was Fâṭimah, the Prophet's daughter, 'Alî's descendants by her (the only descendants of the Prophet) were in particular called Fâṭimids. Descendants of her son Ḥasan are often called *sharîfs*: those of her son Ḥusayn are often called *sayyids*.

'âlim (pl. *'ulamâ'*): a learnèd man, in particular one learnèd in Islamic legal and religious studies.

Allâh: an Arabic (both Muslim and Christian) name for the One God.

amîr (also *emir*): a general or other military commander; after classical 'Abbâsî times many independent rulers held this title; sometimes assigned to members of the ruler's family. *Amîr al-mu'minîn*, commander of the faithful, was the proper title of the caliph; *amîr al-umarâ'* meant supreme commander, generalissimo: used especially of the military ruler during the decline of the High Caliphate.

Anṣâr: 'helpers' of Muḥammad at Medina; name given collectively to the Muslims native to Medina in distinction from the *Muhâjirûn* (q.v.), those who came with Muḥammad from Mecca.

'aql: 'reason', 'reasoning'; in Islamic law systematic reasoning not limited to *qiyâs* (q.v.).

bâṭin: the inner, hidden, or esoteric meaning of a text; hence Bâṭinîs, Bâṭiniyyah, the groups associated with such ideas. Most of these groups were Shî'îs, particularly Ismâ'îlîs.

Dâr al-Islâm: lands under Muslim rule; later, any lands in which Muslim institutions were maintained, whether or not under Muslim rule. It is converse of *Dâr al-Ḥarb*, i.e., lands under non-Muslim rule.

dhimmî (also *zimmî*): a 'protected subject', follower of a religion tolerated by Islam, within Muslim ruled territory, cf. *ahl al-kitâb*. The protection is called *dhimmah*.

dîwân (also *dîvân*): a public financial register; or a government bureau, or council; or its chief officer; also the collected works of a poet.

Falsafah: philosophy, including natural and moral science, as expounded, on the basis of the Greek tradition, in the Islamicate society. A *Faylasûf* (pl. *Falâsifah*) is an exponent of *Falsafah*.

farḍ 'ayn: religious duty such as ritual worship, fasting, etc., incumbent upon every individual Muslim excepting only those incapacitated from so doing; *farḍ kifayyah* is collective duty such as *jihâd* (q.v.) incumbent upon the Muslim community as a whole, but so long as some are fulfilling it, others may be excused.

fatwà: the decision of a *muftî* (q.v.).

fiqh: jurisprudence; the discipline of elucidating the *Sharî'ah* (q.v.); also the resultant body of rules. A *faqîh* (pl. *fuqahâ*) is an exponent of *fiqh*.

ghâzî: a warrior for the faith carrying out *jihâd* (q.v.); sometimes applied to organized bands of frontier raiders.

ḥadîth (pl. *aḥâdîth*; also *ḥadîs*): a report of a saying or action of the Prophet, or such reports collectively. Sometimes this is translated 'tradition', as having been transmitted from reporter to reporter; it has nothing to do with tradition in the ordinary sense of anonymously inherited group lore.

Ḥadîth folk (Ahl al-Ḥadîth): people of the *ḥadîth*, that is, those who concentrated on *ḥadîth* reports as the chief form of learning and source of authority; a particular type of piety was associated with them among the Jamâ'î-Sunnîs.

ḥajj: the annual pilgrimage to Mecca in the month of Dhû-l-Ḥijjah, the last month of the Muslim year; required of every Muslim once in his life if possible.

Ḥanafî: referring to the Sunnî legal *madhhab* (q.v.) ascribed to Abû-Ḥanîfah (699–767 CE).

Ḥanbalî: referring to the Sunnî legal *madhhab* (q.v.) ascribed to Aḥmad ibn-Ḥanbal (780–855 CE).

Hâshimids: members of the family to which Muḥammad belonged; its chief branches were the 'Alids and the 'Abbâsids. Hâshimî usually refers to that family, but may refer to the Shî'î group which regarded the imâmate as passing through Abû-Hâshim, grandson of 'Alî.

hijrah: the flight of Muḥammad from Mecca to Medina; the year it occurred, 622, is the base-year of the Muslim era.

ḥisbah: overseeing of public morals, including especially fair dealing in the market; confided in High Caliphate to a *muḥtasib*; later other terms were also used for such an officer.

ḥiyal (sing. *ḥîlah*): 'legal tricks', legal method of avoiding inappropriate special consequences of general legal principles.

ijmâ': agreement of the Muslim community, as a ground for legal decision; it was debated what constituted the community for this purpose.

'ilm: learnèd lore; particularly, religious knowledge, of *ḥadîth* (q.v.) reports, of *fiqh* (q.v.), etc. In modern Arabic the word is used to render 'science'. Among many Shî'îs it was supposed the *imâm* (q.v.) had a special secret knowledge, *'ilm*.

imâm: leader of the *ṣalât* (q.v.) worship; or the leader of the Muslim community. Among Shî'îs: 'Alî and his descendants as proper leaders of the Islamic community even when rejected by it, are held to have a spiritual function as successors to Muḥammad. Among Jamâ'î-Sunnîs, any great *'âlim* (q.v.), especially the founder of a legal *madhhab* (q.v.), was called an *imâm*.

îmân: religious faith; conviction; that which a Muslim acknowledges both inwardly and outwardly through his actions.

isnâd (also *sanad*): the series of transmitters of a *ḥadîth* (q.v.) report, mentioned to guarantee its validity.

Jamâ'î-Sunnîs: *see* Sunnîs.

jihâd: war in accordance with the *Sharî'ah* (q.v.) against unbelievers; there are different opinions as to the circumstances under which such war becomes necessary. Also applied to a person's own struggle against his baser impulses.

jizyah: commonest term for the 'poll-tax' paid by *dhimmîs* (q.v.) in a Muslim-ruled society, instead of the dues levied on Muslims.

kalâm: discussion, on the basis of Muslim assumptions, of questions of theology and cosmology; sometimes called 'scholastic theology'.

kâtib: a secretary or scribe, specifically one who served in the government bureaus.

Khârijîs (also Khawârij; more properly Shurât): members of a group of puritanical Muslim sects of Marwânî and early 'Abbâsî times.

khuṭbah: sermon delivered (by a *khaṭîb*) at the special Friday midday worship in the mosque; it contained prayers for the sovereign and, being named in the *khuṭbah* and on coins, became a declaration of sovereignty.

madhhab (pl. *madhâhib*): a system of *fiqh* (q.v.), or generally the system followed by any given religious group; particularly, four *madhâhib* were ultimately accepted as legitimate by the Jamâ'î-Sunnîs while Shî'îs and Khârijîs had other *madhâhib*. Sometimes rendered 'sect', 'school', 'rite'.

Mâlikî: referring to the Jamâ'î-Sunnî legal *madhhab* (q.v.) ascribed to Mâlik b. Anas (715–795 CE).

mawlà (pl. *mawâlî*): master or servant, also a man of religious authority; especially in the plural form *mawâlî* it refers to persons associated with Arab tribes otherwise than by birth, particularly in Marwânî times; non-Arab converts to Islam.

miḥrâb: the niche in the inside wall of a mosque (q.v.) showing the direction in which prayer should be performed.

mosque (Ar. masjid): any place of worship for Muslims where the *ṣalât* (q.v.) is performed in a group; a major one, where official Friday services are held, is called *jâmi'*.

muftî: an expert in the *Sharî'ah* (q.v.) who gives public decisions in cases of law and conscience.

Muhâjirûn: those who accompanied Muḥammad from Mecca to Medina.

muḥtasib: see *ḥisbah*.

Murji'îs: name applied to a non-Shî'î school of thought among the Piety-minded opposition of Marwânî times.

Mu'tazilîs: a group among the Piety-minded of Marwânî times who developed a lasting school of *kalâm* (q.v.) stressing human free responsibility and divine justice.

naṣṣ: explicit designation (of a successor by his predecessor), particularly relating to the Shî'î view of succession to the imâmate; it thus comes to confer upon the successor a power of knowledge and understanding that no one else has.

pîr: a Ṣûfî master, able to lead disciples on the mystical way.

qiyâs: the principle of deriving fresh juridical decisions, by way of analogy, from decisions as given in *ḥadîth* (q.v.) or Qur'ân; commonly listed as one of the four *uṣûl al-fiqh* recognized among Jamâ'î-Sunnîs.

ra'y: personal judgment in working out jurisprudence rules.

ṣalât (or *ṣalâh*): the ritual worship performed five times daily, preferably in groups; including the special group prayer of midday on Fridays. In Persian called *namâz*.

sayyid: *see* 'Alid.

Shâfi'î: referring to members of the Jamâ'î-Sunnî legal *madhhab* (q.v.) ascribed to al-Shâfi'î (767–820 CE).

shahâdah: the declaration that there is no god but God, and Muḥammad is His prophet, identifying the declarer as a Muslim.

Sharî'ah (or *Shar'*): the whole body of rules guiding the life of a Muslim. in law, ethics, and etiquette; sometimes called *Sacred Law* (or *Canon Law*), The provisions of the *Sharî'ah* are worked out through the discipline of *fiqh* (q.v.), on the basis of *uṣûl al-fiqh* (basic sources of legal authorities), which Sunnîs commonly list as Qur'ân, *ḥadîth* (q.v.), *ijmâ'* (q.v.), and *qiyâs* (q.v.). Shî'îs commonly substitute *'aql* (q.v.) for *qiyâs* and interpret *ijmâ'* as consensus of the *imâms*.

sharîf: *see* 'Alid.

Shî'ah: 'party (of 'Alî)'; general name for that part of the Muslims that held to the rights of 'Alî and his descendants to leadership in the community whether recognized by the majority or not; or any particular sect holding this position. Shî'î is the adjective, or refers as a noun to an adherent of the Shî'ah. Shî'ism (*tashayyu'*) denotes the attitude or doctrines of the Shî'ah. The most well known Shî'î groups are the Zaydîs, the Ismâ'îlîs or Seveners, and the Twelvers.

shirk: associating other gods—or any objects of regard—with God; the supreme sin.

Ṣûfî: an exponent of Ṣûfism (Ar. *taṣawwuf*), the commonest term for that aspect of Islam which is based on the mystical life.

sunnah: received custom, particularly that associated with Muḥammad; it is embodied in *ḥadîth* (q.v.).

Sunnîs: properly *ahl al-sunnah wa-l-jamâ'ah* ('people of custom and the community'), in this work often Jamâ'î-Sunnîs: that majority of Muslims which accepts the authority of the whole first generation of Muslims and the validity of the historical community, in contrast to the Khârijîs and the Shî'îs (q.v.). Sunnî as adjective refers to the doctrinal position, as noun it refers to an adherent of the position. Sunnism is sometimes referred to as 'Orthodoxy'. The term 'Sunnî' is often restricted to particular positions within the Jamâ'î-Sunnî camp; e.g., often it excludes Mu'tazilîs, Karrâmîs, and other groups which did not survive to command recognition. In older Muslim works it sometimes included only the particular faction of the writer.

taqiyyah: resort to pretence of conformity when avowal of one's principles would be dangerous to oneself or others; used especially by Shî'îs.

'ulamâ': see *'âlim*.

Ummah: any people as followers of a particular prophet, in particular the Muslims as forming a community following Muḥammad.

'ushr: the tenth of the produce, a *zakât* (q.v.) tax leviable on certain Muslim-held lands as recognized by Islamic law.

uṣûl al-fiqh: see *Sharî'ah*.

zakât (or *zakâh*): a fixed proportion of his property that is supposed to be paid yearly by the Muslim of some wealth as a tax for the purposes of a Muslim government, or else as charity to the poor or for other good causes; rendered 'poor tax', or 'legal alms'.

Index

NOTE: Names and terms beginning with the Arabic definite article (al-) are indexed under the letter following the article.